The Dressmaker's Companion

The Dressmaker's Companion

A practical guide to sewing clothes

Elizabeth M Haywood

COOATALAA PRESS 2017

First published in 2017
Second edition 2018
Cooatalaa Press
PO Box 1014
Clare 5453
Australia

Text and illustrations copyright © 2017 by Elizabeth M Haywood
Cover by Stu Nankivell www.bluegoanna.com.au

All rights reserved. This book or any portion thereof may not be reproduced or used in any manner whatsoever without the express written permission of the publisher except for the use of brief quotations in a book review or scholarly journal.

www.thedressmakerscompanion.com

National Library of Australia Cataloguing-in-Publication entry
Creator: Haywood, Elizabeth M., author, illustrator.

Title: The dressmaker's companion: a practical guide to sewing clothes / written and illustrated by Elizabeth M Haywood

ISBN: 978 0 646 98547 3 (paperback)

Notes: Includes index.

Subjects: Sewing.
 Dressmaking--Patterns.
 Dressmaking--Patterns design--Handbooks, manuals, etc.
 Dressmaking--Pattern design--Study and teaching.

Contents

Welcome vii

Acknowledgements viii

Alterations for over 50's 1

Belt loops 5
Belts 9
Bias cut 17
Bias strips 20
Binding 22
Buttons and buttonholes 28

Collars 41
Construction 64
Cutting 67

Darts 85

Facings 97
Front stands and tab fronts 105

Gathering 130
Godets 138

Handsewing essentials 144
Hems 153

Interfacing 164

Linings 170

Measurements and ease 182
Mitres 185

Overlocker FAQs 190

Party fabrics 192
Patternmaking essentials 207
Piping 211
Pleats 213
Pockets 226
Pressing 263

Rouleau 276

Seams 284
Shirt cuffs and plackets 300
Shirt yokes 312
Shoulder pads 317
Sleeves 327
Stain removal 341
Strapless tops 343

Topstitching 349
Tucks 353

Vents and splits 357

Waistbands 370

Zips 402

Glossary 432

Further reading 441

Index 443

Welcome

Hello!

It's my hope *The Dressmaker's Companion* will be a great blessing to you. It's the book I wish I'd had when I was learning to sew and had moved beyond the basics.

This book attempts to illustrate some of the many ways of making clothes, gleaned over the years from knowledgeable teachers and colleagues who generously shared their sewing ideas. The more I learned from them, the more I was astounded by just how many different ways there are to sew clothes! The part I loved the most (and still love) is the transformation of a roll of fabric, by skilled hands, into clothes.

I certainly don't want this book to be seen as a Book of Sewing Rules or that my way is The Only Way. *Your* sewing is how *you* choose to do it and the decisions are yours. Take opportunities to try different methods, examine finished ready-to-wear clothes, talk to others who sew, read sewing books, magazines and websites and try to learn something every time you sew a garment. Continually add to your bank of knowledge and experience.

If you're an absolute beginner, the very best way to learn sewing is to get yourself a teacher. Either join a class or get someone who sews to start you off, then mentor you. Remember, no-one was born knowing how to sew; every professional started in the same place you are now.

You might like to know about me: I trained as a clothing patternmaker in 1990-91 in Adelaide, Australia, however, my first job as a young fresh-faced graduate was as a junior cutter. It was in a ladies wear factory, where we made ski pants, body suits, swing coats, power suits and box pleated skirts by the zillions. After six months they closed down and I got new job in a swimwear and sporting wear factory. It was a remarkable place with very talented staff; they made a huge variety of things out of lycra. They also took on unusual made-to-measure jobs such as unitards for a circus trapeze act.

The early 1990's was an interesting time to work in fashion with many new types of fabrics available. There was microfibre, micro peach, fabric printed with photographic prints, stretch wovens, hologram printed lycra, coolmax fabric, long-lasting polyester swimsuit fabric, UV protection fabric, and I remember seeing my first pair of parachute tracksuit pants (a friend had brought them back from America—little did we know how popular they would become). After the swimwear factory, I did a short stint as a bulk cutter in a school uniform factory, then lived in London working as a temp patternmaker for a fashion agency. I look back on my London era (late 1990's) with special fondness. Not only was it professionally enriching, it was also an exciting time and place to work in fashion.

Back in Australia I went to work at a badly-run bridal studio before they went bankrupt, then five solid years as a clothing cutter, cutting individual garments for corporate uniforms. I estimate I cut 10,000 garments in my time there and actually wore out a pair of scissors. Perhaps unsurprisingly, a wrist injury made me decide to leave and I went to work as a patternmaker at a designer's studio. We did twice-yearly ranges, wedding dresses, mothers of the bride and race wear. Most of her clients were over fifty (apart from the brides) and we used beautiful, expensive fabrics from European fashion houses.

The designer was heading towards retirement and I changed to part-time hours, and began to do patterns seasonally at other places for the next several years; I thrived on the variety. I also began teaching sewing at a private sewing school. It was a steep learning curve because I had never taught before (but I knew my stuff). However, they took a chance on me and I enjoyed teaching and became more confident. Often a student would ask me to recommend a comprehensive sewing book, and the best I could suggest was *The Reader's Digest Complete Guide to Sewing* (a great book, by the way). A sewing book. *Hmm, I could do that*, I naively thought. I started writing this book and much of the material I tested on my classes.

Ten years later, here I am writing the introduction to what I thought might take a year. My life has changed from factories and studios and I now live in the country with my young family.

There isn't really anything new in this book, but I learnt it all the hard way. I hope you enjoy *The Dressmaker's Companion*.

Cheers!
Liz Haywood
January 2017

Thanks

With many thanks I acknowledge the help of Donna Drain, Tom Freebairn, Val Freebairn, Emma Kennedy, Anthea Martin and Helen Sampson who read all or parts of the manuscript. I'm very thankful; your suggestions and corrections made this book so much better.
Stu Nankivell's beautiful cover exceeded my expectations.
I acknowledge my sewing teachers at TAFE and my co-workers at the many places I worked. Everyone was, without exception, generous with volunteering knowledge and answering questions.
I also thank Anthea Martin and the editors of Yarn magazine for their encouragement and taking a chance on my teaching and writing respectively.

This book is dedicated to my husband, who lets me buy any fabric I want.

Alterations for over 50's

Introduction 1	Thick waist 3
More bust shaping (for larger busts) 1	Flat bum/big tum 3
Rounded back 2	Different left and right sides 4
Close in neckline 2	

Does this sound familiar.... *"When I was 20 (and I was thin) I made lots of my own clothes. I would choose a pattern, make it up, and it always fitted perfectly. I never measured anything—I just made it in my size. I'm over 50 now and I still like sewing, but I can never get things to fit properly. I've had disappointment after disappointment, and my confidence in my sewing is so low I'm tempted just to give the whole thing away."* Is this you? (or the person you're fitting?) The reality is, no-one is the same shape as they were when they were 20. Sport, work, children, illness, gravity, diet, menopause—in short, life—have all changed you.

The following are common alterations for women aged 50+. You (or the person you're fitting) might need some or all of them.

Take your measurements and check them against the pattern first, before you cut any fabric. I know you never used to do that, but make it a habit now.

Don't get depressed if you have to sew a bigger size than you think you are. It's a different sizing system and it's only a number, and anyway, the *size* you are *doesn't* define *who* you are!

More bust shaping for larger busts

If you need more shaping, the garment will ride up at the front and there'll be diagonal drag lines from the bust to the side seam.

If the garment has a **bust dart**, make the dart bigger.
Try on the garment or tissue paper pattern and pin a bigger dart.
You might have to change the position of the dart, too.

On the pattern, draw in the new dart. Fold the dart into position and re-draw the side seam if needed. Add onto the lower edge of the front to make the front and back side seams the same length.
If the garment is already cut out, trim the difference off the back to make the hem level BUT do this at the end after all other alterations.

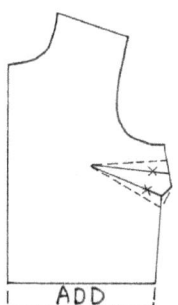

If the bodice is **princess line**, the alteration is a little different.

I think princess line creates the best fit for large busts because of the shaping. I automatically do the following alteration for busts 106cm (42") and bigger:

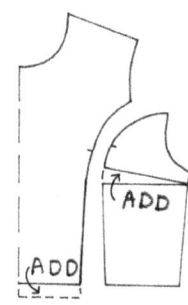

Split the side front panel horizontally at the bust line and spread it 2.5cm (1") where it joins the centre front panel, to nothing at the side.
It's sort of like taking a reverse dart. Usually 2.5cm (1") is about right for most women.

Be sure to spread the pattern from the *stitching* line, *not* the edge of the pattern, otherwise you'll make the side seam longer.

Add 2.5cm (1") to the length of the centre front panel to make the princess line seams the same length. If the garment is already cut out the front will need re-cutting, but if it can be made 2.5cm (1") shorter then you'll only need to re-cut the side panel.

Rounded back

As we get older, our backs and shoulders get rounded and extra length is needed at the centre back. 2.5cm (1") is a common amount, but more rounded people might need more.

If you need more back length, the garment will ride up at the back and diagonal drag lines will appear from the shoulder blades to the sides.

A common solution is to create a centre back seam and spread the pattern at the centre back.

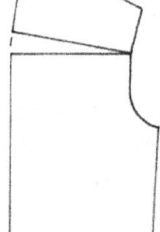

Another solution is to cut and spread horizontally across the back, creating a **shoulder dart**. This is a good solution if you don't want a centre back seam.

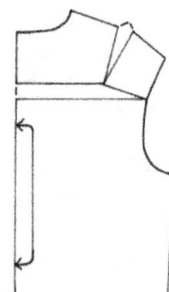
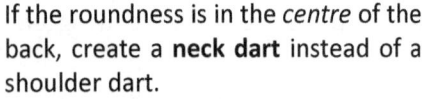

If the roundness is in the *centre* of the back, create a **neck dart** instead of a shoulder dart.

BUT what if you've already cut out the garment and partially sewn it together and there's no more material left?

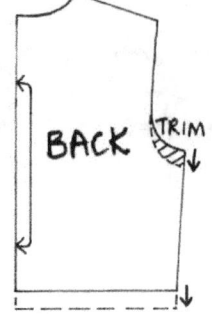

Undo the side seams and remove the sleeve. Pin the side seams back together with the back armhole lowered by 2.5cm (1"). The front will now be 2.5cm (1") longer than the back.
(*Don't* trim the front off yet).

Effectively this is the same as adding 2.5cm (1") horizontally through the back extending into the armhole as well.

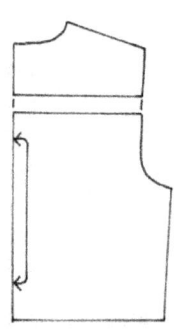

The garment will end up 2.5cm (1") shorter because you'll have to trim this amount off the lower edge of the front to make the side seams match BUT if you had to make the bust dart bigger, the side seams might now be the same length.

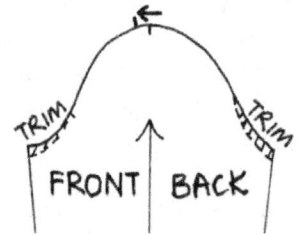

If you have trouble getting the sleeve to fit back in, try lowering the armhole on the sleeve and moving the position of the notch at the top.

Close in neckline

Do wear V necks if they suit you, but the neckline will be more flattering if the back and sides sit close to the base of the neck. Older people are fuller at the back of their neck and often prefer to have it covered.

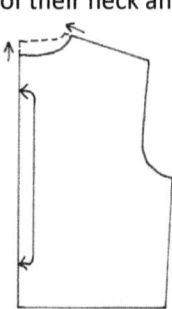

On the back, use a ruler to extend the shoulder and centre back lines the required amount. Change the neckline so it's almost straight and horizontal, not curving.

After changing the back, change the front to match so the shoulder seams are the same length.

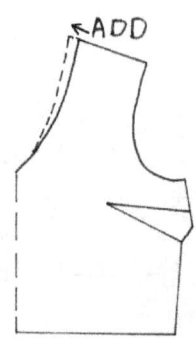

Alterations for over 50's **3**

Thick waist

Every woman mourns the loss of her 18 inch waist, even if it was never as small as 18 inches. With age, the waist thickens as your spinal column compresses, so the waist shaping on your pattern needs to be softer.

Take your waist measurement and compare it to the waist of the pattern.

For dresses, measure the smallest part of your waist. Add the required amount of wearing ease, for example 5cm (2"), and compare this measurement to the pattern.

Most women need to add to the side, about 1.2cm-2cm (½"-¾"), and reduce any darts. The front darts might not even be needed.

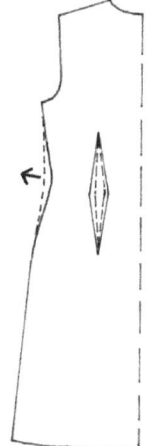

For skirts and trousers with waistbands, measure your waist where you want the waistline to sit. Add ease of 1.2cm (½"), and compare to the waistband pattern. If the pattern has two darts you won't need both. At the front you might not need any, or just small ones. You might need to add onto the side as well.

If there's too much waist shaping (meaning the darts are too big), there'll be puckers at the bottom of the darts.

If the skirt or trousers has a yoke/basque at the top, the basque will need to be made straighter.

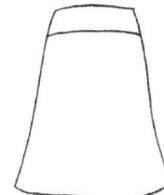

Slash the basque pattern and spread it so the top edge is equal to your waist measurement with no ease. You might need to add a little on the sides as well, so they aren't as curved.

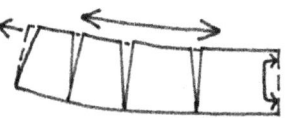

Be sure to pivot the pattern from the *stitching* line, *not* the edge, otherwise you'll make the seam too long.

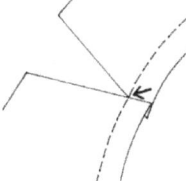

Cut out the new basque and stitch tape to the waist to stop it from stretching. Pin the basque to the skirt, pin the side seams and try it on.

Flat bum/big tum

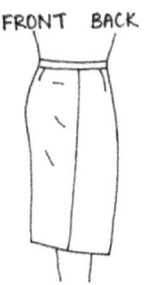

On straight skirts, the side seams won't hang vertically—they'll swing to the front and the front hem will rise up.

Don't wait until the skirt is finished and then trim the excess off the hem. The skirt won't hang right at the side seams.

You'll need a "lift" at the back. Take a horizontal tuck across the top, just below the back waistband, until the hem is level.

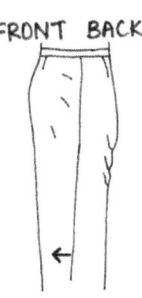

On the pattern, the waist line will curve low. After adjusting, make the top of the dart the same width as it was originally, so the waistband will still fit on.

Naturally, if you have a big bottom, you would take a lift across the *front* until the hem hangs straight and the side seams hang vertically.

Trousers are a little trickier.

On trousers, the side seams will swing forward and there'll be bagginess below the bottom and drag lines across the tummy.

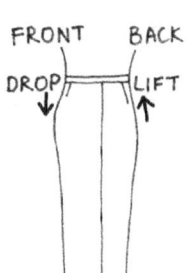

Take a "lift" at the back until the bagginess disappears.

At the front, pull the pants down until the drag lines disappear, to gain extra length over the tummy.

The changes on the pattern will look like this:

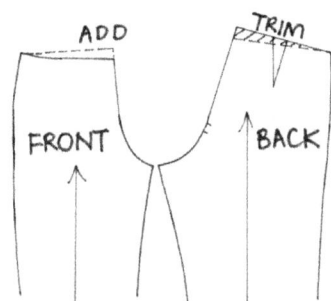

To give more room across the tummy, straighten the centre front parallel to the grainline if it's on a slant.

The back crotch might need straightening and deepening for a low, flat bottom.

You might also need to take in the back inside leg and/or add onto the front inside leg if the inside leg seam is visible from the front when the trousers are being worn.

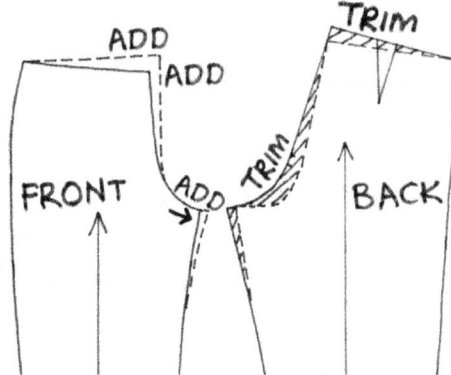

Different left and right sides

It's very common for people of all ages to be different on the left and right sides of their body, and the differences can become more pronounced as you get older.

Differences can also be caused by hip replacements, shoulder injuries, back problems and a lifetime of favouring one side of the body.

While it doesn't matter so much on loose-fitting clothes, the more fitted and simple the garment is, the more the left and right differences will become apparent. Try to fit both sides as similarly as you can, but don't fit too precisely to the differences otherwise you'll amplify them.

If the differences between your left and right side are very great, you'll need to make pattern pieces with a left and right side.

For most people, however, it's adequate to just cut out the garment for the bigger/longer side, then make the adjustment when sewing. You can mark the left and right stitching lines on the pattern with different coloured pens.

Belt loops

Introduction.................................. 5
Thread belt loops........................ 5
    method 1 buttonhole stitch........... 5
    method 2 thread chain 6
Fabric belt loops............................ 6
    no topstitching?........................ 6
    positioning................................ 7
    attaching.................................. 7
Shaped fabric belt loops................. 7

Belt loops, or belt carriers, can be added to any garment you want to wear belted. They're useful for belts that would slip out of place if there were no loops, but they can also be an interesting design feature.

Belt loops may be made from thread or fabric. They can be attached to the surface of the garment or inserted into a seam.

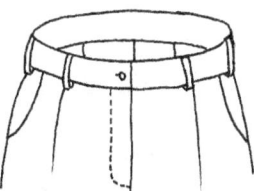

Thread belt loops are barely visible and are most often seen on belted dresses at the side seams.

Fabric belt loops can be wide or narrow and you could make a feature of them if it suits the garment. For example, belt loops can be placed in sets of two or three, or can be adorned with extra topstitching. They can be shaped like a tab or buttoned.

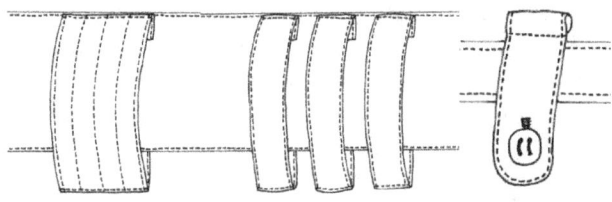

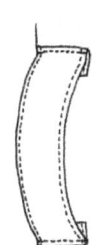

Belt loops are attached with a small amount of play to allow the belt to slip through easily. In other words, they don't lie totally flat next to the garment.

If there's no waist seam on the garment, find the positions for the belt loops by trying on the garment with the belt. Place a pin above and below the belt. Note the position on your pattern for next time.

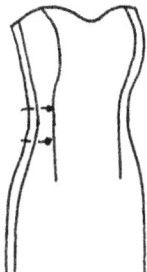

Thread belt loops

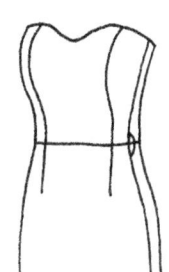

Thread belt loops can look nearly invisible and are usually applied just at the side seams of dresses and coats or jackets. They are made last, after the garment is finished.

Mark the position of the belt loop using pins. There are two ways of making thread belt loops:

Method 1—buttonhole stitch belt loop

1. Thread a needle with four threads (see page 145) and knot the end. Bring the needle up at one end of the belt loop position.

I like to stitch the thread belt loops through the thickness of the side seam allowance, so there's a stronger anchorage than just one layer of fabric.

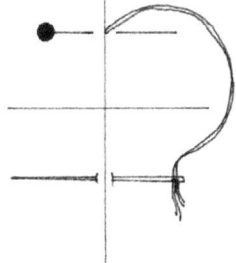

2. Take a tiny stitch at one end, then another at the other end, forming long stitches for the belt loop. Do this three or four times. Remember to leave a small amount of play to allow the belt to slip through easily.

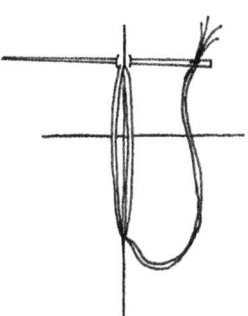

3. Work closely spaced blanket stitches over the loop to cover it, then fasten off the thread on the wrong side.

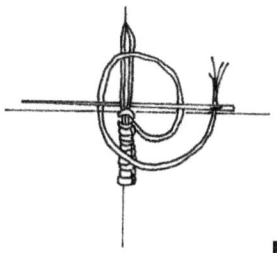

Method 2—thread chain belt loop

This is another method of making thread belt loops. It's quicker but I don't think it's as strong. Try one and see what you think.

1. Thread a needle with four threads (see page 145) and knot the end (illustrated with one thread for clarity). Bring the needle up through one end of the belt loop position and make a tiny stitch, but don't pull the thread all the way through—leave a loop.

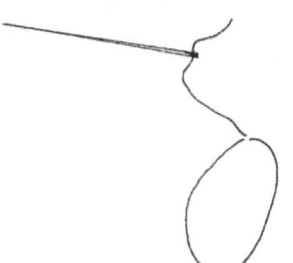

2. Pull a loop of the thread through the loop made by the stitch, and pull so the first loop closes up and forms a knot at the base.
Repeat until you have a chain the length required for the belt loop. Count the loops as you do them so that you can repeat it for the other belt loops.

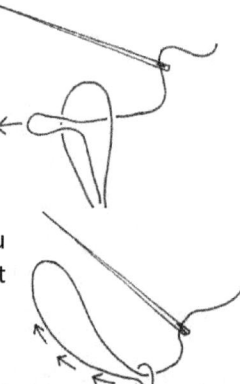

3. To finish the thread chain, pass the needle through the loop and pull until the loop disappears.

4. Lay the thread chain onto the fabric in position. Plunge the point of the needle down through the centre of the last knot in the chain, through the fabric to the wrong side.
Finish off on the wrong side.

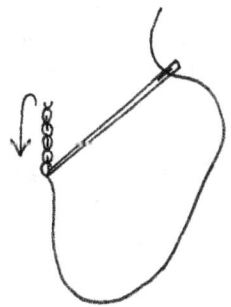

Fabric belt loops

Fabric belt loops are stronger than thread belt loops, but are more visible.
They're cut as a long strip of fabric, sewn to make one very long belt loop, then cut into the individual belt loops.
I usually cut the fabric strip 4cm (1½") wide and long enough to accommodate all my belt loops plus a bit extra.

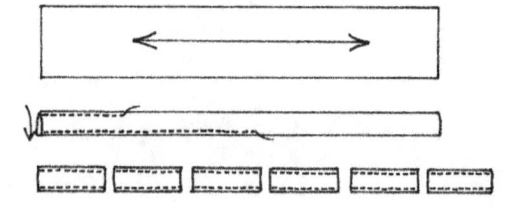

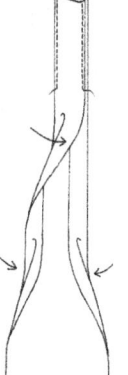

Fold under the long sides nearly to the centre, then fold them together.
Stitch close to the edge on both sides.
Just fold it into position as you sew it—it's quite simple to do without pins or pressing once you get started.
If you aren't confident, press it before stitching.

If the fabric is very thick, here are two alternatives:
✂ (left picture) Cut the strip three times as wide as the finished belt loop, using the selvedge as one edge. Fold the strip in thirds with the selvedge on the outside, and stitch close to the edge through all thicknesses.
✂ (right picture) Cut the strip the width of the finished belt loop plus 1.2cm (½"). Overlock the two long edges, turn them under 6mm (¼") and stitch. Stitch from the right side, and aim to land your stitches in the centre of the overlocking.

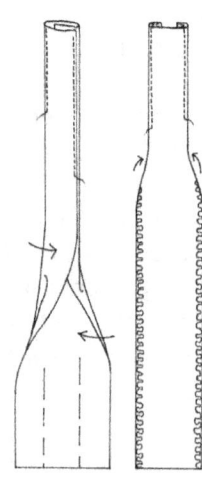

No topstitching?

If you don't want any topstitching on the belt loops and your fabric isn't too thick, you can make your belt loops like a tube, with the seam on the inside.

1. Cut a strip twice as wide as the belt loop plus 1.2cm (½").

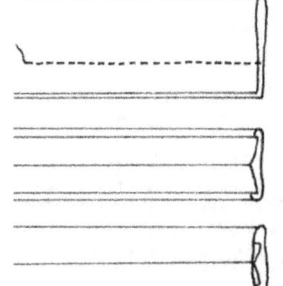

2. Fold the right sides together and stitch along the edge with a 6mm (¼") seam. If possible, press the seam open with the tip of the iron before turning to the right side.

3. Turn through to the right side and press, centering the seam on the underside of the belt loop.

Narrow rouleau cut on the bias can also be used for belt loops, inserted into side seams on dresses, jackets or coats. Rouleau can be attached as a bar or loop. See page 276 for making rouleau.

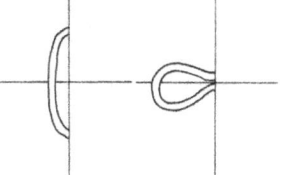

Positioning fabric belt loops

On coats, jackets and dresses, fabric belt loops are usually positioned just at the side seams. Sometimes one is also placed on the centre back. If the belt loops are a design feature, however, they can be more obvious and positioned on the fronts and backs as well.

If the side seams are very bulky, put the belt loops to one side of the seam, so you'll be able to stitch through them.

On waistbands, you'll need one on each side seam, one at the centre back, and one on each front. You can also put one partway along on each back as well, but I don't always. It is traditionally done for men's trousers, though.

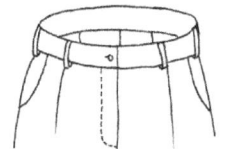 

If you have darts, front pleats or pockets, try to align the belt loops with them.

Attaching fabric belt loops

✂ Belt loops can be attached directly onto the garment after the garment is made. You may have noticed that jeans belt loops are attached this way.

Position the belt loop on the garment, fold under the short ends, and machine stitch across the ends a couple of times for strength. You may need to use a larger sized machine needle to sew through the bulk.

✂ Belt loops can also be inserted into a seam as the garment is being made:

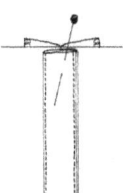

1. Pin or machine stitch the belt loops in position before you sew the waistband on. Put the right side of the belt loops to the right side of the garment.

2. After the waistband has been finished, flip the belt loops up, fold under the short end at the top, and machine stitch in place.

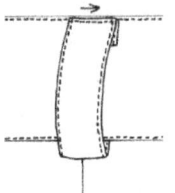

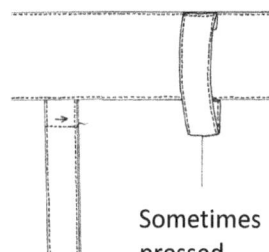

Sometimes the belt loop is stitched down 1cm (⅜") below the waistband before being flipped up, to make a longer belt loop.

Sometimes it isn't stitched, merely pressed.

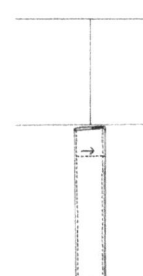 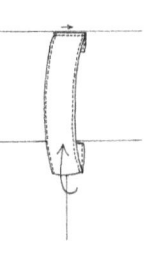

For the centre back belt loop on men's trousers, where you cannot insert the loop into the waist seam, stitch it on separately.

Shaped fabric belt loops

Shaped belt loops require a pattern.

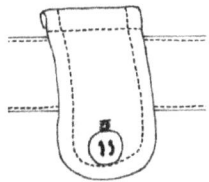

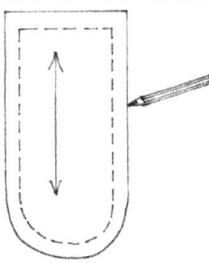

1. Draw the desired shape of the belt loop and add a 6mm (¼") seam allowance all the way around. Cut a pair for each belt loop and one of interfacing. If the fabric is very thick, interfacing might not be needed. Put the interfacing on the outermost piece.

2. Place the right sides together and sew around the edges except for the top edge where it will be attached to the garment.

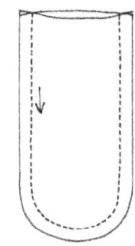

3. Trim any corners and turn it through to the right side and press. Topstitch it now if desired. If possible, stitch the buttonhole before the loop is sewn to the garment.

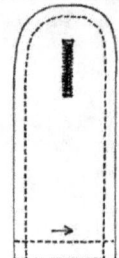
4. Attach the belt loop by laying it right side down on the garment as shown and stitching across the raw edge, taking a scant 6mm (¼") seam. Trim off any stray threads or fraying.

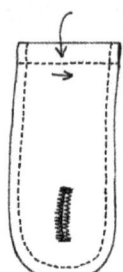
Flip the belt loop down and topstitch 6mm (¼") into position. The raw edges will be encased in the seam.

Finish with a button (and buttonhole if you didn't make one before), allowing some play for the belt to slide through.

Sometimes the button and buttonhole are decorative and don't undo—in this case don't cut the slit in the buttonhole and sew the button through all layers.

Belts

Tie belt/sash 9	securing the belt's pointy end 13
Belts with buckles 10	Some other belt ideas 13
to cut 10	Petal belts 13
to sew by hand 10	Plaited belts 14
to sew by machine 11	4 cord plait 14
Contour belts 11	another 4 cord plait 14
Attaching belt buckles 12	5 cord plait 14
buckle with a prong 12	woven plait for 4-6 cords 15
handmade eylets 12	a plait using only one cord 15
slip-through buckles 12	belt plaited from one strip 16
clasp/interlocking buckle 13	

You can make a belt to add a finishing touch to any outfit you sew. Tie belts give a soft look while belts with a buckle give a more tailored effect.

Tie belt/sash

Tie belts are very easy to make and look good tied in a soft bow or simply knotted.

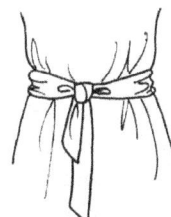

Suitable fabrics:

✂ Close weaves and medium to lightweight fabrics work well.

✂ Try to avoid heavyweight and plush fabrics—they sew up into bulky belts, which is not the most flattering thing around your waist.

✂ Also try to avoid sheer, loosely woven or very fine fabrics that fray easily.

✂ Stretch or knit fabrics are fine to use.

✂ Use a contrasting fabric to make a belt that stands out.

Make a pattern

Determine the **length** of the sash using a tape measure around your waist. Sometimes very wide sashes, 6cm (2½") or more, look better going around the waist twice—starting at the front, crossing at the back then tying at the front.

Cut the sash twice the finished **width** and add seam allowances.

A 6mm (¼" footwidth) seam allowance is adequate. For very narrow ties of 2cm (¾") or less, make the tie the same way as a beltloop (see page 6) or a rouleau (page 276).

Tie belts can be cut on the straight grain or on the bias. Usually they're cut on the straight grain, but if your fabric is a stripe or check you could cut it on the bias for effect. A very stiff fabric will produce a softer bow if it's cut on the bias (see page 17 for bias cut).

Tie belts are not usually interfaced, but if your fabric is very floppy you could iron some lightweight jersey fusing onto all or half of it to give it some body.

To sew a tie belt

1. Fold the sash in half lengthways, right sides together, and stitch leaving a gap in the centre to turn the right way.

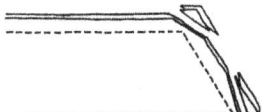

If you're having angled ends, put the pointiest corner on the folded side, so there's less bulk in that corner when you turn it the right way.

2. Trim the corners to within 3mm (⅛") of the stitching line.

3. Before you turn the sash through to the right side, take an iron and press the seam open as far as you can.

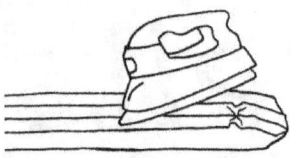
Use the tip of the iron and try not to press folds into the rest of the sash.
You could press the seam over a length of dowel or a pencil to avoid pressing the rest of the sash.

4. Turn the sash to the right side. The end of a wooden spoon or a ruler sometimes helps. Carefully pull the corners out using a pin on the right side.

5. Press the belt flat and slipstitch the opening closed. Topstitch by machine if desired. You won't need to slipstitch the opening shut if your topstitching is right next to the edge.

Belts with buckles

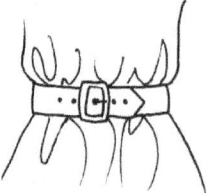

The size of the buckle opening will dictate the width of the belt.

There are three types of belt buckle:

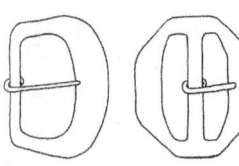

1. The kind with a prong to put through eyelet holes. They're called half tongue or full tongue. Half tongue buckles can be covered to match the belt.

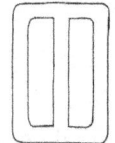

2. Slip-through buckle (no prongs or eyelets).

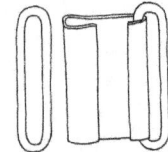

3. Clasp or interlocking buckle.

Second hand shops are an excellent source of interesting and inexpensive belt buckles.
You can buy **covered belt kits** from haberdashery departments. They come with belt stiffening, eyelets, a buckle to cover in your own fabric and instructions. Some people prefer to use a kit for their first belt.
Some shops offer a **belt covering service** if you don't want to make your own.

Belts with buckles—to cut

You'll need some kind of stiffening for the belt, but regular iron-on interfacing isn't stiff enough. Instead, use belting or strips of buckram. Belting comes in different widths, for example 25mm or 30mm wide, and is sold by the metre. Buckram comes on a roll like fabric, sold by the metre.

If the belting or buckram is iron-on, you'll find it easier to cover because the fabric will stay where you iron it.

1. Cut the belt stiffening the **length** of the waist circumference plus 25cm (10"), and **wide** enough to go through your chosen buckle. Don't add any seam allowance to the stiffening—make it the finished width of the belt.

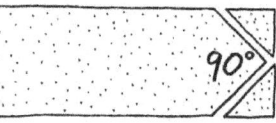

2. Trim one end to a point (not necessary if your belt has a clasp buckle).

3. Cut a strip of fabric twice the width of the stiffening and add seam allowances. 6mm (¼") footwidth seam allowances are adequate, or else 1cm (⅜") if you prefer wider seam allowances.

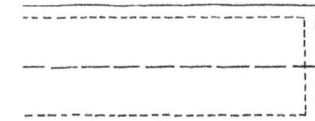

Belts with buckles—to sew by hand

I think this method is the easiest, if you don't mind hand sewing.

1. Cut the fabric and stiffening as described above. The selvedge may be used for one long edge of the belt's fabric (in which case you don't need to add seam allowance to that edge).

2. With the right sides together, sew across one end of the fabric and press it into a point.

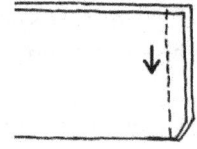 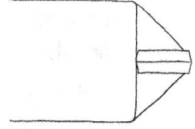

3. At the ironing board, lay the stiffening in the centre with the point inserted into the point of the fabric. If the stiffening is iron-on, place the glue side facing down.

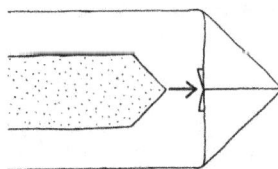

4. Press up the seam allowance on one of the long edges of the fabric, if you haven't used the selvedge.

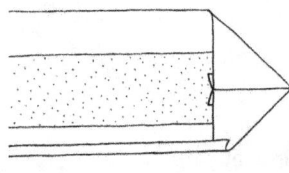

5. Fold over and press each side of fabric over the stiffening.

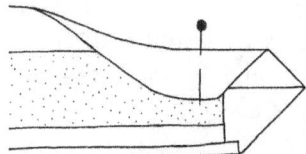

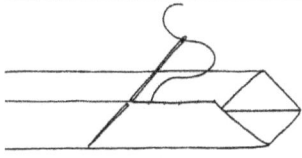
Hand sew them together along the centre.

Alternatively, try gluing the edge down.

6. Attach the buckle as described on page 12.

Belts with buckles—to sew by machine

1. Cut the fabric and stiffening for the belt as described above.

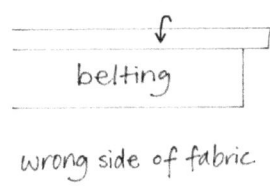

2. At the ironing board, fold over the seam allowance on one side and slot the belting under it. If the belting is iron-on, place the glue side facing down.

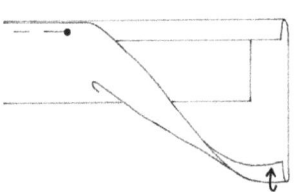

3. Press up the remaining seam allowance and bring it up to cover the belting, matching all the edges. Pin in place. Aim for a smooth, firm fit around the belting.

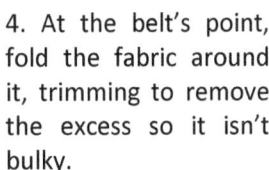 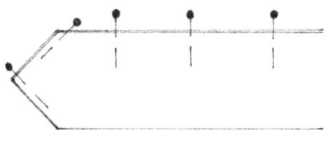

4. At the belt's point, fold the fabric around it, trimming to remove the excess so it isn't bulky.

5. Install a large size needle on your machine to cope with all the thickness. Determine which side to stitch on to achieve the best result (outermost or innermost when the belt is worn). Re-pin the belt if necessary so the pins are easy to remove as you sew.

Edgestitch around the sides of the belt through the fabric and belting. Press.

Contour belts

Contour belts are shaped to fit the curve of the body and are often designed to be worn low-slung or hipster.
These belts have a seam along the top and bottom.

Make a pattern

An easy starting point is to find a skirt or pants pattern with a curved waistband. Maybe you could use the garment you're making the contour belt for.

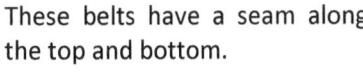

1. Pin the back and front waistbands together at the side seams, matching the *stitching* lines. Trace around them onto a piece of paper, making it the width of the belt. Smooth off the lines to create a pleasing curve and check for a consistent width with a tape measure.

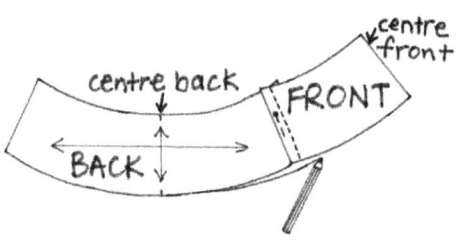

2. Fold the pattern along the centre back to mirror it.

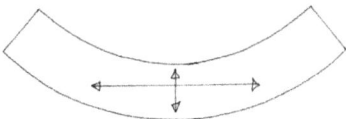

3. On the left, add up to 5cm (2") for attaching the buckle. On the right, add 15cm-20cm (6"-8") following the curves. Add seam allowances where required. Note that the grainline can go either way.

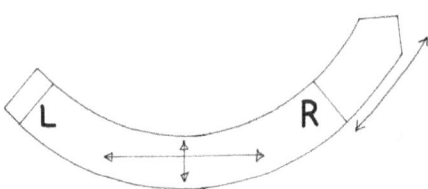

✂ If you plan to attach a **clasp buckle**, the pattern will be symmetrical and both ends will be square.

To sew a contour belt

1. For stiffening the belt, use buckram or a very firm interfacing.
Cut one layer of stiffening the *finished* size of the belt (no seam allowances).

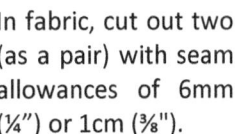

In fabric, cut out two (as a pair) with seam allowances of 6mm (¼") or 1cm (⅜").

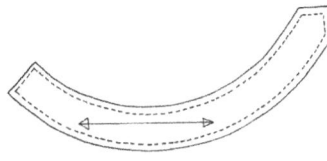

2. With the right sides of the fabric together, stitch the top edge and the end point of the belt. Sew cotton tape along the top edge of the belt to stop it from stretching.

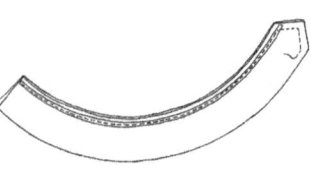

3. Turn the belt to the right side and press. Insert the stiffening and iron it on if it's fusible. Iron it onto what will be the outermost side of the belt when it's worn.

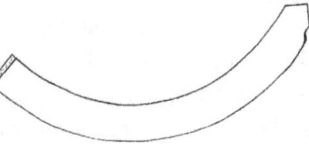

4. Press the lower edges to the inside and hand sew them together.
This part can be fiddly, but persevere.

Alternatively:
If you're confident enough, skip the handstitching and edgestitch around the edge of the entire belt, stitching the lower edges together as you do so.
Either way, if you plan to topstitch the belt, do it now before attaching the buckle.

For ripple-free topstitching, sew in the direction indicated by the arrows.

You're now ready to attach the buckle.

Attaching belt buckles

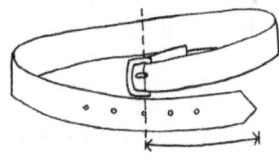

Try the belt on and check the length. The pointy end should overlap about 15cm-20cm (6"-8"). The side to attach the buckle can be up to 5cm (2") long.
If necessary, shorten the belt from the buckle end.
If you haven't topstitched the belt but want to, do it now before attaching the buckle.

To stop the buckle end from fraying you can:
✂ Fold under the end if it isn't too thick. If possible, try sliding back the fabric and trimming the stiffening off, so only the fabric is folded under (not possible if you've already topstitched the belt).
✂ Overlock the end.
✂ Neaten with a close zig zag.

Buckle with a prong
Make a small opening in the belt to attach the buckle prong.

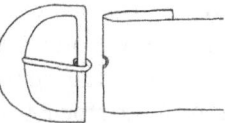

You can use:
✂ a metal eyelet (they come with a tool to attach them)
✂ a small buttonhole
✂ a machine-made eyelet (check your machine's instruction book to see if it has this feature)
✂ a hand made eyelet—see below for how to make

How to make hand made eyelets

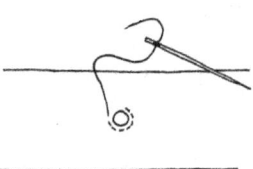

1. Punch a hole with an awl or stiletto. Trim away some of the fabric if necessary to make a neat hole.

2. Reinforce the opening with small running stitches. Use a double strand of thread and wear a thimble.

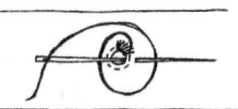

3. Work closely spaced buttonhole stitches over edges of the eyelet (use two or four threads).

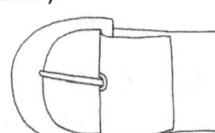

Slip the prong through the eyelet and sew the end down by hand or machine.

Try the belt on and mark the position of the eyelets on the pointy end. Make the eyelets by machine, hand, or use metal ones.

Slip-through buckles
Slip the buckle end of the belt through the middle rung of the buckle and sew the end down by hand or by machine.

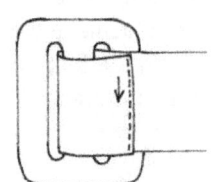

✂ Slip-through buckles can also be used for **soft, crushed belts**.

Make the belt about 2½ times wider than the buckle, following the instructions for a tie belt (page 9). Thicker fabrics will need less width and finer fabrics may need more.
At the buckle end, make three rows of gathering stitches about 2.5cm (1") apart. Pull up the gathers to fit the buckle, slip it through the middle rung of the buckle and sew in place.

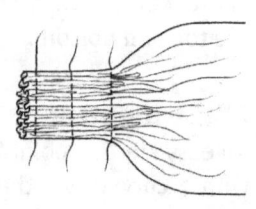

Belts **13**

Clasp buckle or interlocking buckle

Slip the ends of the belt through each side of the buckle and pin them in position.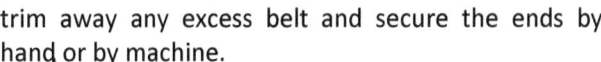
Try on the belt to check the size, then trim away any excess belt and secure the ends by hand or by machine.

✂ These buckles can also be used for **elastic belts**. Buy the appropriate width elastic belting and attach the buckle in same way.

Securing the pointy end of the belt

 The pointy end of the belt can be secured with a dob of velcro, a press stud or with a belt carrier to slip the end through.

The belt carrier is just a length of beltloop seamed to make a ring and slipped over the belt. 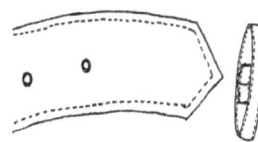 If you're making beltloops for the garment, make a bit extra to use for the belt (see page 6 for making fabric beltloops).

Some other belt ideas:

✂ A belt that does up with large eyelets and ties.

✂ Bind around the edges of the belt.

✂ Embellish the belt with rhinestones, ric-rac, fancy stitching, braid, appliqué or rows and rows of parallel straight stitching.

✂ Instead of making a tie belt, use a length of ribbon. Try crisp grosgrain, glossy satin or several lengths of sheer ribbon. Cut the ends at an angle or a V shape to prevent fraying.

✂ Finish a belt with a flower (or three) on top of a velcro closure.

✂ Make a belt using metal or plastic rings (for example bangles or large washers) joined together with small strips of fabric. Fasten the belt with a tie.

✂ Visit the hardware shop for interesting belt and buckle ideas. Use two D-rings for a belt buckle.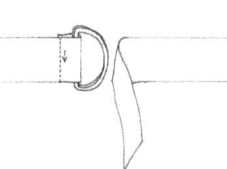

Try a rope belt made by plaiting or macrame. How about a lightweight chain belt fastened with a dog clip?

Petal belts

A petal belt requires no sewing and can be made from small pieces of any non-fraying material, such as leather, vinyl, PVC, oil cloth, suede, boiled wool or thick felt. Fasten it at the front with a concealed giant press stud, or eyelets and ties.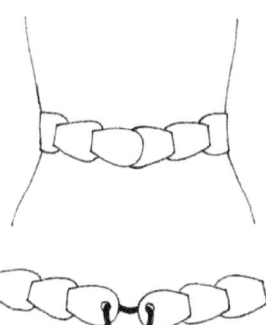
Children aged seven and up are good at making these.

1. Make a cardboard pattern in the shape of the one shown. Accurately cut the slots in the pattern using a craft knife.

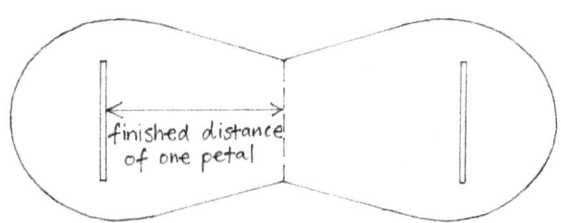

On the wrong side of the material, trace around the template with a biro. Divide your waist measurement by the finished distance of one petal to determine how many you'll need. Cut them out, cutting the slits in all but two of the pieces (these will be at the centre front).
Make sure the slits are cut exactly the right length (children will need help).

2. Place two petals together with the wrong sides facing and line up the slits. These will be at the centre back.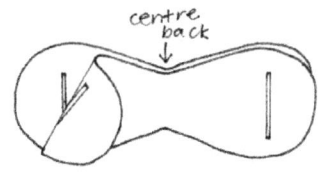
Optional: glue the wrong sides together.

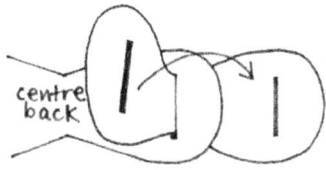 3. Thread a single petal through one of the slits, fold it in half and (optional) glue the wrong sides together.
Continue in this way to the front, finishing with a petal without a slit. Work the same from the other side.

14 The Dressmaker's Companion

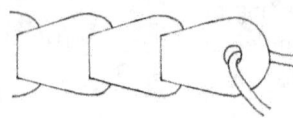

4. Attach a fastening of your choice. You may need to attach the fastening *before* you glue the centre front petals together.

You can invent your own petal designs. Try these:

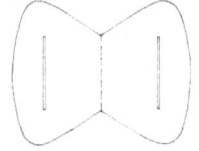 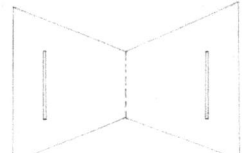

Plaited belts

Belts can be plaited from hobby cord, rouleau, leather strips, lengths of beltloop, thick wool, French knitting/tomboy/I-cord, rope or even ribbon.

The thickness of the cords and the number you use will determine how wide the finished belt will be.

The ends of the plaits can be joined to solid belt ends and do up with a regular buckle and holes. Alternatively, the cords of the plaits could be secured and worn tied with a knot in the front.

Use a bulldog clip to hold the plait if you have to pause during plaiting.

4 cord plait

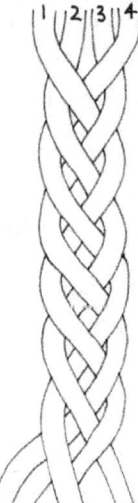

Most people can produce a three cord plait with no worries. Four cords produces a similar but slightly more substantial-looking plait:

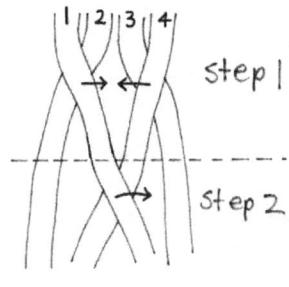

1. Bring the two outside cords to the inside.

2. Cross the left inside cord over the right one.

Repeat Steps 1 and 2.

Another 4 cord plait

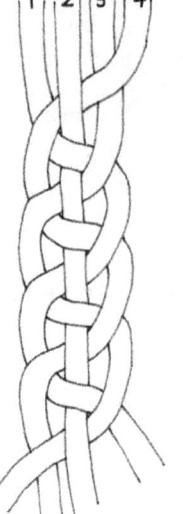

This alternative looks less like a plait and more like an interesting weave.

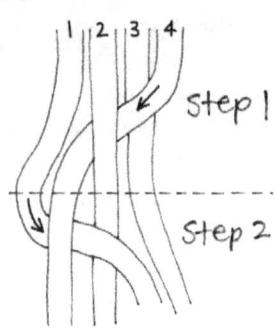

1. Take the right cord over and then under the cords to the left (that is, over 3 and under 2).

2. Take the left cord under and then over the cords to the right.

Repeat Steps 1 and 2, taking the right cord over then under, and the left cord under then over.

Pull the cords tightly or leave the side cords loose and open with a small gap.

5 cord plait

To plait a five cord belt, begin working from alternate sides into the middle:
take cord 1 over 2 and under 3
take cord 5 over 4 and under 1
take cord 4 over 1 and under 2
take cord 2 over 3 and under 5
Alternate taking each side strand over and under, over and under.

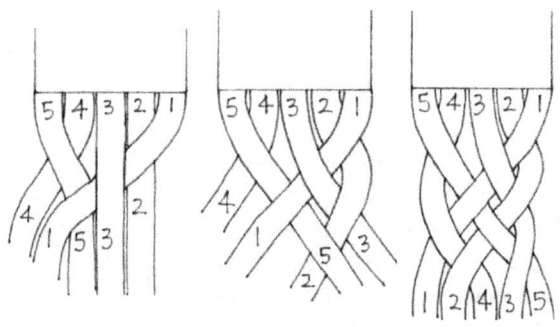

Once you've got going your fingers will fall into a rhythmic pattern.

Belts

Woven plait for 4-6 cords

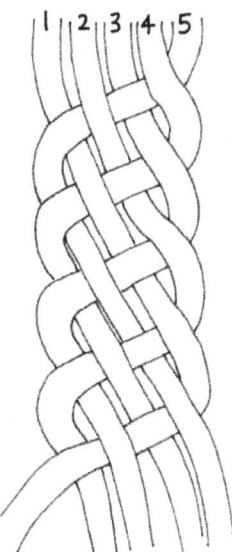 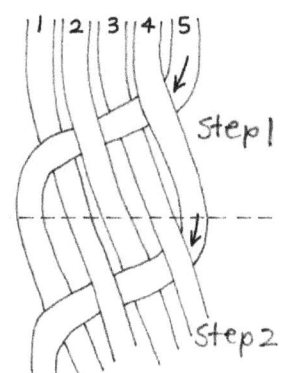

1. Take the cord on the right (cord 5) and weave it through the other cords, heading left. Begin weaving *under* the cord that's immediately to the left.

2. Repeat Step 1, taking the next cord on the right (cord 4) and weaving it through the other strands in the same under-over pattern. Don't forget to include the one on the far left that you wove in Step 1.

Continue on, always using the cord on the far right, and always starting by passing it *under* the next cord. Tighten the plait as you progress.

A plait using only one cord

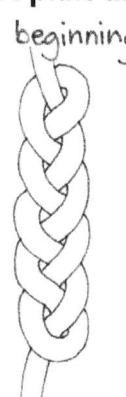

This clever plait uses only one cord to produce a three cord plait with ends to tie. You'll need a fairly long piece of cord—about four times the length of the finished plait, plus extra for the ends.
Try it out with a short length to make a friendship bracelet to get the hang of the technique. A short length will also help you calculate how long to make the first loop.

1. Make a large elongated loop, laid flat on the table, with the curved part at the top.
The length of the loop will be the length of the plaited part of the belt.
Secure the end onto the table with sticky tape and pass the working end *under* the secured end.

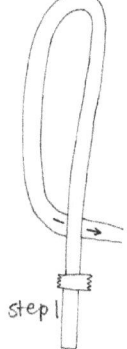

2. Bring the working end through the top part of the loop, passing it under and then over. Secure it just above the loop.

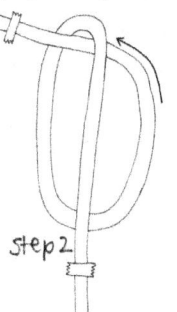

3. Push the right half of the original loop towards the left half.

4. Move the left portion of the original loop *over* the right.

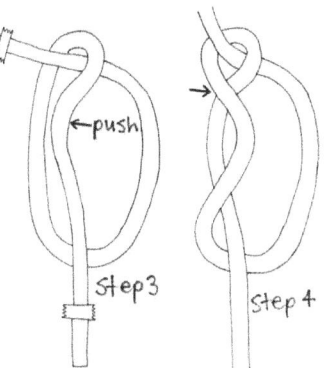

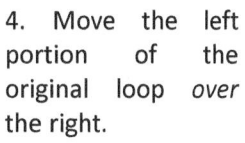

5. Bring the cord on the right *over* the one you moved in Step 4. Can you see what's happening? You're now beginning a regular three cord plait.
It's easier to lift it off the table and hold now as you plait, so undo the sticky tape at both ends.
Keep the plait nice and tight as you make it.

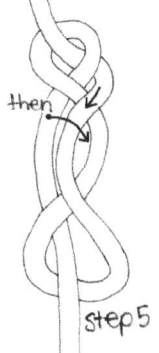

You'll find a sort of reversed plait will happen below the area you're working on that you'll need to undo as you're going along. Pull out the end you secured in Step 1, then straighten out the rest of the loop.

6. Continue on plaiting until you've reached almost the end of the loop. The bottom end needs to be either on the left or the right when you stop.
Insert the end into the loop from the top.
If you need to tighten the plait to remove any slack, do it gradually and work the loose parts through.

Belt plaited from one strip

Many years ago my dad's cousin plaited him a belt from a single strip of leather. At the time it mystified and intrigued us, but later when I actually tried making one it was laughably simple.

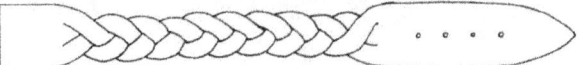

You'll need a long strip with two parallel slits cut along the length. Leave enough at the ends for the buckle and tongue. You'll lose about a quarter of the length when it's plaited, so if the plaited part will be 75cm (30") long, cut the slits about 100cm (40"). Since the plait is only made from three strands it won't be a very wide belt. Choose a thick, firm material such as leather or heavy felt.

With the right side facing up, tape the top end to the table and begin plaiting. Ensure the strands don't twist over—keep them flat. Every few plaits, flip the bottom of the strip through; study it to see which way it wants to go. When you reach the end of the plait, plait as far as you can absolutely go, then distribute any looseness back through the part you've already plaited. Add a buckle of your choice.

Bias cut

Bias refers to a diagonal direction in the fabric. True bias is a 45 degree angle to the lengthwise grain of the fabric. Woven fabric has the greatest amount of stretch along the true bias.

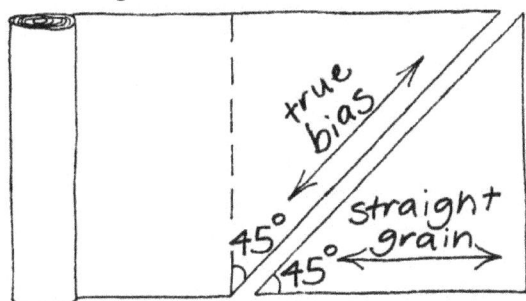

When we say something is cut on the bias, it means that it has a grainline that's 45 degrees to the usual vertical grainline. Bias here always refers to the true bias. Clothing cut on the bias is also sometimes called clothing "cut on the cross" and occasionally "diamond cut" (usually for lingerie).

✂ Note that bias cut clothes generally (but not always) take more fabric, meaning there's more waste.

✂ Bias cut clothing performs in a different way to clothing cut on the straight grain. Clothing cut on the bias falls in smooth drapes and moulds to the figure. It's often used for slinky, figure-skimming dresses in crêpe or satin. The dresses look limp and shapeless until they're put on.

✂ Bias cut is also used to create a chevron or diagonal effect with stripes or checks.

 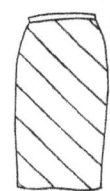 

Cutting and fitting

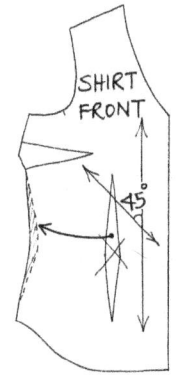

✂ To cut clothing on the bias, draw in a new grain line at 45 degrees to the existing vertical one.
Elimate any waist darts and shape the sides in if necessary. Leave any bust darts.

✂ Whole pattern pieces need to be made for pieces that are cut on the centre front or back fold, so the bias grain line runs across the whole piece. It's easier to position these patterns on the fabric.

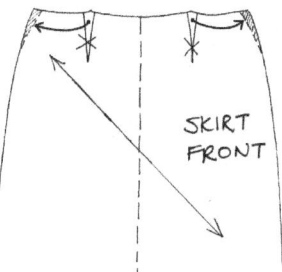

✂ Note that if the garment isn't cut on the true bias, it will hang unevenly on each side and will twist around the body.

✂ Bias cut dresses and skirts in stripes or checks need the back and the front to be the same size, otherwise the stripes won't match at the sides. (Often the front is made bigger than the back so the side seams aren't visible front-on. The amount is anywhere up to 2.5cm (1") on each side, but 1cm (⅜") to 1.2cm (½") is usual.) Equalize the side seams by taking off the front and adding to the back. The side seams should be the same *shape* from the waist down—lay the centre fronts and backs together to see.

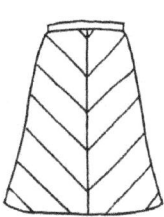

✂ If a pattern piece is very narrow, such as a bias placket or button stand, you can use a transparent ruler with 45 degree markings to help accurately position the piece on the fabric, rather than try to measure the tiny grain line.

✂ The fabric may be too narrow to accommodate bias cut pattern pieces. You can sometimes see this in vintage clothes, when narrow width fabrics were common.

Often there's a join at the side of a skirt, made on the straight grain of the fabric.

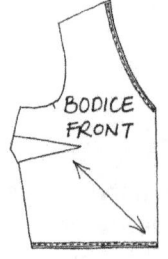

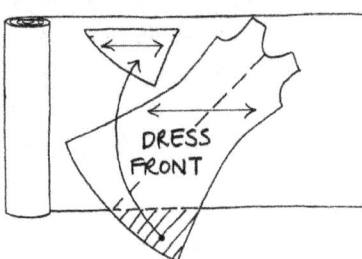

✂ Sections of the garment which are cut on the bias for effect, such as yokes, cuffs and collars on shirts, need light fusing behind to stabilize them. The fusing is cut on the straight grain. This ensures the bias section doesn't stretch compared to the straight section.

✂ Shirts cut entirely on the bias can be cut so the stripes match diagonally across the front (left picture), or cut paired as a mirror image (right picture).

If the fronts are cut as a mirror image, you'll need a separate button stand because the stripes won't match due to the overlap.

✂ Collars cut on the bias won't look the same on both sides—you'll need a centre back seam to give the same look left and right.

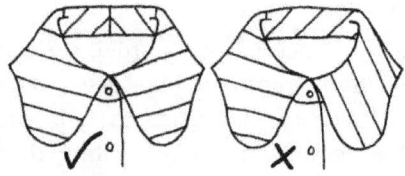

✂ Necklines and other areas such as waists and shoulders need to be taped for support so they don't stretch. You can use 6mm (¼") cotton tape, selvedge cut from the fabric if it's smooth and firm or selvedge cut from silk organza.

✂ Bias cut garments get narrower as the fabric drops.

Armholes, necklines, waistlines and crotches all get longer.

The shoulders may need lifting to raise the neck, bust darts and underarm. The garment's waistline may have dropped down to the high hip and will need letting out.

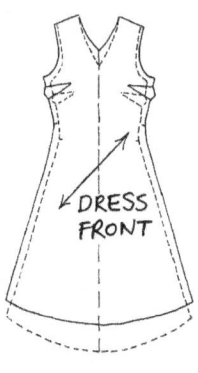

Cut the garment with big side seams in case you have to let out the sides to compensate for the garment becoming narrower.

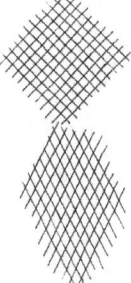

✂ The finer and floppier the fabric, the more it will drop and the narrower it will become. The looser the weave the more it will drop, too.

✂ If the garment is too tight, or if the fabric has dropped and is now too narrow, diagonal drag lines will appear. Undo the side seams and allow the fabric to hang naturally, then re-pin new side seams.

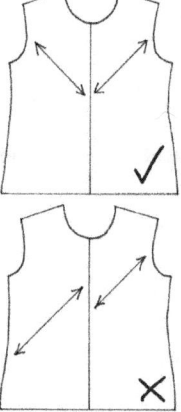

✂ Clothes occasionally need adjusting on one side only, as the lengthwise and crosswise weaves of the fabric perform differently on the bias, causing one side of the garment to hang differently from the other. If there's a central seam, the left and right pattern pieces should be placed so the lengthwise grain is in the same position on both sides (so it's mirrored—top picture).

✂ French seams on the bias can be tricky to do, but not impossible.

I once helped make a georgette bias cut dress with French seams at the side. The seam was perfect on the model when it was sewn as a regular seam, but when a French seam was made it went wavy. We tried pressing it, stretching it, hanging it, re-sewing it—nothing worked.

In the end, we took a measurement of the seam length on the model. The machinist sewed a row of ease stitch and eased the French seam up to the measurement when she sewed it.

✂ Madeline Vionnet, master of the bias cut, brilliantly designed her bias cut garments so that all the seams were sewn on the straight grain.

Zips

Zips in slinky bias cut dresses usually end up wavy, no matter how carefully they're put in.

If the neck opening is big enough, you might be able to eliminate the zip and just pull the dress on over your head, since the bias will stretch.

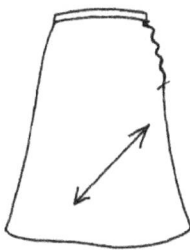

Zips in slinky bias cut skirts usually end up wavy too.

You can eliminate the zip and have narrow elastic at the waist, turning it into a pull-on skirt. Wool and firmer fabrics should be fine, though.

You could also choose a skirt style that has a basque or yoke at the waist, and cut the basque on the straight grain.

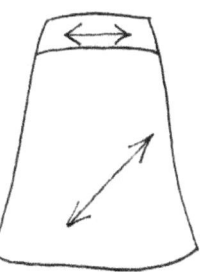

Hems

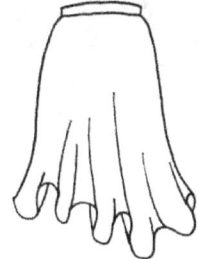

Clothes need to hang for a few days at least to allow the fabric to drop before the hem is levelled. The part of the garment most on the bias will drop the most, and the finer the fabric the more it will drop.

Sometimes individual garment pieces are hung to allow them to drop before they're sewn together, for example skirt panels.

You can achieve frilly lettuce leaf hems by stretching the bias edge as it is hemmed, either roll-hemmed on an overlocker or regular straight stitch machine.

The tighter the fabric is stretched, the frillier the hem.

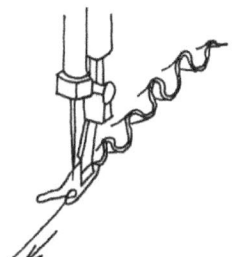

Bias strips

Bias strips are narrow strips of fabric cut at 45 degrees to the straight edge of the fabric. Bias strips have lots of uses: bias binding, piping cord, rouleau button loops and fastenings, spaghetti straps on lingerie and sundresses and as narrow facings around hems, armholes and necklines.

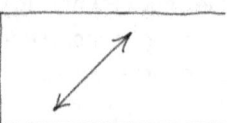

Cutting bias strips

It's important to firstly straighten the cut end of the fabric so it's at 90 degrees to the selvedges. There are three ways to do this:

1. If the fabric is striped or checked, simply **cut along a line**.

2. **Tear** the cut edge to make it straight, by making a snip in one selvedge, grasping both sides of the snip firmly, and ripping across to the opposite selvedge.
If it doesn't look like it's going to tear, don't force it.
Tearing *quickly* is easier and gives better results than tearing slowly, so rip quick.
If the tear runs off to nothing before you reach the opposite selvedge, cut a new snip farther from the end and try again.

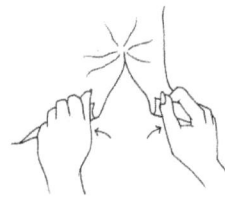

3. If you can't tear it, **pull on a crosswise thread** and cut along the line it makes. Snip the selvedge, find a crosswise grain thread and gently pull it. Ease the fabric along the thread, then cut along the pulled thread.
If the line breaks before you reach the opposite selvedge, cut up to the break, then find a new thread to pull.

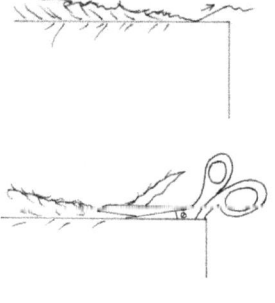

Square up the fabric along the corner of the table.

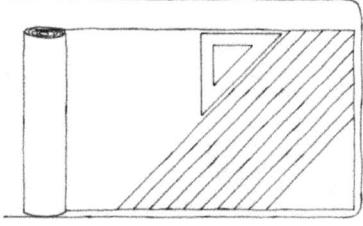

Use an L-square with 45 degrees marked on it to draw the first line, then mark in parallel lines the width of your strips.

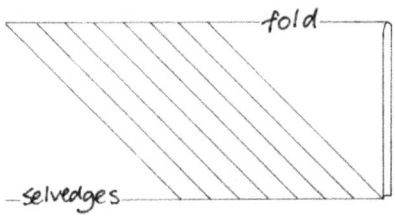

You may prefer to cut bias strips on double folded fabric, rather than a single layer. Obviously the strips will only be half the length but if this is all you need it will be much quicker since you're cutting two out at once.

✂ About 2.5cm-3cm (1"-1¼") is the usual **width** for bias strips, used for making piping, rouleau loops and so on. Note that floppy fabric becomes narrower when it's cut on the bias, so allow extra width for this—maybe 6mm (¼") more.

✂ Ensure the strips are cut at *exactly* 45 degrees to the selvedge, on the true bias, otherwise they'll twist when they're sewn. The result will be rouleau and spaghetti straps with the seam twisting around their circumference, and piping will have a ropey appearance.

✂ On unstable fabrics likely to move and slip on the table, lay some calico under it to stop it moving.

✂ If you have a rotary cutter, mat and a long ruler (preferably the same width as the strips), you can use the rotary cutter to cut the strips instead of using scissors.

✂ Save time: if the fabric is stable enough, you can cut bias strips several layers at a time. Mark, say, the first four strips, cut along the fifth line, then lay this on top of the unmarked fabric and cut out the strips two thicknesses at a time (or even three or four by repeating the steps).

✂ If you're cutting bias strips along with a garment, position the bias strips early on when planning the cutting layout, because they can be difficult to fit in with other pieces. Pin smaller garment pieces in the triangle shaped areas either side of the bias strips.

If the sewing pattern gives an actual pattern piece for strips cut on the bias, for example to finish a neckline or armholes, you can use a transparent ruler with 45 degree markings to help accurately position the pieces on the fabric rather than trying to align the tiny little grainline on the pattern piece.

✂ Recycling tip: old neckties can be unpicked and cut into bias strips. Use the small lengths for interesting binding and piping. Even ugly neckties can make beautiful trim.

Another cutting method
Some people like to cut out their bias strips "pre-joined" in one long length. I think it's a bit slower but you may prefer it.

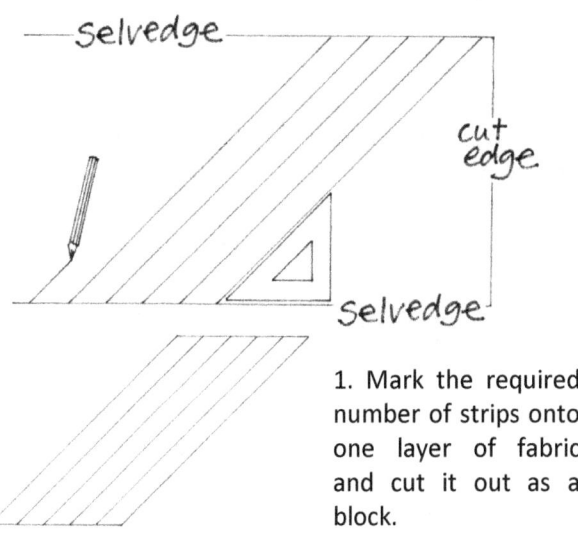

1. Mark the required number of strips onto one layer of fabric and cut it out as a block.

2. Sew the two short ends right sides together, one strip offset. Use a short stitch to help stop the stitching coming undone when you cut it.
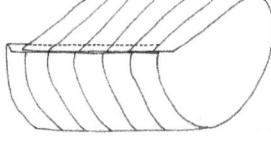
Sew just inside the selvedges, trim the seam back to 6mm (¼") and press it open.

3. Take a pair of scissors and start cutting around and around on the lines until you have one long continuous bias strip.

Joining bias strips
If possible, try to organise enough strips so you don't have to have any joins. If you do need joins, arrange it so they're not in a prominent place on the garment.

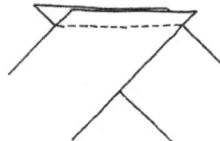
To join strips, cut the ends of the strips so they're on the straight grain. Sew two strips right sides together, taking a 6mm (¼") seam.

Ensure the strips match at the *stitching* line. An incorrect join like this one will not match up when it's opened out.
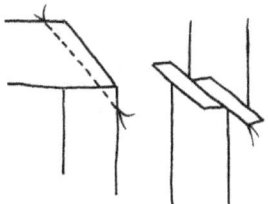

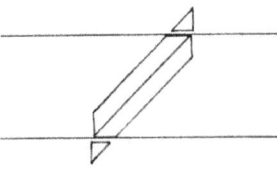
Press the seam open. Trim the corners of the seam allowance.

Another way to join two bias strips is to overlap the ends and stitch diagonally across. Trim the seam back to 6mm (¼") and press open.
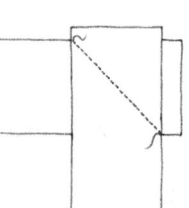

Naturally, match any stripes or checks when you join the strips. You can double-check the match before you sew by pinning *exactly* on the stitching line, then flipping the join open to see what it looks like finished.

Why are bias strips joined diagonally?
If you tried to join strips with an ordinary seam, the seam would stretch when you sewed it because it's cut on the bias.
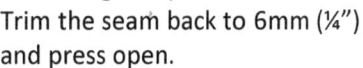

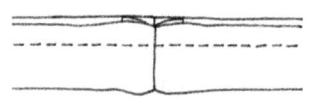
When the strip is folded in half, the seam would create bulk in one spot.

A diagonal seam is less conspicuous, too.

Joining bias strips to a predetermined measurement
Measure the length of the bias strip from edge to edge in the same place, for example the centre. Add seam allowances. Note that the two short ends to be joined will be parallel.
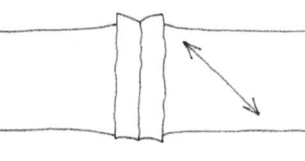

Binding

Introduction 22	Binding around corners 25
Making binding 22	outward corner mitre 25
Applying binding 23	inward corner mitre 25
method 1 visible stitching 23	outward mitre in tape/ribbon ... 25
method 2 no visible stitching 23	inward mitre in tape/ribbon 26
method 3 machine attachment .. 23	Binding a slit 26
Troubleshooting binding 24	Using bias binding as a facing 26
Binding using tape or ribbon 24	curving bias binding facings 27
Binding around curves 24	mitre an outward corner 27
Ends and beginnings of binding 24	mitre an inward corner 27

A binding is a separate strip of fabric that encases the edge of the garment and finishes both sides attractively. The width of the binding should be completely filled with the edge it encases. Binding is frequently used on transparent or sheer fabrics, garments where both sides are seen and on reversible and unlined garments.
Generally, binding is not applied until the garment is almost finished. When sewn to the garment, most bindings are 6mm-12mm (¼"-½") wide finished, but can be as narrow as 3mm (⅛") or as wide as 3cm (1¼"), or even wider.

Bindings can be single folded or double folded.

Single folded binding is made with a single, open strip of fabric and is a good choice for heavy or bulky fabrics and softer edges.

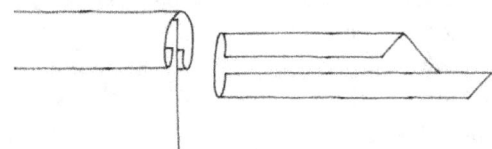

Ready-made bias binding is a single folded binding. It's a narrow bias strip with both long edges pressed under. It comes in many colours, in cotton, satin, printed or plaid fabric, and in several widths. The most common width is 12mm (½") (that's 6mm (¼") when applied). The next most common is 24mm (1") (which is 12mm (½") when applied)—this is sometimes called hem facing on the packaging.

Double folded binding is made with a double layered folded strip and suits floppy, fine, or hard-to-handle fabrics. It's sometimes called French binding or Paris binding.

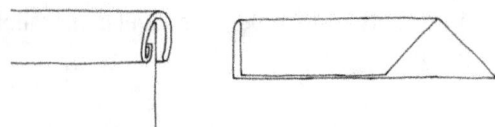

Binding is cut on the true bias (a 45 degree angle to the straight grain) to give it the flexibility to go around curves and shaped edges.
Occasionally, binding is cut on the straight grain when it's being applied to a straight edge only. A good example is binding on the edge of a quilt. Another example might be binding on the straight edge of a short sleeve (although if one area of the garment has binding cut on the bias, then all areas should have it).
It's very important that binding is cut *exactly* on the true bias or *exactly* on the straight grain. If not, the binding will ripple, twist, rope and pucker.

Suitable fabrics for binding are lightweight fabrics, such as thin cotton, satin, georgette, crepe and organza. For heavier edges, thicker fabrics can be used, but it can be difficult to control the bulkiness, especially at the ends and corners.
Important: if using a contrast binding, make sure the colour won't run when the garment is washed.

Making binding
Before you cut the bias strips to make binding, always make a test to see if you've cut the correct width. Unstable or floppy fabrics will get narrower when cut on the bias, so allow extra width for this, maybe 6mm (¼"). See page 20 for cutting bias strips.

Binding

Make **single folded binding** by cutting a bias strip twice as wide as the finished width plus 1.2cm (½"). You can iron the folds into place but I rarely do; I leave it as a flat strip and fold it when I sew it. If you need to press the folds in place, press under each edge 6mm (¼").

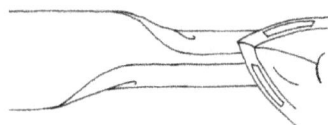

Speed things up by using a bias tape maker tool. Haberdashery and quilting shops sell them.

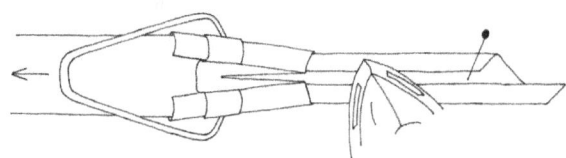

You'll need a different size bias tape maker for every size width. The instructions tell you how wide to cut the bias strip. Pull the strip through the bias tape maker and secure it to the ironing board with a pin. Then, slide the tape maker along while ironing the folded tape.

You can also buy a machine to make single folded bias binding, for example the Simplicity Bias Tape Maker Machine. The touch of a button transforms pre-cut and joined bias strips into pressed and folded bias binding. Changing accessories varies the binding width.

Make **double folded binding** by cutting a bias strip six times the required finished width. Fold or iron it in half lengthways before using, with the right sides facing out.

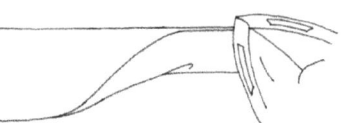

Applying binding

The method you decide to use will depend on what you want the binding to look like and how your fabric behaves. Try a sample first if you aren't sure.

Method 1—visible stitching along edge

1. For **single binding**, place the *right* side of the binding onto the *wrong* side of the fabric. Stitch along the crease.

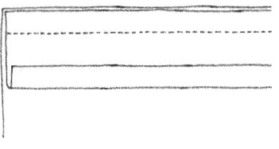

For **double binding**, place the binding on the *wrong* side of the fabric, raw edges together, and stitch.

2. Bring the binding over to the right side and stitch, just covering the first line of stitching.
Hold the fabric firmly towards you and let the binding "sit easy" on top. With practise, both sides of the binding will look the same.

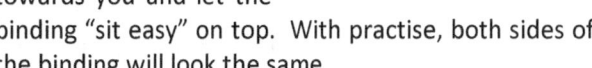

Method 2—no visible stitching

1. Place the *right* side of the binding onto the *right* side of the fabric. Stitch.
For **single folded binding**, stitch along the crease.

For **double folded**, stitch through both layers.

2. Bring the binding over to the *wrong* side and either: Sew by hand, using hidden slip stitch (page 149). Slip the stitches through the fold in the bias binding.

OR

Sew by machine by pinning it first on the right side through all layers, then stitching-in-the-ditch (see page 291) on the right side.
That is, stitching right in the groove between the binding and the fabric.
On the wrong side it should look edgestitched.

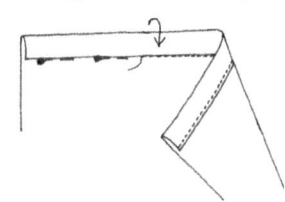

Method 3—machine attachment

Some sewing machines have an attachment that sews on binding in one operation. The binding feeds in around a cone on one side and the fabric feeds in through the centre. It can be fiddly to get started but it's worth it if you have lots of binding to sew. You may need to adjust the needle position to sew the binding in the right spot.

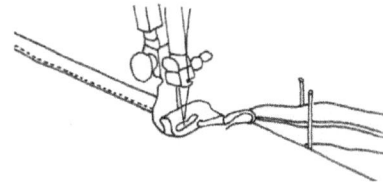

Note that it's impossible to bind around corners using this attachment. Either choose a style with no corners to bind or change the corners to curves.

Troubleshooting binding

How do I stop the bias binding from "roping" as I stitch?

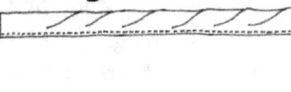

✂ Are you sure the binding is cut on the true bias? Bias strips cut slightly off-grain will twist when you apply them.

✂ For single binding, it might help to iron the binding in half before you start sewing. For double binding, iron it into place after the first row of stitching.

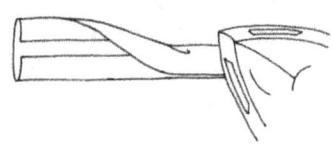

✂ Ease off the pressure on the presser foot if the fabric is thick. There should be a knob to adjust the pressure on the top of the machine—consult your manual.

✂ Try using a walking foot, if you have one.

✂ Understanding how the machine feeds fabric through will help you with your technique. As a sewing machine sews, the presser foot pushes the top layer of fabric forward and the feed dogs feed the underneath layer backwards.

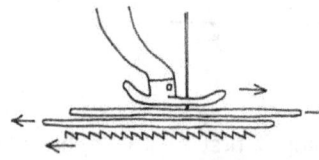

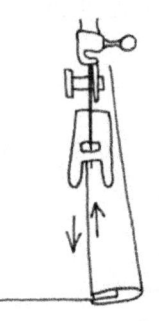

Therefore, if you let a machine just sew naturally, the top layer will be longer by the time you get to the end. When applying binding, this is what causes the roping effect.

To counteract this, hold the underneath layer (the garment) firmly with your left hand, pulling it forward, and let the bias binding "sit easy" on top with your right hand.

Binding using tape or ribbon

Tape and ribbon have no raw edges. They can be made of cotton or synthetic fibres.

Herringbone twill tape is used to bind edges of canvas and is often seen on backpacks and camping gear. It's very strong.

Grosgrain ribbon is sometimes used to bind waists of skirts or trousers instead of a using a waistband or facing. It has a ribbed appearance.

The key to a smooth application is to iron the tape in half longways first.

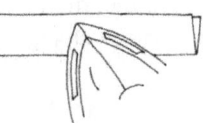

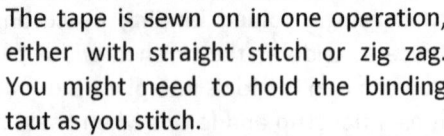

The tape is sewn on in one operation, either with straight stitch or zig zag. You might need to hold the binding taut as you stitch.

You may be able to sew it on using a binding attachment on your sewing machine as pictured on page 23.

Binding around curves

✂ Curves can be inward curves or outward curves. Wide curves will bind more successfully than tight curves. The sharper the curve, the trickier it is to get the binding to lie flat. Front necklines and underarm curves are two places where extra care is needed as you apply binding.

✂ Binding must always be cut on the bias to give it flexibility around the curves. Tape or ribbon is not particularly suited to curves because it's not bias cut, but may work for very wide curves.

✂ When binding is applied to a curve, the *stitched edge* and the *folded edge* will be slightly different lengths:

For **inward curves**, such as necklines and underarms, stretch the binding slightly as you sew the first line of stitching.

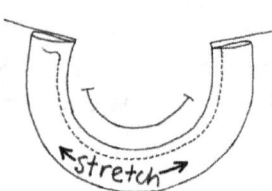

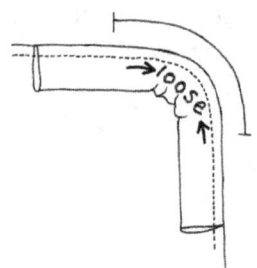

For **outward curves**, apply the binding a little looser around the corner.

Use a steam iron to shrink the binding into shape after sewing.

✂ Pre-shaping the binding into a curve *before* you sew it will help give better results. Pin the folded binding to your ironing board in the curve you want and use a steam iron to shrink out the excess fullness. Leave the binding to dry. It works best on non-synthetics.

Ends and beginnings of binding

To finish binding at the ends, wrap the binding around the end, as shown, and stitch through all the layers as you sew the binding on.

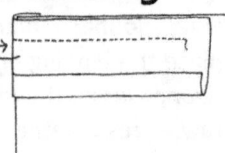

Binding **25**

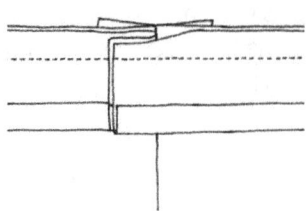

Where beginnings and ends meet, overlap the two ends, but fold back the underneath one so a folded edge is visible when the binding is flipped up.

Put the join in line with a seam and in an inconspicuous place, such as under the arm.

Binding around corners

My advice is to try and avoid binding around corners. Either choose a pattern with no corners to bind, or adapt the pattern and turn the corners into curves.

If you cannot avoid a corner, the neatest way is to make a mitre. Mitred corners can be made at outward or inward corners.

The method is the same for single or double folded binding, applied in either way described on page 23. For crisp, well-defined mitres, it's essential to press the binding at each stage.

Mitre an outward corner

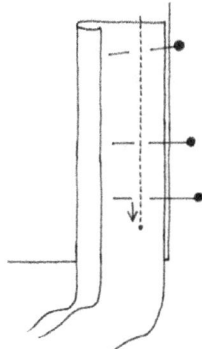

1. Sew the binding along the edge until you reach the *exact* point where the seam lines cross. Back stitch and lift the needle from the fabric.

2. Diagonally fold the binding away from the garment.

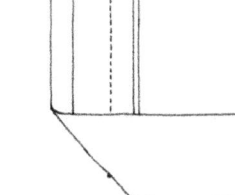

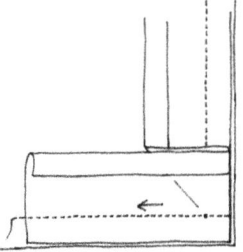

3. Fold the binding straight back towards the garment so the fold is aligned with the binding's raw edge (*not* the previous stitching line). Stitch along the binding.

4. Fold the binding to the other side, at the same time forming a mitre on the corner of the garment.

This is easiest to do in two stages—press one side first, then the adjacent side. Sew the finished mitre fold in place by hand if necessary.

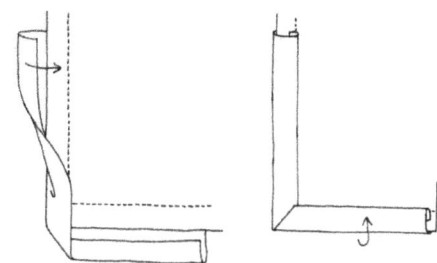

Mitre an inward corner

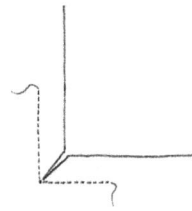

1. Reinforce the inner corner with small stitches on the stitching line. Carefully clip into the corner but not through the stitching.

2. Spread the slashed corner and sew the binding on. Keep the binding stitching line aligned with the garment seam line.

Sew from the garment side to ensure the reinforcing stitches are covered.

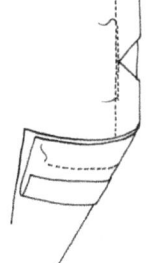

3. Press the mitre in place, keeping the edges at right angles to each other. Put a pin in to hold the mitre in place.

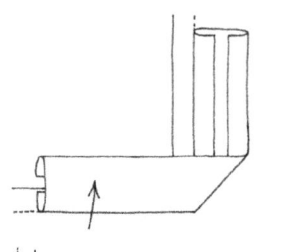
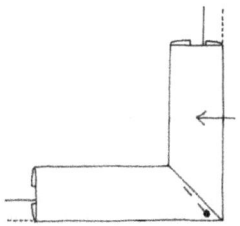

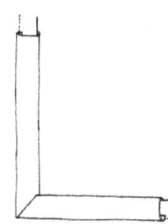

4. Turn the binding down over the seam allowance, forming a mitre on the other side. Press. You'll need to hand stitch the mitre to hold it securely in place.

Mitre an outward corner in tape or ribbon

1. Stitch the binding along one edge of the garment, right to the edge.

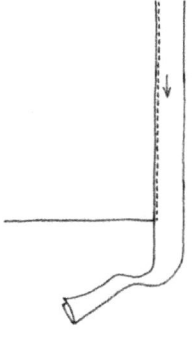

2. Press the mitre into the corner, forming a mitre on both sides.

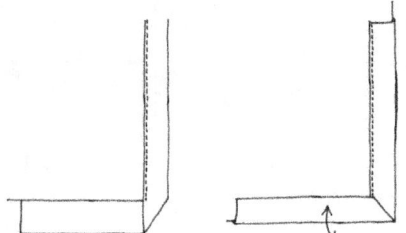

3. Resume stitching.
Handsew the mitred corner if necessary.

Mitre an inward corner in tape or ribbon

1. Reinforce the inner corner with small stitches on the stitching line. Carefully clip to the corner but not through the stitching.

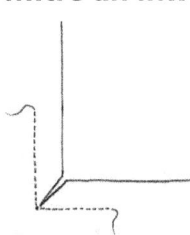

2. Sew the folded binding on exactly to the corner.

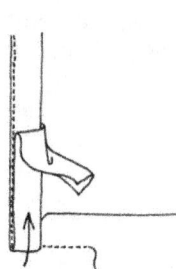

3. Press the mitre into the corner by folding the binding straight back on itself.

4. Fold the binding diagonally and press.

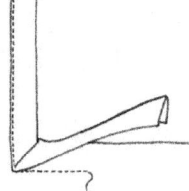

5. Position the binding over the raw edge of the adjacent side of the corner and continue sewing.
You'll need to handsew the mitre in place to keep it secure.

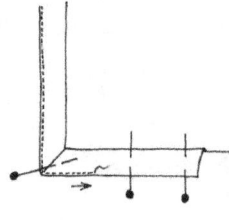

Binding a slit

This is the same method used to make continuous plackets for shirt cuffs.

1. Cut the slit open. Position the binding under the slit with the right sides of both facing up.

Sew the first line of stitching as shown.
Keep the seam allowance on the binding constant, but position the slit so you just catch the point.

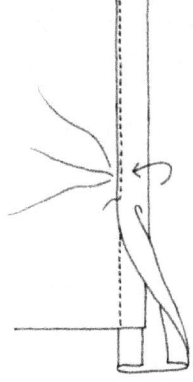

2. Press the seam towards the binding.
Fold the binding over and sew the second line of stitching on the right side.

3. Fold the bound slit right sides together and sew across the corner. Don't sew across the previous stitching, otherwise a pleat will form at the bottom of the V.

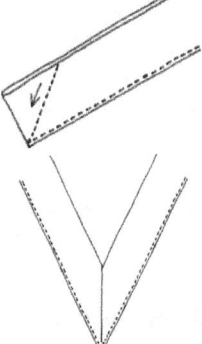

Using bias binding as a facing

Bias binding, either single or double folded, can be used as a facing and is narrower and less conspicuous than regular facings. The binding is shaped, rather than cut, to duplicate the edge.
Narrow 12mm (½") bias binding is generally used, because the wider the binding, the more difficult it is to shape it into a curve. If the edge to be faced is straight, for example a hem, then a wider binding could be used. A 6mm (¼") seam allowance on the garment edge is required.

1. Place the *right* side of the bias binding onto the *right* side of the garment.
If using **single binding** (bias binding), stitch in the crease.

For **double binding**, sew through both layers.

2. Flip the binding up and press the seam towards the binding (single binding shown).

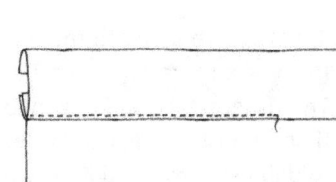

Understitch the binding next to the seam, through all the layers, as you would with a regular facing. This helps the binding stay out of sight inside the garment.

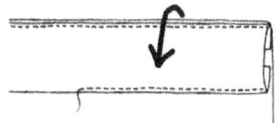

3. Press the binding to the inside and sew in place (single binding shown). If you don't want the stitching to show, sew by hand using hidden slip stitch, however, machine stitching is quicker, more secure, less likely to catch on things and you can make a feature of the stitching.

Curving bias binding facings

If the faced area is curved, such as a front neckline, underarm or pocket edge, it's very helpful to pre-shape the binding into a curve before you sew it. That way you know it's going to lie flat.

Pin the binding to your ironing board in a curve that matches the shape of the garment edge. Use a steam iron to shrink out the excess fullness, leave the binding to dry, then sew the binding to the garment.

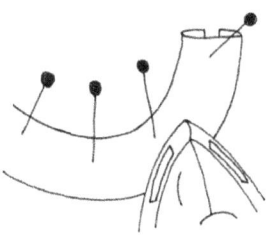

Outward mitre faced in bias binding

1. Locate where the corner will be on the binding and sew a short line of stitching along the stitching line. A factory machinist would skip this step and just snip in at Step 2 as she sewed the corner.

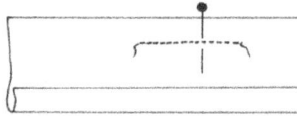

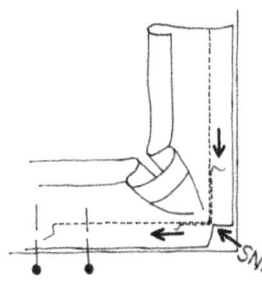

2. Stitch the bias facing along the edge, making a tiny snip in the facing at the corner to make it sit flat. Pivot at the corner and sew the facing along the adjacent edge.

3. Press the facing so it's at a right angle to itself, forming a 45 degree fold in the centre. This crease line will be your guide for stitching.

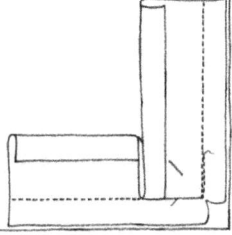

4. Fold the garment right sides together, with the edges of the facing lying on top of one another.
Stitch on the diagonal press line. You may need to use a zipper foot to get close enough.

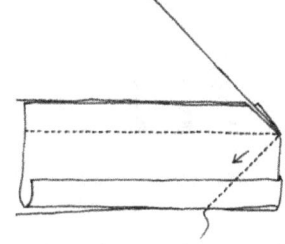

5. Trim the seam back to 6mm (¼") and press the seam allowance open.

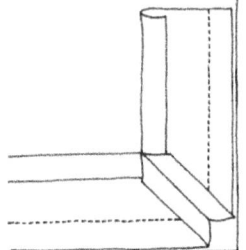

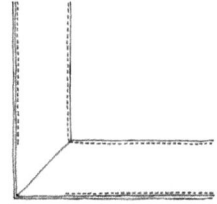

6. Turn the facing to the wrong side of the garment and press. You won't be able to understitch right into the corner—just go as far as you can from each side.

Inward mitre faced in bias binding

1. Pin the facing in place along one edge. At the corner, diagonally fold the facing back and press.

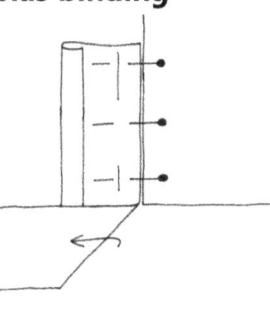

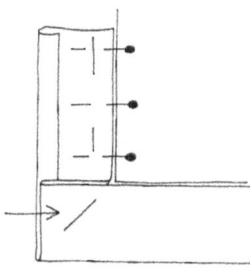

2. Press the facing back towards the corner, aligning the edge of the facing with the edge of the adjacent side.

3. Take the pins out and remove the facing. With the facing right sides together, stitch along the diagonal press line.

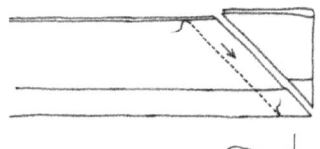

4. Trim the seam back to 6mm (¼") and press open.

5. Sew the facing to the edge, snipping to the corner of the stitching as shown.

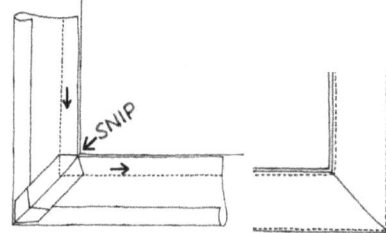

Buttons and buttonholes

Button types 28	Marking button positions 33
To sew on a 2 or 4 hole button 28	Handmade buttonholes 34
to sew by machine 29	Keyhole buttonholes 35
How to sew on a shank button 29	by hand 35
Reinforcement buttons 29	by machine 35
Buttonholes, introduction 30	Slit buttonholes 36
Interfacing behind buttonholes 30	Bound buttonholes 36
Determine the buttonhole length 30	attaching the facing 37
Mark the buttonhole position 30	Buttons and loops 38
in waistbands and cuffs 31	adjusting the pattern 38
in jackets or blouses 31	fabric rouleau loops 38
on shirts 32	elastic loops 39
Cutting a buttonhole 32	handmade thread loops 40
Troubleshooting buttonholes 32	

Q: Which is sewn first, the buttons or the buttonholes? A: The buttonholes are made first then the button positions are determined from them. In clothing factories, the button and buttonhole positions are marked on the garment using templates made from strips of cardboard, so either the buttons *or* the buttonholes can be sewn first.

Button types
Buttons can be made from plastic, metal, glass, wood, horn or bone. There are two main types of buttons:

  **Sew-through buttons** are flat with two or four stitching holes.

Four hole buttons can be sewn on in interesting ways.

 **Shank buttons** have a protrusion with a hole in it, or a metal loop making a shank.

Shank buttons can be covered with your own fabric using a do-it-yourself kit or ordered from button or fabric shops. Covered buttons come in a range of sizes and shapes, for example flat or high-domed.

Another style of shank button is a rivet button, used for jeans, denim jackets, overalls and work clothes.

These aren't sewn on. They come in two separate parts: a button and a pin. The pin is pushed through the fabric and hammered onto the button (button side down). In factories a machine is used.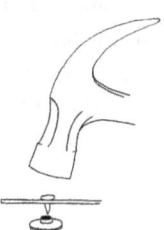

How to sew on a 2 or 4 hole button
Flat buttons require a thread shank to allow for the thickness of the fabric around it in the buttonhole.
The shank looks like a stem between the button and the fabric and is made by winding thread around the stitches after the button is sewn on. A shank also neatens up the stitching on the top of the button—it pulls the stitches to a uniform tightness.
Purely decorative buttons (that won't go through a buttonhole) do not require a shank and can be stitched flat against the fabric.

Buttons and buttonholes

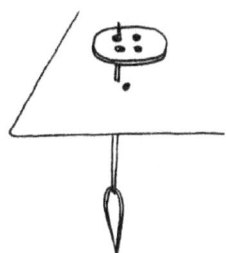

1. Use a hand sewing needle that will fit through the holes on your button. Thread a needle with four threads (see page 145) and knot the end. Centre the button over the placement dot and bring the needle up from the wrong side. Stitch up through one hole in the button and down through the other, checking after each stitch that your thread isn't tangled up.

2. *At the same time*, allow space between the button and fabric to make the thread shank:

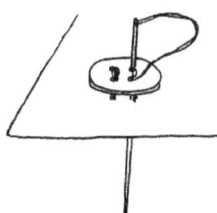

Sew the button on with one stitch through each set of holes. Lift the button away from the fabric the distance of desired shank, say, 3mm (⅛"), then continue sewing the button on loosely.

How many times do you need to sew through the holes? Enough to sew the button on securely. Sewing with four threads on the needle, I would sew about three or four times through a two hole button, or two or three times each through a four hole button.

3. When you're ready to make the shank, bring the needle down through one of the buttons holes so it's between the button and fabric. Wind the thread firmly around the stitches to make a shank (about two or three times), then secure on the wrong side.

Sewing buttons on by machine

Some sewing machines have provision for sewing two or four hole buttons on—check your instruction book.
A zig zag stitch is used, the width of the space between the holes on the button.
A four hole button might have to be sewn on in two steps, for each pair of holes.
Some machines require a button foot for sewing on buttons; other machines don't need a special foot.

How to sew on a shank button

The direction of the shank needs to sit parallel with the buttonhole.

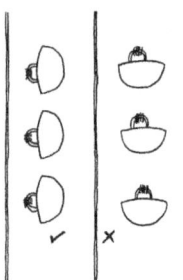

For shank buttons fastened by loops instead of buttonholes, the shank should run vertically up and down the garment, rather than side to side. Otherwise the buttons tend to flop downwards.

1. Use a hand sewing needle that will fit through the hole on your button. Thread it with four threads (see page 145) and knot the end. Centre the button over the placement dot and bring the needle up from the wrong side.

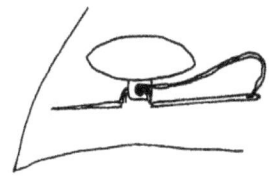

2. Sew the button in place by stitching through the eye of the shank and making a small stitch in the fabric. On bulky fabrics you'll need to stab the needle in and out.

3. Take about three or four stitches, checking after each that your thread isn't tangled up. Finish by securing with a knot on the wrong side.

Making an additional thread shank:
If the button has a short shank and/or the fabric is very bulky, the shank might not be high enough to clear the thickness of the buttonhole, so an additional thread shank will be necessary.
Make this by sewing on the button loosely and winding the thread around the stitches below the button's shank.
When I sew shank buttons on, I always make a thread shank as well, because I think it looks neater.

Reinforcement buttons

Reinforcement buttons are used on heavy fabrics, for example in coats, and where  the button will be under strain. The reinforcement button is sewn underneath and stops the top button from tearing through the fabric.
The top button can be a shank or hole button but the reinforcement button is always a plain flat hole one, with the same number of holes as the top button. The two buttons are sewn on in the same operation.
Occasionally a small circle of felt or fabric is used instead of a button (possibly on fine fabrics, and sometimes on mattresses and quilts).

1. Position the reinforcing button directly under the top button and sew both on at the same time.

2. Make the thread shank on the top button only.

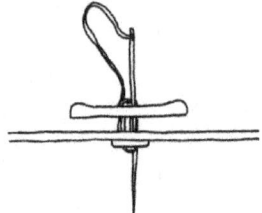

Buttonholes

The most common buttonhole is made by machine. It has parallel rows of close ziz zag and a straight bar of wide zig zag at each end. The slit for the button is cut open after the buttonhole is made.

Most modern sewing machines have a built-in buttonhole stitch. It's usually a four or five step process.

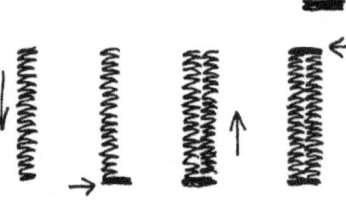

Some sewing machines have a buttonhole attachment that clamps to the presser foot. The button sits in a holder behind the foot and the buttonhole is made in a rectangular frame in front of the foot.

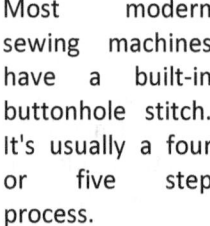

If a buttonhole is being made on thick fabric, for example a jacket, a more substantial buttonhole may be needed. A twice-stitched buttonhole may be the answer. Experiment to see whether you need to cut the slit between making the two buttonholes, or at the end.

If your sewing machine produces second-rate buttonholes with sparse stitching, stitching the buttonhole twice over may be the solution.

Interfacing behind buttonholes

If there isn't sufficient thickness of fabric, for example only one or two layers, or your fabric is very fine or stretchy, your buttonhole will scrunch up or stretch when you sew it. Try making one to check first.

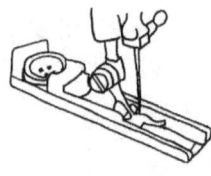

To give stability, apply a piece of interfacing behind the buttonhole position.

Instead of interfacing, I sometimes place a matching piece of firm fabric under the buttonhole position and trim the excess away afterwards. I do this for buttonholes in hoodie top hoods, draw cord buttonholes in swimming trunks and other places where the buttonhole is through one layer of stretch fabric.

Determine the buttonhole length

For **flat buttons**, measure the width of the button. This will be the length of the buttonhole excluding the bars at each end. Add 2mm (a scant ⅛") for the total length.

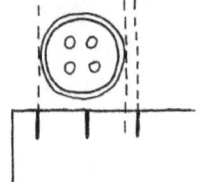

If you're only making one buttonhole, for example on a waistband, you can place the button directly where you want the buttonhole to be and use the button to measure the length.

Thick buttons are measured the same way as flat buttons, but a few extra millimetres are added to allow for the thickness. The amount to add is trial and error—you'll need to make a test buttonhole.

For **high buttons and ball buttons**, measure the circumference by wrapping a strip of paper or tape around it to find the buttonhole length. Once again, add 2mm (a scant ⅛") to allow for the end bars. Make a test buttonhole on a scrap to check it. Make sure the test scrap is the same thickness (fabric and interfacing) as the garment.

Mark the buttonhole position

Mark the position of the buttonhole with three pins, or two dots. If you're using an automatic buttonhole attachment, you'll only need one dot, to mark the beginning.

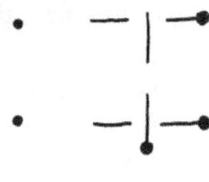

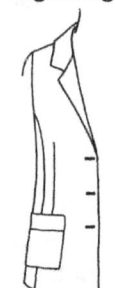

Ladies clothes close right over left (as the garment is worn), therefore the buttonholes will be on the right front. A handy mnemonic to remember this is "women are always right".

Men's clothes close left over right (as the garment is worn), so the buttonholes will be on the left front.

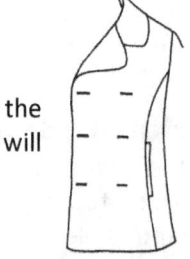

Buttonholes can be positioned horizontally or vertically. Horizontally is the most secure, with the

Buttons and buttonholes 31

direction of the buttonhole in line with the strain. Horizontal buttonholes are made on waistbands, cuffs, collar stands, coats and jackets. Vertical buttonholes are generally used for the front of shirts.

Positioning horizontal buttonholes in waistbands or shirt cuffs

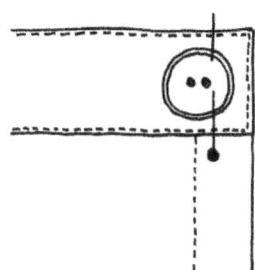

1. Place the button in a pleasing position over the yet-to-be stitched button hole. Put a pin to indicate the start of the buttonhole, usually about 1cm (⅜") from the edge. Note the holes in the button are against the edge of the pin.

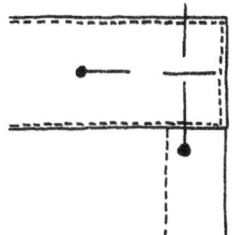

2. Mark the horizontal centre of the buttonhole with another pin.

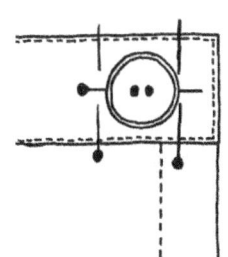

3. Measure the length of the button and mark with a third pin.

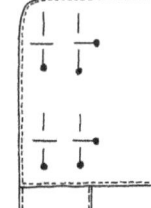

For two buttons, make sure they're the same distance from each edge.

Positioning horizontal buttonholes in jackets or blouses

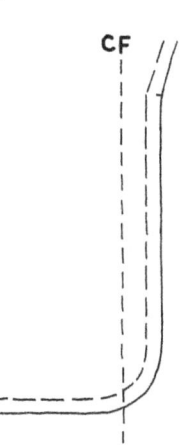

1. Check the pattern and find out where the centre front (CF) line is. Some people like to mark it with a line of hand basting. Usually it's 2cm (¾") from the finished edge for jackets and 1.5cm (⅝") for blouses. This is called the "wrap" (see page 106). It will be more if the garment is designed for big buttons.
A 2cm (¾") wrap will result in a 4cm (1½") double section when the centre front lines are on top of each other when the garment is being worn. A 1.5cm (⅝") wrap will give a 3cm (1¼") wide double section.

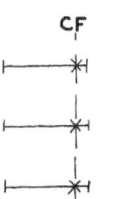

The buttonholes need to start about 3mm (⅛") into the wrap to allow the buttons to sit on the centre front when the garment is done up.

Sit the buttons on the centre front line to see where they'll be when the garment is buttoned up.

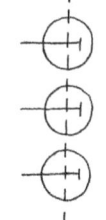

2. Determine where the top buttonhole will be. This may be recorded on the pattern, possibly with a notch, or with a line to indicate the position. Or, you may have a measurement, for example "first button 12cm down from top". Otherwise you could try the garment on and see where it should go, or you could place the button flat on the garment and see where it looks good.

3. Determine the spacing for the rest of the buttons by laying the buttons on the jacket in a pleasing arrangement. Then, measure their average distance apart and use this measurement to mark the buttonhole positions.

Take into account:
✂ Where the last button needs to be, for example on the waist, the same distance from the bottom as the top one is from the top, or above the bulk of the hem.
✂ Any buttons above, below or behind a belt.
✂ If you need a button to be level with a pocket.
✂ If you need a button level with your bust to prevent gaping. Try the garment on and mark the bust line with a pin.

4. Mark the button length of the buttonholes.

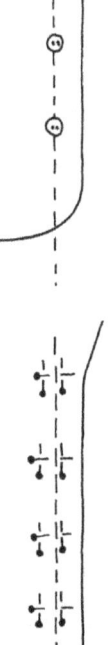

Positioning vertical buttonholes on shirts

The buttonholes on shirts sit vertically in the centre of the button stand. This is also the centre front of the shirt.

The button stand is usually 3cm (1¼") wide but may be 2.5cm (1"), 2cm (¾"), or even 1.5cm (⅝").

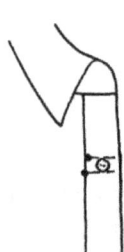

1. Determine the position of the top button. Some people like to have a higher top button to leave undone if they want to, for example 4cm (1½") down from the neck. My own preference is to have the top button 10cm (4") down from the neck and the rest spaced about 8cm (3") apart.

Note that the distance of the top button from the neck doesn't have to be the same distance as the rest of the buttons are apart.

2. Lay out the rest of the buttons in a pleasing arrangement down the front stand, taking into account where the last button needs to be. Measure the average distance between the *centres* of them and use this measurement to mark the positions. You're measuring to the *centre* of each buttonhole— the length of the buttonhole is positioned half either side of this point.

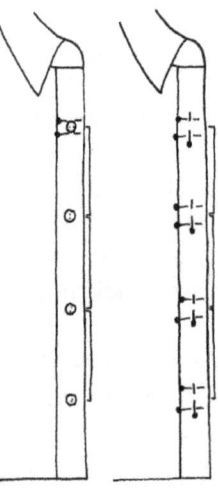

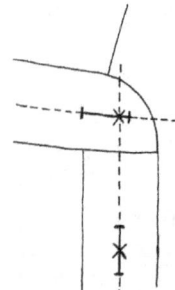

3. The buttonhole on the collar stand is horizontal and runs along the centre of the stand. The button needs to sit in line with the rest of the vertical buttons, so the beginning of the buttonhole needs to be about 3mm (⅛") over towards the edge of the collar stand.

Cutting a buttonhole

There are a few differing views on how buttonholes should be cut—experiment to find your own favourite.

I like to use a pair of very sharp pointy scissors. I fold the buttonhole in half and make a tiny snip, then ease the scissor blades in and cut in each direction to the bar tack.

 Sometimes I use a sharp unpicker to make the first cut, then finish off with scissors.

Some people prefer a tiny pair of sharp embroidery scissors or snippers to cut their buttonholes.
Another option is a block and blade—the wooden block sits under the buttonhole and the blade is used to cut the slit like a chisel. There's a blade pictured on the front cover of this book, at the top.
Whether you use scissors, unpicker or a blade, make sure they're sharp. After cutting, check each buttonhole by sliding a button through it.

✂ When cutting buttonholes in fine fabrics, for example silk satin, cut out all the loose threads from the middle of the buttonhole so they don't catch on the buttons and create pulls in the fabric.

 ✂ On black jackets and coats where the colour of the interfacing shows after the buttonhole is cut, darken the buttonhole slit with a black felt pen.

Troubleshooting buttonholes

If a buttonhole is wrong, it can be unpicked carefully provided you haven't cut the slit. I always prefer to finish making all the other buttonholes, then go back and fix the wrong one.

To unpick a buttonhole, use a very sharp unpicker. Cut the bar ends first, then slide the unpicker under the zig zag sides. Take great care.

Buttonhole too small

✂ Unpick the bar tack at one end and extend the buttonhole.

✂ Is it only a tiny bit too small? Try snipping diagonally into the corners when you cut the slit and see if the button will fit through. 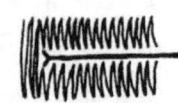 It may only be a matter of a few threads.

✂ If all the buttonholes are too small, see if you can get some smaller buttons.

Buttonhole too big

✂ Is it only a little bit too big? If you haven't cut it yet, don't cut it all the way.

✂ If you've already cut the buttonhole, unpick the bar tack at one end. Handsew the buttonhole at that end until the button fits. Re-sew the bar tack by machine, sneaking it over the top of the two parallel zig zag rows. If the buttonhole is really too big, you might have to do this at both ends.

✂ If all the buttonholes are too big, and you have already cut them, see if you can find some bigger buttons. Alternatively, stitch the buttonholes closed by hand, and sew the buttons over the top. Sew giant press studs underneath, so that the buttons and buttonholes are now decorative.

Buttonhole too close to the edge

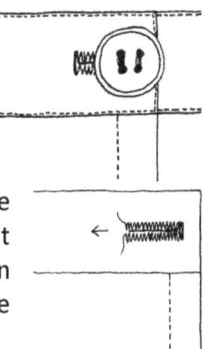

✂ Stitch up (by hand) the end of the buttonhole closest to the edge, then undo the bar tack at the far end and extend the buttonhole by machine. It won't look great, but will look OK when done up. The button will cover the stitched-up part of the buttonhole.

Buttonhole too far away from the edge

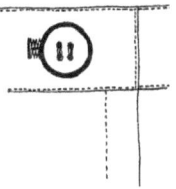

✂ Try the reverse of the above.

✂ You could find a bigger button and extend the buttonhole so it's closer to the edge—do this by undoing the bar tack and re-stitching the end of the button.

✂ if you decide to leave the buttonhole as it is you might need to sew your *button* closer to the edge so the garment isn't too tight when done up.

Zig zag not dense enough on one side of buttonhole

✂ Get your machine serviced and ask if anything can be done. Some machines can be adjusted.

✂ Do a test buttonhole and adjust the stitch length when you do the second side of the buttonhole. Make a note of the stitch length required for each side of the buttonhole and do this manual adjustment when you sew all the buttonholes. It may not work for all machines.

✂ Stitch over your buttonholes twice. I do this anyway for jacket and coat buttonholes, to make a more substantial buttonhole.

Bar ends of buttonhole bunch up

✂ The fabric is too fine or light to support the buttonhole. If you can't stabilize it with interfacing at the back, try using a soluble tearaway behind. You could also try sewing the buttonhole with the fabric in an embroidery hoop to hold it taut, if possible.

Button too big to fit into buttonhole attachment

✂ Make a bound buttonhole or handsewn buttonhole instead.

✂ See if you can override the machine. Some machines have a small arm that comes down and hits a bar on the foot when it's reached the length of the button. For a button that's too big to fit in the buttonhole foot, don't pull the bar down so it will just keep going and going until the buttonhole is the length *you* want it. Then pull the arm down and force it to bump up against something, sew the bar at the end of the buttonhole, turn and do the other side.

✂ Make the button purely decorative—sew the button on the top with a giant press stud underneath, and forget the buttonhole.

✂ Manually make the buttonhole by machine. Find a narrow zig zag for the sides of the buttonhole, and a wide zig zag suitable for the ends (probably the widest one the machine will do). Work out the stitch length so the narrow zig zag is dense enough for a buttonhole and the wide zig zag stitches on the spot. Sew one long side first, then the wide bar at the end, turn the work in the machine and sew the other long side and finish with the another wide bar. This is how I sew buttonholes on my 1964 Singer that has loads of fancy stitches but no buttonholes. With a little practice you can make excellent buttonholes this way and the more you do the better and quicker you'll get.

Crooked buttonhole and you've already cut the slit

✂ Unpick all the stitching, then sew up the slit by hand. Give it a press with an iron then make a new buttonhole over the top.

Marking the button positions from the buttonholes

Vertical buttonholes have the button sitting in the centre of the buttonhole.

Horizontal buttonholes have the button sitting on the side closest to the edge of the garment.

Method 1. Sit the cut buttonhole on top of where the button will go and push a pin through.

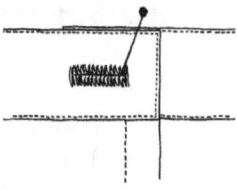

Don't push a pencil through to make a dot, or you'll dirty the buttonhole.

Method 2. Sit the buttonhole on top of where the button will go and peel back the edge. Place a pencil dot or pin to mark the button position.

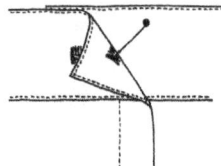

To mark button positions on shirts, blouses and jackets, fold the garment right sides together so the front edges sit on top of each other. Push a pin through the centre of each buttonhole to make a placement dot for the buttonhole.

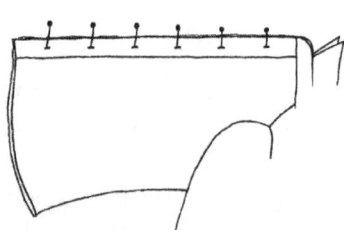

For shirt collar stand buttons, overlap the collar stands the way they'll be worn and mark the button position with a dot.

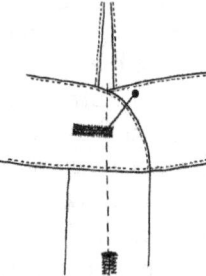

Note that the pin or the pencil dot is a *guide*. You might need to make a slight adjustment to the position using a tape measure or a well-trained eye.

For **horizontal buttonholes on blouse, jackets, and shirt cuffs**, adjust the position so the buttons sit the correct distance away from the edge.

For **vertical buttonholes on shirts**, adjust so the buttons sit in the middle of the button stand.

Handmade buttonholes

I read that Laura Ingalls Wilder once made sixty shirt buttonholes by hand in sixty minutes!

Horizontal handmade buttonholes have a fan-shape worked at the end where the button sits, and a straight bar at the other end.

Vertical handmade buttonholes have either fan shapes at both ends or bars at both ends.

The depth of the stitches is about 2-3mm (⅛" or just under), but can be made deeper for loosely woven fabrics and larger buttonholes.

Unlike machine-made buttonholes, the slit is cut first before the buttonhole is made.

Sew the buttonhole with a single or double strand of matching buttonhole twist (recommended, if you can get some), or else use two or four strands of regular thread that matches the fabric. Don't tie a knot in the end; you'll sew over the tail when you make the buttonhole.

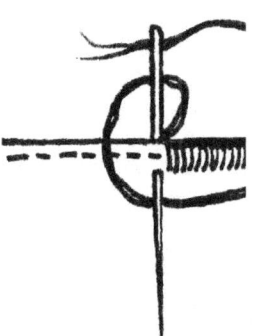

You may like to practise your buttonhole stitch before starting a buttonhole (see page 148). Sew the cut edge of a few layers of fabric together to imitate your garment. Take neat bites of buttonhole stitch over the edge, aiming for consistency and correct size. Experiment with different threads if you need to.

When you're confident, begin a buttonhole:
1. Mark the position with a ruled line the exact length.

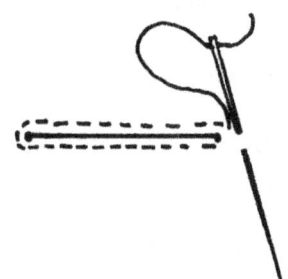

2. Machine or hand stitch running stitch around the edge, then cut the slit. If sewing by hand, use a single or double strand of regular sewing thread for this bit. I sew this by machine, but handsewing will give you more control.

3. **Optional:** overcast the raw edge, if it needs it. You can continue using the thread from the previous step.

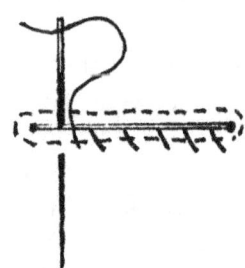

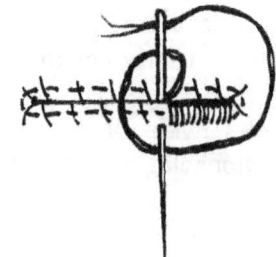

4. Starting furthest from where the button will sit, work buttonhole stitch using the buttonhole thread. Don't knot the thread to start with—leave a short tail and work the

stitches over the top to hide it. Keep the stitches uniform and closely spaced, and don't pull them too tightly. Be careful to pull up both strands of thread evenly with each stitch.

5. Work along the first side, turning the work as the buttonhole progresses.
Work a fan shape at the end, spacing the stitches evenly.

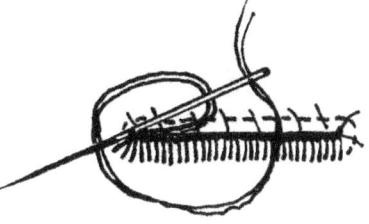

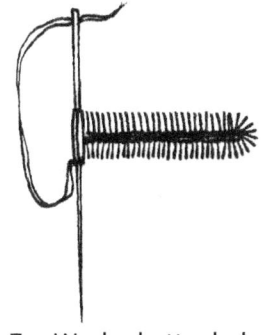

6. Complete the second side. Make a bar tack at the unfinished end by taking long stitches equal to the width of the whole buttonhole.

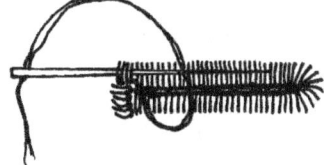

7. Work buttonhole stitches over the bar tack, catching in the fabric underneath. Fasten off the thread at the back.

Keyhole buttonholes

Keyhole buttonholes look like horizontal keyholes, with the stitching fanning out around the tear-drop shaped hole where the button sits. They're a traditional choice for jackets and are smarter and more robust than regular buttonholes.

Handmade keyhole buttonholes

If you have a sewing machine, you'll probably never make buttonholes by hand, however, if you're making a jacket, you might consider making keyhole buttonholes by hand.

These take me about 20 minutes each to make, but when I was beginning they took about 30 minutes. Experienced tailors take about 10 minutes. Practice will give you faster, neater buttonholes.
Use a double strand of matching buttonhole twist (if you can get some in a matching colour), or failing that use four strands of regular thread that matches the fabric. I've also successfully used upholstery thread (two strands).

Thread the needle with enough thread to work the buttonhole in one go. For a 4cm (1½") long buttonhole, try a length that's 65cm (25½").
Keyhole buttonholes are made in the same way as regular handmade buttonholes but with two differences:

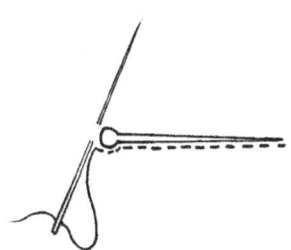

✄ A hole is punched in the end where the button will sit. Use a leather punch to make the hole, about 3mm (⅛") in diameter and work the buttonhole stitches around the hole.

✄ The buttonhole stitches are worked over a cord of some type to give strength and shape. It could be heavy thread, button hole twist, pearl cotton

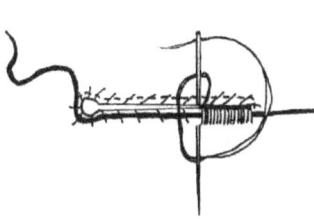

or thin string. The proper cord to use for this is called gimp. Some people like to encase the cord in the overcast stitches if they overcast at the beginning, but I prefer to position it as I sew the buttonhole stitches. To secure the ends of the gimp: at the beginning, after about the first five or six stitches, pull the gimp so that the end lies flush with the first stitch of the buttonhole. At the other end of the buttonhole, when you reach the penultimate stitch, trim the gimp flush, then make one last stitch.

Machine made keyhole buttonholes

✄ You might consider getting your buttonholes made for you by a tailor with a keyhole buttonhole machine.

✄ Some domestic sewing machines come with a facility to make more than one type of buttonhole, and can be programmed to make keyhole buttonholes.

✄ You may also be able to make corded buttonholes on your machine. They're regular buttonholes reinforced with narrow cord under the stitching. The cord sits in a groove under the special foot. Check your instruction manual to see if your machine has this facility. Usually the method is to place the filler cord on the second spool pin of the machine. Pearl cotton or heavy thread make suitable filler cords. Carry the cord through the first thread guide on top of

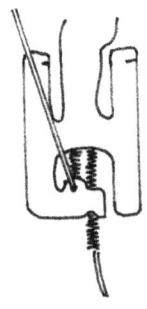

the machine, straight down between the tension discs, into the large thread guide above the needle, then through the eyelet on the special foot. Draw the cord under to the back of the foot. The foot will stitch the buttonhole over the cord.

Slit buttonholes

Slit buttonholes, or in-seam buttonholes, are simply openings in a seam that are part of the garment's design. They're sometimes topstitched as part of the design.

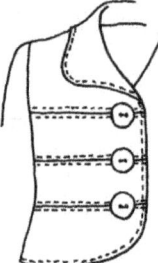

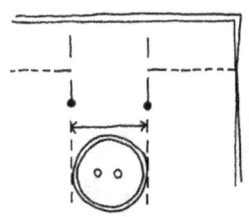

The opening is the same size as the buttonhole. It's important to securely backstitch at each end of the slit.

Sometimes, but not always, the area is stabilized with a patch of interfacing on each side of the seam.

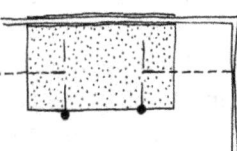

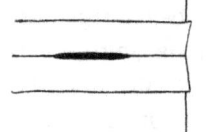

The seam is pressed open.

If there's a facing, the facing has a slit in the same place and the two slits are stitched together.

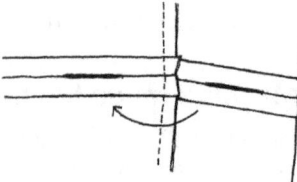

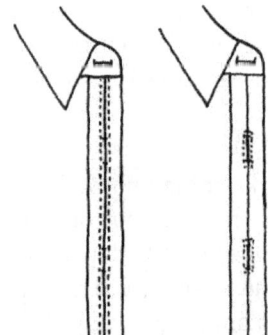

The seam is often topstitched to hold it in place.
It can be topstitched around each buttonhole or along the whole seam.

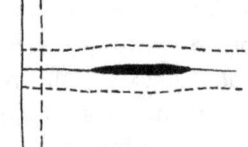

Bound buttonholes

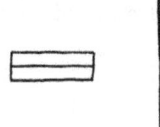

Bound buttonholes were more prevalent in the days before sewing machines came with zig zag stitch.
They really aren't hard to make.
They look extremely smart and may be the best method of making a buttonhole in your particular fabric.

✂ Bound buttonholes are made by stitching a patch of fabric onto the garment. Sometime two strips of fabric are used instead of a patch. The hole for the button is cut, then the patches or strips are turned to the wrong side forming a binding at the edges.

✂ Accuracy in sewing and pressing is extremely important.

✂ The lips of the bound buttonhole are usually about 3mm (⅛") wide each, but can be wider for bulkier fabrics, for example 6mm (¼"), or even 1cm (⅜"). For rounded-looking buttonhole lips, insert a short length of piping cord before stitching them into position.

✂ One of the drawbacks of bound buttonholes is that, ideally, they should be one of the first things made on your garment. However, you may not have chosen the buttons or their positions until the garment is fitted. For ease of sewing, try to make the bound buttonholes as early on as possible. On jackets or coats, definitely make them before sewing the lining in and closing up the jacket.

✂ You'll have more consistent buttonholes if you complete the same step on all of the buttonholes rather than finishing one buttonhole at a time.

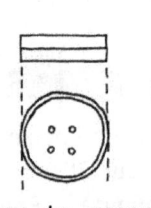

✂ The length of the buttonhole opening will be the total length—you don't need to allow for the end bars that a machine made buttonhole has.
If the button is thick, the buttonhole will need to be longer to accommodate it. Test the proposed buttonhole length by slipping a button through a slit cut in a scrap of fabric.

Mark the buttonhole positions on the wrong side of the garment with two dots indicating each end of the buttonhole. If the garment is not interfaced where the buttonholes will be, iron some small pieces of interfacing on now.

This method is a common one known as the patch method.

1. Cut a patch of fabric 3cm (1¼") longer than the buttonhole and 5cm (2") wide. The patch can be on the straight grain or bias. It can be a different fabric if you want contrasting bound buttonholes. Iron lightweight interfacing onto the wrong side if the fabric needs it. Press a fold in the patch longways.

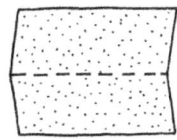

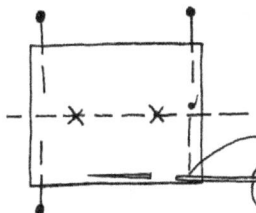

2. Centre the patch over the buttonhole position, right sides together. Tack or pin in place.

3. On the wrong side of the garment, draw parallel lines 3mm (⅛") each side of the buttonhole position (or the width of your buttonhole lips), forming a box shape.

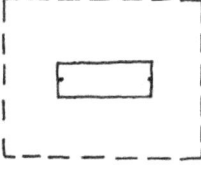

4. With a short 1-1.5mm (1/16") stitch length on your machine, stitch around the box shape, starting and finishing on one of the long sides.

Be extremely accurate:

✂ Pivot on the corners and ensure they're perfectly square.

✂ Take the same number of stitches across each short end.

✂ Measure the distance between the two long sides to make sure they're parallel.

5. Very carefully cut through the centre of the buttonhole to within 6mm (¼") of the ends, then cut into each corner. Cut exactly to, but not through, the stitching.

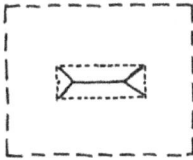

6. Remove the tacking that holds the patch on, and turn the patch through the opening to the wrong side. You should have a perfect rectangular window. Press the seam exactly on the edge of the opening and make sure none of the patch shows on the right side.

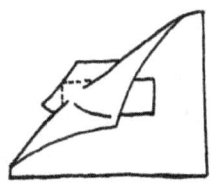

Buttons and buttonholes 37

7. Make the buttonhole lips by folding each long side over the opening so the folds meet in the centre. Check the look of the buttonhole on the right side, then press. The seam allowances around the rectangle should still be pressed away from the rectangle.

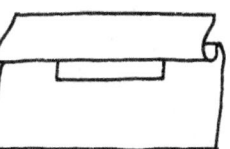

8. Tack the lips together using herringbone stitch and leave them tacked together until the garment is finished.

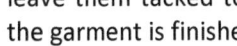

9. With the buttonhole lips facing down, peel back the garment to expose the end triangle. Using a zipper foot on your machine, stitch the triangle to the patch on top of the first row of stitching.

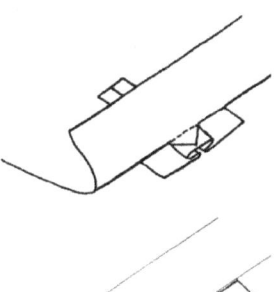

Repeat with the other end, then sew the long sides the same way.

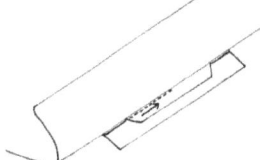

10. Trim the patch to within 6mm (¼") of the machine stitching. Press. On the wrong side, herringbone stitch the outer edge of the patch to the garment, without the stitching showing on the right side.

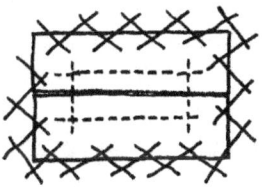

To attach the facing to the back of the bound buttonhole

Here's a quick and commonly used method:

1. Position the facing how it will be worn and tack around the bound buttonhole through all the layers. Insert a pin at each end of buttonhole.

2. Turn the garment over, and on the facing cut a slit between the pins, then remove the pins.

3. Turn under the raw edges of the slit, making an oval shape, and slip-stitch the edges to the buttonhole. It's rather like turn-and-stitch appliqué. Remove the tacking.

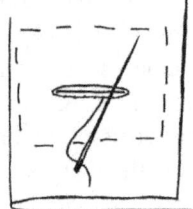

Alternative method
Sometimes, simply a regular buttonhole is made in the facing. The bound buttonhole and regular buttonhole are stitched together by stitching-in-the-ditch around the edge of the bound buttonhole. This is sometimes seen on leather and thick fabrics.

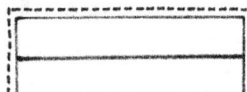

You could also edgestitch around the buttonhole instead, as illustrated.

Buttons and loops

Buttons and loops are good to use for fabrics that can't be buttonholed.

The loops go on the edge of the garment (usually the centre back or centre front), with or without an extension on the button side.

Adjusting a pattern for buttons and loops

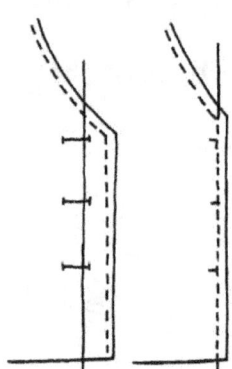

On the **loop side**, you'll need to trim off any button extension that's been added to the centre front or centre back line. It's usually about 2cm (¾") for jackets and 1.5cm (⅝") for blouses, but the centre front or back should be marked on the pattern. Add a seam allowance to the central line; 6mm (¼") or 1cm (⅜") is adequate.

On the **button side**, consider if the garment will always be worn done up, for example a blouse.
If so, then a 2.5cm (1") wide extension on the button side is desirable to stop gaping.
This is usually cut in one with the garment, giving you a different left and right side.

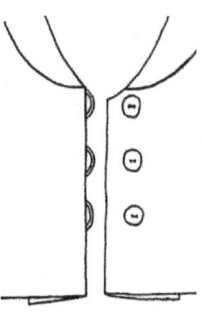

However, if the garment has already been cut without one, a separate double piece of fabric can be sandwiched between the garment and facing.

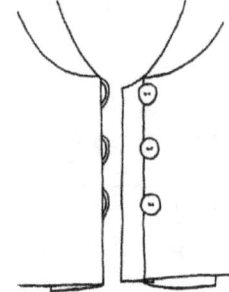

If the garment will sometimes be done up and sometimes left open, such as a jacket, it looks better not to have an extension. In this case, the button side is cut the same as the loop side.

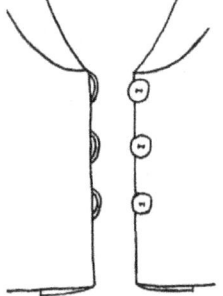

The loops can be made in three ways:
1. Rouleau loops made from fabric
2. Ready-made elastic loops bought by the metre
3. Hand made thread loops

Rouleau loops made from fabric

These are the strongest type of loop and are good for bustier tops, fronts of jackets and side opening skirts. See page 276 for making rouleau. You need tight, skinny rouleau to make the button loops. You can also use cord or tubular braid. If the garment is made from velvet or a fabric unsuitable for rouleau, find a perfectly matching satin to use instead.

Check how big each loop needs to be using your chosen button, and make a test loop. Big flat buttons will have a long, shallow loop.

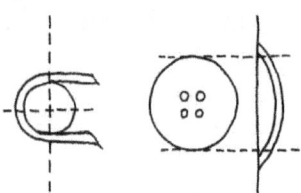

The loops shouldn't extend out past the edge more than 6mm-1cm (¼"-⅜"), otherwise the button placement won't be central. Therefore, avoid making loops like this, unless you intend to use them to thread ribbon through.

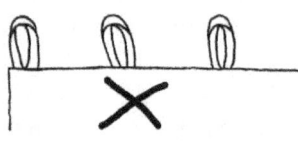

Decide on the spacing of the loops by laying the buttons out in a pleasing arrangement.
A typical measurement for small buttons is 2.5cm (1") apart, measured from centre to centre, but you can space them so the buttons touch or put them in groups of two or three.

Mark the position of the loops using pins or small 3mm (⅛") snips in the fabric.
For small loops, mark the centre of where each loop will be:

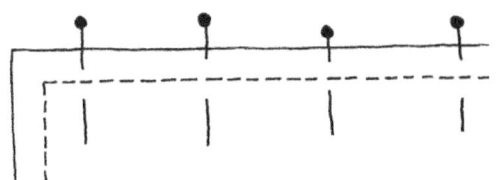

For big loops, mark each end of the loop using two snips or pins:

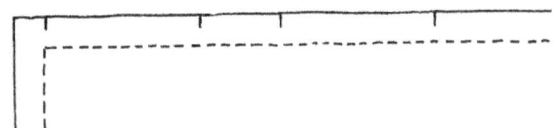

There are a couple of ways of sewing the loops on.
One way is to sew a line of stitching along the seam line (the centre line of the garment) and *at the same time* position and sew each loop as you come to it. With some practise you can do this by eye. Note that the loops are on the *garment* side of the seam, not the raw edge—they'll be flipped over when the seam is sewn. It's a good method for making lots of small loops.

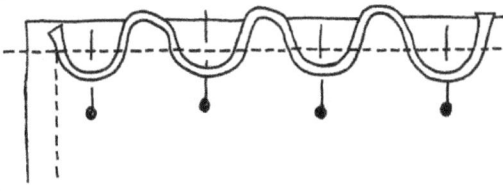

OR
You can pre-cut each loop and position with pins or sticky tape before sewing. This is a better method for making a few big loops.

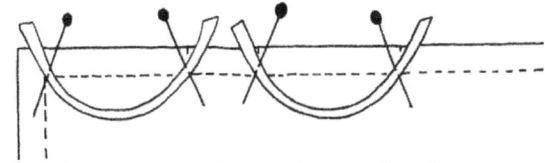

Make the seam in the rouleau tube face *upwards* when you attach the loops to the garment, so when the loops are finished the seam will be underneath.

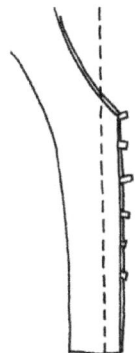

Check that the buttons fit through the loops, then sew on the facing, stitching on *exactly* the same line. The loops will now be sandwiched between the facing and the garment.

Press the seam allowance towards the facing, then edgestitch the facing.
Fold the facing to the inside and press.

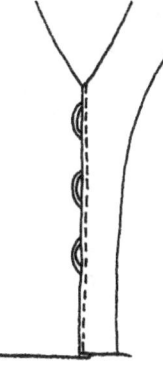

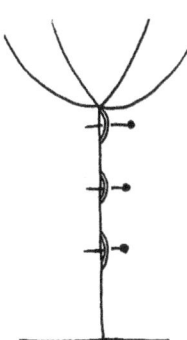

To determine the button positions, lap the loops over the opposite side and mark the button positions with pins. Double-check and correct the spacing using a tape measure, then sew the buttons on at the correct distance from the edge.

Elastic loops

The elastic loops are attached to a tape bought by the metre. The loops come in black, white or ivory.

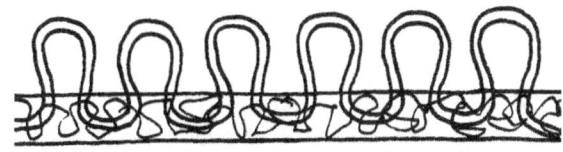

Don't use them for any garment that will strain the loops, such as bustier tops or other tight clothes. These loops aren't really strong enough and they'll stretch. Also, they can't be used for big buttons because the loops only come in a standard size. They're excellent for fronts of blouses, ends of sleeves and backs of wedding dresses that have a zip underneath.

If the loops are too close together for your liking, run a row of stitching down the centre of the tape and fold under every second loop. Don't simply cut off the unwanted loops—it will make the others come undone.

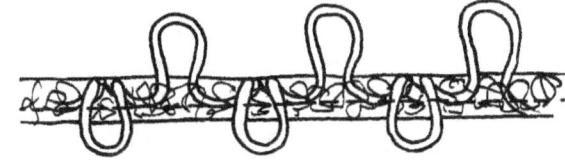

To apply, sew the loop tape on just inside the seam allowance. Note that the loops are sitting on the *garment* side; they'll be flipped over after sewing.

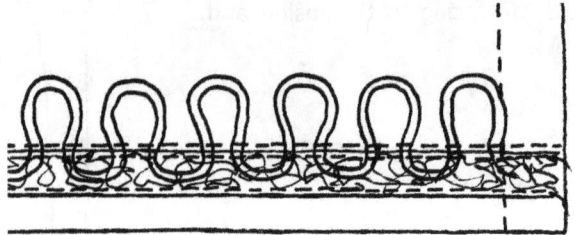

Press under the seam allowance so the loops extend beyond the edge:

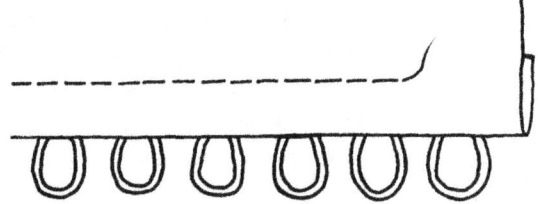

You now can either:
Topstitch the edge to hold the loop tape in position (as shown above).
OR
Apply a facing so the loop tape is sandwiched between the garment and the facing.

Handmade thread loops

These loops are made of strands of thread with blanket stitch worked over the top. They're sewn when the garment is finished and are often used on lace. They're not as strong as fabric loops and will not take strain.

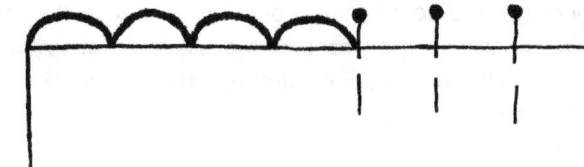

Decide on the button spacing and check how big each loop needs to be using your chosen button. Make a test loop if necessary.

1. Thread the needle with four threads (see page 145) and knot the end. Insert the needle into the top of the first loop, hiding the knot inside the garment. Make a stitch at the bottom of the loop, leaving a strand the size of the finished loop.

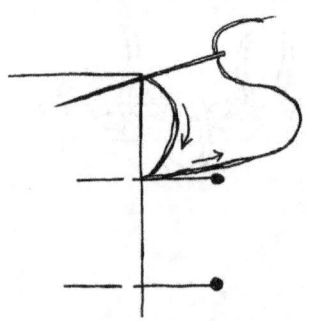

2. Make another couple of stitches over the top in the same way.

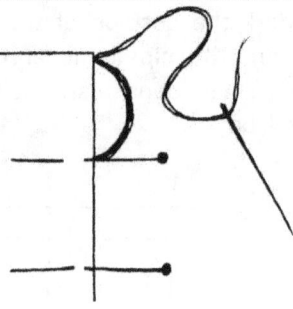

3. Cover all of the strands with closely spaced blanket stitch. At the end, bring the needle to the inside of the garment and secure.

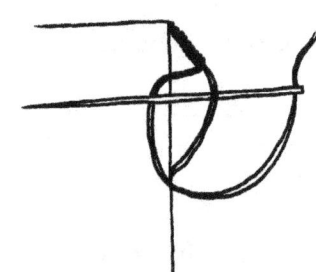

Collars

What makes a good collar?...........................41	one piece shirt collar....................49
Types of collars 41	collar stays 50
Parts of a collar 42	mandarin and wing collars.........51
Ways of attaching a collar 42	Nehru and stand collars 51
Fitting collars..42	Collars cut in one with the garment........52
Changing the collar 43	Collars with revers....................................55
Flat collars 43	on a blouse...................................56
Standing collars 45	on jackets and coats 58
two piece shirt collar.......................46	Eliminating neck darts...............................60
men's two piece shirt collar............48	Tie collars..60
using herringbone twill tape..........48	Knit collars...61
Barbara Hellyer's method...............49	Hoods 62

A beautifully constructed, comfortable collar is the mark of quality workmanship and a thing of joy to behold! With careful sewing, pressing and technique, there's no reason why your collars can't have a professional appearance.

What makes a good collar?

✂ The collar needs to be perfectly symmetrical.

✂ All points should be pointy and rounded edges should be smooth curves. The edges need to be flat and properly pressed. The corners should sit on the garment and not flip up.

✂ Roll lines need to be a smooth soft roll, not squashed flat by the iron.

✂ The back neck seam needs to be covered by the collar.

✂ The interfacing needs to support the style of collar to make it neither too floppy nor too stiff.

✂ The underside of the collar and any facings shouldn't be visible—it makes the collar look sloppy and amateur. Use understitching for control if you aren't topstitching. On the subject of topstitching, the collar's topstitching should match the rest of the topstitching on the garment.

✂ A collar should fit comfortably and naturally around the neck, not too straining and tight nor too sloppy and loose. If it's a shirt collar to be worn with a tie, the shape needs to accommodate the tie knot.

✂ The style and shape of the collar needs to be in proportion to the wearer and the rest of the garment.

Types of collars

In terms of construction, collars fall into one of four categories:

1. **Flat collars** are simple collars that lie against the garment, rising only a little bit above the edge. They're usually seen on dresses and children's clothes.

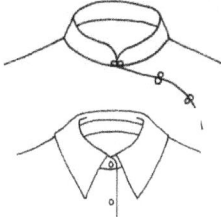

2. **Standing collars** sit as a band around the neck. They may have a collar leaf attached, as in a shirt collar.

3. **Collars cut in one with the garment** are an extension of the garment's front.

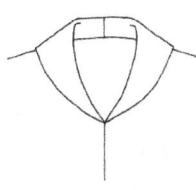

4. **Collars with revers** are used for jackets and blouses, but are constructed a little differently for each. The collar may have a separate stand at the back.

41

Parts of a collar

These names of collar parts aren't just reserved for rever collars as illustrated; all collars have some or all of these parts.

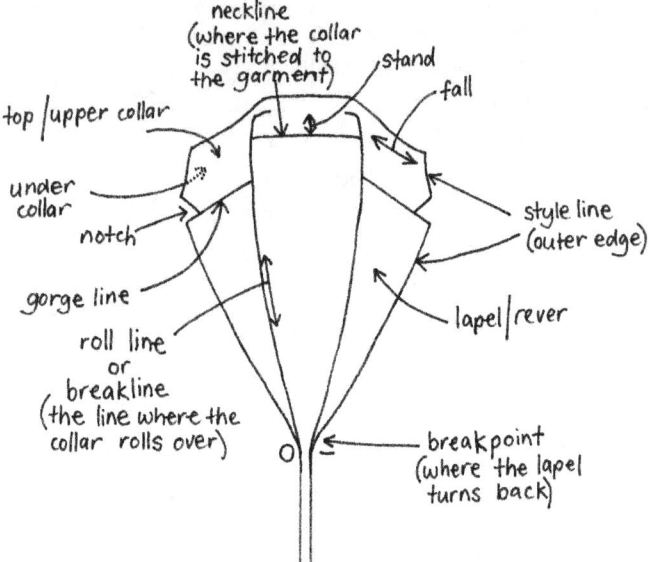

The **break point** is where the lapel turns back. It's identified on the pattern by a notch.

The **roll or break line** may or may not be identified on the pattern (it doesn't matter if it isn't).

The collar's **notch**, **style line (outer edge)**, **fall**, **gorge line** and **lapel** can all tolerate small adjustments to suit your whim and personal taste without affecting the fit of the collar.

The **stand** is roughly 2cm (¾") high on average collars. It's referred to as a stand even if there's no separate stand pattern piece (but if there *is* a pattern piece it's called the collar stand).

There may be separate **upper and under collar** pieces. The under collar is cut slightly smaller to allow for the extra fabric required when one layer of fabric is folded over the other. It's referred to as turn of cloth. The lapel also employs this trick—the facing lapel is cut slightly larger than the garment lapel. The amount is about 3mm (⅛") but thicker fabrics will need more, say, 6mm (¼"). On thin fabrics, for example for blouses, the collars are cut the same using the same pattern piece for upper and under collars. In jackets, the under collar is cut on the bias (in two pieces with a centre back seam) to help the collar roll properly. The reason it's cut in two pieces rather than one (on the bias) is so the left and right of the collar have the same grainline, therefore looking and performing the same.

Ways of attaching a collar

A collar can be attached to a garment in one of four ways. The method you use will depend on the weight and bulk of the fabric and the style of the garment.

1. To a **facing**. Suitable for blouses and unlined jackets in any weight fabric.

2. Using a **bias strip** to cover the seam. Suitable for blouses and unlined jackets in any weight fabric. If the fabric is thick the bias strip should be in a lighter weight fabric. A bias strip can give a more casual, sporty look.

3. To a **lining or part-lining**. Used for jackets in any fabric, but very suitable for thick fabrics.

4. With the **seam allowance turned in out of sight**. Suitable for light weight fabrics only, otherwise the collar will be too bulky. Shirt collars are always attached this way.

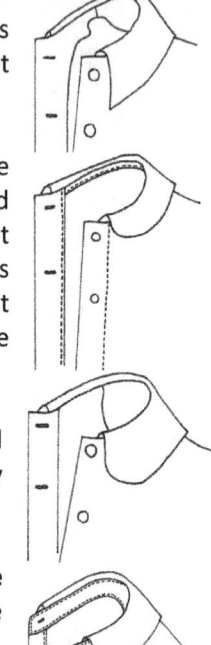

Fitting collars

✂ The collar will stabilize the neck for fittings. If you're doing a fitting and the collar hasn't been sewn yet, either tack or pin the collar on, or else stabilize the neckline in some way, for example tack cotton tape or sew-in interfacing around the neck to the correct measurement. I find that just stay-stitching is inadequate. An unstabilized neckline tends to slip down the shoulders.

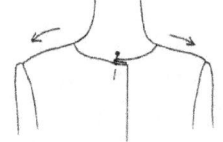

✂ The amount of spread the outer edge of the collar has will partly determine how the collar sits.
For example: if the outer edge of a flat collar is reduced, it sits higher on the neck, increasing the stand. This can be demonstrated on any collared garment you have at home. Pin some tucks in the outer edge of the collar and see how it sits higher on the neck.

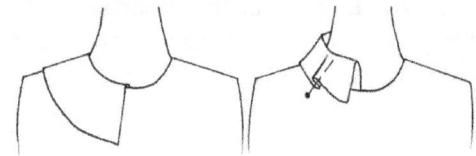

Conversely, if the outer edge of a standing collar is slashed and spread, it sits lower at the neck, reducing the stand.

Note that the *neck edge* of a collar needs to stay the same measurement as the neck of the garment, because they have to be sewn together.

✂ Reducing or adding to the width can affect how high the collar sits up on the neck.

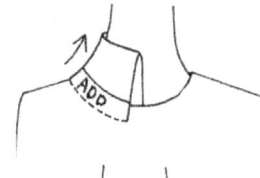

If you make a collar wider it will want to sit up higher.

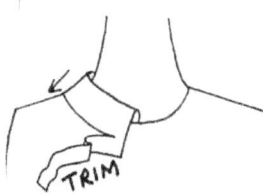

If you make it narrower it will sit lower.

The wider the collar is, the more spread is required at the outer edge to keep the stand constant.

✂ On collars with **lapels**, if you make the break point higher or lower, the width of the lapels will change. Making the break point lower will open the front of the jacket out, causing the lapels to flare out wider. Be aware! If the jacket has a breast pocket or logo it may be partially covered if the lapels are changed.

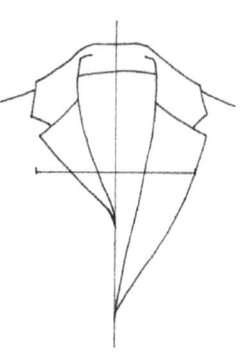

✂ The deeper the curve on the collar's neck edge, and the more the collar's curve corresponds to the shape of the garment's neck, the flatter the collar will lie on the person.

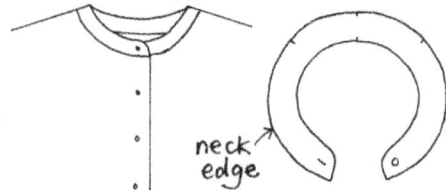

The opposite extreme, a standing collar, will have a straight or only a very slight curved neck edge.

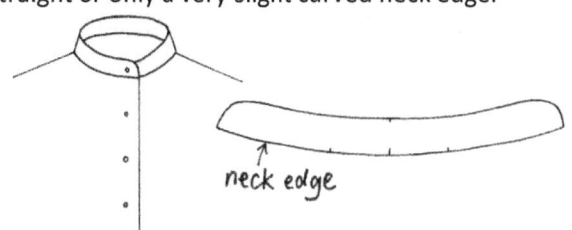

Changing the collar

A collar pattern can easily be switched from garment to garment. As a patternmaker I rarely draft new collar patterns from scratch. More often, I transfer collars from garment to garment and make small changes. I use collar patterns from previous ranges or from our pattern archives. Occasionally I take a pattern off a collar on a garment and use that.

To transfer a collar onto another garment, firstly you'll need to draw in the neckline that goes with that collar.

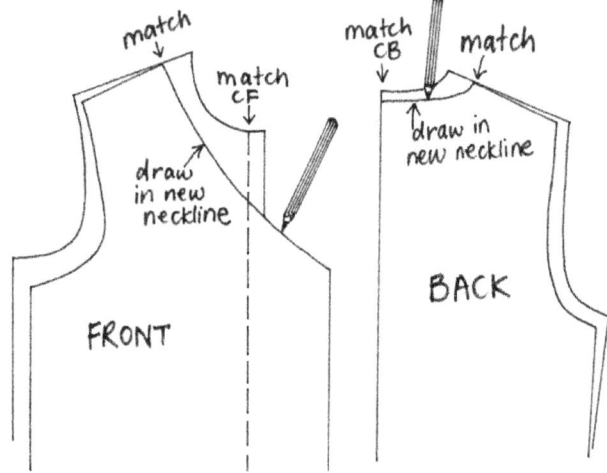

To do this, trace the garment front you want onto some paper. Take the pattern with the neckline and lay it on top. Match the centre front (CF) lines, which should be marked on both patterns. Slide the neckline pattern up until the shoulders touch at the neckline. Draw in the new neckline and front wrap/button stand. Do the same with the back. The collar pieces should now fit the changed neckline. Check the shoulder seams are the same length.

Flat collars

Flat collars sit flat against the garment, slightly rising above the garment's neck edge. They're found on children's clothes, dresses and untailored garments. The garment may have a centre back or centre front opening. The collar may or may not have a centre back seam.

Some examples of flat collars:

Eton Collars look the same front and back.

 **Puritan collars** also look the same front and back.

Peter Pan collars may be curved at the back and front or curved at the front and pointy like an Eton collar at the back. Occasionally the collar is in one piece (straight across at the back), provided the garment opens at the front.

The above three usually have separate left and right collars with a centre front or centre back opening.

Sailor collars open at the front or pull on over the head.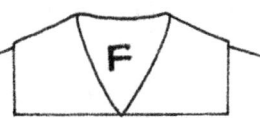

Cape collars open at the front.

✂ A flat collar can be designed with any sort of outer edge shape.

✂ All flat collars are applied by making the collar up first, then sandwiching it between the garment and a facing. The facing could be a regular facing or a strip of bias binding used as a facing. The collar can also be attached using a lining.

✂ The top (outermost) collar is interfaced.

Make a pattern
Patterns for flat collars are very simple to make.
1. Determine how high, low or wide you want the finished neckline to be and adjust the pattern.

2. Lay the front and back together at the shoulders. Match the *seam* lines at the neck and overlap up to 2.5cm (1") at the armholes.

Draw in the shape of the collar. Note that the bigger the overlap, the greater the roll at the back of the collar. A completely flat collar doesn't require any overlap, but an overlap is considered more flattering on adult figures. This collar will lie flat at the front and roll slightly at the back. Eton, Peter Pan, and Sailor collars are made in this way. Cape and Puritan collars usually have no overlap, and the collar is a little wider than the shoulder measurement.

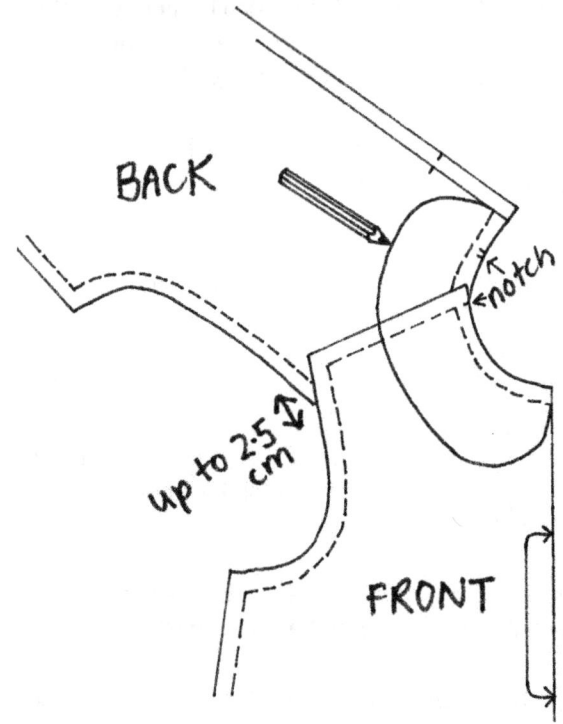

3. Add seam allowances. I prefer only 6mm (¼") for the outer edge and the neck, since the seam allowances will be enclosed. It saves trimming and clipping after sewing and I can accurately and easily sew any curves.

Your pattern piece could look like this: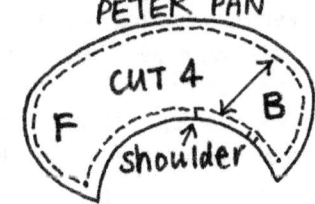

Notch the back with two notches so the back and front don't get confused after the collar is cut.
Make the grainline parallel to the centre back of the garment, but if you're using striped or checked fabric, you can orient the collar so the pattern looks pleasing. The grain line should run in the same direction for all collar pieces.

4. Finish by making some facing patterns for the garment's back and front necklines (see page 97).

Other collar shapes might look like this:

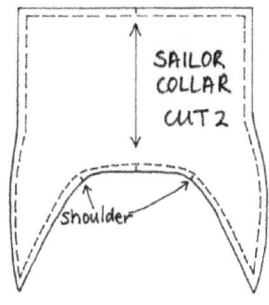
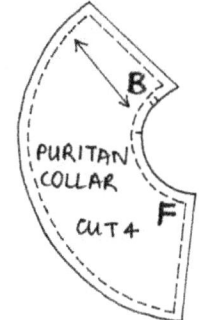

To sew a flat collar

1. With right sides together, sew around the outside edge of the collar. If desired, sandwich piping, lace or frills between the two layers. Trim the seam allowances and clip the corners and curves if required.

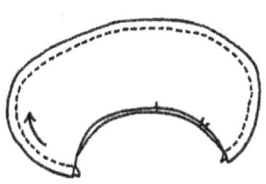

2. Turn to the right side and press. If you plan to topstitch the collar, do so now.

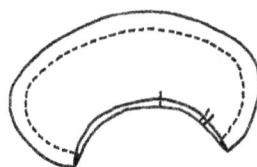
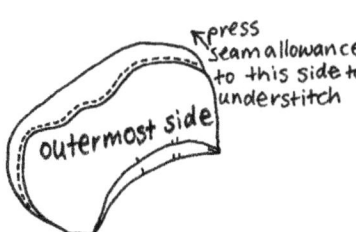

If you *aren't* having topstitching, understitch the collar so the underneath collar will stay rolled underneath.

3. Place the collar on the neckline, matching the raw edges. Pin the centre front and centre back into position. Pin the rest of the collar on, and if preferred you can take it a step further and machine baste it on using a long stitch.

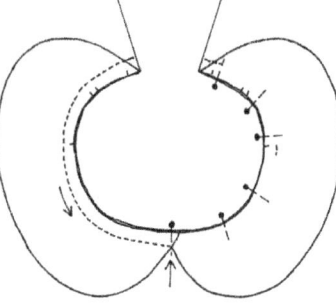

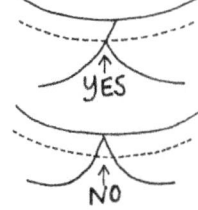

Make sure the centres match at the *stitching line*, not the raw edge, otherwise there'll be a gap between the collars.

4. Prepare the facings by joining the shoulder seams and pressing them open. Overlock the outside edge—there's no need to overlock the shoulder seams because the fusing should stop them from fraying, and they'll be out of sight. If you're using 1.2cm (½") bias binding as the facing, use an iron to steam it into a curved shape to match the neckline's curve.

5. Lay the prepared facing right side down over the collar, pin and sew in place. Trim and clip the seam if required.

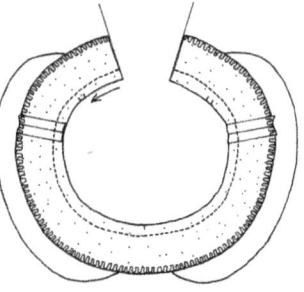

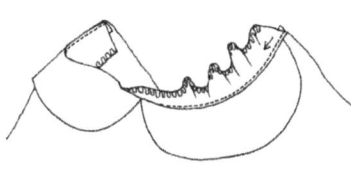

6. Understitch the facing to hold it inside. Secure the facing at the shoulder seams to stop it flapping.

7. To further secure the facing, you can machine stitch through all layers (facing and garment) in the areas that will be hidden underneath the collar. This works very well for bias binding facings.

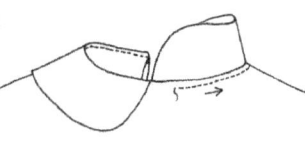

Standing collars

A standing collar should have a slight curve so it stands in at an angle, because our necks angle in slightly. For this, two collars pieces are cut, an inside and an outside, and seamed together at the top edge. Types of standing collars:

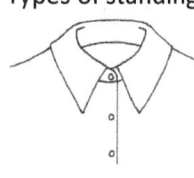 

One piece shirt collar (at left), **and two piece shirt collar** (at right)

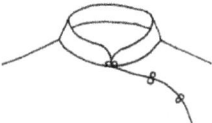

Mandarin collar
A feature of traditional Chinese dress.

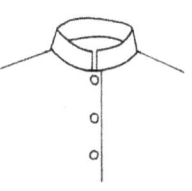

Nehru collar
A feature of the Nehru jacket.

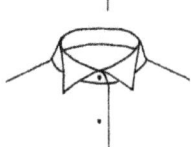

Wing collar

The grainline generally runs longways through the collar. You won't need to measure the grainline if the pieces are positioned near the selvedge, because you can use the selvedge as a guide.

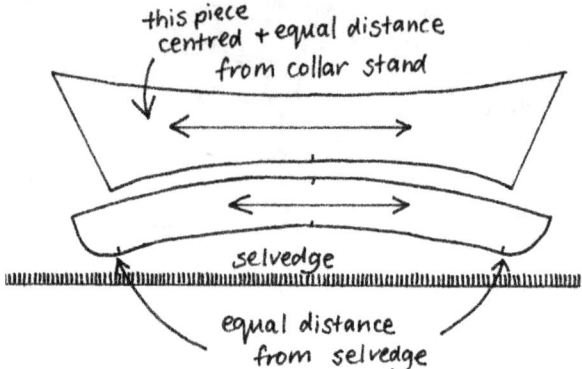

You can also save cutting time by slipping the interfacing under the fabric and cutting them out together.

Two piece shirt collar

It's not hard to guess that a two piece collar consists of two pieces, a collar stand and a collar leaf. The stand can be rounded or squared off at the ends, and the leaf can be rounded or pointy to different degrees. When you find a shirt collar that you like (and that fits well), you can have fun changing the shape of the leaf.

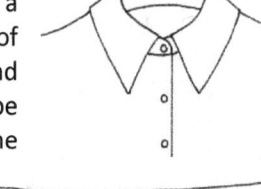

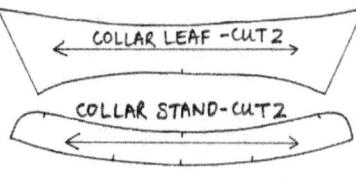

To check a shirt collar pattern for fit, measure the top edge from notch to notch. It should be your neck measurement plus 1.2cm (½") ease.

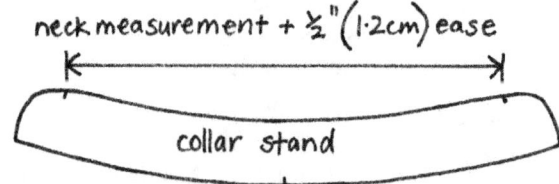

Alternatively, wrap the pattern around your neck and see how it fits. You should be able to comfortably fit two fingers in between your neck and the collar when it's buttoned up.

For ease of sewing, I like to have 6mm (¼") seam allowances on all the shirt collar pieces and also the garment neck edge, although sometimes I make the neck edge 1cm (⅜"). If the seam allowances are much bigger than 1cm, you'll have trouble sewing accurate and consistent curves. Important notches are the centres and each end of the collar stand.

It's much more accurate, faster and easier to make full-sized collar pattern pieces, with no part cut on the centre back fold. If the pattern you're using is cut on the fold, either make a whole pattern piece, or else be very precise when you place the piece on the fold of the fabric.

1. Before you start the collar, you'll need to have sewn the shirt's shoulder seams, overlocked them, and made the front button stand.

2. Cut two of fabric and one of interfacing of each the collar leaf and the collar stand. The *inside* collar stand and the *outside* collar leaf have interfacing on them. To remember this, I picture the collar turned up, with every piece next to the skin interfaced.

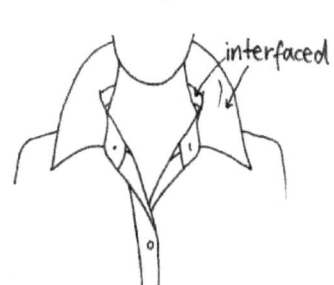

Check the fabric pieces against the pattern after ironing on the interfacing, because sometimes the fusing process causes shrinkage that makes the finished collar a shade too tight. If it has shrunk, see if you can take slightly smaller seam allowances. Otherwise, block fuse the fabric first (see page 166) and re-cut the pieces.

3. Make the collar leaf first. Put the collar leaves right sides together and sew the longest edge and the two short ends.

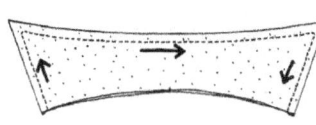

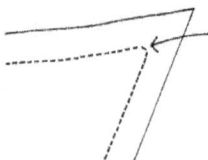

At the corners, instead of pivoting, stitch across one stitch.

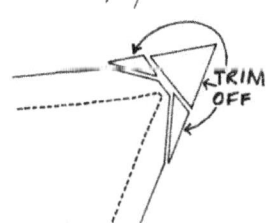

Trim the point of the collar leaf, but don't trim any closer than 3mm (⅛"), otherwise the point may fray out.

Turn the collar leaf to the right side and press.

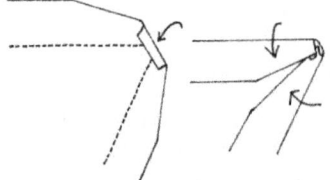

When you turn the point, fold (what remains of) the end in first, then the two sides. Hold it with your thumb as you turn the corner

Collars 47

to the right side. That way, the trimmed seam allowances are sitting folded inside the collar point. Push the point *very gently* from the inside with the point of a pair of scissors, or whatever point-turning tool you prefer, to make a sharp point. If the point still needs some work to make it pointy, carefully pick it out with a pin on the right side. However, it's more important that both sides of the collar are the same *shape* rather than achieving razor sharp points.

If you plan to topstitch the collar leaf, do it now.

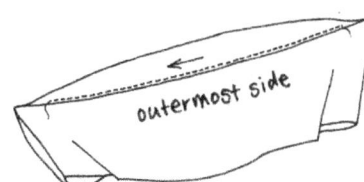

If not, understitch the long edge of the collar as far as you can into each point, to keep the underneath collar underneath. Remember, the side with the interfacing on will be the uppermost side.

Just an aside: some people like to sew the long outside edge first, understitch it, then sew the two short ends. In this way, the understitching extends all the way into the corners. Try it and see if you prefer it.

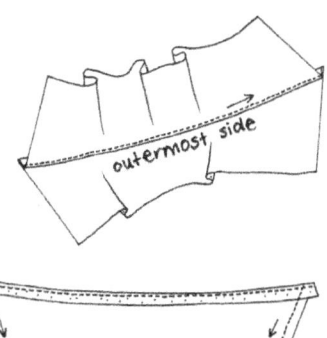

4. Sew the un-interfaced collar stand onto the neck edge, right sides together. Be sure to leave the correct amount of seam allowance hanging over the edge at each end. Flip the stand up and press the seam towards the stand.

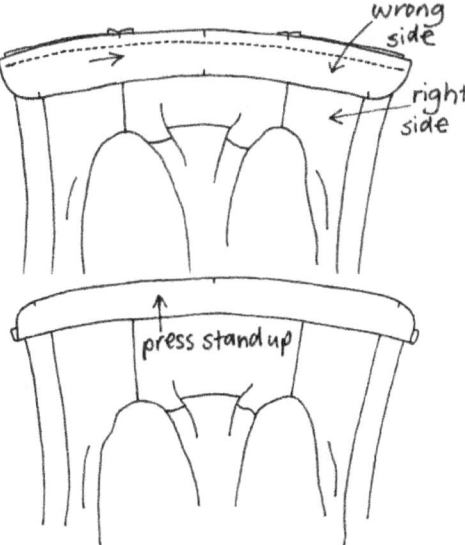

5. Sandwich the collar leaf between the two collar stands. Make sure the *interfaced* collar stand and the *interfaced* leaf are next to each other. At the corners, let the interfaced collar stand lie flat and the un-interfaced one be pressed up. **Very important**: keep the seam allowances correct at the corners.

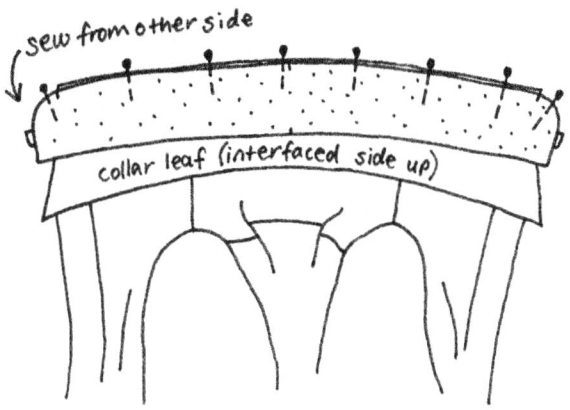

6. With the un-interfaced side facing up, stitch around the stand as illustrated. Begin and end *exactly* in line with the edge of the shirt's button stand. If you sew too far away you'll have a step, and too close will yield a bunched up tight spot.

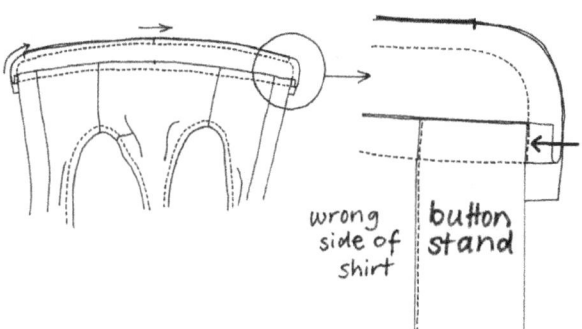

If the fabric is a loose weave, shifts or doesn't sew well with the un-interfaced side on top, flip it over to sew the long straight part in the middle.

7. Trim the seam allowance on the curved ends of the stand back to a generous 3mm (⅛") and fold in each corner neatly as illustrated. Make each fold square and definite. Secure with a pin.

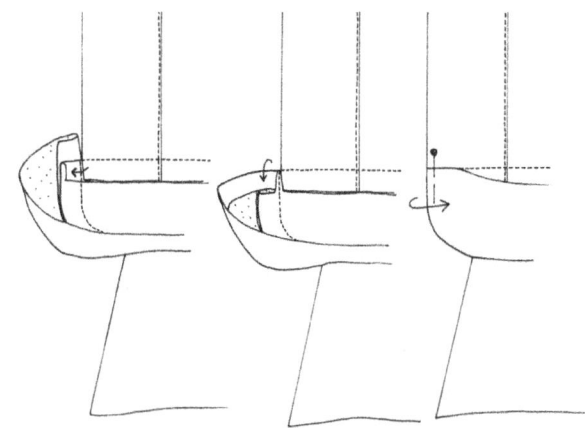

I can still hear my sewing teacher saying: "I've done thousands of these but I always put a pin in the corners to hold them" (she owned a shirt factory and sewed collars without using any pins except for the corners).

8. Turn under the edge of the fused collar stand and pin in position (or not pin, if you're practised enough!). Begin edgestitching next to the collar leaf above one of the shoulder seams. On the neck, the edgestitching should just cover the first line of stitching. As you sew the turned-under edge, prevent rippling by holding the bottom layer firmly and letting the top layer "sit easy" on top. Alternatively, hand sew the collar stand in place.

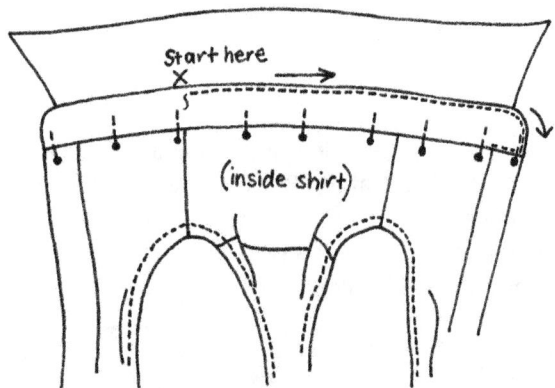

Men's two piece shirt collar

Familiarize yourself with the method for two piece shirt collars described on page 46, because this way is just a slight variation used for men's shirts. You might prefer this way. It can also be used for one piece collars too.

This method results in two visible rows of stitching on the inside collar stand. It requires a 1cm (⅜") seam allowance around the neck edge on the garment and collar. Note that men's shirts can have quite firm interfacing in the collar and cuffs. If you use this method for the collar, sew the cuffs in the same way so they match (see page 309).

1. Make the collar leaf first in the way described above for two piece shirt collars. Attach the un-interfaced collar stand to the neck edge as usual.

2. On the interfaced collar stand, turn under 8mm (it needs to be 2mm less than the seam allowance) along the neck edge and stitch close to the *raw* edge.

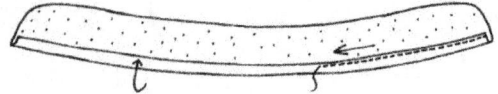

3. Apply the collar as a two piece shirt collar, remembering that only 8mm, not 1cm has been taken, so there'll be a 2mm step at each end when the stands are sewn together.

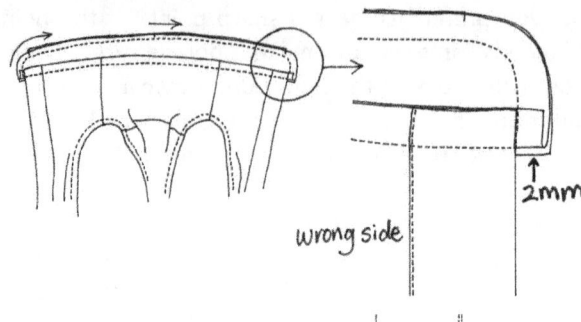

4. Edgestitch the inside collar stand into place along the already-folded-and-stitched-under edge. You'll see two rows of stitching about 6mm (¼") apart on the inside collar stand when the collar is finished.

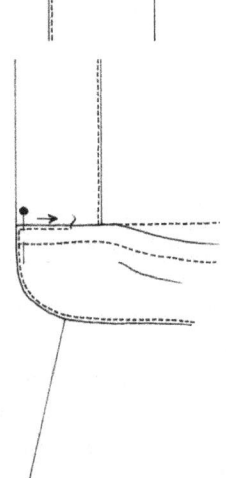

Shirt collar using herringbone twill tape

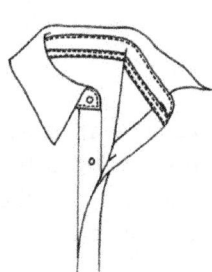

This gives a sporty finish to a collar and looks great on rugby tops where matching tape has been used for the front tab as well. It can be used on a one or two piece shirt collar, although one piece collars are most often used on rugby tops.

You'll need a piece of 1cm (⅜") wide herringbone twill tape the same length as the collar stand.

Familiarize yourself with the method for one or two piece shirt collars (whichever one you're using) described on pages 49 and 46 respectively, because this is just a variation.

1. Make the collar leaf first in the usual way, if the collar is two piece. Attach the un-interfaced collar stand to the neck edge as usual.

2. Attach the tape onto the right side of the interfaced collar stand by edgestitching along the top edge of the tape. Position the lower edge of the tape 2mm below the *seam* line.

So if the seam allowance is 1cm (⅜"), the lower edge of the tape will be 8mm away from the raw edge.

Collars **49**

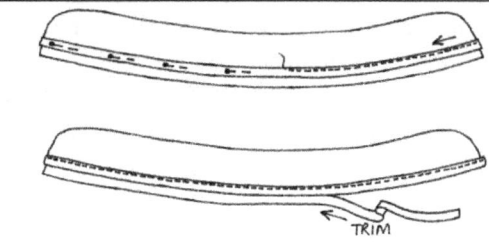

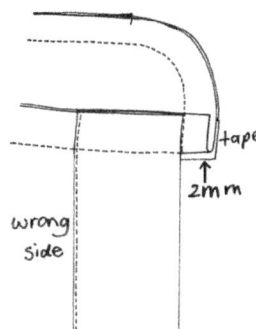

3. Trim away the fabric from underneath the tape.

4. Apply the collar in the normal way, but note that when the collar stands are put right sides together there'll be a 2mm step at each end.

5. Edgestitch the inside collar stand into place along the edge of the twill tape.

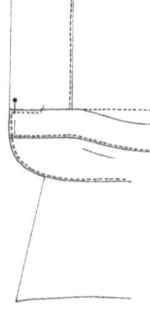

Barbara Hellyer's method
If you really cannot come to grips with the square folding at the corners of the collar stand, you may like to try another way. This ingenious technique of sewing the edges of the collar is from Barbara Hellyer's book *Sewing Magic*.

1. Make the collar leaf first in the usual way (page 46, Steps 1-3). Attach the un-interfaced collar stand to the neck edge as usual (Step 4).

2. Sew the collar leaf onto the stand, placing the un-interfaced sides next to each other.

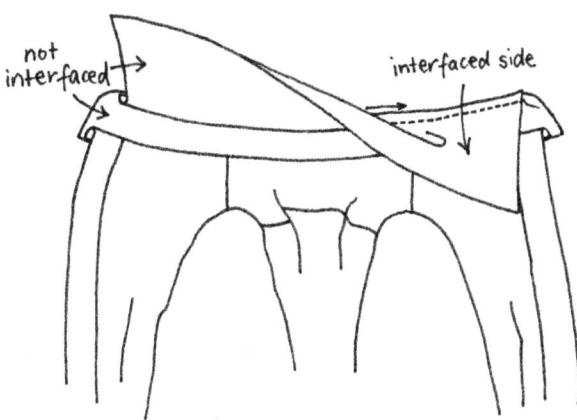

3. Tightly roll each side of the shirt up (shown here without the collar leaf, for clarity) so it will fit into the collar stand for several centimetres at each end. Ensure it clears the neckline stitching—some pins will help.

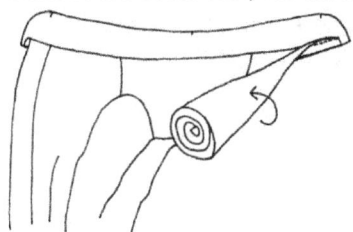

4. Sandwich the collar leaf between the two collar stands and pin.

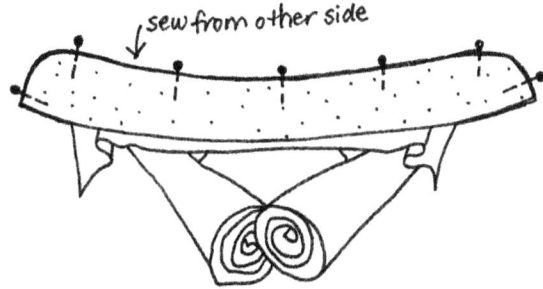

5. Stitching on the un-interfaced side, sew around the collar leaf as illustrated, covering the row of previous stitching. Trim the corners before turning through very carefully. Finally, pin and edgestitch the neck edge of the fused collar stand into place as usual.

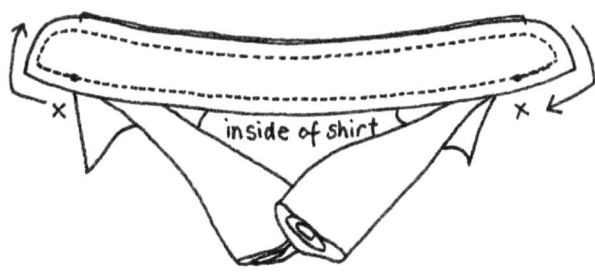

One piece shirt collar
One piece shirt collars have the collar leaf and the collar stand joined together in the same pattern piece. However, you lose the benefit of the shaping in the seam where they join, so a one piece collar will never fit as ergonomically as a two piece. This collar is constructed basically in the same way as a two piece collar, but with fewer steps, so familiarize yourself with the steps for a two piece collar on page 46.

1. Cut two of fabric and one of interfacing. The interfaced side will sit next to the neck.

2. Sew the un-interfaced collar to the garment, right sides together. Be sure to leave the correct amount of seam allowance hanging over the edge at each end.

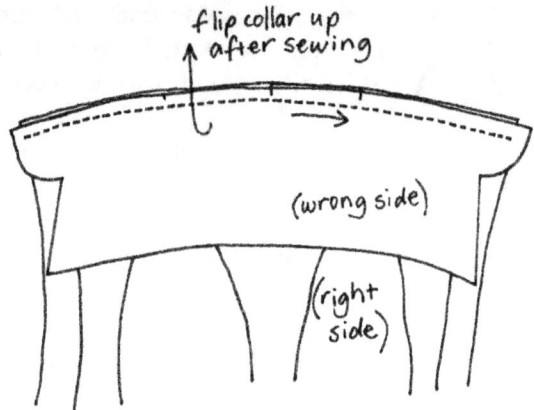

3. With the right sides together, sew the two collars together around the edges. At the corners, let the interfaced collar stand lie flat and the un-interfaced one be pressed up.

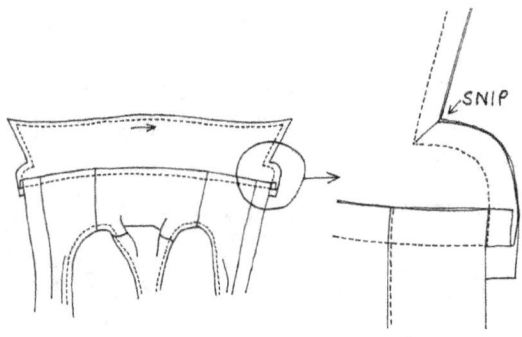

4. Trim the seam allowance on the collar points, cutting no closer than 3mm (⅛") to the stitching. Carefully snip the stand/leaf junction exactly to, but not over, the stitching line.

5. Turn the collar through to the right side and edgestitch in place. You can continue the stitching all around the edges of the collar if you want to. Sometimes the roll line of the collar is also stitched.

Collar stays

Collar stays are an optional detail for men's shirts. They are narrow plastic strips with one pointy end which are used to stiffen collar points to prevent them from rolling upwards. The collar is interfaced as well, as usual. The stay reaches diagonally from the collar point to the roll line. Obviously collar stays cannot be used in rounded or button-down collars.

You may be able to buy some collar stays but if not you can harvest them from old shirts to reuse, or make them if you find some suitable thin, rigid plastic.

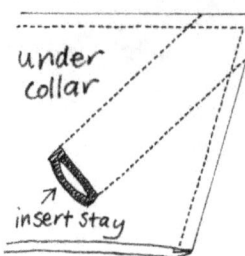

Practically all sewing books say to make a buttonhole in the underneath collar leaf and insert the stay into a channel between the (non-fusible) interfacing and under collar. The stays are removed for laundering.

Ready-to-wear shirts, however, don't use buttonholes. Instead, the stay is put into the collar leaf when it's being made.

One method is to sandwich the stay in between the fabric and fusible interfacing. The stay is held in place by the fusing. On budget shirts and work shirts, the

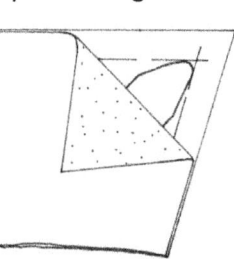

stay is put in the top collar (although the outline of the stay can be visible). However, other shirts have it in the under collar in a small area of fusing just at the points.

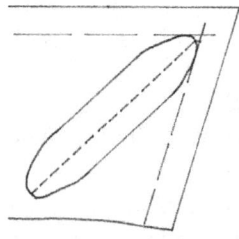

A variation of this is to stitch the stay to the (sew-in) interfacing or the underneath collar.

A common method is to push the stay into the corner of an already-made collar leaf and hold it in place with the topstitching.

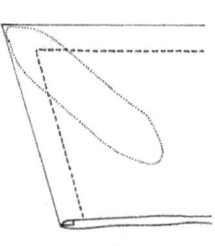

You should be able to stitch through with a regular machine needle without too much trouble.

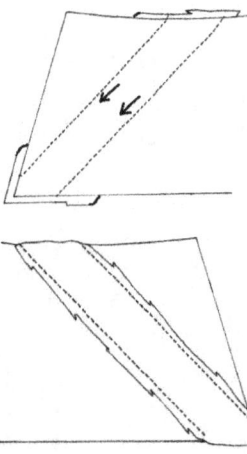

A smart way is to create a permanent channel in the undercollar. Slip a scrap of shirting fabric under the (un-interfaced) undercollar. Stitch a channel 1.2cm (½") wide from point to roll line. Trim away the excess scrap fabric and sew the collar leaf as normal. Slip the stay into the pocket just before attaching the collar leaf to the collar stand.

Mandarin and wing collars

A **mandarin collar** is essentially a two piece shirt collar without the collar leaf. It's a feature of Chinese traditional dress. Softly interfaced it can be used on men's or ladies shirts, where it's called a **grandpa collar**.

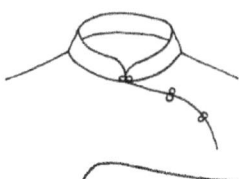
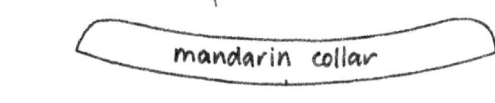

A **wing collar** stands up against the back and sides of the neck and turns down in pointed flaps at the front. Wing collars are seen on men's evening shirts and are worn with a bow tie.

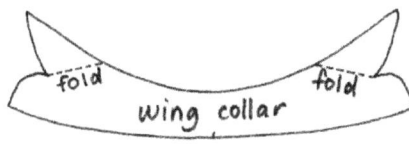

For both of these collars, apply interfacing to *both* collar pieces to make the collar stand up firmly. You can use quite a firm interfacing. I like to apply a firm interfacing (sew-in or fusible) to the outermost piece, and a lighter fusible for the inside. To help the wings on wing collars stay folded, cut the interfacing along the fold line and iron on the interfacing so there's a butted join along the fold line.

The grainline usually runs the length of 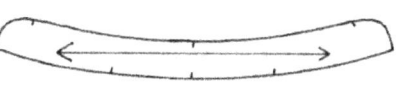 the pattern piece (so it's horizontal when worn), the same as a shirt collar. However, if the fabric is napped the grainline is positioned vertically so it matches the rest of the garment.

Mandarin, grandpa and wing collars are sewn in the same way as a two piece shirt collar (see page 46) but around the other way. That is, the *inside* collar is attached to the *inside* of the garment first, the two collar pieces are sewn together along the top edge, then turned through. The *outside* collar is edgestitched into place on the *outside* of the garment's neck edge.

Nehru collars and stand up collars

A **Nehru collar** is a feature of the Nehru jacket, worn by Jawaharlal Nehru, first PM of India 1947-64. It can be used on men's or ladies clothes.

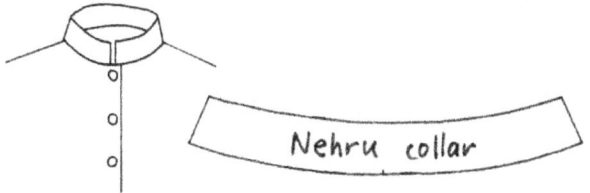

Nehru collars (and stand up collars on coats) are applied using a facing or lining. The facing or lining hides the seam allowance around the neck edge.

Nehru collars always meet in the centre front, with the wrap/button extension forming a step. See page 106 for more on wrap.

Beware of collar patterns cut in one piece with a fold along the top edge. They don't sit as well on the neck, tending to flare out at the top. There needs to be a slight curve on the collar and a seam along the top edge.

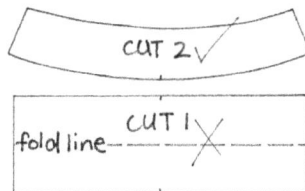

1. To sew a **Nehru collar**, make the collar up first and then sandwich it between the garment and lining (or facing).

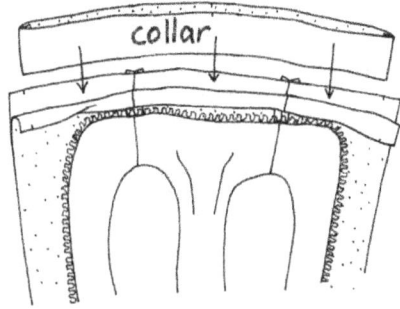

2. Sew on the lining or facing, catching in the collar at the same time.

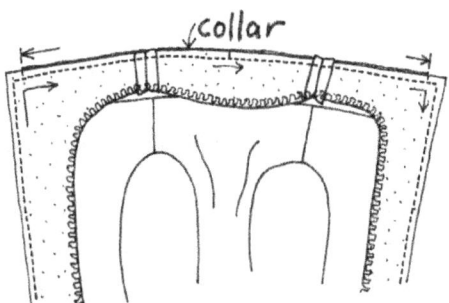

3. Any topstitching around the collar and front edge can be done last.

52 The Dressmaker's Companion

Stand collars on coats where the collar is flush with the button extension are sewn a little differently from Nehru collars.

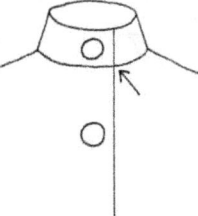

This method avoids forming a bulky little step where the collar and front meet each other

1. Sew the *outside* collar to the *garment* and the *inside* collar to the *lining (or facing)*. Press the seam allowances open.

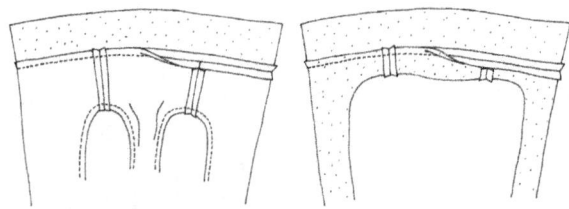

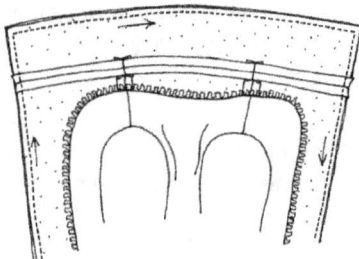

2. Stitch the collars and garment and facing together around the outside edge. Turn through to the right side.

3. Stitch together the two neck edge seams from the inside so they don't pull apart. Go as far as you can into each corner.

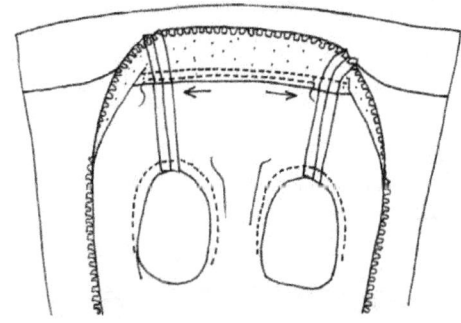

Collars cut in one with the garment

Collars cut in one with the garment are also called roll collars, shawl collars or continuous roll collars.
The outside edge of the collar can be any shape. A classic roll collar has gently curving edges. A shawl collar has a wider, curved edge. Collars cut in one with the garment can be used for jackets or blouses; the construction method is the same for both.

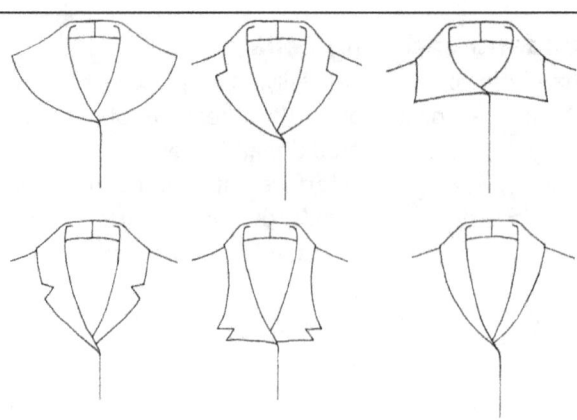

The pattern pieces might look something like this:

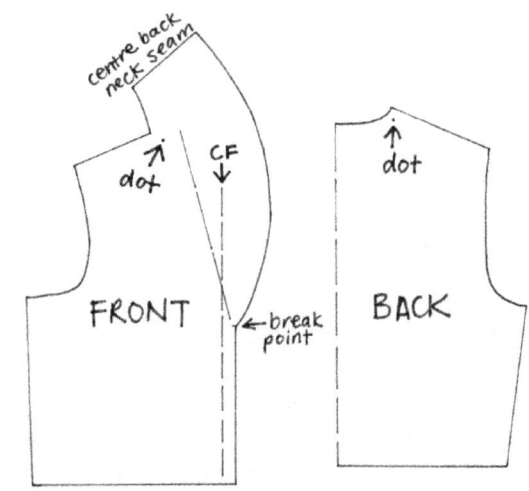

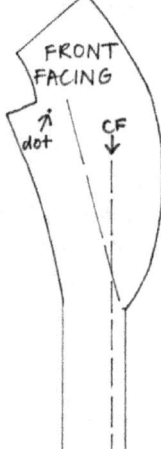

There's also a front facing to form the lapels.

There's also a back neck facing too, although some garments, usually lightweight blouses, don't have one (the back neck is finished a little differently). Also note that sometimes lined jackets use the back lining in place of a back neck facing.

If you need a back neck facing, simply trace around the back pattern and draw in the shape of the facing. Ensure the shoulders are the same length as the front facing.

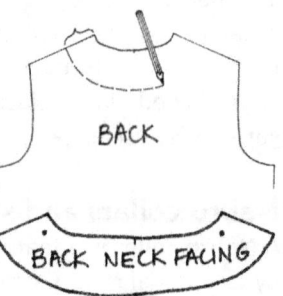

Collars **53**

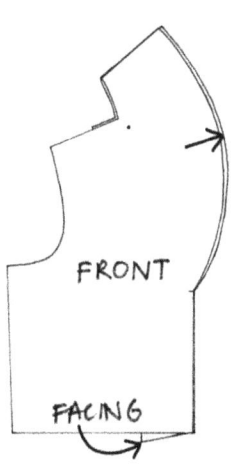

✂ Sometimes the front has a **dart** next to the collar, which is sewn first. The dart is hidden underneath the collar and its purpose is to hollow out the neck. It's possible to eliminate the dart—see page 60.

✂ If you lay the front on top of the facing, the outside curve of the facing should be slightly larger by at least 3mm (⅛"), and up to 6mm (¼") for thicker fabrics.

This accommodates the slight extra fabric required for the top collar to roll over the underneath one so the underneath one remains out of sight. It's referred to as turn of cloth.

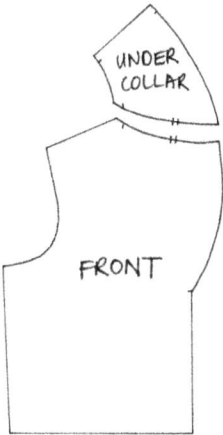

✂ Sometimes there's an under collar cut separately—the pattern pieces might look like this. The sewing order is a little different for this type of pattern—it's described on page 54.

✂ When cutting out the pattern pieces, don't neglect to snip the notch indicating the break point—it's the point at which the collar should start to roll back.

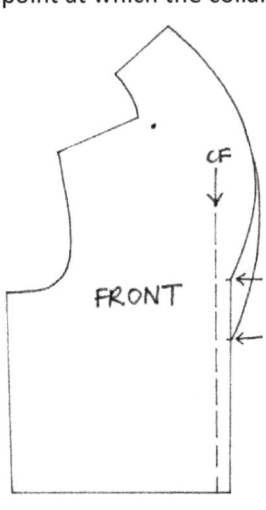

If desired, you can adjust the break point on the collar, but note that lowering the break point will cause the lapels to flare out wider, so you might need to adjust the lapel width as well.

✂ The front facing is interfaced and if there's a back neck facing it's interfaced too. Some jackets have the whole front interfaced as well.

To sew a shawl collar

1. Sew any neck darts first, if you have them. Press. Often the darts are slit along the fold line and pressed open, to reduce bulk.

2. On the facing and the front, stay-stitch the corners of the collar a few centimetres either side of the dot. Stitch on the stitching line. I like to use a smaller stitch (1 or 1.5) for strength. Pivot exactly on the point.

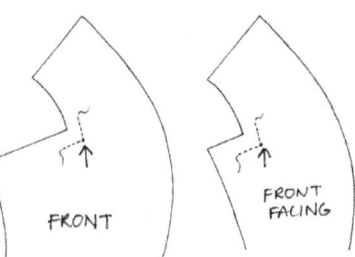

You may like to identify the point with a dot on the wrong side, but I prefer to use the seam guide on the machine—when I think I've reached the pivot point, I pivot and check the second side using the seam guide.

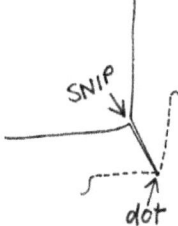

Snip diagonally exactly to, but not over, the stitching. The collar won't sew together properly if you don't snip far enough.

3. With the right sides together, sew the fronts together across the centre back seam. Do the same with the facings. Press the seams open. There's no need to overlock—the seams will be enclosed.

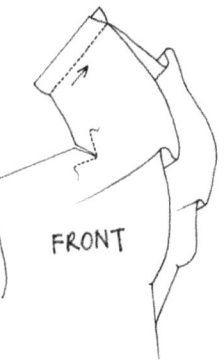

4. Place the fronts onto the back, right sides together, matching the shoulders and back neck.

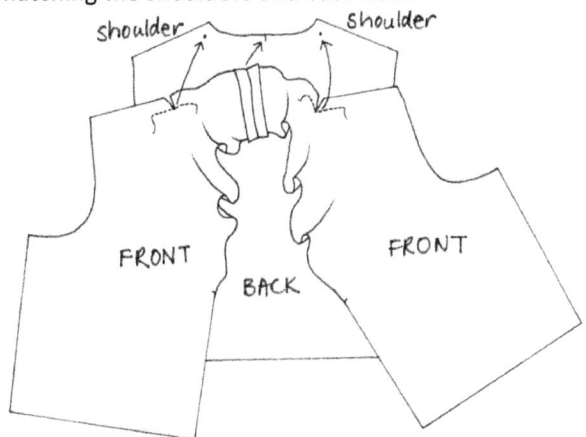

Plunge a pin into each of the pivot points on the front, matching to the points on the back.

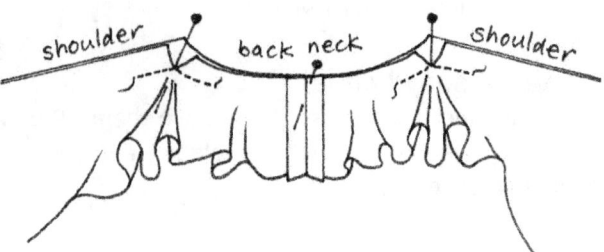

It will be difficult to pin the whole seam before you sew it, so don't try. Beginning at the shoulder with the front on top, pin the first section and sew it to the pivot point. Pin the next section while the first is still in the machine.

Stitch just outside the stay-stitching so it doesn't show on the right side. Pivot at the point of the first pin, then re-arrange the folds of the fabric to sew the back neck to the next pin. Pivot again, re-arrange the fabric and sew the final shoulder. Many people find this part difficult. Take the time to be exact.

If you're doing a fitting, you can sew the garment up to this stage.

If there's a **separate under collar**, the sewing order is a little different (and a bit easier, I think). Sew the front and back together at the shoulder seams. Sew the centre back seam of the separate under collar. Press all the seams open. Sew the under collar onto the garment in one fell swoop. Press the seam open and snip the seam allowance if necessary to make it lie flat.

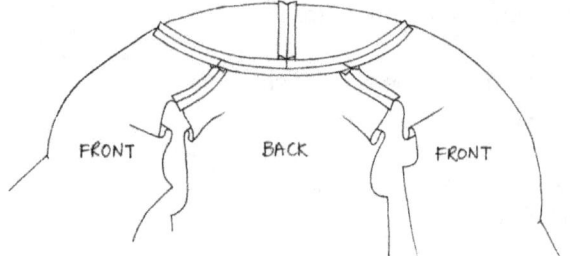

5. Join the facing to the front along the long, curved edge.

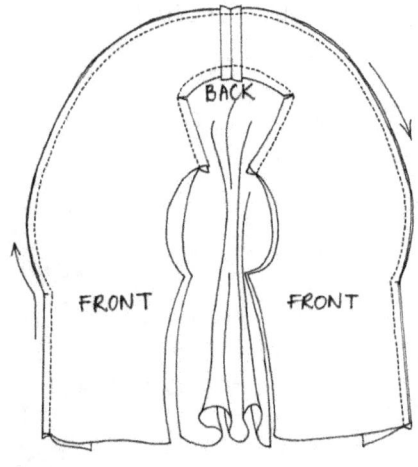

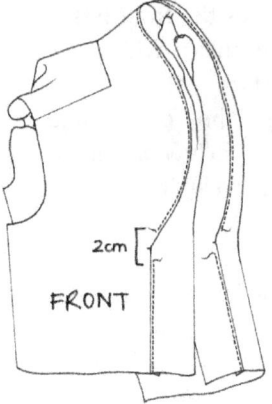

6. Under stitch around the edge of the seam. Stitch on the *facing side* for the fronts and the *undercollar* side for the collar. Leave a 2cm (¾") gap at the break point notch where the understitching changes sides.

7. If the garment has a **lining or a back neck facing**, join the collar facing to it in the same way as you joined the fronts and back in Step 4. Press the shoulder and back neck seams open. At the pivot points, press the seams open and fold the seam allowances neatly over the tops of each other.

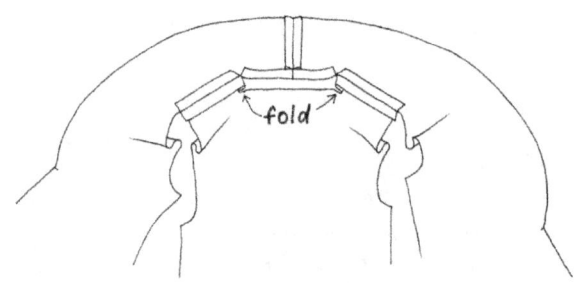

8. Mould the collar around a tailors ham, a dressmakers model or a person's neck. Pin the back neck seams together.

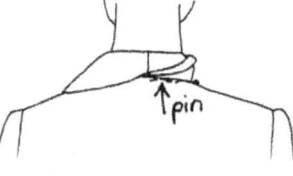

To keep the collar in place, flip up the lining and machine stitch the back neck seams together. Since you've pressed the seams open, you'll be stitching the back lining to the back.

Sometimes the neckline seams don't meet exactly—it depends on how thick the fabric is and how much turn-of-cloth was allowed. Don't force the raw edges to meet, but stitch them where they lie—they do need to be parallel though. The finished collar needs to lie smoothly over the neck seam. The top collar shouldn't curl up.

Collars **55**

9. On a garment with **no lining or back neck facing**, turn the back neck under and stitch. Overlock the long edge and shoulder seams of the facing. Press the back neck seam *up*. Press under the back neck edge of the facing and either hand or machine sew into position.

The shoulder seams of the front facing can be either overlocked and stitched flat (good for bulky fabrics) or folded under and stitched at the same time as the back neck (a neat finish for fine fabrics).

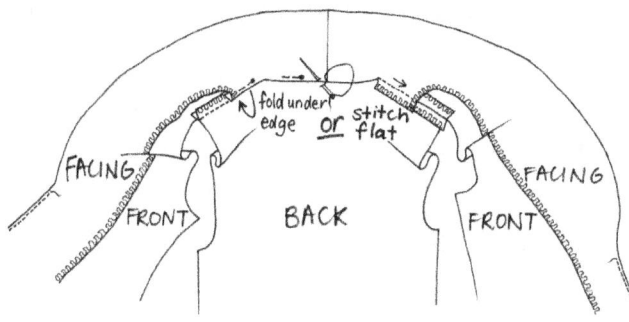

Collars with revers

Rever collars are considered the hardest type to make and certainly sloppy sewing will yield an amateur-looking collar. Take your time and finish each step accurately before continuing and a beautiful collar will be your reward.

The lapels can be notched (left) or peaked (right).

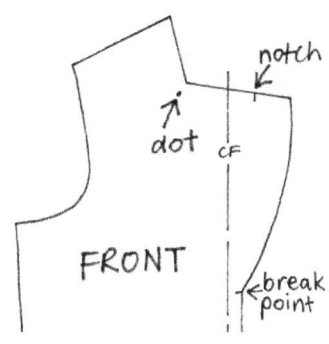

The pattern pieces might look something like this:

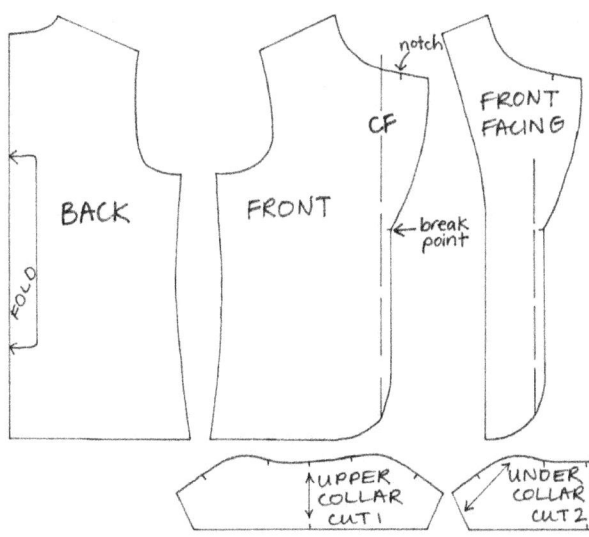

✂ The centre front (CF) line is always indicated. There'll be a notch on the lapels to indicate where the collar is sewn to. On commercial tissue patterns it might be shown as a dot.

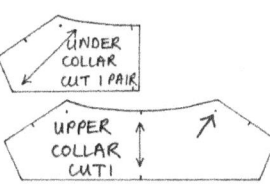

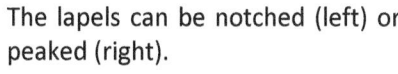

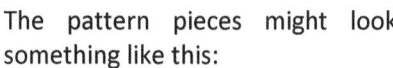

The dot on the front and front facing indicates a pivot point. If you're lucky, the pattern will have been made with a neckline curve (which is quicker to sew) instead of an angle and pivot point. The collar will have a corresponding curve, rather than a matching pivot point dot. The front in the previous column has a curve; this one has an pivot point.

✂ 1.5cm (⅝") seam allowances as featured on commercial patterns are fine. Factory patterns often have the outer edges of the collar and lapels pre-trimmed back to 6mm (¼"). You might find it helpful to do this on your pattern if you have curved corners on the collar or lapels. The narrower seam allowance will give you a more accurate and consistent curve, because with 6mm (¼") seams you can use the edge of the presser foot as a guide.

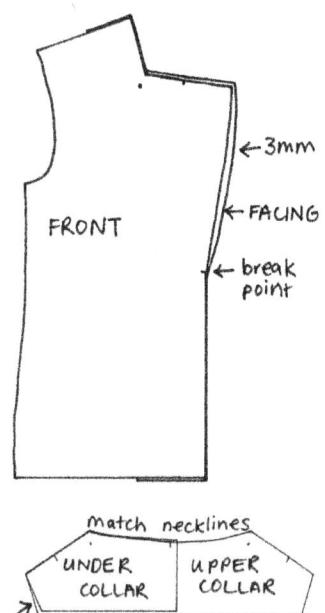

✂ To accommodate the slight extra fabric required for the top collar and lapels to roll over the underneath ones (referred to as turn of cloth), the facing and top collar are cut about 3mm (⅛") wider. Thicker fabrics will need more than this, say, 6mm (¼"). You can lay the collars and front/front facing on top of each other to see this.

Under collars on blouses are often cut exactly the same as the top collar (not even with turn of cloth), and with the same grainline.

✂ Under collars on coats and jackets are cut on the bias with a centre back seam to give a better shape and help the collar to roll. If there's no under collar pattern piece, it's easy to make one. Trace the top collar, cut it in half down the centre back and add a seam allowance. Draw in a new grainline at 45 degrees to the centre back. Trim off 3mm (⅛") along the outside edge to allow for turn of cloth.

✂ **Interface** the facing and top collar for blouses. On coats and jackets, interface the facing, top collar and under collar. The under collar fusing has the same bias grainline as the fabric. Often on jackets the entire fronts are also interfaced.

✂ Rever collars on jackets have a lining or back neck facing. On blouses they may or may not have a back neck facing.

To sew a rever collar on a blouse

1. Sew the shoulder seams of the blouse and overlock.

2. Make the collar first: place the right sides together and sew along the outside edge. Trim the corners to 3mm (⅛") from the stitching. Turn to the right side and press.

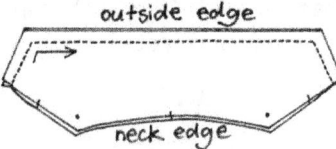

3. If you're not having topstitching on the collar, understitch along the outside edge to stop the undercollar (un-interfaced side) from showing.

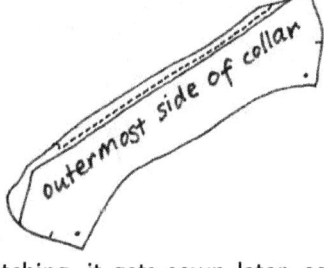

If you *are* having topstitching, it gets sewn later, so ensure the collar is well pressed at this stage. The seam should be sitting perfectly on the edge of the collar. An easy way to do this is to press the seam flat before you press it folded. You can choose to understitch first as well as topstitch if you find it makes topstitching easier.

Some people like to sew only the long outside edge first, understitch it, then sew the two short ends. This makes the understitching run all the way into the corners, which is better if you aren't planning to topstitch.

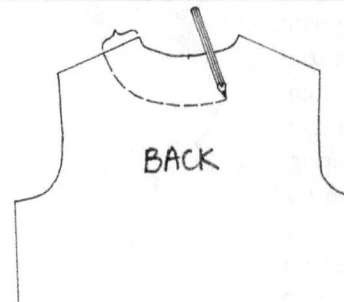

4. You may or may not have a back neck facing—it's easier if you do and simple to make one. On the back pattern piece, trace around the back neck and shoulders, then draw in the line where you'd like the facing. The shoulders of the back facing should be the same length as the shoulders of the front facing (because they have to be sewn together).

5. Prepare the facings: apply the interfacing and overlock the long outer edge. If you have a back neck facing, join the shoulder seams of the facings and press them open. Don't overlock these seams—the fusing will prevent fraying.

6. If the fronts and front facings have pivot points, stay-stitch a few centimetres on either side *on* the seam line, pivoting on the dot. I like to use a smaller stitch length (1 or 1.5), for strength. Snip diagonally exactly to, but not over, the stitching.

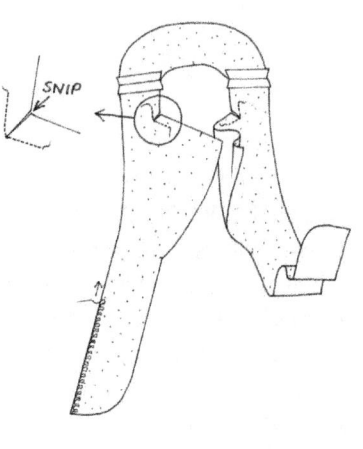

7. If you have a **back neck facing**, sandwich the pre-made collar between the garment and the facing, matching the notches and pivot points if you have them.

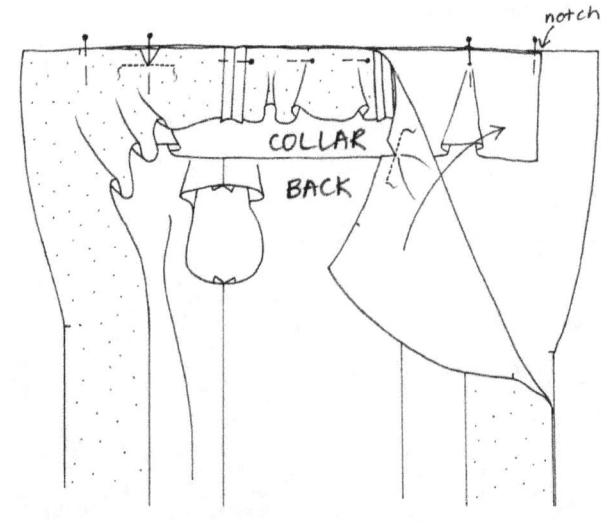

Plunge a pin through all the matching pivot points to keep the layers together. If you have curves instead of pivot points, you might need to strategically snip them a few times if the curve is tight and you have a wide seam allowance. Snip half way into the seam allowance to allow the curve to spread—the tighter the curve the more snips you'll need, but start with about two. Sew, then turn the collar to the right side. Secure the facings at the shoulder seams.

I like to stitch through all layers (garment, facing and seam allowances) around the back neck, 6mm (¼") away from the seam, to hold everything in place. The collar covers the stitching. Proceed to Step 8.

Overlock, or press under, the shoulders of the front facing. Sandwich the front sections of the collar between the fronts and the front facings and stitch. If you have pivot points, plunge a pin through all the matching pivot points to keep the layers together. If you have curves instead of pivot points, you might need to strategically snip them a few times if the curve is tight and there's a wide seam allowance. Snip half way into the seam allowance to allow the curve to spread. Sew the seam then turn to the right side and press.

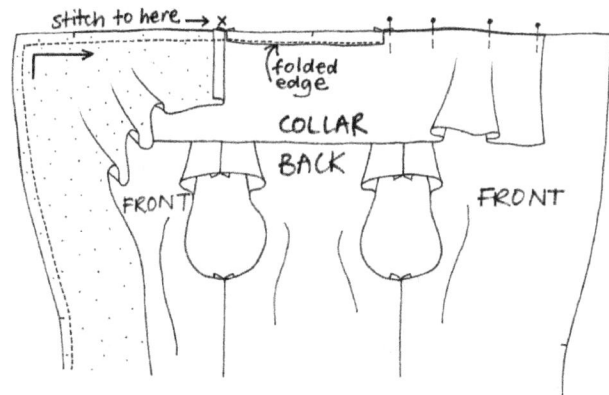

Secure the back neck of the collar by either edgestitching by machine or handsewing it in place.

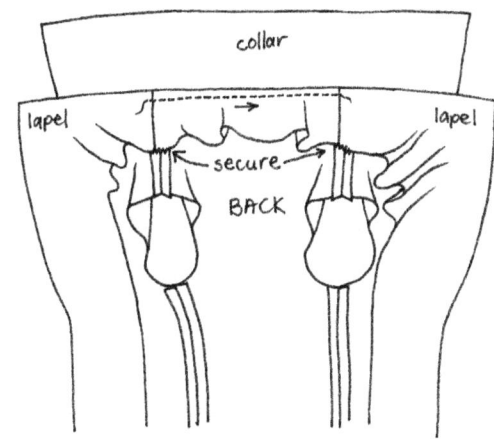

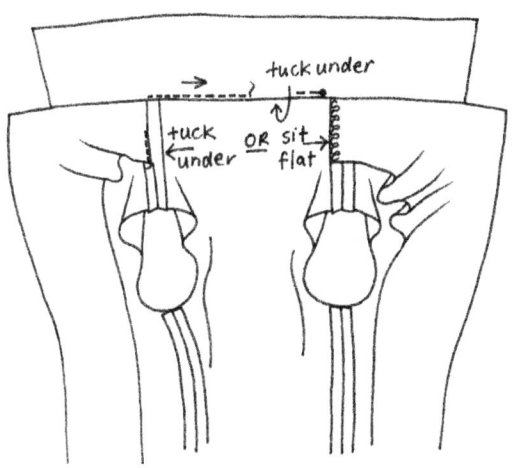

If you **don't have a back neck facing**, snip the shoulder seam points of the outermost (interfaced) collar to the depth of the seam allowance. Press under the seam allowance on the outermost collar.

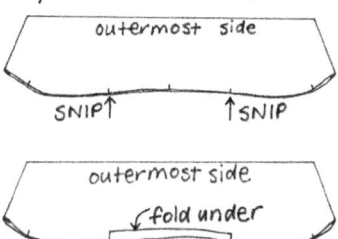

Stitch the un-interfaced back neck portion of the collar to the garment. You can stitch slightly beyond the shoulder seams. Snip into the seam allowance at the shoulder seam points, right up to the stitching, through all layers. Press this seam towards the collar.

8. **For all collars regardless of back neck facings**, understitch the lapels and the front edge. Leave a 2cm (¾") gap at the break point notch where the understitching changes sides.

If you sew the lapels separately before attaching the collar, you can make the understitching continue all the way up into the point of the lapel.

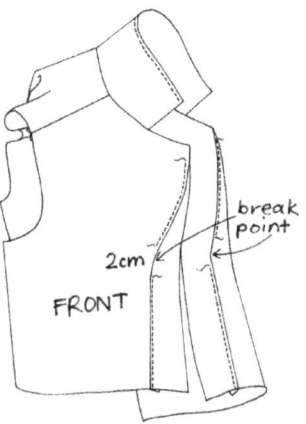

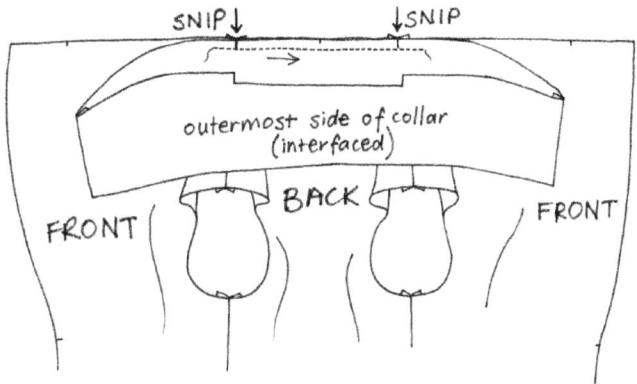

To sew a rever collar on jackets and coats

A rever collar on a jacket is sewn a little differently to a blouse. Instead of making the collar and sandwiching it between the facing and garment, each side of the collar is sewn to its respective front/back and facing/lining, then joined along the entire outside edge. This way allows all the collar seams to be pressed flat and opened to reduce bulk. Blouses can be sewn this way, too, but it's more work and not necessary since blouse fabric is finer.

1. Interface everything that needs it. On coats and jackets, the facing, top collar and under collar are interfaced. The under collar fusing follows the fabric's bias grainline. Often on jackets the entire fronts are also interfaced.

2. Join the jacket's shoulder seams and press them open. Make the jacket's lining, joining it to the front facing. If the jacket is unlined but has a back neck facing, join the shoulder seams of the front and back facings and press open. Sew the centre back seam of the under collar and press it open.

If the collar has pivot points instead of a curve, stay-stitch a few centimetres on either side on the seam line, pivoting on the dot. I like to use a smaller stitch length (1 or 1.5), for strength. Snip diagonally exactly to, but not over, the stitching.

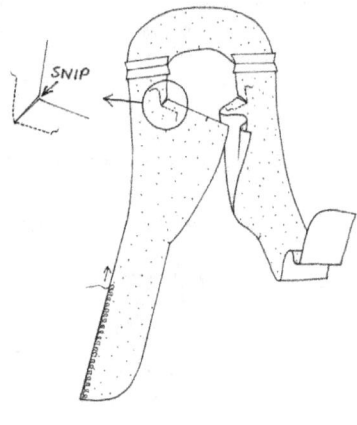

3. With the right sides together, sew the under collar to the garment and the top collar to the lining. Pin together the centres, the dots at the beginning and end and any pivot points.

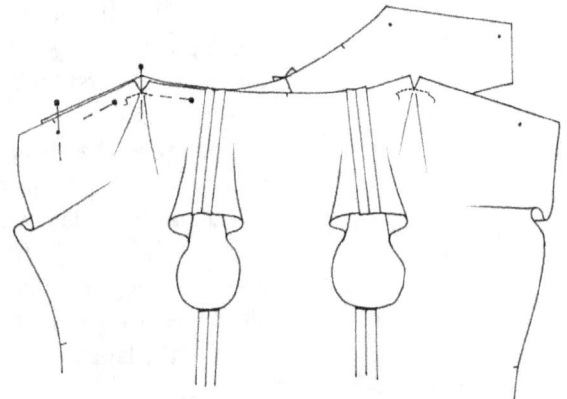

To start sewing, plunge the needle *exactly* into the point indicated on the pattern, ensuring that the backstitching doesn't go over the dot. Accuracy here is very important.

If your pattern has pivot points, plunge a pin into each point and match it with the corresponding point on the collar. Sew with the collar underneath, so you can see the pivot point. Sew just outside the stay-stitching so it doesn't show on the right side.

If the collar has curves instead of pivot points, you might need to strategically snip them a few times if the curve is tight and you have a wide seam allowance. Snip half way into the seam allowance to allow the curve to spread.

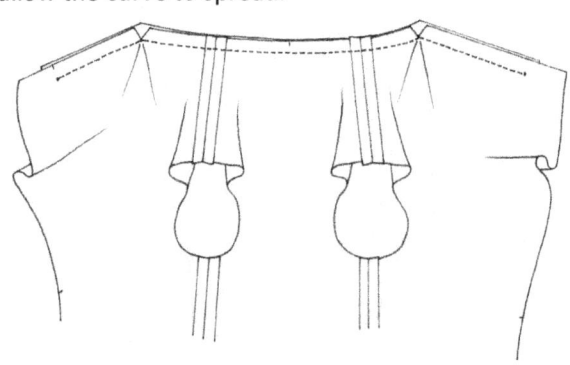

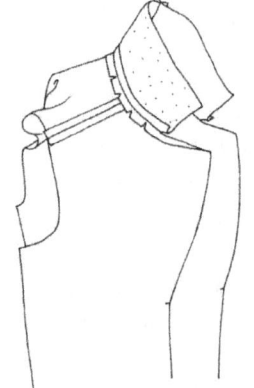

4. Press the collar seams open. Snip any curves if necessary to make them lie flat. At the corners where you pivoted, press the seam allowances into a neat square folded over each other. If you're doing a fitting, you can sew the collar up to this stage.

5. Sew the collars together: at each end, flip the seam allowance towards the lapel so you can see the starting point. It's more accurate to begin sewing at this point on each side and sew away from it, meeting in the middle of the collar.

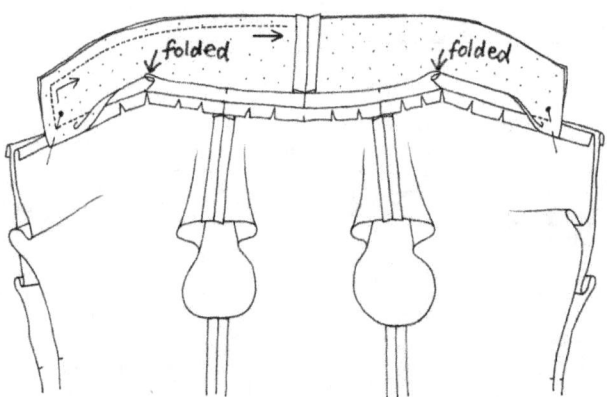

Collars

Plunge a pin through the exact point where you'll begin stitching and start with the needle down in that point. Back stitch carefully at the point, so you don't sew past the dot. After sewing, trim the corners of the collar and turn them temporarily through to the right side to understitch. Understitch along the long edge as far as you can into the corners of the collar.

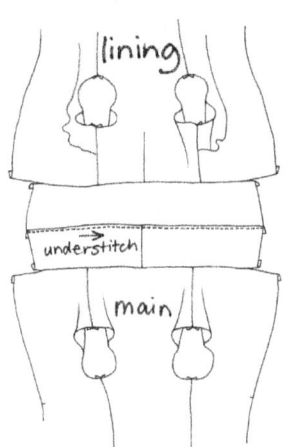

Some people prefer to stitch the long edges of the collars together, then press the seam allowance towards the under collar and understitch. They then sew the two shorter sides. The advantage with this is the understitching reaches right into the corners, which is better if you aren't planning to have any topstitching on the collar.

6. Sew the lapel seams, flipping the seam allowance towards the collar this time. Begin sewing at the dot point once again, with careful backstitching. Insert a pin through the layers so you know exactly where to position the needle, then begin the seam by plunging the machine needle into the point and whipping out the pin. After sewing, trim the corners and turn the collar and lapels through to the right side.

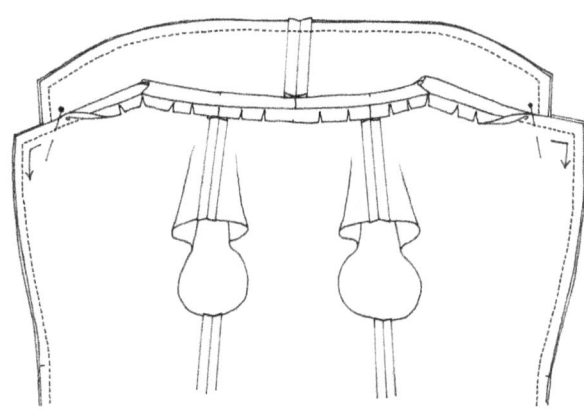

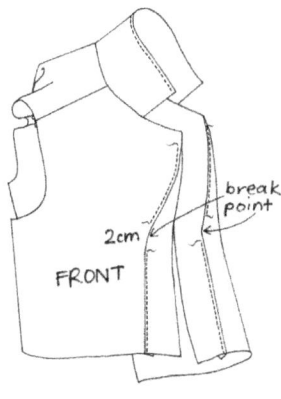

Press and understitch the lapels, leaving a 2cm (¾") gap at the break point notch where the understitching changes sides. If you sew the long edge of the lapels first before sewing the short horizontal part of the notch, you can make the understitching continue into the point of the lapel.

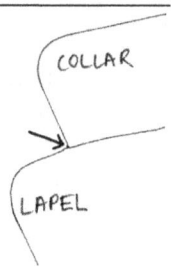

7. There might be a little hole at the four-point junction of the collar/lapels where you began the seams—it's OK, the hole will disappear after the collar and lapels are pressed. Carefully press the collar and lapel, rolling the under collar and under lapel out of sight.

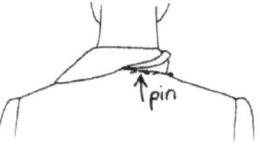

8. Mould the collar around a tailors ham or the neck of a dressmakers model. Pin the back neck collars together in the ditch of the seam.

Flip up the lining and stitch the seam allowances of the back lining and the back together along the back neckline between the shoulder seams.

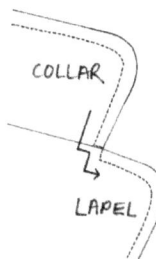

9. Topstitch the collar if desired. To correctly stitch around a lapel notch, stitch around the collar and pivot 90 degrees at the seam (or gorge line, as it's technically known). Stitch-in-the-ditch for a few stitches along the groove in the seam line, then pivot 90 degrees again at the corner and stitch for 6mm (¼") or the whatever the width of your topstitching is. Pivot a final 90 degrees and continue topstitching the lapel.

If you're using special **topstitching thread** in the needle only (and regular thread in the bobbin), be sure to switch sides at the break point where the right side becomes the wrong side. Stitch the upper collar and lapel, stopping at the break point. Cut the thread leaving long tails. Flip the jacket over and continue the stitching on the right side. When you're finished, take a hand sewing needle and invisibly sew in the thread tails at the break point.

If you **aren't using topstitching thread**, make sure your machine tension is adjusted properly so that the stitching looks the same on both sides. When you topstitch, try to roll the edge slightly so that (what will be) the wrong side is out of sight.

Eliminating neck darts

A neck dart is used to give the collar a better fit in both roll and rever collars. It gets rid of excess fabric bulging at the base of the front neck so the collar sits properly around the neck with a well-defined roll line. Not all collars have or need neck darts.

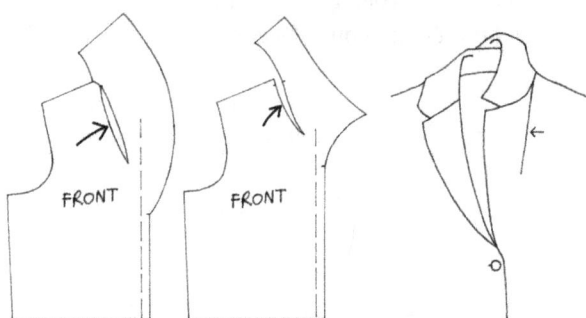

While neck darts are a perfectly legitimate fitting tool, where I worked we always removed them. The entire jacket was cut in calico for the first fitting, then it was ripped apart, pressed and used as the pattern for cutting the good fabric. It was *at* the fitting, rather than before, that we saw if the jacket needed neck darts. The darts got pinned in the calico at the fitting. After the fitting, we undid the front but left the dart

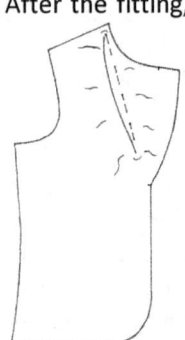

sewn or pinned in (using the type of pins without heads). The dart was pressed using an iron with steam, squashing it as flat as possible. It was pressed on the reverse side so the pins didn't scratch the surface of the iron. We used this as the new front pattern and made new front facing patterns, because the shape changes slightly.

Some commercial patterns have neck darts in them—if you're careful, you could pin the dart in the tissue paper and press it out in the same way. Use a dry iron so the paper doesn't get wet. Otherwise, cut the front in calico, sew or pin the dart, and press that. Don't forget to make new facing patterns.

Tie Collars

A tie collar is basically a stand collar ending in ties. The ties can be slim, almost a binding, a flowing luxurious bow or a wide simple knot. The collar can fold over or ruche around the neck, resulting in wider ties.

Make a pattern

The tie pattern is a long rectangle. Cut it on the bias to allow the ends to tie softly and sit around the neck smoothly. Tie a tape measure around your neck to decide how **long** to make the ties.

Stand a tape measure on edge to measure around the *stitching* line of the garment's neck, then mark on the tie pattern the section to be sewn to the neck.

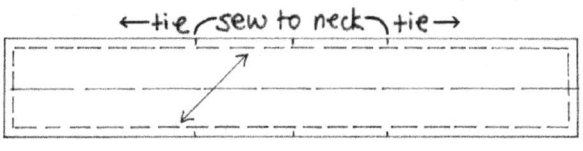

The tie collar will need a gap to accommodate the knot or bow.

For the collar's **width**, multiply the desired finished width by two (or by four for a fold-over tie) and add two seam allowances. The seam allowances you add should be the same as the neck of the garment.

The neck line will need a front facing to finish off the edge.

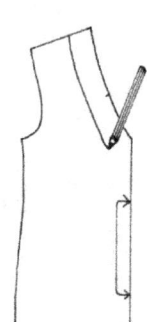

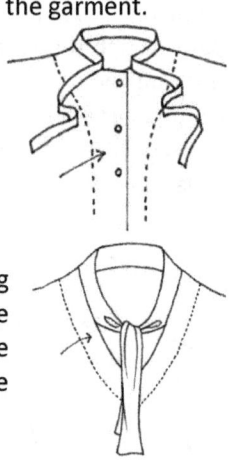

You can make a front facing pattern by tracing around the garment's neckline and drawing in the facing line.

Don't interface the tie collar—it will add bulk and make the ties hard to tie. The facings, however, will need to be interfaced.

If there's a centre back seam on the garment the tie collar will be in two parts. The back of the collar can fasten with a zip, hooks and eyes, or buttons and loops.

To sew a tie collar

1. With the right sides together, sew the prepared front facing onto the garment, to the parts of the neck *not* joined to the tie collar.

Collars **61**

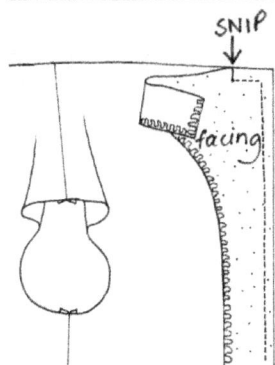

Stop exactly where the collar begins, backstitching securely. Snip into the seam allowance at the end of the stitching, exactly to the stitching. Clip any curves or corners, turn to the right side, press and understitch the facing.

2. Sew the shoulder seams of the garment and overlock. Overlock the shoulders of the front facing. Tack, using a long machine stitch, the remaining neck edges of the facing onto the neck edges of the garment (this part will be sewn to the collar).

3. With the right sides together, stitch one edge of the collar to the outside of the neck.

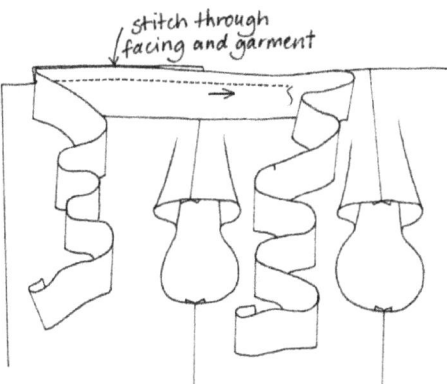

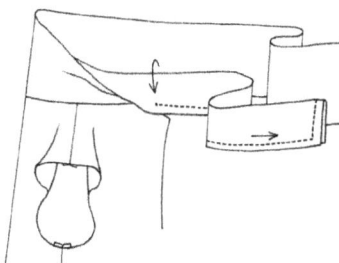

4. Fold the ends of the collar (the ties) right sides together and sew. Trim the corners, turn through and press.

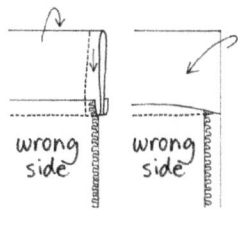

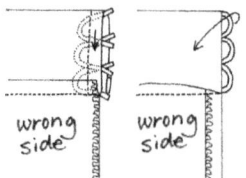

5. **If the collar has a centre back opening**, decide on the fastening before finishing the ends.
For hooks and eyes, bag out the ends before stitching down the collar.

If you're planning buttons and loops, insert the loops as you bag out the ends.

If you've opted for a back zip, finish stitching down the collar *after* sewing the zip in.

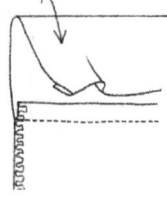

6. On the inside of the neck, turn under the seam allowance on the tie and stitch the folded edge down. You can either do this by hand on the inside, or, by pinning the edge carefully, you can stitch-in-the-ditch on the outside by machine.

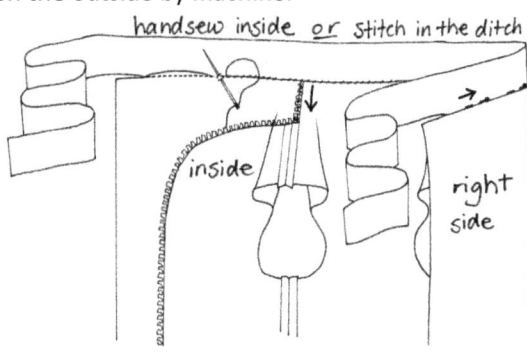

Knit collars

Standing collars intended for knit fabrics (such as skivvy necks) have a rectangular pattern piece, with a fold line through the centre and the greatest amount of stretch going around the neck.

A **polo collar** is two thicknesses when worn. It's  different from the polo *shirt* collar (see pages 116-120 for these).

A fold-over **skivvy neck** is designed as a double width to fold back down on itself (as in a "roll necked" skivvy), making the collar four thickness when worn.

T-shirt necks are made in exactly the same way, with a narrower band that's cut *smaller* than the neckline.

These are all easy to construct. The fabric can be the same as the garment if it's stretchy enough, or a matching rib.

For **polo necks**, the pattern is cut twice as wide as the finished width plus two seam allowances. The pattern is as long as will comfortably fit over the head and around the neck plus two seam allowances.

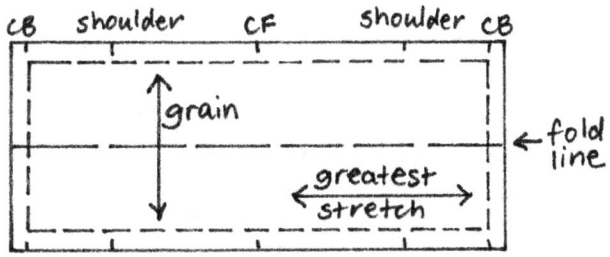

A **fold-over skivvy neck** pattern is constructed in the same way but twice as wide, to accommodate the turnover.

Mark the centre front (CF) point on the collar and if possible the shoulder points, to help sew the collar on evenly stretched. Note that the collar may be smaller than the neckline to which it will be sewn, or it may be the same size, but it's never bigger.

A **t-shirt neck** will be around 5cm (2") smaller than the neckline. Since all knits stretch to a different degree, trial and error is the only way to get a perfectly fitting collar. See page 188 for a V-necked band with a mitred V.

To sew a knit collar

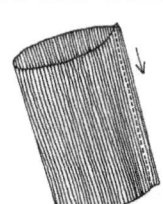
1. Sew the centre back seam to make a tube and press the seam open or to one side.

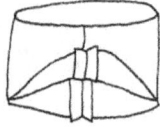
2. Fold the collar wrong sides together, matching the raw edges.

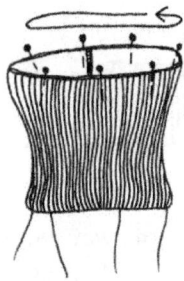
3. Pin the collar onto the neck of the garment, right sides together, matching the centre back, centre front and shoulder notches. Stretch it to fit the neck as you sew it on, between these points.

Hoods

Hoods aren't really a collar but they *are* a type of neckline finish. They can be applied to tops, jackets or capes. A hood on a t-shirt or fleecy top can be a good solution if you can't find any matching rib trim.

The neckline of a hood needs to be the same measurement as the garment's neckline, however, the hood can be gathered or pleated onto the garment depending on the style.

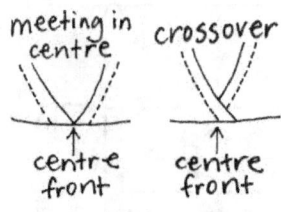

The front edges of the hood can cross over at the neckline or meet in the centre front. Obviously hoods on jackets and capes would meet at the centre front.

The very simplest kind of hood is a rectangle folded in half to form each side of the hood. These work best in knitted fabric. Pixie hoods, as they're sometimes called, can be attached to the garment or made to be worn separately as a hat, buttoning or tying under the chin. The point of the hood sticks up and looks cute on children.

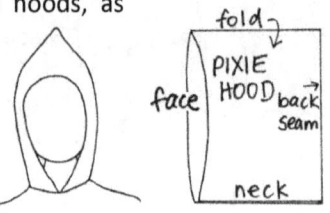

Most hood patterns have a more refined shape to fit the head and neck better. There's usually a seam running through the centre of the hood, from the forehead to the back of the neck, but sometimes the top is on the fold so you can't see a seam from the front.

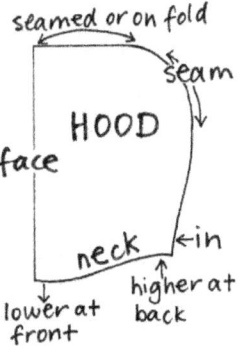

The most fitted type of hood has a gusset and high neck to fit snugly around the head.

It must be made from knit fabric to stretch. Track and field athletes sometimes wear hoods like this on their race gear. Cathy Freeman in the Sydney 2000 Olympics comes to mind. The pattern might look like this:

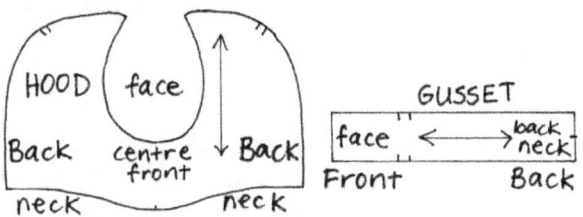

At the opposite end of the spectrum are the hoods worn in period costume dramas or Star Wars movies, usually attached to capes. The hood droops at the sides and can hide the wearer's face. It's gathered or pleated onto the garment's neckline. The pattern might look like this:

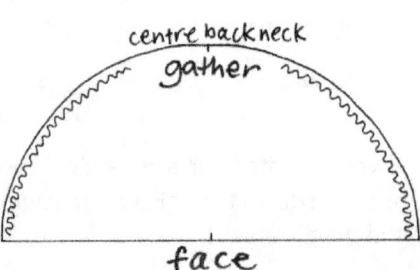

Collars **63**

A hood can also be made from a very high skivvy or cowl collar, pulled up to make a hood or snood. The pattern is simply a tube. This type of hood collar was very popular in the 1970's on knit tops and dresses.

Hoods can be made to fit deep V or scooped necklines.

Make a pattern

Hood patterns are simple to make with a few measurements, but rely on trial-and-error to get the look you want. Usually the neckline of the garment is determined first and then the hood made to fit. The garment doesn't have to have a high neckline—some elegant hoods are designed to fit scooped or wide necklines.

1. Measure the exact neck circumference of the garment by standing the tape measure on its side around the pattern's *stitching* line. Note the measurement of the shoulder seam position.

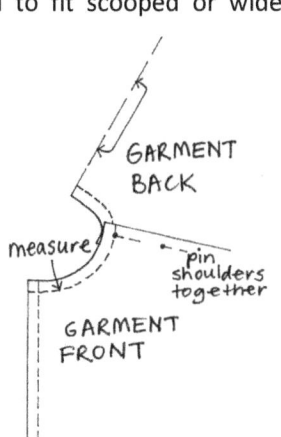

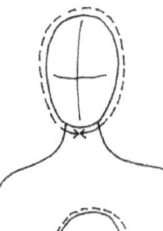

2. Take three measurements around the person's head:
(1) Measure around the face.

If the hood will be droopy, adjust the tape measure to imitate its looseness.

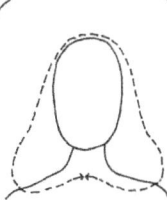

(2) Over the head from forehead to nape of neck, and (3) around the head from temple to temple.

3. Draft a hood shape on paper. I like to start with a rectangle or square using the measurements I've taken, then draw a hood shape that I think looks right. If the hood has a gusset I don't put it in yet—I like to get the basic shape right first. I sew one up in some suitable fabric to check it.

To make a **gusseted hood**, take a finished hood pattern and remove half the width of the gusset from the edge (dash line). Make a straight gusset to fit the exact length.

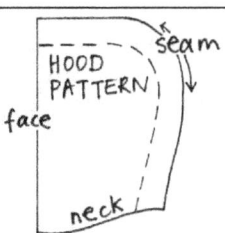

For example, for a gusset that is to be 10cm (4") wide finished, trim 5cm (2") from the long edge of the hood pattern. Make a straight gusset 10cm (4") wide *plus* two seam allowances (the seam allowances for the *hood* are already on there; you just have to add them onto the gusset). To find the length the gusset needs to be, measure around the *stitching* line of the now-trimmed hood.

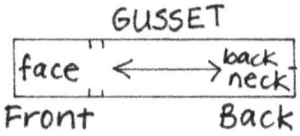

Gussets don't necessarily have to be the same width all the way along—yours could be wider at the centre and tapered at the front and back, for example, just as long as the hood and gusset match up.

When you make a hood pattern, think about how you would like to finish the front edge.

Hoods can have a casing for a drawcord or elastic. A drawcord will need buttonholes or eyelets in the casing for the ends of the cord—mark these on the pattern and transfer to the fabric when cutting out. They will be the first thing to do when sewing the hood.

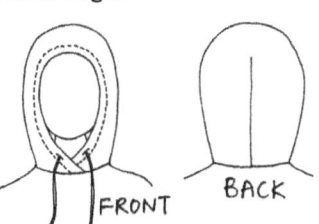

A hood can be all or partially elasticised to make it sit close around the face—some hoods have elastic for a short way just at the top.

Binding is effective on jackets and capes. The hood and front edges can be bound in one operation, then a zip can be inserted or buttons and loops or toggles added.

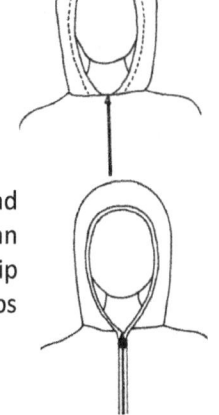

The edges can be trimmed with fur, feathers or braid. The hood can be lined in the same fabric if it's light enough, or else a matching or contrast lining. The lining and main fabric can be stitched together at the edge, or the main fabric can extend in a little.

Construction

(or "When I make a garment, what order do I sew things in, and why?")

Although commercial patterns come with step-by-step instructions, sometimes you might need to make a garment without any directions. You might have made a change to the style of a pattern you bought, or selected a fabric that requires different handling. Some patterns come with no or very few directions (or confusing ones!), or you might have drafted your own pattern.

There are lots of different ways to make garments, and the often the answer is "it depends".

The order and methods you choose will be dictated firstly by the type of fabric you're using, and then by the machines you have available, your own skills, the overall look of the garment, how much money you have to spend, the time factor and (in industry) the price the garment will sell for.

Each time you make a garment you'll build on the knowledge and skills acquired from the previous one.

I can recall the satisfying feeling at the end of a production run of a season's clothing range. Every garment had been perfected in fit and construction, as all the problems had been sorted out...and then it was time to start on the next range.

Think first and make some decisions before you begin:
- Seams open or closed?
- Topstitching?
- How are you going to apply any bindings, facings or linings?
- How and when will you apply any trims?
- Decide which edge finish you're going to use before sewing. There are lots of ways to finish the edges of facings, seams, hems and pockets.

A general sewing order:

1. Cut out all the pieces of fabric, lining, interfacing and any contrasting fabric. Mark all the darts, notches, and placement lines so you don't have to keep referring to the pattern. If I have a lot of sewing to do, I do all the cutting out in one session—it's quicker.

2. Apply interfacing to all pieces that require it. While you're at the ironing board, press in folds, press up hems and press waistbands or cuffs in half.

3. Sew all the garment details: linings, ties, collar, pockets, tabs, belt loops and so on.

4. Sew anything that can be sewn flat on the main garment sections. For example, darts, pleats, cuff plackets, gathering and pockets that don't go through seam lines.

5. If there are any seams on the front or back (for example princess line seams or design lines), sew and press the seams before sewing the completed front and back together.

6. Complete complicated sewing tasks on pieces before joining them to the main garment, for example sew plackets and cuffs on a shirt sleeve before setting the sleeve into the armhole.

7. Things to sew last: waistbands, hems, inserting linings, buttons and buttonholes.

When I was a fashion student learning to sew, our teacher asked us to find some ready-made garments and write out the order they were sewn in. We also had to write out our intended sewing order for garments we made in class (we had drafted the patterns ourselves). After a while it became easy to "make" the garments in our heads before we sat down to actually make them, and we didn't need written directions anymore. It was a good exercise and now I find my mind does it automatically.

Sewing flat versus sewing-in-the-round

There are two ways to sew intersecting garment seams: flat or in-the-round. Each has its advantages and disadvantages.

Generally, the **flat** method is fast, efficient and easier, but can be bulky where seams intersect. It's great for oversized, loose fitting garments with simple shapes.

In-the-round is considered a better quality method. It's more ergonomic to the body's shape because the seam forms a continuous curve, and is the best choice for sewing fitted garments.

Crotch seam on trousers

In the flat method, the front and back crotch seam gets sewn first, then the inside leg seam is sewn in one fell swoop.

Jeans are sewn this way, because in factories the inside leg gets sewn on a flat felling machine that topstitches at the same time.

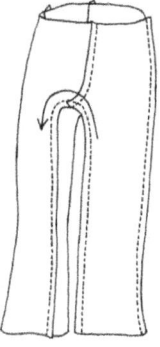

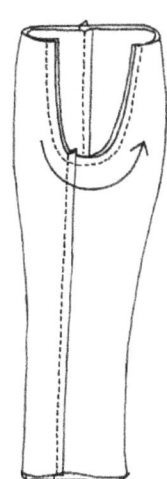

To sew a crotch seam in-the-round, the inside leg seams get sewn first, then the crotch seam is sewn in a continuous curve. It's easier to do this when one trouser leg is placed inside the other, right sides together. I sew all of my trouser crotch seams in-the-round. If there's a centre back or centre front zip, I sew a little bit of the crotch seam, enough to put the zip in, then sew the rest of the crotch seam later. By the way, I always sew crotch seams with two rows of stitching, one on top of the other, for strength.

Sleeve and armhole seams

In the flat method, the sleeve is sewn into the armhole first, then the underarm/side seam is sewn in one seam. This method is used for sleeves where the sleeve head is flatter and there is little or no ease, for example men's shirts, drop shoulders, children's sleeves and doll's clothes.

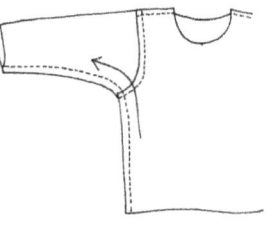

When sewn in-the-round, the seam is sewn in a continuous curve around the armhole.

The side seam of the garment and the sleeve underarm seam are sewn first, then the sleeve is set in (sewn) to the armhole.

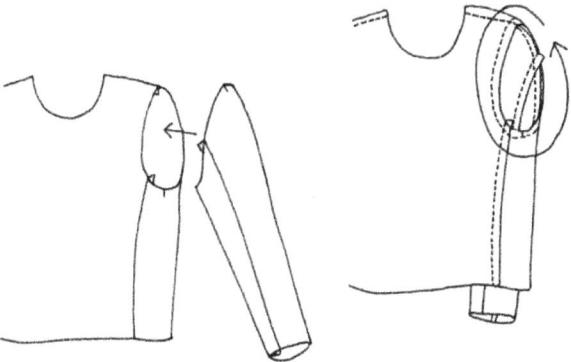

This method is always used for fitted jackets and coats, and also for blouses and dresses.

You'll *have* to use this method for garments with a side panel instead of a side seam, because there's no underarm seam.

Waist facings

To sew a waist facing using the flat method, first the front and back facings are attached to the respective front and back. The side seams are then sewn all the way through the garment and facing. The facing is then folded down and secured to keep it in place.

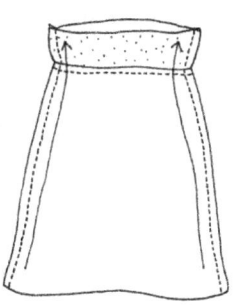

The big advantage of this method is being able to adjust the waist measurement easily, without a great deal of unpicking. You can fine-tune the fit of the waist when the skirt is nearly finished. I like to use this method if I'm making a garment for someone whose weight fluctuates. The disadvantage is slight bulk around the top of the side seams, even if the side seams are pressed open.

When the waist facing is sewn on in-the-round, first the side seams of the garment are sewn together and the side seams of the facing are sewn together. The facing is then sewn on as a ring around the waist. This is my preferred method because I think it looks better on the inside.

See page 382 for more on sewing waist facings.

Fittings

The construction order will be slightly different if fittings are required. Even if the garment is made in calico first and checked, you'll probably need to do a check in the fabric as well, as all fabrics perform differently.

✂ Always fit the garment right side out. Put on the type of shoes and underwear that will be worn with the garment to get the full effect. Do up the garment accurately, matching the centre lines and seam lines, and insert shoulder pads if they're going to be used.

Fit both sides of the garment as similarly as you can—it's almost impossible to pin the left and right sides exactly alike while the garment is on the body, but do the best you can. Slight differences can be evened up when the garment is flat on the table.

✂ First check the overall effect—silhouette, balance and proportions—before attending to the minor details.

✂ Try and do as much construction as you can between fittings (without having to unpick and backtrack too much if it's wrong) so that your fitting time is maximised. You want to be able to check as much as possible at each fitting.

✂ As you prepare for fittings, check the garment as you go using a dressmakers model (if you have one).

✂ Try to limit the number of fittings to no more than four, otherwise the garment starts to look worn and creased and begins to take up too much of everyone's time.

✂ Immediately after a fitting I like to make notes on what changes to make, while things are fresh in my mind. When I make the changes I mark them on the pattern as well.

✂ If you're fitting **stretch fabrics**, use safety pins instead of regular pins. Sew up the garment for the fitting using a long straight stitch, a stretch needle and matching thread. After the fitting you can overlock straight over the top of the long stitches without unpicking. Give the seam a stretch to pop the stitches.

Streamlining construction

In construction, time is saved by completing as much as possible at each "station" (sewing machine, overlocker and ironing board) before moving to the next. Begin every component of the garment at the same time and continue until pressing is required. Press everything, then resume sewing until pressing is required again.

Usually in factory production, all the pressing is left until the end (with the exception of garments with closed linings, such as jackets, which have to have the seams pressed before the lining is attached). The machinist machines, and the presser presses.

For single garments, it's better to press-as-you-go; it's easier to press smaller sections, it makes sewing easier and more accurate and there's less work to do at the end.

Cutting

Understanding fabric..............................67	scissors and shears......................74
Do I prewash the fabric?.......................68	cutting and scissor tips...............74
how to prewash..................68	Estimating fabric........................75
interfacings and trims.......68	skirt layouts 75
what do factories do?........68	trouser layouts 76
how to test for shrinkage......69	tops and shirts layouts.............77
Straightening the fabric ends................69	dress layouts 78
3 ways to straighten an edge 69	recording layouts 78
Check the fabric....................................70	Transferring pattern markings............78
one way fabrics....................70	Cutting knits.............................79
Check the pattern pieces.......................70	Stripes, checks and geometrics............80
Folding the fabric.................................72	analyse the stripe or check........80
Positioning the pieces..........................72	styles that work....................80
guidelines for layouts 72	where to match the pattern.......81
other layout tips..................72	sleeve checks on jackets.............82
chalk and pins......................73	cutting details.......................82
thrifty and time saving tips..........74	alternatives to matching.............82
Cutting..74	laying out pattern pieces 83

The usual procedure for cutting is to fold the fabric double, right sides together. Pin all of the pieces on, aligning the grainlines, and cut them out. Transfer the pattern markings (notches and dots) before removing the pattern pieces. Hmmm....sounds nice and simple when you say it like that, so why are people afraid of plunging in with the scissors?

Understanding fabric

Before preparing to cut, it may help to understand how fabric is structured. Did you ever do weaving with piece of cardboard at school? You created warp threads by winding wool through cuts in the ends of the cardboard, then wove the wool under and over the warp (if you weren't careful the weaving always got skinny in the middle from pulling the weft too tightly).

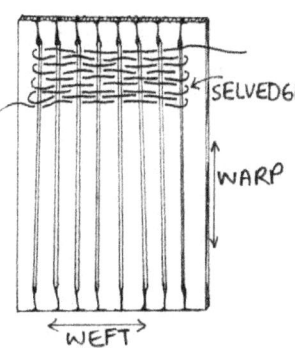

Fabric is constructed in just the same way, but on a larger and finer scale.

Woven fabrics are made from two sets of yarns, the **warp** and the **weft**. They intersect each other at right angles. When the fabric is woven, the warp threads are positioned first on the loom and the weft threads are interlaced over and under them.

The **selvedge** is the firm, woven strip at the edge. Each piece of fabric has two selvedges, one on each side.

The **grain** refers to the direction the threads run in. The lengthwise grain is the direction the warp threads run in (it's parallel with the selvedge) and the crosswise grain is the direction of the weft.

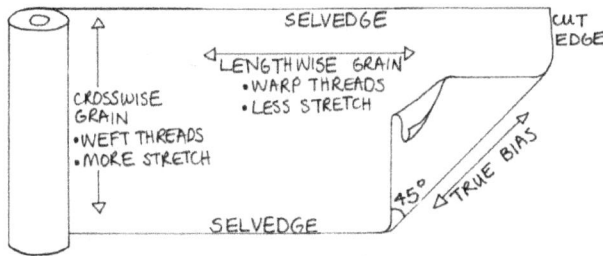

The **grainline** is a line printed on the garment pattern piece to align with the lengthwise grain and help position the pattern correctly on the fabric.

Fabric tends to have more give or stretch on the crosswise grain than the lengthwise.

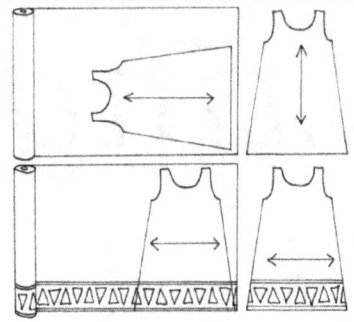

In most cases, the lengthwise grain hangs vertically when you're wearing clothes. The exception is to achieve a design feature, for example to position a border print.

In that case the crosswise grain will hang vertically when you're wearing the garment.

The **bias** is any diagonal that intersects these grains. True bias is a 45 degree angle to the grain. The bias has the most stretch and makes an unstable edge when cut.

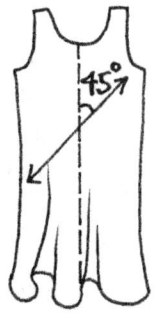

Bias cut clothing has a grainline which is 45 degrees to the usual horizontal grainline (even though technically it's cut on the true bias, it's referred to as simply "cut on the bias"). Bias cut clothing performs in a different way to clothing cut on the straight grain—it falls in smooth drapes and moulds to the figure, although the garment looks limp and shapeless until it's put on.

Bias cut is also used to create a chevron or diagonal effect with stripes or checks.

Clothing cut on the bias is also sometimes called "cut on the cross" and occasionally "diamond cut" (usually for lingerie).

Do I prewash the fabric?

When you buy a length of gorgeous new material, you probably feel like running straight home and cutting out a garment immediately. But, do you need to prewash it? Prewashing guards against possible fabric shrinkage after construction and dye running.

Prewash the fabric when:

✂ You think the fabric might shrink a lot when you wash it. I like to prewash corduroy, cotton, linen, rayon and washable (non-drycleanable) silk.

✂ The fabric is dirty or it smells.

✂ You're using two or more different fabrics in the same (washable) garment.

Don't prewash when:

✂ You plan to dryclean.

✂ You don't think the fabric will shrink. I don't wash synthetic fabrics (unless they smell like plastic).

How to prewash

✂ Some people simply wash the fabric in whichever way they'll wash the garment when it's finished.

✂ Other people hot machine wash, dry in a hot dryer, then repeat the process. The theory is to give the fabric the worst treatment to maximise the shrinkage before beginning to cut and sew. I don't recommend this for any but the toughest fabrics (if at all), in case the fabric is ruined before you even start!

✂ I dip the fabric in a bucket of really hot tap water (or warm water for silk and wool), swish it around, then spin it damp in the machine and line dry.

Try not to wring the fabric by hand—it will stretch it. You can spin it damp in the washing machine or wrap it up in towels and stand on it to blot the excess moisture. Ironing the fabric before you cut it will make cutting easier and more accurate.

What about interfacing and trimmings?

Personally, I never do, and I've never had a problem, but it is recommended for some interfacings, for example woven, weft and knit fusibles, especially those containing rayon. Ask when you buy it. Soak the interfacing in a basin of hot water without agitating for ten minutes, roll up in a towel to blot excess moisture, then line dry. Store labelled.

What do factories do?

It may come as a surprise (although not really when you think about it) to hear that fabrics, interfacings and trims are not prewashed in clothing factories, even though the fabrics and trims come from the same suppliers that fabric shops use. Apart from the added cost and inconvenience, washing removes the size that the fabric is finished with after it's woven. Size is kind of like starch. It makes the fabric firmer, and easier and faster for the machinists to handle and sew. It also makes a better-looking finished garment.

So what do clothing factories do about fabrics that might shrink? The fabric supplier might say how much the fabric will shrink or the manufacturer will test it themselves. Large factories have dedicated testing facilities, but smaller factories just use a bucket and soap (kept under the sink in the lunch room) or an employee will take it home on the weekend to chuck in with their weekly wash.

A preliminary test might be to cut a square of fabric *exactly* 10cm by 10cm and wash it by hand. A further, more accurate, test is to cut a square 1m by 1m to wash and then measure.

Another test is to make up a sample garment in the fabric and wash it, then measure it. This gives a good indication as to how the fabric performs as a garment. If the fabric does shrink, either the manufacturer will decide not to use it, or else will build a shrinkage allowance into the pattern.

To allow for shrinkage, extra length is added onto the pattern. Most fabrics, if they shrink, will shrink on the lengthwise grain, that is, parallel to the selvedge, or vertically if you're wearing the garment. If a fabric shrinks on the crosswise grain at all it tends to also shrink a greater amount on the lengthwise grain. Manufacturers usually decide not to use these fabrics, because the total shrinkage is so great it's not worth the hassle.

Here's an example of building a shrinkage allowance into a pattern: corduroy trousers made from corduroy that shrinks 5% (which is quite a lot). Therefore every 100cm will shrink 5cm. A leg length is about a metre, so 5cm will be added onto the length of the trousers. Special care labelling might be used to tell the customer how much shrinkage to expect. Or, sometimes garments are washed/shrunk after sewing them. Stone washed jeans are a good example of this. Shrinkage doesn't only happen from washing the fabric. It can also be caused by pressing, steam, heat applied transfers, a fusing press, heat used to set screen printing, or lots of stitching (for example quilting or embroidery).

Some knits actually get larger in one or both directions as the fibres relax.

How to test for shrinkage

Cut a square of fabric *exactly* 10cm by 10cm (metric is easier than imperial for this). Mark the grain direction. Press with a steam iron, dampen it, wash it, put it through your fusing press—do all the things that the garment will have done to it in manufacture or afterwards. Measure the square and determine how much it has shrunk and in which direction. For example, it may now measure 9.6cm in the lengthwise direction, which means it has shrunk by 4%.

Straightening the fabric ends

On many fabrics (but not all), the cut end must be straightened so the fabric can be folded evenly for cutting out. I only straighten one end and then begin at that end when I place my pattern pieces. The straightened end and the selvedge can then be squared up on the corner of the table.

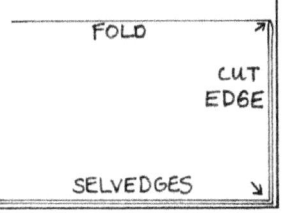

If you don't straighten the end, you won't have a reference point for the horizontal edges of your garment.

You'll need to straighten the end if:

✂ The fabric has woven checks, or crossgrain stripes, pattern or weave. Otherwise the design will be crooked when you cut the garment out.

✂ The fabric is fine, floppy and unstable. Otherwise the hemline will hang unevenly.

After the fabric end has been straightened, the straightened ends should sit on top of each other when the fabric is folded perfectly in half, selvedge on selvedge.

For all other fabrics, including knits (but excluding horizontally striped knits), **let the cut edges sit where they want to**. It's far more important that the *selvedges* sit on top of each other rather than the cut edges, otherwise the garment will twist around the body when it's finished. If you stretch the fabric on the bias to attempt to align the cut edges, it will only be temporary—many fabrics have permanent finishes and won't remember the new alignment.

3 ways to straighten a cut edge (in order of trying)

1. **Cut on a prominent line**, if the fabric has a woven stripe, check or geometric design.

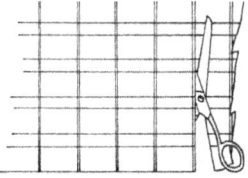

2. **Tear off a strip**. Make a snip in one selvedge. Grasp both sides of the snip firmly and rip across to the opposite selvedge.

Tearing *quickly* is easier and gives better results than tearing *slowly*, so rip quick. If the tear runs off to nothing before you reach the opposite selvedge, cut a new snip farther from the end and try again.

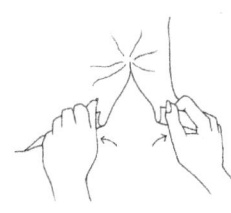

3. For fabrics that won't tear, **draw a thread**. Snip the selvedge, find a crosswise grain thread and gently pull it. Ease the fabric along the thread, then cut along the pulled thread. If the line breaks before you reach the opposite selvedge, cut up to the break,

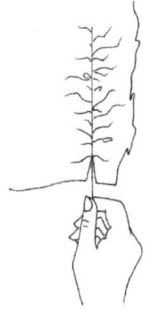

then find a new thread to pull. You can also do this along the lengthwise grain if you have a piece of fabric with no selvedge.

Check the fabric
The right side, or face, of the fabric is usually obvious, but sometimes careful inspection is needed.

- Printed fabrics are sharper, clearer and more defined on the right side, and blurrier on the wrong.
- Smooth fabrics are shinier or softer on the right side.
- Fabrics with texture are more so on the right side. The texture may be more defined or outstanding.
- There might be irregularities on the wrong side, for example, lumps of thread.
- Fancy weaves such as brocade are smoother on the right side, with uneven or loose floats of thread on the wrong side.
- Knits tend to roll towards the right side when stretched along the crosswise grain and the wrong side when stretched along the lengthwise grain.
- In the fabric shop, look at the other fabrics of the same type. The other colours might give you a clue about the intended right side. Ask the sales assistant's opinion.
- If the right and wrong sides still look the same, take a look at the selvedge. Generally, the selvedge is smoother and the pinholes face *up* on the right side.

If you prefer the look of the wrong side, there's no reason why you can't use it. The main rule is *consistency*—stick to the side you've chosen.

After cutting out, if it's difficult to tell the wrong side from the right, identify the wrong side in some way. I use a small chalk mark or a dot in one corner. Some people use a piece of sticky tape.

One-way fabrics
While you're looking at your fabric, look and see whether it's a one-way fabric. One-way fabrics are sometimes referred to as directional fabrics, because they need to be cut with all the pattern pieces laid in the same direction. Sometimes, but not always, more fabric is required to do this. One-way fabrics are described as "with nap" on the pattern envelope.
Included in this category are:

- Fabrics that actually do have a nap—a pile or brushed surface. Velvet and corduroy are a good examples of short naps, and fake fur an example of a long nap. To determine if the fabric is napped, run your hand over the surface as if you were stroking an animal. It should feel smooth with the nap running down and rough with the nap running up. Short naps give a richer, darker colour if the nap runs up the garment, and a lighter coloured, smoother effect if the nap runs down. Long naps are best cut with the nap running down, because they look better. Napped wool coating (short nap) also looks best with the nap running down.

- A pattern or design that doesn't reverse. See which way you like it best according to the design. Note that plants and flowers grow *up*!

- Surfaces that reflect the light in different directions, for example satin. To check, arrange the fabric so you can see it going up and down in each direction next to each other. Look at it in different lights and try holding it up to yourself in the mirror. If the opposing directions look different, the fabric is one-way.

On patterned fabrics, note any prominent patterns and think about where you'd like them positioned on the garment. Or, where you *wouldn't* like them positioned. It helps to hold up the fabric against you while looking in the mirror at a distance.
Consider:

- You don't want a bullseye over your breast.
- Does the pattern need to be centred? Patterns should be *either* centred perfectly *or* not centred at all, but not placed a little bit off-centre.
- The design should balance visually on each side of the garment.

Lastly...
Mark any flaws in the fabric so you can avoid them when you're placing the pattern pieces. Look for slubs, printing errors, dirty marks, holes, snags and permanent wrinkles. If the fabric came from the beginning of the roll, check for slits and holes accidentally made when the roll was unwrapped. If the fabric came from the end of the roll, look for wrinkles, folds and the manufacturer's printing.

Check the pattern pieces
Look at your pattern pieces before laying them on the fabric. Recognise the shapes of the pattern pieces and how they go together, checking the sewing instructions if you need to. Identify the top and bottom of each piece and the side seams.

The **place on fold** symbol means "place this edge on the fold of the fabric". Fold the fabric and place this edge *precisely* on the fold. If you're a little bit off the

Cutting **71**

edge, that means you're adding or subtracting double that amount of fabric to the pattern, so be exact.

The purpose of **notches** is to help you match the seams together when you sew. The fastest and most accurate way to mark them is with a tiny snip in the seam allowance, about 3mm (⅛") long. A snip is much quicker than cutting around the triangles on commercial patterns. Cut the triangles off and snip 3mm (⅛") into the seam allowance instead.
So, this: rather than this:

I also like to mark the garment centre front and centre back with a tiny snip—it helps to position the corresponding pieces centrally.

I learnt early on in my career, as a fresh-faced junior cutter, just how much time is wasted getting the pattern out and checking where missed notches should be. The factory machinists would get *extremely* upset when notches weren't snipped—one machinist used to dump the whole order back on my table in a messy heap (for me) to sort out. So take a tip and make sure you snip all the notches when you cut out, then you won't waste precious time going back to the pattern.

The **grainline** arrow is the key to positioning each pattern piece correctly. The grainline needs to be positioned *exactly* parallel to the selvedges. Pin one end of the grainline first to hold it, then measure from the grainline to the selvedge. Repeat at the other end of the grainline, adjusting the pattern so the measurements are the same.

If you're cutting vertical stripes or checks you won't need to measure, because the grainline will be parallel to the stripes, making positioning the pattern pieces quick and easy.

Sometimes the grainline has only one arrow at the end. It's a symbol for a one-way fabric and denotes the top/bottom direction the pattern piece should be placed in. All the arrows must point in the same direction.

The grainline determines how the fabric will hang when the garment is worn, because the grainline is aligned with the warp threads in the cloth.

To illustrate, here's a four gore flared skirt with three different grainlines. None of these three variations are wrong (although I would choose the first one), rather, they show how the grainline can affect the style and silhouette.

1. If the skirt has the grainline running down the *centre* of each panel, it will cause the centre of the panel to fall flat, with flaring at the sides and centre of the skirt.

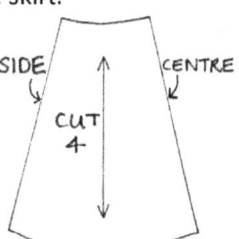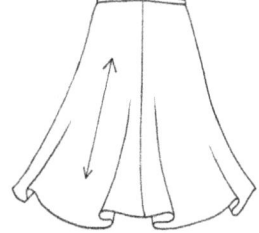

2. If the grainline is aligned with the *centre front* of the skirt, the skirt will hang flat in the middle and flared at the sides.

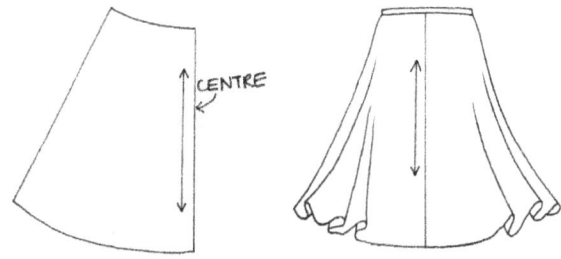

3. If the grainline is aligned with the *side seam* of the skirt, the skirt will have flare in the centre and hang straight at the sides.

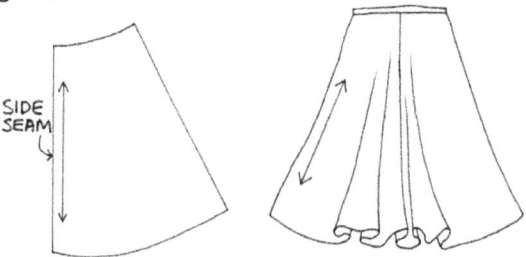

There are many things in sewing that you can fudge (if you know what you're doing) but when placing pattern pieces on the fabric, **the grain line is non-negotiable.** A garment that is cut off-grain will hang incorrectly and the seams will twist around the body and there is *nothing* you can do to fix it. ***Never ignore or guess the grainline—always measure it exactly.***

Tops have the grainline through the centre, so the left and right sides hang in the same way. Tops cut with a centre fold will automatically have the straight grain running through the centre, provided the fabric was folded correctly.

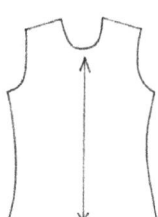

The front of **trousers** cut on-grain should hang flat and smooth.

Trouser legs cut off-grain look terrible. The trouser leg twists around the body and falls in folds, either towards the outside of the leg or into the centre.

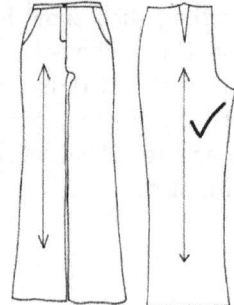

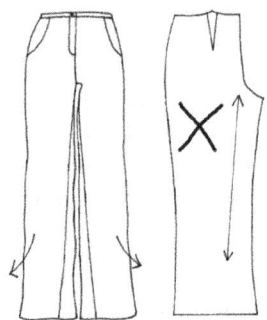 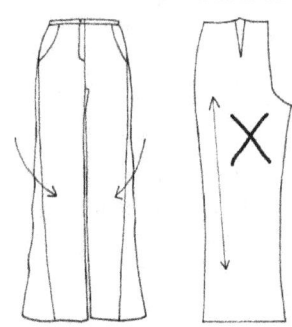

The grainline of a **sleeve** is through the centre. A sleeve cut off-grain will twist around the arm. When the pattern is folded along the grainline, the underarm seams should be parallel and the underarm points level.

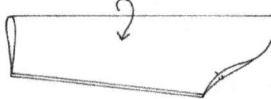

Folding the fabric

Be consistent with the way you fold the fabric. When I do it, I always fold fabric with the right sides together. If I'm cutting only one layer of fabric I cut it with the right side face up. That way, when I go to sew I instantly know which side the right side is.

Fabric can be folded in five different ways:

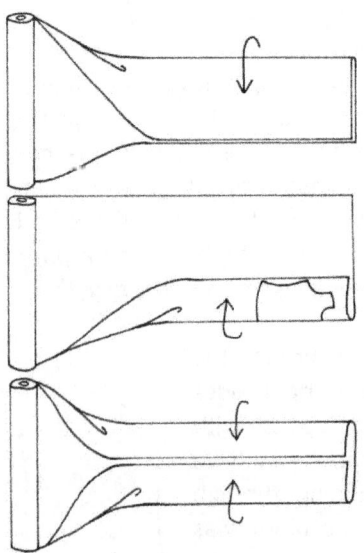

1. **Selvedge-to-selvedge** is the most common. Fold this way first to see if the pieces fit.

2. **One selvedge to the centre**. The widest pattern piece determines the amount to fold.

3. **Both selvedges to the centre** is used for garments with a centre back *and* centre front fold. It's also used if there's an irremovable crease down the centre of the fabric. Often knits get folded this way.

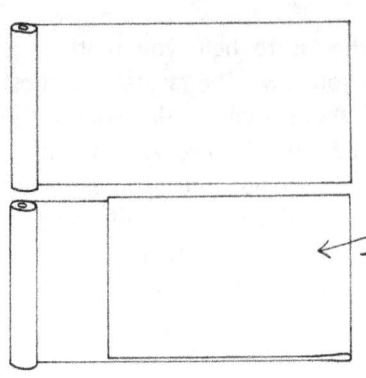

4. **Open (single layer)** is used for bias cut garments and asymmetrical garments.

5. **Open (double layer)** is often used for trousers in narrow width fabrics, or garments with no centre back or centre front fold. Note that for fabrics with a nap or one-way design, the fold will have to be cut and the top layer turned 180 degrees so that both layers run in the same direction.

Sometimes the fabric is folded one way to cut some of the pieces, then re-folded to cut out the rest. Make sure enough fabric remains for the second cut.

Positioning the pieces on the fabric

Commercial paper patterns come with a cutting guide in their instructions. The guide has layouts for each view in different fabric widths: 115cm (45"), 150cm (60") and occasionally 90cm (36"). Don't feel that you have to follow the cutting layouts given. If you've always used them, why not try putting them aside? You'll be stretched to think beyond the instruction sheet and your confidence and skills will grow too.

Guidelines for laying out pattern pieces (in order)

1. Lay out all the large and long pieces that are cut on the fold—this determines which way you'll fold the fabric
2. Arrange the other large or long pieces
3. Fill in the gaps with smaller pieces
4. Account for all the pattern pieces

Other layout tips

✂ If the patterns are made of tissue paper, it can help to iron the pieces before you begin. You can use a fairly hot iron but don't iron any sticky tape or get the pieces wet or they'll distort.

✂ Begin laying out the pieces at the (straightened) cut end of the fabric and put the large end of the pattern piece(s) at the cut end so all the remaining fabric is in the same area.

Cutting

✂ Place the pieces as close together as you can to use the fabric economically. Leave no unnecessary unused cloth between pattern pieces—let the edges of the pattern pieces touch one another and try to interlock the pieces together by placing the narrow parts of one with the wide parts of another.

✂ Butt straight edges next to each other—as well as saving fabric, you'll only need to cut the line once, not twice.

✂ Remember to flip any pattern pieces where a pair is required.

✂ Place the straighter edge of a pattern next to the straight edge of the fabric (either the selvedges or the fold) to help maximise fabric usage.

✂ Don't be tempted to use the selvedge for one of your long edges; it can perform differently to the rest of the fabric. It sometimes shrinks after washing. As usual there are exceptions to this "rule", for example: curtain lengths, the bottom edge of kilts, the edge of the front fold-back facing of some men's shirts and maybe the sides of skirt lengths on gathered waist skirts that take a whole width of fabric.

✂ Pay attention to the grainlines. They must be perfectly parallel to the selvedge. Align the grainline first, then pin the rest of the pattern.

An easy way to do this is to pin a tiny amount at one end of the grainline. Measure the distance between this end of the grainline and the selvedge, keeping your finger on the spot on the tape measure.

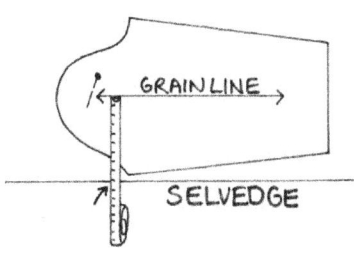

Now hold the tape measure at the other end of the grainline and pivot the pattern piece until it's in the right place. Pin this end of the grainline, then go ahead and pin the rest of the pattern piece.

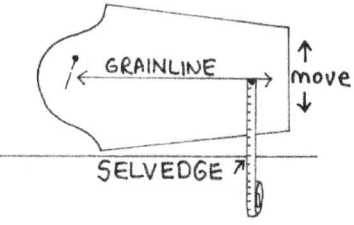

✂ If you need to add extra length or seam allowance to the pattern pieces when you're cutting out, put pins sticking out beyond the cutting line to remind you to add on (even if you've drawn a line on the fabric). I *always* do this. It's very easy to get distracted and accidentally cut on the wrong line. It's usually on the very last piece, too.

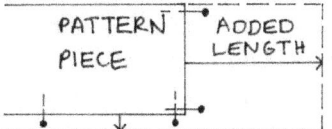

✂ Sometimes folding and positioning the fabric can take longer than the actual cutting. For very slippery or hard-to-handle fabrics, lay a length of calico or paper under the fabric to stop it from moving.

✂ Plan the entire layout in the most economical way before actually pinning anything to the fabric. When you're satisfied with the layout, pin the pieces on beginning at the cut end of the fabric where the layout was started.

Chalk and pins

Patterns made from heavy paper or cardboard are held in place with weights and traced around with **tailors chalk**, pencil, biro, or even felt pen. The pattern is then removed and the traced line is cut.
Most people don't like using tailors chalk because it's difficult to get a fine line. The key is regular sharpening. You can buy chalk sharpeners but you can get a finer edge if you do it yourself. Take an opened pair of paper scissors and stand over a bin. Scrape the blade of the scissors along the edges of the chalk to sharpen it, on both sides.
The beauty of using chalk is that it can almost always be rubbed off the fabric. White chalk usually shows up on white fabric, however, the most versatile colour is yellow. Use red or blue chalk sparingly, only if you absolutely have to, because it tends to be permanent.

Paper and tissue paper patterns require **pins** to hold them in place on the fabric. You'll need at least one pin in each corner of the pattern and more on longer edges. Too many pins and the pattern won't lie flat. Too few and the pattern will move when you cut it out. I like to pin the folded edges or grainlines first, then smooth the pattern out from there. Sometimes I use a large transparent ruler as a paperweight.
Place the pins only within the seam allowances if the pins leave holes.
Don't be afraid to spend money on good quality pins; cheap pins will snag the fabric. Most people prefer to use pins with heads, but my favourite pins have no heads and are 34mm long by .60mm. I think the longer and finer the better for pins. Make it a habit to pick up a pin as soon as you've dropped it (you will if you've spent money on top quality pins).

Some thrifty and time-saving tips

✂ If you think ahead, you can save some time by cutting things out together. Can you lay the lining or interfacing under the main fabric and cut out the pieces together? Even if this means trimming or cutting down the lining, it's still quicker. If the fabric is stable, you can hack around the pieces requiring interfacing and transfer them to the interfacing to cut out together.

✂ If you're making several garments, it's more time efficient to do all the cutting out for everything in one session—fabric, lining, interfacing and trimmings. Then you can clear the decks and start sewing.

✂ Try to have scraps left in one large piece rather than two or more. To do this, you may have to re-fold the fabric so the lengthwise fold is off-centre and exactly the width of the pattern piece. Or you can position a piece which isn't on the fold next to the selvedge so the uncut portion is next to the fold.

✂ I always keep all the significant scraps until the garment is totally finished "just in case" a piece is ruined and needs re-doing, or I want some fabric to test sew. Mark the scraps for the right or wrong side and for lengthwise grainline, if you need to.

✂ Double check that you haven't made any mistakes by systematically checking through all the pattern pieces at the end. Get a friend to check for you, too, if you're worried about it.

Cutting

The actual cutting is really the easy part after all the preparation, but most people are nervous when it comes to plunging their scissors into the fabric. Fear not! Confidence will come with practice!

What's the difference between scissors and shears?

Scissors have blades that are 4"-6" (10cm-15cm) in length, and are more lightly constructed than shears. They have sharp points and slender blades.
Shears have blades 6"-12" (15cm-30cm) with bent or straight handles.
I find shears too heavy to use. I like to use scissors with 5" (13cm) blades and lightweight ergonomic plastic handles. I have a pair for me, a pair to lend and a pair to cut paper with.

Some cutting and scissor tips

✂ For right-handers, have the pattern piece on your right and pull the trimmings away with your left hand as you cut. It makes it easier to cut a smooth line. Don't lift the fabric from the surface of the table and keep the bottom blade of the scissors in full contact with the table. Stop cutting each stroke before the blades fully close to avoid a choppy edge. It's easier to continue each cut slightly beyond the desired stopping point, but I prefer to cut exactly in case I need the scraps (I've been caught out in the past).

✂ To cut around corners, try not to flex your wrist—it's very bad for it, especially if you do a lot of cutting. Angle your whole arm instead, keeping your wrist straight, and try to move around table to cut from a more natural angle, if you can.

✂ If you traced around the pattern pieces, you need to cut the line off as you cut the piece out.

✂ Cutting large pattern pieces if you're a short person is a problem, since it's hard to reach the middle of the table. Try having paper or calico underneath the fabric, so you can slide the whole thing towards you without disturbing it.

✂ Keep your scissors sharp. When I used scissors all day every day I got them sharpened annually. Avoid dropping them on a hard surface because, apart from damaging the tips, they might not cut properly afterwards—they'll need to be taken back to the scissor shop to be re-set (usually just after you've had them done—groan!). I have a personal "no scissors on the ironing board" rule because of this. Also, avoid running sharp scissors through the fabric without moving the blades—it tends to blunt one spot on the blades (even though it's a really quick way to cut a length of fabric).

✂ Wipe the blades before and after using them, since dust and fluff will dull the blades. To keep them moving freely, now and then apply a drop of sewing machine oil near the screw.

✂ Don't use pinking shears or thread snips for cutting out. That's not what they're designed for.

✂ If your scissors have a serrated edge, check before cutting fine fabrics—the blades can catch. They're OK to use, but cutting will be more difficult. The answer is, of course, to buy another pair with smooth blades. When I worked in a studio that made evening wear,

Cutting

we had a pair of designated "chiffon scissors" with smooth blades, as well as our own regular scissors.

Estimating the fabric needed and some common layouts

The yardage (if it's in yards) or meterage (if it's in metres—although yardage generally means either) on commercial pattern envelopes tells you how much fabric to buy. In the clothing industry, this is sometimes called a costing because it forms part of calculating how much the garment will cost.

If you've made your own pattern and/or don't have a yardage, you'll have to do your own. There are no magical formulas or industry secrets with this—you lay out the pattern pieces within the width of the imaginary folded fabric and take a measurement.

However, what if you're in a fabric shop and you've forgotten your pattern, or you've fallen in love with a piece of fabric but only have a vague idea of what you'd like to do with it? If you know the fabric width and a few key body measurements, you can make a pretty good estimate.

Fabric generally comes in widths of 115cm (45") or 150cm (60"). It might not be exactly that width; 115 can vary from 110 to 118, and 150 can range from 146 to 152 or more, but it's fine as long as the width is within 5cm (2"). (As usual, there are exceptions to standard fabric widths: vintage fabrics are often 90cm (36"), and lace, lining, hand-loomed fabric, sheeting and embroidered fabrics can be all sorts of widths.)

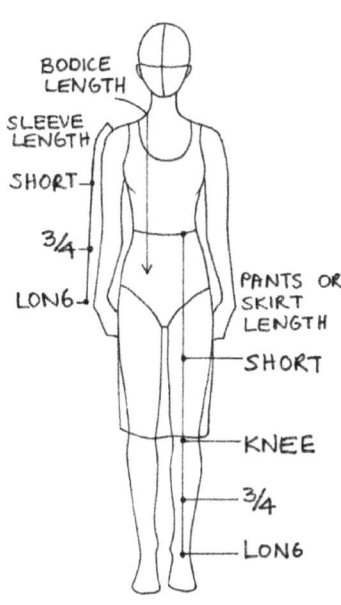

Measure yourself to find each of the length measurements on the illustration. You'll also need your largest body circumference (usually the hip).

To estimate the yardage for a particular garment, note the width of the fabric, then take a look at the layouts described below.

Determining the yardage in this way automatically takes care of the small pattern pieces like pockets and collars because they'll fit between the larger pieces.

With a bit of experience, you'll be able to hold up a length of fabric to yourself and say: "Yep, I can get a (dress, top, skirt, whatever) out of this".

Skirts

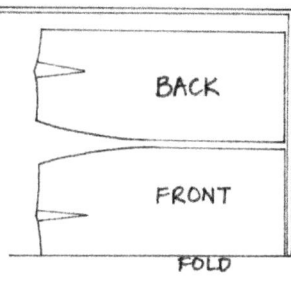

For **straight skirts**, if your hip circumference plus 15cm (6") is *less* than the fabric width, you'll need one length.

If you're a small size you *might* be able to squeeze a skirt out of 115cm (45") wide fabric.

If your hip circumference plus 15cm (6") is *greater* than the fabric width, you'll need two lengths.

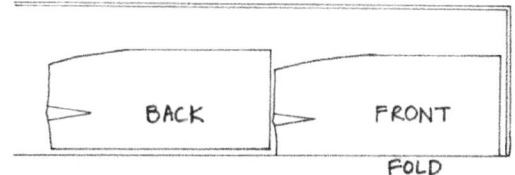

For **flared skirts**, you might be able to position the pieces side-by-side or interlocking on 150 (60") wide fabric.

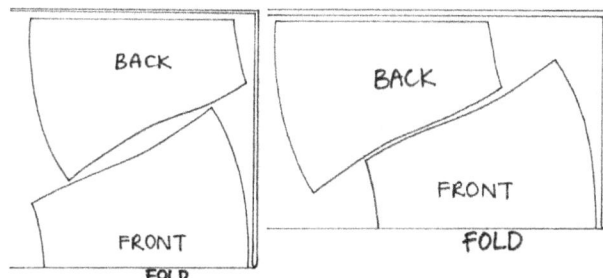

If not, you'll need two lengths of either 115cm (45") or 150 (60") wide.

You'll need two lengths if the skirt only has side seams, so the centre front and centre back can be placed on the fold. You'll also need two lengths if the fabric is one-way.

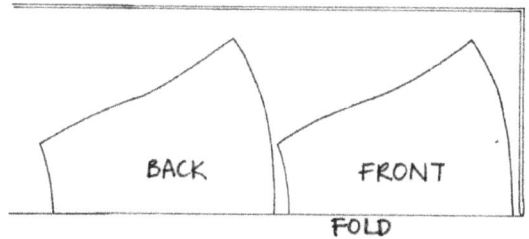

Running short of fabric?
✂ Can you make smaller seam allowances? Reducing the side seams by .5cm will give you an extra 2cm.

✂ On flared or A-line skirts, can you reduce the flare? If you only need a couple of centimetres, you can skim it off the side. If you need more and the skirt is very flared, pin in some of the flare evenly across the skirt.

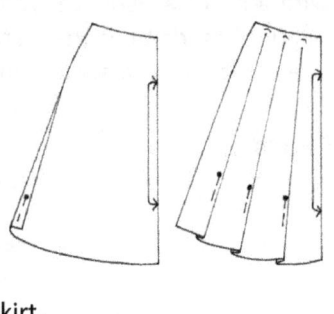

✂ A false hem will create a little extra length.

✂ On straight, untapered skirts, can you eliminate the side seams? Overlap the back and the front pattern pieces on the stitching line, and cut as one piece. The tops of the side seams will become shaped darts. This could yield an extra 6cm (2⅜") if the side seams are 1.5cm (⅝").

Trousers

For 115 (45") wide fabrics, you'll need two lengths.
For 150 (60") wide fabrics, you'll need one or two lengths depending on your size and if the fabric is one-way.

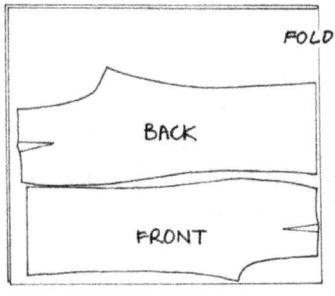

You may only need one length of 150 (60") wide fabric if you're a small size and the trousers are a slim cut. Add 30cm (12") extra to cut pockets and details. Experiment flipping the pattern pieces to make them fit in the width.

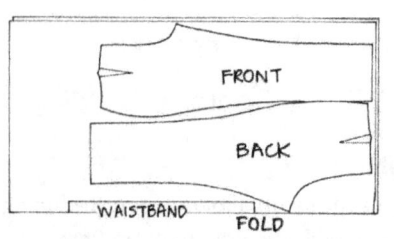

I find the illustrated arrangement suits me and I can fit the waistband on the folded edge.

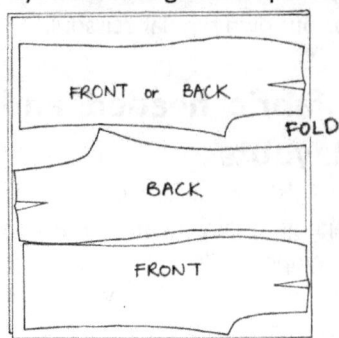

If you're cutting several pairs of trousers in the same fabric, three "legs" can easily fit across 150 (60") wide fabric (therefore, four lengths will yield three pairs of trousers, or three lengths will yield two pairs with a bit left over).

Running short of fabric?

✂ On a length of 150 (60") wide fabric, the most economical layout is to mark each leg singly, interlocking them with each other to take up all the space. Be sure to flip each piece so you have a pair.

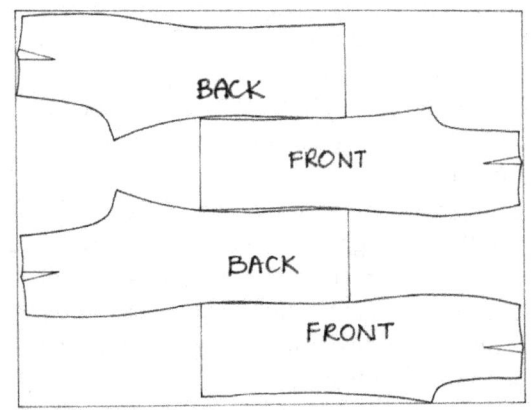

✂ If you're really pushed for fabric, or the fabric is very narrow, consider piecing the back crotch curve, or fork. It's a totally legitimate (although Old School) solution. The seam will be hardly noticeable, especially if the fabric is checked or patterned and (naturally) you've matched the design at the seam.

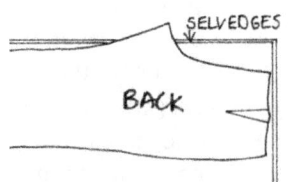

1. Let the back crotch curve hang off the selvedge edge by up to 5cm (2"). Cut out the back.

2. Sew a selvedge scrap onto the missing area, right sides together, enough to cut the absent fork.

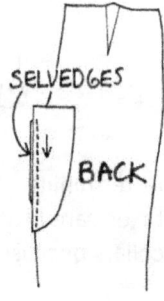

3. Press the seam allowance open, put the pattern back on and cut the fork.

Tops and shirts

For 115 (45") wide fabric, you'll need one sleeve length and two body lengths.

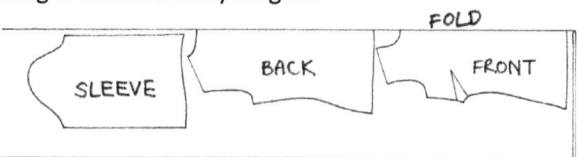

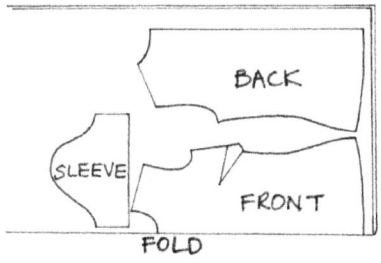
For 150 (60") wide fabric, you'll need one sleeve length and one body length.

In any width, fitted styles on slim people might only need one sleeve length and one body length, since the front and back bodies can be cut next to each other.

Running short of fabric?

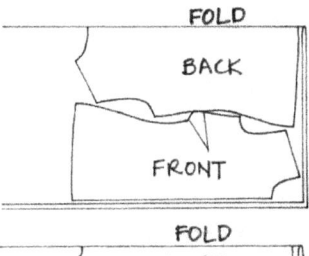

✂ Can you flip either the front or the back so they interlock more closely?

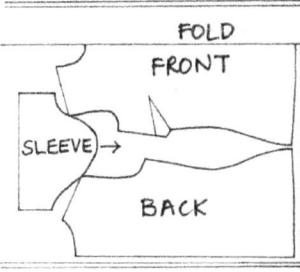

✂ Can you position the sleeve so the sleeve head fits between the front and back armholes?

✂ Can you interlock the back and front at the armholes and cut the sleeves separately afterwards?

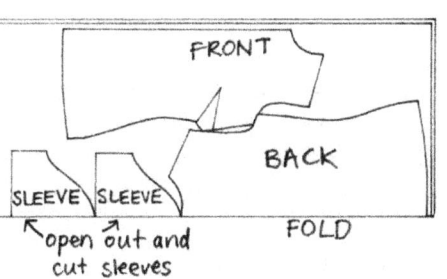

✂ If the top has a front button band, can you omit it and cut a separate front band, OR cut the front on the fold and have a placket opening? (See pages 105-126.)

✂ Can you cut any facings in a different fabric?

If you're cutting **shirts** with wide flat sleeve heads, you might not be able to fit the sleeve across a folded length of 115 (45") wide fabric.

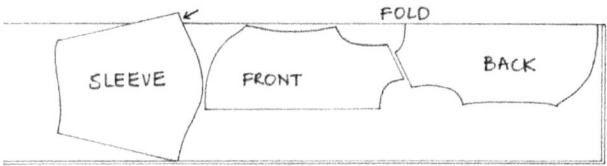

There are a couple of solutions:

✂ You could cut the back and the front first, then open out the fabric and cut the sleeves singly, top-and-tailing them. Don't forget to flip the sleeves so you have a pair.

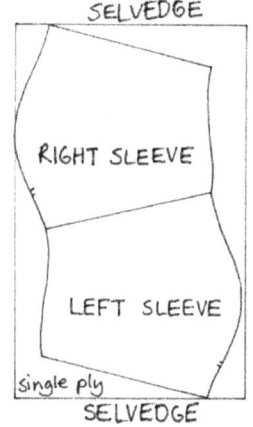

✂ If the sleeves still won't fit, try cutting them next to the fronts. Cut the back first, then re-fold the fabric to cut the sleeves and the front.

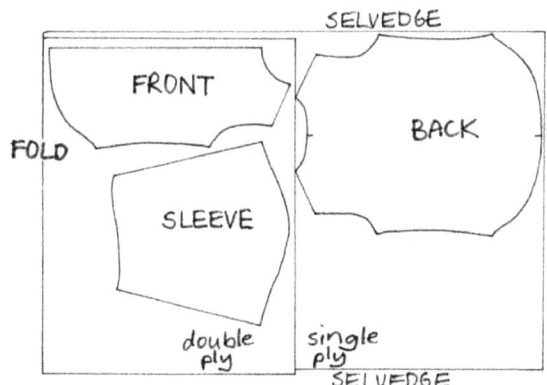

✂ The last option is to piece the underarm section at the back. There's no shame in this—it's how some shirts were made in the olden days when narrow fabric widths prevailed.

Dresses
For any width fabric, add together the lengths needed for a top and skirt.

Recording fabric layouts
By the way, if you want to draw a sketch of a layout to remember it for the future, and easy way is to first draw two sides of the fabric.

Draw in the pattern pieces, then draw in the top edge of the fabric.

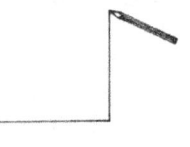

Transferring pattern markings
All the pattern markings like notches, darts and placement lines need to be marked *before* you remove the pattern. Most sewers like to leave the pattern pieces pinned onto the fabric until it's time to construct that part of the garment, but I like to have everything cut and marked, so I can sit down and just sew when I'm ready. After removing the pattern, I fold all the front pieces together and all the back pieces together. I put all the pieces needing fusing with their fusing and leave them out separately to iron on.

You'll need to mark:
- Dart positions
- Pleat positions
- All the pattern notches
- Placement lines (for pockets or trims)

And possibly:
- The centre front line (for coats and jackets)
- The right or wrong side of the fabric

You *don't* need to mark:
- Regular stitching lines for seams and darts
- Grainlines
- Hemlines

Mark the pattern notches with a tiny snip as you cut the pattern out, making the snips no deeper than 3mm (⅛") into the seam allowance. I do this as I cut out each piece.

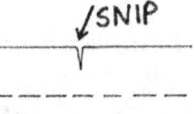

You can also use tiny snips to mark fold lines (for turning up hems, for example) and selected seam allowances (for example the seam a zipper is inserted into). Snipping each end of a fold line helps it fold up easily and saves time having to measure it.

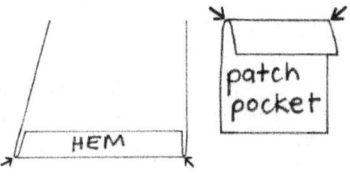

I also like to mark the centres of pieces, such as the centre front neck and centre back neck, centre of the collar and the centre front/back waist.

When the piece is cut on a centre fold, instead of inserting the scissor tip down the fold to snip, factory machinists nick the double fold to make a V shape.

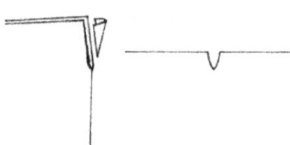

The dots for darts, tucks and pocket placements can be marked in several different ways:

✄ An easy way is to mark with **pencil**. Push a pin through each dot, going squarely through the pattern tissue and all the layers of fabric. Use the type of pin with no head.

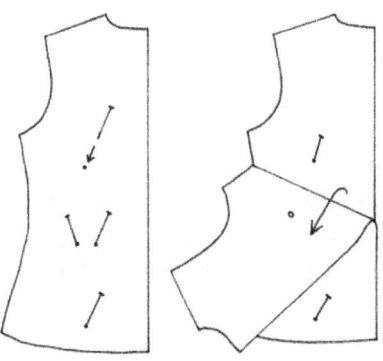

With gentle persuasion, push the pin through the pattern tissue as you remove it.

The pin will leave a tiny hole in the tissue paper where you popped it through. You now have a pin connecting all the layers at each dot. Mark the dots on the wrong side of the fabric with a chalk pencil, chinagraph pencil, regular pencil or water soluble texta and remove the pins. Did you cut the garment with the right sides together? If so, it's easy to draw the dot where the pin enters and exits (as illustrated). If not and the wrong sides are together, peel the layers apart to draw the dots.

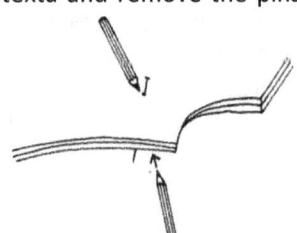

✄ If the pencil will show through the fabric, it's best to mark with **pins** (or thread—see below). To mark with pins, take a tiny "stitch" at each dot on the wrong side.

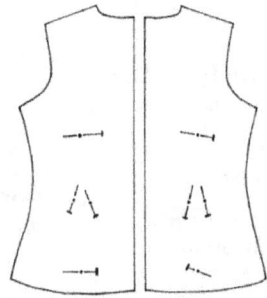

✂ To mark with **thread**, thread a needle with a double strand of contrasting thread and take a tiny stitch at each dot on the wrong side. Cut the thread leaving a V of double thread at each dot. I use thread on lace or mesh fabrics where the pins are likely to drop out.

If marking with thread, you may prefer to make proper tailors tacks. Tailors tacks are made before the pattern is removed and are accurate but time-consuming to make.

1. Thread a needle with a long double strand of thread and no knot. Sew through the pattern tissue and the two layers of fabric using long running stitches, making a loop at the dots you're marking.

2. Cut the middle of the loops and each stitch and carefully lift off the pattern.

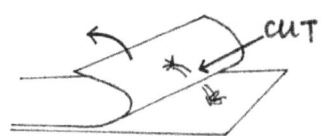

3. Gently pull the two layers of fabric apart so that some of the thread remains in each layer, and cut to separate.

✂ **In factories,** dots are marked by drilling through the layers using a special drill. On a few layers, an awl might be used. It creates an actual hole in the fabric which the machinists will cover (with the dart, pocket or trimming). That's why if you alter ready-to-wear clothes you may come across a hole.

In the olden days before drills, clothing cutters threaded a needle with two long strands of thread and pulled it through the dot. They separated each layer and cut the thread leaving a short strand of double thread in the fabric. Some high end factories still do this on request so clothes can be altered later (but the cutters sure don't enjoy it!).

Cutting knits

Cutting knits requires a different approach to positioning pieces on the straight grain. Knits have fine ribs running lengthwise, parallel to the selvedge, instead of warp threads like woven fabrics. It's more accurate to align the pattern grainline with the ribs rather than measure from the selvedge like woven fabrics.

With the rib side up, get down next to the fabric, close one eye and look along. Follow along a continuous rib of the fabric. The ribs are usually visible on the right side of the fabric (for t-shirt knits and cotton lycra), but some (nylon lycra for example) are visible on the wrong side. Still others (such as tubular ribbing) have the ribs visible on both sides. You can lay a ruler along a rib and draw a line with chalk as an easy reference, or check visually (as just described) each time you position a pattern piece.

Fold the pattern along the grainline and align the folded edge with a rib. Pin the piece on, correctly aligned, then flip down where you folded and pin the rest of the pattern.

If the ribs aren't matched to the grainline on the pattern pieces, the seams of the garment will twist around on the body. The beauty of visually placing the pieces according to the ribs is that if the knit is skewed (and even expensive knits can be), the pattern is accurately positioned. You can also use the ribs as a guide to folding the fabric as you prepare to place the pattern pieces, instead of folding according to the selvedge.

✂ Curly edges on knits can be tamed by sticky taping them to the table while you lay out and cut (don't do it if the table is French polished).

✂ Some knits like rugby top and t-shirt fabric have a stiff selvedge. It's glue to stop the edge from curling. Don't place pattern pieces on this edge—the stiffness doesn't come out even after washing.

✂ Some knits, such as cotton lycra, have a line running through the centre, more noticeably on light colours. Avoid it completely or else position it in a discreet place at the back of the garment.

✂ Cut knits supported—don't let them hang off the table and stretch. I let the excess fabric lie on a chair next to the table, or you could set up your ironing board next to the table. When you fold the knit to cut it out double, be careful not to stretch it. Try to let the knit relax and sit where it wants to.

✂ If the knit fabric has been tightly rolled on a roll, allow it to relax before cutting. When I worked in a swimwear factory, we would unroll the whole roll of fabric onto the cutting table and leave it overnight before cutting it the next day.

✂ Check to see if the knit ladders when it's pulled. If it does, it will ladder in only one direction. Pull tightly on a crosswise cut edge to see. Cut the garment so that the knit ladders *up*. Why? The hem (where the ladder will originate from) is less prone to being stretched than a neckline or armhole and therefore less prone to laddering.

✂ Regular pins are fine to use on knits, but when doing fittings (especially on underwear and swimwear), use safety pins instead. They won't pop out and stick into the person when the fabric is stretched.

Cutting stripes, checks and geometric designs

Striped and checked fabrics take a little longer to cut than plain fabrics, but the results can be very rewarding. Curiously, striped garments can be difficult to sell and are avoided by some fashion designers. Plaids, checks, tartans, stripes and other geometric designs are generally handled the same for cutting purposes. You'll usually (but not always) need extra fabric to match the pattern, anywhere from 25cm (10") to a metre (40") depending on the size of the pattern repeat and the garment you're making.

Before laying out the pattern pieces, straighten the end by cutting on a prominent line.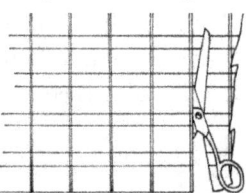

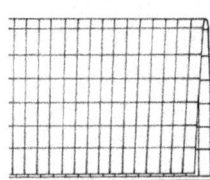 Sometimes checked fabrics and horizontal stripes do not align at the cut edges even though the edges are cut on grain.

To re-align, stretch the fabric on the bias to pull it into shape, so all the corners form right angles.
Sometimes giving it a blast with the steam iron helps.

Avoid like the plague printed checked fabrics which 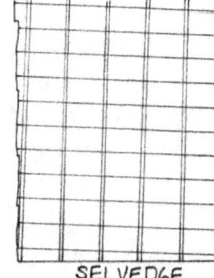 are printed off-grain. The fabric will seem crooked even if the garment's grainlines have been aligned properly and can never be corrected.
If you have to use it, cut it out in a single layer (see page 83 for how), and give the check pattern priority over the straight grain.

Analyse the stripe or check
Stripes and checks can be balanced or unbalanced.

Balanced, or even, stripes or checks are composed of symmetrical repeats, so the pattern is the same in either direction. To see if the design is balanced, fold back a corner and see if the design mirrors itself.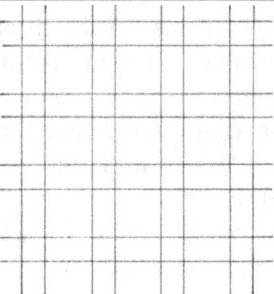

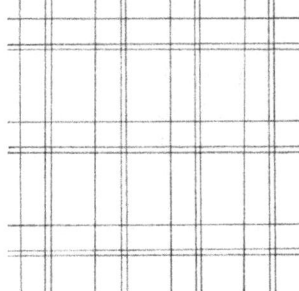 **Unbalanced**, or uneven, stripes or checks are asymmetrical in one or both directions. Extra care needs to be taken when cutting, because although the pattern will be asymmetrical on the garment, it still needs to *look* balanced. This can be achieved by placing the dominant part of the stripe or check at the centre of the garment, or evenly on the left and right. The visual centre or dominant part of each stripe or check can be hard to identify. Try holding the fabric up in the mirror and standing some distance away. Glance quickly at the fabric (or take your glasses off) and see which part stands out the most.

Styles that work with stripes and checks

✂ Select designs that use darts for shaping, rather than seams. For example, choose darted bodices over princess line.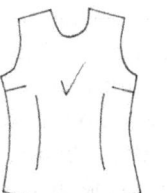

✂ Look for commercial patterns where the sketch or photo on the envelope is in stripes or checks. The pattern should tell you how much extra fabric to buy, too.

✂ A-line or gored skirts, or even straight skirts for that matter, should have the front and back the same width, so the stripes will meet in a V at the side seams.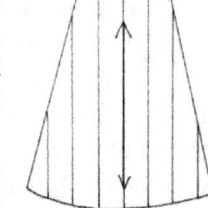
Skirt patterns are often made with the front slightly bigger than the back so the side seams aren't visible from the front. It's usually about 1cm (⅜") to 1.2cm (½") each side but can be up to 2.5cm (1"). You can't have this difference if you want the pattern to match, so shift the seam line so the back and front are the same.

If you centre a stripe down the middle of each panel, every vertical seam will have the same V pattern.

✂ T-shirt style tops should have the shoulder and side seams in the same place on the back and the front, so the pattern will match there.
If you put the back and the front on top of one other, the shoulder and side seams should lie together:

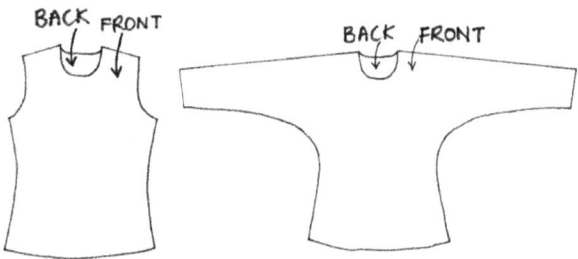

Where to match the pattern
The general rule for matching is to match vertical stripes at horizontal seams and horizontal stripes at vertical seams. You might not be able to match the stripes at every seam, but some seams matter more than others.

✂ Match or mirror the design at the **centre front**. If you only match in one place, make it here. Even budget garments match at the centre front.

 ✂ Match the **shoulder seams** if you can.

✂ Try to position stripes or checks **centrally** at the front or back. Position centrally down sleeves, too. Even when the stripe is unbalanced, put the most dominant part of the design in the centre, so the eye registers approximate symmetry on the garment.
If for any reason it isn't possible to centre the design, place a dominant stripe an equal distance either side of the centre, so the garment still looks symmetrical.

✂ **Low on the priority list**: underarm seams on sleeves, hidden facings, under collars, side seams above bust darts, cuff plackets, trouser inseams.

✂ For **horizontal stripes**, match the stripes at the side seams and if possible match the sleeves to the body.

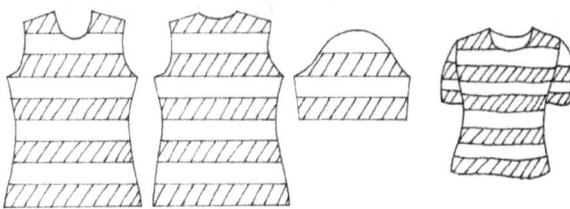
Try to place dominant horizontal stripes at the garment's edges, so the hem folds up along the edge of a stripe. If this leaves you with a stripe in an unflattering position, move the pieces around to find a more pleasing effect. Exceptions: for A-line or flared skirts, place dominant stripes *away* from the garment's edge, so the curved hemline is less conspicuous.

✂ On a **dress with a waist seam**, place the bodice so the waistline falls on the same crosswise stripe as the waistline of the skirt, making the progression of crosswise stripes unbroken from neck to hemline. Avoid placing heavy crosswise stripes at the waistline; it's more flattering if the dominant stripe falls above and below, not on, the waistline.

✂ On a **jacket and skirt**, note the waist position on the jacket when you fit the pattern. When cutting the checks, place the jacket so the stripe along the lower edge coincides with an identical stripe under it on the skirt, making an uninterrupted progression of crosswise stripes from the top of the jacket to the hem of the skirt when the outfit is worn.

✂ On **facings**, match the plaid in the facing horizontally and vertically to the part faced.

✂ In factories, sometimes part of the stripe pattern is drawn onto the pattern piece to help placement.

✂ Men's shirts (and women's, too) have the stripes or checks positioned in a particular way that not only breaks up the pattern for the eye, but is economical on fabric too. The front, back, pockets, sleeves and cuff placket all have the stripes vertically (on the lengthwise grain) and the yoke, collar pieces and cuff have the pattern running horizontally.

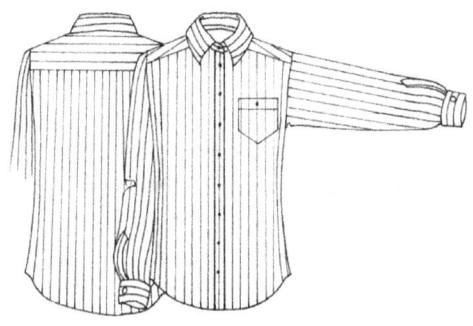

Pieces to match are the cuff placket on the sleeve, the pocket on the front, and (if you can) the stripes on the yoke to extend down the sleeve.

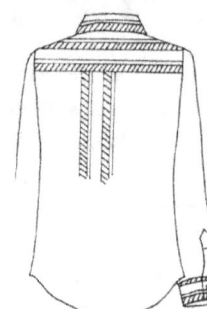

With directional stripes and checks, choose a direction and cut all the pieces running the same way. This applies to any garment, not just shirts.

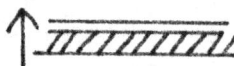

Try and place edges of yokes, cuffs, waistbands and other details on the edge of a stripe, so the seam doesn't cut the stripe pattern in half. Position stripes and checks symmetrically on the details, too.

✂ **Very narrow stripes and tiny checks** don't need to be matched.

✂ To match stripes or checks on a **patch pocket,** cut out the garment first, marking the pocket position with one or two dots at the pocket's top corners. In industry, pocket positions for checks are marked with only one dot (the dot is a hole drilled into the fabric that's *just* covered by the corner of the pocket), so the machinist can shift the pocket if needed to make the checks match and cover the dot hole. The dot should be the one closest to the centre front of the garment.

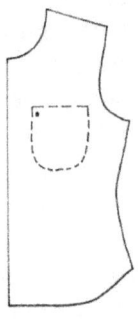

To match the pattern, lay the pocket pattern onto the garment in the correct position and use a pencil to draw key stripe positions onto the edge of the pattern piece. Flip back the seam allowance or pocket facing to find the stitching line, if you need to. Use the marks as a guide when you cut out the pocket.

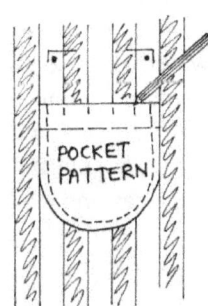

For checks, mark the check position on the top *and* the side, so the vertical and horizontal lines will match. Note that for some checks, the left and right pockets will be different. If there's a dart under the pocket, match the pocket edge nearer to the centre front.

Consider cutting patch pockets on the bias to avoid matching difficulties. It can look more interesting, too. To do this, simply draw in a new grain line at 45 degrees to the old one. Interface the whole pocket for stability, if required.

Matching sleeve checks on jackets

Matching the check on the sleeves of tailored jackets poses some problems: if you match at the underarm points of the sleeve and body, the pattern won't match across the chest and sleeve cap due to the ease in the sleeve.

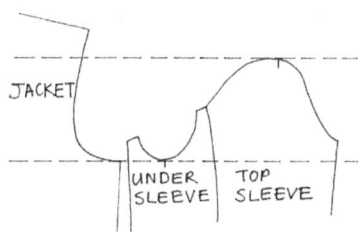

The pattern needs to match across the chest flowing onto the sleeve.

Here's a method for matching the sleeve from Valentino:

1. Cut out the garment but not the sleeves—leave a place to cut them later.

2. Assemble the garment and accurately baste or pin in a calico sleeve head. Pin a scrap of the plaid fabric to the calico, matching the pattern. Alternatively, use a pen to draw where the pattern should fall.

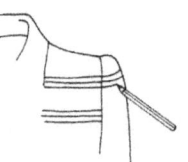

3. Remove the calico sleeve, lay it flat on the fabric and align the fabric scrap with the plaid pattern.

Cutting fashion details

Position on the fabric all the main pattern pieces first, then decide how to position the details like facings, pocket pieces, flaps, collars, cuffs, yokes and tabs. You might decide to delay cutting some of these pieces until you fit the garment. Experiment with scraps to see what looks best—either cutting details on the bias or perfectly matching the pattern, and deciding where the pattern should be positioned.

If you can't match perfectly, don't match at all

If you can't match the pattern, consider cutting some pieces on the perpendicular grain or on the bias for a

Cutting **83**

more interesting effect. It's a great opportunity to be creative with a design. Stripes and checks aren't as harsh and tailored when cut on the bias—a bias cut can give a completely different look to the fabric.

To cut a piece on the bias, draw in a new grainline at 45 degrees to the existing one. If the fabric is very unstable, consider fusing details with a light interfacing to give stability and make sewing easier.

Note that bias *stripes* don't work on collars and yokes without a centre back seam to mirror the pattern on the left and right of the garment.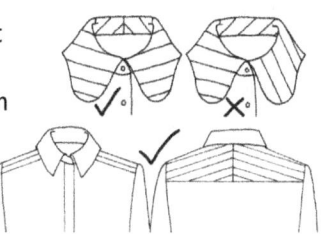

For a perpendicular grainline, simply draw a new grainline at 90 degrees to the old one. While a perpendicular grainline might solve your seam matching problems, you'll still need to position the piece carefully so the stripe or check falls in the right spot on the garment to achieve balance.

Try a bias or perpendicular grainline for
- Patch, welt, or jet pockets
- Yokes on shirts and skirts
- A-line skirts
- Plackets and front bands
- Collars and cuffs (note that collars will need a centre back seam for stripes cut on the bias to look the same on both sides)
- Tabs
- Side panels of princess seamed tops and jackets
- Godets
- Whole garments

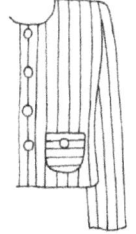  

Laying out the pattern pieces
The big plus when working with stripes and checks is not having to measure the grainline on the pattern—simply align it with the nearest stripe. However, the pieces must be perfectly placed.

The fabric can be cut in a single layer or folded double. A single layer is more accurate but folded is faster. I prefer folded wherever I can.

To cut the fabric folded, fold it along a dominant stripe or between two stripes, so the pattern on top matches the pattern underneath. Note that the selvedges may not sit perfectly on top of each other, but they should still be parallel.

Pin the intersections of the checks (or stripes) 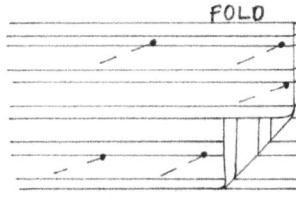 together to stop the layers shifting, making sure the pin goes through the underneath layer in the exactly same part of the check.

To cut checks in a single layer of fabric, pin and cut out each pattern piece once, matching the pattern where you want to match it. Remove the pattern and 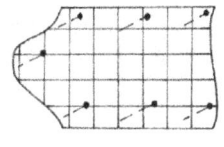 lay the garment piece face down on the remaining fabric, so the right sides are together. Pin, matching the pattern so you have a perfect pair.

Essentially you're using the first piece as a pattern for the second one.

You can't use this method for pieces to be cut on the fold, but you can use a combination of folded and single layer cutting. I cut checked fabric in a single layer when I can't get the checks to sit on top of each other perfectly when the fabric is folded.

It's *important* when matching the pattern to match 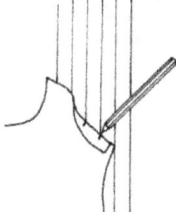 the *stitching* line, not the edge of the pattern. To help match the pattern, use a pencil to draw key stripe positions onto the edge of the pattern piece before you place it. Flip back the seam allowance to find the stitching line, if you need to.

Obviously I cannot show every cutting scenario (that would be boring to read!), but here's some examples.

Balanced stripes or checks are fairly straightforward to cut. Fold the fabric along a stripe so the stripe on top sits on the stripe underneath. Position anything on the fold first (the back or the front) and note where the prominent checks or stripes lie on the shoulders and/or side seams. Position the corresponding pieces to match.

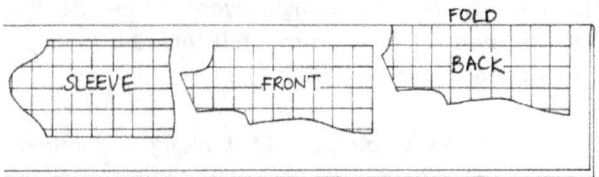

If you have to choose between matching the pattern at the shoulders or a harmonious design across the front, pick the front.

Unbalanced stripes or checks can be cut in two different ways, depending on where and how you want the pattern to fall on the garment.

The first way is asymmetrical, with the design going around the body in one direction only. Identify the centre of the dominant stripe and fold the fabric along this centre. The selvedges might not sit on top of each other, but should be parallel. The centres of the dominant stripes must sit on top of one another, just like cutting balanced stripes. You can pin the intersections to make sure they match. If the fabric has a nap and must be cut in one direction, you'll need to cut it out using this method to keep the nap running in the same direction.

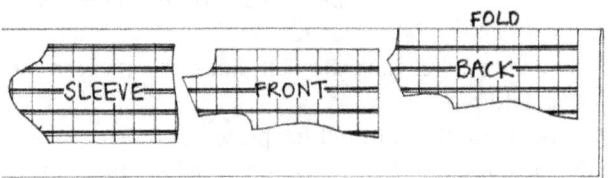

If the fabric isn't napped (a two-way fabric), you can flip the back so the stripes match at the shoulders.

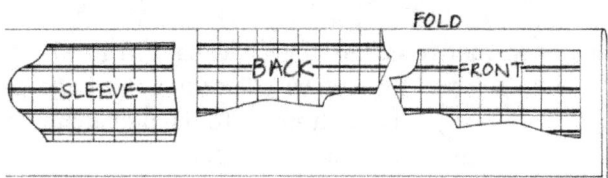

The second way is to have the stripe repeat mirrored at the centre front and centre back. This arrangement requires the fabric to be cut in a single layer. It doesn't work for pieces that have to be cut on the fold, so add a seam allowance along any centre fold lines and cut them in two pieces.

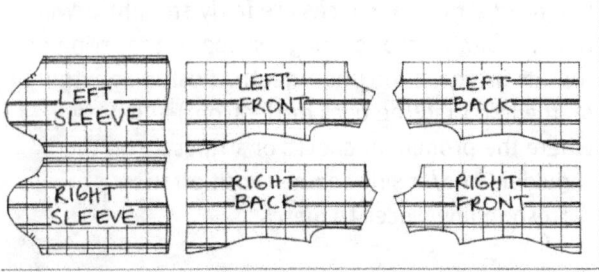

However, you might be able to cut it double by folding the fabric in half and cutting along the fold

so that you have two pieces. Turn one piece 180 degrees and align the centres of the dominant stripes so that they sit on top of one another.

Check first before you do this—if the fabric has a large repeat you might be better off cutting it in a single layer so you can fit all the pieces in easily.

Darts

Introduction...85	Moving darts.......................................91
To sew a dart..85	Making a dart bigger or smaller............92
Troubleshooting darts............................86	Adding a bust dart 92
Pressing darts 86	Getting rid of bust darts........................92
Double pointed darts 87	Making a dart longer or shorter..............93
Topstitched darts 88	Add/remove double pointed darts........93
French Darts 88	Shoulder and neck darts 93
Overlocked darts 88	Gape darts 93
Darts in two layers of fabric 88	what if I forgot them?..................94
Shaped darts 88	Getting rid of small darts 94
Darts in interfacing 88	Darts in design.....................................94
Darts in stripes......................................89	seams 94
Changing darts on a pattern..................89	tucks or pleats 95
Moving alterations from the garment onto the pattern 90	ease 95
Transferring a dart 90	flare 95
another method..................91	gathers 96
	elastic 96

A dart is a triangular fold of fabric sewn in place, used as a way of shaping the garment to fit the curves of the body. Darts are used more often in women's clothing than men's.

Darts most often occur at the bust and waist, but on some garments darts are used at the back neck, back shoulder or elbow to give a closer fit.

The **dart value** is the width of the dart at its widest point. The bigger the curve on a body, the bigger the dart value needs to be. The dart always points to the most prominent/fullest part of the curve. The sides of the dart are always the same measurement, whether curved or straight.

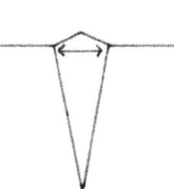

To sew a dart

Mark the dart position with two tiny 3mm (¼") snips at the top, and a dot for the point on the *wrong* side.

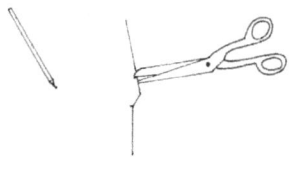

You can mark the dot with a pencil, chalk, or a pin.

On lace, mesh, or fabric where pins drop out and dots don't mark, make a thread tack. Use double thread and make two tiny stitches at the point.

In factories, the point is marked with a hole made by an awl or a drill. The hole is *just* covered when the dart is sewn.

Therefore, in factories all the dots are stepped back 6mm (¼") from the actual point of the dart.

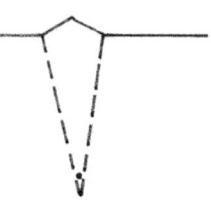

Sew the dart by folding it through the centre, right sides of the fabric together, matching the snips at the top. Start sewing from the wide end of the dart. Run off to nothing at the point.

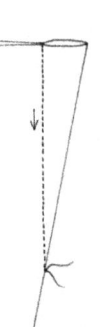

I backstitch at the beginning and end of the dart, but some people like to leave long threads at the point and tie them off. Both ways are fine. Backstitching sure is quicker though!

Troubleshooting darts

Most people have trouble keeping their stitching in a straight line and judging the angle to run off to achieve a smooth point.

The key to a smooth dart is an acute angle at the point, running off to nothing. As you're sewing, start to run off sooner than you think you need to.

If you draw a straight line from the snips to the point, your stitching should be *on* or *slightly inside* the line—*not* outside the line.

A pimple point is the result of not running off at an acute angle, or stopping short of the point.

Short, fat darts are harder to get a smooth point on than long, narrow darts, because the angle is less acute. If you're having problems keeping your stitching straight, you could draw the stitching line in with chalk, or use a strip of sticky tape as a guide.

With practice, practice, practice, you'll be able to sew a perfect dart every time. I would say it took me about ten years before I was able to sew a perfect dart first time every time.

Roping happens when the two sides of the dart aren't the same length but one side has been stretched to fit

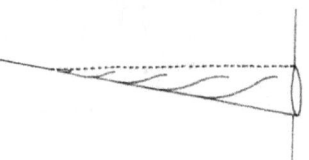

when the dart was sewn. There only needs to be a few millimetres of difference. Usually pressing will remedy the situation. Roping happens easily on long, wide darts that aren't on the straight grain. To avoid this, take care with your pattern and cutting out, and before you sew the dart you could iron the fold in the dart instead of just folding it. You can also measure the dart on the pattern to see if both sides are same length.

Pressing darts

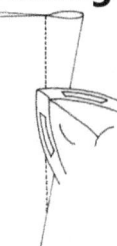

1. Press the dart flat as it was stitched, on the wrong side.

2. Turn the fabric to the right side and press the dart to one side. Slide the tip of the iron into the point of the dart—don't squash it.

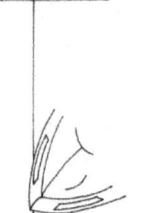

To mould curves, press darts over a tailor's ham.

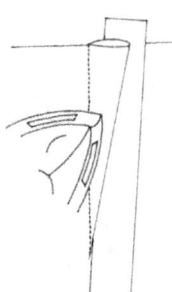

If you think the dart will imprint through, press from the wrong side and slip a piece of light cardboard under the dart's fold.

Horizontal darts are usually pressed down.

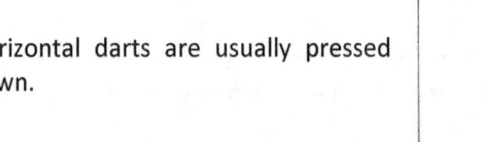

Vertical darts are pressed either both to the sides or both to the centre (but *not* one dart one way and one the other).

I always press my darts towards the side seams and if the lining has darts in it, I press the lining the opposite way to reduce bulk.

If the dart is particularly deep or bulky, it can be slashed, trimmed and pressed open. Cut the dart open to within about 2.5cm (1") of the point.

Darts in **leather** are treated this way, and the slashed edges are glued down.

In fabric, generally the slashed edges are not overlocked or neatened in any way, because after trimming they're slightly on the bias and therefore unlikely to fray. High quality vintage clothes sometimes have the slashed edges overcast by hand.

Double pointed darts

These are sometimes called contour darts.

The widest part occurs at the waist, and tapers in either direction towards the bust and hips (on the front), or the fullest part of the back and seat (on the back).

Double pointed darts look a diamond, with four dots to mark the position.

Sometimes double pointed darts have a straight part in the middle. There are six dots to mark the position.

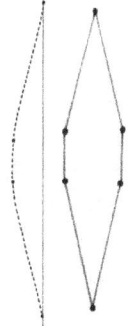

Double pointed darts can also be marked on the pattern with only three dots—one at each end and only one for the centre. Some clothing factories do this. The three dots get lined up and the machinist has instructions on how far away to sew from the centre dot (for example 1cm). This makes sewing the dart quicker and it's quicker for the cutter who has one less hole to drill.

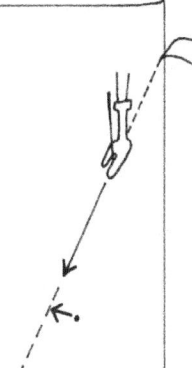

Double pointed darts can be sewn in one operation, despite having two points. Fold the dart longways through the centre, lining up the centre dots on top of each other. Pin to hold in position. Begin sewing at the bottom dot. Sew to the centre dots, but don't pivot on them—what we want is smooth rounded curve, not a point, in the centre.

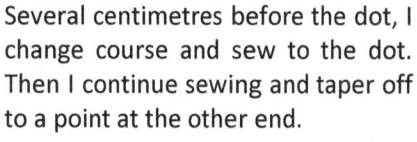

To get a good shape, when I begin sewing I aim the machine foot about 1cm (⅜") to the left of the centre dot.

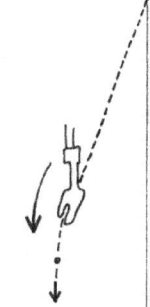

Several centimetres before the dot, I change course and sew to the dot. Then I continue sewing and taper off to a point at the other end.

You might need to snip the centre to make the dart lie smoothly if there's strain.

Of course, you *could* sew double pointed darts in two steps—from the middle out to each point. But, if you can manage to sew the darts in one step as described above, it will save you a lot of time.

Topstitched darts

Darts may be topstitched after sewing as a design feature.

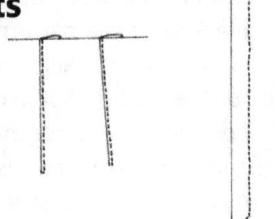

French darts

French darts are bust darts that extend diagonally from the side seam to the bust point. They can be curved or straight. They are only found on the front, never the back. Garments with French darts don't have front double pointed waist darts as well. French darts look smart and give a slimming effect because they're more vertical.

French darts are sewn like an ordinary dart, but sometimes they're slashed with a seam allowance—in other words, they're pre-trimmed.
This is because:
✂ French darts can be very deep darts, and the more vertical they are the deeper they'll become. Trimming will reduce the bulk.
✂ Curved sides of a dart are easier to sew trimmed.
Important: Don't cut away for the dart until you've done your fitting, otherwise you'll have no fabric to adjust the dart if needed.

Can I sew darts on my overlocker?

Mostly no. It's difficult to get a smooth point and you only get one chance with an overlocker, because it trims away. Overlocked darts are sometimes seen on budget ready-to-wear clothes, both for woven and stretch fabrics. If you want to try, use a four thread overlocker and sew the darts as usual, trimming off the dart as you sew. At the dart's point, thread the tail back or overlock over the top of it to stop the point from coming undone (see page 190).
It works best on fabrics with a busy print, to hide any imperfections at the point. You'll need to be confident with your overlocker and dart sewing.

Darts in two layers of fabric

You might encounter a darted garment with two layers of fabric, for example a sheer overlay with a solid fabric underneath.

Sometimes the darts are sewn together and the side seams sewn separately. This stops the dart showing through to the outside on the sheer.

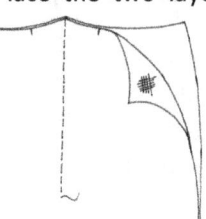

Place the two layers on top of each other as they would be worn, matching the dart points and snips. Before you sew the dart, stitch a row of long machine stitches through the centre of the dart. This stops the layers from moving. Sew the dart as usual.

Shaped darts

Darts are usually stitched almost straight from the edge to the point. However, some darts require shaping when they're stitched to match the body they'll be worn against.

 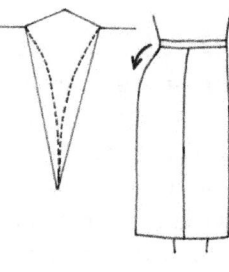

For example, some bodies increase in size suddenly from the waist.

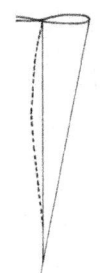 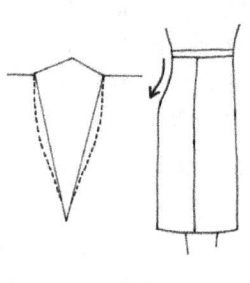

Other bodies are concave before increasing.

Mark the stitching line on the pattern and refer to it when you sew the dart.

Darts in interfacing

Usually, the fabric is interfaced first, then treated as one piece when the darts are sewn.
Note that the dart's dots will need to be marked on the *interfacing*, not the fabric, otherwise they'll be lost when the interfacing is applied.

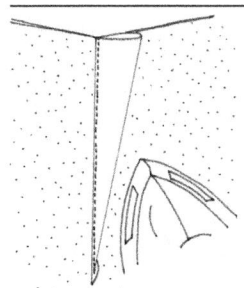
One way to reduce bulk in interfaced darts is to sew the dart in the fabric first. Cut the dart out of the interfacing and iron on the interfacing around the dart.

When using sew-in interfacing, sometimes the darts are sewn separately. An example might be the shoulder darts on a back jacket stay.

Sew the dart as usual in the fabric. In the interfacing, cut along the centre of the dart to the point.

Overlap the stitching lines and zig zag or straight stitch through the two layers. The interfacing can be trimmed back next to the stitching.

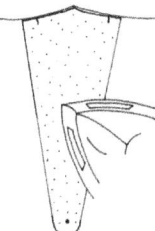
Sometimes on very loose weaves, metallics or fabrics liable to distort, the dart is interfaced before it's sewn.

Alternatively, the dart can be taped as it's sewn. Use a lightweight tape, such as the selvedge cut from silk organza. Press the dart to one side with the tape on top.

Darts in stripes

If you're sewing darts in striped fabrics, you may need to adjust the dart positions to fit the stripes. Lay the pattern onto the fabric and consider where the darts will lie in relation to the stripes.

For **vertical darts in vertical stripes OR horizontal darts in horizontal stripes**, the darts need to run in the same direction as the stripes.

If they don't, the stripes will appear to be broken when the dart is sewn, like this:

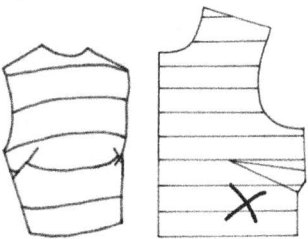

To adjust the dart to the stripe, match up one side of the stripe with one side of the dart. Then make sure both sides of the dart are the same measurement and add to the length of the shortest side if required.

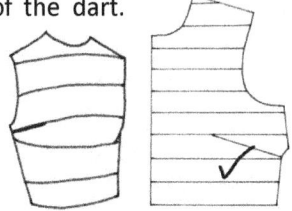

The same principle can be used for skirt darts:

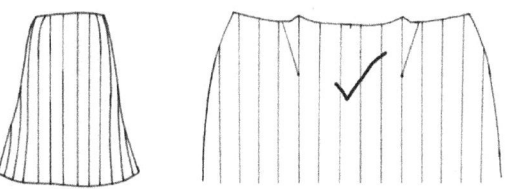

For **vertical darts in horizontal stripes**, the centre of the dart needs to be perpendicular to the stripes.

If it isn't, the stripes won't meet when the dart is sewn up, like this:

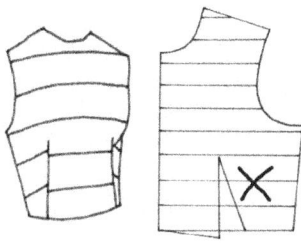

To adjust the darts, use an L-square to make the centre line of the dart exactly vertical.

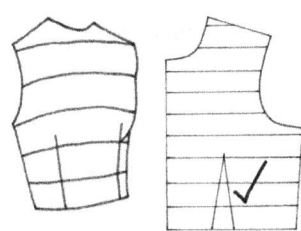

In factories, sometime part of the stripe pattern is drawn onto the pattern piece for placement reference.

Changing darts on a pattern

Darts follow a few important rules:

✂ The dart points to the most prominent/fullest part of the body's curve.

✂ The dart value is the widest part of the dart (the part that gets sewn into the seam). The bigger the curve, the bigger the dart value needs to be.

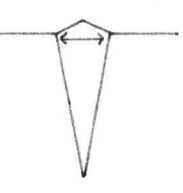

✂ The dart value can be divided between two or more darts, provided the total value remains the same. The dart value can also be converted into pleats, tucks or gathers.

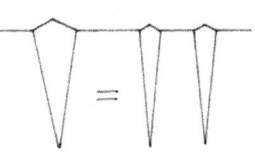

✂ The dart *has* to go into a seam, unless it's a double pointed dart.

✂ Both sides of the dart need to be the same length, whether curved or straight, otherwise you won't be able to sew it together (or you'll end up with a step at the top of the dart). Measure both sides of the dart and add onto the shorter one.

Here the sides of the dart are uneven lengths:

Here both sides are the same:

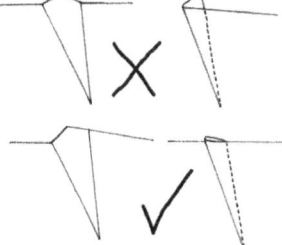

✂ Bust darts stop at 2.5cm (1") before the point of the bust, otherwise the result is pointy boobs.

After changing darts on a pattern, you'll need to check the dart and the seams to make sure they'll sew together properly. This is very important and should always be done. You'll need to add an extension or jog on the end of the dart to make sure it gets caught in when you sew the seam. This is called truing, as in "truing the seam".

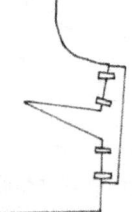

1. Stick a piece of paper onto the edge of the pattern as shown.

2. Fold the dart the way it will be sewn, with the dart value pressed in the correct direction. Position the point over the corner of a table and pin the dart in place. Trim off the excess paper in line with the edge.

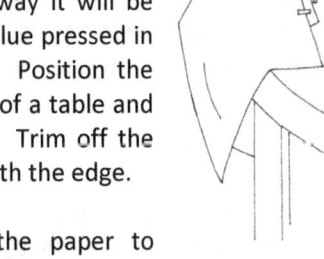

3. Unfold the paper to reveal the new shape.

Note that the shape of the jog depends on the direction the dart is pressed in.

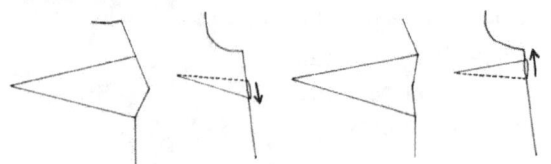

4. Finally, compare the seam with the dart to the one it will be sewn to, to make sure it's the same length. Add extra length on the bottom if necessary.

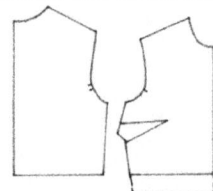

Moving alterations from the garment onto the pattern

So, you've altered a dart during a fitting and you now have a garment full of pins. How do you mark the changes on your pattern so you don't have to re-fit if you intend to use the pattern again?

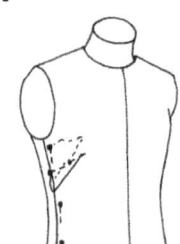

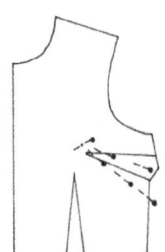

1. Undo and re-arrange the pins so the fabric will lie flat, with the pins marking the dart position. Remember, you only need three pins to mark a dart—one for the point and one for each of the snips.

2. Compare the left and the right by laying them on top of each other. Are they very different or a pair? If they're very different you'll need to make a pattern with left and right sides.

3. Lay the garment onto the pattern and transfer the new lines. I usually push pins through to make holes in the pattern, then draw the lines in.

Then, as described on this page, fold the dart as it will be sewn and true the seam. Compare the seam with the dart to the one it will be sewn to, to make sure it's the same length. Add extra length where necessary.

Transferring a dart

Transferring darts was the first thing we learnt when I was training to be a patternmaker.

Once you get the hang of it, whole new worlds of changing patterns will open up to you. You can transfer the dart value to any edge. You can also transfer part of the dart value to one place and the rest of it to another.

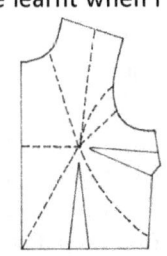

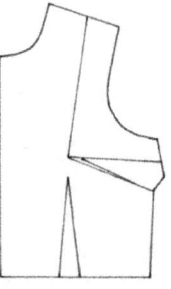

1. Extend the existing dart to the actual bust point (remember, darts stop 2.5cm (1") short of the bust point). Draw a line where you'd like the new dart to be, for example, to the shoulder.

Darts **91**

2. Cut along this new line to the bust point. Fold closed the old dart, and the new one will open up. Stick a piece of paper behind the new dart.

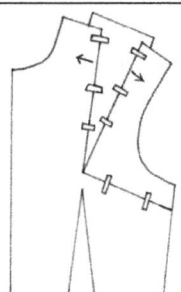

3. Draw a point 2.5cm (1") away from the bust point and draw in the new dart. True the seam as described on page 90, to create a jog on the end of the dart.

Another method to transfer darts

Actually, patternmakers transfer darts using a quicker method, but the theory is the same. It creates a new pattern piece, instead of changing the old one. It's very easy to do if the pattern is made of cardboard because you can just trace around the edge. Follow the steps in order or it won't work.

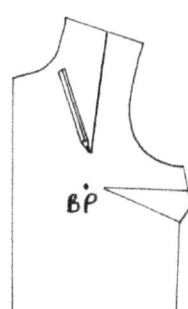

1. Identify the bust point (BP) on the pattern and poke a hole in it big enough to fit your pencil point.
Draw in the position of the new dart—in this example it's on the shoulder.

2. Trace around the pattern, from the new dart to the old one. Place a mark on the edge to indicate the dart lines of the new and old darts.

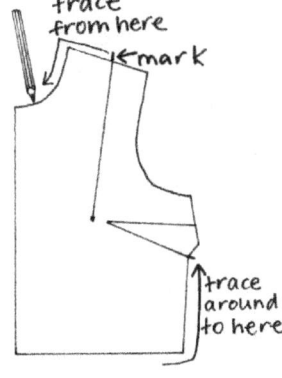

3. Place your pencil point through the BP and use it to pivot the pattern. Close the old dart by bringing the second side to match the mark.

4. The new dart (on the shoulder) will open up. Place another mark where the new dart line is now and trace the remainder of the pattern.

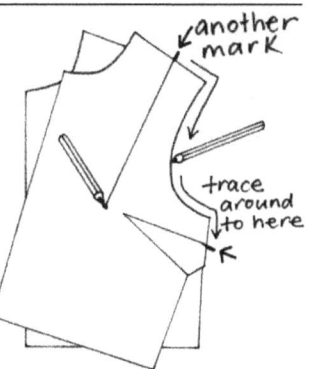

5. The new pattern should look like this. Draw the new dart and true the seam to create the jog, as described on page 90.

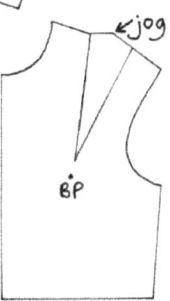

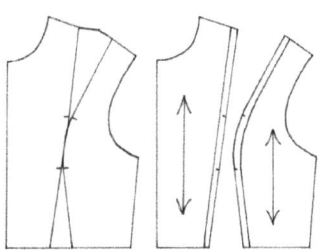

If you want to, you can go one step further and incorporate the darts to be part of a seam.

Smooth off any points and draw in notches that you'll match when you sew the seam.

✂ Try not to have the waist and bust dart values all in one dart. It results in a very pointy bust.

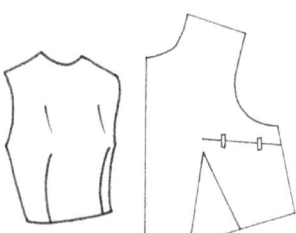

Moving darts

Usually, *transferring* a dart is done for design purposes, and *moving* a dart is done to get a better fit.

1. On the body, undo the side seam and unpick the dart. Pin the dart in the correct position. The garment should fit smoothly with no wrinkles or drag lines.

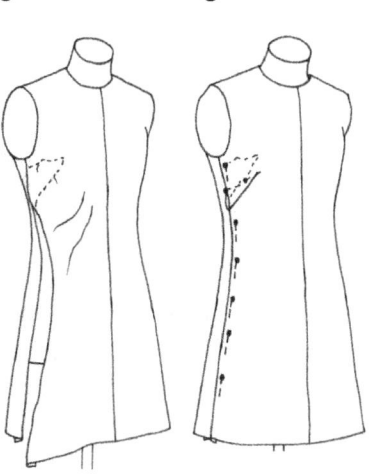

If you can see the dart is the right size but simply needs to be a little higher or lower, you don't need to unpick and re-pin. You can mark it straight onto the pattern in relation to the old dart.

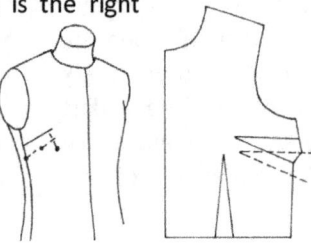

2. Fold the new dart into position and true the seam as described on page 90.

Making a dart bigger or smaller

A bust dart needs to be bigger if the garment rides up at the front and there are drag lines coming from the bust.

It needs to be smaller if there is too much fullness at the bust.

1. On the body, decide how much bigger or smaller the dart needs to be. If the dart needs to be bigger, you can usually just pin a bigger dart on top of the old one. If the dart needs to be smaller, unpick the old dart and side seam and pin a new, smaller, dart.

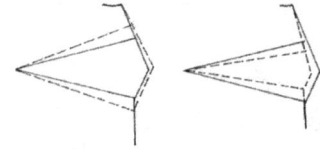

2. Transfer the dart to the pattern.

3. Compare the back and front side seams. If you've made the dart bigger, the front will now be shorter than the back. If you've made the dart smaller, the front will now be longer than the back. Add onto the bottom of either the back or front to make them the same length.

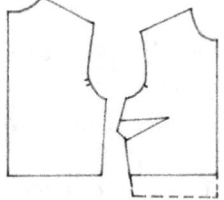

On **skirts or trousers**, the lower the waistline the less dart value is needed. On very low waisted skirts or trousers, you may not need any front darts at all and only small back ones.

If the dart is too big, there'll be fullness at the bottom of the dart. If there's only a little fullness, it means the dart just needs to be longer—check and see.

If the dart is too small, drag lines will be visible.

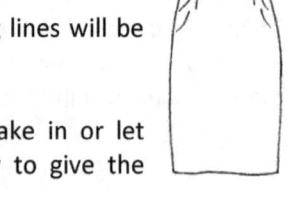

After adjusting the darts, take in or let out the side seams equally to give the correct waist measurement.

Adding a bust dart where there isn't one

Adding a bust dart eliminates drag lines and stops the garment riding up at the front.

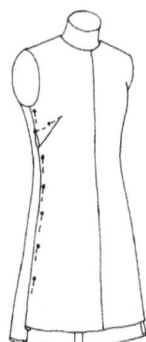

Try on the garment or the paper pattern and pin a dart where you need it. You'll need to undo the side seam of the garment.

Transfer the position of the dart to the pattern and true the seam, both as described on page 90.

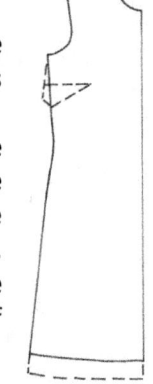

The front will now be shorter than the back, so add the dart value onto the bottom of the front pattern so the side seam is the same length as the back. Alternatively, trim the difference off the back instead of adding it onto the front, if you don't need the length.

Getting rid of bust darts

You may wish to eliminate the bust dart on your pattern for

✂ Large, loose styles
✂ A very flat chest
✂ Knits—if you're converting a pattern for woven fabric into a pattern for knits. The stretchier the knit, the better the garment will fit without darts. Very large busts might still need a bust dart.

Transfer the bust dart to the side seam (see page 90), then simply straighten off the side. The front will now be longer than the back, so add onto the back to make the side seams the same length.

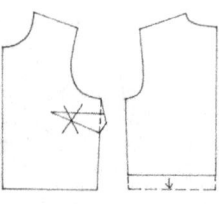

Making a dart longer or shorter
Very easy—simply draw in the new point of the dart on the pattern.

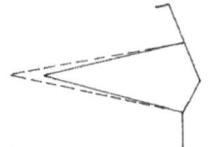 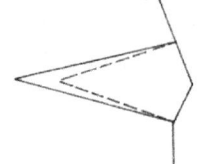

Adding or getting rid of double pointed darts

Sometimes adding double pointed darts to the back is all that's needed to give a garment a flattering fit. Getting rid of double pointed darts is even easier—just don't sew them in.

Double pointed darts can be added without truing the seams or adding length. They can even be added when the garment is finished, if necessary.

Shoulder and neck darts

Shoulder darts on the back give a smooth fit over the shoulders.
You may require shoulder darts if you are:
- Round-shouldered
- Over 50 (see page 2)
- Broad-backed
- Obese
- Making a fitted jacket or other garment with a natural shoulder line (that is, without shoulder pads)

To add a shoulder dart, add 1cm-1.5cm (⅜"-⅝") onto the edge of the back shoulder, then draw in a 1cm-1.5cm (⅜"-⅝") dart on the shoulder. Make the dart about 6cm (2⅜") long. Fold the dart into position and true the seam as described on page 90.

To remove a shoulder dart, the reverse is done. Take the dart value off the shoulder, then straighten the shoulder seam with a ruler. Shoulder darts can also be converted into ease—see page 95.

Neck darts will also give a smooth fit. They are usually about 1cm (⅜") wide.

To convert a shoulder dart into a neck dart, transfer the shoulder dart to the neck and draw in a new dart point.

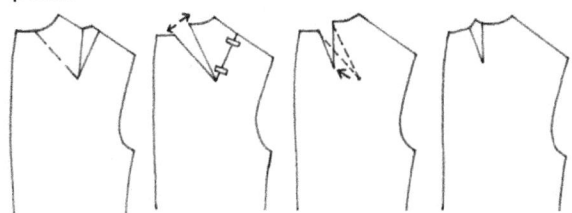

True the seam as described on page 90.

Another way to add neck or shoulder darts is to undo the garment's shoulder seams and pin the darts in place at the fitting, then transfer the darts to the pattern.

Gape darts

A gape dart is a tiny dart made on the neckline of the *pattern only* to stop a low neckline from gaping. You'll *always* have to do this when you change a high neckline to a low neckline on a pattern.
Sometimes commercial paper patterns need a gape dart—try on the tissue paper and see if the neckline gapes. Pin one in if required.
A gape dart's value is usually 6mm-1cm (¼"-⅜"), that is, 3mm-5mm (⅛"-scant ¼") on the double. Sometimes more than one is needed.

Gape darts can run off to a seam, for example a princess line (pictured at right) or the armhole (pictured at left).

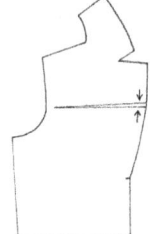

Gape darts can be taken through collars.

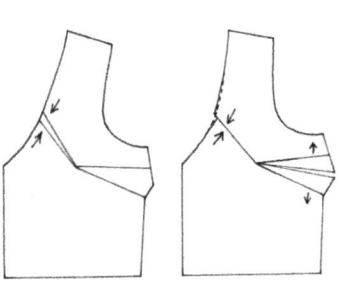

Gape darts can also run off to the bust dart. When the gape dart is closed, the bust dart will be slightly bigger.

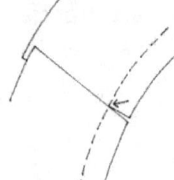 When you adjust the pattern be sure to run the dart off to the *seam line—not* the edge of the pattern.

You can also run gape darts off to nothing (see this page).

When you've closed a gape dart, smooth off the neckline.
Don't forget to do the same alterations to any facings.

What if I forgot to put gape darts in my pattern and now it gapes?

✂ Re-cut new pieces if you have the time, fabric and inclination.

✂ Sew tiny gape darts in the garment, topstitch them if desired, and call them a feature.

✂ Sew tiny gape darts in the garment, then sew a braid or some sort of trim over the top to disguise the gape darts and help pull the neckline in.

✂ Try taping the neckline with 6mm (¼") cotton tape to a smaller measurement and steaming out the excess fabric with an iron. It works well on sleeveless armholes, too. Here's how:

1. Find out the measurement the cotton tape needs to be by trying on the neckline and pinning in gape darts.

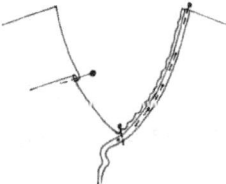

2. Cut the cotton tape to fit the pinned-in measurement.

3. If the neckline has yet to be sewn, sew the tape on first and steam out the excess fabric. Apply the facing, to which gape darts have been sewn in.

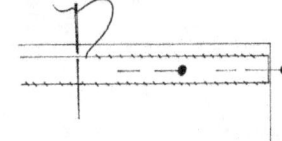

4. If the garment is already finished, handsew the tape to the inside edge. Press.

Getting rid of small darts

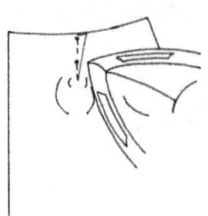 This comes under "creative patternmaking". Small darts on the *pattern* can sometimes be eliminated by pinning the dart in position and ironing it flat.

There'll be sort of a bubbly wrinkle at the dart's point, but press it flat with the iron.

I wouldn't try this on a dart bigger than 1.5cm-2cm (⅝"-¾").

Examples of where I would do this are:

✂ Tiny darts on the front of a skirt, as pictured above.

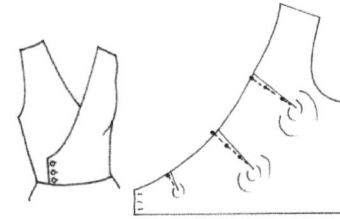

✂ A gape dart taken to stop a low neckline from gaping. See page 93 for more on gape darts.

✂ A dart under a lapel, taken to make the collar sit better—see page 60 Eliminating neck darts.

Darts in Design

As you may know, darts are only one way of shaping a garment to fit the curves of the body. The dart value can be transformed into other design features in a garment. Here are some very simple ones:

Seams

The dart value can easily be incorporated into a seam, as in this example of princess line seams. See page 91 for a shoulder princess.

A colleague of mine never used darts—his signature look was to always convert them to seams.

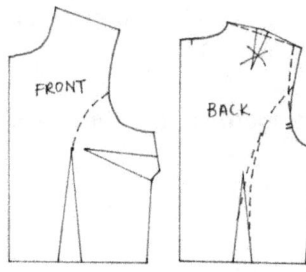 1. Draw in the lines of the princess seam (broken lines). In this example, the shoulder dart has been removed, too.

Darts 95

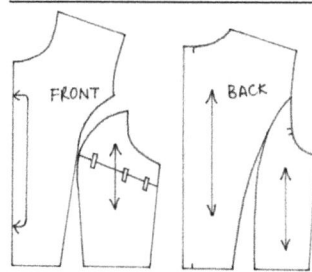

2. Close the bust dart to form the side front panel. Draw in grainlines on the side panels. Separate the pieces and add seam allowances.

Tucks or pleats

Tucks or pleats are really darts that haven't been sewn all the way. In linings, sometimes the darts are sewn as tucks to allow more movement.

Here's the pattern for the blouse pictured:

1. Draw in a yoke (broken line) on the blouse front. Draw a line from the yoke to the bust point. You'll transfer the bust dart to this line.

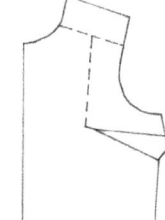

2. Close the bust dart, opening up a dart to the yoke.

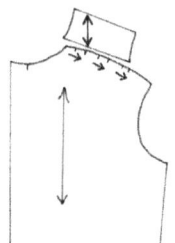

3. Change the new dart to tucks coming from the yoke.

Ease

Converting darts to ease depends on the fabric and the size of the dart. It isn't successful for big darts or for fabrics that don't mould or shrink well.

Shoulder darts can be converted to ease. Ignore the dart and curve the back shoulder seam slightly.
Burda patterns often employ this technique.

Elbow darts on sleeves can also be converted to ease. Mark in notches on the side seam so all the ease is isolated in the elbow area; the area between the notches will be eased. See page 332.

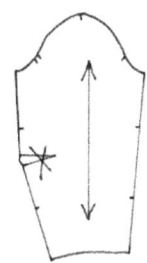

Bust darts don't convert to ease particularly well, because they're big darts and no-one wants loads of ease in their side seams. However, in this example a small bust dart remains after a side panel is drawn.

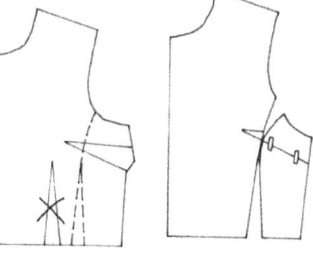

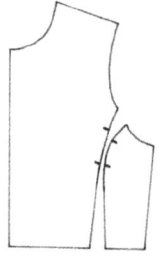
At this point, the small dart could be sewn in as normal.

Or, the small dart could also be converted to ease:
Mark in notches to isolate the ease in the bust area; the area between the notches will be eased.

This styling is often seen on wool coats, because the fabric eases well.

Flare

A flared skirt can be made by folding out the dart at the top to create flare at the bottom. Smooth off the waist and hem to a pleasing curve.

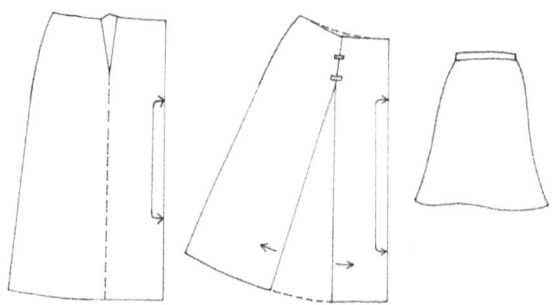

You might need to take excess curve off the hip for a smooth fit.

You can make a skirt with more or less flare depending on how wide you spread the hem.
Make sure you keep the waist measurement the same.

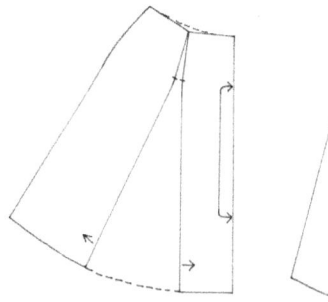
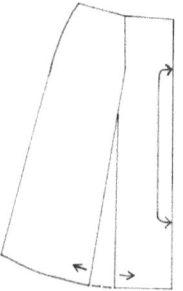

Bust darts can be converted into flare to make a tent dress, pinafore or maternity top.

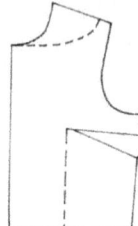 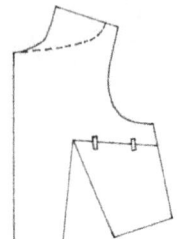 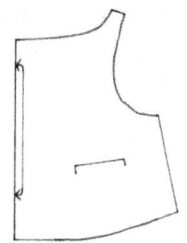

Gathers

In this example, the bust dart has been transferred to the neckline, then changed to gathers. If more gathers are needed than the dart can provide, extra width can be added onto the side. For this example, I would add extra onto the centre front.

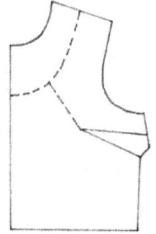 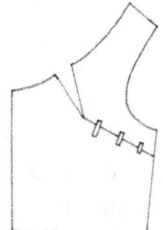 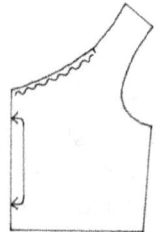

Elastic

To make a skirt with darts into a skirt with an elastic waist, ignore the darts and square up from the hip line.
Add double the width of the elastic to form a casing plus a seam allowance onto the top. See page 385.

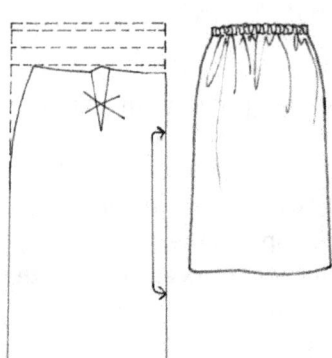

This is a good skirt solution for very large figures.

Facings

Introduction..97	Waist facings....................................... 100
Make a pattern.....................................97	using tape 101
no-pattern facing..................98	using tear away stabilizer......... 101
extended facings..................98	All-in-one facings..................................... 101
facings on areas with darts...............98	Troubleshooting all-in-one facings 103
To sew a facing....................................99	Faced scallops 104
Troubleshooting facings................................100	

A facing is a piece of fabric that's used to cleanly finish the edge of a garment and support the garment's edges.

Facings can be found at necklines, armholes, front and back openings, edges of pockets and at lower edges of sleeves.

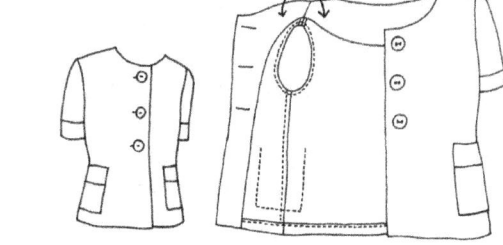

Facings are also used at the waistlines of skirts and trousers.

✂ A facing is cut the same shape as the edge it will finish. After a facing is attached to the garment's edge, it's turned to the inside of the garment and secured. It doesn't show on the right side.

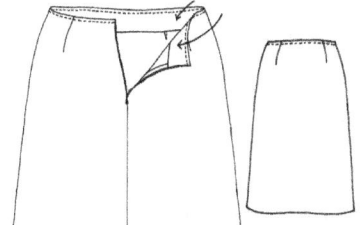

✂ Usually facings are separate pieces stitched on, but if the edge is straight, the facing can be cut in one with the garment and simply folded inside. These are called extended facings, self-facings or cut-on facings.

✂ A facing is usually cut from the same fabric as the garment, but can be cut in a lighter weight fabric to reduce bulk, or in a different fabric if you don't have enough of the garment fabric left.

✂ If the fabric is a sheer print or a sheer that's embellished with beads or embroidery, use a sheer fabric as a facing—either skin toned or matched to the background colour of the sheer print. You could use organza, voile or netting, or you could unpick the embroidery or beads on the sheer to make it plain. Lace is often finished with a soft tulle facing. Match the colour of the facing to the wearer's skin tone so it doesn't show through.

If the garment has extended facings you'll need to change them to separate facings—see page 98.

✂ In lightweight, sheer or light coloured clothes, you can prevent the facing from showing through to the right side by matching the facing to the wearer's skin tone—not the garment fabric.

Make a pattern

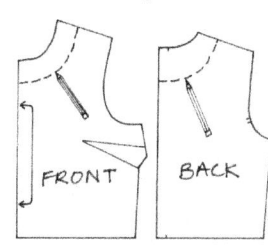

Simple! Make a pattern piece by tracing the edge of the pattern onto a piece of paper. Draw in the width of the facing, generally 5cm-7cm (2"-2¾") wide. Facings have the same grainline as the garment.

Although the facing is usually cut a uniform width all the way around, it's often made deeper at the centre back. I own a pajama top with a very deep back neck facing of 20cm (8"). It's 5cm (2") at the shoulders.

✂ If the garment has a centre that's cut on the fold,

make complete pattern pieces for the facings. That is, don't make the facings "Cut on the fold". It will give you more accurate pieces when cutting out, because there isn't such a small edge to place on the fold (that could possibly be placed at the wrong angle).

✂ In industry, the edges of the facing sewn to the garment have a 6mm (¼") seam allowance, and obviously the garment has the same. This makes the facing easy to sew on and gives accurate curves, because you can use the presser foot as guide. It also eliminates any need for trimming back or clipping the seam allowance after sewing (although on very tight curves I might trim back to 3mm (⅛") or clip the curves). Consider pre-trimming the edges of your pattern back to 6mm (¼"). The other seam allowances on the facing, such as the side seams or shoulder seams, are the same as the garment.

✂ If any alterations have been done to the garment, make sure the same alterations are done to the corresponding facings.

✂ Facings have **interfacing** in them to help support, define and reinforce the edge.
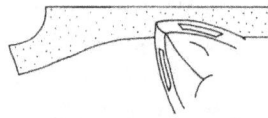

Some people like to trim all or most of the seam allowance off the interfacing to reduce bulk and help prevent it sticking to their ironing board cover. I rarely do, because if I can, I like to cut the interfacing out with the facings to save time. Lay the interfacing under the main fabric and pattern and cut them out together.

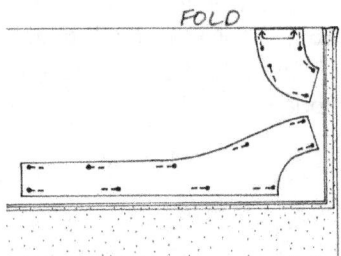

No-pattern facing
If the facing pattern is uncomplicated (with no darts to fold out) and the fabric is fairly stable, I don't make facing patterns for my own clothes. I lay the pattern onto the fabric and draw around the edges to be faced.

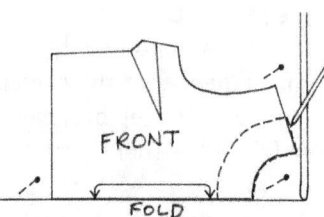

Then I draw in the width of my facing. If I can, I'll slip some interfacing underneath and cut them out together.

Extended facings
An extended facing is cut as an extension of the garment, then it's folded back along the edge it finishes. It's used for centre back and centre front openings, and is often seen on shirts and pajama tops. It's still interfaced like a regular facing. It's important to notch with tiny 3mm (⅛") snips the top and bottom of the fold line so you can accurately press the extension back.
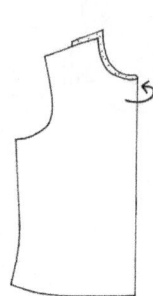

Some designers prefer extended facings wherever possible, because having no seam means reduced bulk, resulting in a lighter garment.

An extended facing can easily be turned into a separate facing (or back again). Simply cut along the fold line and add a seam allowance to both sides.
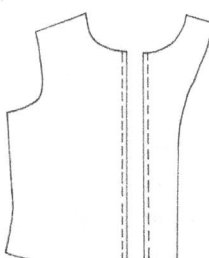

Facings on areas with darts
Facings don't have darts in them; the darts are folded out of the paper pattern before the facing is drawn in.

There are two ways to go about making a pattern:

✂ On the pattern, fold the dart into position and secure it with a pin. Lay it over the corner of a table to accommodate the point.
Draw in where you want the facing, then trace it off to make a separate pattern piece. This is the method I use.
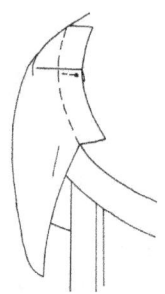

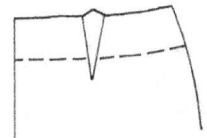
✂ The second way is to draw in the facing across the dart while the pattern is flat.

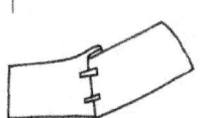
Trace off the facing and fold out the dart, taping it in place.

Whichever method you use, smooth off any angles on the facing.
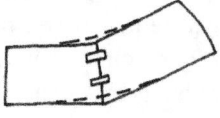

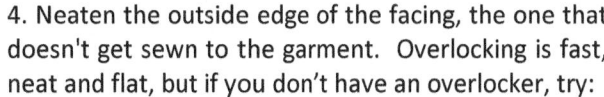

If the facing is cut on the centre back or front fold, make a full-sized pattern piece, for accuracy.

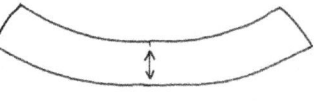

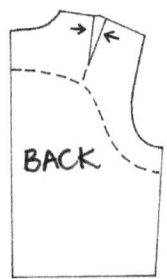

On a top or jacket with **shoulder or neck darts**, the dart is folded out of the facing in the same way.
Extend the point of the dart to the edge of the facing if necessary.

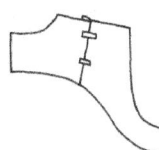

As before, smooth off any angles and straighten the shoulder seam.

If there's a **lining** attached to a horizontal back facing, fold out the shoulder dart but keep the lower edge of the facing horizontal.
This will make the top edge of the lining curved. Essentially the dart has been transferred to the lining side of the seam.

To sew a facing

Facings are usually applied *after* the zip has been put in. If you need to sew the facing first, leave a space for the zip.

1. Cut out all the pieces and iron interfacing onto the facings.

2. On the garment, sew any side or shoulder seams, and any darts. Neaten the edges of the seams and press. Apply tape to the top edge of skirts or trousers to stabilize (see page 101).

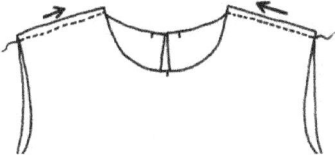

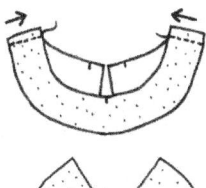

3. On the facing, sew the corresponding seams. Press the seams open to reduce bulk. The seam allowances aren't neatened because the fusing will arrest any fraying and besides, they'll be tucked away inside.

4. Neaten the outside edge of the facing, the one that doesn't get sewn to the garment. Overlocking is fast, neat and flat, but if you don't have an overlocker, try:

✄ Zig zag or similar neatening stitch on your regular machine.

✄ Straight stitch 6mm (¼") from the edge, then trim with pinking shears.

✄ Turn the edge under once about 3mm-6mm (⅛"-¼"), then straight stitch close to the folded edge. An Old School treatment often seen on vintage clothes.

✄ Bind the edge with bias binding or a lightweight seam binding. This looks smart from the inside but press the garment carefully to avoid a ridge showing on the outside.

5. Place the facing and garment right sides together, matching any seams or notches. Match the centre fronts and centre backs. Sew together, taking the correct seam allowance.

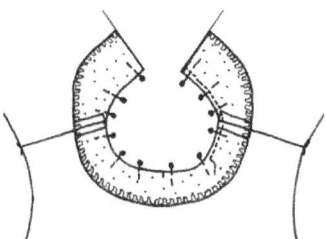

6. If your seam allowance is bigger than 6mm (¼"), you'll need to clip any curves to make the facing sit flat. The tighter the curve, the more snips you'll need.

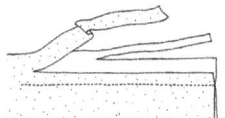

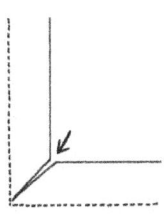

You may also trim the seam allowance to reduce bulk. Sometimes the seam allowance is graded, that is, each seam is trimmed back to different widths, with the seam allowance that falls closest to the garment being cut the widest. The idea is that you won't get a bulky ridge (just a less bulky one). If you own duck billed (appliqué) scissors, you can use them to grade the seam.

Trim any outside corners so they aren't bulky. Trim no closer than 3mm (⅛") to the stitching.

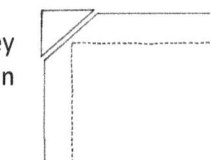

Clip any inside corners *exactly* to the stitching, to make them sit flat when turned to the right side. I sometimes stitch inside corners with a shorter stitch length (1.5) to make them stronger, since they're made weaker by having to clip them.

100 The Dressmaker's Companion

7. Press the seam allowance towards the facing. To keep the facing from rolling towards the outside of the garment, understitch the seam.

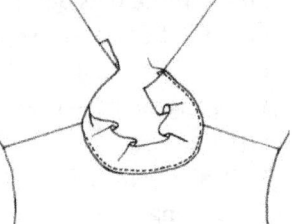

To understitch, have the right side up and sew about 2mm (a scant ⅛") away from the seam on the facing, through the seam allowances as well. Pull the seam flat as you sew. Some people like to press the seam before understitching, to make it easier to do. If you've snipped any curves, make sure all the little sections between the snips are pushed to the same side.

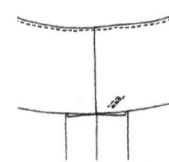

8. Turn the facing to the inside of the garment and press. Catch the facing to the garment at the seams. You can do this by machine (I always do) if you hold the facing and one seam allowance together to stitch. Be extremely careful not to catch the outer fabric.
Or, sew by hand using herringbone stitch (page 149).

9. Topstitch the facing if desired.

✂ If the facing is used to apply a **collar**, the collar gets made first, then it's sandwiched between the facing and the garment. To help the back neck facing sit flat, stitch it to the garment through *all* layers, stopping at the shoulder seams. The stitching will be hidden by the collar.

✂ Facings are used not just for necklines but also for the **opening edges** of a garment.
Sew the facing around the whole edge—up one side of the opening, around the neck and down the other side. Trim the corners and turn through to the right side. Understitch the facing as far as you can into each corner.

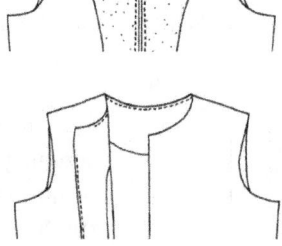

I think a **better way** is to attach the facing in two steps: sew the long straight edges of the garment opening first, press and understitch.
Then sew the neck edge, trim the corners, press and understitch.

It produces superior corners because the first row of understitching goes right up into the corner.

Troubleshooting facings

You might find that the garment edge has stretched slightly and the facing, which is held firm with interfacing, now doesn't fit. *Don't* stretch the facing onto the garment.
There are two ways to help it fit:

✂ Pin the facing on, matching the seams. Distribute the extra fabric between more pins placed perpendicular to the edge. Sew with the facing on top and the garment underneath. The action of the feed dogs on the machine should take care of the extra fullness by pushing the bottom layer backwards and the top layer forwards. Check afterwards to make sure there are no pleats. In most cases this will be enough to help attach the facing.

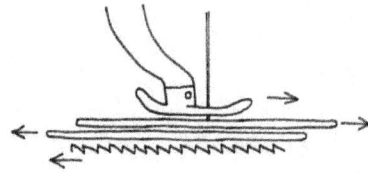

✂ Unpin the facing. Sew a line of staystitching, using a long stitch, along the garment edge, with your middle finger held firmly behind the presser foot. When the fabric has bunched up (5cm (2") or so along, depending on how thick the fabric is), take your finger away and release the built up fabric, then put your finger back. A concertina-like effect results. This should pull in the garment's edge enough for you to attach the facing. I find I often need to do this when sewing stretch corduroy or other stretch wovens, particularly on waists.

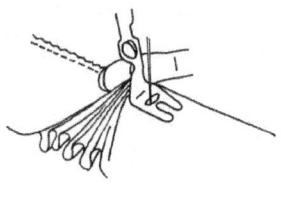

Waist facings

If you're facing the waist of a skirt or trousers, you'll need to tape the waist to stop it from stretching when you wear it. Even though the facing has interfacing in it, it won't be enough to stop the waist from stretching. Ever put on a pair of freshly laundered jeans that feel nice and firm, then noticed them get looser as the day progressed? The same will happen to an untaped waist. The waist will stretch bigger as you wear it.

You can stabilize the waist using 6mm (¼") cotton tape, a 6mm (¼") strip cut from the fabric's selvedge if it's smooth and firm, the selvedge from some organza or tear-away stabilizer. I prefer 6mm (¼") cotton tape, available in black or white. I don't preshrink the tape, and neither do clothing factories; it just gets used straight from the roll.

Using tape

Apply the tape to the waist *before* you do a fitting—otherwise you won't know what size the waist should be.

Tape can be applied to the back and front waists separately, or sometimes the tape is cut as one long piece for the whole 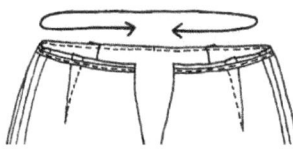 waist and applied after the side seams have been sewn. I prefer the former—it makes it easier to fine-tune the waist measurement and easy to alter later, because the side seams don't have tape over them.

You'll find it's easier to apply waist tape when the waist seam allowance is only 6mm (¼").

1. To cut the tape, use the *pattern* as a guide, rather than the garment which may have already stretched. Place the tape along the *stitching* line and cut it to the correct length. Mark the centre front or centre back 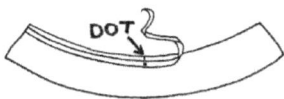 with a pencil dot. Be exact. Include the side seam allowance.

✂ In industry, a measurement is given for cutting the tape and recorded on the garment specs, rather than measuring it on the pattern each time.

2. Sew any darts in the garment. Pin the tape around the waist on the *stitching* line and sew with a long stitch.

3. Sew on the facing, stitching *on* or *just outside* the tape stitching line, so it won't show on the outside.

Using tear-away stabilizer

Tear-away stabilizer looks like a thick sew-in, non-woven interfacing. It tears easily in one direction and not in the other. Apply tear-away to the front and back separately.

1. Cut a strip about 2.5cm (1") wide in the same shape as the edge (you can use the facing pattern for this). Since tear-away tears in only one direction, orientate the strip it so it will tear horizontally as the garment is worn.

2. Sew any darts in the skirt or trousers.

3. Sew the tear-away onto the garment's edge on the wrong side  of the fabric. Use a long stitch within the seam allowance. Attach the facing and understitch (it's **very important** to understitch).

4. Tear away all the excess tear-away you can see. A  narrow strip of tear-away will remain in place held by the seam and understitching.

All-in-one facings

These are sometimes called combination facings, because they combine an armhole and neck facing into one. They're used for sleeveless garments.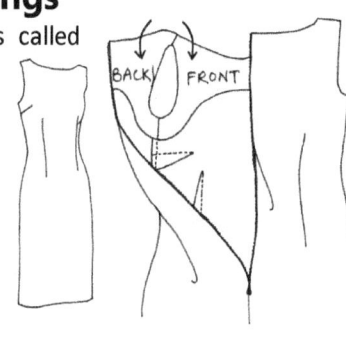

Make a patten

Trace around the pattern and draw in the facings. Aim for a smooth flowing line, with no sharp angles. At the underarm, make the facing 5cm-7cm (2"-2¾") wide. Make sure the 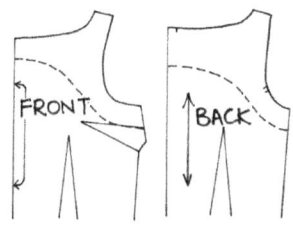 back and front facings are the same width at the side seams. The back facing can be deeper at the centre back if you like.

If the garment has seams in it, such as princess line seams, pin the pattern pieces together at the *stitching* line, then draw in the facing.

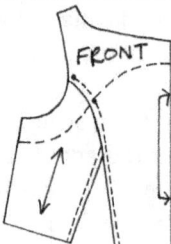

✂ I always snip the centre front and centre back of the neckline with a tiny 3mm (⅛") snip. On the front, it helps position the facing centrally when sewing it. On the back, it helps identify which way around the piece goes—once the pattern is taken away, it's an easy shape to get confused.

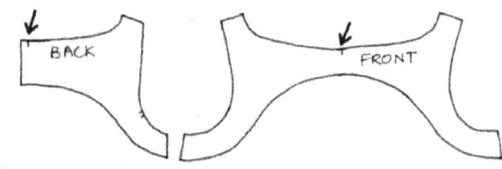

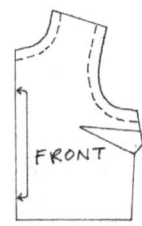

✂ An alternative to all-in-one facings is to make separate, narrow neck and armhole facings, only 2cm or 3cm (¾"-1¼") wide. The facings can be topstitched on the right side to hold them in place.

I sometimes make narrow armhole facings to finish the edges of sleeveless summer shirts.

To sew an all-in-one facing

1. Cut out all the pieces and apply interfacing to the facings. Neaten the lower edge of the facing.

2. Sew the shoulder seams of the garment and the facing but leave the side seams undone on both.
This is **very important**—it won't work if the side seams are sewn.

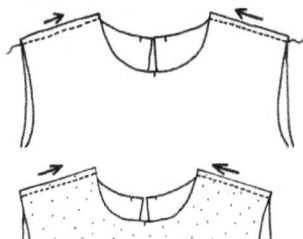

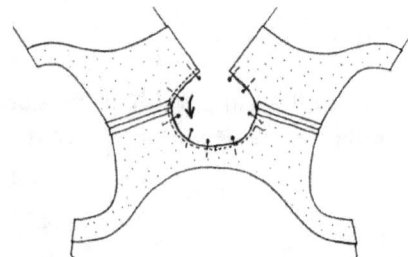

3. Sew the facing to the neck edge first, press and understitch.

If the garment has a back zip, sew the zip in and attach the facing around the zip. Otherwise, leave several centimetres unstitched at the ends of the facing and sew the zip in later.

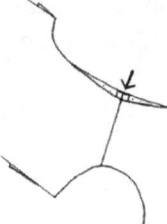

When the facing is turned inside, you'll notice that, due to the understitching around the neck, the shoulder seams of the facing are now slightly wider than that of the garment.

You can trim it off now
OR
When you sew the armholes, let the facing shoulder seams sit 6mm (¼") out past the garment's shoulder seams, then blend the edges back together for the rest of the armhole (that's what I do).

4. If there's a centre seam on the garment that isn't sewn up yet, sew the armholes, right sides together. Remember to step the facing shoulder seam out by 6mm (¼"), if you haven't trimmed. Trim or clip any curves then turn the facing through to the right side.

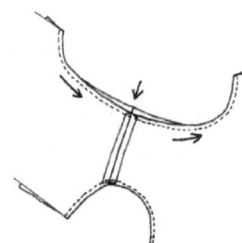

If there's no centre seam, or if it's already sewn up, for example to put the zip in, each armhole needs to be sewn separately in this way:

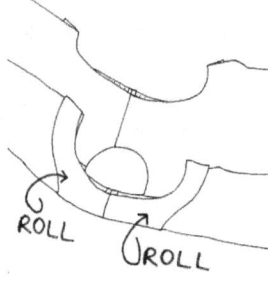

Lay the garment out flat, then begin rolling it up, starting from one armhole across to the other.

When the rolled up side is sitting on top of the opposite shoulder, hold it there and flip the facing so the right sides are together at the armhole edge.

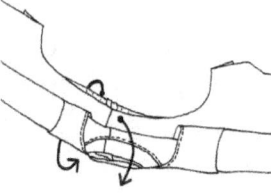

The rolled up side is now encased in the opposite shoulder. You can now stitch the armhole, remembering to step the facing out by 6mm (¼").

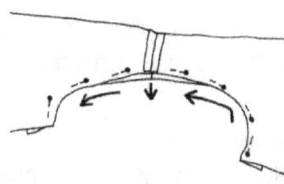

Facings **103**

Trim or clip any curves before pulling the garment through the shoulder to turn it the right way, then repeat with the other shoulder.

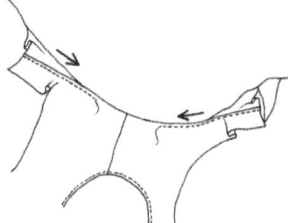

5. Press the seams towards the facings and understitch them. Start the understitching at the side seam and sew as far as you can towards the shoulder. Repeat on the other side.

There may be an area in the middle with no undersitching, but that's fine. On wide shoulders you might be able to make the understitching meet at the shoulder.

6. Sew the side seams of the garment all the way through the facing in one fell swoop. If there's a lining attached to the facing, join it onto the facing *before* sewing the side seams.
Press the side seams open and neaten the edges.

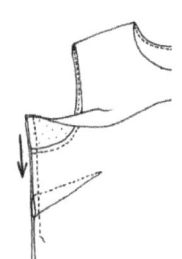

7. Catch the facing to the garment at the side seams either by hand or machine. A neat and invisible way to do this is to sew the seam allowances together *underneath* the facing.

You can only use this method where the facing is stitched on *before* the seam to secure it to is sewn, as it is here.

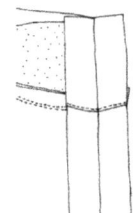

Press the side seam open.

Fold the facing down in place as it will be when finished.

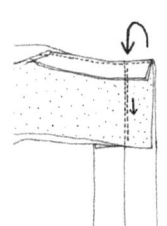

Reach under the facing, grasp the seam allowances of the facing and garment together and peel back the facing. Sew a line of machine stitching through both seam allowances, close to the seam line.

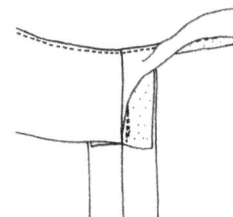

Bring the facing back to cover the seam.

Troubleshooting all-in-one facings

The shoulders are too narrow to pull the garment through, or the garment is too voluminous or creases too much to pull it through.

✂ Sew each half of the armhole separately. First sew the neckline as usual, then, starting at the underarm, bring the edges around so the right sides are together. Sew the seam as far as you can towards the shoulder, then sew the other side in the same way, meeting at the shoulder.

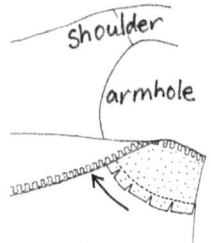

OR

✂ If the shoulders are narrow and strappy and you don't mind a bit of edgestitching, another idea is to stitch them from the right side. First sew the neckline as usual. Press and fold under the seam allowances around the armholes, snipping into the seam allowances around the curves so you can turn them under. Place the wrong sides together and edgestitch around the edges of the armholes to hold them together. Edgestitch around the neckline to match.

I forgot to leave the side seams undone.

✂ If the shoulders are wide and the neckline is high, it's possible to sew the armholes without having to unpick the side seams. Sew the neck first as usual. For the armholes, reach in between the facing and the garment to get to the armhole seam. Sew each half of the armhole separately by sewing the front of the armhole, and then turning the garment around and doing the same to the back of the armhole. Trim or clip the seam allowance and understitch, stitching as far as you can around. The understitching will have to be done in two stages, the same as sewing the armhole seam.

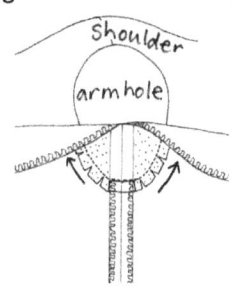

OR

✂ If the neckline of the garment is low and the shoulder seams are narrow, unfortunately you have no choice but to undo the side seams before you can attach the facing at the armholes. Sorry.

I forgot to step the edge of the facing when sewing the armhole and now the facing peeks out. The garment is finished.

✂ Press the neck and armhole edges thoroughly *exactly* on the seam lines, then topstitch 6mm (¼") around the edges to hold the seams in place.

OR

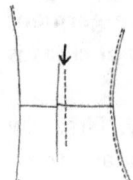

✂ On the facing, take a tiny tuck perpendicular to the shoulder seam to take up the excess fabric.

Faced scallops

To sew a faced, scalloped edge, use a narrow 6mm (¼") seam allowance for accuracy.
A pencil dot at the apex of each scallop will help make them all the same size.
Alternatively, make a cardboard template the finished size of the scallops to help stitch each one the same.

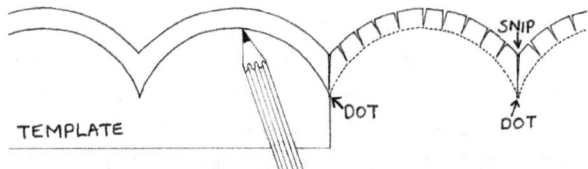

After sewing, snip exactly to each apex so the scallops can be turned through neatly. Depending on how tight the scallops are, you may also need to snip around the curves too.

Front stands and tab fronts

Introduction.. 105	Neck binding for knitted collars............ 116
"Wrap" explained 106	A simple tab front....................................... 116
Fold-under button stand............................ 106	Simple tab front variation 1 118
Double folded button stand 107	Simple tab front variation 2 118
Separate front button stand 107	Tab front with facing 119
Separate stand with a facing 108	Troublehooting tab fronts........................ 120
Men's shirt front stand............................... 109	Adding piping to a tab 120
Concealed fronts 110	Tab fronts from slit..................................... 121
Concealed front for a shirt......................... 110	Tab from a slit using twill tape 121
Concealed front with a facing 110	Tab from a slit using fabric tabs............. 122
Concealed fronts for jackets 112	Tab from a slit with a 1pce facing 123
1. Concealed front on extended facing .. 112	Tab from a slit using a rectangle 124
2. Concealed front with separate (folded) facing..................................... 113	Free-hanging tab 125
	Placket with a pleat below....................... 125
3. Concealed front with separate facing 114	All-in-one placket 126
Tab fronts 116	All-in-one placket as a hand opening. 127
Interfacing tab fronts.................................. 116	

Most clothes need some sort of opening to get them on, which then fastens closed. Tops and shirts usually open at the front either all the way with a buttoned front stand, or partially with a tab front.
Sometimes the front stand or tab front is referred to as a placket or placket opening. A placket is simply the name for a strip of fabric that finishes an opening or slit in a garment, in this case the centre front.

✂ Men's clothes fasten left over right and women's right over left (as you wear them). This means the buttonholes are on the left front for men's clothes and the right for women's. A mnemonic I use to remember this is "women are always right".

✂ When making patterns, note that wide button stands will be curved for the neck at the top of the stand. To get the correct curve, fold the pattern piece, securing with a pin if necessary, and position it back on the shirt front pattern. Trim the top to follow the neck curve.

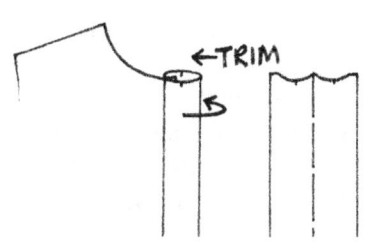

✂ The style of the front band on any garment is easy to change without making a whole new pattern. Make a template of the desired front band with a piece of card. When you cut the garment out, use the template to match the centre front (CF) to the garment's centre front and draw in the new front band directly onto the cloth.

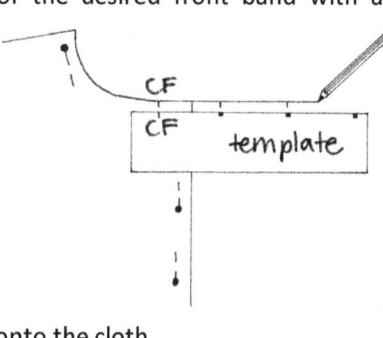

✂ If necessary, try out the front stand using a strip of paper to understand how it's constructed before making the pattern.

"Wrap" explained

The wrap is an extension of the garment's edge to allow the buttons and buttonholes to lap over each other.

The button stand or placket is *double* the amount of wrap, so the centre front of the garment remains in the centre. For example, if a 1.5cm (⅝") wrap is added, then the button stand will be 3cm (1¼"). For a 2cm (¾") wrap, the stand will be 4cm (1½").

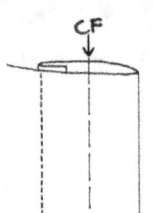

On **shirts and blouses**, the amount of wrap is normally 1.5cm (⅝") yielding a 3cm (1¼") wide stand. However, the wrap can be as narrow as 6mm (¼"), or much wider if the garment is designed for big buttons. Some men's shirts have a 2cm (¾") wrap (= 4cm (1½") wide stand) to allow for 6mm (¼") topstitching either side. For a **jacket**, 2cm (¾") is the usual amount of wrap. Naturally, a seam allowance is also added to the edge if required.

If the collar has a stand that overlaps at the neck, the stand will have the same amount of wrap on it.

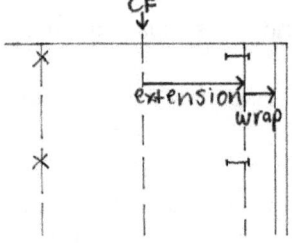

For **double breasted** garments, an extension for the double breasted part is added first, then the wrap and seam allowance. The centre front (CF) is always marked on the pattern.

Fold-under button stand

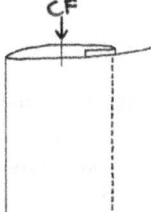

A very simple front edge for shirts is an extension that folds under and is stitched in place. The top of the placket is caught in the collar stand, sewn on later.

This is my most often-used method.

This type of button stand is good for:
- Classic shirts with a collar leaf and collar stand
- Shirts and blouses in sheer fabric
- The right (underneath) front of a man's shirt

Don't use it for open necked blouses unless the fabric is sheer. A faced opening is a better choice because a facing looks nicer when the blouse is worn open at the neck.

Make a pattern

1. Add a 1.5cm (⅝") wrap to the centre front (CF) line, to yield a 3cm (1¼") wide finished stand.

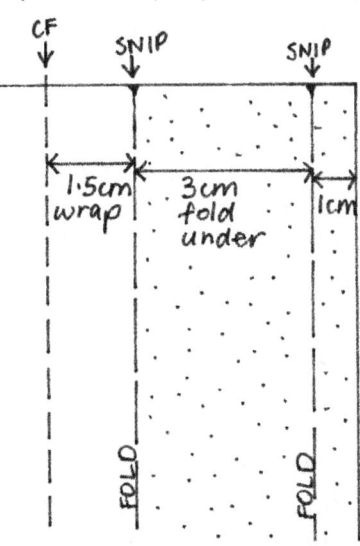

2. Add a 3cm (1¼") fold-under (that is, double the amount of wrap).

3. Add a 1cm (⅜") seam allowance.

4. Notch each end of the fold lines with a tiny 3mm (⅛") snip so you know where to fold.

To sew a fold-under stand

1. On the wrong side, iron a 4cm (1½") wide strip of fusing to the edge (shaded area, above).

2. Press the stand along the fold lines, pressing under the 1cm (⅜") seam allowance, then the 3cm (1¼") fold-under.

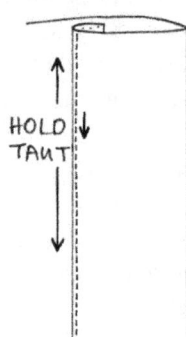

3. With the wrong side up, stitch the button stand into position along the edge. It's very important to hold the button stand taut as you sew it, to prevent it puckering or bunching up slightly from the stitching. No amount of ironing will be able to flatten it later.

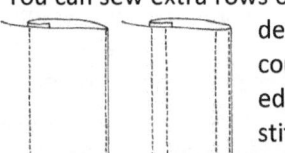

You can sew extra rows of topstitching on the stand, if desired. For example, you could edgestitch the folded edge, or have two rows of stitching on either side of the stand.

If the fabric looks the same on both sides, you could iron the interfacing onto the right side and fold the stand *over* instead of *under*, if you like the look of a stitched edge instead of just a row of stitching.

Front stands and tab fronts **107**

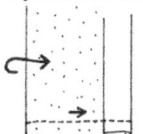Optional: bag out the hem before stitching down the button stand, by folding the stand right sides together back on itself, and stitching across the bottom the depth of the hem.

Overlock or double roll the hem before turning the corner through.

Double folded button stand

This button stand is even simpler than the fold-under stand described above. It has no interfacing, because the three layers of fabric provide enough support. It works best on firmly woven fabrics that fold crisply. It's a useful method if you don't want any stitching down the front of the shirt.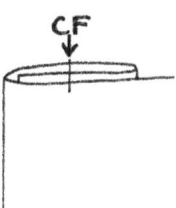

Make a pattern

1. Add a 1.5cm (⅝") wrap to the centre front (CF) line, to yield a 3cm (1¼") wide finished stand.

2. Add the finished band width, in this case 3cm (1¼").

3. Add slightly less than the finished band, about 3mm (⅛") less = 2.7cm (1⅛"). This accommodates the fabric thickness when it's folded.

4. Notch each end of the fold lines with a tiny 3mm (⅛") snip so you know where to fold.

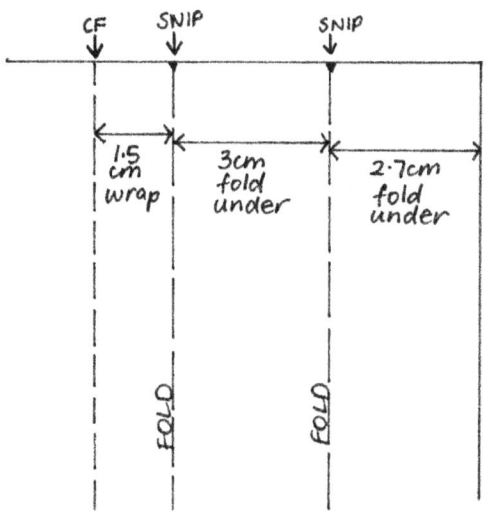

To sew a double folded stand

The button stand is simply ironed along the foldlines into position. The buttons and buttonholes keep the stand folded correctly.

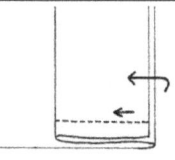Optional: bag out the hem by folding the stand right sides together back on itself, and stitching across the bottom, the depth of the hem. Overlock or double roll the hem before turning the corner through.

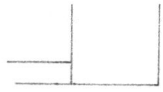

Separate front button stand

Sometimes a separate front button stand is necessary, for example, if there are gathers coming from the button stand, or if the front band is cut in a different fabric, or on the bias in a checked or striped fabric.

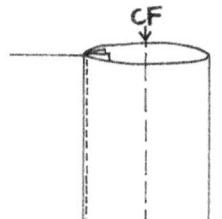  

It's also a handy solution if you'd planned a fold-under stand but ran out of fabric, or made a mistake when cutting or ironing on interfacing.

Make a pattern

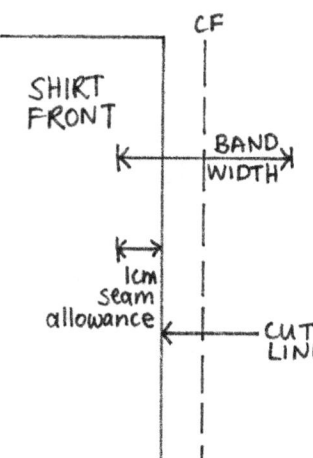

1. Locate the centre front (CF) line on the pattern.

2. Decide how wide to make the front band, for example, 3cm (1¼") finished.

3. Remove half the width of the band from the centre front (1.5cm or ⅝"), then add a 1cm (⅜") seam allowance.

Rather than trim this off, if I'm making a pattern for myself I simply fold the paper under. That way, I still have the centre front marked on the pattern and can easily adapt it to other styles.

4. To make the separate band, double the width of the finished band and add two seam allowances. In this case: 3cm + 3cm + 2cm seams = 8cm wide (1¼" + 1¼" + ¾" seams = 3¼"). Notch each end of the fold line with a tiny 3mm (⅛") snip so you'll know where to fold.

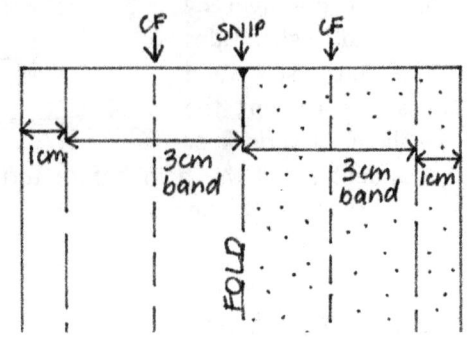

To sew a separate front stand
1. Apply interfacing to either the entire band or only half the band. If you interface only half, make the interfaced side outermost when you sew it to the shirt. Test the interfacing and the fabric to check the band doesn't become too stiff.
If the band is cut on the bias, find a suitable interfacing and fuse the *whole* piece so it's all stabilized *and* cut the interfacing on the straight grain to stop it stretching.
While you're at the ironing board, iron a central fold down the length of the band.

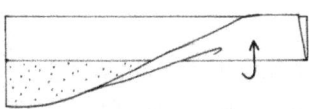

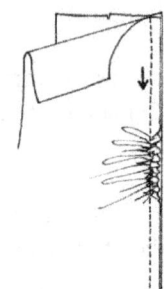

2. If the garment has gathers, as the illustration has, stitch them first. Then, place the *right* side of the (innermost side of the) band and the *wrong* side of the shirt together and stitch down the long edge. Press the seam allowance towards the band.

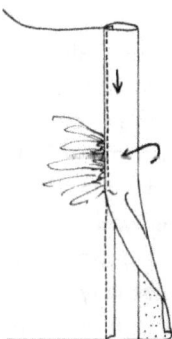

3. Bring the band over to the right side of the shirt, press under the seam allowance, and edgestitch into position.
To stop the band rippling when edgestitching, hold the garment firmly and let the band "sit easy" on top. If desired, you could edgestitch down the folded edge of the stand to match—I usually do.

Separate front stand with a facing

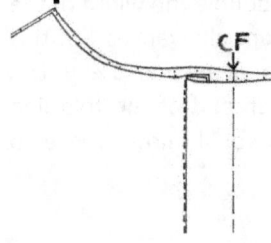

This is a variation of the Separate front button stand on page 107. It looks good if the shirt or blouse is to be worn open at the neck.

Make a pattern
1-3. Follow steps 1-3 of the Separate front stand on page 107 to make the pattern for the shirt.

4. To make the stand with the facing, trace around the shirt's front neckline and top of the shoulder, including the centre front (CF) line. Add a 1.5cm (⅝") wrap to the centre front (CF) line, to yield a 3cm (1¼") wide finished stand. (See sketch below)

5. Add the 3cm (1¼") band width.

6. Add a 1cm (⅜") seam allowance. Draw in the rest of the facing with a smooth flowing line as illustrated. Notch each end of the fold line with a tiny 3mm (⅛") snip so you'll know where to fold.

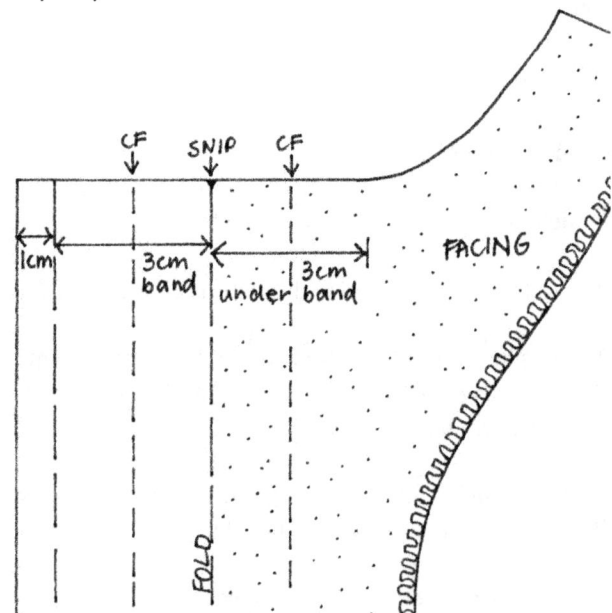

To sew a separate front stand with facing
1. Apply interfacing to either the whole band pattern piece (recommended if you have a suitable fusing), or just the facing and underneath part of the band. While you're at the ironing board, press a lengthwise fold in the band along the foldline.

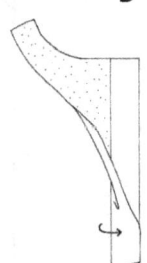

2. Place the right sides of the shirt and band together along the long front edge and stitch. Press the seam allowance towards the band.
Alternatively, if the fabric is very thick, press the seam allowance open (you'll then need to neaten the raw edge because now it won't be enclosed in the band). Overlock the long curved edge of the facing, since once the band is stitched down you won't be able to.

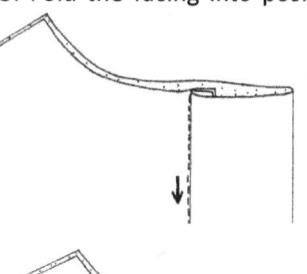

3. Fold the facing into position, ensuring the band is an even width the whole way down. Stitch-in-the-ditch along the edge of the band to hold the facing and band in position.

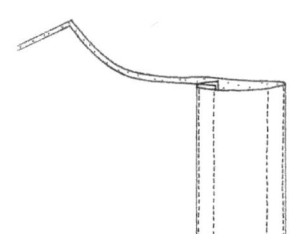

For an alternative finish, edgestitch the band instead and finish off with some extra topstitching.

If the shirt has **no collar** (just a faced edge), or a **collar inserted into the facing**, you'll need to finish the neckline or collar *before* stitching-in-the-ditch.

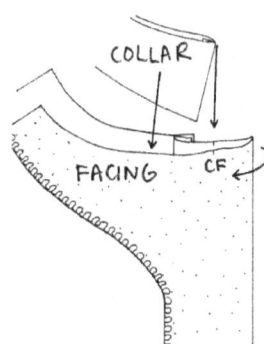

Fold the facing back on the shirt so the right sides are together.

For a collarless faced neckline, stitch around the neck then turn through to the right side.
For the collared version, sandwich the prepared collar between the two.

Match the centre fronts of the collar, facing and front band. Note that the underneath side of the collar needs to sit next to the shirt, and the outermost side against the facing. Sew around the neck, then turn it to the right side.

Finally, stitch-in-the-ditch down the seam of the front band, as described before.

Men's shirt front stand

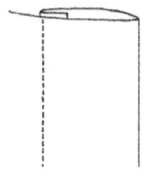

On men's shirts, often the left and right sides are made differently, with the right hand side (underneath) made as a simple fold-under button stand (see page 106).

On some shirts the underneath stand isn't even interfaced; it's just the selvedge edge folded under once.

The left hand side (top) is craftily constructed to hide the raw edge.
Although this finish is often used for business or dress shirts, it's also seen on casual shirts, too.

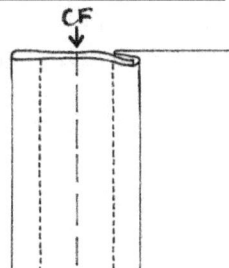

Make a pattern

Make separate left and right pattern pieces for the shirt, clearly labelled with "cut fabric right side up". On the reverse side, write "PTO" (Please Turn Over). Here's how to make the left (buttonhole) side:
1. Add a 1.5cm (⅝") wrap to the centre front (CF) line, to yield a 3cm (1¼") wide finished stand.

2. Add a fold-under the width of the finished stand 3cm (1¼").

3. Split the pattern as shown and add in 1cm (⅜").

4. Notch each end of the fold lines with a tiny 3mm (⅛") snip so you know where to fold.

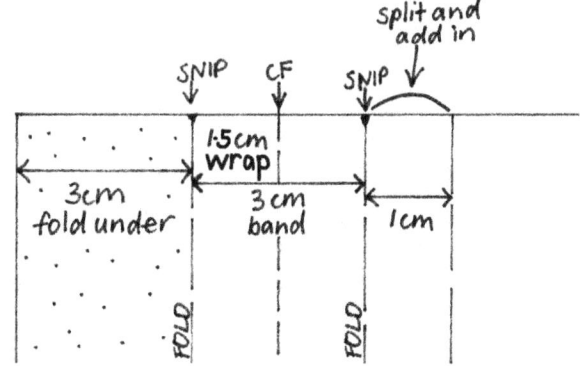

To sew a men's shirt front stand

1. Cut a strip of fusing the width of the finished stand (3cm or 1¼") and iron it onto the wrong side of the fold-under, as shown (shaded) in the pattern sketch.

2. Press under the interfaced fold-under section, then fold under and press again so it's three thicknesses.

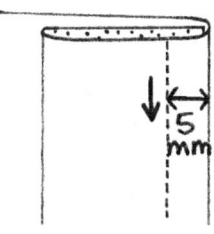

3. Sew *exactly* 5mm away from the fold line as shown. When the stand is opened out the raw edge is concealed in the stitched fold. To complete the stand, stitch exactly 5mm away along the other folded edge so it matches.

✂ If you prefer a 6mm (¼") stitched edge on each side of the stand, simply add in 1.2cm (½") when you split the pattern instead of 1cm (⅜"), and stitch 6mm (¼") away from the edge.

✂ If the shirt has short sleeves, the **sleeve hems** can be finished in the same way.

Concealed fronts

A concealed front, or concealed placket, hides the buttons and gives a clean finish to a shirt or jacket.
On women's shirts (right over left), the right hand side is a concealed front and the left hand side is made as a regular fold-under front of matching width. On men's it's the opposite.
When I cut out a concealed front shirt, I like to save time by cutting a pair of concealed fronts, then trimming one to make the other side, rather than cutting two separate fronts. Cutting the left and right separately, however, will save fabric.
There are lots of ways to design a concealed front for a shirt or a jacket. The first two presented are good for shirts and the next three for jackets.
If necessary, try out the concealed front using a strip of paper to understand how it's folded into place before making the pattern.

Concealed front for a shirt

Use this method if the collar will be attached to the neck *after* the front stand is finished. This method works well on medium to lightweight fabrics that fold crisply. It looks good in sheer fabrics, too. Beware of 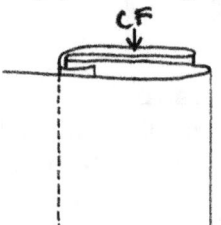 using a fabric that's too thick, because the stand is five layers thick in one place (six if you count the interfacing), and an unsightly ridge will show on the right side next to the stitching line.

Make a pattern

1. Add a 1.5cm (⅝") wrap to the centre front (CF) line, to yield a 3cm (1¼") wide finished stand.

2. Add the width of the stand (3cm or 1¼"), the width of the stand minus 3mm (⅛") *twice* (that is, two lots of 2.7cm or 1⅛"), and finally a 1cm (⅜") seam allowance.

3. Notch each end of the fold lines with tiny 3mm (⅛") snips so you know where to fold.

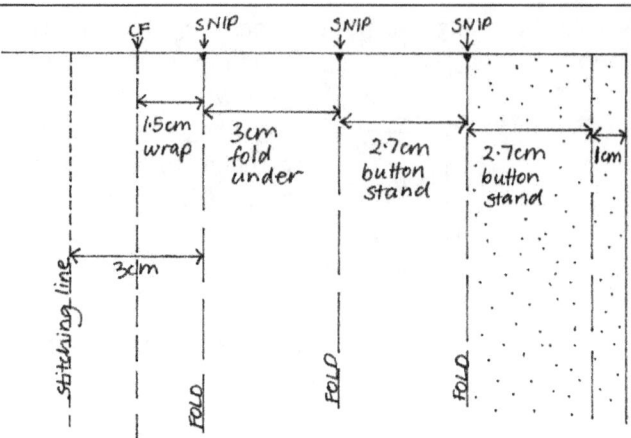

To sew a concealed front for a shirt

1. Cut a strip of interfacing 3.7cm (1½") wide and iron it onto the wrong side of the edge as shown in the pattern sketch (shaded area).

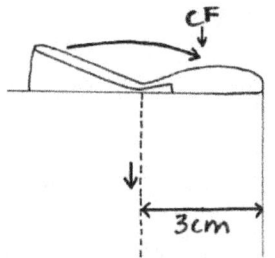

2. Iron the folds into position very precisely, measuring as you fold, then sew one row of stitching as shown. Be accurate—the stitching shows on the right side so it must be straight and even the whole way.

3. Make the top buttonhole before attaching the collar, otherwise you won't be able to get the machine in there. Sometimes the top buttonhole goes through all the layers and does up with a feature button, or sometimes a feature button is sewn on top for decoration. Plain flat buttons are used for the rest of the concealed front.

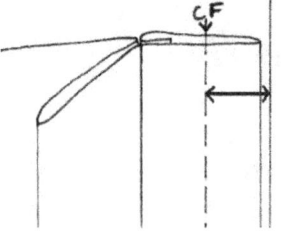

Important: note that the position of the centre front and buttonholes will be 3mm (⅛") *in from the edge*, that is, not sitting in the centre of the stand.

Concealed front with a facing

Use this method if the shirt or blouse has a collar that needs to be inserted *into* the top of the neck (instead of being sewn on afterwards). You can also insert a button and loop at the top and bag out the 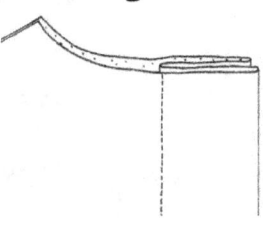 hem before finishing the stand. This method can also be used for a shirt with no collar, just a faced neckline, and it also looks good if the neck is worn open.

Front stands and tab fronts

Make a pattern
1. Trace around the shirt's neckline and the top part of the shoulder.

2. Add a 1.5cm (⅝") wrap to the centre front (CF) line, to yield a 3cm (1¼") wide finished stand.

3. Add a fold-under the width of the stand (3cm or 1¼")

4. Add a button stand 3mm (⅛") *less* than the width of the stand (2.7cm or 1⅛") *twice*.

5. Fold the pattern so the stitching lines shown sit on top of one another and trace off the neckline and part of the shoulder for the facing. Note the position of the centre front (CF) on the facing.

Draw in the outer edge of the facing as a smooth flowing line and allow a 1cm (⅜") seam allowance from the stitching line. Notch each end of the fold lines with tiny 3mm (⅛") snips to denote the foldlines.

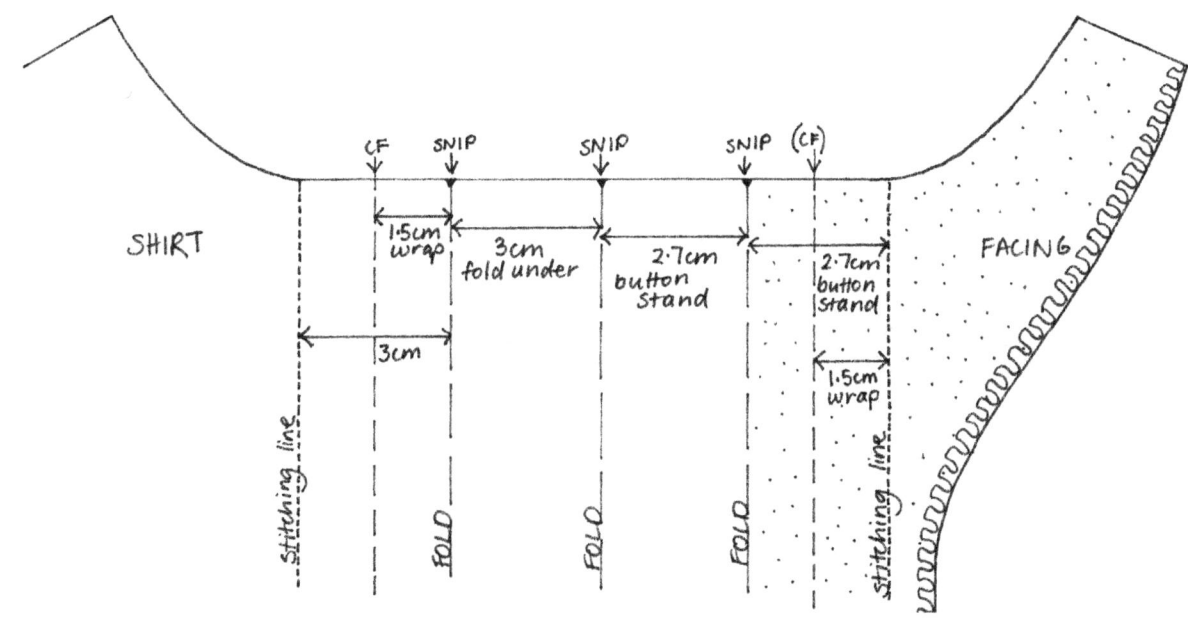

To sew a concealed front with a facing
1. Apply interfacing to the facing and one of the 2.7cm (1⅛") wide button stands as shown in the pattern sketch (shaded area).

2. Iron the folds into position, measuring as you go, taking care to be *very* accurate. The edge of the button stand will sit 3mm (⅛") behind the front of the stand.

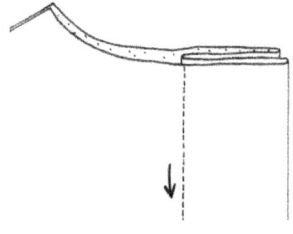

3. If the shirt has **a shirt collar that will be sewn over the top of the stand later,** you can go ahead and stitch the stand. Sew a very straight line of stitching down the length of the stand, just catching the fold of fabric inside. If the fabric is loosely woven or tends to creep as you sew it, try sewing from the wrong side where the interfaced layer will be on the top.

If the shirt has **no collar** (just a faced neckline) **OR a collar that's sandwiched into the facing,** press the stand into position but don't stitch it yet.

4. Make the top buttonhole before stitching across the top of the stand and facing *or* attaching the collar, otherwise you won't be able to get the machine in there. Sometimes the top buttonhole goes through all the layers and does up with a feature button, or sometimes a feature button is sewn on top for decoration. Plain flat buttons are used for the rest of the concealed front.

Important: note that the position of the centre front and buttonholes will be 3mm (⅛") *in* from the edge. Therefore, the vertical buttonholes will sit 1.2cm (½") from the edge, not 1.5cm (⅝").

5. **If the shirt has no collar:** with the right side up, take the top layer (the shirt) and fold it back around on itself, so the folded

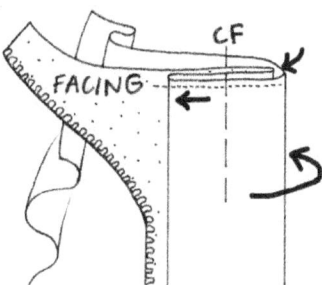

edge is opposite to what you've pressed in, and the right sides of the shirt and facing are together. ***Important:*** ensure the 3mm (⅛") step between the front and the button stand is still there.

Stitch across the top through all layers, then fold the shirt back again to the right side. Finish stitching the stand as described above in Step 3.

If the shirt has a collar that's sandwiched into the facing: with the right side of the stand facing up, take the top layer (the shirt) and fold it back around on itself, so the folded edge is opposite what you've pressed in and the right sides of the shirt and facing are together. ***Important:*** ensure the 3mm (⅛") gap between the front and the button stand is still there.

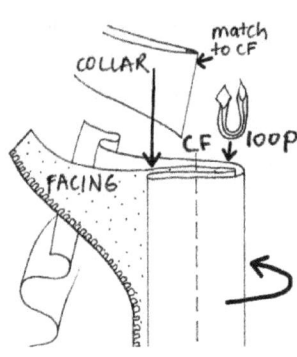

Insert the prepared collar in between the shirt and facing, matching the centre front of the shirt to the corner of the collar at the *stitching line*, not the raw edge, particularly if the collar is very angled.

Note that the underneath collar will sit against the shirt. You may also decide to insert a button loop in the top as well—insert it right in the corner of the fold. Sometimes the button loop doesn't have a button (or is never done up if it does), but it can be a nice feature if the shirt neck is worn open. Both the collar and button loop should sit in between the right sides of the shirt and facing. With the raw edges matched, stitch across the top through all layers, then fold the shirt back again to the right side. Go ahead and finish stitching the stand as described above in Step 3.

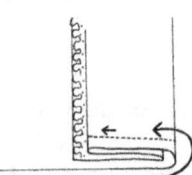

Optional: bag out the hem by folding the stand right back on itself and stitching across the bottom, the required depth of the hem.

Ensure there's a 3mm (⅛") step between the front and button stand. Overlock or double roll the hem before turning the corner through.

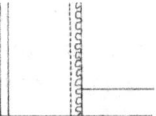

Concealed fronts for jackets

As already mentioned, there are lots of ways to design a concealed front. The method you choose will depend on what type of collar the garment has, how bulky the fabric is and where the buttons are positioned. The usual 3mm (⅛") step between the edge of the garment and the concealed stand can be as great as 6mm (¾") if the fabric is very thick. These methods can also be used on tops as well as jackets.

1. Concealed front on an extended facing

This is an easy-to-construct concealed front that doesn't interfere with the collar or hem. It has a placket sewn onto the facing with the buttonholes in it. The button side is cut exactly the same but without the placket. The separate placket doesn't have to be cut in the same fabric as the rest of the garment—you could use something lighter in weight.

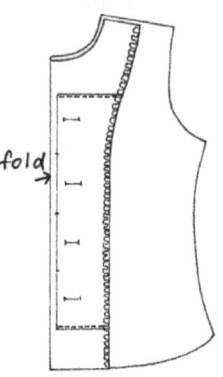

Make a pattern

1. Add a wrap and mark the buttonhole positions on the jacket front if it doesn't already have them. If there's a very top buttonhole on the garment it cannot be concealed, since the placket won't extend right up to the neckline. However, the top button can be a regular button visible on the right side.

2. Make an extended facing for the jacket front (see page 98).

3. For the placket, trace around the long edge of the facing as shown, marking a fold line for the placket 3mm (⅛") from the facing fold line. At each end, clear the buttonholes by half the distance between them plus a 1cm (⅜")seam allowance.

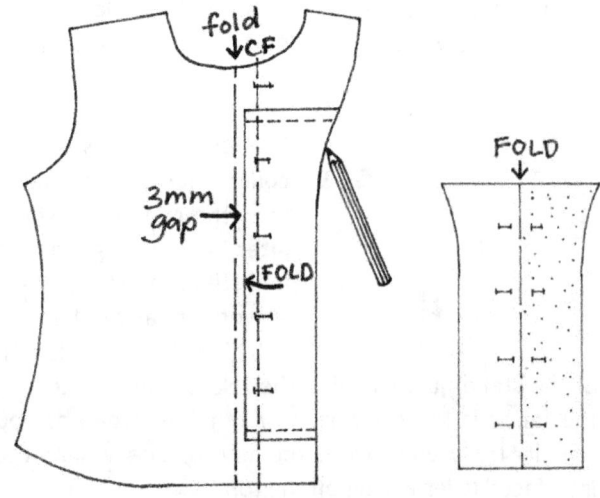

4. Make a separate pattern for the concealed placket, with the buttonhole positions marked on it.

Front stands and tab fronts **113**

To sew a concealed front on an extended facing

1. Interface one half of the placket—the one that will be outermost when the jacket is worn.

2. Fold the placket in half lengthwise with the right sides together and stitch across the top and bottom, taking whatever seam allowance you allowed. Trim the corners, turn to the right side and press. Machine baste the long raw edges together using a long stitch.

3. Make the buttonholes in the placket.

4. Position the concealed placket onto the (already interfaced) extended facing. Edgestitch all but the folded edge of the placket to the of the facing, as shown, leaving the front of the garment free. Make sure the placket is set 3mm (⅛") back from the foldline of the facing—it will help if you press the facing's fold in first.

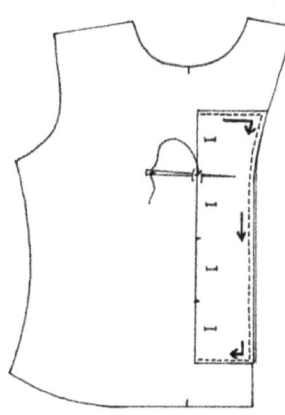

5. Hand or machine stitch small tacks between the buttonholes to anchor the edge of the concealed placket to the facing. You can do this at the very end when the jacket is finished.

2. Concealed front with a separate (folded) facing

This method is suitable for jackets or tops that button all the way up to the neck. These instructions are for the buttonhole side. The button side is made plainly but with the same amount of wrap, which is 2cm (¾") in this example.
The garment may or may not have a collar.

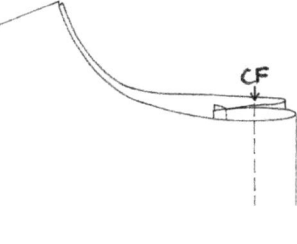

Make a pattern
(See the diagram at bottom of this page).
1. On the front, add to the centre front (CF) a 2cm (¾") wrap.

2. Add a 4cm (1½") fold-back (double the wrap).

3. Add a 1cm (⅜") seam allowance.

4. To the facing, reduce the amounts by 3mm (⅛") to allow for a 3mm (⅛") step back (add a 1.7cm wrap, 3.7cm fold-back and 1cm seam allowance).

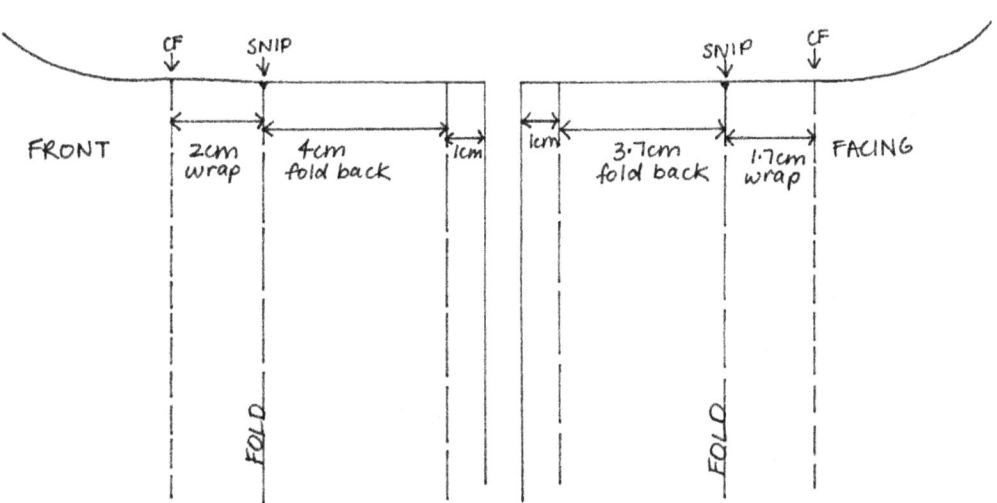

To sew a concealed front with a separate (folded) facing

1. Interface the entire facing.

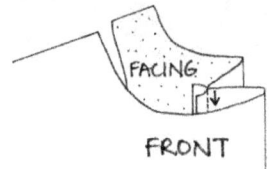

2. Accurately press the folds in the front and facing. Lay the front and facing right sides together and stitch down the long edge, taking the 1cm (⅜") seam allowance.

3. Mark and make any buttonholes now in the concealed stand, because you won't be able to get the machine in there if you leave it until last, particularly if the top button is concealed as well. Sometimes the top buttonhole goes through all the layers and does up with a feature button, or sometimes a feature button is sewn on top for decoration. Plain flat buttons are used for the rest of the concealed front.
Important: Note that the position of the centre front and buttonholes will be 3mm (⅛") in from the edge, that is, not sitting in the centre of the stand. Therefore, vertical buttonholes will be 1.7cm (⅝") from the folded edge, not 2cm (¾").

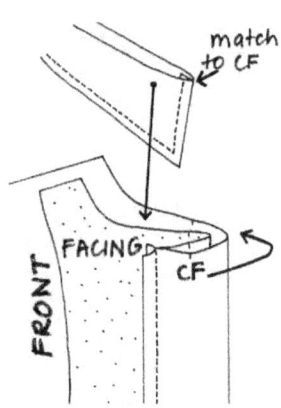

4. To finish the neckline, fold back the jacket front on the foldline, in the opposite direction the fold was pressed in. The right sides of the facing and front are now together. If there's a collar, insert the prepared collar in between the facing and front, matching the edge of the collar to the centre fronts of the jacket. Ensure there's still a 3mm (⅛") concealed step at the top. Stitch through all the layers around the neck, then turn through to the right side.

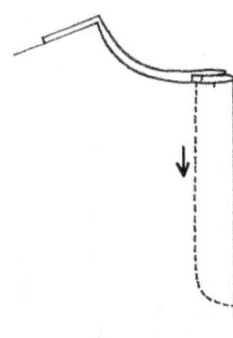

5. After the neckline and hem have been sewn, stitch the concealed front into place last of all. You can use a contrasting thread or more than one row of stitching if you intend to highlight this feature. The stitching can be curved at the end of the buttonholes or go all the way straight down to the hem, but either way make sure it's sewn perfectly straight. If the fabric is loosely woven or tends to creep as you sew it, try sewing from the wrong side where the interfaced layer will be on the top.

6. To finish off, hand tack the edge between the buttonholes to stop gaping.
This can be done at the very end when the jacket is finished.

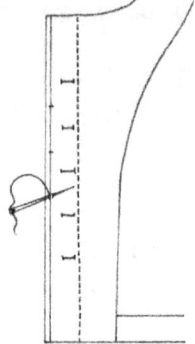

3. Concealed front with a separate facing

This method is suitable for jackets with lapels and jackets made in thick fabric, because the placket doesn't extend all the way to the top and bottom, and involves as little bulk as is possible. Unlike the other two methods, the edge are flush with the edge of the jacket, not stepped back 3mm (⅛").

Make a pattern

1. Add a wrap to the centre front (CF), for example 2cm (¾"), and add a seam allowance to the front (buttonhole side) edge of the jacket if it doesn't already have one.

2. Determine where the buttonholes will be and mark them in.

3. Add an extension at least double the width of the wrap plus 1cm (⅜") seam allowance. The extension should clear the top and bottom buttonholes by half the distance between the buttonholes plus a seam allowance. Cut the facing the same shape.

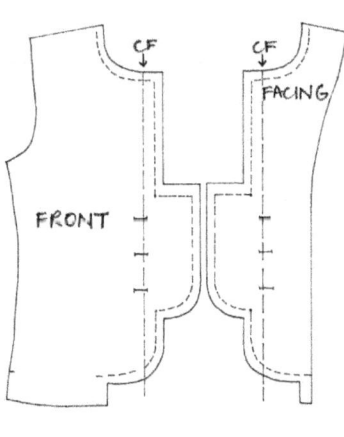

If the fabric is very thick, the extensions can be cut separately in a thinner fabric, or a contrasting one. Cut a pair of the extensions—one for the front and the other for the facing.
Mark with a dot where the stitching lines of the jacket meet the corners of the extensions.

Front stands and tab fronts **115**

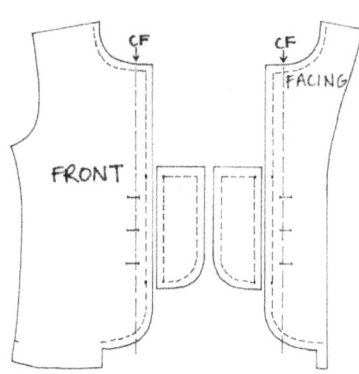

4. The other side of the jacket (the button side) is cut plain.

To sew a concealed front with a separate facing

1. Interface the entire facing with extension. If you're interfacing the jacket front as well, include the extension.

2. If the extension is cut in one with the front, stay-stitch the corners. Snip diagonally in to, but not over, the stitching. Do this for both the front and the facing. Press the extension to the underside accurately along its foldline.

If the extensions are separate, stitch one to the front and the other to the facing, right sides together. Stitch *exactly* from dot to dot, and backstitch securely at each end.

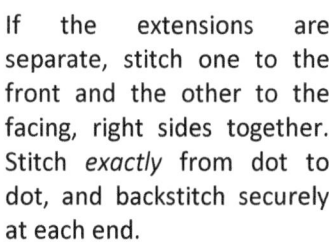

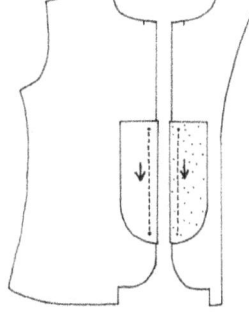

Diagonally snip to the stitching, angling the snip towards the centre as shown. Accurately press the extension to the wrong side. For a perfect crisp fold, press the seam open first, then press the extension into position. Press the edge very flat.

3. Mark and then make the buttonholes on the facing, since when the concealed front is finished you'll be unable to get the machine in there.

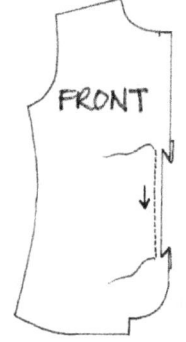

4. If you've decided to topstitch the front edge of the jacket, do this now on the part with the extension only, leaving long threads at each end to tie off later (don't backstitch at each end—just leave the long threads).

If the facing edge needs help staying flat, you can also topstitch that edge as well.

5. Place the facing onto the front, right sides together and sew the centre front seam *exactly* above and below the extension. Backstitch securely at both ends of the extension.

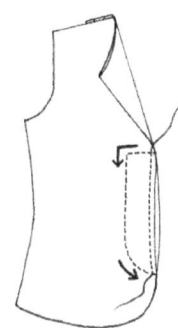

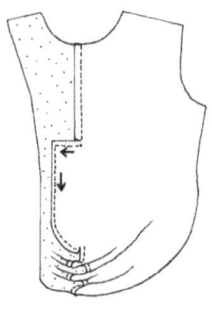

6. You can finish the concealed front in one of two ways. The first is to topstitch through all the layers around the edges of the extension. You can do this very last of all when the jacket is finished.

The other is to flip the front towards the facing and stitch both extensions to it. Note that if the front edge of the jacket is topstitched, you won't be able to flip the front extension back fully, so pin carefully and stitch where you can.

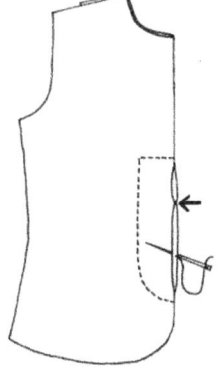

7. Catch the two layers together by hand at the edges between each buttonhole.

Tab Fronts

A tab front is a type of placket—a band of fabric that finishes an opening or slit in a garment. It consists of a strip of fabric sewn to each side of a slit opening, which are then lapped on top of each other.

✂ A tab front could be a good solution if you're cutting out a shirt and running short of fabric. Cutting the front on the centre front fold and designing a separate tab may mean you can fit all of the large/main pattern pieces across the fabric easily.

✂ How **long** should a tab front be? 15cm (6") is a common length for adults, down to 10cm (4") for children, but provided the opening is long enough to get the garment on, it can be any length.

How **wide** is a tab front? Your average tab front on a polo shirt is typically about 3cm (1¼") wide, but tab fronts can be made very narrow or wide, or even double-breasted. Choose a size to suit the proportions of the garment.

✂ Although it's the classic opening for polo shirts, tab fronts can be used on regular shirts, sleeves, side openings and side splits in skirts and trousers. The garment can be made of woven or knitted fabric. A woven tab can be applied to a knitted or woven shirt.

✂ Most people find that the difficult part of a tab front is getting the end neat and pucker-free with square corners. The key is accuracy and taking the correct amount of seam allowance.

There's more than one way to cut and sew a tab front. The method you choose will depend on the finished look you want and the type of collar the top has—some tabs are only suitable for regular shirt collars (sewn on afterwards) while others are designed for knitted polo shirt collars as well. Why not make all of them over the next several shirts you sew?

Interfacing tab fronts

The tabs need to be interfaced for support and to stop the buttons and buttonholes from tearing out. You can interface all or just one side of the tab—test your interfacing and fabric and decide. It can be easier to sew if the whole tab is fused with a lighter interfacing rather than a heavy one for half. If only one side of the tab is interfaced, the interfaced side should be uppermost when the tab is worn. While you're at the ironing board, iron the folds in the tabs to make them easier to sew.

Neck binding for knitted collars

A binding is a neat way of covering the seam allowance around the neckline of a knit shirt and can be used in place of a facing on knit fabrics.

1. To make the binding, cut a strip of knit fabric *across* the grain (the stretchiest way) about 4cm (1½") wide. Fold it in half longways, wrong side inside. Lay the collar onto the shirt the way it will be worn and lay the folded strip on top, matching all the raw edges.

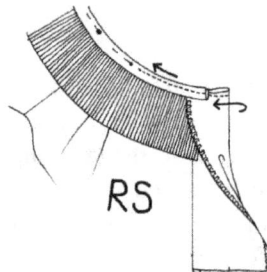

2. Stitch the binding around the back neck of the polo shirt at the same time as attaching the collar.

Note the right side (RS) and wrong side (WS).

3. Flip the binding down and stitch along the folded edge to conceal the raw edge of the neck.

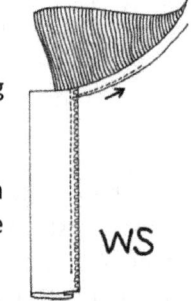

✂ Sometimes a length of (possibly contrasting coloured) **herringbone twill tape** about 1.2cm (½") wide is used instead for a sporty look.

✂ If you prefer, you can cut a **back neck facing** instead of using a back neck binding strip. The facing is typically deeper at the centre back than at the shoulders, and is stitched down so it doesn't flap up when the shirt is put on. Sometimes it's cut in a contrasting colour, and sometimes it's cut in a woven fabric to use on a knit shirt to provide stability and interest. See page 56 for how to make one.

A simple tab front
(regular shirt collars only)
This basic method looks neat when the tab is worn open and is a good

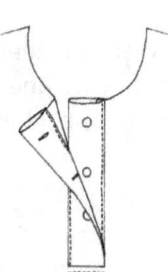

Front stands and tab fronts

one for sheer fabrics. The tab can be cut from the same fabric as the rest of the garment, or a contrast. The fabric can be woven or a knit.

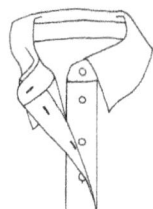

Note that it's only suitable for regular shirt collars that are sewn on *after* the tab is finished, not knitted polo shirt collars.

Make a pattern

1. On the front pattern, draw in the finished shape of the tab front, with the centre front (CF) running through the middle. The tab can be as wide or as long as you like, but 3cm (1¼") wide is a common width.

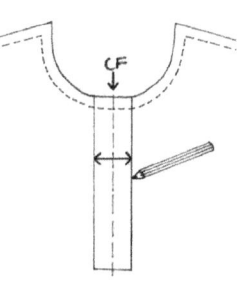

2. Add a seam allowance all the way around. I usually make my seam allowance 1cm (⅜"), but it can be as small as 6mm (¼"). If you prefer working with all 1.5cm (⅝") seam allowances, for a 3cm wide tab you would simply cut a slit down the centre, stopping 1.5cm from the end.

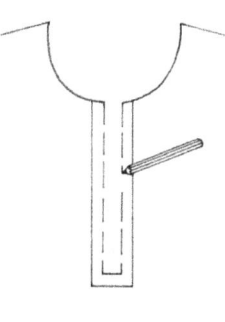

3. Make a pattern for the tab twice as **wide** as the finished width, plus two seam allowances (for example 3cm + 3cm + 2cm seams = 8cm wide).
Make the **length** of the tab the proposed length plus one seam allowance for the bottom (for example 15cm + 1cm seam).

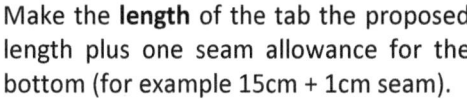

Often, extra seam allowance is added onto the length, for example 2.5cm (1") instead of 1cm (⅜"), to permit an overlocker to easily neaten the bottom seam.

The top of the tab should have the same seam allowance as the neck edge. The tab should be straight across the top, but if the tab is very wide it might need to be curved at the top to make a smooth neckline curve. To do this, lay the tab pattern onto the front neckline and trace the curve onto the tab. If the tab has a collar, mark the centre front (CF) position on the tab with a small 3mm (⅛") snip.

To sew a simple tab front

1. Interface half or all of both tabs, then iron them in half longways, with the wrong sides together.

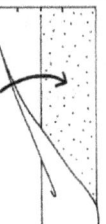

2. **Optional**: stay-stitch the lower corners of the tab window exactly on the stitching line, pivoting at the corners. Use a smaller stitch on you machine, such as 1 or 1.5, for strength. Snip exactly to, but not over, the stitching. I would stay-stitch if the fabric is a loose weave, frays, or is hard to handle.

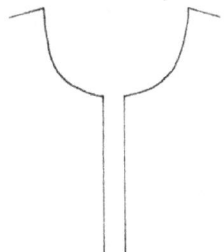
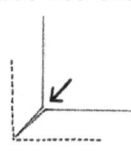

Factory machinists don't bother with the stay-stitching and they snip in *after* sewing the tabs on (Step 3). You may like to try that instead.

3. Lay the (uninterfaced, if you only fused half) right side of a tab on the wrong side of the garment and sew from the pivot point to the top.
If you sew with the garment side up you can see where the stay stitching and pivot point is. Sew *just* outside of the stitching so it won't show. It's vital to take the correct amount of seam allowance, otherwise the tabs won't fit on top of each other at the end. Repeat with the other tab.

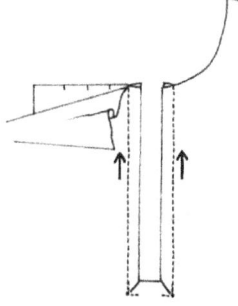

If you're sewing as a factory machinist, sew with the tabs uppermost and eyeball the ends of the tabs to check the stitching is level on both sides. Snip very carefully into the corners and try not to stretch the lower part of the tab window when you handle it.

4. Press the seam and tab *away* from the garment.

5. Fold the tab into position, and topstitch in place close to the edge. As you sew, hold the garment firmly and let the folded edge of the tab "sit easy" on top, to help stop the tab from rippling. Repeat with the other tab. You can also edgestitch the folded edge to match, so both sides of the tab have matching stitching.

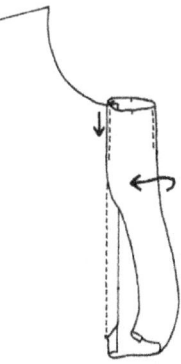

6. Lap the tabs over each other the correct way (men left over right, and women right over left, as the garment is worn) and hold with a pin.

The entire tab can be topstitched around the edge, on the garment side, to hold it flat.

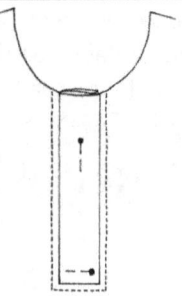

7. Flip up the bottom of the garment. Position the bottom flap over the lapped ends of the tabs. Pin it first, then carefully stitch across from point to point. Try to keep your stitching straight and the ends square, covering the stay-stitching. Use a zipper foot so you can get in close.

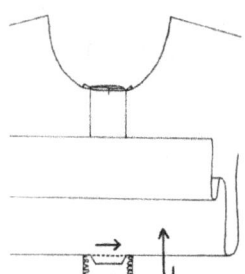

A simple tab front—variation 2
(regular shirt collar *or* knitted shirt collar)
This variation has no visible stitching on the tabs. The pattern and method are exactly like the Simple tab described on pages 116-118, except the tabs are sewn onto the *right* side of the shirt, then brought around to the *wrong* side.

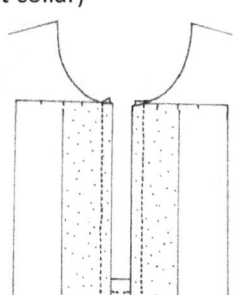

8. Overlock across the end. This will be easier to do if you allowed a 2.5cm(1") seam allowance across the bottom to accommodate the width of the overlocker foot.
Sometimes after overlocking, the end of the tab is topstitched down on the right side, to hold it flat.

Overlock the remaining long side of the tabs.
Secure on the right side by stitching-in-the-ditch or edgestitching.
Instead of overlocking the underneath long side, you could fold under the seam allowance. It would look neater, but overlocking would be flatter. Note that the overlocking will be visible if the tab is worn open.

A simple tab front—variation 1
(regular shirt collar only)
This variation has no visible stitching on the tabs. It's faster, less bulky and easier to do but doesn't look quite as neat when the tab is worn open because the overlocking shows. The pattern is made exactly the same as the Simple tab front (pages 116-118).
Sewing Steps 1 and 2 are the same as the Simple tab front on page 117.

3. Sew the folded tabs onto the right side of the garment, matching the raw edges and sewing through all layers. If you've stay-stitched the inside corners, sew with the shirt side up so you can see where the pivot points are.

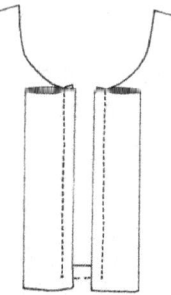

If you're planning to use a **knitted collar**, you'll need to insert the collar into the tab *before* you ditch stitch down the edges on the right side.

The ends of the collar should meet in the centre of the tab, so they touch when the tab is done up (even if it's never worn done up).

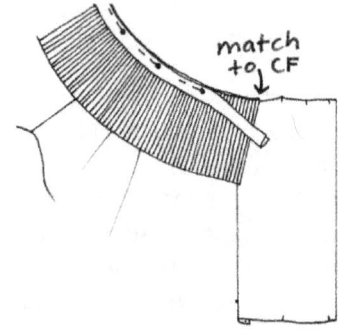

1. Lay the collar on the right side of the shirt, matching the end to the centre front (CF) of the tab. Lay the neck binding (see page 116) over the top, matching all the raw edges.

4. Press the seams towards the *shirt* and overlock them.

5. Follow Steps 6 and 7 of the Simple tab front, on page 118.

Front stands and tab fronts

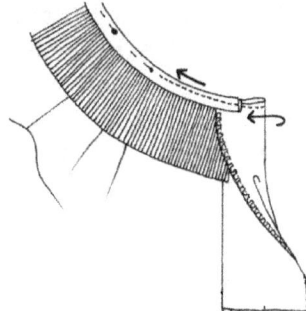

2. Fold the tab back along its lengthwise fold, sandwiching the collar inside. Lap the end of the binding over the top. Stitch around the neck through all layers.

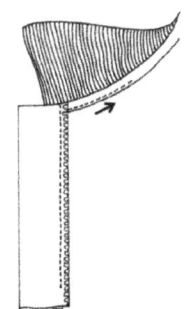

3. Trim if required and turn the tab to the right side. Check that both sides look the same, then topstitch the tab into position.
Stitch the neck binding down around the neckline last of all.

Tab front with facing
(regular shirt collar *or* knitted collar)
A facing inside the tab front makes the inside of the tab look neat when it's unbuttoned.

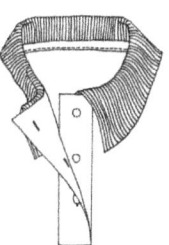

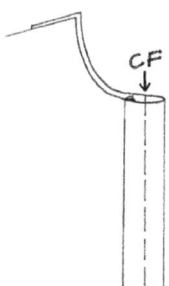

I worked in a factory that made tab front polo shirts by the zillions. The tabs were faced like this one and 2.5cm (1") wide finished. A machinist told me she could make fifteen faced tabs in an hour, but her personal best was twenty one.

Make a pattern
Make the pattern for the opening on the shirt in the same way as a Simple tab front, on pages 116-118.
1. Make a pattern for the faced tab by tracing around the centre front line (CF), neck and shoulders of the shirt. Draw in the shape of the facing. Add half the width of the finished tab to the CF line, which is 1.5cm (⅝") for a 3cm (1¼") tab (this is the wrap, by the way). The tab folds along this line.

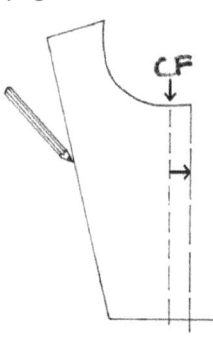

2. Add one width of the finished tab (3cm), then a 1cm (⅜") seam allowance.
Make the **length** of the tab the same as the finished tab plus a seam allowance for the top and bottom.

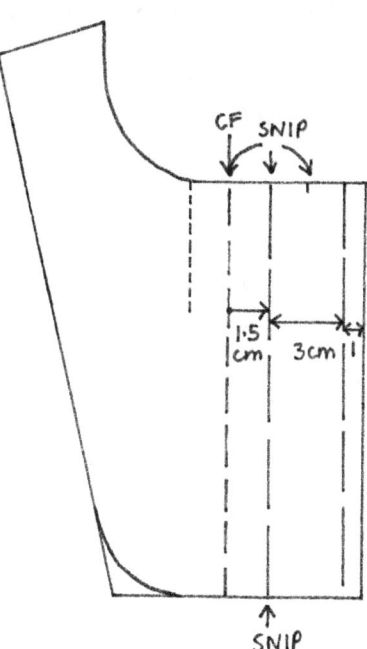

The seam allowance for the top should be the same as the neck. The bottom seam allowance can be up to 2.5cm (1") to allow easy overlocking. The lower corner of the tab can be curved or squared. Snip small 3mm (⅛") notches at the top and bottom of the fold line and at the top of the centre front (CF).

To sew a tab front with facing
1. Cut a pair of the faced tab and interface all with lightweight interfacing.

2. **Optional:** stay-stitch the lower corners of the tab window exactly on the stitching line, pivoting at the corners. Use a smaller stitch on your machine, such as 1 or 1.5, for strength. Snip exactly to, but not over, the stitching.

I would recommend stay-stitching if the fabric is a loose weave, frays or is hard to handle.

In factories, machinists don't stay-stitch; they snip in after sewing on the tabs on (Step 3).

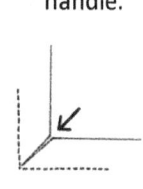

3. Place the tab and shirt right sides together and stitch the long front edges together. If you stay-stitched, sew outside of the stay-stitching so it doesn't show on the right side.

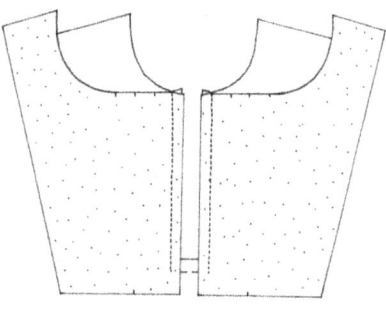

It's easier to stitch with the shirt side up so you can see the pivot points.

If you *didn't* stay-stitch, sew with the tabs uppermost and eyeball the ends of the tabs to check the stitching is level on both sides. Snip very carefully into the corners, and try not to stretch the lower part of the tab window when you handle it.

4. Press the seams and tabs *away* from the shirt. Press the tabs into position along the fold lines.

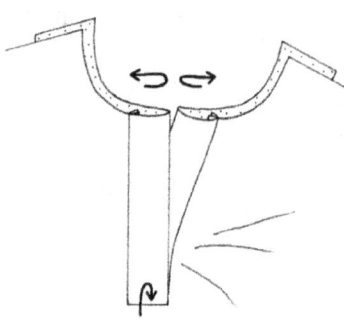

Overlap the ends, left over right for men and right over left for women (as the garment is worn) and tuck them into the bottom of the tab window. Secure with a pin.

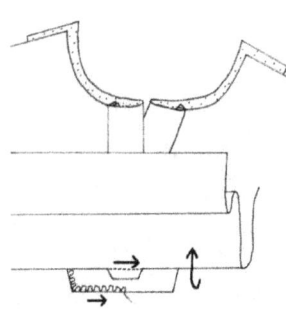

5. Flip up the bottom of the shirt and sew across the ends of the tabs to secure, making sure you cover any stay-stitching. Try to keep your stitching straight and the ends square. A zipper foot will help you get in close if the edge is bulky.

6. Overlock around the sides, bottom and shoulders of the facing. Sometimes after overlocking, the bottom of the tab front is topstitched down on the right side (say, 6mm (¼") below the horizontal seam), for strength.

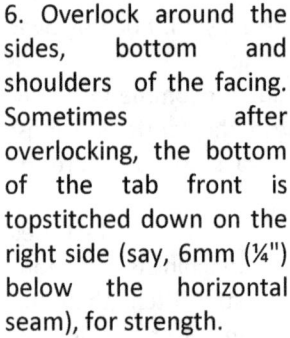 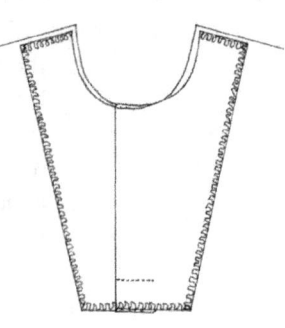

7. Sew the shoulder seams of the garment in preparation for attaching the collar.

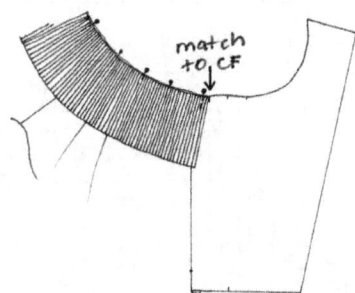

8. Apply the knitted collar by laying it onto the right side of the shirt and matching the end of the collar with the centre front of the tab.

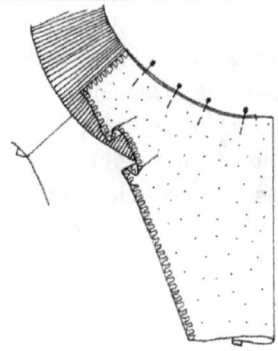

9. Fold the tab back on itself, opposite to the pressed-in foldline, so the collar is sandwiched between the garment and the tab facing. Note that the collar should finish 1.5cm (⅝") short of the fold at the centre front, so that when the collar is done up it will meet in the centre while the tab overlaps.

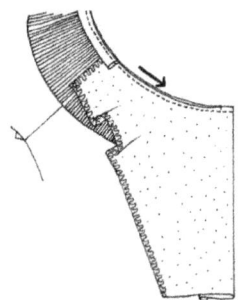

10. Lay the back neck binding strip (page 116) over the collar around the back of the neck, lapping the ends a little onto the facing. If you're using a back neck facing instead, sew the shoulder seams and sandwich the collar between the facing and shirt.

11. Stitch around the entire neck. Trim the seam allowance if necessary and turn through to the right side. Finish off by flipping down and stitching the back neck binding to conceal the seam allowance. Secure the shoulders of the facing to the shoulders of the garment. Sometimes the vertical edges of the tab are stitched-in-the-ditch to keep it in position, but since the buttons and buttonholes will hold things in place it isn't always done.

Troubleshooting tab fronts
Stuffed up the bottom of the tab? OR Has the bottom point of the tab frayed out?
If you have some fabric or twill tape left over, cover the bottom of the tab with a "designer patch" and make a feature of it. Enhance it with some creative topstitching.

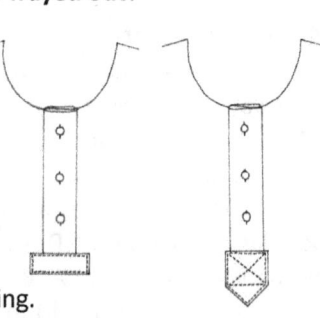

Adding piping to a tab
Piping can be applied to all three sides of a tab front. The piping is first sewn to the shirt before the tab is attached. Allow the correct seam allowance on the tab window (and tab) for the piping.

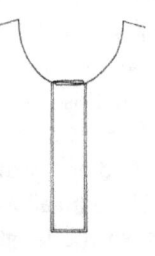

Front stands and tab fronts

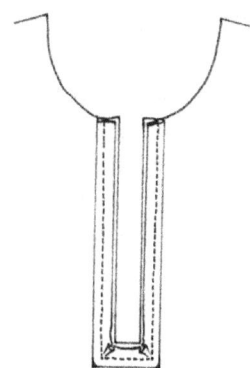

Sew the piping around the tab window, matching the raw edges and snipping into the flat part of the piping to take it around the corners. You won't need to stay-stitch the lower corners of the tab window because the piping stitching will do the same job. Snip as usual into the two pivot point corners after sewing, then apply the tab.

For tabs made from a slit (see immediately below for how to make), stitch the piping to the strip before sewing it to the tab.

Tab fronts from a slit

A tab front can be made from a single slit in the fabric. These are a feature of rugby shirts, which are made from heavy knit fabric with a woven one or two piece shirt collar, applied afterwards. The placket may have press studs instead of buttons and buttonholes.

These type of tabs can be used for any shirt, woven or knit. They aren't suitable for vertically striped fabric because the seam allowance around the slit interrupts the stripe, however they look great in horizontal stripes.

Make a pattern

An adjustment is required on the garment's front to allow for the seam allowance along each side of the slit. If you neglect to do this, the collar will be too large for the neck on one side.

1. Split the front down the centre and add in 1cm (⅜") at the neck, tapering to nothing at the hem.

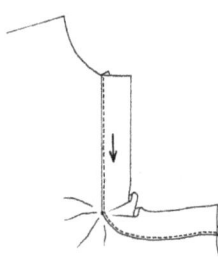

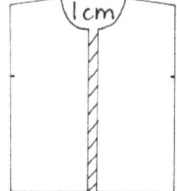

If the top is very square and boxy, you may prefer to add it all the way through.

2. Draw in the new centre front (CF) line. Then draw in the line for the slit, which is usually 2cm (¾") away from the centre front.

Tab from a slit using twill tape

Twill tape tab fronts are often teamed with a (woven) one-piece shirt collar. Sometimes the collar has 1cm (⅜") wide matching twill tape on the inside edge for a sportier look (see page 48 for how to do this).

Make a pattern

Make the slit on the shirt front as described on this page. The slit's distance from the centre front (CF) depends on the width of the twill tape you're using; it should be half the width of the tape.

To sew a very simple tab with twill tape

1. Cut one length of twill tape the twice the length of the slit plus 6mm (¼").

2. Lay the tape onto the front, both right sides up. Edgestitch the tape on, taking a 5mm seam on the shirt and ensuring you catch the point of the slit. Sometimes factories sew this with a narrow twin needle.

3. And that's it. Fold the tab into position.

For a very casual sports top, this can be left as is, but it will be stronger at the bottom point if the layers are stitched together. You can also stitch along the folded edge and the overlap side can be stitched to the garment's front.

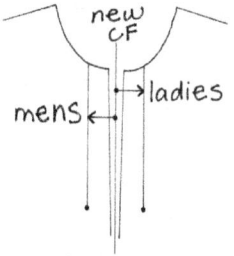

To sew another tab with twill tape

1. For a more sophisticated (if that's the word) tab, cut three lengths of tape the same length as the slit plus 2.5cm (1").

2. With the right side facing up, edgestitch a pre-cut length of tape to each side of the slit, taking a 5mm seam allowance on the shirt. Leave 2.5cm (1") free at the bottom of the slit. Take care to stitch right down to the end of the slit. The stitching on each piece of twill tape should meet at the point at an acute angle.

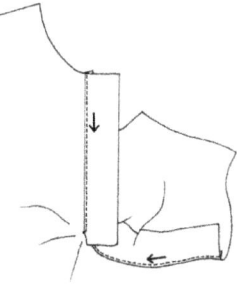

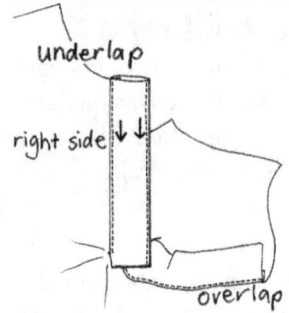

3. On the underlap (button) side, stitch the third piece of tape on *behind* the piece stitched to the slit, matching the edges and stitching exactly over the first row of stitching.

✂ For a **concealed tab**, cut a fourth piece of twill tape. Sew it to the overlap side, stepping it back from the edge by 3mm (⅛"). Sew the buttonholes in this piece now, in line with the centre front. The buttonholes are normally vertical.

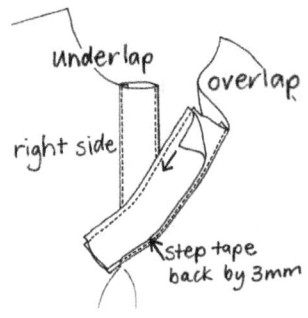

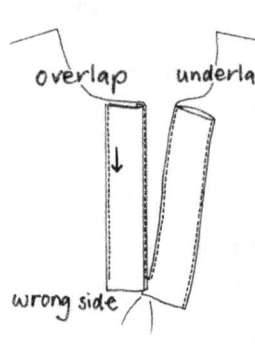

4. Lay the overlap side into position on the wrong side of the front and stitch down the free edge, attaching the tape to the shirt. Stop 1cm (⅜") from the slit's end. It's easiest to sew with the tape facing up, so match the bobbin to the shirt's colour.

5. Overlap the two sides and stitch through all layers to secure the bottom of the tab. Do whatever stitching takes your fancy here—I favour a square with an X in the centre. The stitching should come part way up the slit, to secure the weak point at the bottom.

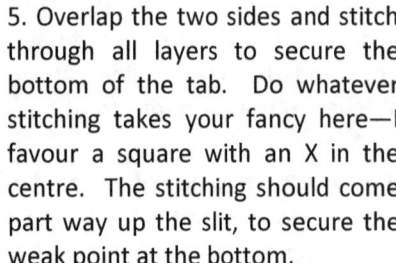

6. Flip up the bottom of the garment and overlock the lower edges of the twill tape together to neaten them. Sew the buttons on.
Optional: for a concealed front, add some extra stitching between the buttonholes, for example horizontal rows.

Alternatively, stitch a bartack between the buttonholes, either by hand or by machine.

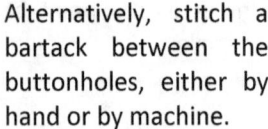
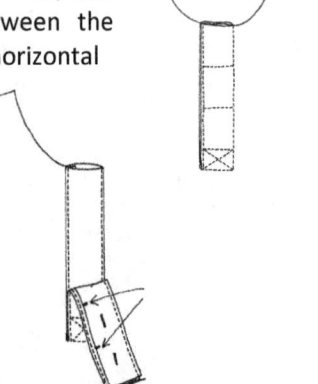

Tab from a slit with fabric tabs

A tab can be made with a strip of woven fabric instead of twill tape, often using the same fabric as the shirt collar. It's made in exactly the same way as a continuous bound placket on a shirt cuff. This type of opening can also be used with buttons on the back of dresses or skirts, where there's no central seam.

Make a pattern

1. Make a pattern for the front as described on page 121. Cut the slit for the tab 2cm (¾") away from the centre front.

2. For the tab, cut a strip of fabric 7.5cm (3") wide. It will be 3cm (1¼") wide when finished. Cut it twice as long as the slit plus 6mm (¼") (a little extra is taken up when sewing the point of the slit). Sometimes the strip is cut longer and the excess is trimmed afterwards. Interface half or all of the tab.

To sew a tab with fabric

1. Lay the tab underneath one side of the slit, matching the raw edges. If you've interfaced half, match the *un*-interfaced side. Have the right sides facing up for both. Begin sewing, taking a 5mm seam allowance.

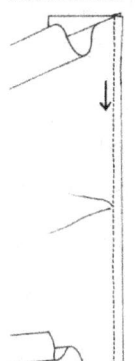

As you approach the point of the slit, spread the slit so it's straight and just catch the point with the stitching. A small stitch length (1 or 1.5 instead of the usual 2.5) will make it stronger.
Press the seam towards the tab, and press under 6mm (¼") along the other long edge of the tab.

2. Fold the pressed edge of the tab over to encase the raw edge. Edgestitch it in place, just covering the previous stitching line. In a perfect world (and with some practice) the back and front should look the same. To prevent the tab from rippling or twisting as you sew it, hold the bottom layer firmly towards you and let the top "sit easy".

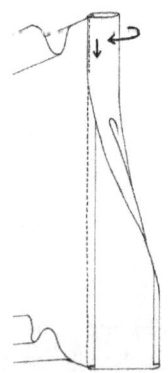

3. Arrange the tabs how they'll be worn. Bar tack, straight stitch or sew a box across the end to hold it in place, making the stitching come part way up the slit

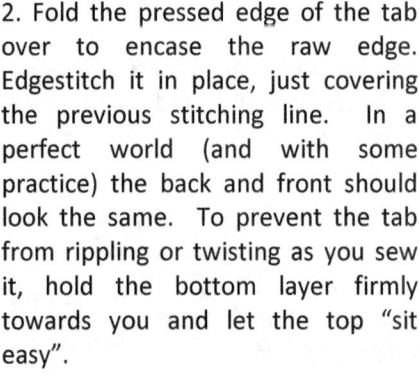

to secure the weak point at the bottom. When you sew the collar on, make sure both sides of the tab are the same length when the collar is done up.

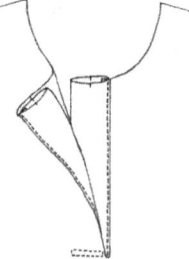

Tab from a slit with a 1pce facing

This is suitable for rugby tops or polo shirts, in woven or stretch fabric. Once you've made the pattern, this is a very quick and easy tab to sew. It's **very important** to mark clearly on the pattern which way up to cut it because the tab is asymmetrical. If you accidentally flip the pattern piece and cut it out the wrong way, it won't work.

Make a pattern
1. Make a pattern for the front as described on page 121. Mark the slit for the tab 2cm (¾) away from the centre front.
If the neck is very curved and the top of the slit finishes higher than the centre front, draw a horizontal line across level with the slit.

2. For the facing, turn the front over, so the slit is on the other side. Trace around the pattern—the whole neckline, shoulders and slit. Draw in the shape of the facing. The shoulders can be about 5cm (2") long and the bottom can be about 10cm

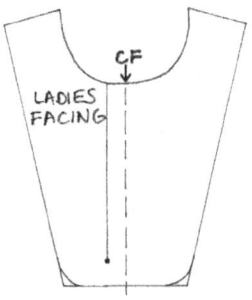

(4") wide. The lower corners can be curved or square. Cut the lower edge of the facing 2.5cm (1") longer than the slit.
Then, add in 6.5cm (2½") next to the slit, as shown.

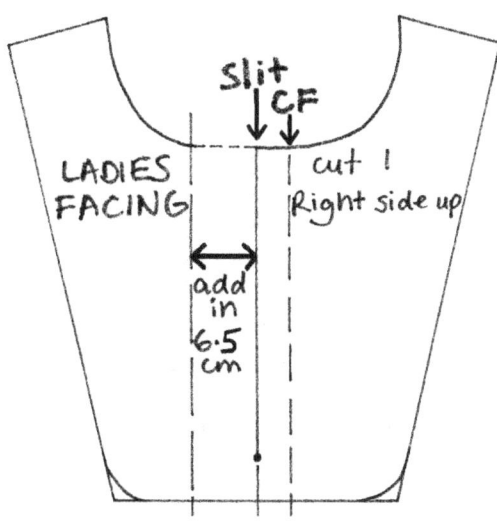

This is a ladies facing; a men's facing is a mirror image. Mark the "right side up" on the facing and write "PTO" (Please Turn Over) on the reverse side. Do the same on the garment front, too.

To sew a tab with a one piece facing
1. Cut out the shirt front, but don't cut the slit yet. Mark the top of the slit with a tiny 3mm (⅛") snip and the bottom with a dot on the wrong side. Also mark the top of the centre front (CF) with a tiny snip. **Optional:** (depending on the fabric's stability) iron on a strip of fusing 2cm (¾") wide over the slit line.

2. Cut one of the facing, with the right side of the fabric facing up, and interface with a light fusing (the fusing needs to be cut sticky side up). As with the shirt, don't cut the slit yet, but mark the top of the slit with a tiny 3mm (⅛") snip and the bottom with a dot on the wrong side, then join with a ruled pencil line. Also, mark the centre front (CF) with a tiny 3mm (⅛") snip.

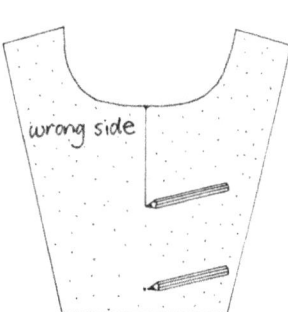

3. Overlock around the lower edge and shoulders of the facing.

4. Place the facing on top of the shirt, right sides together, matching the slit positions. Note that the shoulders and neck won't sit on top of one another. Match the raw edges

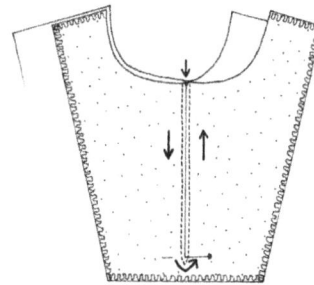

at the neck first, then line up the slit by pushing a pin through. With the facing on top, stitch 5mm either side of the slit line, pivoting at an acute angle at the bottom point. Use a small stitch (1 or 1.5) for extra strength around the point. Cut the slit line, cutting exactly to, but not over, the pivot point.

5. Turn the facing through to the wrong side and press into position, forming 3cm (1¼") wide tabs on each side. Trim up the neckline of the tabs to match the

garment's, if required. Stitch a box at the bottom of the tab to hold it in place, stitching a little way up the slit to secure the weak point at the very bottom.

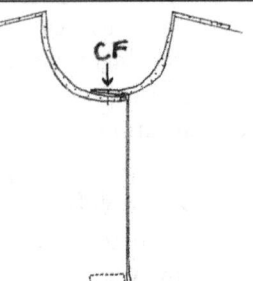

6. When attaching the (knitted polo) collar, sandwich it between the right sides of the facing and shirt (you'll have to flip the facing back along the tab's fold line), with the collar beginning at the centre front on each. Lay the back neck binding (page 116) over the top.

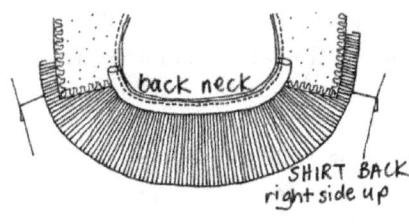

Tab from a slit using a rectangle

The one-piece faced tab front described above can also be made *without* a facing. The pattern is simpler and is easily transferable to other sizes or garments since it's just a rectangle.

Make a pattern

1. Make a pattern for the front as described on page 121. Mark the slit for the tab 2cm (¾") away from the centre front.

2. The tab pattern is a rectangle with a slit line, as shown below.

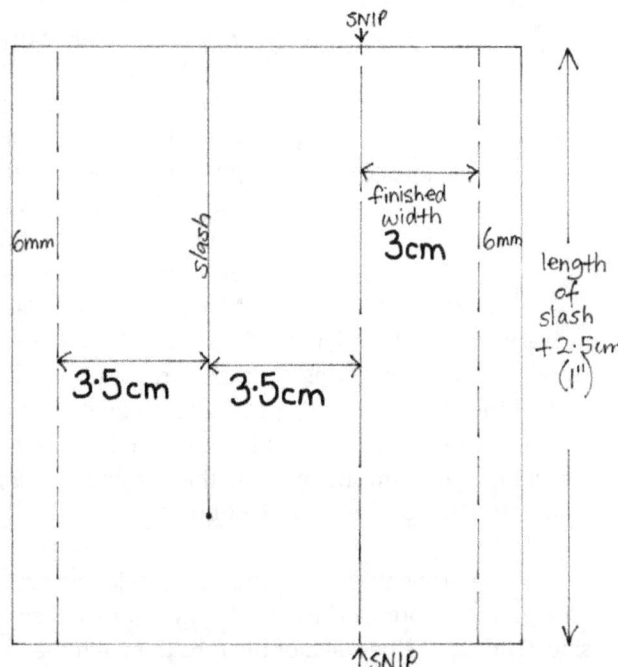

This is a men's tab—cut one right side up as illustrated. For ladies, flip the pattern over then cut one right side up.

To sew a tab using a rectangle

1. Cut out the shirt front, but don't cut the slit yet. Mark the top of the slit with a tiny 3mm (⅛") snip and the bottom with a dot on the wrong side.

2. Don't cut the slit yet on the tab. Fuse the tab with a suitable interfacing. Mark the slit with a tiny 3mm (⅛") snip at the top and a dot at the bottom. Rule a pencil line to join the two. Overlock the sides and lower edge of the tab.

3. Lay the tab face down onto the front, right sides together. Match the top raw edges and the slit position. Push a pin in to align the bottom points of the slit. Taking a 5mm seam allowance, stitch along the edges of the slit, pivoting with an acute angle at the bottom 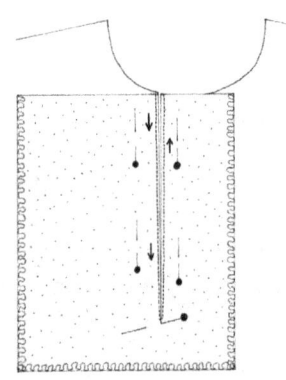 point. Use a shorter than normal stitch length for strength (1 or 1.5 instead of the usual 2.5) at the pivot point. Using a very sharp pair of scissors, snip exactly to the pivot point, being careful not to cut the stitching.

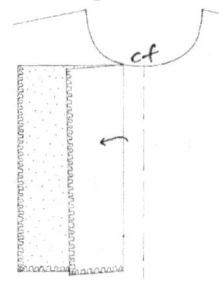

4. Turn each side of the tab back and press, pushing the seam allowance towards the slit.

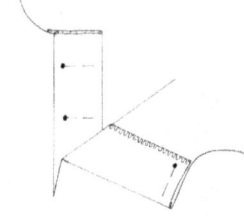

5. Turn the tab to the wrong side of the front. Fold the tab piece along the fold line (denoted by a snip at each end) to form the underlap and press. You may like to edgestitch the folds.

6. With the tab accurately folded into position, horizontally stitch through the bottom of the tab, through all the layers. You can make one or two rows of stitching, or a box with an X in it. Take the

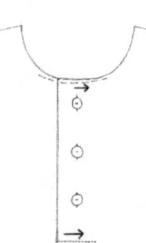

stitching a little way up the slit to secure the weak point at the very bottom. If you're planning to attach a regular shirt collar, machine baste the top edges of the tab pieces to each side of the neck edge.

Free-hanging tab at end of placket
Familiarize yourself with sewing the Simple tab front (pages 116-118); this is a fun variation to the bottom of it. Note that this can't be used for the tab front with a facing.

Make a pattern
1. Make a new pattern for the overlap side of the tab, making it a little longer, for example 3cm (1¼"), and shaping the end if you want to. You could make it pointed, rounded or just leave it square.
Important: mark the end of the actual placket stitching line on the pattern with small 3mm (⅛") snips, so you know where to sew to.

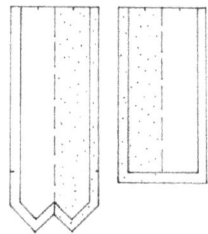

You'll have two pattern pieces for the tab: the longer overlap and shorter underlap.

To sew a free-hanging tab
1. Interface half of the tab, so the outermost side will have the interfacing on it when the garment is worn.

2. Bag out the bottom of the overlap side by folding it with the right sides together and stitching around the end to the snips. Snip in to the stitching, then turn to the right side.

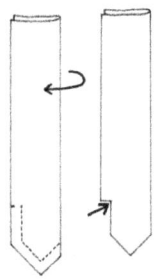

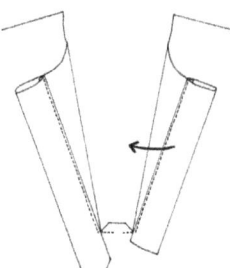

3. Sew each side of the tab onto the shirt. If desired, you can edgestitch around the whole tab.
Then sew the *underlap* side to the bottom of the opening.

4. Stitch horizontally across the bottom of the tab to secure the overlap, leaving the end hanging loose. Sometimes a button and buttonhole is sewn to the free hanging part as a design feature.

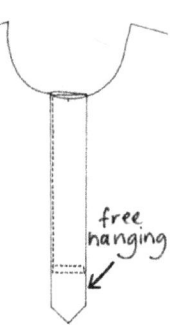

Placket with a pleat below
This type of opening for a shirt was very popular in the early 1900's. I've also seen it used for the back opening of smocked baby's dresses. It's a very simple idea and the pattern is easy to make. This placket is intended for fabrics with the same wrong and right sides. You can use it for one-sided fabrics but it's not quite as neat (see afterwards for adaptation).

Make a pattern
The pattern has no separate placket pattern pieces—the actual fronts form the plackets. It needs no interfacing.
Add in a section through the middle of the shirt:

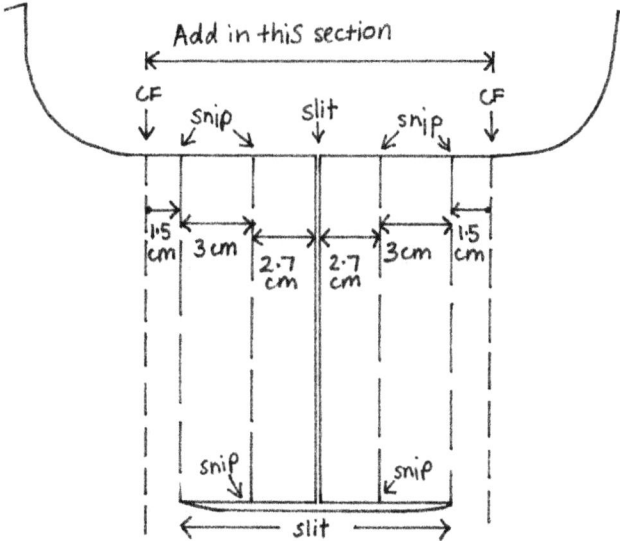

For a 3cm wide finished placket, first add a 1.5cm (⅝") wrap (half the finished placket) to the centre front (CF), then add 3cm (1¼") (double the wrap), and finally 2.7cm (1⅛") (double the wrap less 3mm (⅛")). Snip small 3mm (⅛") notches at the tops of the fold lines. Note on the pattern where the fabric is slit.

To sew a placket with a pleat below
1. Fold each side of the vertical slit twice to form a placket on each side. The overlap side (that will be on top with the buttonholes in it) folds *under*, and the underlap side (that will be underneath with the buttons) folds *over*, exposing the wrong side of the fabric. You can stitch down each side to hold it, or just leave it as a double folded placket and let the buttons and buttonholes hold the folds in place.

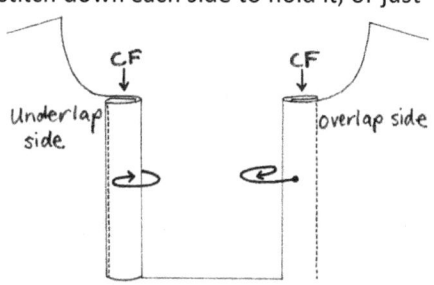

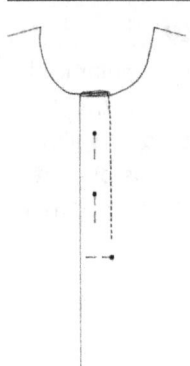

2. Lap the overlap over the underlap, neatly pleating the excess fabric below the placket. Sandwich the raw edges of the top of the pleats between the two plackets and stitch through all layers to hold it.

If the fabric is single-sided, fold both sides of the placket *under* before pleating and lapping them over each other.

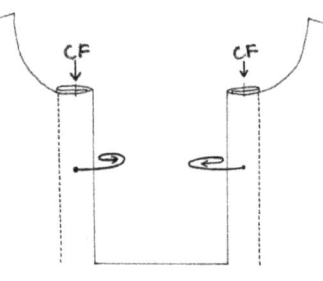

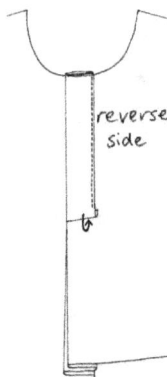

Hide the raw edge of the underneath placket by turning it under and stitching across on the right side. It will result in two parallel rows of stitching at the bottom of the placket.

✂ If you're making a **maternity shirt**, add at least 5cm (2") length onto the lower edge, tapering to nothing at the side seams. Make more room across the front by adding more fabric in the centre to be pleated.

All-in-one placket

This is simply a classic shirt cuff placket turned upside down and the finished dimensions altered slightly. It makes a front tab that's wonderfully neat on the outside and inside. The bottom can be squared or shaped.

Make a pattern

1. On the shirt pattern, draw in a slit line on the centre front (CF), the length of the intended opening. The actual finished placket will sit 5cm (2") longer on the surface than the finished slit.

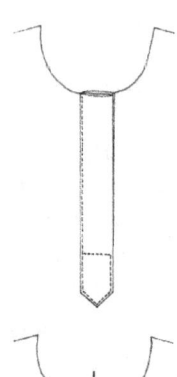

2. The pattern for the placket looks like an upside down house with a chimney. Make the slit the same length as the shirt's slit. Write on the pattern which way up to cut it. The illustration show a ladies placket. For men, cut it as a mirror image.

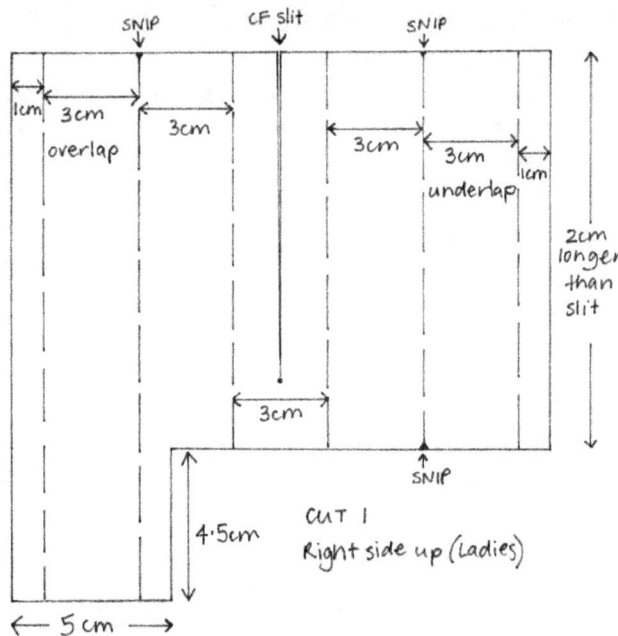

To sew an all-in-one placket

1. Iron a 4cm (1½") strip of light fusing onto each vertical end of the placket (as shown in the sketch in Step 3, below). While you're there, press under the 1cm (⅜") seam allowance at each end.

2. Don't cut the slits yet. Mark them on the wrong sides of the shirt and placket using a ruler and pencil.

3. Lay the right side of the placket onto the wrong side of the shirt (so both wrong sides are facing *up*) and match the slits with a pin. Stitch around the slit, taking a 1.5cm (⅝") seam allowance on each vertical side, and 1cm (⅜") across the bottom, pivoting cleanly at the corners. I like to shorten the stitch length at the corners to 1 or 1.5, instead of the usual 2.5, for extra strength.

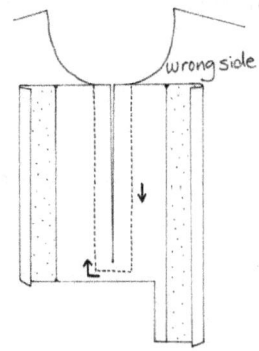

Important: ensure the two vertical lines of stitching are *exactly* 3cm (1¼") apart all the way down, especially at the corners.

Front stands and tab fronts **127**

4. Cut along the slit line and snip into each corner exactly to, but not over, the stitching. Trim back the 1.5cm (⅝") seam allowance if the fabric is thick.

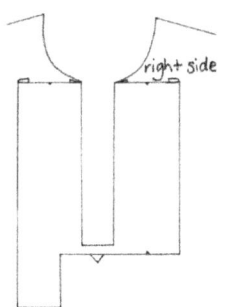

5. Bring the placket through to the right side of the shirt, forming a neat window.

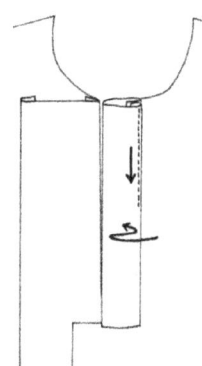

6. Fold the underlap into place as illustrated so it exactly fits into the 3cm (1¼") wide window. Lay the 1cm (⅜") folded edge over the previous line of stitching, just covering it, and stitch down. To avoid ripples, hold the underneath layer firmly as you sew, and let the folded edge "sit easy" on top.

7. If you're having a **pointed peak** at the bottom of the placket, stitch it now: fold the chimney in half vertically, right sides together, and sew across the top of the chimney taking a 6mm (¼") seam allowance.

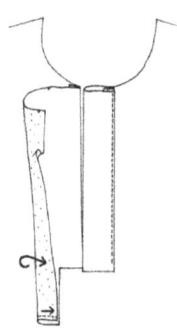

Press the little seam open and centre it behind the (now pointed) chimney.

8. Fold the overlap over the underlap, again laying the 1cm folded-under edge over the previous line of stitching. If you're having the end of the placket squared, simply fold it under 1cm (⅜").

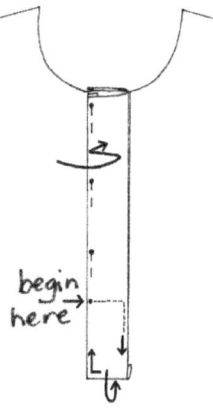

Pin the placket in place so the overlap covers the underlap and everything is neat and correct—press with an iron if necessary. Begin stitching horizontally making sure you catch all the layers. Make sure the underlap is out of the way for the final leg of stitching.

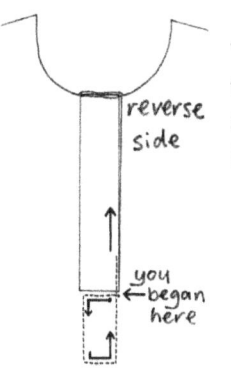

The reverse side should look like this. The start of the stitching should just catch the edge of the horizontal fold.

Extra: All-in-one placket as a hand opening

The same all-in-one placket can be adapted slightly to use as a hand opening for capes and overalls. Positioned either vertically or angled, it looks very neat on the inside of unlined garments.

It can be used as an opening in (rainwear) overtrousers to reach the pockets of the clothes underneath.

If the opening faces the opposite way, the hands can reach out of a cape.

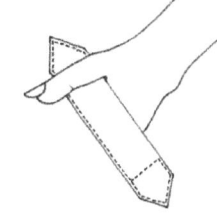

Make a pattern
Determine the finished shape and size of the placket and its position on the garment, and draw it in on the garment pattern. The ends can be squared or pointed. The finished placket will need to extend at least 2cm (¾") beyond either end of the slash.

The **length** of the *slash line* needs to be a minimum of 15cm (6") for women, or 17.5cm (7") for men, to enable a hand to fit through.

The finished **width** of the placket needs to be at least 2.5cm (1") wide to cover the 2cm (¾") wide underneath strip of the placket.

Draw on the garment:

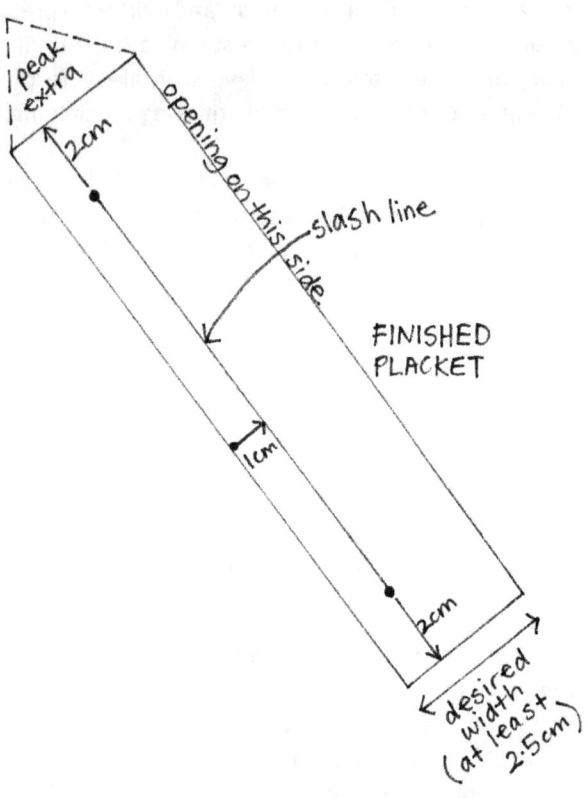

Make a pattern for the placket:

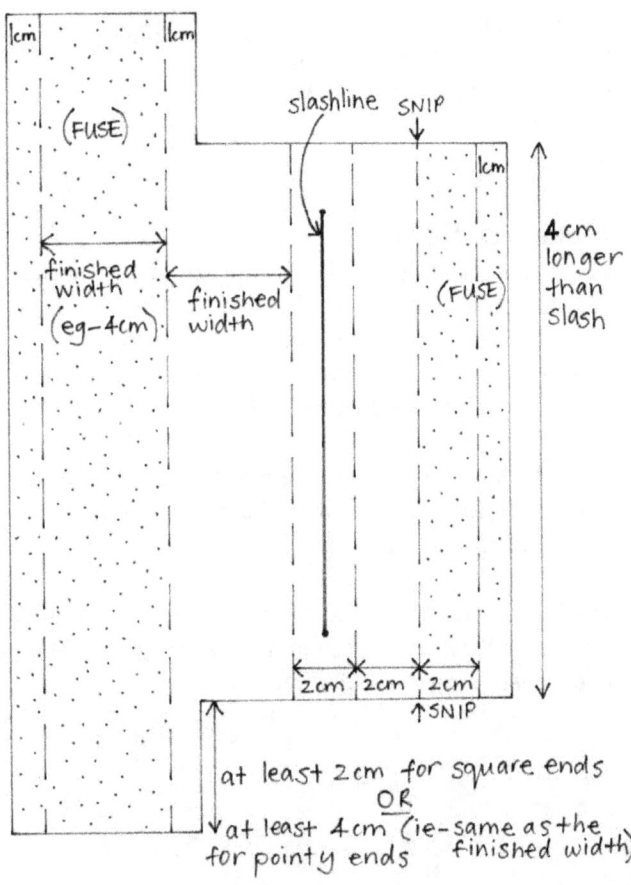

To sew a placket hand opening

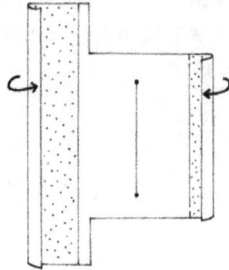

1. Interface the placket, and while you're at the ironing board press under the 1cm (⅜") seam allowance at each vertical edge.
Mark the slash lines on the wrong sides of the placket and garment using a ruler and pencil. Don't cut them yet.

2. Lay the right side of the placket down onto the wrong side of the garment, so the wrong sides of both are facing up. Align the slash lines by placing a pin through all layers at the top and bottom of the slash.
Very important: note the orientation of the placket on the garment.

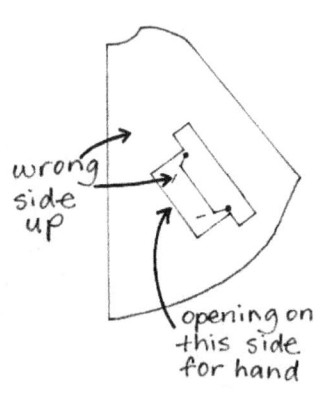

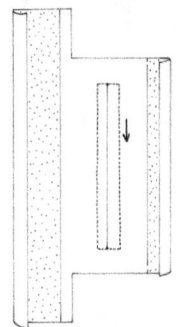

3. Sew a box around the slash line, stitching 1cm (⅜") either side of the line and across the top and bottom level with the top and bottom of the slash position.
The stitched box should measure 2cm (¾") wide and be the length of the slash line long.

4. Carefully cut along the centre of the stitched box to within 1cm (⅜") of the ends. Cut into each corner forming a triangular flap of fabric.

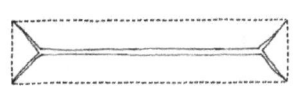

5. Bring the placket through to the right side of the garment, forming a neat window.

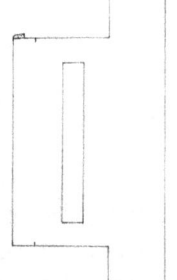

Front stands and tab fronts **129**

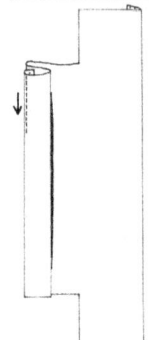

6. Fold the underlap side into place so it fits exactly into the 2cm wide window. Lay the edge along the previous stitching line and edgestitch it into place.

7. If you're having **pointy ends** on the placket, make them now. Fold each long part in half lengthwise, right sides together, and sew across the end, taking a 6mm (¼") seam allowance.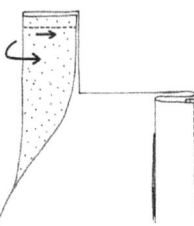

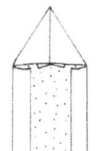 Press the seam open and centre it in the placket end.

8. Fold the overlap over the underlap, laying the 1cm (⅜") folded-under edge over the stitching on the "window".
If you're having a placket with **squared ends**, fold them under 1cm (⅜").
Press and pin the placket in place so the overlap covers the underlap and everything is neat and correct, ready to sew.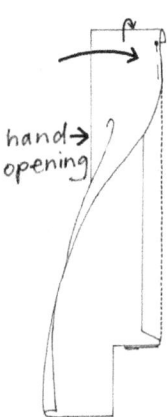

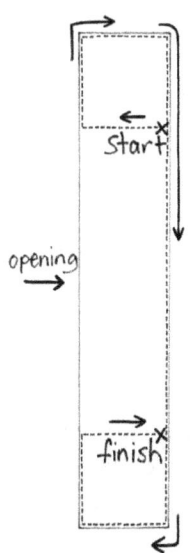 9. Begin stitching across the placket as shown, making sure you catch all the layers. Make sure the underlap is out of the way as you stitch. Finish up at the other end, stitching across the placket again.

Gathering

Introduction 130	shirring 133
Gathering with 2 rows of stitching 130	channel gathering 134
Pressing gathers 131	Ruffles 134
Gathering over a cord 132	Ruching 135
Gathering with a gathering foot 132	Zig zag ruching—a decorative trim 135
Gathering on an overlocker 132	Adding gathers to a pattern 136
Smocking 132	sleeves 136
Making gathers on gathers 132	shirts 136
Gathering with elastic 132	pockets 136
stitching elastic to the fabric 132	skirts 137

Flamboyant, prissy, cute or voluminous, gathering is a way of creating soft fullness and volume in a garment and can give a variety of looks depending on the fabric and garment. Gathering is used to create puffed sleeves of any type, fullness from a yoke, ruching, ruffles, ruffled trims and dirndl skirts (simply a length of fabric gathered onto a waistband) or similarly made trousers.

Gathering is often used in women's and children's clothing, but men's clothes can feature gathering as well–think of English farm smocks, pirate shirts and Regency period costume. Gathering is also used extensively in dance and folk costumes, such as Cossack dancers, flamenco, peasant and gypsy.

✂ The minimum amount for gathering any fabric is 1½ times the finished width, but twice the finished width is usual.

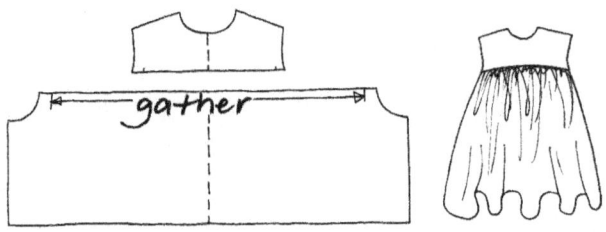

✂ The fabric used will affect the appearance of the gathers. Soft fabrics will drape and cling to the body, whereas crisp or thick fabrics will stand out from the body on their own. Very soft, fine fabrics like chiffon or soft tulle require three or four (or more) times the finished width to make the gathers look substantial. The heavier the fabric the less gathering is needed.

✂ There are many ways of gathering fabric. Choose the best method to suit the amount of gathering required, the fabric, the design, the time you want to spend and the machines or accessories you have available.

Gathering with two rows of stitching

The most common way to gather is to sew two parallel lines of stitching, with the machine set on the longest stitch possible.

1. Make the first row *on* the seam line and the second row 6mm (¼") away from the seam line, within the seam allowance. Leave long ends. Don't be tempted to stitch only one row—you need two, otherwise the gathers won't sit flat when you sew the seam. Two rows also helps to distribute the gathers evenly, resulting in superior gathers.

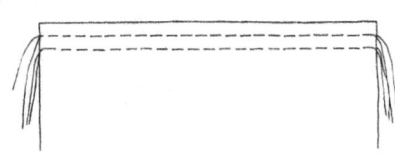

✂ On **heavy fabrics**, if you intersect a previously sewn seam, you'll find it difficult to pull up the gathers through two thicknesses. A flat spot in the gathering may result. The solution is to gather the seam on each side, leaving the seam allowance free.

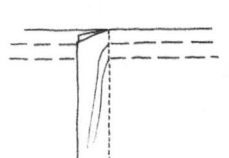

✂ The gathering threads can also be done **by hand** using running stitch. Use a length of thread long enough for the distance to be gathered. Begin with a knot and try and make as many stitches as possible without drawing the needle out of the fabric. It helps to keep the fabric taut as you sew—you could pin it to your lap. Work two rows as above.

2. With the right sides together, pin the gathered section on, matching the notches and seams.

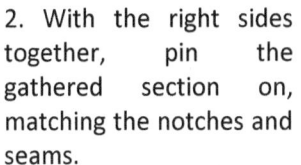 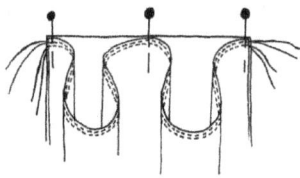

If you have a very long area to gather (or even a medium long area), it helps to mark the halves, quarters, eighths, sixteenths and so on of each section to allow easier and more even distribution of gathers.

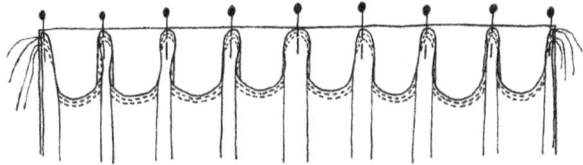

There's a danger of the gathering threads breaking over long areas while you're drawing up the gathers, especially on thick fabrics. To avoid this, try making several shorter sections of gathering instead of one long one.

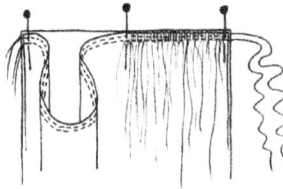

3. Pull on the bobbin threads with one hand, and with the other hand slide the fabric along the two threads to form the gathers.

Don't panic if one of the threads breaks—see if you can get by with just one, or else catch it before it undoes too much. Make the gathers even and neat by stroking across them with a pin, parallel to the stitching. You can also hold the gathered edge in one hand and pull firmly on the lower edge to "set" the gathers.

4. When the gathered edge matches the straight edge, you can secure the thread ends by winding a figure eight around the end pins. Distribute the fullness evenly and secure with extra pins if necessary.

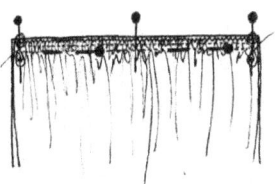

✂ Sometimes, to give gathering extra pouf and support, a strip of gathered net is sewn behind the gathering.

A good example is big puffy sleeves on wedding dresses like Princess Diana's. The strip can be held together with the sleeve and gathered at the same time, or else gathered separately and sewn on behind afterwards.

5. *Remember to change the stitch length back on your machine!* Stitch the seam on the seam line, placing your fingers either side of the gathering stitches as you sew, to make sure you don't end up with 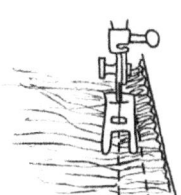 pleats instead of gathers. Flip the seam to the right side and check for any flat spots or uneven gathering. An experienced machinist can pull up the gathers as she sews. I've done this myself and it's much quicker than pinning everything. It works well on short sections like shirt sleeves gathered into cuffs. Place the seam under the presser foot and begin sewing to anchor the fabric. Lift the foot and draw up the gathering threads, stroking across them with a pin to make them even. When the gathered section is the correct length, sew the rest of the seam.

6. Neaten the seam allowance after sewing the seam. Gathered seams are closed seams. That is, both layers are neatened together and pressed to one side, not opened out.

Pressing gathers

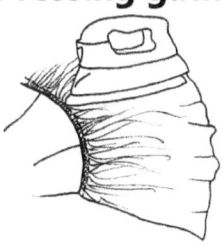

When pressing gathers, be careful not to put the iron across the gathers, or you'll flatten them. Instead, slide the point of the iron *into* the gathers.

Almost always, seams are pressed *away* from the gathers, but there are exceptions.

Press seams on puffed sleeves *towards* the gathers and away from the body for perky, puffed gathers.

Press *away* from the gathers, towards the body, for a flatter look. You'll have to secure the seam at the top of the armhole to make the gathers stay— either topstitch the armhole seam or anchor by hand inside.

Gathering over a cord

This is ideal (and fast) for making bridal veils. I use dental floss for the cord because it's strong, but you could use cord, thin string or crochet cotton.

1. Place the cord in the seam allowance, just inside the stitching line.

2. Set your machine to a wide and long zig zag stitch, and zig zag over the cord so the stitch is just inside the stitching line.

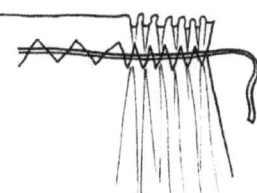

3. Pull up gathers by sliding the fabric over the cord. Secure one end and stitch the seam, being careful not to catch the cord. You can pull the cord out and re-use it when you've finished.

Gathering with a gathering foot

You can buy a gathering foot for most sewing machines that will gather as you sew. The longer the stitch, the denser the gathering. A gathering foot is a great idea if you have lots of gathering to do.

Gathering on an overlocker

Your overlocker can do gathering. It works best on fine to medium weight fabrics. You can use a three or four-thread overlocker. Note that the seam allowance will be trimmed to 6mm (¼") as you gather.
1. Set the stitch length to 3mm-5mm (⅛"-¼") and the width to the widest possible.

2. Set the needle thread tension(s) to very tight. For more gathers, tighten the needle thread tension(s). For less gathers, loosen the needle thread tension(s).

3. After overlocking, adjust the density of the gathers by pulling the needle thread(s) along gently.

You can also overlock over a cord then pull up the cord to make gathers:
1. Set the stitch length to 2mm-3mm (⅛") and the width to the widest possible.

2. Use dental floss, topstitching thread or crochet cotton for the cord.

3. If the foot on the machine has a hole in the front, thread the cord through the hole from front to back. Put the cord under the foot at the back. If the foot doesn't have a hole, guide the cord over the front of the foot then under the back of the foot.

4. As you overlock, the stitches will form over the cord and the seam allowance will be trimmed to 6mm (¼"). To form the gathers, slide the fabric along the cord.

Smocking

Smocking is another type of gathering and can be simple or very elaborate. Parallel rows of identical gathering stitches are pulled up to form a fine concertina effect, which are then are held in place by decorative embroidery. It's often associated with cute little girl's dresses and heirloom sewing, but has much more design potential. If you're interested, dip into the loads of books, magazines and classes already available.

Making gathers on gathers

Sometimes gathering cannot be held in place by a straight piece of fabric because both sides of the seam are gathered, for example:

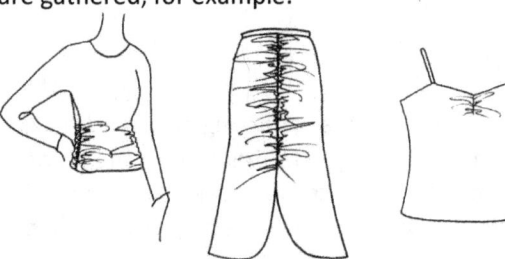

The gathering needs to be sewn to a stay of some sort. The stay can be a strip of cotton tape, ribbon, seam binding or even a piece of the fabric's selvedge, cut to the right length.
1. Place the two edges right sides together and stitch the gathering threads through both layers at the same time.

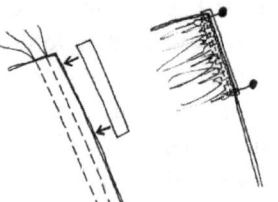

2. Pull up the gathers to the specified length and sew it to the stay.

3. Neaten the edge and press it to one side with the stay uppermost.

Gathering with elastic

Gathering using elastic produces stretchy, flexible gathers and can be used on knitted or woven fabrics.

Stitching elastic directly onto the fabric

A very simple and quick way to gather using elastic is to stitch a cut length of elastic directly onto the fabric with straight or zig zag stitch. The elastic is stretched to fit the fabric during sewing. A drawback with this method is that the amount of gathering is limited by how far the piece of elastic will stretch.

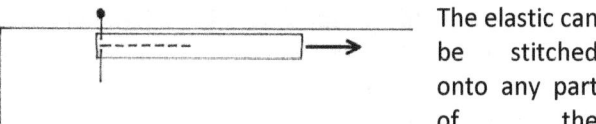

The elastic can be stitched onto any part of the garment to gather it—seams, edges or in the centre of the fabric. Regular or plastic elastic can be used.

If the elastic is to gather an edge, the fabric can be folded under first then the elastic stitched on top:

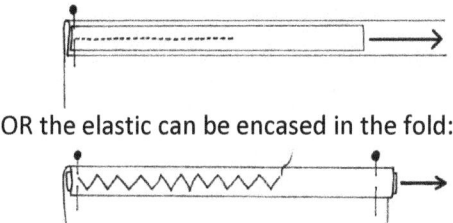

OR the elastic can be encased in the fold:

Motor bike leathers use this idea in a slightly different way. A wide piece of elastic is stretched onto the wrong side of the leather and stitched *perpendicular* to the stretch in parallel lines. When the elastic is relaxed the leather folds into even grooves.

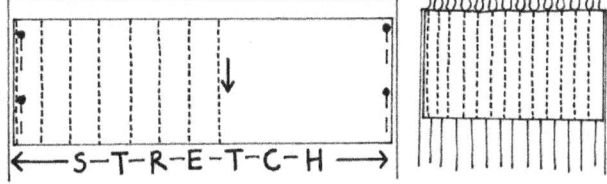

Shirring

Shirring elastic has a fine elastic core around which is wound thread. It comes in black or white on a spool same as a reel of thread. Because the elastic is fine, shirring works best on light to medium weight fabrics only. The finer the fabric the more it will gather. See the next page for shirring on thicker fabrics.
Shirring makes clothes cling gently wherever you decide to put it. It gives a softer cling than elastic in a casing and is very simple to do by machine. Shirring self-adjusts to many sizes due to the softness of the gathers and the amount of fullness it can hold in.
Soft skirt and dress waists, sundresses, wrist edges of long full sleeves, headbands and children's clothes are just some of the applications.
You can make shirring decorative by where you use it on the garment, using a contrasting coloured thread or by experimenting with zig zag-style embroidery stitches on your machine.

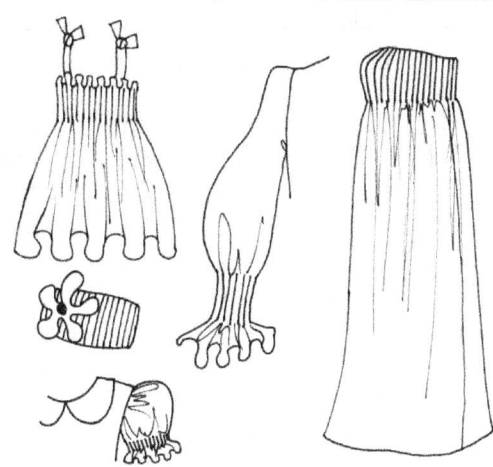

To use shirring elastic:
1. Wind the elastic by hand onto a machine bobbin without stretching it. Use regular thread on top.

2. Set the stitch length for a long straight stitch.

3. Tighten the top tension (for example, on my machine, 4 is normal and 6 or 8 is shirring). Sew a test piece to determine the tension—adjusting it can make slightly tighter or looser gathers.

4. Work with the right side of the fabric facing up. Simply stitch along and the fabric will gather up by itself. Knot the elastic and thread together at the beginning. Multiple rows are easy to sew a footwidth (6mm or ¼") apart by using the edge of the presser foot as a guide along the previous row. When one row is completed, turn it 180 degrees and go straight onto the next one without cutting the threads.

Shirring generally gathers fabric to slightly less than half its original width. For example, 90cm of fabric shirrs in to around 40cm, sewing 10 rows 6mm apart. You can control the amount of gathering by how you set the tension, the weight of fabric you choose to gather and also by how you wind the bobbin. For very tight stretchy gathers, wind the bobbin at *full stretch* of the elastic. Set the machine to a long stitch and tighten the top tension as usual. The fabric can gather to about ⅓ its original width. So, 90cm will gather in to 30cm.

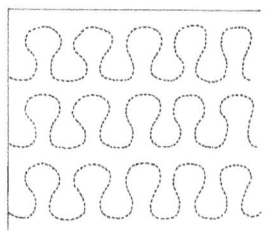

You don't need to shirr in straight lines. Interesting and creative effects can be achieved by shirring in a pattern, but the degree of stretch may not be as great.
Make a cardboard template of the stitching line and mark it on the fabric using

chalk or water soluble pen before you begin, or else try "freeform" shirring.

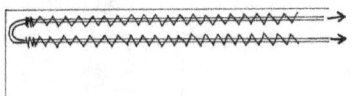 **Another way** to achieve a shirred effect is to catch cord elastic inside a zig zagged seam. This can work on heavier fabrics where regular shirring with shirring elastic can't. The elastic can be hat elastic or a fatter tubular elastic; the heavier the fabric the stronger the elastic should be.

Fit your machine with a grooved cording foot to allow the elastic to sit underneath and set the stitch to a wide zig zag. Sew over the elastic with the wrong side of the fabric facing up. Check that the zig zag tension looks OK underneath, since that's the part everyone will see. After stitching, pull up the elastic to gather the fabric and secure the ends.

You can stitch single or multiple rows anywhere on the garment, next to an edge, or even on a regular seam joining two parts of the garment together. The gathers can be adjusted when the seam is complete—just pull the elastic tighter through the zig zag.

Channel gathering

Channel gathering involves a casing or tunnel stitched to the fabric then elastic (or cord, tape or ribbon) threaded through the casing. This method has two useful features: the gathering can be re-adjusted at any time, and the elastic or cord can be removed to return the fabric to its ungathered length.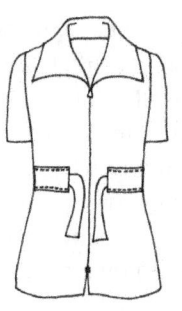

Channels are used when the fullness needs to be adjustable. The channel is a straight or shaped band stitched along both edges to the wrong or right side of the garment, and is only just wide enough to accommodate the elastic, cord, ribbon or belt that's threaded through. The channel can be cut in the same fabric but sometimes it's cut in a thinner fabric so it's less bulky when gathered. Sometimes for convenience pre-folded bias binding or wide ribbon is used.

1. Cut the channel the desired **length** plus a seam allowance to turn under on all sides. The seam allowances on the short ends should be at least 1.5cm (⅝") to prevent untucking when the cord goes through, especially on wider channels.

The seam allowance on the long straight sides need only be 1cm (⅜") or even 6mm (¼"); too much bigger and it will interfere with the cord going through the channel.

The finished **width** needs to be a little wider than the cord, because the channel will be edgestitched in position and you'll lose some width, so add another 6mm (¼") to the total.

Usually the channel is straight, but if the channel needs to be curved, cut it on the bias and curve it to fit.

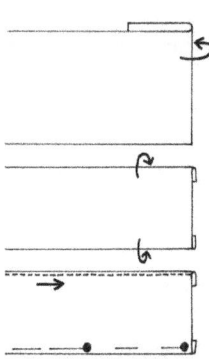 2. Press under all the edges and pin the channel in position. It's not necessary to overlock the edges of the channel unless the fabric frays really badly.

Edgestitch along the long sides. Thread the cord through using a safety pin. To save time, you may be able to stitch the channel with the cord already inside the channel.

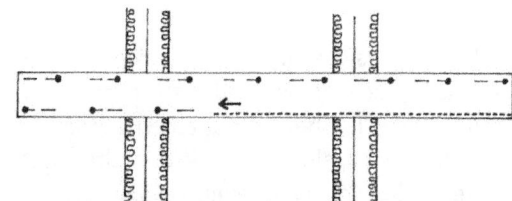

If the channel is applied to the inside of the garment, a buttonhole at each end of the channel allows the cord to come through to the right side. You could also leave a short gap in the seam allowance if the channel finishes at a seam.

3. The ends of the cord or elastic can be stitched to hold them at each end of the casing, making the gathering non-adjustable
OR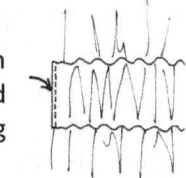

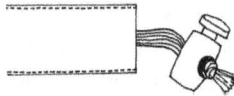 can have long ends that are knotted or have a toggle at the end.

Ruffles

A ruffle is a hemmed strip of fabric gathered either down the centre or to one side of the centre, then 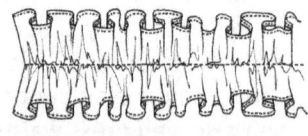 stitched on top of a flat piece of fabric. The hem finish of the ruffle will affect how it sits. A firm finish such as binding (using ribbon or bias binding) will make the edges of the ruffle stick out.

A ruffler foot attachment on a sewing machine can gather or pleat the strip for you.

Gathering **135**

If you don't own a ruffler, you can quickly sew a ruffle with a regular machine foot:
1. Set the machine on a long stitch.

2. Start sewing along the ruffle to gather it up *and at the same time* hold the thread tightly as it comes off the spool at the top of the machine. The tighter you hold it the more the fabric will ruffle up.

3. At the end, leave long threads. Move the ruffling along the threads to give the amount of ruffling desired.

Ruching

Ruching is a gathered panel applied on top of a plain foundation, secured on all sides by seams. It's often found on evening and bridal gowns.
The foundation needs to fit firmly and can be a strapless top or skirt basque/yoke. Ensure the foundation fits accurately, since alterations after the ruching has been applied are difficult.

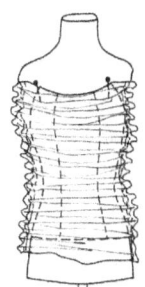

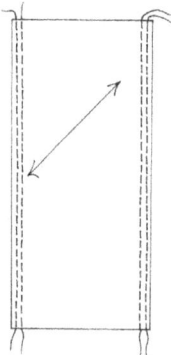

Fabric for ruching can be anything, really, but fabrics that drape well without creasing work best. Sheer fabrics are fine to use.
The foundation fabric needs to be a firm fabric, and if the ruching fabric is sheer it needs to look OK underneath. If the ruching fabric is opaque, you can use a firm woven sew-in interfacing for the foundation instead of fabric. If you don't think it will be firm enough, iron on a layer of fusing to firm it up.

1. Cut out the garment pieces and sew any seams in the foundation that will have ruching over the top of them, such as bust seams. Generally, the fronts and backs are ruched separately, so don't sew the side seams yet.

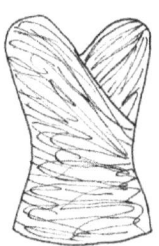

2. For the ruching, buy plenty of fabric to give you artistic freedom. Cut the piece on the *bias* and at least twice as long as the foundation it will lay over. If the fabric is fine and sheer, for example chiffon or georgette, cut it 3 to 3½ times longer. Sew gathering stitches on each side.

Pull up the gathers to the length of the foundation.

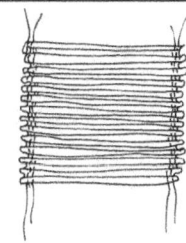

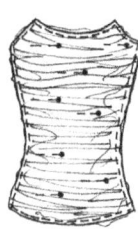

3. Pin the foundation to a dress model and work on one piece at a time, either the front or back. Pin the gathered panel over the foundation, arranging the gathers and pinning it at the sides. It will look best if it's pulled quite tightly over the foundation; when off the model it will collapse into the middle. When you're happy with the look, strategically pin the gathers in spots in the centre of the piece for catching by hand later.

4. Take the ruched foundation off the dress model and stitch around the edges of the piece with a large machine stitch to secure the gathers, then trim off the excess ruching hanging over the sides. Treat the ruched panel as the single piece it now is and carry on sewing the garment.

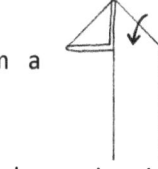

Zig Zag ruching—a decorative trim
Try it!
1. Use ribbon OR cut a strip of fabric on the straight or bias grain and press under 6mm (¼") on each side

2. Using an iron, fold the band diagonally to give stitching guidelines for the gathering stitching you'll be doing.
At one end, fold down a corner and press.

Then, make a second fold to form a triangle.

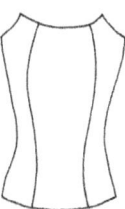

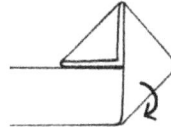

Continue folding and pressing in this manner to give zig zag triangle shaped folds along the length of the strip. Unfold the strip.

3. Sew a line of gathering stitches along the folds, pivoting where the fold changes direction at the edges of the strip. Use a long machine stitch or sew by hand. On really wide bands, use two rows of stitching

close together. Draw up the thread and adjust the fullness, evenly spacing the peaks.

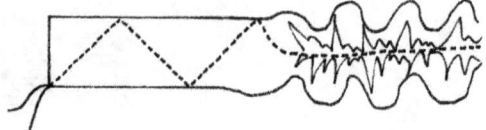

Adding gathers to a pattern

Gathering can be added to patterns by either "slashing and spreading" to add in the gathers, or by simply adding onto the sides, depending on how full the gathers need to be.

Here are just a few patternmaking ideas. Consult a patternmaking textbook for more.

Sleeves

To make a puffed, gathered sleeve head, raise the height of the sleeve head, say, 2cm (¾"), 4cm (1½") or more. Add notches to indicate where the gathering should occur. See page 331 for further notes.

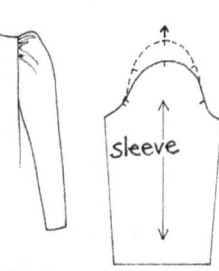

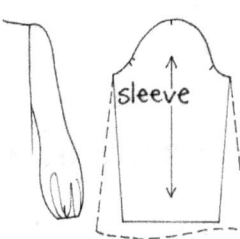

For a sleeve gathered at the wrist, sometimes it's enough to add onto the sides. Add a little extra length for more "pouf". Note that the lower edge is curved with more length at the back.

For more volume, slash and spread the pattern and re-draw the line.

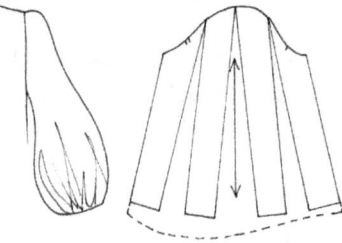

Shirts

Back gathers on a shirt look best falling from a yoke rather than the back neck, which tends to gives a hunchbacked appearance.

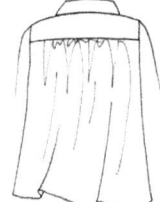

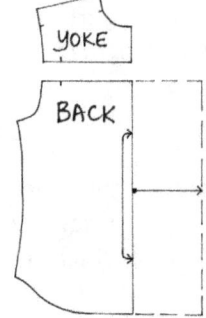

See pages 312-316 for making a shirt yoke.

Add the back gathers onto the centre back.

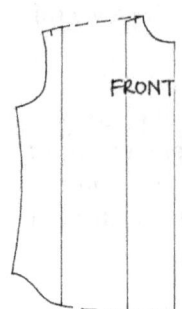

For front gathers, slash and spread the front as illustrated.

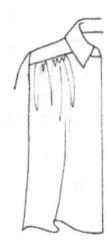

If the shirt has a bust dart, it can be incorporated into the gathers:

1. Trace around the front and draw a straight line from the bust point to the shoulder (broken line). Cut along this line.

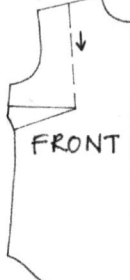

2. Fold out the bust dart and secure with a pin. You can leave the pattern as it is if you just want gathers from the shoulder but no extra volume. Stick a piece of paper behind the wedge that's opened up to give a completed pattern piece.

For more gathers and a roomier shirt, draw a straight line from the bust point to the hem. Cut along this line, separating the front into two pieces. Move the two pieces apart to give the amount of volume desired, then stick a piece of paper behind the gap to complete the pattern.

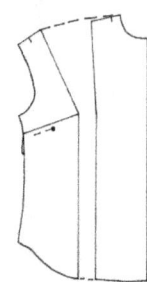

3. Smooth off the shoulder and add notches to indicate where the gathering should start and finish.

Pockets

Slash and spread a patch pocket to make it gathered. Support the gathers with a plain facing, a binding, or a casing with ribbon or elastic in it.

1. Draw the shape of the finished pocket, and note the finished length of the top edge.

2. Cut the pattern through the centre and spread the top a little or a lot depending on the thickness of the fabric and the amount of gathering desired. It's trial and error how much to spread

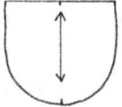

it but it should match the degree of gathering on the rest of the garment (for example, double the finished width).

3. Stick a piece of paper under the spread section, and draw in a pleasingly smooth line to finish the pattern.

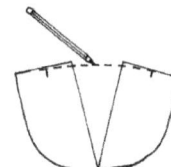

Add seam allowances if you haven't yet. Add notches to indicate where the gathering should start and finish, and note the finished measurement on the pattern.

Skirts

For many gathered skirts you may not need to make a pattern, because the skirt can be made from rectangles of fabric marked straight onto the fabric. Just make a sketch and note down the measurements of the pieces to cut.

A skirt gathered onto a waist band or yoke is simply a rectangle, and can be two widths of 112cm or 150cm (45" or 60") fabric—one for the front and one for the back. The only pattern pieces will be the waistband or yoke, and you can thieve these from an existing skirt pattern.

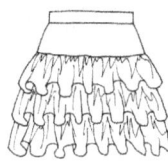

"**Ra ra**" **skirts** are an A-line skirt with gathered strips either sewn on top or inserted into horizontal seams.

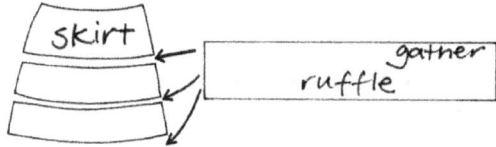

Gathered **tiered skirts** have one strip of fabric gathered onto the next, so each successive tier gets wider and wider, doubling each time.

The bottom tier can get very long, wider than the fabric's width. To avoid joins, the tiers are often cut parallel with the selvedge and run the length of the fabric.

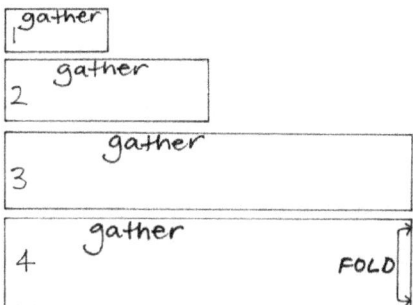

Godets

Introduction 138	Pleated godets 140
Make a pattern 138	One godet at the centre back 141
To sew a godet into a seam 139	Godets with rounded tops 142
another way 139	Godets with square ends 142
To sew a godet into a slit 139	Troubleshooting godets 142
Linings 140	

A godet (pronounced "*god*-ay", or some people say "*go*-day") is a triangular shaped piece of fabric sewn in a garment to increase fullness around the hem. Godets are most often seen on skirts, but can also be used on jackets and other garments.

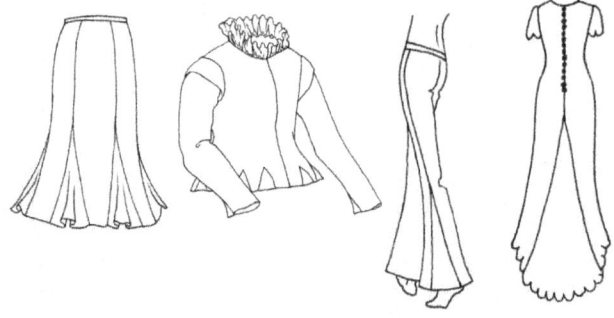

✂ A godet can be sewn into a seam *or* a slit in the fabric.

✂ The size of the godet is dependent upon the fabric and the design. In general, narrower godets suit thick or firm fabrics, whereas wider godets are required for sheer, floppy or drapey fabrics. Slimmer godets suit shorter garments and fuller godets suit longer ones. For example, a knee-length skirt with very full godets would look unbalanced and awkward, but a long sheer evening skirt would need generous wide godets to balance the length.

Make a pattern

1. Decide how tall you want the godet to be and mark the measurement on your garment's pattern. Notch the pattern where the point of the godet will be.

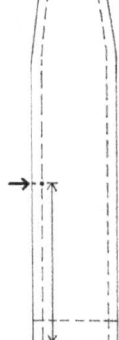

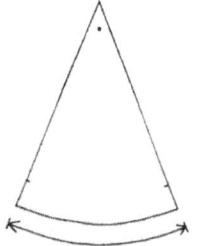

2. Decide on the width of the godet. It can be any size from a slim wedge to a quarter circle, and I suppose you could have a half or even full circle godet, although I've never had call to make a godet bigger than a quarter circle.

No idea what size to start with? Make it at least ⅛ of a circle, then test it by cutting it out in calico or tracing vilene and pinning it in position on the garment. You could even pin the actual pattern to the garment to get an idea.

3. Draw a symmetrical triangle with the left and right sides the same as the measurement on the garment. Draw a dot at the top of the godet where the stitching lines cross. When you cut the godet out of fabric, mark this dot on the wrong side.

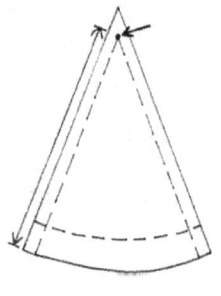

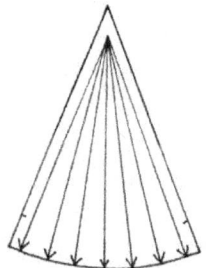

The lower edge of the godet should be the same length from the dot all the way around, making the edge curved.

The seam allowances on the godet need to be the same as the garment's and so does the hem allowance. However, the wider the godet is, the curvier the lower edge will be, requiring a narrower hem that can be easily turned up. Therefore, you might need to change the hem allowance on the garment.

Godets **139**

4. Draw in a vertical grainline. You can find this by folding the godet in half.

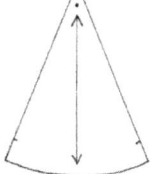

Sometimes godets hang better if they're cut on the bias. Stiff or thick fabrics tend to hang better with a bias godet, and striped or checked godets cut on the bias give an interesting effect. Large godets (for example, a quarter circle godet for a long skirt), might not fit on the fabric width unless they're cut on the bias. To change the pattern, simply draw in a new grain line at 45 degrees to the vertical one.

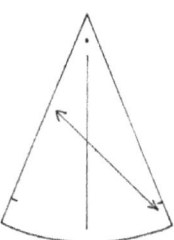

To sew a godet into a seam

1. Sew up the seam leaving a gap where the godet will go. Make sure you backstitch securely at the end. Press the seam open. Don't neaten the edge just yet.

2. With the right sides together, match the dot on the godet *exactly* to the top of the seam—push a pin through the dot on the godet and the end of the backstitching on the previous seam. When you begin sewing, plunge the machine needle in exactly where the pin is, whip the pin away, put the presser foot down and start sewing. Be sure to backstitch securely and accurately at the point. Sewing from the dot, stitch one side of the godet to the garment. Repeat with the other side, once again sewing from the dot to the hem.

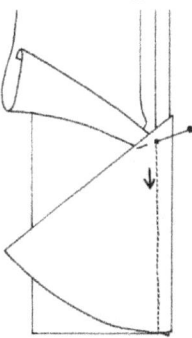

3. Press the godet seams away from the godet so it sits flat. Overlock each side of the godet and the garment's seam.

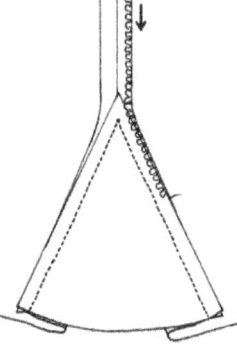

4. If desired, you can topstitch the seam either side of the godet, or stitch around the godet only.

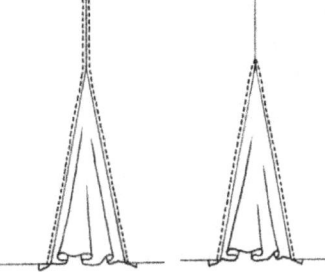

Another way to sew a godet into a seam

A slightly quicker method. The godet sits just off-centre at the top and can look quite interesting and modern. Be sure that each godet is stitched on the same side, so they hang the same way. If you're sewing a knit garment entirely on the overlocker, with only a 6mm (¼") overlocking seam allowance, you can overlock the godet on using this method.
Fast results guaranteed!

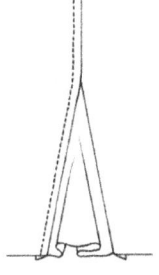

1. Sew one side of the godet to the garment *before* sewing the garment's seam. Don't sew beyond the dot.
If you're sewing by overlocker with 6mm (¼") seams, overlock the entire side of the godet onto the garment.

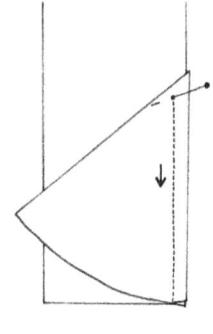

2. Neaten the entire length of the godet and press the seam towards the godet

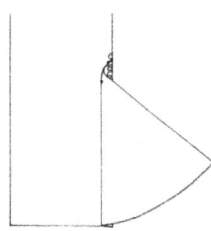

3. Sew the garment's seam and the other side of the godet in one operation, pivoting slightly at the dot. Neaten the seam. This seam can be topstitched for emphasis.

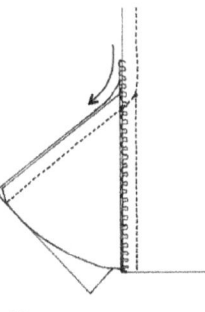

To sew a godet into a slit

A godet inserted into a slit isn't quite as strong as one inserted into a seam because the point is weaker. However, it's an excellent solution if you want fullness with no seams. You might have a fabric with a large, flowing pattern that you want to leave uninterrupted by seams.

1. Make the godet pattern as described on page 138. Give the side seams a 6mm (¼") seam allowance.

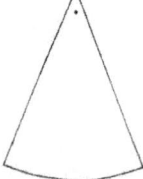

2. On the wrong side of the garment, draw in the slit with a pencil and ruler and mark the top with a dot. Don't cut it yet.

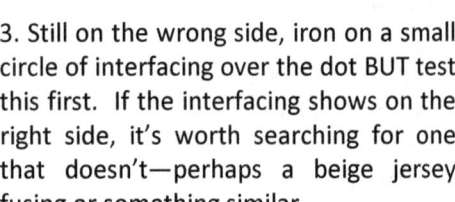

3. Still on the wrong side, iron on a small circle of interfacing over the dot BUT test this first. If the interfacing shows on the right side, it's worth searching for one that doesn't—perhaps a beige jersey fusing or something similar.

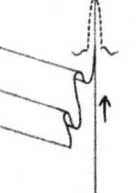

4. Reinforce the top of the slit by staystitching 6mm (¼") away from the slit, pivoting at the dot. I like to use a very small stitch, say 1mm-1.5mm, to make it stronger.

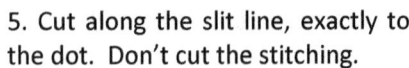

5. Cut along the slit line, exactly to the dot. Don't cut the stitching.

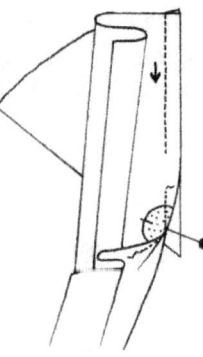

6. Lay one side of the godet and the slit right sides together, with the slit side uppermost. Match the hem edges. Match the dots by pushing a pin exactly through the top of the slit (on the stay stitching) and the godet's dot.
Sew from the hem edge to the dot, stitching exactly *just to one side* (not the raw edge side—the other side) of the stay stitches. Again, change the stitch length to 1mm-1.5mm just at the point, for strength. When you reach the dot, leave the needle plunged in, pivot, re-arrange the top layer (slightly tugging the fabric will help move it around the needle) and sew down the other side of the godet.

Press the seam allowance away from the godet and carefully overlock to neaten.

7. The godet will be stronger and will sit flatter if you topstitch around the edges on the garment side.

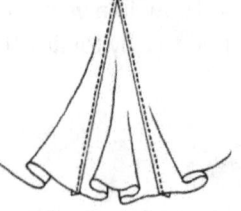

Linings

If the garment has godets, often the lining doesn't—it makes the lining far quicker to sew and less bulky without the seams.

A lining can just have hemmed slits where the godets are. Often this is used when there's just one godet in a seam at the back of a skirt. You can use the garment pattern pieces for the lining, just omit the godet.

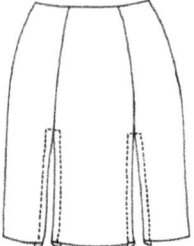

More often, flare is added to the lining. The amount of flare is usually less than the godet but still enough to allow movement for walking.

The flare is added in equal amounts to each side of the seam.
If the godet is inserted into a slit, it's fine for the lining to have a seam with flare added.

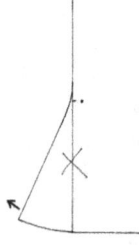

Pleated godets

Godets can be professionally **sunray pleated** before inserting. Lightweight, synthetic fabrics hold pleats the best. The godet should be at least a quarter circle because the pleats narrow the width. Hem the godet before sending it to the pleaters.

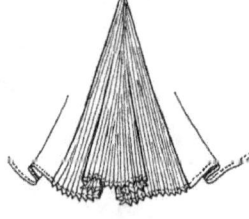

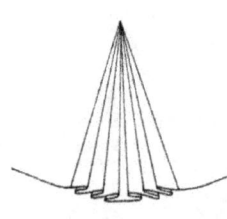

Knife pleats can successfully be incorporated into godets, but they work best on lightweight fabrics because the top of the godet becomes very thick from all the pleated layers on top of each other.

Godets **141**

Make a pattern

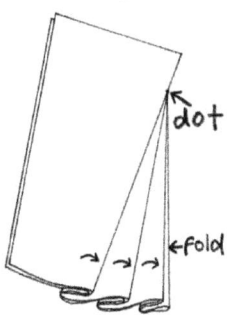

1. Take a piece of paper and fold it in half vertically. The fold will become the centre of the godet. Pleat the paper in the way you'd like the godet pleated, angling the pleats so they all meet at the same point at the top.

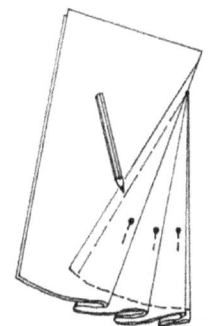

2. Draw the godet shape over the top of the pleated paper, add the seam allowance onto the side and cut it out.
Mark the dot position at the top of each pleat.

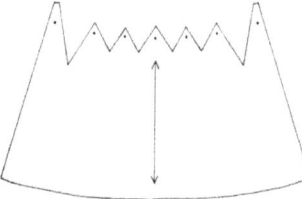

3. Open out the paper—you now have your pattern.

To sew a knife pleated godet

1. Form the pleats in the godet, matching the dot at the top of each pleat. Take great care to get the point of all the pleats perfectly lined up with the point of the godet. Stay-stitch the pleats in position.

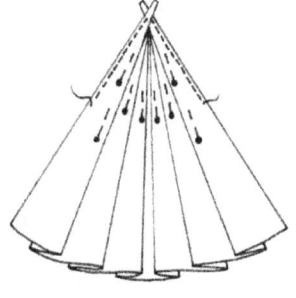

2. Proceed to insert the godet as normal, either into a seam or a slit. You can press the pleats, or leave them unpressed. The back view of the pleated godet should look something like this:

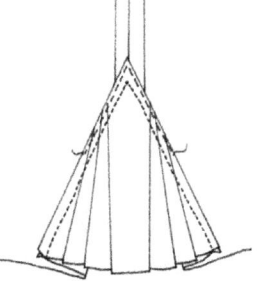

One godet at the centre back

A single godet in the back of a skirt or dress is a glamorous alternative to a vent or split. Sometimes the godet is made a little longer in the centre to dip down at the back.

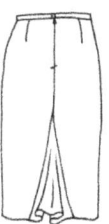

A single godet is ideal at the centre back of a wedding dress to form the train. It allows the train to spread more at the hemline and means there won't be a seam running through the centre of the train. A godet is also perfect for achieving a mermaid skirt silhouette.

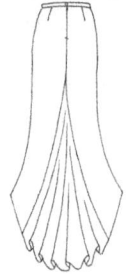

These godets look better if they're inserted into a slightly triangular shaped opening, rather than a straight seam or slit.

You can check if a triangular opening will improve the godet by pinning the godet in this position *before* trimming away the fabric. It can be in a seam (top illustration) *or* a slit (lower illustration). The triangular opening should be narrower than the size of the godet, so the godet still hangs flared. Note that the godet will need to be made slightly longer because the diagonal seam is longer than the vertical seam.

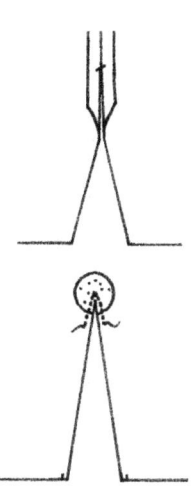

Make a pattern

1. Use a long straight skirt pattern.

2. Add flare on the side seams if you're making a mermaid skirt shape. If you want a straight skirt, I suggest tapering the side seams in by 4cm (1½") at the hem (= 16cm in total around the hem of the skirt).

3. Draw in the triangular opening for the godet, extending it past the end of the skirt to form part of the train. Join this point back up to the side seam.

This skirt has flare on the side seams for a mermaid shape.

4. Make a godet pattern as described on page 138 (I suggest a quarter circle size), but extend the lower edge to make the train. Pin the godet pattern to the skirt pattern at the hem to check for a good flow-through line where the seams meet.

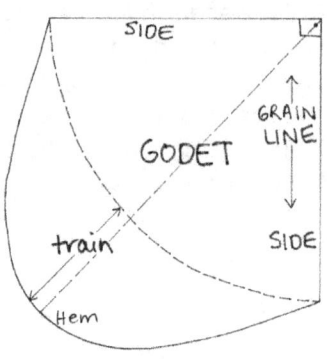

If you aren't having a train, the centre back of the godet will still need to be hemmed a little longer to look right.

Godets with rounded tops

Godets with rounded tops are an interesting "twist on a classic" and are no more difficult to execute than pointy godets. They're sewn in one operation because there's only one seam.

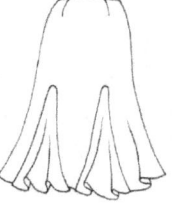

Make a pattern

1. Decide where to insert the godet on the garment and draw in two parallel lines about 2.5cm to 5cm (1"-2") apart. The distance between the lines depends on how tight you want the curve at the top to be. A wider curve will be easier to sew. Draw in the curve at the top, folding the pattern vertically to make the curve symmetrical. Add a 6mm (¼") seam allowance and place a notch at the top of the curve to match to the godet. You can add a few notches (symmetrically) either side, too, to help sew the godet in accurately.

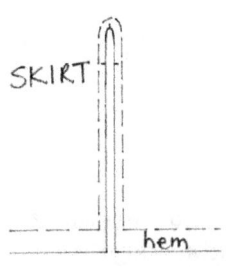

2. Take a tape measure and, holding it on its side, measure the *stitching* line from the top notch to the bottom of the hem. Note down this measurement—you'll need it to draft the godet.

3. For the godet, draw a large quarter circle (actually, it doesn't have to be a quarter circle, it can be a smaller wedge) and round off the top point. Draw in a notch at the top. Determine the length by measuring the side of the godet from the notch down to whatever the measurement was on the skirt. Draw in the curved hemline by measuring down from the original top point of the wedge and marking in the same point all the way along. Join the marks to form a smooth curved line. Add a 6mm (¼") seam allowance and any extra notches to correspond with the skirt. Fold the godet in half vertically to find the grainline. You may choose to cut the godet on the bias, in which case draw in a new bias grainline at 45 degrees to the vertical one.

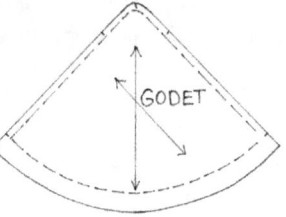

To sew a godet with a rounded top

Stitch the seam with the godet underneath and the skirt on top. Overlock the seam allowances together and press towards the godet. Topstitch if desired.

Godets with square ends

A godet pattern can be simply a square, resulting in a handkerchief hemline.

If you find the hanky hem too long it can be trimmed to suit.

Actually, you can make the lower edge any shape you like, and it can be changed after the garment is finished.

Troubleshooting godets

The godet is longer than the opening

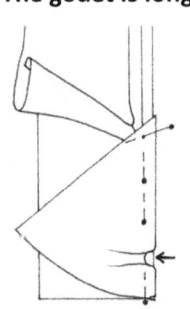

This might be caused by:

✂ An incorrect pattern—do you have a hem allowance on both the garment and the godet? Is the dot in the right place?

✂ The godet stretching or dropping, particularly if it was cut on the bias or in a flimsy unstable fabric.

Possible solutions:

✂ If it's a patternmaking error, correct the pattern and trim or re-cut the godets.

✂ If the godet has stretched or dropped, don't try to ease the godet into the space. Just let it sit where it wants to sit, making sure both sides have the same amount of overhang at the hem.

I recommend pinning both sides of the godet carefully before sewing.

Top of the godet doesn't sit right
This might be caused by:
- Taking an inconsistent or wobbly seam allowance.
- Not lining up the dot at the top exactly.
- Being sloppy with backstitching at the dot.
- The fabric stretching or being over-handled.

Possible solutions:
- Try pressing the top of the godet. If the top is bubbly, you might be able to shrink the fullness in. Otherwise, your only alternative is to unpick that section, press the pieces and re-sew. Pin along the stitching lines to check before re-stitching. The dot may not match its correct position, but pin the top of the godet so it sits flat.

Top of the godet (inserted into a slit) is fraying
This might be caused by:
- Loosely woven fabric.
- Fabric not bonded securely to interfacing.
- Not stitching the top of the godet correctly.
- Repeated launderings or rough handling.

Possible solutions:
- See if you can repair the godet by hand, using a fine needle and one strand of perfectly matching thread. You could apply some fray stopper to the seam allowance to stop future fraying.
- If the area is beyond repair, secure the fabric and experiment with sewing something over the top. For example, a circular ruffle, a bow, a stitched triangle of fabric or machine embroidery. It could turn out to be the creative feature your garment needs!

Handsewing essentials

Choosing a needle and thread 144	method 3 147
How to hold the needle 144	7 Basic hand stitches 147
Do I need a thimble? 144	running stitch 147
Threading a needle 145	backstitch 148
How many strands of thread? 145	blanket and buttonhole stitch 148
Threading four strands easily 145	hidden slip stitch 149
Knotting the end 145	herringbone stitch 149
method1 145	blind hem stitch 149
method 2 146	whipstitch 150
"no knot" knots 146	Sewing on fastenings 150
Twisting and knotty thread 146	press studs 150
Finishing off 147	hook and eye 150
method 1 147	mini or trouser hook and bar .. 152
method 2 147	

It's hard to imagine that pre-1860, all garments were completely sewn by hand. Women devoted a great deal of time to making and repairing the family's clothes, curtains and household linen, all without a sewing machine. Many sewers now will do just about anything to avoid hand sewing—and why not? Machine-made stitches are neater, quicker, stronger and more consistent. However, there are times when you'll need hand sewing, and hand sewing is necessary for all sewers. Practise will bear the fruit of neat, consistent hand stitches with balanced, even tension.

Choosing a needle and thread

Hand sewing needles come in different sizes and types. Needles vary according to:
- The eye shape (long or round)
- The length
- The point (sharp, blunt, ballpoint, wedge)
- Size. The needle size refers to the needle's diameter, or thickness, just like machine needles.

Always use a clean, well-pointed needle and dispose of any blunt or rusty ones. The best criteria for choosing a needle is to use the one that feels the most comfortable in your hand. Try to find a balance between the most comfortable needle and the finest needle possible for your thread and fabric.

Use the same good quality thread you would use for your sewing machine. Gütermann, Mettler, Coats and Rasant are all brands I enjoy using.

How to hold the needle

Try to relax your hand as you hold the needle. Hold the needle close to the eye end, between your thumb and first two fingers. Your fingers will act as pivot, controlling the direction and size of the stitches. If you hold the needle too close to the point, you'll loose movement and control.

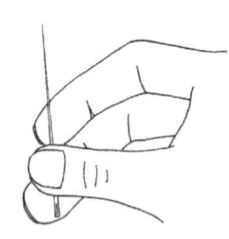

Do I need a thimble?

I never used to wear a thimble—I found them clumsy and annoying. That is, until I met a lady in her 50's who worked in theatre wardrobe. She'd done sewing most of her life, and she, too, had never worn a thimble.

Handsewing essentials 145

She showed me her finger, the top of which had to be removed because it had become poisonous from pushing a needle through fabric all of those years. Eeek! She wears a thimble now, and so do I.

I prefer a plastic or metal thimble, but use whichever thimble feels comfortable and fits your finger best. There are several soft, flexible leather and rubber thimbles available, and if you suffer from sweaty thimble finger try stick-on disposable thimbles.

Threading a needle

Freshly cut the thread using sharp scissors so you have a clean, unfrayed end. Some people also like to moisten the end of the thread in their mouth (I do sometimes). Hold the end of the thread quite close to the end (less than 5mm) between your forefinger and thumb, and, holding the needle in your other hand, accurately drop the eye of the needle on top of it.

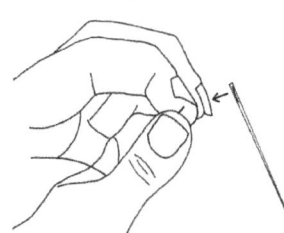

Using large eyed (crewel) needles will help.

If you find needle threading difficult, invest in a needle threader. Simple needle threaders consist of a pointy loop of wire inserted into a holder. Pass the point of the wire through the eye of the needle, then pass the thread through the wire loop. When you pull the needle off the wire loop it should be threaded. The wire might not fit through the eye if you're using small-eyed needles.

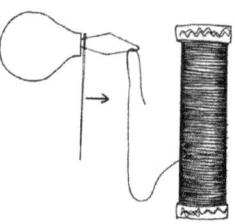

Larger contraptions for needle threading (for example, the Desk needle threader by Clover) are expensive but make needle threading very easy when you have bad eyesight. To use, you insert the needle into the gadget, lay the thread across, hold gently and push the lever down. Pull out a perfectly threaded needle.

How many strands of thread?

Use a single strand when you want your stitches to be as invisible as possible, for example when hemming.

Use a double strand when you want strength, for example stitching a stuffed toy closed.

Use four strands when attaching any kind of fastening, making thread chains or (depending on the thread) sewing buttonholes by hand. It makes the work go faster, although some people still prefer to use two strands.

For **tacking**, I use one strand if the fabric is very fine, otherwise I use two strands.

Threading four strands easily

1. Pull a double strand of thread the desired length off the spool.

2. Thread the needle close to the spool with a folded-over loop of the thread.

3. Pull the loop through the eye until you have four strands the same length.

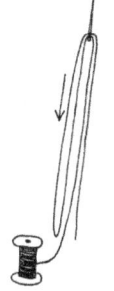

Knotting the end
Method 1

This forms a substantial, slightly messy, knot. I like to use this method and I can make a knot very quickly.

1. Hold the threaded needle in your right hand.

2. Lick the index finger of your left hand.

3. Hold the end of the thread between middle finger and thumb of your left hand.

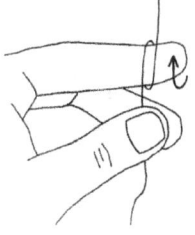

4. Wrap the end of the thread once around your wet index finger.

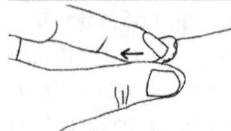
5. Roll the loop off between your index finger and thumb, tightening it into a knot.

Method 2
Sometimes known as a quilter's knot. This yields a very neat, polite knot. It's favoured by quilters who bury their knot into the batting to begin quilting. Try this if you can't get the hang of the first method.

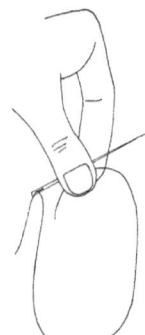
1. Make a large ring of the thread, holding the end and the needle in one hand.

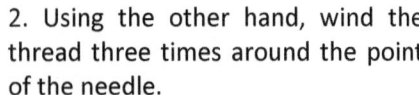
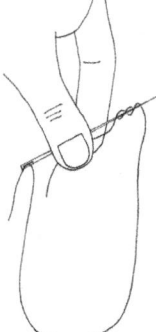
2. Using the other hand, wind the thread three times around the point of the needle.

3. Grasp the thread you've wound around the needle firmly between your thumb and forefinger.

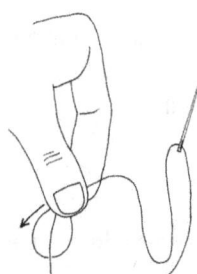
4. Slide it off the needle and down the length of the thread until it reaches the end.

"No-knot" knots
You don't have to use a knot at the beginning of a row of stitching, although I tend to. Instead, you can sew a few short secure backstitches.

Sometimes this is preferable to a knot, for example when the fabric is very fine and the knot would show through to the right side after pressing.

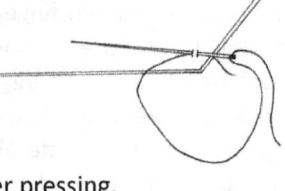

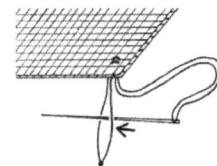
If you're sewing with thick thread or wool, you can omit the knot and stitch through the tail when you begin sewing, to secure the end.

If sewing mesh, net or an open fabric where the knot will pass through, use double thread and pass the needle between the threads to hold the knot.

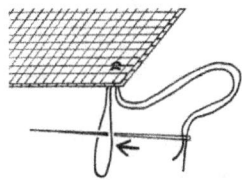

Even better is to thread the needle with the loop at the bottom. Pass the needle through the loop to secure the first stitch. Embroiderers do this for a perfect beginning.

Twisting and knotty thread
The working length is the thread length from needle to knot. Ideally, it should be about 45cm-60cm (18"-24") long, no longer. After making a stitch you should be able to pull the thread through in one motion.

It's better to work with a slightly shorter length of thread than a longer one. Shorter lengths keep twisting and knotting problems to a minimum. Shorter lengths also reduce abrasion on the thread. Every time you make a stitch, the thread abrades slightly, particularly at the eye of the needle, and (obviously) weak thread makes weak stitches.

If the thread twists while you're sewing, let the needle dangle down freely from the work so it untwists itself. Help the thread not twist by running it through your hands a few times before you start sewing.

Some people say that thread twists itself less if the needle is threaded straight from the spool, with the knot closest to the spool end, but I have tested this and it appears to make no difference.

Knots can form in the thread, usually with a small loop coming from them.

Mostly you can remove these by inserting the tip of the needle into the loop and pulling gently on the thread either side of the loop. Try one side first, then the other, holding the loop in tension with the tip of the needle. Hopefully the knot will slide out. If you can't remove the knot, you've no choice but to cut the thread and re-knot the end to continue stitching.

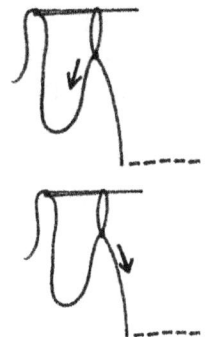

Ways to finish off

Always use scissors to cut the thread. If you bite the thread off with your teeth it causes uneven dental wear and is bad for your teeth. Also, if you are wearing lipstick it will mark the thread or fabric.

Method 1

Make three tiny stitches on top of each other. This is a good idea for fine fabrics where you don't want a knot to show.

Method 2

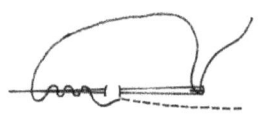

1. Insert the needle into the fabric to make a tiny stitch and wind the thread around the needle three times.

2. Push the wound-around threads down the needle and carefully pull the needle through, completing the stitch and forming a knot.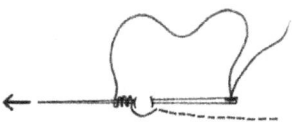

This is my preferred method. If I'm using four strands of thread, I only wind the thread around the needle once or twice, otherwise the knot becomes too big. I then make another (tiny) stitch to bury the thread in the fabric before cutting it.

Method 3

A related method to Method 2 is to take a small stitch and pass the needle through the loop once as you pull the thread through. I think it's a good quick method if you're using four strands.

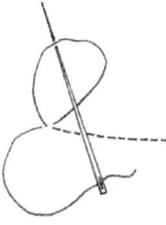

An added refinement is to pass the needle back through its own loop again.

I like to take one tiny stitch before cutting the thread, to bury the end.

7 Basic hand stitches

For smooth, even, good-looking hand stitches, consistency of stitch size and tension are the key factors. Practise taking stitches of consistent size with even spacing, even if it means taking larger stitches. Consistent stitch size will improve the overall appearance of your hand sewing. Regulate how tightly you pull up the thread after making each stitch, to control the tension. If the tension is too loose the stitches won't anchor the fabric, and too tight will appear puckered and homemade looking.

There are plenty of books and resources with hand stitching glossaries, but I consider these to be the Top Seven basic stitches you need to know.

Running stitch

This is THE simplest hand stitch.
It's used for:
- ✂ Visible hemming
- ✂ Quilting, craftwork
- ✂ Decorative stitching
- ✂ Gathering and easing fabric
- ✂ Basting/tacking seams together temporarily

Work from right to left. Insert the needle in and out of the fabric, while maintaining desired spacing and stitch length. The tinier the stitches, the stronger the seam.

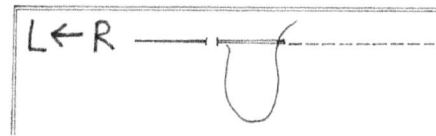

For left handers, the stitch is worked from left to right:

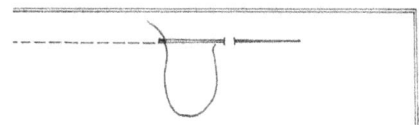

To make a tacking stitch, make the running stitches longer. Finish off the row of tacking stitches by working one backstitch. When you undo the tacking, unpick the one backstitch, grasp the knot at the beginning and pull it out in one motion.

I use hand tacking to tack together velvet or velveteen for a fitting, because machine tacking stitches (a long machine stitch) show when they're unpicked.

Backstitch

If you're going to be sewing seams by hand, backstitch is a much stronger (although slower) choice than running stitch. As with running stitch, the tinier the stitches, the stronger the seam.

It's used for:
- Sewing seams by hand
- Repairing broken machine-stitched seams
- Understitching by hand
- Decorative stitching
- Sewing zips by hand (see page 411)
- Securing the beginning or end of a row of stitching

Work from right to left. Insert the needle a stitch length *behind* where the thread emerges and bring the needle out the same distance in front.

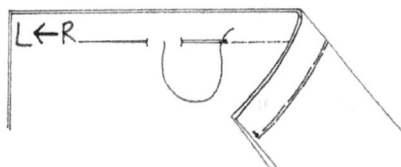

From the top side, the stitches look similar to straight machine stitching. Underneath, the stitches are twice as long and overlapping.

For left handers, the stitch is worked from left to right:

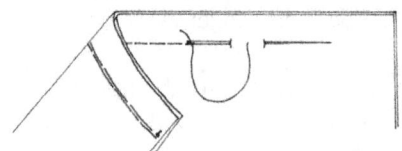

Blanket stitch and buttonhole stitch

Blanket stitch and buttonhole stitch look very similar but are made in a slightly different way. Some people (including me) like to work either of these stitches at a 90 degree angle, so experiment and work in a way that feels comfortable to you.

Blanket stitch is used for:
- Decoration and edging for blankets and garments
- Decorative edging for appliqué
- Thread bars for hooks
- Making thread beltloops
- Swing/French tacks and bar tacks

Blanket stitch is worked from left to right. The edge of the fabric can be folded under or left raw. Have the point of the needle and the edge of the work both pointing towards you. Insert the needle through the fabric from the right side and bring

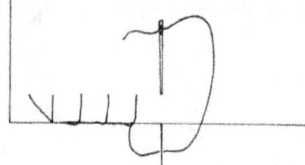

it out at the edge. Keep the thread from the previous stitch *under* the point of the needle as you draw the needle and thread through the fabric. The spacing and size of the stitch can be varied or uniform.

Bar tacks, thread beltloops, swing tacks and so on are made by working blanket stitches over threads.

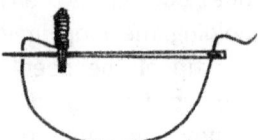

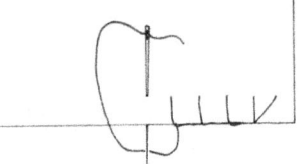

For left handers, blanket stitch is worked from right to left.

Buttonhole stitch is used for:
- Decoration and edging for blankets and garments
- Sewing around the edges of hand-worked eyelets
- Making buttonholes by hand

Buttonhole stitch is worked from right to left. Have the point of the needle towards you and the edge of the fabric away from you. Insert the needle from the *underside*, into the fabric a distance away from the edge. Loop the thread behind the needle, under both the eye and the point of the needle. Pull the needle out through the fabric, then away from you to place the stitch on the fabric's edge. The stitch size and spacing can be large or small.

When making buttonholes or eyelets by hand, the stitches are 3mm (⅛") deep with no space between them.

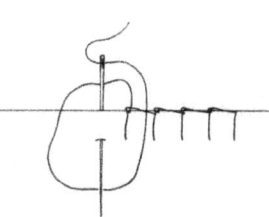

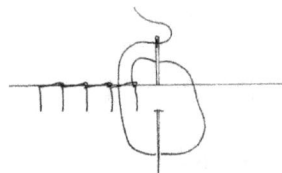

For left handers, the stitch is worked from left to right.

What's the difference between buttonhole and blanket stitch?

In buttonhole stitch, the needle and thread form a loop with a single twist which pulls up to form a purl at the end of the stitch. In blanket stitch the needle and thread come through an untwisted loop, with one stitch slipping into the next although no actual purl is formed at the end of the stitch.

Buttonhole stitches form a heavier edge with more firmly locked threads that have less tendency to slip.

Hidden slip stitch

If you only learn one hand stitch, make this the one. It's very useful and I use it often. It's an almost invisible stitch formed by slipping the needle through a fold of fabric. The threads lie in the fold. When it joins *two* folded edges, it's known as ladder stitch, invisible stitch and (for knitting) mattress stitch. It's a good choice for practising your stitch consistency, since the stitches can't be seen.

It's used for:

✂ Joining a folded edge to a flat surface
✂ Joining two folded edges (ladder stitch)
✂ Invisibly closing openings (ladder stitch)
✂ Applying trim, sewing down binding, mending, appliqué, sewing on patches

Sew from right to left. To sew a folded edge to a flat surface (as you would for a hem), take a tiny stitch in the garment, just one or two threads, then slip the needle through the folded edge of the hem.

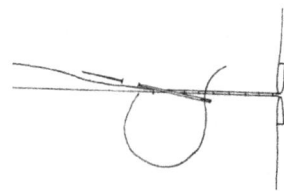

To sew two folded edges together, alternately slip the needle inside the fold of one side and then the other.

For left handers, the stitch is worked from left to right:

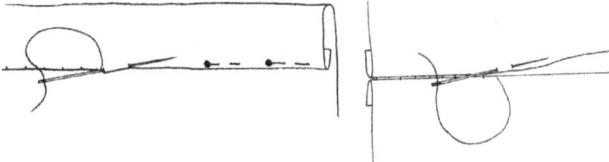

Herringbone stitch

Herringbone stitch is my favourite stitch. It's good for hemming knits, because the stitch has a bit of stretch in it. It's also good for fabrics that tend to curl and/or fray. Because the thread crosses over itself, the raw edge is covered and lies flat.

It's used for:

✂ Hemming
✂ Holding down facings and other seamed edges

Herringbone stitch is one of the few stitches worked from left to right. Take small stitches alternately in the hem and garment. Make the stitch on the *garment* side very small, just one thread if you can.

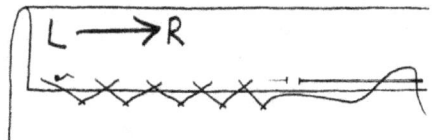

The thread lies on top of the hem edge, neatly encasing the raw edge. Although this seems to expose the thread to potential abrasion, it's actually quite a strong stitch.

For left handers, herringbone stitch is worked from right to left:

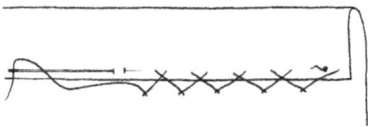

When sewing trouser hems, I prefer herringbone stitch to blind hem stitch (see below) because there's less chance of catching your toes in the hem when you get dressed.

I use herringbone stitch for hemming light fabrics, but when I sew heavy fabrics I use blind hem stitch because the herringbone stitches tend to press the hem edge into the garment causing a ridge to form on the outside. Blind hem stitches sit in between the hem and garment. However, you can also sew herringbone stitch *between* the hem and the garment (it's known as blind herringbone stitch). Work from left to right as before.

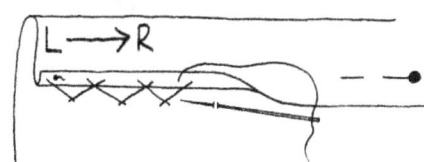

Blind hem stitch

Also called catch stitch. Blind hem stitch lies hidden between the hem and the outer layer of fabric. The advantage over herringbone stitch is that the raw edge of the fabric isn't pressed into the garment by the stitches. Consistent spacing, tiny stitches on the outer fabric and matching thread all help ensure an invisible finish on the right side.

It's used for:

✂ Invisible hemming

Work from right to left. Fold back the hem edge about 6mm (⅛") and take alternate stitches between the hem and the garment.

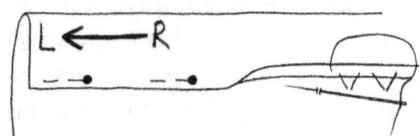

Make the *garment* stitches very small, just one thread. The tension should be loose. The stitches can be small or quite large depending on where you're using the stitch. I use large blind hem stitches to loosely secure the hem inside a lined jacket.

For left handers, the stitch is worked from left to right:

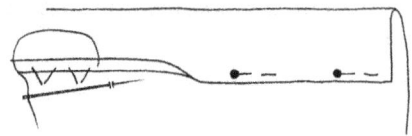

Whipstitch

This stitch results in visible stitches, requiring neatness and consistency.

It's used for:

✂ Closing openings

✂ Overcasting edges to prevent fraying (referred to as overhand or overcast stitch in this situation)—see page 287

Sew from right to left. Insert the needle at a right angle and close to the edge, picking up a few threads on each side. The thread tension is important—if you pull it too much you'll get a hard ridge. Slanted floats will be produced between the tiny stitches. The stitch spacing can be wide or narrow.

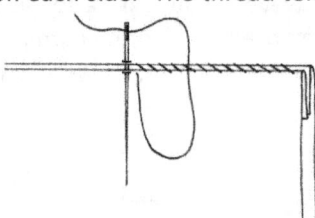

For left handers, whip stitch is worked from left to right: I'm right handed but often I prefer to whipstitch from left to right like this.

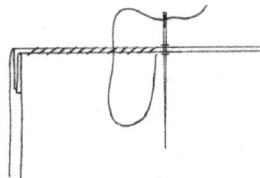

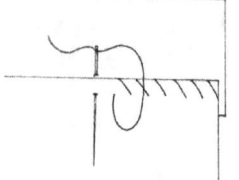

Whipstitch can also be used to hold a raw edge neatly against a flat surface, for example for appliqué.

Sewing on fastenings

I was initiated into (speedily) sewing on fastenings during a stint at the hand-finishing table of a large fashion workroom. Four strands of thread were always used. Each stitch had to be robust and neatly made on the back and front.

When sewing on fastenings, check after each stitch to make sure it's neat and correct on both sides before making the next one.

Press studs

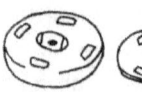

Press studs consist of two halves—a ball and a socket—which snap into each other. The halves are sometimes referred to as male and female. You can use press studs behind buttons when you're unable to make a buttonhole. They're also used to make lingerie strap holders. Press studs have less holding power than buttons and buttonholes or hooks, but large sizes (20mm+) can be pretty sturdy.

Sizes range from 4mm to 20mm and bigger and they come in silver or black metal, clear nylon or coloured plastic.

The ball side of the press stud is sewn on uppermost, and the socket side goes underneath.

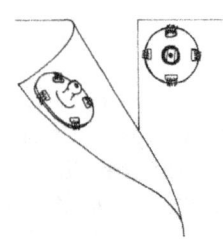

Both sides have a hole in the centre, allowing you to push a pin through to hold it in place while you stitch.

Use four strands of thread (see page 145) to sew press studs on, for speed. Conceal the knot under the press stud, and sew up through each hole several times. The stitches on the ball side (uppermost) must not show on the right side of the garment. To move from one hole to the next, take the needle between the fabric layers. Make sure each stitch is neat on both sides before progressing to the next one.

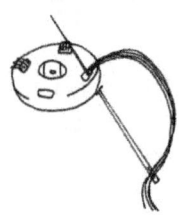

Hook and eye

Hooks are a surprisingly strong fastening. Often a hook and eye is used at the top of a zip; by doing up the hook first the zip is supported as it's zipped up. Hooks come with a matching metal eye, or you can make one of thread. A thread eye isn't as strong as a metal one, but it's almost invisible.

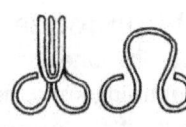

The hook goes on the uppermost layer and the eye is sewn on the underneath layer.

Thread eyes can be used where there's an overlap in the garment opening.

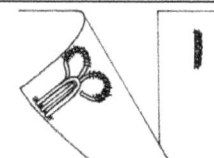

Metal eyes can be used when the edges of the opening butt against each other, and are sewn on inside, so no-one sees the two loops of wire.

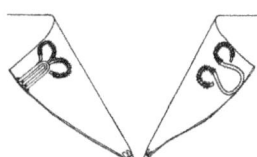

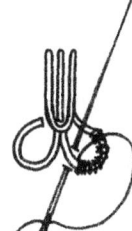

The hook gets sewn on first. Use four strands of thread (see page 145). Conceal the knot under the hook to begin. Sew stitches through each wire hole, fanning out the stitches to cover the wire all the way around.

After completing both holes, pass the needle through the fabric to the end of the hook. Make several stitches to hold the end of the hook flat against the garment, then finish off.

The metal eye is easier to sew on. Simply sew through the two holes, fanning out the stitches to cover the wire in the same way as the hook.

Thread eyes can be made in one of two ways. Use four strands of thread for both methods (see page 145). The thread chain method was used at the fashion workrooms when I worked at the hand-finishing table. It's a little faster, I think, but I've seen both methods used at various workrooms and factories.

Either of these two thread eye methods *could* also be used for making thread button loops and thread belt carriers, however I prefer the blanket stitch method for these two things, because it's stronger. I only use the thread chain for hook eyes.

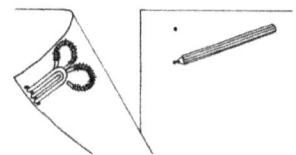

Sew the hook on first, then determine the size and placement of the bar. Mark with a pin or a pencil dot.

Thread chain eye
(Illustrated with one thread for clarity).

1. Bring the needle up through one end of the eye position. Make a tiny stitch, but don't pull the thread all the way through, just leave a loop.

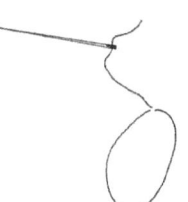

2. Pull a loop of the thread through the loop made by the stitch, and pull so that the first loop closes up and forms a knot at the base.

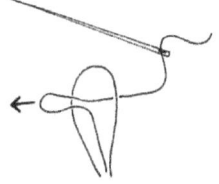 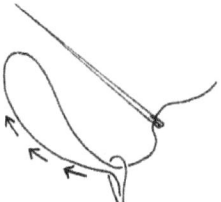

3. Repeat until you have a chain the length required for the thread eye. About four or five repeats should do it.

4. To finish the thread chain, pass the needle through the loop and pull until the loop disappears.

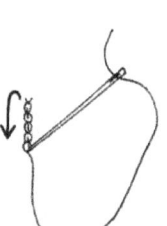

5. Lay the thread chain onto the fabric in position. Plunge the point of the needle down through the centre of the last knot in the chain, through the fabric to the wrong side. Secure the thread on the wrong side.

Blanket stitch eye
(Illustrated with one thread for clarity)

1. Insert the needle into the fabric the length of the intended eye. Make two or three stitches on top of each other in the same way, forming a bar.

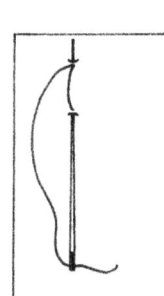

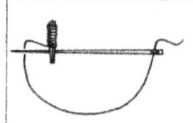

2. Cover the length of the bar with closely spaced blanket stitches, being very careful not to catch the fabric. Finish off on the wrong side.

Mini hook and bar/Trouser hook and bar

Mini hooks and bars are strong and flat, bigger than 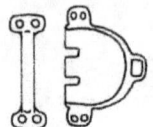 wire hooks and eyes, and designed so the hook "clicks" into the bar so it can't easily come undone. They're used to do up waistbands instead of a button and buttonhole.

Trouser hook and bars are more elongated but are sewn on in the same way. They're not quite as flat. They're used for men's trousers.

Trouser and mini hook and bars are sewn on in the same way.

The hook goes on the uppermost layer and the bar is sewn on the underneath layer. I like to sew on the hook first.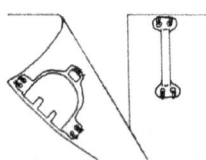

1. Use four strands of thread (see page 145). Position 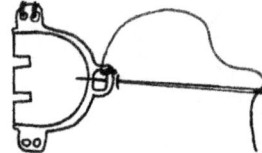 the hook fairly close to the edge. Conceal the knot underneath the hook. Sew through each hole several times.

To move to each set of holes, pass the needle between the layers of fabric. Finish off on the wrong side.

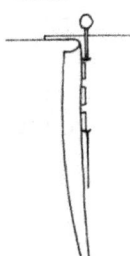 2. Determine the position of the bar after the hook has been sewn on. Lap the edges of the garment over each other and lay the hook on top of where the bar will be sewn. Insert a pin into the fabric the width of the hook.

Slip the edges of the bar underneath the pin, which will hold it in the right place for you to sew it on. Note on which side of the pin to put the bar—it's the side closest to the hook.

 3. Sew the bar on in the same way as the hook, sewing through each hole several times. Pass the needle between the layers of fabric to move to each set of holes.

Hems

Introduction 153	rolled hem by hand 158
What makes a good hem? 153	Other hems 159
Hem allowance 154	blind hem by machine 159
how much hem allowance? 154	twin needle hem 159
Determining the hemline 154	deep hem on a curved edge ... 159
tops and jackets 154	fancy machine edges 160
skirts 154	hemming pleats 160
trousers 155	fast hems 160
Truing the side seams 155	hems in jackets 160
Sewing a hem 155	hemming leather 160
Single folded hem 155	hemming fur 160
by machine 156	shortening jeans 160
by hand 156	rock 'n' roll t-shirt hem 160
Double folded hem 157	chain weighted hem 160
by machine 157	Trouser cuffs 161
by hand 157	separate cuffs 161
Narrow hems 157	separate cuffs on thick fabric . 162
rolled hem by machine 157	Trouser hems for wheelchair users 162
using a rolled hem foot 158	False hem 162
rolled hem by overlocker 158	using lace or bias binding 163

A hem is a finish for the bottom edge of a garment. With a few exceptions, it's the last thing sewn on a garment.

✂ A hem can be sewn by hand or by machine. As always, use a good quality sewing thread. For sewing hems by hand, use a single strand so the hem will be as invisible as possible.

✂ You may like to trim the seam allowance in the hem area to eliminate bulk before hemming, although I rarely do (I might on very thick fabrics). It isn't usually done in clothing factories.

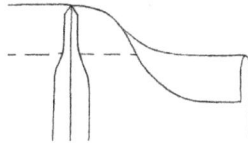

✂ When pressing up a hem, don't press over the top edge—press only the fold. Otherwise a ridge will show through on the right side, very noticeably on thick fabrics.

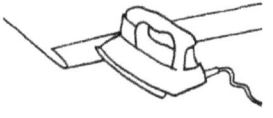

✂ Is the fabric too difficult to hem attractively? Substitute bands, ribbing, braid or binding.

✂ A **blind hem** has no visible stitching on the right side. A blind hemming machine is used in factories and while it's possible to sew a blind hem on your machine at home, the best way is to do it by hand.

What makes a good hem?

✂ It should hang evenly each side, back and front.

✂ The hem should not be conspicuous unless it's intended to be decorative.

✂ Any visible stitching should be straight and a consistent distance from the fold.

✂ The amount of hem allowance should be suitable for the fabric and type of garment.

✂ Once turned up, the hem allowance should lie smoothly inside the garment, with no lumps or gathers.

✂ The fold should be crisp and definite.

✂ The hem stitching should be as close as possible to the *cut* edge so the edge is held fast and doesn't fold back on itself.

Hem allowance

The hem allowance is how much gets turned up. The amount depends on the fabric, the garment and the style.

How much hem allowance?

Generally, the thicker the fabric, the deeper the hem needs to be. A deep hem may be a design feature of the garment, regardless of the fabric thickness. A deep hem on a straight garment (for example, a skirt, caftan or wide trousers) will add weight and body. Cheaper clothes tend to have less hem allowance, but a small hem allowance doesn't necessarily indicate a cheap garment. Here are my own preferences:

Garment	Hem allowance	Type of hem
Trousers and ¾ length trousers A-line skirts Straight skirts	4cm (1½"). If the hem is very curved it will need to be smaller, for example 2.5cm (1")	Single folded hem. Sew by hand for wool and suitings; by hand or machine for everything else.
Jeans	2cm (¾")	Double folded hem by machine
Shirts	1cm-3cm (⅜"-1¼"), but often 1.5cm (⅝")	Single or double fold by machine
Jackets	4cm (1½")	Single fold
Coats	At least 4cm (1½"). I like 5cm (2") for the body and 4cm (1½") for the sleeves, but you could allow up to 7cm (2¾") for the body.	Single fold
School trousers, dresses and skirts Children's clothes	Deep hems to allow for growth. Up to 10cm-12cm (4"-5") sometimes.	Single or double fold

Determining the hemline

The first step in hemming is to determine the length and mark the hemline if you don't already know it.

If you already know where to fold up the hem, you may consider pressing up the hem allowance right at the start, before sewing the pieces together. Mark the fold line of the hem allowance with tiny 3mm (⅛") snips at each end. Use the snips to accurately fold up the hem without measuring and as a reminder as to how much hem has been allowed. The snips should still be visible after overlocking providing you don't trim anything off.

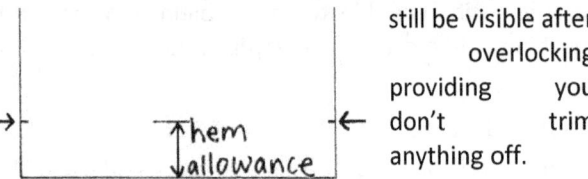

Tops and jackets

Check the pattern and see how much hem allowance it has. Turn up the specified amount and try the top on. If possible, try the top on with the skirt or trousers you'll wear with it, to get an overall look at the proportion. For tops being worn untucked with jackets, ensure the top is not longer than the jacket. Adjust the length if necessary. Take off the top or jacket and note the amount of hem allowance. If you had to make the garment considerably shorter, trim off any excess now and level up the hem allowance all the way around. If you had to make the garment longer and you now don't have enough to turn up a hem with, see the section on False hems (page 162).

Skirts

If the skirt is flared, circular or cut on the bias, the hem will need to be levelled. Hang the skirt for at least a few days to let the fabric drop. You can also hang individual skirt panels before they're sewn together.

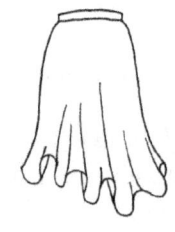

Try the skirt on with the shoes you'll wear. If possible, try it on with the top you'll wear too to get an overall look at the proportion. Stand straight while a friend moves around you measuring up from the floor. (Or you could stand on a table to make it easier for your friend). Use a long ruler, L-square or special skirt hem marker.

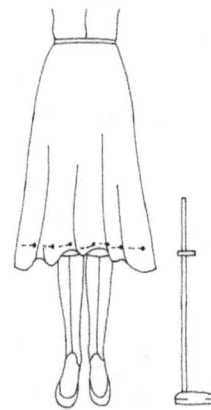

If you're alone, you could use a chalk puffer skirt marker, if you have one. Another idea is to dip a length of string into powdered chalk, tape it across a doorway at the correct height, then wear the skirt and let the chalked string brush against it as you slowly rotate.

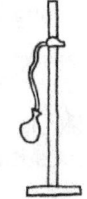

Hems

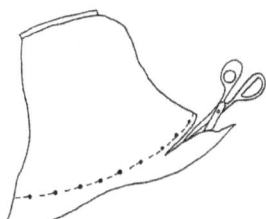

Take the skirt off and lay it flat on the table. Note how much hem allowance you need and trim off any excess, making a smooth flowing line as you cut.

Note that **straight skirts** should not need levelling. If the back hem is higher than the front or vice versa, you should adjust this from the waist (see page 3). (Great! *Now* she tells me after I've finished the skirt.)

Trousers

Try on the trousers with the shoes and belt you plan to wear with them. The length you decide on will depend on the width of the trouser leg and the type of shoe. The longer the trouser leg, the longer your legs will look. Note that summer trousers worn with open shoes can be made slightly shorter and look fine.

Narrow trouser legs need to be shorter so they sit over your shoe. They can be slightly longer if you plan to wear high heels.

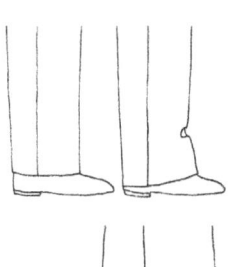

Straight leg trousers can touch to top of your shoe in front (left picture). However, your legs will appear longer if the trousers cover the back of your heel and break over the front of your shoe (right picture).

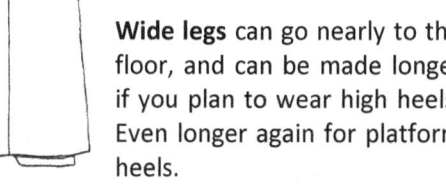

Wide legs can go nearly to the floor, and can be made longer if you plan to wear high heels. Even longer again for platform heels.

Pin up an approximate amount of hem allowance on both legs and check the length in the mirror, standing up straight. Adjust the length until you're happy with it. Remove the trousers and measure the amount you took up. If it varies, find an average and try the pants on again to check. Note how much hem allowance you need and trim off any excess. If you don't have enough to turn up a hem, see False hems (page 162).

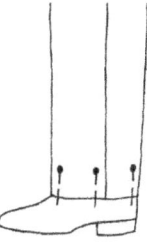

Truing the side seams

If the garment side seams are flared or tapered you'll need to true the side seams of the hem, so the hem folds up perfectly inside. This applies to *any* hem on any garment. If the sides 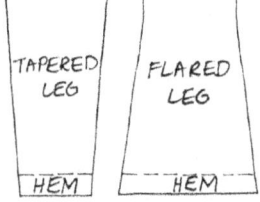 are straight you won't need to worry about it. You can do this on the paper pattern pieces if you already know the length, or on the actual fabric pieces if need be.

1. Fold up the hem allowance and trim the sides (for a flare) or add onto the sides (for a taper). If you're unable to add on (because you don't have fabric there), note where the *stitching line* will be for the seams.

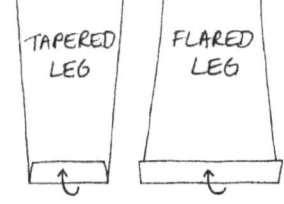

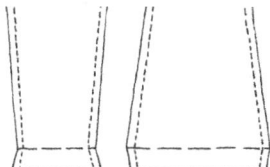

2. When you sew the side seams, pivot the stitching at the jog you've created at the hem fold line.

Now when you turn up the hem it will fit the garment.

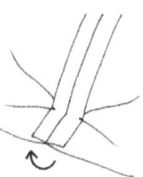

Sewing a hem

If the hem has been pinned up at a fitting, remove the pins and place them *on* the fold line so the hem is unfolded and the garment is flat. Adjust the pins to create a smooth pleasing line. Check the distance with a tape measure if needed. Decide on the amount of hem allowance and trim off any excess.

Single folded hem

This is an easy, useful hem for all sorts of garments. The raw edge is neatened and the fabric is turned up once and stitched by hand or machine. It's very suitable for thick fabrics. Consider a double folded hem (see below) for very fine or sheer fabrics.

1. Neaten the raw edge in some way.

Some possibilities are:
- ✂ Overlock the raw edge (highly recommended).
- ✂ Do nothing if the fabric doesn't fray.
- ✂ Zig zag using a long wide zig zag stitch.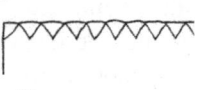
- ✂ Cut the edge using pinking shears.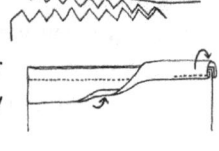
- ✂ Bind the edge with fine net or lining fabric—suitable for very heavy fabrics.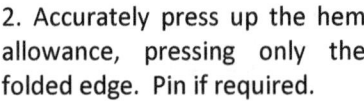
- ✂ Use seam binding, bias binding or lace to cover the raw edge. Stitch it flat on top of the raw edge.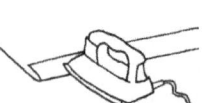

2. Accurately press up the hem allowance, pressing only the folded edge. Pin if required.

To sew a single folded hem by machine

Begin sewing the hem at a side seam or back seam. The stitching needs to be an even distance from the *bottom of the garment*. Therefore, use the seam guide on your machine to line up the *folded edge* as you sew, rather than using the overlocked or cut edge as a guide. If there's no seam guide, stick a piece of tape on. You may find it easier to sew with the hem underneath (I do).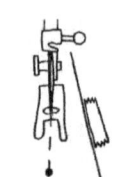
Aim to have your row of machine stitching finish in the centre of the overlocking or very close to the cut edge, otherwise the edge will flip back on itself when the garment is washed.
Optional: make a feature of the hem by sewing two parallel rows of stitching. I like to do this for casual trousers.

To sew a single folded hem by hand

This is referred to as a blind hem, because the stitching doesn't show on the right side. Use it for heavy fabrics, wool or anything where you don't want the stitching to show. You can use it on lightweight fabrics, too.
Sew the hem using a single thread and a fine needle. I find it comfortable to sew the hem with the fold of the hem at the top, that is, upside down to how the garment is worn.

There are several choices of stitch:
Herringbone Stitch is my very favourite hemming stitch—I use this one the most. It's great for fabrics that tend to curl, because the stitching holds the edge flat. Because the thread crosses over itself, it helps stop the edge from fraying—you may not need to neaten the raw edge at all. Herringbone stitch has a bit of stretch in it, so it can be used for hemming knits. I like to use herringbone stitch for trouser hems because there's less chance of catching your toes on the hem when you get dressed.
Use it on light to medium weight fabrics.
Work from left to right:

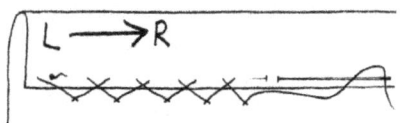

Take small stitches alternately in the hem and garment. Make the stitches in the garment side very small, just one or two threads.

Some people prefer **blind hem stitch (also called catch stitch)** because it's said that herringbone stitch wears out quickly because the surface of the stitches is subject to abrasion, although personally I haven't found any evidence of this.
Blind stitch can be used for any blind hem. It has an advantage it has over herringbone stitch: the stitches actually sit between the two layers. This stops the edge of the hem pressing into the garment and leaving a visible ridge on the right side.
Work from right to left:

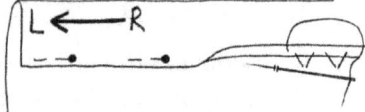

Lift back the hem edge about 6mm (¼") and take alternate stitches between the hem and the garment. Make the stitches in the garment side very small, just one or two threads.

You can also mix the two and sew **blind herringbone stitch**. It's simply herringbone stitch sewn between the hem and the garment. It's good for very heavy fabric as it tend to be stronger than blind hem stitch.
Work from left to right:

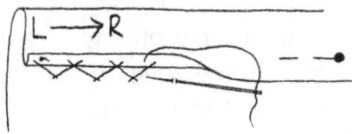

Hems **157**

If you've use bias binding to cover the raw edge, you can sew the hem using **hidden slip stitch**, as described further along on this page.

Double folded hem

A double folded hem is folded up twice to conceal the raw edge. It's considered a higher quality hem than one which is simply overlocked and turned up, *provided* it doesn't create bulk. Double folded hems are used for light weight and sheer fabrics, shirts, summer dresses and nighties. I always use a double folded hem for linings.

Press under the raw edge 6mm (¼") with an iron. Accurately press up the hem allowance minus the 6mm and pin if required.

To sew a double folded hem by machine

Begin sewing at a side or back seam. Have the hem side facing up. Note that the stitching needs to be an even distance from the *bottom of the garment*, **not** the edge of the 6mm (¼") turn-up (so you need to be accurate with your hem folding up). Line up the bottom fold with a seam guide on your machine, rather than stitching next to the 6mm fold. Your row of machine stitching should finish right next to the 6mm folded edge, otherwise the edge will flip back and/or the 6mm will come unfolded when the garment is washed.

With experience and a calibrated eye, you can sew these hems without measuring them—just folding as you sew (although it always helps to press under the 6mm first). You can also measure as you sew using the end of a tape measure or sewing gauge.

✂ If you're sewing **jeans**, allow a 2cm (¾") hem allowance. Turn up 1cm (⅜"), then another 1cm, then stitch.

To sew a double folded hem by hand

You can sew a double folded hem by hand using **hidden slip stitch**. This is a very useful stitch to know, and I find I use it often. As well as sewing a double folded hem by hand, it can be used to sew any folded edge where you don't want the stitches to show. The great thing about hidden slip stitch is that it's almost invisible because the thread lies within the fold of the hem.

Work from right to left. Take a *tiny* stitch in the garment, just one or two threads, then slip the needle through the folded edge of the hem.

Narrow hems

A rolled hem is a very fine double folded hem. The usual hem allowance is 6mm (¼") or less, depending on the method used to make the hem. There are several ways of making them depending on your equipment and skill. Rolled hems are used for fine and sheer fabrics, on lingerie, handkerchief and scarf edges, and ruffles and frills.

✂ Rolled hems fold best on a cut edge, not a torn edge. If you need to tear the edge to make it straight, trim off the ragged edge first. Likewise, trim the edge if the cut edge has frayed so you have a cleanly cut raw edge to hem.

✂ Practise the hem on a scrap to find out how your fabric handles a rolled hem. Crisp fabrics such as organza or fine cotton are easier to hem than soft slippery fabrics.

✂ If your garment is a knit fabric or cut on the bias, by stretching the 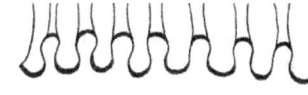 bias edging as you sew you can create a frilly lettuce leaf edge. The tighter you stretch the edge, the frillier it will be BUT don't do this on knits that ladder—if the knit *does* ladder, cut it so the ladders run from top to bottom.

✂ If you're hemming frills to be applied to a garment, it's up to you whether to hem first then apply the frill, or to apply the frill first then hem it.

✂ After sewing the hem, **press** carefully. Use a steam iron to shrink in any stretching that has occurred, or to stretch out a frilly lettuce leaf hem.

To sew a rolled hem by machine

You'll need a 6mm (¼") hem allowance. You may find your first attempts are a little clumsy and thick, but practise, practise, practise will yield slender, 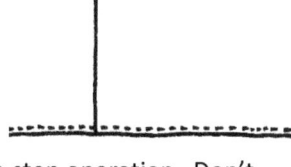 fine hems. This hem is a two-step operation. Don't be tempted to sew the hem in one operation to save time—the best results are achieved by sewing two rows of stitching.

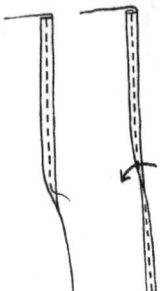

With the wrong side of the garment facing up, take a 3mm (⅛") hem, stitching down the centre. Turn the edge over with your fingertips as you sew, holding the fabric taut if necessary.
Repeat the process, taking another 3mm (⅛") hem to make a double roll.

Another method

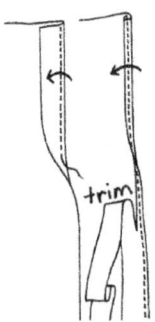

You'll need a wider hem allowance of 1.2cm (½"). Make the first hem 1cm (⅜") and stitch close to the fold. Trim back close to the stitching before sewing the second row. This makes the first row easier to sew, but you may not enjoy the trimming—duckbilled or appliqué scissors might help.

Using a rolled hem foot

Superb fine hems can be achieved using a rolled hem foot on your regular sewing machine. A hemmer rolls under 6mm (¼") of raw edge, making a 3mm (⅛") hem. The rolled hemmer won't go over side seams easily, so you'll need to make your hems before sewing the seams.

1. Form the rolled hem by hand for the first couple of centimetres, and place it under the rolled hem foot as if it were a normal foot. Position it so the needle will land where you want it (it shouldn't be necessary to adjust the needle position).

2. Sew normally for a few centimetres, then stop with the needle down and raise the foot. Wind the raw edge of the fabric into the spiral of the foot, using long tweezers if this helps.

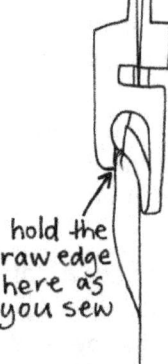

hold the raw edge here as you sew

3. Lower the foot and continue sewing, letting the foot roll the hem. Feed the fabric through holding the raw edge in the same spot.

To sew a rolled hem on an overlocker

An overlocked rolled hem gives a different looking hem than the other methods—it's more of a rolled edging.

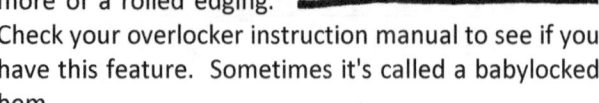

Check your overlocker instruction manual to see if you have this feature. Sometimes it's called a babylocked hem.

✂ Overlocker rolled hems typically take a 3mm (⅛") hem allowance.

✂ You could use a contrast or varigated thread.

✂ An overlocker rolled hem has the advantage of being suitable for knits and lycra as well as woven fabrics.

✂ If you use this type of hem frequently and you have a spare overlocker (or spare $$), you may consider setting up a dedicated rolled hem machine rather than constantly changing the settings on your regular overlocker.

To sew a rolled hem by hand

This requires some practise and I recommend making a sample before attempting to hem the garment, to get a feel for how your particular fabric handles.
Before you begin, sew a line of machine stitching as close as you can to the raw edge.

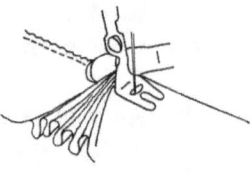

If the fabric is likely to stretch as you machine stitch, for example if the edge is on the bias, hold your middle finger firmly behind the presser foot as you stitch. When the fabric has bunched up, 10cm (4") or so along, take your finger away and release the built up fabric, then put your finger back.
Trim off leaving 1mm-2mm of fabric next to the stitching BUT do this in sections as you handsew the hem, not all at once now. This will give you a clean freshly cut raw edge to roll under.
Work from right to left. Use a single strand of thread and a fine needle. With your left hand roll the edge finely between your thumb and forefinger. Prepare several centimetres at a time in this way and then hem finely using hidden slip stitch, taking only a single thread of the garment before sliding the needle through the rolled edge. Don't attempt to pin it and don't baste.

Hems **159**

You can use the point of the needle to slip under the turning just ahead of the hemming to push under the edge and roll the hem. After hemming several centimetres, pin the hemmed part to your lap or something solid on the table so that the edge can be kept taut to keep the hem narrow. I like to sit with my feet hooked into a chair and my knees up, and pin the work to the knees of my trousers to keep it tight.

Other hems
Blind hem by machine
It's possible to sew a blind hem by machine, if your machine can make the stitch shown. Study the picture closely to make sure you've folded the fabric correctly. If you're sewing a curved edge, it's easier to fold and pin the entire hem first, to match up the differing curves.

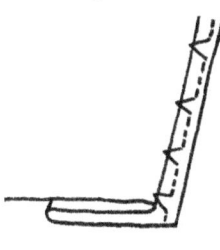

For a single folded hem you'll need to neaten the raw edge.

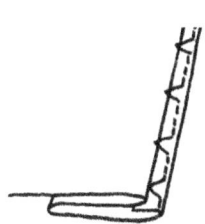

For a double folded hem, press under the raw edge 6mm (¼") first.

✂ It's possible to buy a blind hem foot for your machine and some machines come with them. They require a little trial and error to set up but make sewing the hem soooo much easier. I worked for a dressmaker who had a dedicated machine for blind hemming; it was a domestic machine set up permanently with a blind hem foot.

✂ Check your overlocker's manual—by changing the presser foot, your overlocker threaded with three threads can sew blind hems in the same way.

Twin needle hem
I love my twin needle! A twin needled hem is a great solution for hemming knits. It has give and stretch, is easy to do and looks smart. The finished hem has two parallel rows of straight stitching on the right side, and underneath is zig zag.

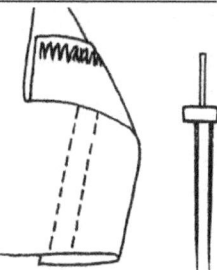

A twin needle can be used for woven fabrics too, but I tend to just make two rows of regular stitching.

Twin needles come in different sizes (for sewing light, medium or heavy weight fabrics), stretch or universal (for sewing knits or woven fabrics respectively) and the needles come different distances apart (2mm, 3mm and 4mm being the most common). Some older machines have provision for inserting two regular needles side-by-side in the shaft, instead of a twin needle. You can also buy triple needles.

1. Install the twin needle in your machine. Make sure it's a stretch twin needle if you're sewing knits.

2. Thread the machine with two spools of thread on the top. If you don't have two spools the same, wind an extra bobbin and use that instead. Hold the two strands together as you thread the machine in the normal way. Thread the twin needles separately. Thread the bobbin as usual.

3. Do a test sew first to check the tension. If the two parallel rows of stitching form a ridge between them, experiment tightening the top tension to give a flat row of stitching.

4. Sew the hem with the hem side underneath. Match the folded edge to a seam guide on your machine so the stitching is an even distance from the edge.

Deep hem on a curved edge
Sometimes it's necessary to make a deep hem on a curved edge, for example, a flared skirt. The problem is that the raw edge is fuller than where it is to be stitched.

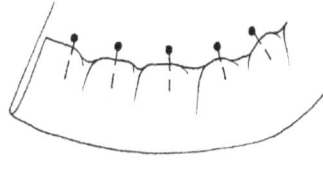

If the fabric is a wool or wool blend, you might be able to shrink in the fullness with a steam iron. It will help to run a line of hand stitches along the raw edge to help ease in the fullness.

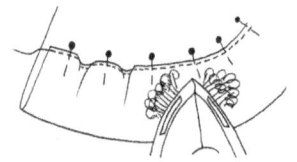

If you're unable to shrink in the fullness, it's perfectly OK to take small pleats along the hem. This idea is often used for hemming cotton school dresses that have deep hems, giving them provision for being let down later on.

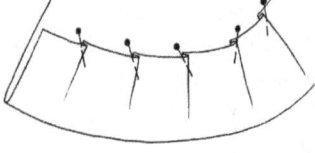

Fancy machine edges such as scallops

Check your machine's instruction manual to see if it does any suitable fancy edgings.

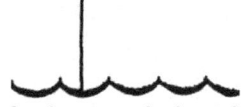

Fancy machine edges are used for lingerie, little girls dresses, sheer fabrics and fine blouses. They can be an alternative to a rolled hem.

After sewing scallops or similar edgings, trim closely with embroidery scissors.

Hemming pleats

Hemming is done *before* the fabric is sent away to the pleaters, so the hem gets pleated in the same direction as the rest of the garment. Otherwise when you go to hem the already-pleated fabric, the pleats will fold in the opposite direction.

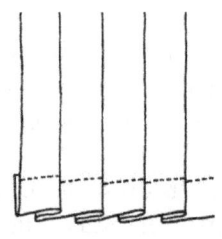

An exception is if you desire a fluted edge as a feature of the design. Finely pleated sheer fabric hemmed afterwards with a fine rolled hem makes superb ruffles or an interesting voluminous hem to a skirt.

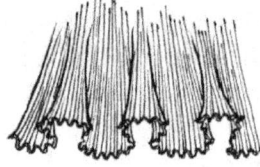

Fast hems

Use fusible web for a fast hem. Test it on a scrap of fabric first to make sure it won't be too stiff. Cut the fusible web 1cm (⅜") narrower than the hem allowance.

Sticky tape makes an excellent emergency hem on heavy fabrics.

Hems in jackets

Hems in jackets and coats have interfacing in them, even if they aren't lined. Cut a strip of iron-on interfacing the same width as the hem allowance. Iron it onto the hem allowance, then press up the hem. Do this before sewing.

If the jacket piece is interfaced all over (the front often is), then you don't need to iron extra interfacing on the hem—it's already there. Simply press up the hem.

If you have yet to decide the finished length, iron the interfacing on the hems *after* your fitting, when you do know the length.

Hemming leather

There are a couple of possibilities for hemming leather. You can:

✂ Leave the edge raw.

✂ Press the hem up using a dry iron and piece of heavy paper as a press cloth. Hammer the fold lightly, then glue the hem into position.

✂ Same as above, then topstitch from the right side.

Hemming fur

Fur is best hemmed by hand to avoid catching the fur in the stitching.

Shortening jeans—preserving the hem

It can be difficult or impossible to replicate the hem on jeans that need to be shortened, especially if a frayed look is desired. Instead of cutting and re-hemming to shorten, take a horizontal tuck around the leg, just above the original hem stitching, with the tuck of the fabric on the inside. You'll need a zipper foot to stitch closely to the existing hem.

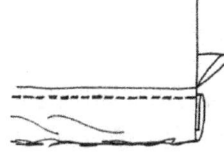

Trim the tuck to a generous 6mm (¼") and overlock to neaten. If your overlocker won't accept the thickness, neaten the edge with zig zag stitch.

Rock 'n' Roll t-shirt hem

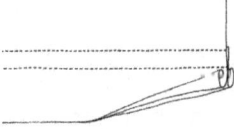

A distressed hem on t-shirts can be achieved by sewing a twinneedled hem, then slitting it along the fold. The knit fabric will curl on both edges.

Chain weighted hem

Chanel used them in her suits, and I have heard the Queen has them in her skirts so they don't fly up when helicopters land nearby. Chain weights are used in jacket and skirt hems to weigh them down so the garment hangs straight and doesn't bounce up. Chain weights look like chain necklaces and are sold by the metre (or yard). Like necklaces, they come in different weights. Cut the chain to the correct length with pliers and handstitch it to the already-sewn hem. On jackets it sits above the hem fold right next to the lining seam. It can be sewn on last of all when the jacket is finished. The chain gives a heaviness to the garment, but you really don't notice it. Most jackets and skirts don't need chain weights, but it's a good solution to know about if they ever do.

Trouser cuffs

Trouser cuffs go in and out of fashion, but are always a smart finish to the bottom of trouser legs. Note that cuffs can make your legs appear slightly shorter than a plain hem, because the eye will stop at the horizontal line.

Make a pattern

A trouser cuff is actually a deep hem which is then turned up, hiding the hem stitching.

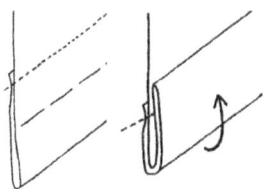

1. Determine the finished length of the trousers (left picture, long dash line).

2. Decide on the finished cuff depth. 3cm (1¼") is a usual amount.

3. Add to the finished length one cuff depth (3cm). This is the fold line; notch the edge of the pattern or fabric with tiny 3mm (⅛") snips to indicate where to fold. Then add 1½ times the cuff depth (3cm + 1.5cm = 4.5cm). Grand total = 7.5cm.

4. You'll need to true the side seams to make sure the cuff fits the leg when it's turned up: turn under 1½ times the finished cuff depth (4.5cm), then turn up the finished cuff depth (3cm).

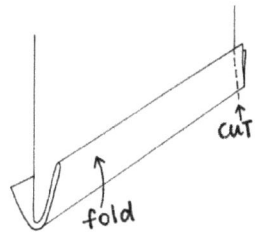

Trim any excess off the sides. If you're doing this on an actual pair of trousers and there's nothing to trim off (on tapered leg trousers there won't be), note where the *stitching line* will be for the seams.

To sew trouser cuffs

1. Sew the side seams of the trousers, following the shaped edge by pivoting at the angles. Overlock the side seams and the bottom edge.

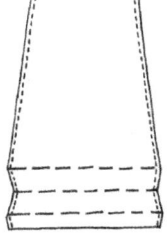

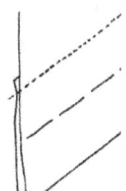

2. Turn under 1½ times the finished cuff depth (4.5cm) as indicated by your 3mm (⅛") snips. Lightly press and hem, either by machine or by hand.

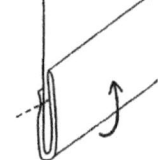

3. Turn up the cuff and press into position.

4. Secure the cuff at the side seams by hand or by machine. With the right side facing up, stitch-in-the-ditch along the seam line, stopping just short of each end.

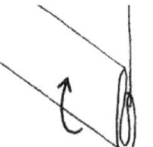

Separate cuffs

If you don't have enough length available to make cuffs, they can be added separately. This method looks very neat inside because all the raw edges are in the cuff. There's no fear of catching your heel on the hem.

I have also used this method to rescue trousers that were hemmed too short to wear (but we had spare fabric).

1. Determine the finished length of the trousers, then decide on the finished cuff depth. 3cm (1¼") is a common depth.

2. On the trousers, cut off from the finished length: half the cuff width less 1cm (⅜") seam allowance (1.5cm - 1cm seam allowance = .5cm).

3. For the cuffs, cut four pieces of fabric three times the cuff depth plus 2cm (¾") for seam allowances (9cm + 2cm seam allowance = 11cm deep).

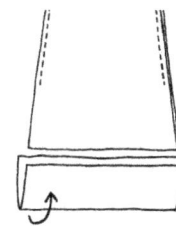

Make them slightly wider than the bottom of the trousers because you'll need to true the the side seams to make sure the cuff will fit the leg when it's turned up.

To do this, iron the cuff pieces in half horizontally. Pin the cuff onto the bottom of the leg along the seam line and fold up the cuff depth. Trim the excess off the sides.

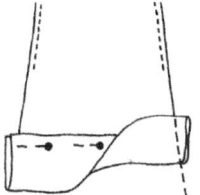

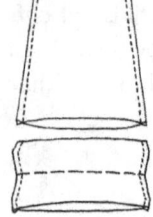
4. Sew the side seams of the trousers and the cuffs. Press the seam allowances of the cuffs open. Neaten the seam allowances of the trousers but not the cuffs.

5. Place the *right* side of the cuff onto the *wrong* side of the trouser leg and sew one edge of the cuff to the trousers. It's easier to do if your sewing machine converts to free arm.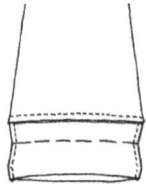

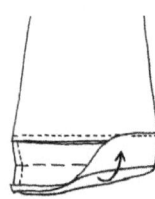 6. Fold under the seam allowance of the remaining edge of the cuff, then bring the folded edge up to the trousers and stitch. Some people like to sew this by hand but I do it by machine.

7. Turn up the cuff and press into position.

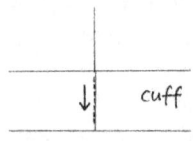 8. Secure the cuff at the side seams by hand or by machine. With the right side facing up, stitch-in-the-ditch along the seam line, stopping just short of each end.

Separate cuffs on very thick fabrics
Follow the above instructions up to Step 4.

5. With *right* sides together, sew the cuff to the trouser leg. Press the seam open. Neaten the seam allowance on the trouser side.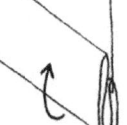

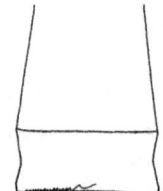 6. Neaten the remaining edge of the cuff.

7. Turn under the neatened edge. Stitch the neatened edge in place by stitching-in-the-ditch of the previous seam.

8. Turn up the cuff and press.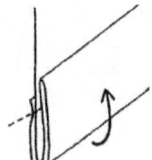

9. Secure the cuff at the side seams by hand or by machine. With the right side facing up, stitch-in-the-ditch along the seam line, stopping just short of each end.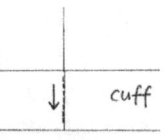

Trouser hems for someone in a wheelchair all the time
Often hems taken up in the usual way are fine. However, sometimes extra adjustments are desirable to have the hemline parallel to the floor and sitting neatly over the shoe.

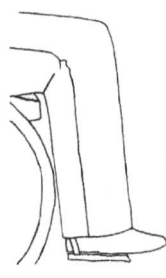 Sew a tuck behind the knee to level the hemline. This works well if the trousers have cuffs or a fancy hem.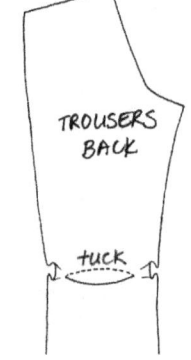

If this isn't enough, or makes the trousers too awkward to put on, adjust the hem to make the back higher. For example, the sides could be 1.2cm (½") higher than the front and the back could be 4cm (1½"). Curve the hem so it's flowing line. Don't worry about truing the side seams—the back and front will balance each other.

To turn up the hem, slit the centre back hem allowance and take one or more small pleats in the front allowance. If the trousers are wool, you might be able to shrink the front pleats flat.

False hems
A false hem is a type of facing. It's a separate strip of fabric stitched to the lower edge, then turned up inside like a regular hem. The strip of fabric can be the same as the garment, a lighter weight fabric, a bias strip or lace.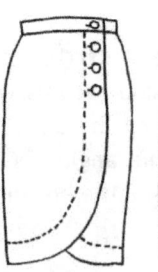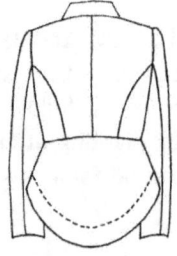

False hems are used when:
- ✂ The hem is curved, for example in the jacket and wraparound skirt pictured.
- ✂ You want to remove bulk from a hemline. For example, heavy wool might have a lighter weight fabric false hem or you might use a length of lace in a matching colour.
- ✂ You've run out of fabric and don't have enough length for a hem.
- ✂ The hem is piped (see pages 211-212).

False hems generally don't have interfacing in them, but there are some exceptions. A false hem for a jacket would, because jacket hems normally have interfacing in them. The wraparound skirt pictured above would have fusing in the curved fronts, because the false hem needs to support the shape of the curves and it has buttonholes going through it. It wouldn't have fusing in the back hem. The back hem might be a regular turned-up hem the same width as the false hem.

Make a pattern

1. Trim the pattern's hem allowance to 6mm (¼").

2. The facing needs to be the same shape as the hem. Trace around the lower edge of the garment, and draw a facing. The width depends on the garment; it can be a very narrow facing or a wide one. The grainline is usually the same as the garment's.

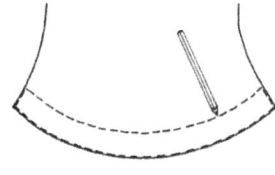

To sew a false hem

1. Join the facing's side seams taking the same seam allowance as the garment. Press them open. The seams aren't neatened because they'll be enclosed in the hem.

2. Neaten the top long edge or turn it under 6mm (¼").

3. With the right sides together, sew the false hem to the garment along the lower long edge, taking a 6mm (¼") seam.

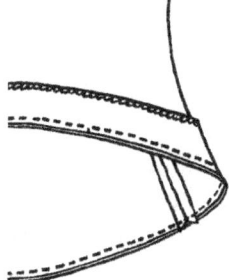

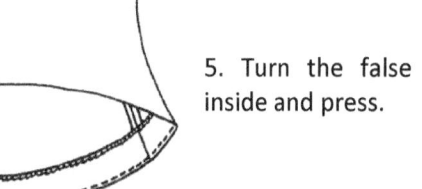

4. Press the seam allowance towards the false hem and understitch the false hem through all the layers. This row of understitching will help the false hem stay tucked inside.

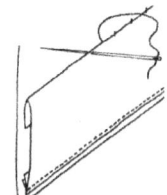

5. Turn the false hem to the inside and press.

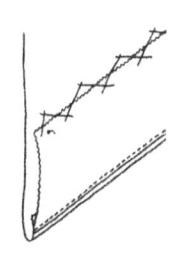

6. Hem by hand or by machine as you would a regular hem.

False hem using lace or bias binding

A false hem can also be made from a bias strip, ready-made bias binding or a strip of lace that has one straight edge.

Sew it straight on top of the raw edge. If you're using a bias strip and the edge is curved, pre-curve the strip using an iron before sewing it on.

This can be a good solution to hemming difficult-to-handle fabrics that won't hem neatly in any other way.

Interfacing

Introduction 164	fusible interfacing 166
Types of interfacing 164	Troubleshooting fusing 167
Where to interface 165	Buying and storing interfacing 167
Make a test sample 165	Pre-shrinking interfacing 167
Cutting out interfacing 165	Specialty interfacings and stabilizers ... 168
Applying interfacing 166	My favourite interfacings 168
sew-in interfacing 166	Fusing jackets and coats 168

Interfacing is essentially an extra layer of fabric applied to the inside of a garment to give body, shape, support and strength.

Interfacing is applied to the wrong side of the fabric on what will be the outermost layer.

Very occasionally an entire garment will be interfaced, but interfacing is generally applied to certain areas and details. Collars, cuffs, lapels, necklines, facings, pockets, hems, opening edges, belts, waistbands and behind buttons and buttonholes are all interfaced. You can use more than one type of interfacing on a garment and choose the type according to where it will be used and the desired effect.

Be prepared to spend money on quality interfacing, the same as choosing quality fabric and thread. Don't spoil good quality fabric with cheap, unsuitable interfacing.

Types of interfacing

✂ Interfacing can be woven or non-woven or knit.
Woven interfacing behaves like woven fabric. It has lengthwise and crosswise grains and also bias grain.
Non-woven interfacing is made from fibres bonded together. It *does* have a grain and it stretches more in the crosswise grain than the lengthwise.
Knitted interfacings stretch in at least one direction, and if used on a knit fabric will allow it to stretch slightly. It can be used on woven or knitted fashion fabric.
Woven and knitted interfacings will shape better than non-wovens. All three interfacing types come in a variety of weights, so select a weight that's compatible with your fabric. Slip a piece under the fabric and drape it over the back of your hand to get an idea of how the two layers will feel together.

✂ Interfacing can be sew-in or iron-on.
A fusible or fusing refers to an interfacing which is ironed on, or fused, to the fabric. The adhesive on one side creates a bond between the fabric and the interfacing. You can tell which side of the fusing to iron onto the wrong side of the fabric because the fusing has a rough side with dots of adhesive on it. If both sides are smooth, the shiny side when you hold it up to the light has the adhesive on it.

With few exceptions, I use fusibles wherever possible. They're quick and easy to use and can be used with nearly every fabric. They're great for stabilizing small areas such as buttonholes, slashes and pockets. Fusibles are an excellent choice for fabrics that fray badly because the weave bonds to the fusible.

Don't use fusibles on:
✂ Textured fabrics like seersucker (fusing would change the texture)
✂ Beaded, sequined or re-embroidered fabrics
✂ Transparent fabrics such as organza
✂ Fake furs and velvet (the fusing process would crush the pile)
✂ Most brocades
✂ Leather, vinyl and PVC
✂ Open fabrics such as lace and mesh

Why? Some fabrics cannot stand the heat fusing requires and some fabrics refuse to bond with the fusible. If you use a fusible on sheer and open fabrics, the interfacing and/or adhesive would be visible. For these, a sew-in must be used.

Which interfacing you use will depend on the weight of the fashion fabric, the area to be interfaced and the amount of shaping or stiffness required. The interfacing shouldn't be heavier in weight than your fashion fabric, although it can be crisper. Ideally, it should be slightly lighter in weight.

Where to interface

✂ Commercial patterns specify the garment pieces to be interfaced. It's written on the pattern, for example "Cut 2 of fabric and 1 of interfacing".

✂ Facings. These are always interfaced with very few exceptions (the exceptions might be *very* thick or firm fabrics). I use a woven or non-woven fusible on facings with the fabric weight dictating the firmness.

✂ Details. For example, collars, cuffs, pocket flaps, patch pocket top facings, welt pockets, epaulettes and tabs. Generally, only one side of the detail is interfaced, and it's the outermost one.

✂ Belts. Any belt with a buckle and/or eyelets will need interfacing to support it and stop it creasing.

✂ Behind areas to be slashed. For example, welt pockets and bound buttonholes. The interfacing reinforces and supports the slashed edge and stops it from fraying.

✂ Behind buttons and buttonholes. Fusing stabilizes buttonholes making them much easier to sew. It also adds strength so the buttons and buttonholes don't rip out with wear.

✂ On jackets. The hem allowance, any vents (sleeve vents, back vents), top and under collar, often the entire front, across the back shoulders, around the armholes to stop them stretching and any other places mentioned above. See the extra notes on interfacing jackets and coats on pages 168-169.

Make a test sample

Your own experience is a good guide to choosing an interfacing, however, a test sample is always a good idea for a new fabric or interfacing. If using a fusible, test a piece on your fashion fabric, following the instructions for applying interfacings on page 166. Do the fabric and fusing feel good together? Is it too...stiff? crisp? soft? floppy? bulky? Is there a colour change or does the fusing show through?

Cutting out interfacing

✂ The interfacing pieces should be cut out using the same grain line as the garment, unless the interfacing is stabilizing an area so it doesn't stretch, for example a strip across a shoulder.

When a piece is cut on the bias like this jacket undercollar, the fusing is also cut on the bias to maintain the drape.

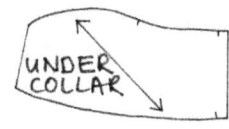

If the fabric piece is cut on the bias for effect, like a shirt cuff in checked fabric, the interfacing should be cut on the straight grain to stabilize it.

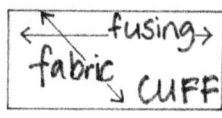

✂ It's important to transfer any pattern markings such as darts onto the back of the *interfacing* rather than the fabric. Otherwise, when the interfacing is applied you won't be able to see the markings.

✂ If you have to fuse a piece of interfacing onto the back of the garment for reinforcement, for example to make a welt pocket, *rounded* corners are less liable to peel off than *square* ones.

✂ For a greater drape and natural handle, experiment with cutting woven or knit fusing on the bias and applying to fabric cut on the straight grain.

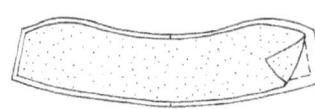

✂ I prefer to cut the fusing the same size as the pattern, but some people like to cut it a little smaller, say, 5mm or more, or just a little less than the seam allowance. The idea is so the edges don't accidentally get fused to the pressing surface. Another reason might be to reduce bulk in the seam allowances, or just the corners, although interfacing isn't very bulky.

I find it easier and more accurate to position interfacing if it's the same size as the fabric, particularly if the fashion fabric is floppy and unstable, because you can go by the interfacing for the correct shape.

Usually in Australian manufacturing, fusing is cut the same size as the fabric to keep the costs down, otherwise separate pattern pieces would need to be made for each piece in each size and the fusing and fabric then cannot be cut together.

✂ You can save time by cutting out the interfacing and fashion fabric together, provided the layers aren't too thick to cut through.

Some ways to go about it:

Lay the fusing under the fabric. Pin the pattern on through all the layers and cut them out together. This is very convenient if all, or most, of the garment is interfaced, or if all the pieces to be interfaced can be positioned next to each other.

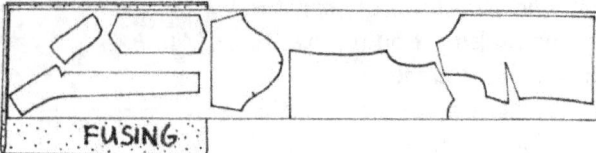

OR

If the fashion fabric is stable, cut it out as normal, but roughly hack around the pattern pieces to have interfacing. **Lay the pieces on top of the interfacing**, pin, and cut them out properly together.

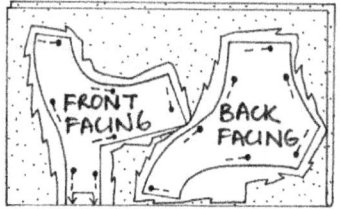

OR

If the fabric is very unstable and floppy, you can **block fuse** a section, then cut out the pattern pieces. Cut a piece each of fabric and fusing big enough to accommodate the pattern pieces. It's very important to make sure the sides are squared up so the fabric and fusing will both be on grain. One corner should be 90 degrees and the adjacent sides cut perfectly straight. Although it uses more fabric, by fusing the fabric *before* cutting it's much easier and more accurate to cut out.

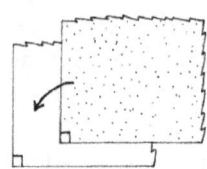

Applying interfacing
Sew-in interfacing
Accurately place the sew-in interfacing on the wrong side of the piece and pin around the edges. I like to do this at the ironing board and press each piece flat before pinning them together. Set your sewing machine to a long stitch and, sewing within the seam allowance, stitch around the whole piece. Iron flat (if your fabric can be ironed) to marry the layers before assembling the garment.

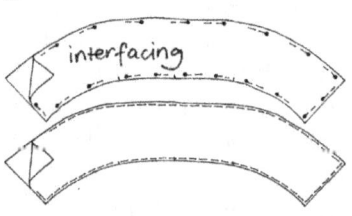

Fusible interfacing
Do a test swatch first if you need to. Use a wool setting on your iron, and steam. Lay the fabric right side down. Position the fusing adhesive side down on top of it. If the fabric is unstable and has stretched or changed shape, gently coax it back to the shape of the fusing (which should be the original shape).

Press with an up-and-down motion so the layers don't shift. Fuse each area for 7-15 seconds, overlapping your iron to avoid missing areas. You may need to follow up with a press on the right side—but check the iron's soleplate first in case it has glue on it.

For light weight fusings, you might need a dry iron instead of steam, and a damp press cloth.

For heavy fusings, a combination of heavy steam and damp press cloth may be required with a longer fusing time. Pre-test the fabric to ensure the extra steam won't shrink the fabric.

When cool, the fusible interfacing should be firmly bonded. Try picking off a corner to check. If you're able to peel it back, it hasn't bonded properly. Try again, this time increasing the temperature, pressure or length of time.

If the glue from the fusing transfers itself to the soleplate of your iron, you can:

✂ Use a special silicone soleplate cover for your iron.

✂ Use a press cloth (damp or dry) over the interfacing to protect the iron. I do this. I keep a dedicated press cloth for interfacing with the "up" side marked so I don't get glue on the iron. I have separate ones for light and dark interfacing.

✂ Use a sheet of kitchen greaseproof paper instead of a press cloth to protect the iron.

✂ Iron on all of your interfacing, then clean the soleplate of the iron using an iron cleaner. However, the fumes can be noxious, so have the door open. It's better not to get the iron dirty in the first place.

If the glue from the fusing transfers itself to your ironing board cover, sometimes it can then re-transfer itself to the surface of your fashion fabric when you fuse the next piece. To avoid this, cut your interfacing accurately, so you don't have interfacing hanging over the edge of your fabric piece. Residual glue will come off the ironing board cover when you wash it. You can also buy a non-stick appliqué mat to protect the ironing board cover; try quilting shops. Baking paper is a good substitue.

To use **fusible fleece**, trim off any seam allowances to eliminate bulk at the seam line so the fleece is the exact finished size of the pattern piece. Place the fusible fleece glue side up and the fabric wrong side down over it. Cover with a lightweight dry press cloth and steam press with the iron on "wool" setting, and press lightly for 10-12 seconds. When the piece has cooled, check for adhesion. If the fleece will be covered by stitching, you'll only need a light bond to keep things in place while you stitch. If you need a firmer bond, flip the pieces over and press on the fleece side. Note that the more steam and pressure you apply, the flatter and less lofty the fleece will become.

To **fuse large areas**, lay a blanket on a table a couple of layers thick and spread a sheet over the top to create a smooth surface big enough to hold the pieces to be fused. You might need an extension cord for the iron. Alternatively, see if you can take the fabric and fusing to a dry cleaners and get them to do it for you. I'll admit I find applying lots of fusing a bit of a snore, but set aside an evening, pour yourself a glass of wine and turn the TV on while you do it.

Factories apply interfacing with a fusing press, similar to a domestic Elna press but bigger. Some factories use a large machine where the fabric pieces, laid with their fusing, go in and out on a wide conveyer belt. Whole rolls of fabric can also be fused at one time.

Troubleshooting fusing

Bubbles in fusing
The iron was not hot enough or not applied for long enough. Sometimes you'll notice bubbles after you've been handling a fused piece for a while—you'll need to re-fuse it. It often happens on very textured or very smooth fabrics.

Bubbles in fabric
The iron was too hot and you've caused the fusing to shrink. I've noticed this is very easy to do on silk. If you can manage to peel the fusing off you can reuse the fabric, otherwise you'll need to cut a new piece of fabric and fusing and be more careful next time.

Dots showing through the fused areas of fabric, sometimes appearing after laundering (when it's too late)
You've used the wrong fusing. It happens more so with smooth or lightweight fabrics and also seems to happen with cheap, non-woven fusing. Next time try a different fusing or use a sew-in.

Accidentally ironed interfacing to incorrect side of fabric
Sorry to say, you won't be able to restore the surface of the fabric, even if you manage to remove all the interfacing. The adhesive makes a bond between the fabric and the interfacing. The only solution is to re-cut the piece. If the piece is a facing or a piece no-one will see, you could leave it if you don't have any fabric left.

The fusible interfacing won't bond properly
Some fabrics, in particular those with very rough or very smooth surfaces, won't bond well, no matter how you apply them. In those cases, you'll have to use a sew-in interfacing instead.

Running short of interfacing
You'll probably need to have joins in the interfacing. Try to organise the joins either in an inconspicuous place or centrally, for example at the centre back.
With lightweight fusible interfacing, you can overlap the edges 3mm-6mm (⅛"-¼"). Cut it with pinking shears to avoid a ridge, and if you're using light coloured fabrics check first in case the overlap shows as a dark line on the right side.

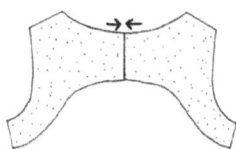

For heavier fusibles, cut the pieces so the edges butt together.

For sew-in interfacing, lap the two (pinked) edges over each other by 6mm (¼") and stitch down the centre, using straight stitch or zig zag.

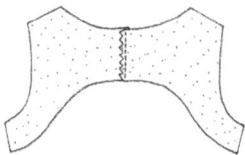

Buying and storing interfacing
A good tip: don't buy exactly the amount of interfacing the pattern calls for; buy several metres. Then you won't have wastage and you'll always have it in the cupboard ready. If you have the means, buy a whole roll of your favourite interfacing. It will last for years and you'll always have it on hand.
Store the interfacing neatly folded or on a roll, because you won't be able to press creased fusible interfacing flat! I store short lengths of interfacing neatly folded in a plastic bag. I keep small pieces in there too to use for reinforcement behind buttonholes and the like.

Pre-shrinking interfacing
Some fusings are recommended "pre-shrink" by the manufacturer, due to the rayon content of the fusing (notably Whisperweft and Armoweft by McCalls). To preshrink, soak it in hot tap water for ten minutes, then drip dry on a towel.
I must confess I've never pre-shrunk interfacing and never had a problem. The shrinkage is minimal. Interfacings and fabrics are not pre-shrunk before clothing manufacture.
However, if you don't want to take the chance, pre-shrink if recommended, then *label* the pre-shrunk piece before you store it.

Specialty interfacings and stabilizers

Stabilizer is just that: interfacing used to stabilize a particular area to stop it from stretching or distorting. Machine embroidery requires a stabilizer behind the fabric.

Waistband interfacing has perforations to indicate the fold line and 1cm (⅜") seam lines. It's an non-woven and comes in different widths and in dark or light. It's sometimes called ESL tape.

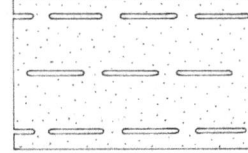

Stay tape is a continuous, narrow strip of fusing with reinforcing threads running through it. It's used to stop edges from stretching, for example necklines and shoulders. It's very handy when sewing stretch wovens and knits. It comes in different widths.

Graduated interfacing is used for the fronts of men's tailored jackets. It's sold on a roll by the metre.

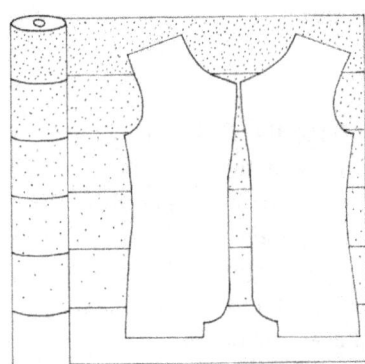

On one edge is heavy interfacing (used up at the shoulders where it's needed), graduating to lighter interfacing (to be used lower down on the jacket). If you can't find it in the shops, a tailor might be able to sell some to you.

Fusible web bonds two layers of fabric together. It's available on a roll by the metre, or as a narrow tape in different widths. It can be used to:
- ✂ Bond sew-in interfacing to fashion fabrics
- ✂ Put up hems
- ✂ Hold appliqué in place
- ✂ Secure patches before stitching

Vlisofix is a fusible web with paper on one side, used for appliqué. The web side is ironed onto the appliqué fabric and the shape of the appliqué is drawn on the paper. It's cut out and the paper peeled off, then the shape is ironed onto the background fabric.

Tear away is a firm, non-woven, sew-in stabilizer. It tears easily in one direction. A shaped strip of tear away can be stitched in with a seam (such as a neckline or waist) to stabilize it, then the excess torn away after the seam is understitched or topstitched.

Water soluble tear away is used to stabilize the back of machine embroidery or buttonholes. After sewing the embroidery or buttonhole, the tear away is dissolved by spraying it with water or washing it.

Some of my favourite interfacings

Light weight knit (jersey) interfacing (such as McCall's Sheerweft) is very versatile. I like it for blouses and dresses in light-to-medium weight woven fabrics. Sometimes I use it on the fronts of jackets to give body and use a heavier fusing for the facings, collar and everything else. It's also excellent for completely bonding nubbly Chanel/novelty tweed and other very fray-ey and loosely woven fabrics before sewing them.

Sew-in Shapewell, a stiff woven interfacing. I use it for the back stays of jackets, strapless tops and the waist facings of skirts and trousers. In a light weight it's good for leather, PVC, heavily embroidered fabrics, fake fur and other fabrics that can't be fused.

Heavier weight knit interfacing (such as McCall's Armoweft) for jackets and coats.

Silk organza can be used as a sew-in interfacing for organza, silk, sheer fabrics and fine embroidered fabrics. A skin tone helps keep the colour of the interfaced sections consistent with the colour of the rest of the garment. If silk organza makes the garment too expensive, try using a suitable weight nylon net.

None for lace, mesh and broiderie anglaise.

Fusing jackets and coats

Interfacing is an important part of jackets and coats to give durability, structure and body. Edges get a lot more wear than in a shirt, and collars require more support to give them structure.

✂ Hem allowances. Cut a strip as wide as the hem allowance. It's not necessary to cut it on the bias. After fusing the hem, press up the hem allowance.
If the sleeves have vents, the vent is interfaced too—see pages 338-339.

✂ Entire fronts. On coats and long jackets, just the upper front is fused. Sometimes a lighter fusing for the whole front is preferable.

Interfacing 169

You can save time by cutting out the front and front facing with their fusing. Lay the fusing under the fabric, mark the front and front facing next to each other and cut out together, through all layers. If the entire back is fused as well, you can position it there too.

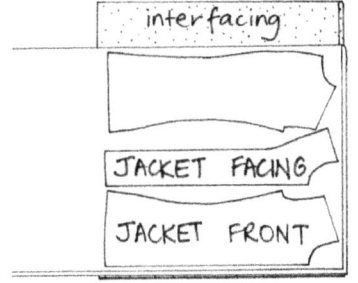

Remove the fusing and cut out the rest of the jacket, then cut any other fusing pieces required from the fusing off-cuts.

✂ Upper back and armhole. It stops the jacket from stretching across the back and around the armhole. If the jacket is a light colour, the entire back can be fused so there's no horizontal line showing through. Often, instead of fusible interfacing, a back stay (or saddle, as it's called) is cut from sew-in woven interfacing such as Shapewell. It's cut on the fold at the centre back (even if the jacket has a centre back seam) and continues to the side. I usually extend it 5cm (2") down each side seam. Any shoulder or neck darts are slit down the middle, overlapped and stitched before the stay is applied. Any seams such as princess line seams are overlapped and eliminated on the pattern before the stay is cut. A sew-in back stay is usually done for custom-made jackets; factories tend to fuse everything.

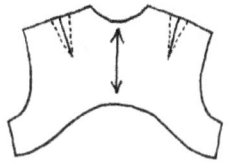

Here's an example of a jacket and a coat and their pattern pieces, with the areas to be interfaced shaded. These are examples only; the fabric may dictate more or less or different interfacing.

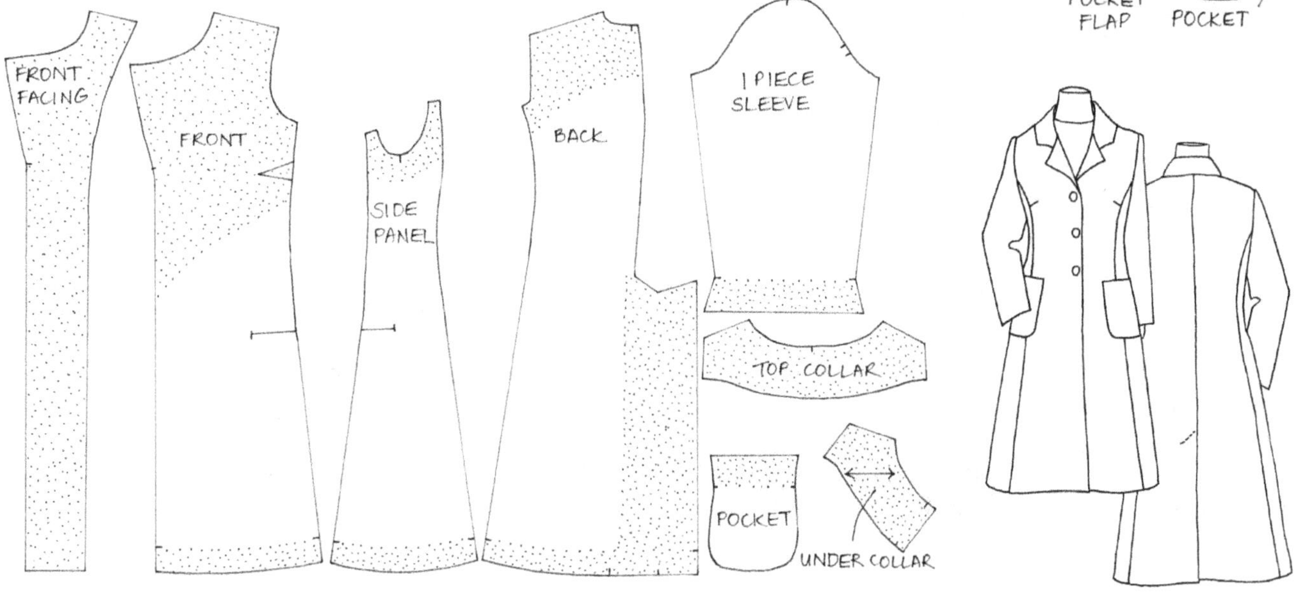

Linings

Introduction 170	lining sleeves 173
Suitable fabrics 171	lining faced neck/armholes 174
What is an interlining? 171	Lining pleated skirts 174
What is an underlining? 171	Closed linings in skirts and dresses 174
Making patterns for linings 171	Lining a vest 175
Lining skirts and trousers 171	Lining a jacket 176
lining pattern for trousers 171	Where lining hem meets front facing . 180
lining pattern for skirts 172	method 1 conventional 181
to sew 172	method 2 European 181
Lining faced waists 173	free hanging linings 181
Lining dresses and tops 173	

Linings give a professional finish to the inside of a garment and stop the garment coming into direct contact with the body. While linings improve many garments, resist the temptation to line *every* garment you make. Not every garment needs one. Sometimes a petticoat, camisole or natural coloured underwear will do the same job, and sometimes adding a lining will inhibit the drape and flow of the fabric.

A lining...
- Covers the inner construction and makes the insides look neat.
- Helps the garment to slip on and off easily where the main fabric might catch or cling, for example coat sleeves.
- Feels nice to wear against the body and protects the skin from rough fabrics such as wool or the inside of leather.
- Makes a garment warmer.
- Helps the garment hang smoothly with flattering lines and prevents it from clinging to the body.
- Helps stop the garment from stretching.
- Gives body to limp fabrics.
- Helps a garment keep its shape.
- Reduces wrinkling in the outer fabric.
- Gives a higher quality finish.
- Adds durability and prolongs the life of the garment since the skin is not in contact with the outer fabric. A garment can be re-lined if necessary.

- Linings in skirts and trousers are usually free hanging, meaning they're attached to the garment at the waist only and have a separate hem. This gives more movement to the lining. The seam allowances in free hanging linings need to be neatened to stop fraying.

The opposite of a free hanging lining is a closed or bagged out lining. Closed linings are frequently used in jackets and coats, handbags, hats and occasionally skirts and tops. A closed lining is attached to the garment at every edge, enclosing all the wrong sides and giving a very neat finish to the inside of the garment. The seam allowances do not require neatening unless the fabric frays badly.

- Double-faced or a self-lining is where the garment is lined in its own fabric.

- Seams in linings are closed seams wherever possible. That is, pressed to one side rather than pressed open. A closed seam in thin lining fabric creates little extra bulk. Darts in the garment become tucks in the lining to give more movement, but you can sew them as darts if you want to.

- It's OK, even desirable, if the lining is a little bigger than the garment. You can cut the lining the same size as the garment, but sew it with a slightly smaller seam allowance, say, 3mm (⅛") smaller. It is ***not*** OK if the lining is smaller than the garment.

- Before a lining is stitched into a garment, the lining and garment are stitched separately. Both are pressed before sewing together.

Linings

✂ The length of a lining is cut at the *finished* length of the garment. Simply trim the hem allowance off your main fabric pattern. Sometimes, to save time, you may be able to cut the main and lining out together, then trim any difference off the lining.

✂ When making an alteration on a lined garment, I don't bother altering the lining too, unless I'm making the garment bigger or the alteration is a lot.

Suitable fabrics for linings

Lining fabrics are relatively slippery to make it easy to take the garment off or put on. They are also lighter in weight than the garment fabric. The lining can match the garment colour or be a contrasting colour, but make sure the colour doesn't show through to the right side. If you're lining a garment to stop it being see-through, check the lining and garment fabric together to make sure it's opaque enough. You can make a lining special by using satin, printed satin or silk.

The fibre content matters when choosing a lining. Linings can be silk, polyester, acetate, cotton, knit fabric, flannelette, fleecy or quilted. The most common fabrics sold as lining are polyester or acetate. They are both fine to use. To tell the difference, acetate will dissolve in acetone nail polish remover, and polyester will melt and form a hard bead when burnt.

When selecting a lining fabric, ask:

✂ Will it be warm enough?

✂ Will the lining make the wearer too hot and sweaty? Some people find polyester lining too much like wearing plastic.

✂ Is the lining light enough for the garment, or is it too thick and heavy?

✂ Will the lining be strong enough? For example, in trousers.

✂ Does the lining have the same care requirements as the fashion fabric? For example, if you're making a silk skirt, you may like to line it in silk as well. Note that many linings need a cooler iron than the fashion fabric.

✂ Is an anti-cling lining required?

✂ Is the lining fabric the same type as the outer fabric? For example a knit fabric needs a knit lining, or a stretch woven fabric might require a stretch polyester lining.

What is an interlining?

An interlining's main purpose is warmth. It's an extra layer of fabric, usually brushed cotton or flannelette, applied to the garment or the lining. Some linings also work as interlinings, for example quilted lining and fleece-backed lining.

Sleeves are not usually interlined. I once interlined the sleeves of a coat as well as the body, and although it was very warm to wear, it made the coat far too bulky and I looked huge when I wore it.

Confusingly, interfacing is sometimes referred to as interlining.

What is an underlining?

An underlining is a fabric applied to the wrong side of the garment primarily to give extra strength, support or opacity. You could say that it's a backing. Each main garment piece is mounted onto its underlining by stitching around the edge, then it's treated as one layer and the seams of the garment are sewn as usual. An underlined garment can have a lining as well.

Some examples of underlining are:

✂ Dupion silk mounted onto silk organza to give extra body and crispness.

✂ A bustier top mounted onto stiff woven interfacing to give rigidity and support.

✂ A sheer fabric mounted onto an opaque backing to stop it being see-through.

Making patterns for linings

If your garment pattern doesn't have a lining pattern, it's not difficult to make one. Lining patterns are drafted using the original garment patterns. Sometimes cut lines for the lining are marked on the garment patterns, so no new pattern is required.

Plan any facings before you make lining patterns. The lining will cover the areas remaining beyond the facings.

Transfer all the original grainlines, notches and pattern markings onto the lining patterns. Add notches to the facing and lining patterns to match together when you stitch them.

Differentiate between the lining pattern pieces and the garment pieces in some way, so you don't accidentally cut out the lining in garment fabric. When I make patterns I boldly underline the word <u>lining</u> on my lining patterns. Some patternmakers write "lining" in red pen and others use a different coloured cardboard for the lining pattern pieces.

Lining skirts and trousers

Lining pattern for trousers

A trouser lining helps stop the bottom and knees from stretching and sagging out. Lining also stop light coloured trousers being see-through. It stops woollen trousers being itchy and makes them warmer, although some people find lined trousers too hot to wear. Sometimes trousers are half lined. The lining only goes down to the middle of the leg. A disadvantage with this is that the lining and main fabric can't be cut out together.

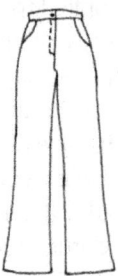

1. Cut the length of the lining the same as the *finished* length of the trousers (just fold up the hem allowance on the pattern).

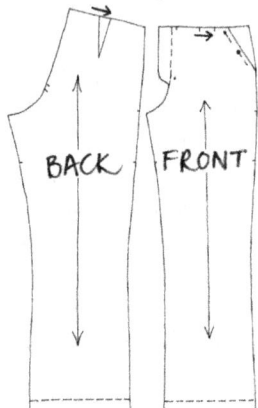

2. Cut the back lining the same as the back and make the back dart a tuck.

3. If the front has cutaway pockets, pin the pocket back in place to make a whole front.

4. Remove any fly front zip extensions and notch the centre front to denote the length of the zip opening.

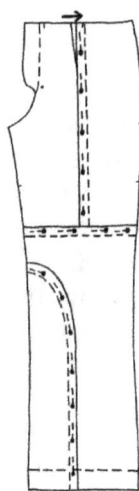

If the trousers have design lines, pin the pattern pieces together flat along the stitching lines to make a whole pattern piece. If the waist dart has been incorporated into the design lines, leave it as a tuck.

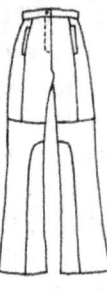

Lining pattern for skirts
The lining is cut the same as the skirt, with the darts becoming tucks.

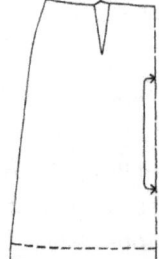

Cut the length of the lining the *finished* length of the skirt (fold up the hem allowance on the pattern). For straight and A-line skirts, make the lining 2cm (¾") shorter again. This stops the lining peeking out when you sit down.

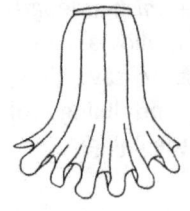

Flared skirts often have the lining cut a little less flared than the main.

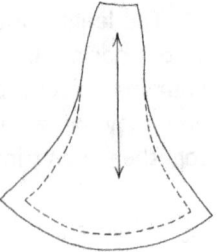

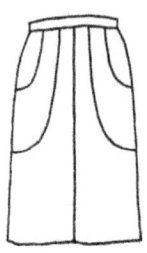

If the skirt has design lines, pin the pattern together flat before cutting the lining. Any waist darts that were incorporated into the design will become tucks.

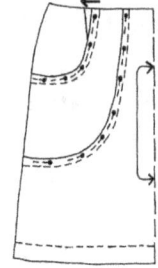

If there are cutaway pockets, pin the pocket back in place to make a whole front.

To sew skirt and trouser linings
Often the lining is sewn a little larger than the garment, even though they're cut the same size. This helps stop the lining from tearing if the main fabric stretches, especially around the seat and knees. To sew the lining larger, take smaller side seams. For example, if the seam allowance is 1.5cm (⅝"), take a 1cm (⅜") seam. Make the waist tucks (formerly the darts) larger to take in the excess around the waist.

1. Assemble the lining. Assemble the fashion fabric trousers or skirt except for the waistband.

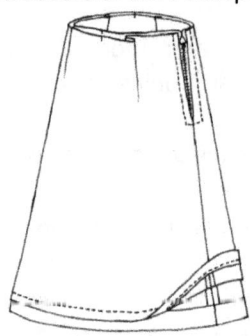

2. Place the trousers or skirt and lining together at the waist, with the wrong sides together. That is, as the garment will be worn.

3. Attach the waistband as normal through all thicknesses.

Sew the lining around the zip by hand or by machine. See page 414 for options.

In trousers with a fly front, the lining and main fabric are tacked together at the crotch seam.

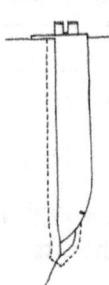

Alternatively, the lining is hemmed and sits around the fly shield.

Linings

Another method is to sew the waist of the trousers or skirt to only the outermost side of the waistband. Sew the lining to the waistband's innermost side taking a seam allowance that's 3mm (⅛") *less*. Finish off the ends of the waistband, then bring the lining and main together and stitch-in-the-ditch through all layers of the waistband on the right side.

This is a good way to reduce bulk at the waist because you can open the seams flat. The disadvantage is a lot of unpicking if you want to make an alteration.

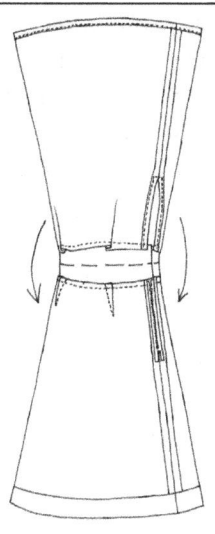

✂ Occasionally in high quality skirts, the lining is attached to the side seams at the hem with a long bar tack about 2cm (¾") long. Thread a needle with four threads (see page 145) and make a 2cm (¾") long tack between the skirt and lining. Work blanket stitches over until the tack is covered, then secure and cut the thread. This is called a French tack or a swing tack. It's a higher class finish but I don't do them in my own skirts—it makes ironing the skirt harder.

Lining faced waists

If the skirt or trousers has a faced waist, it looks far better to have the lining attached to the bottom edge of the facing, rather than the facing hanging unattached over the lining.

Make a pattern

1. Lay the facing onto the pattern, matching the waists, and trace around it.

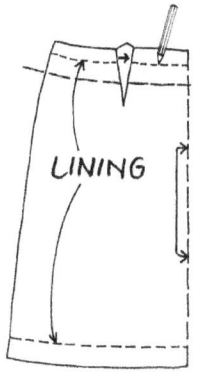

2. Add two seam allowances above this line to make the lining cutting line. Any remaining darts will become tucks in the lining.

You can make separate lining pattern pieces if you like, but I just mark the cut line on my existing pattern because it makes it easier to cut out the lining and main fabric together (and saves making another pattern piece).

To sew a faced waist

Attach the front and back linings to their respective facings, then proceed to sew the garment as normal.

On skirts, you can eliminate the facing if you want to and bring the lining up to the waist. This is a good solution if the skirt fabric is thin and you want to avoid a ridge from the facing pressing through. It's also useful if you don't have enough fabric to cut facings. A disadvantage is that tops may come untucked easily due to the slippery lining.

I never use this method for trousers—I always have a facing.

1. Cut the lining up to the top of the skirt and cut an "interior facing" out of a firm sew-in interfacing (I use Shapewell). This will support the top of the waist.

2. Sew the darts in the lining (don't leave them as tucks for this), then sew the interfacing to the *wrong* side of the lining around the edges, so it becomes one unit.

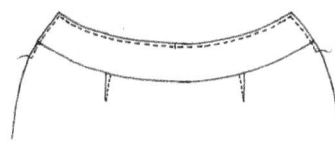

Lining dresses and tops

The above section on skirts applies to the skirt part of the dress. Linings in dresses and tops are generally free-hanging linings. The length of the lining is cut to the finished length of the dress and sleeves (simply fold up the hem allowance on the pattern).

Lining sleeves

Are you going to line the sleeves? If the fabric is sheer, it can look good to leave them unlined.

If you *do* line the sleeves, the lining tends to sit better if the sleeves and body are lined as separate units. Stitch them together around the armhole seam and overlock. This means the sleeves get sewn in last of all.

A higher end finish is to sew *only* the main sleeve on and press the seam towards the sleeve. Turn under the edges of the sleeve lining and hand sew the lining in place around the armholes. This is a good, if time-consuming, solution if the fabric is scratchy.

Usually the sleeve lining is not a free hanging lining. It's attached at the sleeve hem, even if the rest of the garment is free hanging.

For **short sleeves**:
1. Allow a 1cm (⅜") hem allowance on the sleeve.

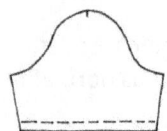

2. Cut the lining 1cm (⅜") shorter than the sleeve. That is, the sleeve without the hem turning.

3. Sew the underarm seams of both sleeve and lining.

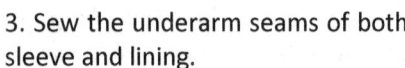

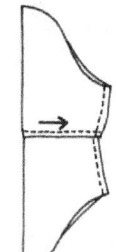

4. With the right sides together, sew the sleeve and lining together at the hem with a 5mm (scant ¼") seam allowance. If you have a free-arm sewing machine it will be easy to tuck one inside the other and sew around the hem.

5. Press the seam allowance towards the lining and understitch the lining.

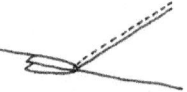

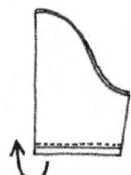

6. Bring the wrong sides together and match the raw edges at the top to the sleeve. Press. A 5mm border of main fabric will be visible on the lining side.

If the sleeves are long, have a 3cm-4cm (1¼"-1½") hem on the sleeve and cut the lining the *finished* length of the sleeves.

When they're sewn together, a pleat will form to allow movement (this is called a jump hem, by the way). You can then hem the sleeve invisibly by hand as usual, or by machine through the main fabric only.

Lining faced neck and armholes
If the neck or armholes (or both) are faced, cut the lining so it attaches to the bottom of the facing.

1. Lay the facing onto the pattern and trace around the facing.

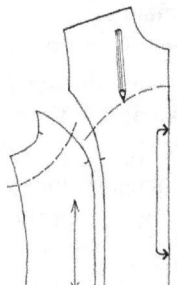

If the dress has seams (such as princess line) trace around the facing on each piece and indicate on the facing where the princess seam will lie.

2. Add two seam allowances above this line to find your lining cutting line. You can make separate lining pattern pieces if you like, but I just mark the cut line on my existing pattern. It makes it easier to cut out the lining with the main fabric.

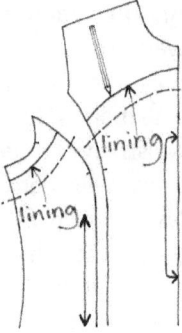

To sew, attach the linings to the facings, then proceed to sew the garment as normal. On princess line dresses, sew the princess seams in the lining before sewing the lining to the facing.

Alternatively, you can decide not have any facings, and bring the lining right up to the neck and/or armhole edges. This is a good idea if the lower edges of the facing show through the dress. It maintains an even colour throughout. It's also very handy if you've run out of fabric.

1. Cut the lining the same as the fashion fabric.

2. Cut some firm sew-in interfacing the same size as the facing pattern (I use Shapewell).

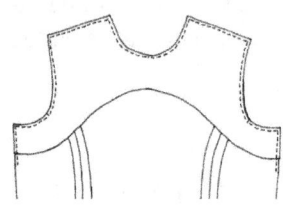

3. Sew the interfacing to the wrong side of the lining around the edges, then treat it as one piece.
The interfacing will sit between the main fabric and lining and add stability.

Lining pleated skirts
You can line pleated skirts, but the lining shouldn't be pleated. An A-line skirt pattern can be used to cut the lining. Sometimes the lining has side splits to allow extra movement.
Another method is to half-line the skirt. Cut the lining about 30cm (12") long using an unpleated skirt pattern, so that only the top of the skirt is lined.

Closed linings in skirts and dresses
A closed lining is sometimes referred to as a bagged out lining, since the skirt and lining create a bag. The method is actually the same as lining a short sleeve, described on this page. Closed linings are often used for wedding gowns, particularly ones incorporating a train, so if the

train flips over everyone sees a neat lining. Skirts lined in this way work best if the fabric is stable, crisp and non-stretchy. The lining must be the same size as the skirt.

An advantage of this method is that no hem stitching is visible. A disadvantage is that the skirt cannot be lengthened by taking down the hem.

Unless the fabric frays excessively, it isn't necessary to neaten the raw edges, since they'll all be enclosed inside. If you leave a gap in the side seam of the lining, you can perform this whole operation last, then sew up the gap in the lining.

1. Determine the length of the skirt and trim off any excess leaving a 1cm (⅜") hem allowance.

2. Cut the lining 1cm (⅜") shorter than the skirt. That is, the skirt less the hem turning.

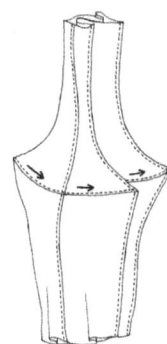

3. Sew all the seams in the skirt and lining and press them.
With the right sides together, sew the skirt and lining together at the hem, taking a 5mm (scant ¼") seam allowance.
Press the seam towards the lining and understitch the lining.

4. Fold the lining into the skirt and align the top edges. Press. A 5mm border of main fabric should be visible on the lining side.

Lining a vest

A lining neatly finishes all the edges on a vest. A vest can have fabric fronts with a satin back and regular lining throughout OR be made all of fabric with satin lining throughout OR it can be reversible with a different fabric inside and out.

1. Assemble the main fabric and the lining separately, *but leave the side seams undone* on both (**very important**). If there's a front facing, attach it to the lining so you have two vests the same shape—the inside and the outside.

2. Place the vest and lining right sides together and sew around the edges, leaving the side seams open.

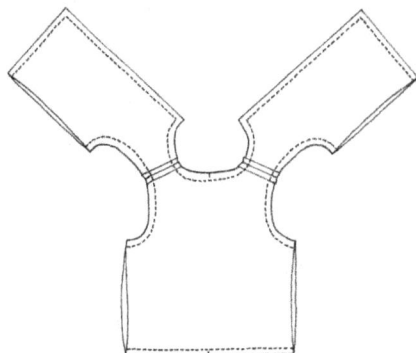

Unless the vest is reversible (where you won't be understitching), do this in stages for a higher quality finish:

First, sew the **centre front edges** and the **back lower edge** and understitch. The reason I suggest doing the centre fronts first is to make the understitching easier to do—you'll be able to understitch the entire length without trying to get into the corners. When the vest is finished, the front understitching will extend all the way to the corners.

Second, sew the **neckline** and understitch as far as you can go around.

Third, sew the **armholes** with the lining underneath. At the shoulder point, extend the lining out 6mm (¼"), blending it back in about 10cm (4") either side. Keep the

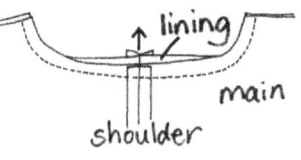

stitching line the correct distance from the main fabric raw edge. The purpose of this is to ensure the lining doesn't show at the shoulder and the shoulders are flat and smooth. Understitching will tuck the underneath layer (the lining) further under, away from sight. On a narrow area like the shoulder seam that has understitching at each end, you'll end up with an excess of lining fabric if you don't make the lining smaller. To solve the problem, either it slide away (as described) or actually trim 6mm (¼") off the lining on the armhole side.

Understitch each armhole from the underarm towards the shoulder seam on each side as far as you can sew. It doesn't matter if there's a small section with no understitching at the top of the shoulder.

Fourth, sew the **lower edges of the front** and understitch them as far as you can.

3. Turn the vest through to the right side and press. All the understitching should make pressing the edges

very easy. I often understitch even if I plan to topstitch as well later.

4. Sew one of the side seams, matching main-to-main and lining-to-lining, accessing the seam through the opposite back side seam. You'll be sewing the seam in a circle.

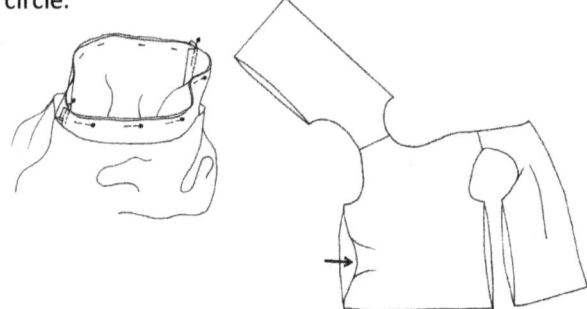

5. Sew the remaining side seam, again in a circle, but leave a gap in the lining so you can get to it. Close up the gap by handsewing it closed or simply press the two edges together like a pair of lips and machine sew on the edge. If the vest is reversible, invisibly sew the gap by hand.

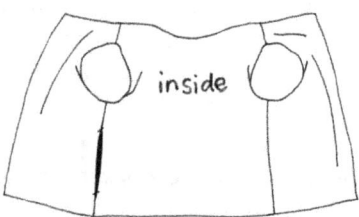

6. Topstitch the edges of the vest if desired. On a reversible vest, ensure the tension is perfect and looks good from either side, especially if you're using different coloured threads in the top and bobbin.

Lining a jacket

✂ You may not need to make separate lining pattern pieces for your jacket. With a bit of experience, and depending on the style, you can just use the jacket pattern.

In large manufacturing, complete sets of lining pattern pieces are often made, sometimes on different coloured cardboard to avoid mix-ups. This is time consuming but eliminates confusion and mistakes particularly if the cutting and sewing is done elsewhere.

In smaller operations and especially if the making is in-house, cutting lines for lining pieces are indicated on the main jacket pieces where possible. Separate pieces are made where the lining is different, for example the centre back or side front.

In small workrooms making one-offs and made-to-measures, no separate lining pattern pieces are made. The main jacket pieces are used to make a lining pattern as it's marked and cut out. Often the same person makes the pattern and does the cutting.

✂ Sometimes only the sleeves of jackets are lined, for example on school blazers, to help arms slide into the sleeves on what is mostly an unlined jacket. Sometimes the body of the jacket is lined in brushed cotton for warmth and the sleeves are lined in satin, once again to help arms slide in easily.

✂ Consider using a *satin* lining for a jacket or coat—satin costs only a little more than regular lining but feels luxurious. Satin also gives a more substantial lining for coats. A jacket can be lined in satin or a special lining for the body, and the sleeves (which are less visible) can be lined in regular lining or a plain colour.

✂ When choosing a contrasting or patterned lining, it looks best if it *relates* in some way to the jacket fabric, incorporating the same tones or colours. The exception is strong contrasts in plain fabrics, for example a bright yellow lining in a dark grey jacket, or a red lining in a black opera cape. Ensure that a brightly coloured lining doesn't show through the jacket fabric.

Make a pattern

✂ The lining is cut to the *finished* length of the jacket, so that way you'll never see the lining hanging longer. It forms what's called a jump hem. You can use the jacket pattern pieces with the hem allowance removed or just folded up.

✂ Seam allowances are the same as the main jacket, but often slightly less is taken when sewing. For example, for 1.2cm (½") seams, the lining is sewn with a 1cm (⅜") seam. It's fine if the lining is a little bigger than the main, but not if it's smaller.

Front lining pattern

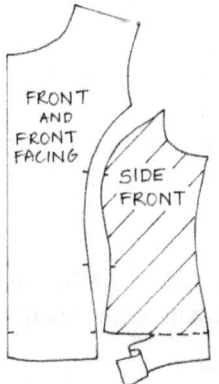

On **princess line jackets**, cut the centre front panel as the front facing. Cut the side front panel (with the hem allowance removed) in lining.

Decide now how you're going to finish the area at the bottom of the fronts where the facing joins the lining, as this will affect how you make the side front pattern (see pages 180-181 for options).

On **jackets with a seamless front or side panels**, make a separate front lining pattern:

Linings **177**

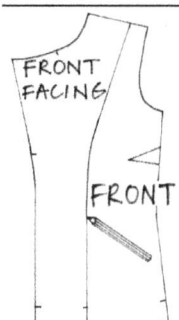

1. Trace around the front. Lay the facing on top, matching the centre fronts, and draw in the long edge of the facing.

2. Add two seam allowances to the facing line—so if you've decided on 1cm (⅜") seams, add 2cm (¾"). Cut along this line.

3. Draw a grainline parallel with the facing and turn any darts into tucks. Before you trim off the hem allowance, decide how you're going to finish off the area where the facing meets the lining—see pages 180-181 for options.

Back lining pattern

The back is cut with a centre pleat. Add 2cm (¾") to the centre back *stitching* line, rule straight and place it on the fold. Remove the hem allowance and notch the top and bottom *stitching* line to indicate the pleat.

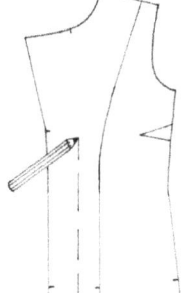

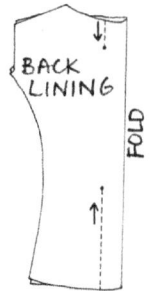

The pleat is stitched about 4cm (1½") down from the top and also from the hem up to the waist, forming an action back across the back between the armholes. Sometimes the back lining is cut with a central seam rather than on the fold, to save fabric (I never do this, but it's an option).

If the jacket has a back vent or is long, the back lining has a seam in it with the pleat starting above the waist. Add 2cm (¾") to the centre back *stitching* line, then add a seam allowance and rule straight. The pleat is stitched in about 4cm (1½") down

from the top. The rest of the seam follows the edge of the fabric.

Sometimes the back lining has a **back neck facing**, rather than the lining going all the way to the neck. The facing can be rounded or horizontal. A back neck facing makes the jacket look good on a coat hanger and also gives a smooth surface to sew the garment's label on. A horizontal facing (see below) provides extra stability across the shoulders, especially if coupled with a front facing from a princess line jacket, resulting in the entire shoulder being faced. A back neck facing is essential for collarless jackets. However, a facing has drawbacks: the facing's colour or seam line may show through the jacket. A facing takes longer to cut and sew, and takes slightly more of the fashion fabric. More time is needed to make pattern pieces for it, rather than just adding to the back piece when cutting out. I tend not to use a use a back neck facing unless I have to.

For a rounded back neck facing:

1. Trace around the jacket back and draw in where you'd like the facing to be. The facing can be deeper in the centre than at the shoulders.

2. Trace off the facing and add a seam allowance (for example 1cm (⅜")). Remove the seam allowance from the centre back and cut it on the fold. Cut one of fabric and one of interfacing.

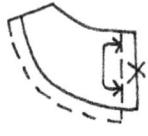

3. Add a seam allowance (same as you added to the facing) onto the lining. Create a back pleat as described on this page. Remove the hem allowance.

Sew the pleat in the back lining first, then sew the facing to the back lining with the lining uppermost as you sew. You can then treat the back lining as one unit.

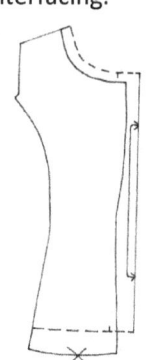

For a horizontal back neck facing:

1. Trace around the jacket back and rule a horizontal line in for the facing.

2. Trace off the facing and add a seam allowance (for example 1cm (⅜")). Remove the seam allowance from the centre back and cut it on the fold. Cut one of fabric and one of interfacing.

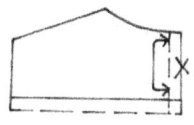

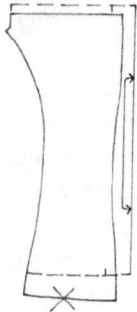

3. Add a seam allowance (same as you added to the facing) onto the lining. Create a back pleat as described on page 177. Remove the hem allowance. Sew the pleat in the back lining first, then attach it to the facing. You can then treat the back lining as one unit.

Sleeve lining pattern
As with the body, cut the sleeve lining to the finished length of the sleeves.

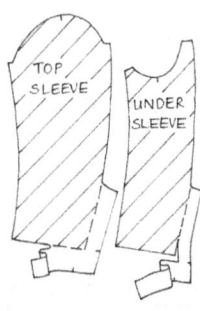

On two piece sleeves, remove any vent extensions.

School blazers and uniform jackets sometimes have a stitched-in pleat in the sleeve lining for lengthening them. The pleat might be about 2.5cm (1") deep when finished, meaning an extra 5cm (2") gets added to the sleeve lining length. This is coupled with a deep hem allowance of 7cm-10cm (3"-4") on the actual sleeve so it can be let down for growth. Note that you cannot do this if the sleeve has vents (but you can sew buttons on the sleeve to simulate vents). Add the pleat value straight onto the bottom of the sleeve lining pattern.

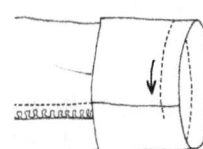

Sew the seams in the sleeve linings first. Stitch the pleat by folding up the end as illustrated and stitching around. You could make two smaller pleats instead of one big one, but the total pleat value needs to remain what you added onto the pattern. A free arm machine is helpful when stitching around.

Some people like to **raise the lining underarm** to bring the lining over the seams of the underarm. I admit I never do this, but you may like to try it on your next jacket and see if it improves the hang of the sleeves. On a 2pce sleeve, raise the underarm on the undersleeve by 1.5cm (⅝"). On a 1pce sleeve, raise the underarm by 1.5cm (⅝") and out by 6mm (¼"), and blend the new line back to the original. Raise the front and back body by a matching amount.

Pocket lining pattern
Pockets in jackets or coats often require lining, even if the jacket is an unlined one. Cut lining for:
- ✂ The top layer of in-seam pockets
- ✂ Lined patch pockets
- ✂ Welt/jet/flap pocket linings
- ✂ Underneath pocket flaps—these are sometimes cut in lining to reduce bulk

See the following page for an example of a jacket and a coat lining.

To sew a jacket lining
There's no need to neaten the raw edges of the lining unless it frays terribly. As with the main fabric, all the seams will be enclosed inside the jacket. The lining seam are generally pressed to one side because it's quicker and the lining fabric is so thin it doesn't create any noticeable bulk.

Assemble the lining
1. With the right sides together, stitch the pleat in the lining back. If the lining has centre back seam, sew that too. Attach the back facing if you have one.

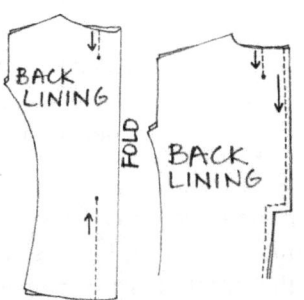

2. Sew the front facing to the front lining, then assemble the rest of the lining pieces so you have a jacket made out of lining.

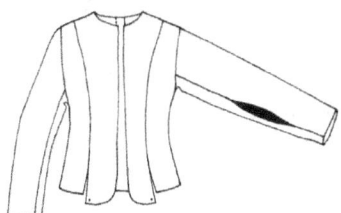

Leave a gap in one of the sleeves approximately 20cm (8") long or large enough to get your fist through. This is how you'll access the last part of the jacket/lining assembly.

Another way is to leave a gap in the lower back edge to be closed up by handsewing, or some people like to leave a gap in the lining's side seam. I favour the sleeve gap, but the lower back edge is the least obvious.

Depending on how you plan to finish the lower front lining/facing area, either sew the lining and facing together *all* the way down, or *stop* 10cm (4") short of the end. See pages 180-181.

Here's an example of a jacket and a coat lining:

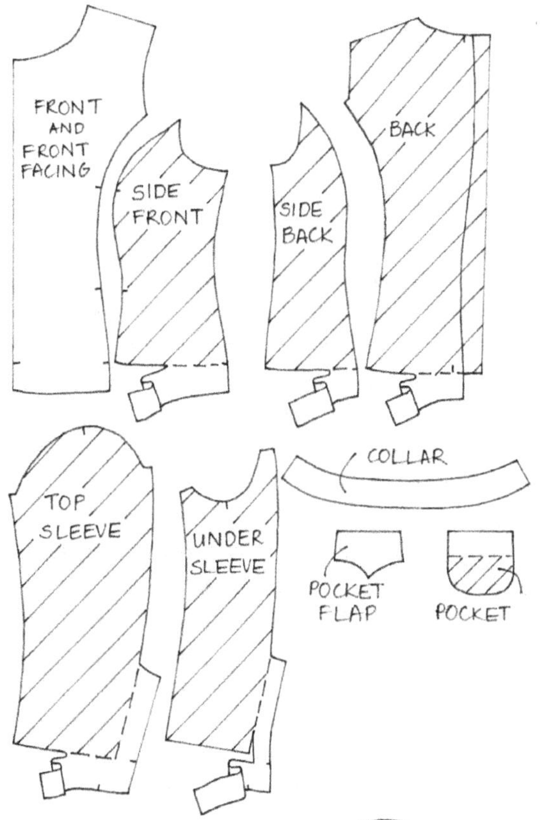

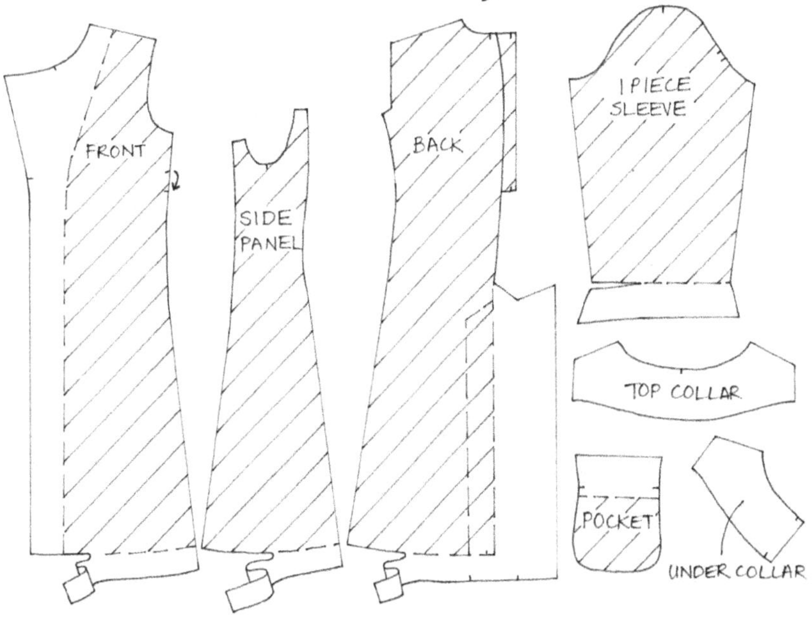

180 The Dressmaker's Companion

3. If the jacket has revers, sew the top collar to the lining neck so you can make the collar.

4. Fully press both lining and jacket before you start to sew them together. The jacket should have all the hems interfaced and already pressed up. Press the pleat in the back lining. Store both on a coat hanger or over a dressmakers model until you're ready.

Sew the jacket and lining together

5. With the right sides together, sew the lining unit to the body at the front edge and finish making the collar. Press. Understitch the front edge/collar if required.

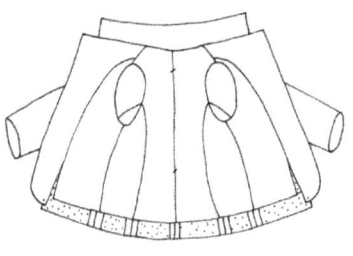

Turn everything the right way so the lining is sitting inside the jacket the way it will be worn, including the sleeves. It's **very important** that you don't try to attach the lining simply by placing the right sides together and sewing the edges, because it won't work. You won't be able to turn it through.

Instead, the edges to sew together need to be accessed from *inside* the jacket, which is why you have the gap in the sleeve lining to get to the last part.

6. Attach the sleeve linings at the wrists. Reach them from *inside* the jacket (**very important**). Take a 6mm (¼" footwidth) or 1cm (⅜") seam—it's inconsequential which. Note that the sleeve lining will not be sitting neatly inside the sleeve. Instead, you'll be bringing the edges together and stitching around.

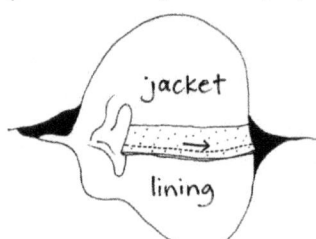

7. Secure the sleeve hem by machine stitching at the sleeve seam allowances on the inside. You can do this by hand using herringbone stitch (left picture), or by machine (right picture) but be extremely careful not to catch the outside part of the sleeve with the stitching. I do mine by machine.

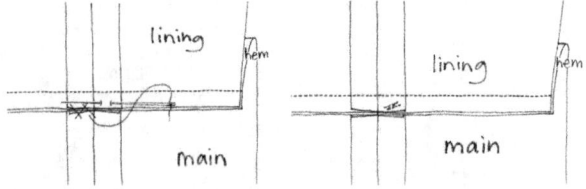

For one piece sleeves you'll need to catch up the hem by hand as well, because there's only one point where you can machine the seams together. Use a single strand of thread and take large, invisible stitches inside. I use blind hem stitch (on page 149).

8. Sew "That controversial area"—where lining hem meets front facing. See further on this page and next.

9. Finish sewing the bottom of the lining to the hem, once again with a 6mm (¼") or 1cm (⅜") seam. You'll have to use the gap in the sleeve to reach this area, and from now on. Secure the hem at the seams the same way as you did for the sleeves. Catch the hem up by hand if necessary (jackets with only side seams will need this—princess line jackets have enough seams to hold the hem in place).

10. Inside, attach the underarm point of the jacket to the underarm point of the lining by machine, ensuring both seams point towards the *sleeve*, not the body. Also inside, attach the top of the jacket sleeve to the top of the lining sleeve by hand with 2.5cm (1") long loose stitches. This stops the lining pulling out with your arm when you take the garment off.

11. Close up the gap in the sleeve lining—press the edges together like lips and machine along the edge. If you chose to leave a gap in the back hem instead, close it up by handstitching the jacket hem and lining together. The lining will sit over the stitches.

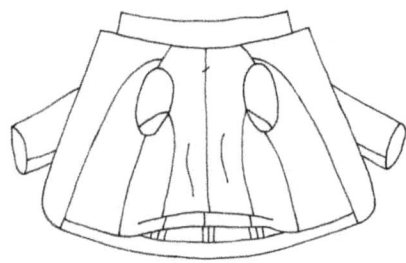

12. Sew any topstitching around the collar or front edges.

"That controversial area"—where lining hem meets front facing

There are two methods to finishing off this controversial area. They are both good methods. The first is the most conventional. The second is easier and is very good for fur coats and jackets. It's used in Australia but is often seen on European jackets. There's a third way if your jacket or coat has free-hanging lining.

Linings

Method 1 Conventional

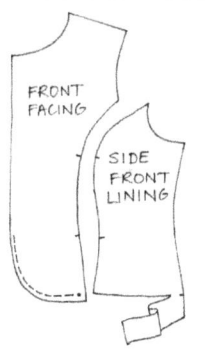
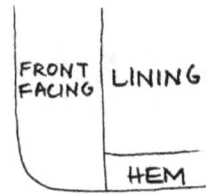

1. Make the lining pattern by removing the hem allowance from the front lining. The front facing only requires a seam allowance at the lower edge.

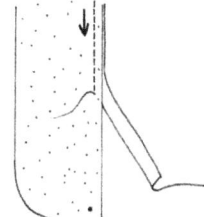

2. Sew the lining to the facing, but finish 10cm (4") short of the end.

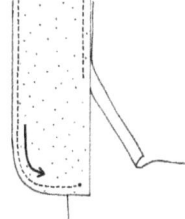

3. Stitch the facing to the front *exactly* to the end of the seam *and not over* (**important**).

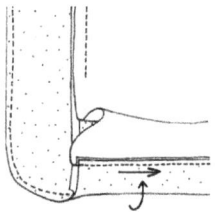

4. Sew the bottom of the lining and jacket together, taking a 6mm (¼" footwidth) or 1cm (⅜") seam (doesn't matter which).

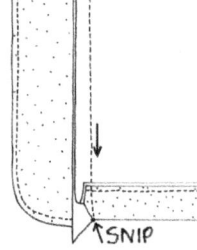

5. Clip the jacket front seam allowance *only*, to where you finished sewing the facing in Step 3. Stitch the lining to the facing through this point, creating a horizontal pleat in the lining as illustrated.

Method 2 European

This method is easier and it kind of does itself, but it needs the jacket lining to be cut in a particular way.

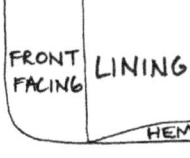

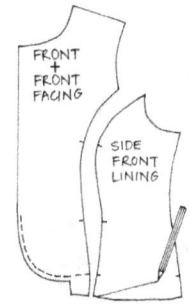
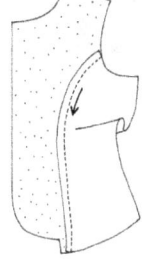

1. Make the lining pattern by cutting the side front lining the same length as the jacket *with* a hem allowance, then sloping back to the normal lining length at the side seam. The facing must also have a hem allowance.

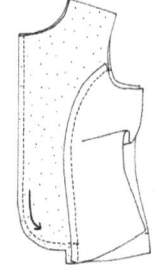

2. Sew the side lining to the facing all the way through.

3. Sew the front facing to the jacket front, taking the correct seam allowance. Stop sewing at the previous stitching line. Understitch if required.

4. Sew the hem of the jacket to the lining, taking a 6mm (¼" footwidth) or a 1cm (⅜") seam. A pleat will automatically form in the lining.

For **fur jackets**, the lower edge of the facing and front can be caught together by hand to stop fur getting caught in the seam.

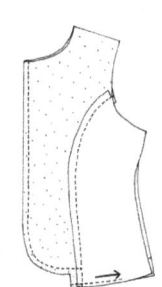

Free hanging coat linings

Some coats and jackets, particularly long coats and swing coats, may have a free hanging lining.

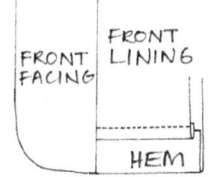
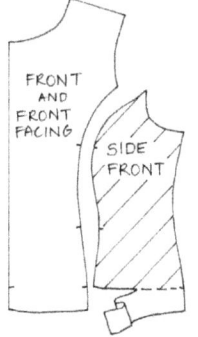

Make the lining pattern by removing the hem allowance from the front lining.

The sewing order is:
1. Hem the lining
2. Attach the lining to the front facing
3. Stitch the front facing to the front
4. Stitch the hem on the actual jacket

Measurements and ease

Selecting a commercial paper pattern size based on your retail/ready-to-wear size is destined to end in disappointment because pattern companies and clothing manufacturers use different size charts. The most reliable way to choose a size is to take *your* measurements and compare them to the pattern pieces.

Taking measurements

Measurements are a guide to choosing a pattern size. You'll still have to fit the garment, because measuring is only a guide to *size*, not *shape*. Two people can have the same measurements but be completely different shapes.

Take measurements over regular clothes, but try to wear the underwear intended to be worn with the garment, for example push-up bra, control-top knickers, pantihose.

Note the date when the measurements are taken, and record the date and measurements on the pattern. I also jot mine down in a book—it's interesting to look back and see what's changed.

I would say bust, waist and hip are the three most important measurements, but certainly take other measurements if you expect them to be smaller or larger than average.

Bust
Measure around the fullest part of the bust. Be sure to keep the tape measure level at the back.

Waist
Don't suck your tummy in. Your actual waist is the smallest circumference around your middle. However, if you wear skirts and pants lower than this, also take a measurement where the garment's waist will be.

Hip
Hip is more accurately described as a seat or bum measurement. It's the fullest part around your bottom, not where you would put your hands if asked to "put your hands on your hips". I ask the person I'm measuring to stand side-on to me, so I can see to measure around the fullest part. The fullest part is usually about 20cm (8") below the waist.

Neck
If the style has a fitted collar, for example a shirt, take a neck measurement.

Across back and across front
Everyone seems to measure this differently. Measure across the back or chest about 10cm (4") down from the shoulder. Try to imagine where the sleeve seams will sit and measure from seam to seam.

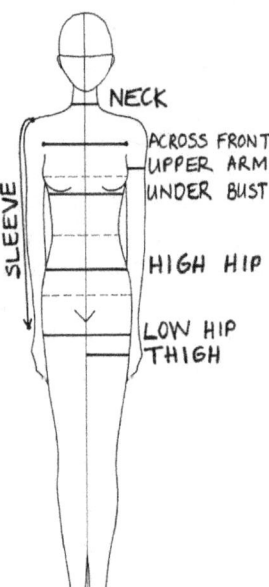

Upper arm
If you have large upper arms and suspect the pattern might be too tight, take this measurement.

Under bust/rib cage
A good measurement to check against the pattern when making strapless tops.

High hip
Your high hip is about half way between your waist and hip, therefore about 10cm (4") down from your waist.

Low hip
A low hip measurement could also be called an "around thighs" measurement; occasionally some people are wider on their legs below their hip measurement.

182

Measurements and ease

Thigh
Large thighs and making trousers? Take this measurement.

Length
You can measure the desired length with a tape measure, or simply by holding the pattern up to the person (or yourself in the mirror) and checking. Make sure you don't bend over to see where the measurement is!

Measure sleeve length from the top of the shoulder to the desired length with the arm *straight* and vertical. If you measure with the elbow bent the sleeve will end up too long.

On men's shirts or drop shouldered garments, the sleeve length is measured from the middle of the back to the wrist.

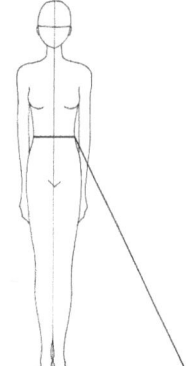

For skirts that stick out with petticoats, such as wedding gowns, take an angled length measurement.

Full U and half U
A full U measurement is useful for one-piece swimsuits and jumpsuits. Begin with one end of the tape measure on one shoulder, pass it between your legs, then up to your shoulder again.

A half U measurement can be used for trousers or knickers. It's taken like a full U, but only from the waist. Place the tape measure at your waist, pass it between your legs, then to the other side of your waist. If the garment sits lower than the waist, place the tape measure lower too.

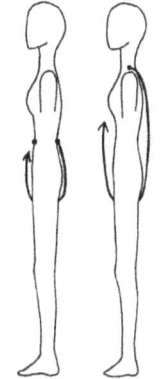

Ease
If you made a garment to exactly the same measurements as your body, it would be skin tight. Ease is the extra room in a garment to allow for comfortable wearing and movement. It's the difference between the wearer's measurements and the finished garment's measurements. Confusingly, "to ease" also refers to how a seam is sewn when one side is longer than the other—we say one side of the seam is eased into the other side (we're not talking about that kind of ease here).

To illustrate ease, try the pinch test. Try on a garment and pull all the fullness to one side. If you can take a 2cm deep pinch of fabric, you have a total of 4cm ease since you're pinching a double thickness of fabric.

Wearing ease is the *minimum* amount of ease required for movement in a fitted garment made from woven fabric. It varies for different parts of the body. Some examples of minimum wearing ease are:

- Bust 4cm-6cm (1½"-2⅜")
- Waist for a waistband that sits on the actual waistline 1cm-1.5cm (⅜"-⅝")
- Waist for a lower faced waistline none
- Hip 6cm-8cm (2⅜"-3⅛")
- Upper arm 5cm (2") for woven fabrics or 2.5cm (1") for stretch fabrics
- Neck 1.2cm (½")

The amount of ease you find comfortable is personal preference. Some people like tight fitting clothes and some like loose clothes. To get an idea, try measuring some of the clothes you already have.

The amount of ease also varies for the *type* of garment. Naturally, outer garments will have more ease than underwear, because they have to fit over other clothes. Here are some examples of bust ease from my own wardrobe:

- Bias cut full slip 2.5cm (1")
- Loose summer nightie 25cm (10")
- Fitted blouse 6.5cm (2½")
- Fitted winter coat 20cm (8")
- Ribbed skivvy negative 20cm (8") (see below about negative ease)

Design ease is added in addition to wearing ease according to the style and whims of fashion.

Some patterns are designed with **no ease**, for example tight jeans, because the garment is designed for stretch denim. The pattern must only ever be made in the fabric it's designed for otherwise it won't fit.

Negative ease is where the garment is smaller than the wearer's measurements, for example in stretch swimwear. Paper patterns designed for stretch fabrics have a guide on the envelope to tell you how stretchy the fabric should be. If you've drafted your own pattern or are substituting fabrics, it can be hard to predict the amount of ease or negative ease needed on stretch fabrics without actually making the garment in the correct fabric.

Mostly, as a patternmaker, I use the correct fabric. I cut it out with no ease allowed for, then take the garment in if needed.

In summary: body measurements + wearing ease + design ease if any = finished garment measurements.

Comparing measurements to pattern pieces

Try to get the paper pattern as correct as you can before cutting any fabric, even if it's only test fabric. Compare your measurements plus ease to the finished garment measurements. Either measure the pattern yourself or see if it's written on the pattern. Some commercial patterns even tell you how much ease it's designed with.

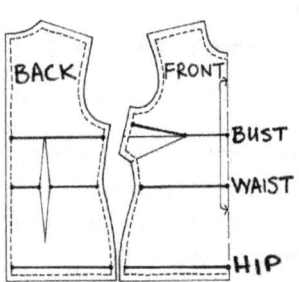

To measure the pattern, take a tape measure and measure from the centre front to the centre back, excluding seam allowances and darts. Then, double over the tape measure to find the total measurement.

If you own a garment similar to the one you're making, compare it to the pattern (or, better, if you have the garment's pattern, compare that). If you frequently use a certain brand of pattern, you'll come to expect what size you are and even what alterations you'll need to do for a good fit. If you frequently fit a certain figure type you'll become familiar with the alterations required, and with experience you'll be able to see if the pattern *looks* right.

What if the measurements don't match the pattern's? Pick the closest size and add where required.

If the pattern is made of paper or tissue, try pinning the pieces together and trying it on over your clothes. It's very good for checking design proportion and length. Pin the centre front and centre back to your clothes (you'll only have half the garment). Pin the side seams together if you can, or note where you need to add. Check: shoulder width, neckline depth, dart position, waist and underbust seam position and length. Pin the underarm seam of the sleeve and slide it onto your arm to check the sleeves.

Mitres

Introduction.................................... 185
Mitring a trim or braid 185
Mitring a hem 185
Mitring a hem using a template............ 186
Mitred edges, borders and bands 187
Mitred edgings 187
Mitred borders............................. 188
Mitred bands—inside corners............... 188
Mitred bands—outside corners 189

A mitre is a diagonal join of two edges at a corner. It's an elegant solution to eliminating the bulk caused by folding the two edges over each other.

The corner can be an outward corner (the mitre goes *around* the corner), OR

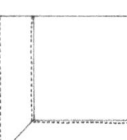

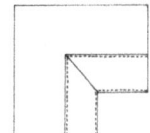
It can be an inward corner (the mitre lies *within* the corner).

Successful mitres require:
- Accuracy in measuring, cutting, sewing and pressing. One millimetre makes a difference.
- Pressing the folds of the mitre as you make them.

Mitring a trim or braid

1. With the trim and garment both right side up, lay the trim on the garment and stitch them together along the edge, stopping at the corner.

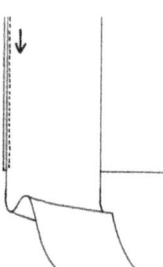

2. Press the trim straight back on itself, so the fold aligns with the adjacent edge.

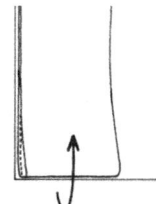

3. Fold the trim down creating a diagonal fold across the centre.

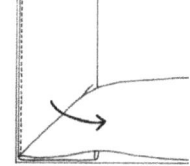

4. Lift up the trim and stitch along the diagonal fold line, through all layers including the garment. Trim the corner off.

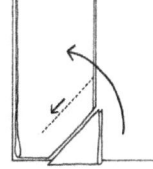

If you think this will create too much bulk along one side of the mitre (by having both seam allowances on one side), stitch through the trim only and press the seam open.

5. Fold the trim back, align the edges with the garment, and continue stitching.

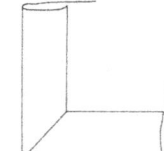

Mitring a hem

If required, overlock the raw edge *before* you sew the mitre, otherwise it will be too hard to get the overlocker in. If the hem isn't overlocked but will be turned up twice, press up the first amount and leave it like that as you sew the mitre.
Both sides of the mitre need to be the same depth.

Method 1
This is quick and easy to do at the ironing board.

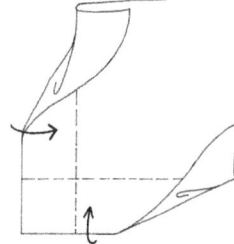

1. Press the hem allowances up to form creases. Open them out.

2. Fold the corner up diagonally, aligning the creases and press.

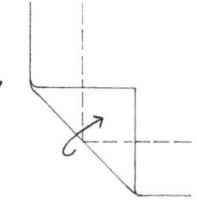

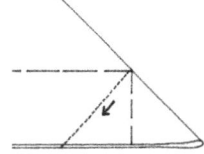

3. Open out the corner. Fold the fabric diagonally, right sides

together, and stitch on the diagonal press line.

4. Trim the seam back to 6mm (¼") and trim the corner too. Press the seam open and turn it to the right side.

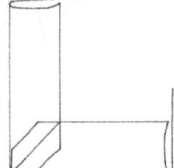

Method 2
1. Press up the hem allowance on both sides.

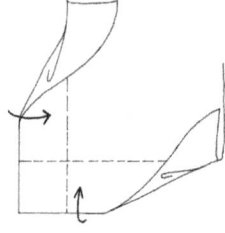

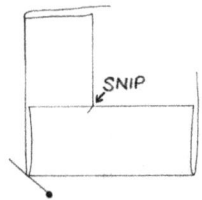

2. Make a tiny snip where they intersect.

If you don't want to snip the fabric (say, if you've already overlocked the edge or if the edge is turned under), insert a pin in each hem allowance where they intersect. Pin or mark the corner. Unfold.

If you haven't overlocked the edge but plan to, this is your last chance. You should still be able to see the snips under the overlocking.

3. With the right sides together, stitch from the snips to the corner point.

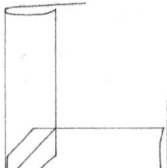

4. Trim the seam to 6mm (¼") and trim the corner too. Press the seam open. Turn to the right side and press.

Mitring a hem using a template
If you have a lot of corners to do, for example if you're making tablecloths and serviettes, a cardboard template is the quickest way to go. You'll need an L-square, pencil and some cardboard. It's important to be very accurate.

Make a pattern
1. Create a perfect 90 degree corner on the cardboard and rule in the fold lines of the hem. Mark twice the hem depth along both edges.

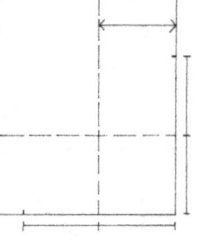

2. Rule a line connecting these two points, which should run perfectly through the centre of the intersecting hem folds.

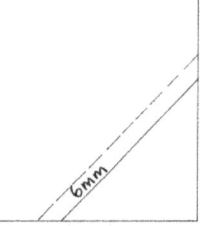

3. Add a 6mm (¼") seam allowance to the line—you'll be able to quickly sew the mitre using the edge of a 6mm (¼") foot as a guide.
Score the cut line of the template with a biro so you can flip up the corner.

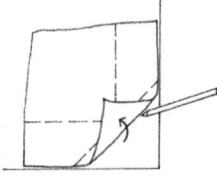

To use the template, position it on the corner of the fabric. Flip up the corner of the template and draw in the cut line. Trim the corner off the fabric. Speed things up by trimming three or four layers at a time.

To sew a mitre using a template
1. Before you sew the mitre, either overlock or press under 6mm (¼") along the straight edges of the fabric. I just measure this using my calibrated eye as I press, otherwise it takes too long. Leave the mitre part as a raw edge.

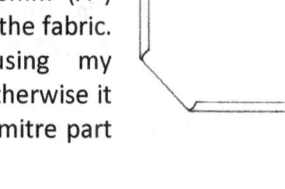

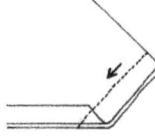

2. Place the right sides of the fabric together and sew accurately across the corner, taking the 6mm (¼") seam allowance.

3. Press the mitre seam open.

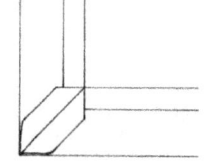

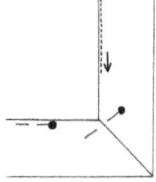

4. Turn the mitre to the right side and press the hem in place, securing with a few pins. Sew the hem.

✂ The same method is a lovely way to finish an **embroidered baby blanket or lap rug**. The blanket must have perfectly square corners and straight sides, so measure and trim it up if required.

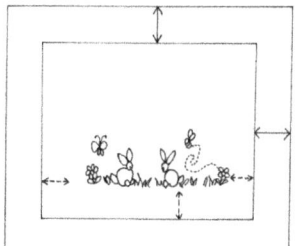

1. Cut a backing fabric 10cm (4") bigger than the blanket all the way around. Ensure that any embroidery is at least 10cm (4") away from the edges.

2. Trim off the corners using a template made for a 10cm (4") hem allowance. Press up 6mm (¼") on the straight edges.

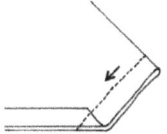

3. Sew the mitres, press the seams open and turn through to the right side. Press the border hem up.

You now have a "window frame", of which the outside edge is the same size as the blanket. Slip the blanket into it and sew the hem through all thicknesses. The result will be a mitred border for the embroidered blanket, with a matching backing to hide the embroidery's back.

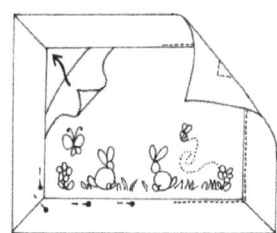

Mitred edgings, borders and bands

An **edging** is like a binding but is not filled by the edge it's attached to.
The reverse side is the same as the front.

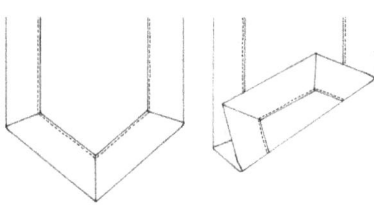

A **border** looks like an edging from the front, but it sits on the top like a picture frame.
The main fabric acts as a backing to the border on the reverse side.

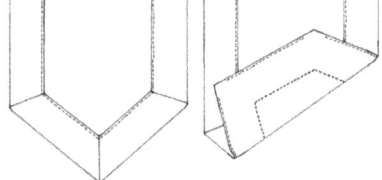

Ribbed or plain **bands** are a usual way to finish knitwear.

For all of these, you'll need to make a pattern incorporating the mitred corner. Start by drawing the finished shape with the seamlines and mitred corners. Trace off each separate piece and add seam allowances and grainlines.

Mitred edgings

The front and reverse sides of the mitred edging are the same.

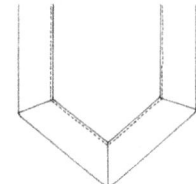

Make a pattern

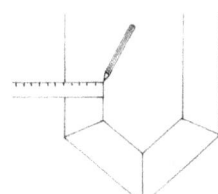

1. Draw the edging onto the pattern.

2. Trace off the separate pieces.

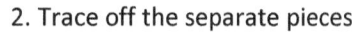
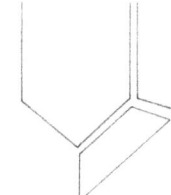

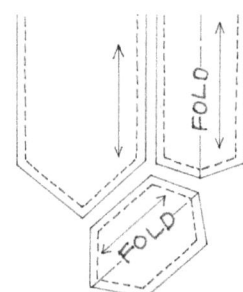

3. Add seam allowances to the pieces. Mirror the pieces requiring a folded edge, as shown.
If the edging is curved, there will need to be a *seam* instead of a *fold* on the outer edge.

To sew a mitred edging

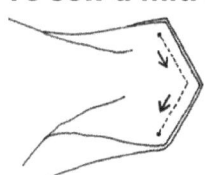

1. Join the mitres together first, but don't sew beyond the seam allowance. Backstitch securely at each end and be accurate.

2. Press the seams open and turn the edging to the right side. Press a fold in the outside edge. The edging is now ready to be applied.

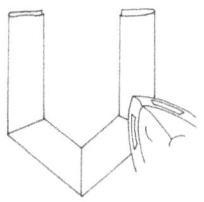

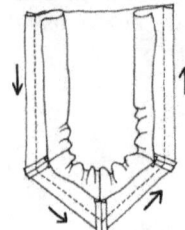

3. Lay the prepared edging on the *wrong* side of the edge and stitch through one layer, pivoting at the corners. Press the seam towards the edging.

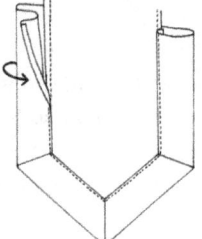

4. Bring edging around to the right side. Press under the raw edge and sew the edging in place by machine.

If you wish to **handsew** the edging in place, lay the prepared edging on the *right* side of the edge in Step 3, stitch, then bring it around to the *wrong* side and handsew down (so you're handsewing what will be the underneath).

Mitred borders

Borders sit on top of the main fabric, with a seam all the way around the outside edge.

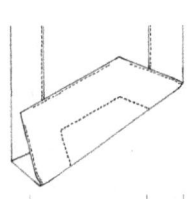

Make a pattern
1. Draw the border onto the pattern.

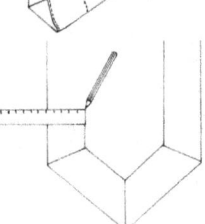

2. Trace off the separate pattern pieces.

3. Add seam allowances and grainlines to the pieces.

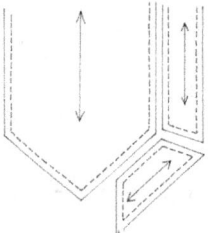

To sew a mitred border

1. Sew the mitres first but don't sew beyond the seam allowance. Backstitch securely at each end. Be very accurate.

2. Press the seams open.

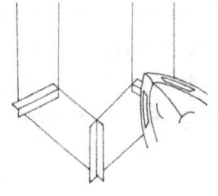

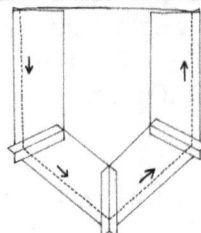

3. Lay the right side of the border onto the wrong side of the main fabric, and sew around the outside edge, pivoting at the corners.

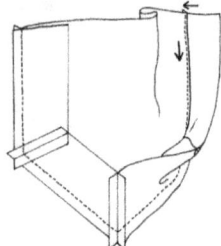

4. Trim the corners if required, and press the seam towards the main fabric. Understitch as far as you can into each corner.

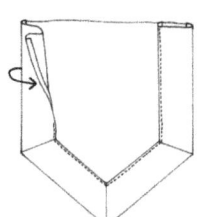

5. Bring the border over to the right side. Press under the raw edge and sew in place by machine.

Mitred bands—inside corners

The most usual place to see an inside mitre is at the bottom of a V-neck on a knit top.

Make a pattern

1. On the garment pattern, draw the shape of the *finished* band in the neckline.

2. Make a pattern for the finished band. The **width** should be twice the finished width plus two seam allowances. The **length** should suit the edge it's to be sewn to.

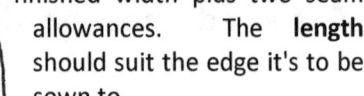

3. To get the correct angle of the mitre, fold the band pattern in half longways and lay it on top of the neckline pattern.

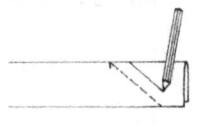

Draw in the shape of the mitre, then add a seam allowance and cut off the excess pattern paper.

Mitres **189**

To sew a band with an inside mitre

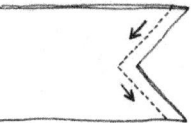
1. Sew the mitre in the band first. Fold the band right sides together and stitch the two ends together, pivoting in the middle.

2. Turn the band to the right side.

3. On the garment, stay stitch the point of the V neck, stitching on the seam line. Pivot at the point. You can use a shorter stitch length, such as 1 or 1.5, for strength. Snip exactly to the stitching.

4. Set the mitre into the corner: With the mitred band underneath, put a pin exactly through the corner to match the point up with the centre of the mitre. Stitch to the corner, pivot on the point, then continue sewing.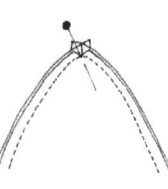

5. Overlock the seam, and press it away from the band. You may like to sew a row of topstitching on the garment side to keep everything flat and in place.

Mitred bands—outside corners

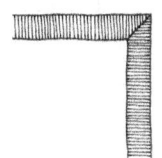
Outside corners in knitted bands are rare, but any fabric, knitted or woven, can be used to make an outside corner this way. The point of the band is 90 degrees.

Make a pattern

1. The **width** of the band should be twice the finished width plus two seam allowances. The **length** should suit the edge it's to be sewn to.

2. To make the mitred corner on the band, fold the band pattern in half longways. Mark the corner point on the seam line. Draw a 45 degree line from the folded edge to the corner point. Add a seam allowance to this line to create the cutting line. Trim off the excess pattern paper.

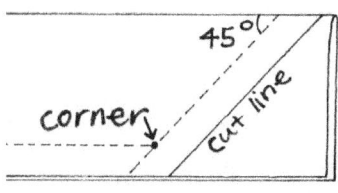

To sew a band with an outside mitre

1. Sew the mitre in the band first, but don't sew beyond the seam allowance.

2. Trim the point and turn the mitre the right way. Press the seam allowances open inside. Press the fold along the outside edge.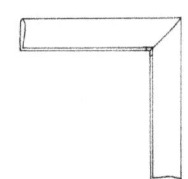

3. Position the band along the edge with the band uppermost. Place a pin exactly through the mitre and the corner. Stitch the band to the edge, pivoting at the corner.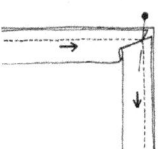

4. Overlock the seam. Press the seam away from the band to help it lie flat. At the corner, press the seam allowances neatly folded over each other. You may like to topstitch on the garment side to keep everything in place.

Overlocker FAQs

Or serger, for US readers. Overlockers are fabulous machines that sew seams, trim the edge and neaten it all in one operation. Some people find overlockers intimidating, especially the threading, but mastery will bring confidence!

Do I really need an overlocker?
AND
If I have an overlocker, do I need a straight stitching machine anymore?
You don't really *need* an overlocker (I didn't have one for years) but it sure makes it easier to sew a neat, professional-looking garment!
Yes, you will need your regular machine to use with your overlocker. I tell people an overlocker is like buying a microwave for your kitchen; it makes life easier but you still need your regular oven and hotplate.

What do I do with the ends? Do I just leave them or cut them off?
If you leave the ends long they'll undo and you'll have threads. Cut them off; overlocking doesn't undo readily when it's stitched through fabric. In most cases an intersecting seam will hold the ends and stop them fraying. In situations when you need to secure a tail end, you can:

- Thread the tail onto a tapestry needle or loop turner and thread it back through the just-overlocked seam.
- Use a liquid fray stopper at the end of the seam. When it's dry, cut off the tail.
- Secure the tails as you overlock. This might require practise to get neat results.

At the beginning of a seam, sew for one or two stitches, then raise the presser foot. Bring the tail to the left, towards you, around and under the presser foot, and between the needle and the cutter. Lower the presser foot holding the tail in position. Sew over the tail, then swing it off to the right so it gets cut off.
At the end of a seam, stitch past the end by one stitch. Raise the presser foot and needle. Turn the fabric over carefully to sew back the way you came and align the edge with the cutter. Lower the presser foot and turn the handwheel so the needle goes in at the end of the seam. Stitch over the previous stitching a short distance then run off the edge.

Is it OK to trim as I overlock?
It's better not to, if you want to prolong the life of the cutting blade. Trimming blunts the cutting blade much more quickly and turns the edge into a chewed rag instead of a crisply cut line. Rather than trimming off a strip of fabric, aim to only graze the edge to cut off the fraying threads. Grazing the edge should still allow you to see any 3mm (⅛") notches you've snipped. If you're overlocking an edge before you've sewn the seam, you certainly *won't* want to trim because you won't know where the stitching line is.

I just can't seem to get the tension right. Is it that important?
Yes, the tension *is* important. The overlocking stitch should sit smooth and flat, and will be much easier to unpick should you need to. Your manual should hopefully offer solutions to fixing the tension.

How do I stop that blasted lower looper from coming unthreaded all by itself, especially starting off?

- Check to see if the thread is caught on any of the spools or thread holders above the machine.
- Are you using a good quality thread? OR is the thread old? OR has it been stored in a sunny place? Thread becomes brittle with age and this is hastened by sunlight. Cheap or old thread can have weak spots that will abrade and break as the thread passes through the machine.
- When you re-thread the machine (for the millionth time), pull all the threads through to sit neatly under and behind the presser foot. Cut the bottom looper thread so it's only about 5cm (2") long—I don't know why but sometimes it helps. Start sewing slowly. You could also try holding the thread behind the needle for a short way and see if that helps.
- Some machines need to be re-threaded in a certain order; check the manual.
- More suggestions: start off with a few turns of the handwheel, or start off with fabric under the foot rather than running onto it.

Why shouldn't I use pins?
You can use pins; just be careful to keep them out of the way of the presser foot and cutter otherwise you'll damage your machine and the cutting blade. Some people find the experience of not using pins freeing and find that it improves the rest of their sewing.

Overlocker FAQs

The overlocker isn't grabbing the whole edge of the fabric; there's overlocking hanging off the edge.
Make sure the fabric is well under the needle(s). The weight of the garment may be pulling itself out from under the presser foot. Support the weight as you sew and hold it in place with your left hand.
If that doesn't resolve things, check that the stitch width isn't jammed.

What is differential feed? Do all overlockers have it?
Differential feed consists of two sets of feed dogs—one at the front and one at the back. The differential feed automatically stretches, gathers or eases the fabric when the amount of feed of the front feed dog is changed in relation to that of the back. It can be used to prevent puckered or stretched stitches on fabrics such as sheers, knits and bias cut fabrics. Not all overlockers have differential feed. Refer to your overlocker's manual.

Is there a right and wrong side to overlocking?
Yes there is. The right side comes out uppermost when you're overlocking.

You can identify the right side because it looks loopy.
The wrong side looks triangle-y.

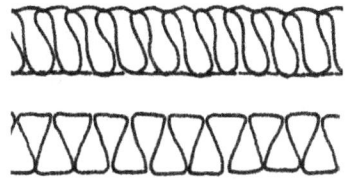

Preferably, the right side of the overlocking should be on display in the interior of the garment.
For open seams, hems and the edges of facings, overlock with the *right side* of the fabric facing up.
For closed seams to be pressed towards the back of the garment, overlock with the *front facing up*, so when it's pressed the right side of the overlocking will be seen.

For both open and closed seams, this means beginning the overlocking at opposite ends of the seam for the right and left of the garment, so you've got a pair.

For underarm/sleeve seams, begin overlocking at the wrist for one seam and the hem for the other. For open seams the right side faces up while overlocking, and for (already stitched) closed seams the front faces up.

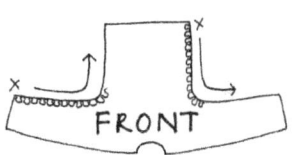

Side seams and shoulders can be conveniently overlocked in an anticlockwise direction, again with the right side facing up for open seams or the front facing up (already stitched) for closed ones.

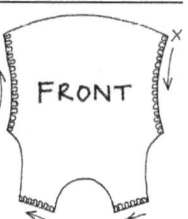

What if I don't have all the same colour threads?
Colours can be mixed on the overlocker if you don't have all the same shade. Use the closest matching thread in the upper looper, since that one forms the right side of the overlocking. Use the next matching for the needle thread and the remaining one for the lower looper. By the way, cream or ecru thread suits most pastel coloured fabric.

I have trouble overlocking curves—the fabric slips out.
Overlockers don't sew curves easily because the presser foot is long. Try and straighten the curved edge with your hands as you sew it and watch where the machine is actually sewing, not where the fabric enters.

How often should I get my overlocker serviced?
It depends on how much you use it but it's easy to forget about if you don't use it much. You can go a long time between services if you clean and oil your machine regularly. A vacuum cleaner is ideal for getting the fluff out of the insides.

What else can my overlocker do apart from neatening edges?
Overlockers (but not all) can:
- make a narrow rolled hem
- gather
- sew and hem knits
- be used as an embellishing tool (for example using water soluble stabilizers)
- do decorative overlocking with decorative thread and stitches
- blind hem
- pin tuck
- flatlock hems
- make a lettuce leaf hem on knit or bias cut fabrics

Party fabrics

Introduction	192
Fabrics for figure flattery	192
Dupion silk	193
Novelty tweed	193
Satin	194
Lace	195
Brocade	197
Velvet	198
Sheers	199
Taffeta	200
Metallics	200
Fur	201
Beaded and sequined fabric	202
Introduction to beading	203
requirements	203
plan the design	203
start beading	203
sewing single beads	203
sewing more than one bead	204
couching—a line of beads	204
parallel rows of beads	204
clusters of beads	204
lazy daisy 3D effect	204
Sequins	205
single sequins	205
rows of seqins	205
Paillets	205
Other general beading/sequin tips	205

Special occasions call for special clothes. Whether it's a wedding, party or important dinner, making your own special occasion garment is totally achievable. Although it can be intimidating to make the first cut into that (maybe expensive) fabric, nothing beats the confidence-boosting moment of saying *Thank you, I made it myself*.

Picking a fabric is the key to getting the look you want. If you're on a budget, buy a small amount of expensive material to use for accents. If you're designing a range, using stunning fabrics in simple styles is a good way to lessen your manufacturing costs and speed production.

✂ When mixing fabrics in the same garment, a good design rule is to match the colour *or* the texture. For example, trim a red velvet dress with perfectly matching red satin.

✂ Store your fabric rolled onto a long tube to prevent wrinkles and creases. Ask for a tube at the fabric shop when you buy the fabric.

✂ Install a fresh, sharp needle in your sewing machine and throw that old, dull needle away! You may want to change the needle two or three times for one garment.

✂ Don't wear lipstick if you habitually put pins in your mouth. It leaves red dots on the fabric where the pins have been. Alternatively, don't put pins in your mouth if you habitually wear lipstick.

✂ Test! Test! Test! your machine stitching and pressing on spare fabric first.

Fabrics for figure flattery

✂ All shiny fabrics reflect the light and make you look heavier. Dull-faced fabrics which absorb the light add less visual weight.

✂ Knits with weight and drape tend to be more slimming than wovens.

✂ Short haired furs look less bulky than long haired furs.

✂ Keep bulky fabrics such as wool, leather and chunky knits away from areas of your body that you want to look smaller.

✂ Since stiff fabrics stand away from the body they can be used to hide figure irregularities, but they make the figure appear larger when used for exaggerated silhouettes. Most soft fabrics flatter heavier figures, but if you fit them too tightly they'll emphasize bulges.

Dupion silk

Also called dupioni or douppioni, it's a silk with a lustrous yet slight slubby texture. It comes in a huge range of colours, from vivids to pastels.

Styles and fitting

Dupion silk lends itself to crisp, fitted designs such as jackets and skirts. It's also used for garments with volume, intended to stand away from the body, such as ball gowns and party dresses.

It looks good with piping to define the edges. Styles with gathering and pleats look terrific, as does ruching, ruffles and buttons and loops.

A good fit is very important since dupion silk is unforgiving. Any differences in the left and right sides of the wearer's body will show, particularly on simple, fitted clothes. You may need to adjust the garment differently on each side to get a perfect fit, or even make left and right side pattern pieces if the difference is great.

Dupion silk doesn't work for garments designed with soft drape. It doesn't ease particularly well, either, so take care on areas such as set-in sleeves.

As with all fabrics, cheap and low quality silk will be harder to sew into a good-looking garment.

Interfacing and lining

Iron-on interfacing tends to make the silk "papery" and stiff—try it and see. A soft, jersey (knit) fusing may work. Otherwise, use a sew-in interfacing or silk organza. For out-of-sight facings and waistbands, you can use regular fusible interfacing.

Beware of using a too-hot iron when ironing interfacing on, as it will cause the silk to bubble.

Ideally, each piece of the garment should be mounted onto silk organza before sewing together, to stop creasing and give support when it's worn. This can make a garment quite expensive. As an alternative, firmly fitted areas like dress bodices can be mounted onto a light woven, sew-in interfacing (such as Shapewell) and medium weight bridal net used for the rest of the garment.

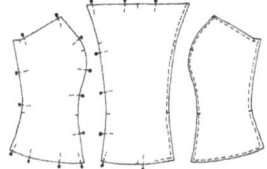

Cutting

First, make sure the silk is perfectly smooth. Mist with water and dry iron if required.

Pull the silk into shape if it isn't square, so the slubs will be perfectly horizontal, parallel to the hem, when the garment is worn. Straighten the cut edge by pulling a thread and cutting along the pull—see page 69.

When positioning pieces on the fabric, avoid big slubs landing in obvious places (such as the centre front).

You can cut the silk out at the same time as any lining or interfacing—simply slip the extra layers underneath.

Use sharp scissors to prevent the edges ragging and getting chewed up.

Stitching

Dupion silk frays easily. Watch that your seams don't fray away to nothing from handling. If you have to do a fitting, at the very least overlock the lower edge to stop fraying.

If the garment has buttonholes, check to see if they look OK. If not, consider zips or buttons and loops instead.

Dupion silk doesn't ease too well, so sew with particular care eased areas like sleeve heads. Any tiny pleats accidentally caught in a seam will not press out. If you have to do alterations, the stitching holes from the unpicking will show and so will any folds that have been pressed in. To remove, dip your thumb into some water and rub the line of holes or the crease with the back of your thumbnail. Use a very sparing amount of water only where you need it, to prevent watermarks. You can also wet the area with a spray bottle; the mist of a spray bottle produces a less definite watermark line. Either way, check first. Press with steam until it dries. The stitching holes won't come out as well if the area is pressed with steam first. See pages 298-299 for more on unpicking.

Pressing

Turn the dial on the iron to silk setting. Be very careful with moisture. Dupion silk is particularly prone to watermark or waterspot, that is, the water will leave a tide line or spots. You can usually use a steam iron, provided that the iron doesn't spit water or leak onto the fabric. It may give more control to use a dry iron and a damp press cloth.

Check if you need to press before overlocking seams in case the overlocking imprints through.

Press curves over a ham. Pay special attention to bust curves to get a smooth seam.

Novelty tweed

This is sometimes called fashion tweed, modern tweed or Chanel tweed. It's a loosely woven, slubby plaid favoured by Chanel. It appears to be a "love it or hate it" fabric for people. Popular for wedding guest attire or race wear, it can be 100% silk, synthetic, wool or a blend. It comes in all colours, from subdued to vivid, and may have shiny or metallic threads woven into the plaid.

It's typically made into Chanel-style suits, with neat little jackets and knee length slim skirts. A feature is a special braid or fringed edge made from the fabric and stitched around the collar and front edge, wrists and pocket flaps.

Novelty tweed isn't usually cut on the bias but details such as pocket flaps can be.

Novelty tweed moulds well to the figure and is fairly pliable and forgiving. The main challenge when sewing it is controlling the fraying.

Styles and fitting
Choose a fitted style. Novelty tweed is generally too thick for pleats and gathers.

Novelty tweed is prone to abrasion and snagging due to the loose weave.

If you're making a fringed edge, experiment with the fabric to see if the lengthwise or crosswise grain makes a more interesting one (the colours will be different).

Interfacing and lining
The big drawback of novelty tweed is that it frays like mad even if you only look at it! Bond every piece of the garment with lightweight fusible jersey (knit) interfacing before you begin to handle it. For skirts, instead of interfacing the whole skirt, you can fuse 2.5cm (1") strips onto every edge—these will get stitched in when you sew the seam. For the hem, iron on a strip the depth of the hem allowance.

Novelty tweed doesn't have to be lined, but usually is since it's used for suits. Regular lining is fine.

Cutting
If you're planning to make fringing, cut the strips for it first.

Match the plaid pattern when you lay the pattern pieces out, just like you would for any checked design. See pages 80-84.

Save time by slipping the interfacing under the tweed and cutting them out together, if it isn't too thick.

Stitching
After cutting, fuse all of the pieces with lightweight jersey interfacing, then overlock around the edges of all the pieces, even if the inside of the garment will be enclosed in a lining. *Then*, when all the pieces are stabilized, you can start sewing.

Take care to match the plaid pattern as you sew the seams.

To make **fringing**, cut strips the depth of the finished fringe plus one seam allowance. Iron a strip of fusible interfacing onto the seam allowance so it doesn't fray. As an extra anti-fray precaution, overlock the edge of the seam allowance and sew a line of regular machine stitching between the fusing and the fringing to stabilize. Fray away to make the fringing.

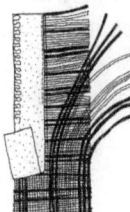

Pressing
Novelty tweed is easy to press with a steam iron set to the fibre content of the fabric.

Satin
Satin refers to the fabric's weave. The fibre could be anything, but silk or polyester are often used for evening wear.

Satin weave has lots of floats so you see more of the thread's surface. That is, instead of the threads being woven "under-over-under-over", they're woven "under-over-over-over-over-under". This makes the fabric shiny, but less durable and more prone to abrasion.

Satin can be high gloss or matt.

Satin can be stiff and heavy, for example duchess satin. It can also be thin, floppy and drapey. Crêpe-backed satin has an equally useable crêpe finish on the reverse side, providing its own tone-on-tone coordinating fabric.

Styles and fitting
Heavy satins look good in structured, fitted designs, for example strapless tops or formal wedding dresses. Floppy satins suit drapey, flowing, bias cut or loose-fitting garments. Gathers and pleats work in either type of satin. Satin is sometimes used behind lace, with either the shiny or dull side out. Crêpe backed satin can be used with the satin side as a contrast *or* the satin side used with the crêpe side as a contrast.

Interfacing and lining
Check that fusible interfacings aren't too "papery", crisp or stiff. Match the weight of the interfacing with the weight of the satin.

Heavy satins are often lined, but floppy satins aren't if the lining will interfere with the drape. A lining will give a floppy satin more substance.

Cutting
Use quality pins to avoid snagging.

Check if the satin is a one-way fabric, or can be cut in either direction. Most are two-way though.

Folding and positioning floppy satin can often take more time than actually cutting it. To prevent it slipping around, lay it out on calico or a sheet.

Straighten one end of floppy satin by either tearing it or pulling a thread—see page 69. Drawing a thread is preferable to tearing if you really need to use every last centimetre of fabric, because you have more control over how much of the end you remove and the cut edge is neater. After straightening the edge, square up the fabric at the corner of the cutting table. If you don't make a straight, square edge before you begin, when the finished garment is worn the hem will be wavy.

Stitching

Install a fresh needle in your machine to prevent snagging.

If the seam puckers along the stitching line, hold it taut while sewing. To do this, hold the fabric in front of and behind the needle as the seam is sewn. Hold the fabric firmly without stretching it and just let it feed through the machine on its own. Keep repositioning your hands as you sew each section.

Pressing

Check if you need to press before overlocking seams in case the overlocking imprints through. Press curves over a ham, particularly with heavy satin.

Lace

Ahhh, lace. Romantic, elegant and often exquisitely beautiful, laces are sheer or semi sheer fabrics composed of motifs on a mesh background. Rather than being knitted or woven, laces are constructed with twisted and knotted threads and do not fray.

Lace can be made from a variety of fibres, for example silk, cotton, nylon or polyester.

Sometimes lace is re-embroidered with a cord or ribbon outlining the design. It may be beaded or sequined (or both).

Look at lace against a contrasting background to see the pattern better.

Fine lace can be expensive, so look for bargains. You might find reduced prices online. You also might find lace in second hand shops, either as pieces or as garments that can be cut up.

Lace can be:

✂ A fabric with an all over repeating motif. It may have one straight edge and one scalloped edge, both edges scalloped or both edges straight. Sometimes the two edges have different sized scallops. Lace fabric comes in a wide variety of widths and weights.

✂ A trim. Sometimes lace trims are made to match lace fabrics. **Lace edging** has one straight and one scalloped edge. **Lace insertion** has two straight edges and is used between seams as a decorative join. **Galloon** has two scalloped edges. **Ruffling** is pre-gathered or pleated lace.

✂ An appliqué. This is a single lace motif. It can be cut from lace fabric or bought individually.

Styles and fitting

If the lace fabric is narrow, choose a style with pattern pieces that will fit onto the lace. Bring the pattern pieces with you when you buy the lace. A trial layout is the best way to work out how much you need. You won't be able follow the yardage listed on the pattern envelope; laces come in all widths.

With one or both edges scalloped, you can incorporate the scalloped edge in the design. The scallops can go around the hem and sleeve hems—this means you'll need to determine the correct length before you cut.

On the subject of length, note that some heavily beaded laces may drop and become longer due to their own weight. Determine the amount of drop by measuring the length of the lace flat on the table, then measuring the lace hanging up and deduct the difference from your pattern length. A large amount of drop will make the garment narrower, so allow big seam allowances in case you need to let the sides out.

Decide on the construction method before you begin. Lace can be quite a weak fabric and cannot support heavy flounces or a tight fit. The more seams of the lace that are stitched in with an underlining or backing, the less susceptible it will be to tearing. An added benefit is that the seam allowances and darts won't show through the lace.

Consider closures. Use buttons and loops instead of buttonholes. The loops can be made of satin rouleau or thread. Zippers work fine on most lace. I prefer invisible zips (because...they're invisible). When sewing a zip in, sew it in through both the lace and the underlining if you have one, so you won't see the seam allowance through the lace.

Is the lace scratchy? Or does the wearer have sensitive skin? I once backed the throat and shoulders of a lace wedding dress in flesh coloured chiffon to stop the bride breaking out in an instant rash.

Facings don't look good in lace because you can see them. Try cutting them in a skin-toned organza or net. You could also try binding the edges with satin binding, a binding made from net or even binding with the lace itself.

Interfacing and lining

You cannot use interfacing on lace because it will show.

Lace can have an underlining (essentially, a backing) as well as a lining.

An underlining is where each lace piece is individually mounted onto the chosen underlining fabric by stitching them together around the edge. *Then* the garment's seams are sewn, treating the pieces as one layer. It gives strength and opacity to the lace.

A lining is sewn separately and then attached to the garment. Like an underlining it also provides opacity, but gives no support to the lace. It makes the inside of the garment feel comfortable and look neat.

Cutting

The right side of the lace generally has a pronounced thread outline around the motif pattern. Because of the construction of lace, either the lengthwise or crosswise grain can be used.

Layout and planning are the most important steps, so try to relax and take your time. Cut the lace over a contrasting surface so you can see the motif pattern easily. A garbage bag works well under white lace.

Make sure the motifs run in the same direction and try to maintain symmetry between the right and left halves of the garment.

Have the bust point marked on the pattern to avoid placing prominent motifs directly over the bust.

Use pins you can see. I recommend 4cm (1½") long colour headed pins, such as flower headed pins or quilting pins. The ones sold as lace pins are short with no heads (not recommended).

Match the scallops at the hem so the seams fall on the top of a scallop. You may need to slightly add or subtract to make things match, but lace is fairly flexible and (up to a point) can be manipulated to fit the pattern. The lace scallops can be slightly curved to fit a curved hemline.

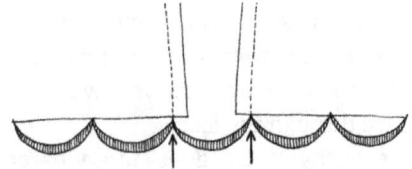

Mark notches and dart points with thread, because snips and dots will be invisible.

Decide on the seam treatments before cutting (see Stitching, below).

Here's a possible layout for a lace gown and a lace top.

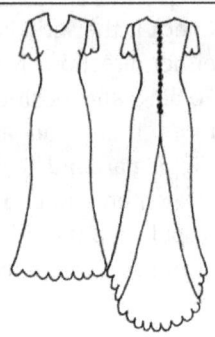

You can see that the width of the lace dictates the maximum length of the garment. You can also see that the pieces don't necessarily have to be cut on the straight grain.

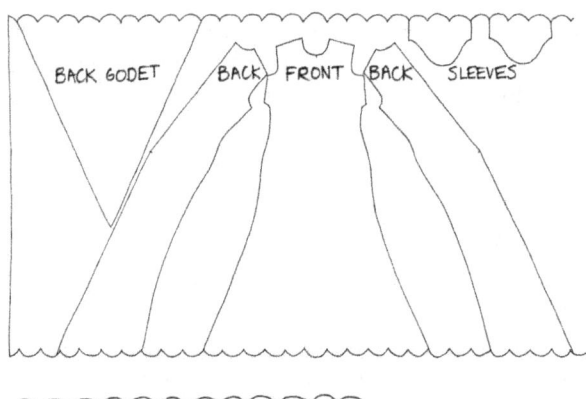

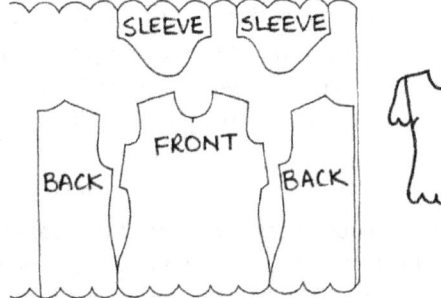

Stitching

There are two ways to sew the seams in lace: conventional seams and lapped seams.

Conventional seams are just that: place the right sides together and sew the seam as usual. Most seams in lace are sewn conventionally. Use a conventional seam if the lace has been mounted onto an underlining or backing, if the seam is in an out-of-the-way place or if the lace has widely spaced, non-touching motifs. Sleeve and armhole seams are conventionally seamed.

The more open the lace, the shorter the stitch length should be. If the machine's presser foot catches on the mesh, wrap tape around the front of the foot.

You won't need to overlock lace seams, because they don't fray. Trim them back neatly to 6mm (¼") after stitching.

Lapped, or invisible, seams are special and take more time. The lace is trimmed around the motifs closest to the seam or dart and then overlapped so you can't tell there's a seam there. It's used on heavy re-embroidered laces where the motifs are outlined by cord. Lapped seams can be sewn by machine using a small zig zag, but are often sewn by hand using whipstitch. Often lapped seams and darts are used for the front and back of a gown and all the other seams are sewn conventionally.

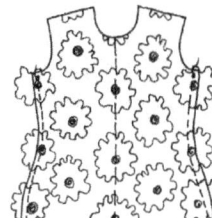

To cut **lapped seams**, lay the pattern piece onto the lace and trim around the motif edges that straddle the seam.
Mark the actual seam line with contrasting thread.

Use this as a guide to cut the pattern piece with the corresponding seam, continuing the motif pattern across the garment.

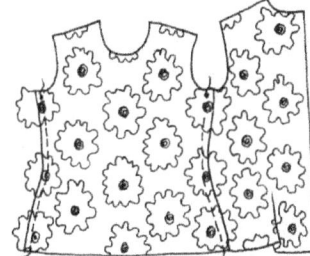

To sew, lap the trimmed motifs over the top with the marked seam lines aligned. Sew the seam around the edge of the motif and trim the excess lace away underneath.

Lapped darts are made in a similar way. In the vicinity of the dart, define a route that follows the corded edge of one or more motifs. Cut open the dart along this line and overlap it according to how long or wide the dart is. Pin the dart closed and sew it by hand, stitching through all the layers along the corded edge. Underneath, trim away the underlap of the dart fairly close to the stitching.

To fashion **fragile lace** into a fitted style, back it onto a strong but sheer underlay such as silk organza. Cut sheer pieces for each pattern section. Sew the hem of the underlay first by folding the hem allowance to the wrong side and hand sewing it to the lace—line it up with the tops of the scallops.
Align the two layers carefully and anchor the underlay to the lace by hand tacking through the most prominent motifs. Baste together along the seam lines. For lapped lace seams and darts (see explanation above), sew the underlay separately. For conventional seams, stitch the underlay and lace as one. To neatly finish the seam allowance, trim both lace seam allowances and one underlay allowance. Use the untrimmed underlay allowance to wrap and bind the seam.

On **beaded laces**, remove the beads from the seam allowance first and then sew the seam using a zipper foot, so you can get in close. You can remove the beads by unpicking them and securing the threads, or if the lace is heavily beaded they can be gently smashed with a hammer. Don safety glasses and sit the lace on a clean hard surface. Break the beads with the hammer—don't get too enthusiastic or you'll damage the lace. Vacuum the floor afterwards.

To attach lace trim, insertion or a motif, position the trim on the right side of the garment and pin it in place. Stitch along the edge using a tiny zig zag. Cut away the fabric underneath close to the stitching line. Scalloped edging can be trimmed off lace fabric and applied to the edge of the garment, for example around the neckline. It works well for trimming curved edges of garments. Cut the lace along the scalloped pattern. Fit the strip around the edge and stitch along the lines of the lace pattern. Trim away the excess lace behind.

Pressing
Take care to avoid snagging the lace on the tip of the iron—use a press cloth.
Check first that the lace doesn't shrink with heat or steam.
Press textured, beaded or re-embroidered laces face down on a soft surface to prevent flattening the detail.

Brocade
Brocade is a rich, Jacquard weave fabric that has a raised design usually of flowers or figurines. It sometimes has metallic threads woven into it.

Styles and fitting
Choose simple dresses or tunics without lots of seams to interrupt the pattern. Brocade is very suitable for evening coats or jackets. Brocade is a forgiving fabric; it moulds well to the figure and hold seams and creases well. Careful—it has a snag-sensitive surface.

Interfacing and lining
A sew-in interfacing will work best if the raised design is likely to be flattened when fused.
Brocade may be lined or unlined.

Cutting
Have large seam allowances—brocade frays easily.
Make sure the fabric pattern runs in the same direction and match the pattern motifs.

Stitching

To arrest excessive fraying, overlock around the edges of all the pieces before you begin.

Try a sample buttonhole if the garment has them. If buttonholes don't work, try buttons and loops or sewing large press studs behind the buttons. Avoid bound buttonholes if the fabric frays badly.

Metallic threads will make the needle blunt quicker, so change them when necessary.

Heavy brocade may not ease well because it's so thick, so take extra care when sewing sleeve heads and other eased areas.

Pressing

Press lightly with a cool iron, with a towel underneath the fabric to stop the raised design being flattened. Avoid over-pressing and handling.

Velvet

A winter evening fabric, velvet refers to the weave. It's a closely woven fabric with a short, dense pile and soft, rich texture. The word velvet is from the Latin *vellus*, meaning fleece or tufted hair. Velvet can be made from silk, polyester, acetate or rayon. Silk velvet is often softer than synthetic velvet. Synthetic velvets are usually slightly crisper with more structure and less drape.

Velveteen is made of cotton to imitate velvet. It's not as plush as velvet, but easier to handle and less expensive. It has a shorter, denser pile than velvet.

Panne velvet is a velvet-like fabric with the pile pressed flat in one direction, giving a shimmery surface with almost a wet look.

Velour, the stuff of science fiction uniforms, is a highly stretchy soft plush knit. It can also be a woven fabric, often used for upholstery and stage curtains. It's much cheaper than velvet and often dyed in outrageous colours. Sometimes velour has a panne finish.

Corduroy, a daytime cousin of velvet, is a durable, usually cotton, winter fabric with velvety, parallel, lengthwise cords or ridges called wales. Corduroy can have narrow or wide wales, with wider wales being more durable.

Styles and fitting

Choose simple styles. Gathers and darts work fine, but avoid pleats.

Velvet can add visual weight to a figure.

Satin and heavy lace work well as accents.

Topstitching doesn't work well on velvet (but does on velveteen and corduroy—in fact, it really helps collars, pocket flaps and the like sit flat since you can't press them hard).

Forget buttonholes (yay!). Buttons and loops work well; make the loops from satin rouleau or cord. Bound buttonholes look smart as a design feature on short pile velvets.

Invisible zips work well with velvet, but as with sewing seams they will slip unless hand basted in first. If using a regular zip, insert by hand (see page 411).

Interfacing and lining

Use a sew-in interfacing so the pile isn't crushed when the fabric is fused.

Match the weight of the interfacing to the weight of the velvet.

Satin lining looks gorgeous next to plush velvet and doesn't cost much more than regular lining.

Cutting

Prior to cutting, store velvet hanging on a skirt hanger, not rolled up or folded, so the pile isn't damaged. Check the fabric before cutting for spots of damaged pile, especially at the beginning and end of a piece.

For velvet with a very deep pile, cut pieces singly to avoid the layers slipping against each other by the scissor blades.

Lay the pattern pieces so the pile runs in the same direction on all pieces. If the pile runs *upwards* on the finished garment the colour will be much richer and deeper.

Be prepared to vacuum after cutting and sewing. Velvet produces fluff and crumbs. Try to do all your cutting and sewing in one session and then have a clean up.

Stitching

The biggest challenge when sewing velvet is preventing the layers from slipping against each other. It's worth it to hand baste the seams with small stitches before machine sewing. Pin seams in both directions, that is, parallel and perpendicular to the seam line.

Machine stitch in the direction of the pile.

Overlock carefully—your overlocker may also slip.

Instead of overlocking seams, zig zag might work better, or binding the seam allowances with satin bias binding. Of course, if the inside of the garment is fully enclosed in a lining, you won't need to neaten any seams.

Consider using a matching satin for unseen facings and under collars. Also consider making a false hem using lace trim that has one straight edge, to reduce bulk around the hem.

Note that stitching lines in velvet will show if they have to be unpicked, so if you need to do a fitting, hand baste the seams using one strand of thread. Don't press until you're sure of the seam.

Clean your machine and overlocker with a vacuum cleaner and brush after sewing, to prevent the fluff transferring to your next project. You might need to vacuum the next day, too, after the fluff has settled.

Pressing

First remove any tacking threads or pins, otherwise they'll leave marks.

Hang the garment in a steamy bathroom to remove slight wrinkles.

A needleboard is often recommended to press velvet so the pile isn't flattened. It's made of wire bristles ("needles") on a canvas backing. Needleboards are expensive and hard to get (to be honest I've never met anyone who owned one), but an alternative is a Velvaboard—it's a piece of fabric with a stiff, bristly pile. However, I always use a scrap of the same velvet placed pile side up. Whatever you're using, place the seam pile-side down on top and press lightly with steam.

For velveteen, velour and corduroy, you don't need to do this. Just press these flat but lightly with steam or through a damp cloth.

Sheers

Sheers are transparent fabrics in natural or synthetic fibres. They can be crisp or soft. Examples of crisp sheers are organza and net. Soft sheers include chiffon, georgette, gauze, handkerchief linen and Swiss cotton. Crisp sheers are easier to handle than soft sheers.

Styles and fitting

Choose airy, floaty styles. Patterns should allow plenty of ease—at least 25cm (10") around the hips. Tight fitting styles will pull and crease around the body.

Three choices for modesty:

- Interline (mount) the sheer onto a solid fabric
- Make a lining
- Make a slip to wear underneath

Consider using two or more layers of sheer fabric to give more substance to the garment, particularly on evening gowns. Sleeves are generally cut from a single, unlined, layer of fabric. Sheers can also be used under lace as an underlining.

Gathers work well on sheers but you may need extra fabric or more than one layer to make them look substantial. Fine sheers require three or even four times the finished gathered length.

Tucks look lovely on sheers and are easier to make on crisp rather than soft sheers.

You can eliminate facings (which will show through) and bind the edges with the same fabric. Alternatively, cut the facings in a flesh-coloured sheer. The fabric may be too fine for buttonholes—consider buttons and loops, ties or press studs sewn behind buttons.

Interfacing and lining

Interface with another layer of the same fabric or use skin-toned organza as a sew-in interfacing.

Sheers can be lined with the same fabric or a skin-toned fabric. Alternatively a separate slip, petticoat or camisole can be made.

Cutting

Some soft sheers, notably silk georgette, are prone to shrink when pressed with steam. Check and see. It's worth pre-pressing the fabric for small areas, such as bodice pieces, before you cut them out.

Sheers can be slippery or filmy to handle. If so, lay a length of calico or a sheet on the cutting surface first.

Note that folding and positioning sheers, particularly soft sheers, can often take much longer than the actual cutting, so be patient.

Make a straight edge across the end of the fabric by either tearing or pulling a thread. See page 69. Most sheers (except net) will tear. Drawing a thread is preferable to tearing if you really need to use every last centimetre of fabric, because you have more control over how much of the end you remove and the (cut) edge is neater.

When the end is straight, square up the fabric in the corner of the cutting table. If you don't make a straight, square edge before you begin, the hem will hang wavy when the finished garment is worn.

If the sheer is printed with a non-random design, and the fabric doesn't tear along the line of the pattern, it's better to go by the pattern rather than the cross grain of the fabric. Neatly cut along the edge of the pattern, then square that up in the corner of the table.

Allow large seam and hem allowances if the fabric frays.

Place pins within the seam allowance to avoid marking the fabric, and use fine, good quality pins.

Stitching

Use a new, fine (size 10/70) needle in your machine.

The inner construction of a sheer garment must be neat because it shows through. For a high quality finish, use French seams. For sleeves, see page 338. For a lesser quality finish, trim back the seam allowance to 6mm (¼"), or 1cm (⅜) at most, and overlock. Use perfectly matching overlocking thread to minimise the overlocking showing through.

Experiment with your machine tension and stitching. Some fine fabrics may pucker and require holding taut as you sew. Overlocking may also need holding taut or it will gather up. To do this, hold the fabric in front of and behind the needle as the seam is sewn. Hold the fabric firmly without stretching it and just let it feed through the machine on its own. Keep repositioning your hands as you sew each section.

If the fabric doesn't fray, for example net, consider just trimming the seam allowances back to 6mm (¼") and leaving them, rather than adding bulk to the seam by overlocking.

For hems, sheers lend themselves to wonderful fine, narrow hems. Try narrow hand or machine sewn hems, or rolled hems on your overlocker. Alternatively, make a feature of deep hems. Hems on sheers look smartest if they're double folded hems, rather than overlocked and turned under once.

Self-fabric can be used for binding edges, facings and interfacings.

Pressing

Take care not to over-press. Set your iron temperature according to the fibre.

Silk georgette will shrink if you use steam.

Press embroidered sheers face downwards on a soft towel so the fabric doesn't wrinkle around the embroidery.

Taffeta

Taffeta is fine, stiff fabric woven from silk or synthetic fibres. It has a sheen on the surface and rustles when you walk, and is available in a wide range of weights, colours and patterns. It was hugely popular for formal and debutante dresses during the 1980's.

Moiré taffeta has a water wave pattern on the surface.

Styles and fitting

Gathering, ruching and pleats all work well. Taffeta works wonderfully for crisp bows, full gathered sleeves and sticking-out skirts. It combines nicely with velvet and other soft fabrics like wool.

Taffeta can be used as an economical underlay for sheers and laces. The fit shouldn't be too tight; taffeta is prone to perspiration stains.

Taffeta doesn't ease well.

Interfacing and lining

Fusible interfacing is fine to use, but use a good quality one. Set the iron at a low temperature to avoid shrinking the taffeta and consequently bubbling the surface.

Taffeta can be lined or left unlined. Regular lining is fine to use. Taffeta is sometimes used as a lining for other fabrics.

Cutting

Taffeta can slip when cutting (and sewing).

Place pins within the seam allowance so the holes don't show.

Stitching

Change machine needles if necessary during sewing; a blunt needle will punch through the fabric.

Stitching holes will show if unpicked, so be sure your seam lines are correct before you sew them. Place pins within the seam allowance.

You might need to hold the fabric taut as you sew the seams to avoid puckering. To do this, hold the fabric in front of and behind the needle as the seam is sewn. Hold the fabric firmly without stretching it and just let it feed through the machine on its own. Keep repositioning your hands as you sew each section.

If you're using an overlocker or zig zag to neaten the seam allowance, check to see if you need to press the seams *before* neatening to avoid a shiny overlocking or zig zag imprint on the right side. Consider neatening the seams using pinking shears instead.

Pressing

Use an iron set on a low temperature. Do not over press, or all the interior construction (seam allowances, darts and facings) will leave a shiny imprint on the right side.

Metallics

A metallic fabric is any fabric that has metal threads knitted or woven into it, from sheer flimsy silks to heavy brocades.

Metallic fabrics that contain copper may, under some circumstances, turn bluish green or black in reaction to the wearer's sweat. If you see this starting to happen, try dusting talcum powder on the area then brushing it off with a clothes brush. This unfortunately happened to my wedding dress. The ivory silk with gold flowers had developed a decidedly greenish tinge around the wrists and neckline by the time I returned from my honeymoon. It darkened to a blackish/greenish shade in the following weeks.

Styles and fitting
Depends on the fabric.

Interfacing and lining
Fusible interfacing is usually fine but test it first. Line garments if the metallic will irritate the skin.

Cutting
Place fabric pieces running in the same direction. Leave large seam allowances if the fabric frays badly.

Stitching
The metallic threads make machine needles blunt quickly, so change needles when necessary.

Pressing
Test the effect of heat and steam on a sample of fabric before you start your project.

Fur
Does anyone sew with real fur any more?
Fake furs are also called faux furs, synthetic furs or simulated furs. They're easy to cut and sew, and available in a huge variety of patterns, piles and colours, from imitations of real animal fur to "fantasy" furs.
The fibres of fake furs are manufactured from synthetic materials such as acrylic or polyester, with either a knitted or woven backing. Knitted backed furs feel more flexible and are less costly. As with other textiles, better quality furs are finer, softer and have more fibres per square inch. They are usually richer looking and come in more up-to-the minute fashion colours and patterns.
The length and thickness of the pile varies from long and shaggy to short and sheared. The thicker and longer the pile, the heavier the fabric.
Short piled furs can be cut and sewn in much the same way as velvet, on page 198. Long piled furs require slightly different handling.

Styles and fitting
Faux fur is best suited to outerwear with very few seams. Fur garments tend to be boxy, with few or no darts, single-breasted, with simple collars and minimal details. Sleeves are cuffless and one piece, pockets are in-seam pockets (not patch pockets) with no welts or flaps. There are no pleats or tucks on such a bulky fabric. Buttonholes are replaced with large press studs or special fur hook and eyes. Fur garments are lined to hide the scratchy backing.
You can buy patterns designed especially for fur, but you can also use regular patterns—just look at the illustration to analyse the overall shape and omit or modify some of the details to accommodate the bulk. Where facings do not show, cut them in a smooth fabric to eliminate bulk. Sometimes the lower part of a front facing is cut in a smoother fabric and the lapel is cut in fur, with a join below the break point. Where possible, convert centre front facings to extended facings rather than separate ones.
On collars, put a join in the centre back so the nap on each half runs evenly towards the garment's front.
If you haven't sewn with fur before, consider starting with something small, such as a shrug, caplet or fur collar and cuffs on a coat.

Interfacing and lining
Use a sew-in interfacing; fusible interfacing will crush the pile when ironed on.
Line the garment to hide the unattractive and scratchy backing. Satin lining looks and feels luxurious and its slightly heavier weight goes well with fur.

Cutting
Have the vacuum cleaner ready! Try to cut and sew in one session and then have a clean up at the end. Sometimes you'll need to vacuum again the next day after the fluff has settled. If the fur is very long and fluffy, consider wearing a mask so you don't inhale the fibres.
Make sure the nap smooths *down* the garment. If the fur has vertical indentations or channels, treat these like stripes and match them at the shoulders if possible. Centre them at the centre front, centre back and the centre of the sleeve.
Cut out the fur in a single layer, with the wrong side facing up. Some people like to make extra pattern pieces so they don't have to unpin and flip those "Cut 2" and "Cut on fold" pieces.
Forget pattern weights. Use long pins with large visible heads to pin the pattern pieces to the wrong side of the fur, or stick the pieces on with sticky tape. Cut short piled furs with regular sewing scissors. For long piled furs, avoid cutting the pile by using very sharp scissors and lifting the fabric with one hand, so you cut through the fabric backing only. You could also try using a safety razor or craft knife to slice through only the backing and if necessary following up with small sharp scissors to clip any remaining threads.

Stitching

For knit-backed furs, you may need a ball point needle. Otherwise use a large (14 or 16) needle and a longish stitch length (3 or 4). A standard machine foot is fine.

Release the presser foot pressure on your machine to accommodate the bulk of the fur. There should be a knob or lever at the top of your machine to adjust this—consult your manual.

Always sew seams in the same direction as the fur runs.

Push the fibres away from the cut edge as you sew, forcing them to the garment's right side.

After sewing a seam, brush the fibres from the seam on the garment's right side using a fine plastic comb or a pin. Repeat on the wrong side. On long piled furs, clip the fur from the seam allowance with small scissors to reduce bulk.

If you have darts, slit them after sewing and hand stitch each side flat.

If you find the fur slipping or creeping as you sew the seam, hand baste the seam before machine sewing. You can also try using lots of pins in both directions (parallel and perpendicular to the seam allowance).

Zips work well on short haired furs, but tend to catch on long-piled furs. However, if you want to use a zip on a long-piled fur, sew the zipper to a band of fabric or leather so the zipper teeth are away from the fur. Alternatively, you could insert the zip so the teeth are exposed, then topstitch 6mm (¼") either side with the fur pushed out of the way. See page 431.

Finally, after sewing, brush and clean out your sewing machine. Use a vacuum cleaner or compressed air to blow out the fluff. Brush yourself down with a clothes brush.

Pressing

Don't press the fur if you don't think it needs it. If you do need to press, prevent flattening the pile by placing it face down on to a scrap of the same fabric. Steam lightly, holding the iron above the fabric. After pressing, brush lightly in the direction of the nap.

Alternatively, finger press the seams open and rub them on the inside with a thimble to make them lie flat.

Press linings before sewing them to the fur.

Beaded and sequined fabrics

Glamorous, eye-catching and expensive!

Beaded or sequined fabric may be lightly or heavily encrusted and can have a knitted or woven base.

If you're transporting sequined garments by car, keep the fabric covered. The hot Aussie sun coming in through the car window can melt sequins or cause them to loose their shine (can you hear the voice of regretful experience?).

Styles and fitting

Let the fabric do the talking. Choose a style that's as simple as possible, with a minimum of seams. It will make it easier to sew, too.

Interfacing and lining

Use a sew-in interfacing, matching the weight of the interfacing to the weight of the fabric. Choose a lining fabric that matches the garment in weight, too.

Consider lining the entire inside of the garment right up to the edges of the neck and arms (thus avoiding facings). See page 173 for skirts and 174 for dresses. Alternatively, cut facings from satin and interface them with sew-in or fusible interfacing.

Cutting

Don't use your best fabric scissors! Use an old pair or buy some cheaper scissors to use.

I suggest cutting and fitting the lining before cutting the sequined fabric.

Wear safety glasses if you don't already wear ordinary glasses.

If the fabric looks like it will slip around, secure a sheet or length of calico to the cutting table first, and spread the fabric on top of it.

Cut a single layer of fabric at a time and position any beaded motifs carefully.

Keep all the beads that fall off when you cut. It's good to have spare beads for the garment, and you might need to re-bead small sections after sewing.

Put sticky tape over unravelling bead or sequin threads until you can secure them by sewing.

Stitching

Wear safety glasses while you machine sew and have loads of spare machine needles handy.

Tack seams by hand first if you're doing a fitting. When you're sure of the fit, remove the beads from the seam allowances and darts before sewing. If there are few beads, unpick the sections of beading in the seam allowance and secure the threads. If the beads are many and close together, lay the fabric on a hard, clean surface and use a hammer to smash the beads (while wearing safety glasses). Don't get too carried away with the hammer or you'll damage the fabric with it. Fasten the threads to stop the rest unravelling. You can then machine sew the seams using a zipper foot. Re-apply spare beads over the seam on the right side afterwards, if necessary.

Party fabrics **203**

To keep the fabric from ravelling you probably won't be able to overlock (unless your seam allowances are very wide), because the overlocker foot won't go over the textured surface. Instead, zig zag with a long, wide zig zag stitch, or overcast by hand. You could also bind the seam allowances with net or satin bias binding.

For all-over evenly sequined fabric, don't remove the sequins in the seam allowance. Sew the seams carefully and slowly using a thick needle (size 16) and wearing safety glasses. Neaten the seam allowances using a long, wide zig zag. You might need to hand sew the seam allowances down afterwards to get them to sit flat inside. Line the garment to stop the sequins scratching. Bind the edges of the garment instead of using facings. Alternatively, cut the lining so it extends to the edge of the garment and insert a fine piping to provide separation between skin and sequins.

Pressing

Use a cool iron so you won't melt the beads.
Press on the wrong side using a press cloth over a soft, padded surface.
Don't press all-over sequined fabric but *do* press the lining before attaching it.

Introduction to beading

Beads can enhance lace motifs, embroidered or printed designs, and add "bling" and sparkle to plain fabrics.
Beading stitches are similar to traditional embroidery stitches, except beads are picked up on the thread as you go.
Beading is done on finished or partially finished garments.

Requirements

✂ Beads. Seed beads are the small beads. Bugle beads are like thin tubes, available in a range of lengths up to 3cm (1¼"). Handle the longer lengths with care because they're vulnerable to snapping. Seed beads and bugle beads are sewn on in the same way.

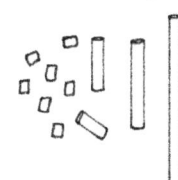

✂ Thread. You can buy beading thread but many beaders just use a double strand of regular (good quality) thread in a colour matching the fabric's background (note that the illustrations here are shown with a single strand of thread for clarity).

✂ Sewing needle. Regular sewing needles are fine provided they fit through the hole in the bead.

✂ Beading design, paper, water soluble marking pencil or chalk.

✂ Embroidery hoop (optional). An embroidery hoop will keep the fabric taut while you bead, and is especially good for lightweight fabrics to prevent the stitches from puckering. Don't leave it on for extended periods because it will stretch and distort the fabric.

Plan the design

Look in hand embroidery books for designs or create your own. Draw your idea out on paper first, then transfer the design onto your fabric using a water soluble marking pencil or chalk.

Make a small sample of your design on swatch of fabric to see how it looks. It's good to have to refer to later and also helps you estimate how many beads you need to buy.

Start beading

Thread the needle, knot the end and bring the needle up from the wrong side of the fabric to begin. If you're beading mesh or open weave fabric which won't hold the knot, make a tiny stitch and pass the needle through the two strands of thread to hold it fast.

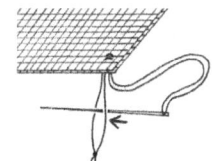

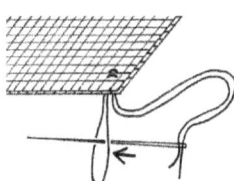

Even better is to thread the needle with the loop at the bottom. Pass the needle through the loop to secure the first stitch.

To load beads onto the needle, I like to tip some onto a dinner plate. Other people spread them out onto velvet or a soft surface. Position your needle point next to the bead hole and pick it up with the point.

Backstitch—for single beads

1. Pick up a bead on the needle and let it fall down the thread.

2. Lay the bead on its side.

3. Take the needle back down into the fabric a bead length away, behind the bead.

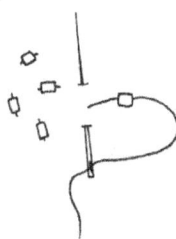

Running stitch—for more than one bead

1. Pick up two or three beads and let them fall down the thread.

2. Lay the beads on their sides with the holes parallel to the surface.

3. Take the needle back down into the fabric right next to the last bead.

Couching—sewing a line of pre-strung beads

Sewing pre-strung beads is much quicker than sewing them on a few at a time. You can buy beads pre-strung onto strong thread or thread them yourself. You'll need two needles.

1. Bring one threaded needle up from the wrong side of the fabric and string the beads. If you're using pre-strung beads, thread one end onto a needle, take the needle through the fabric from right side to wrong side, then remove the needle and knot the end.

2. Let the beads fall down the thread onto the fabric.

3. Lay the thread along the fabric, leaving spaces between the beads and temporarily secure the needle in the fabric.

4. Thread a second needle. Stitch over the beaded thread between every three or four beads. Add more beads to the first thread if needed.

5. To finish off, insert both needles into the fabric and secure on the wrong side.

✂ It's also possible to sew a line of threaded beads down using a sewing machine. The string of beads is zig zagged over using a grooved presser foot. It's worth experimenting with if you have a lot to do.

1. String the beads onto lengths of thread leaving long unknotted tails on both ends. Loop the ends into a loose knot to prevent the beads from sliding off. To start, thread one end of the strand of beads onto a hand needle and secure it with a knot on the wrong side.

2. Choose a grooved presser foot with a groove large enough to make a little tunnel for the beads to pass through. If the beads are very small, try a satin stitch or buttonhole foot. A pintuck or cording foot could also work.

3. Thread the machine with regular thread and set the stitch to a zig zag. Do a trial run on a scrap to get the setting right. Adjust the tension and foot pressure as needed.

4. Slide the beads along the thread to touch the fabric. Position the fabric and strand of beads so the presser foot straddles the beads. Zig zag over the beads guiding them as you sew. When you reach the end, remove the work from the machine and thread the tail of the beaded thread onto a hand needle. Stitch through the fabric and secure on the wrong side.

Satin stitch—sew parallel rows of beads

Satin stitch is made by sewing long stitches next to each other.
Zig zag or float the thread under each row to start the next row.
The rows should butt up against each other.

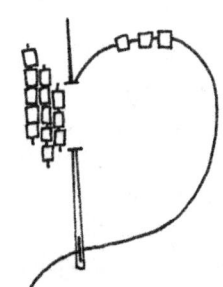

Cluster—one large bead surrounded by smaller beads

1. Sew the middle bead on first.

2. Sew the smaller beads around it, two at a time. The holes of the beads should run around the middle bead like a tunnel.

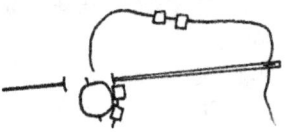

3. When the middle bead is surrounded by the smaller beads, pass the needle through all the holes of the smaller beads again to tighten the circle. Fasten off on the wrong side.

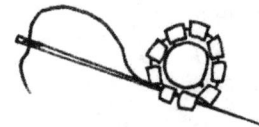

Lazy Daisy stitch—a three dimensional effect

1. Pick up about a dozen beads, then insert the needle back into the fabric at the same point where it came out.

2. Pull until a loop of beads forms on the right sided of the fabric.

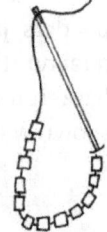

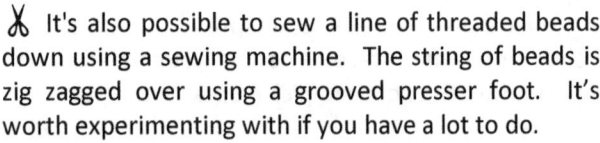

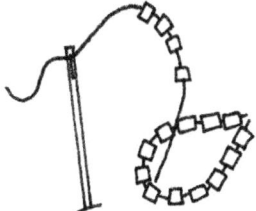
3. Holding the loop in place, bring the needle from the wrong side back up through the beaded loop, at the loop end.

4. Pick up enough (possibly contrasting coloured) beads to straddle the loop, then re-insert the needle through the fabric on the outside of the loop.

Sequins
Sequins can be flat or cupped, but are both sewn on in the same way. Cupped sequins have facets around the hole and generally they're sewn so the cup sits up.

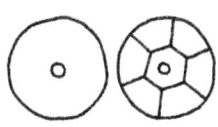

Single sequins
Single sequins are sewn on with a bead in the centre.
1. Bring the needle up through the fabric.

2. Place a sequin on the needle, then a bead.

3. Slide both sequin and bead down onto the fabric, then stitch back through the centre of the sequin.

Row of sequins
A row of sequins can be used to outline a design.
1. Bring the needle up to the right side of the fabric and pick up a sequin.

2. Hold the sequin flat and take a stitch over the edge. Bring the needle to the right side, half the width of the next sequin.

3. As you continue sewing, the edge of each sequin will be overlapped by the next.

Paillets
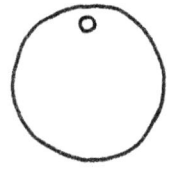
Paillets are flat oversized sequins, with the hole in the top instead of the centre. Like sequins, they come in lots of colours, sizes, shapes (circular, oval) and finishes (metallic, iridescent, clear).
Sew them on with a thread that matches the paillet.

✂ You can stitch them on densely, scattered, orderly or random.

For example, they can be densely overlapping for a mermaid, fish scale effect.

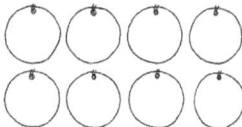

 Or, line them up in rows all over the garment for a 1960's mod look.

Paillets can be sewn on densely overlapping at the top of the garment, then scattering randomly towards the hem.

✂ For a subtle look, try tone-on-tone. For example, white paillets on white fabric. You can also pick up two or three colours from a printed fabric and sew on matching paillets.

To sew on paillets, bring the needle up through the fabric into the hole of the paillet. Take two stitches, then secure underneath with a knot.

To get a hanging coin effect, don't make the stitches too tight. Unless the paillets are being sewn on close together, don't float the thread behind the paillet because it can cause the background fabric to pucker.

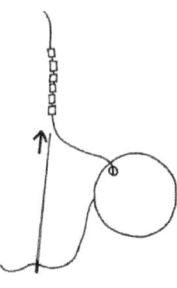
To sew on paillets for movement, add a short chain of seed beads. Pick up six seed beads (or five, or four, or however many you like), then the paillet. Take the needle back through the seed beads and into the fabric at the same point you began. Secure behind.

Other general beading/sequin tips
Secure the beads
While beading, guard against bead loss if a thread breaks within the bead work.
Loop and pull: make a tiny stitch with one or two threads of fabric, then pull the needle until a loop forms. Pass the needle through the loop and pull to form a knot.
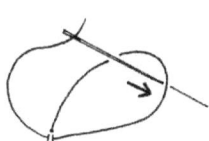

Keep it neat
If the thread must cross 2cm (¾") or more on the underside to get from one beading spot to another, take a tiny stitch in between, ideally next to another bead to camouflage it. This stops long floats of thread on the underside.

Health and safety
Look after your eyes by working in good light, preferably daylight. Gaze up often to give your eyes a rest.
Don't sit hunched over your work; watch your posture.

Gluing beads
Beads can also be glued on. It's not as strong as sewing, but it sure is quicker! Use a craft glue that stays clear and flexible after drying.
Set out your pearls or beads, and squirt a gob of glue onto a piece of card. Use scissor-style tweezers to pick up a bead and dip it in the glue. Allow it to dry for a few seconds before placing it on the fabric. Don't move it until the glue has dried completely.

Patternmaking essentials

Making a pattern 207
Patternmaking tools 207
Patternmaking tips and advice 208
Making a test garment 209
    save time and fabric 209
2 alternatives to test garments 210

Making patterns is an activity that brings me great satisfaction. Patternmaking requires skills such as an eye for proportion, ability to envisage flat shapes as three dimensional ones, knowing *how* a garment will be constructed and making actual pattern pieces to bring it about, sewing skills and fitting. Although I was formally trained, I found that most of these developed over time with experience (especially my fitting skills). It helps if you enjoy maths, drawing and clothing construction, and have a certain persistence to "get it right".

When I was a student, a senior patternmaker gave me some good advice. She said make every pattern as accurate as you can get it; millimetres count. Because the pattern is the first step in producing a garment, any mistakes in the pattern are amplified as the garment goes into production and is cut and sewn. If there happens to be a problem with the fabric, cutting, or sewing, you'll know that your pattern was as correct as it could be.

Making a pattern

There are many ways to go about making a pattern, for example:
- draping fabric on a model
- drafting a pattern from a diagram
- drafting a pattern using a block as a base
- taking a pattern from an existing garment
- adapting an existing pattern
- using a patternmaking system (either on paper or software), for example Lutterloh, Telestia, PatternMaker or Wild Ginger.

Draping fabric on a model is referred to as *draping* and all the others are referred to as *flat patternmaking*. All these routes have the same destination which is a pattern for a garment. Whichever method you choose, you'll still have to make a test garment to check it. Draping is sometimes viewed as the superior method over flat patternmaking, but actually draping isn't suitable for every pattern. Either flat patternmaking or draping or a combination of the two may be the way to go, but it really depends on the kinds of patterns you're making.

The best way to learn patternmaking is to have a teacher, even if it's only to get you started. Making patterns isn't rocket science; it's just a skill you learn, and the more you practice it, the better you'll get at turning your creative visions into reality. Learning to fit patterns isn't hard either, but experience, a reliable text on the subject and a good teacher really help.

Making patterns requires concentration and discipline. If you meet a creative block or can't find a resolution to a design problem, try taking a break and doing something else. Don't worry; your mind will keep ticking over the problem without you thinking about it and when you come back to it you'll have a fresh perspective.

Understanding garment construction is the key to making useable patterns that work. The more you know about sewing, the more you can expand your patternmaking. As well, set yourself patternmaking goals and let them grow as you become more proficient.

Don't worry about making mistakes; value them because they're part of the creative process. Mistakes challenge us to search for a different and better way.

Patternmaking tools

Paper. At home, I use kitchen greaseproof paper to make my patterns. It's cheap, available, strong enough and easy to trace through. It comes in a 30cm

(12") wide roll from the supermarket. For small patterns, I sometimes use A4 printer paper, which is firm enough to trace around and thin enough to put pins through easily. In industry, patterns are made on cardboard. Small fashion studios sometimes use heavy paper.

Pencil. The best pencils to use are mechanical ones, because they yield a consistent line thickness. I favour .5mm in HB or 2B. For sketching I still like to use a mechanical pencil, but I prefer a .7mm 2B. Get an eraser too.

Rulers. You'll need an L-square at the very least. Mine has a French curve built it to it, but I find I don't need a French curve very often. A metre long metal ruler is also very useful. The ruler I use most is actually a transparent quilting ruler, 20cm (8") long and 5cm (2") wide with a grid of ⅛" marked on it. I use it for grading patterns (making many sizes from a single pattern), adding seam allowances and general patternmaking.

Paper scissors, tape measure, sticky tape, pins, paper weights and a calculator.

If you're making **cardboard patterns**, you'll require a pattern notcher, stapler, tracing wheel, 3mm (⅛") hole punch and clear packing tape instead of regular sticky tape. You'll also need a large hole punch and wire hooks for hanging patterns.

For **checking patterns** you'll need a sewing kit, cheap fabric, sewing machine and a full length mirror.

Patternmaking tips and advice

✂ This sounds basic, but *rule* your lines, cut the patterns out accurately and make sure *all* corresponding seams and notches match.

✂ Another basic one: always make a test garment in an inexpensive fabric to check the pattern before you cut into your fashion fabric. Don't be disappointed if it isn't right on the first attempt; it rarely is. The toile allows you to make changes, correct the pattern and work out how it will be sewn together.

✂ Have plenty of paper and sticky tape. Don't be tempted to shorten a pattern just because you've run out of paper and can't be bothered to stick a piece on.

✂ To make a symmetrical pattern piece, fold the pattern in half down the centre when you cut it out (leave enough paper for this). Pin the paper together to hold it, or staple it together outside the line if the paper is too thick for pins.

✂ Write on the pattern: the garment type, size, name of piece (back, front, etc) and cutting instructions (Cut 2 or Cut 2 as a pair, etc). Depending on the pattern, you may also choose to write the date, wearer's name, seam and hem allowance, or the pattern number or name. Remember to mark the grainline.

✂ Not only does the pattern have to be accurate, it also has to be foolproof, especially if someone else will be using it either to cut out or sew or both. You need to make the pattern as clear and easy to use as possible, so there can be little chance of error.
Some of the things I like to do are:
I use a thick felt pen to write on my pattern pieces so it can be read at a glance. For multiple sizes I use a different colour for each size (for example green for 8, black for 10, blue for 12, red for 14 and brown for 16). I circle the size so it gets noticed. If the piece is cut out of lining, I underline the word lining. Some patternmakers use a different coloured cardboard for their lining patterns, but brown is all that's available in Australia.
If the piece is to be interfaced, I write fuse, underlined, in red (unless I've used red for that size, in which case I'll use another colour).
I make whole pattern pieces, not "Cut on the fold" ones. If a piece is to be cut "Right side facing up", I write this clearly and then write "PTO" (Please Turn Over), circled, on the reverse side in case the pattern is accidentally flipped.
I write "Cut 1 pair" rather than "Cut 2" if we need a pair, "Cut 2" if it doesn't matter if it's paired or not, or I may write "Cut 2 NOT a pair" if that's how the pattern needs to be.
Ideally there should be as few notches as possible to make cutting out quicker, but not at the expense of clarity for the person sewing it. You might need to add some extra notches to prevent pieces being sewn together wrongly. If you're making patterns for a range, bear in mind that the person who sews in a factory might not have access to the pattern pieces.

✂ How are you going to catalogue and store your patterns? At home I put each pattern into an A4 envelope (recycled) with a diagram on the front and store it in a box. Some people like to store patterns in a clear plastic sleeve in a folder. In factories, cardboard patterns have a hole punched through them and are hung on wire hooks on a rail. They are numbered and sometimes named (with girls names, for example).
Cataloguing patterns can get messy when the same pattern is used in several ranges, or has variations, so

often the pattern has two numbers: a pattern number and a style number. The pattern number is usually just a sequential number used for cataloguing the actual pattern so it can be found. The style number (or name) might refer to the range or collection it's in, for example Donna dress Spring 17. A style sheet will tell which pattern/s to use for that particular style.

In factories where the same patterns are used over and over with slight variations (notably menswear), *each pattern piece* is given a number. Managing this makes it possible to create new styles by recombining existing pattern pieces in new combinations.

In industry, a pattern will be stored with a **specification sheet**. The spec sheet is typically an A4 sheet of paper in a plastic sleeve that's hung up with the pattern pieces. Sometimes a copy of the spec sheet is kept in a separate folder so all the patterns can be conveniently looked up.

The spec sheet contains manufacturing information: the pattern number, a back and front sketch, information such as seam and hem allowances, specifications for elastic, hanging loops, zips, velcro, buttons, interfacing, amount of fabric, sometimes some finished measurements and any other information the patternmaker deems necessary. I like to note how I graded the pattern on the reverse of the spec sheet, to save time if I need to make extra sizes.

A **style sheet** also may contain specifications, but relates to the garment being made from the pattern, rather than the pattern itself. Every garment in a range will have its own style sheet.

A style sheet typically has a style number, a reference to the pattern number(s), back and front sketch, fabric swatch and fabric and notions required. It may also have a breakdown of the fabric, notions and labour costs so that a garment price can be determined.

Making a test garment

Test garments are sometimes called muslins, calicos, fitting garments or toiles. Calico is the most oft-used fabric, but if the garment is a knit try and find something similar to use. Likewise, if the intended fabric is slinky, floppy or very fine, find an inexpensive fabric that behaves similarly.

Get the pattern as correct as you can on paper before cutting any fabric.

So, how much detail do you sew in a test garment? Well, as little as you can get away with! It's still very important to cut it out accurately and snip all the notches.

✂ Trousers and skirts. Sew the outer and inner leg seams and crotch seam for trousers. Sew the side seams for skirts. Some people like to install a zip but I just leave an opening to pin closed. You may like to write FRONT or BACK on it to avoid confusion.

✂ Waistbands. Iron the waistband in half and pin it onto the waist, right sides together, through all three thicknesses. Put the pins on the garment side then flip the seam allowance down to hide the pins OR sew it on using a big stitch.

✂ Necklines (and faced waists). Support the edge in some way so it doesn't stretch. I like to sew cotton tape on, measuring the tape on the pattern not the garment which might have already stretched. You could also get some heavy interfacing or even paper, and accurately cut out the shape of the neck, 2.5cm (1") wide. Sew it to the neck with a big stitch.

✂ Pockets. Draw pockets on in texta, or cut out a pocket in calico and pin it on.

✂ Sleeves. You only need one.

✂ Hems. Iron up the hem allowance before sewing, or else trim it off when you cut the test garment out.

Save time and fabric

✂ If you want to just check the look and proportions, consider sewing only the front and holding it up to the body. I would sometimes do this for skirts to see if the designer wanted to go ahead with it.

✂ Try and re-use test garments if you can; you don't need to make a whole new one after doing each fitting. It might be enough to sew the changes in it and re-use it. If the test garment uses a lot of fabric, recycle the fabric for a different test garment.

✂ When I was a fashion student, we would sometimes cut it out in calico, staple it together and iron it. It works very well if you're in a hurry or don't have a sewing machine handy (or you're too lazy to thread one up, or you left your sewing kit at home).

✂ If there's only one part of a garment to test, for example the sleeves of a jacket or a pocket shape, cut out the garment in fashion fabric and leave fabric for the pieces you're testing. Cut the test pieces in calico and pin or sew them in for a fitting.

✂ Don't spend forever tweaking and fine tuning the test garment. Sometimes it feels as if you could go on and on. At some point you'll have to move onto the fashion fabric, which will perform differently anyway.

Two alternatives to test garments

If you're reasonably sure the pattern is OK, you could:

✂ Cut the garment out in its lining fabric. Sew it up in a regular stitch and you can use it for the lining when you've fitted it.

✂ Cut the garment in a cheaper fabric that you could finish off and wear. This has the advantage of actually wearing the garment to test it.

Piping

Introduction 211	Applying piping 211
To make piping 211	Double piping 212
Joins in piping 211	Flat piping 212

Piping is a trim made from a strip of fabric cut on the bias, wrapped around a cord and stitched to hold the cord in place. It's inserted into a seam (or sometimes a hem) and is used to accentuate the line of the seam.

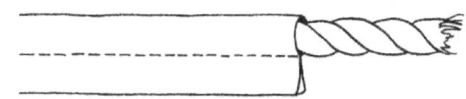

Piping can go around collars and cuffs, necklines, yokes, sleeveless armholes, in vertical or horizontal seams, around pockets, around hems, in fact, anywhere where there's a seam or edge to apply it to.

You can buy piping ready-made or you can make your own. Ready-made comes in a limited range of colours and sizes, so it may be preferable to make your own. It's very simple to make.

Important: test the colour fastness of the piping if you're using colours likely to run. Reds and maroons are particularly prone. I remember a uniform company who made some hotel uniforms with maroon piping on the jackets, of which the colour ran as soon as the jackets were cleaned. It cost a large amount of money to fix.

Also important: check the piping cord for shrinkage, whether you've made your own or bought ready-made.

To make piping

1. Select some piping cord in a width proportional to the garment. For example, use a fine piping cord on children's clothes and a chunky cord for cushions.
The sizes are numbered. Size 000 is a very fine piping cord. Size 14 is fat and chunky. Size 0 is most commonly used for adult clothes.

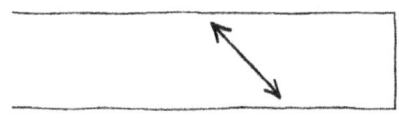

2. Cut some bias strips of your chosen fabric (see pages 20-21). 3cm (1¼") wide is usual for piping cord sizes up to about size 1. It needs to be the circumference of the cord plus two seam allowances.

3. Encase the cord in the bias strip and stitch close alongside it using a zipper foot on the machine. You can use a long stitch.
If the zipper foot on your machine is the type with a wide back, you may not be able to stitch close enough. Use a specially designed piping foot. If your zipper foot is the adjustable type (a universal foot) you'll have no worries.

Joins in piping

For single garments, avoid joins by making lengths of piping cord to suit the lengths of the seams.

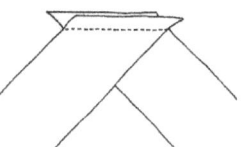

When large amounts of piping cord are required, make joins in the bias strips and sew continuous metres of piping. It's OK to have joins in the piping on the garment, but try not to have them in the centre front.

Applying piping

Piping is applied in two stages. It's sandwiched in a seam, or between a garment and its facing.

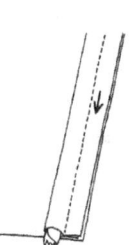

1. Stitch the piping to the right side of the garment. Use a long stitch and a zipper foot. Hold the garment firmly and let the piping "sit easy" on top.
The stitching should be *on* the seam line, so adjust the distance of the piping from the edge if necessary.

212 The Dressmaker's Companion

2. Place the other side of the seam (or the facing) on, right sides together. Pin. The piping is now sandwiched between the two layers. Stitch the seam with the first row of stitching *uppermost* 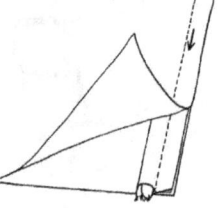 (*not* as illustrated, for clarity), so you can see where to sew. Use a regular length stitch and a zipper foot.

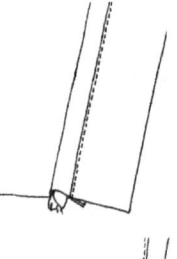 3. If the piping is between the garment and a facing, understitch the facing as you normally would.

You can topstitch the garment next to the piping if desired.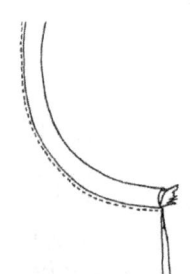

✂ To apply piping to a **hem**, make a facing (see page 97) and sandwich the piping between the facing and the hem.

✂ If the piping goes around **corners or curves**, snip the piping to shape.

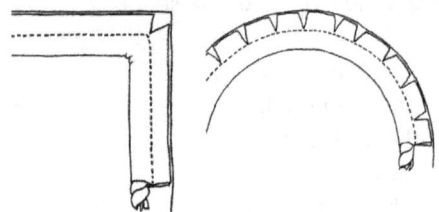

✂ The **ends** of the piping usually end up sewn into another seam. Where they don't, for example hems, just run the piping ends off to nothing where they overlap. Make them overlap at a side seam or inconspicuous place.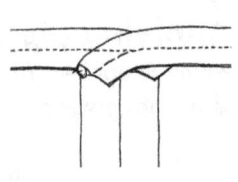

✂ Another way to deal with the ends of piping is to seam the piping to itself at the end of an existing seam. Press the seam open and handsew down the ends of the piping. As you can tell, it's slightly bulkier and it's important that the piping seams match exactly.

✂ On cushions with piping around the edge *and* a zip in the edge, sometimes the piping starts and finishes at each end of the zip. In other words, there's no piping along the zip.

Double piping
Double piping features two lengths of piping, which don't necessarily have to be the same width or same fabric.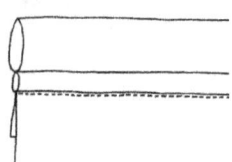

If using double piping on an edge, for example around the edge of a jacket, you might need to trim back the edge of the garment to allow for the extra distance the piping will take up.

1. Make two separate lengths of piping. Use a wider bias strip for the outside one.

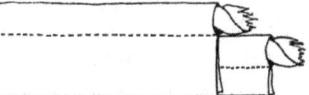

2. Sew the two pieces of piping on top of one another to make one unit.

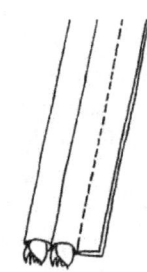

3. The piping is applied in the same way as described above.

Flat piping
Flat piping is simply piping made without the cord inside. Press the bias strip in half longways before applying.

Pleats

Types of pleats 213	Inverted pleats with an underlay 218
Choosing a fabric 213	Installing zips in pleats 218
Grainline 214	Patterns and calculations for pleats 218
Lining pleated garments 214	pleat a strip of paper 218
Making unpressed pleats 214	pleat the pattern or fabric 219
free hanging 214	pleat to a plaid or stripe 219
stitched down 214	using maths 220
Hemming pleats 214	using a pleating tool 221
Topstitching pleats 215	Other types of pleating 221
Making pressed pleats 215	sunray pleats 221
professional pleating 215	cartridge pleating 222
pleating at home 215	pipe organ pleating 224
Joining pleated pieces 216	broomstick pleating 225
Tapering the waist of a skirt 216	contortion pleaing 225
Fitting notes for pleats 217	

A classic fashion perennial, pleats can be used on a whole garment, for example skirts, or parts of a garment, such as pleated trims. However, pleats are used on skirts more than any other garment.

A pleat is a fold in the fabric used to control fullness, made by folding fabric along a specified line (the *fold line*) onto another line (the *placement line*). The *underfold* is the fabric behind the pleat.

Types of pleats

Knife pleats have all the folds facing the same direction. The depth of pleat may or may not be equal to the distance between the folds—it could be more or less. Traditional kilts have knife pleats with underfolds that overlap. That is, the depth of the pleats is *more* than the distance between the pleats, and up to seven yards of fabric are pleated for one kilt. It's important to note that knife pleats aren't symmetrical, and sometimes a box or inverted pleat, or a space, is used at the centre so the knife pleats hang symmetrically on the garment.

A **box pleat** looks like two knife pleats facing away from each other. The folds behind the pleat may or may not meet each other in the centre.

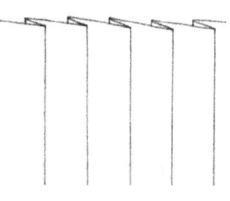

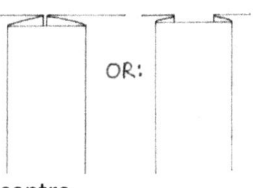

Inverted pleats look like the reverse side of box pleats—two knife pleats facing inwards, but the folds always touch. Inverted pleats can be made with a separate underlay that forms the back of the pleat, so instead of two folds at the back there are two seams. From the right side, the seams look like very crisp folds under the pleat.

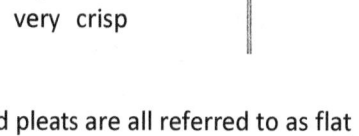

Knife, box and inverted pleats are all referred to as flat pleats.

Choosing a fabric

Unpressed or **soft-fold** pleats are allowed to fall in the fabric's own folds. Almost any fabric is suitable for unpressed pleats.

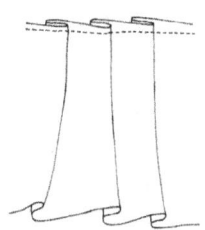

Pressed or **sharp-fold** pleats are pressed in crisp, sharp folds along the entire length of the pleat. The best fabrics for pressed pleats are ones that are smooth, crisp, hold a crease, light to medium in weight and firmly woven. Thick fabrics and knits are unsuitable.

Lightweight fabrics generally pleat well into any size and type of pleat. Thick fabrics can create too much bulk if the pleats are too deep and close together. Synthetics fabrics such as polyester hold the creases in pressed pleats longer because the heat changes the shape of the fibres. The pleats will be permanent and wash-proof.

Grainline

Pleats hang best if the pleats fold along the straight (preferably lengthwise) grain, at least from the hip down.

Conveniently, skirt lengths can be cut from a roll of fabric with the selvedges used for side seams.

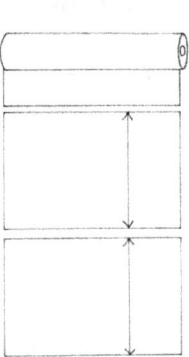

Lining pleated garments

The lining on pleated garments shouldn't be pleated but should provide enough room to move. Skirt linings should be free-hanging from the waist. Some skirt lining possibilities:

✂ Half-line the skirt to just below the fullest part of the hips.

✂ Use an A-line skirt pattern for the lining (my preference).

✂ Use a straight or A-line skirt pattern for the lining and leave long side splits in the side seams, to allow for walking.

Making unpressed pleats

Pleats can be held in place at the top by a seam (**free-hanging pleats**) or stitched down from the top to a certain point (referred to as **stitched down** pleats).

Stitching down the tops of pleats looks more flattering over the tummy, because the pleats don't fall open at the widest area. The sewing 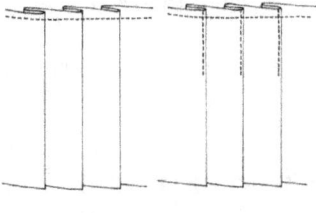 pattern will show if and where the pleats are to be stitched down. Either way, the pleats may be unpressed or pressed pleats.

Free-hanging, unpressed pleats

These are very simple to make.

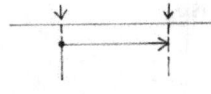 1. Mark the position of each pleat by making a tiny 3mm (⅛") snip at the top of each pleat.

2. Using the pattern as a guide, bring the snips together, exactly matching them. The arrows on the pattern will tell you which way to fold the pleat. Usually the fold line 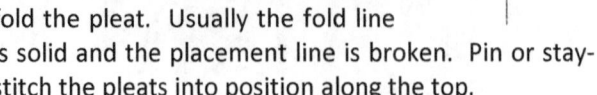 is solid and the placement line is broken. Pin or staystitch the pleats into position along the top.

If the edge is curved or shaped, there will be an angle 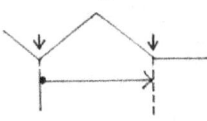 or jog at the top of each pleat which will fold neatly together as each pleat is made. You'll still need to snip the pleat positions.

Stitched down, unpressed pleats

These are a little more time consuming than free-hanging pleats. They're a bit like sewing a dart with an open end.

1. Mark the position of each pleat by making a tiny 3mm (⅛") snip at the top of each pleat and a dot (on the wrong side) at the points the pleat will be stitched to. The stitching lines often splay out at the top, rather than being the same width from top to bottom, so the top will be stitched like a dart with no point.

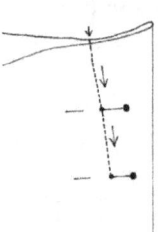 2. With the right sides together, match the snips and the dots. Stitch along the line formed by them, beginning at the snips. Backstitch at each end.

Press the seam. Sometimes the pleat is topstitched.

Hemming pleats

✂ Garments with unpressed pleats can be hemmed whenever.

✂ Pressed pleats are hemmed *before* pleating, so the folds of the pleat at the hem are creased in the right direction. If you're unsure of the length, you could press in the pleat folds to just short of the bottom edge. After hemming, press in the pleat folds the rest of the way.

✂ Fabric that is to be sent to professional pleaters is always hemmed first Afterwards any excess length is trimmed off the *top* before sewing the garment.

✂ The exception to the "hem-first" rule is if you want a fluted, ruffled lower edge. It looks wonderful on finely pleated organza for evening wear. If so, hem after pleating.

✂ Real Scottish kilts use the selvedge as a hem.

Topstitching pleats

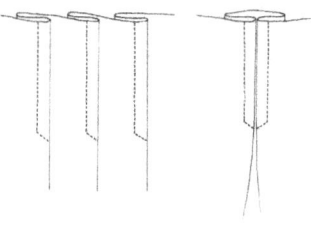

The tops of pleats can be topstitched or edgestitched, giving a tailored effect.

If the top of the pleat is shaped, sew the pleat as usual and topstitch it afterwards.

You can also use edgestitching only to stitch the pleat into position, eliminating the previous sewing step. Fold the pleat into position and stitch it down from the front. The pleats on the fronts of trousers can be sewn this way. This works best with edgestitching only—for wider topstitching, sew the pleat first and then topstitch, otherwise the fold doesn't sit flat against the fabric (unless you want that look).

Edgestitching both the front *and* underfold of each pleat not only gives really crisp looking pleats, but makes ironing *far* easier for clothes washed at home. Pleats need to be re-pressed every time the garment is laundered. Dry cleaners will charge extra for the time it takes.

When edgestitching the front folds, you can stitch just the top part of the pleat, or the entire length. If you plan to stitch the entire length, decide where you want the pleat to be stitched down to and stop there leaving long threads. Continue sewing *just the edge of the fold* all the way to the end of the pleat. Invisibly tie off the threads afterwards to hide where the stitching is joined.

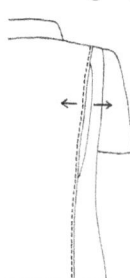

Topstitched down pleats are also a feature of action backs in overalls and school dresses. The stitching on every pleat fold encourages the pleat to return to the closed position each time.

Making pressed pleats

Fabric can be professionally pleated at custom pleaters (highly recommended) or pleated at home, requiring a steam iron and patience.

Professional pleating

If you decide to have a length of fabric professionally pleated, phone the pleaters first and ask them what types and sizes of pleats they offer and how they require the fabric. They usually charge per piece of fabric to pleat. They'll probably say:

✂ Hem the lengths of fabric before sending them.

✂ Don't sew any side seams, just send the hemmed lengths (there's no guarantee where the seams will end up in relation to the pleats).

✂ Choose a fabric with a synthetic content for best results. If you send them, for example, a 100% wool fabric, the pleating won't be as permanent.

For a skirt professionally pleated all around

1. Decide on a skirt length and add a hem and waist seam allowance.

2. Measure your hip circumference and add ease, for example 97cm hip + 7cm ease = 104cm. This gives the hip measurement for an *unpleated* skirt. Note this measurement.

Pleating usually uses three times the fabric of the finished measurement. Each pleat, whether knife or box, touches but doesn't overlap the preceding one. Therefore, multiply the noted measurement by three (in my example 104cm x 3 = 312cm). Measure the width of the fabric you plan to use to see how many lengths you need—it's usually two or three. For example 312cm ÷ 112 wide fabric = 2.78 which would be three lengths. 312cm ÷ 150 wide fabric = 2.08 which would be three lengths as well. Make sure you have some spare width allowed to sew the panels together when they come back from the pleaters. You'll need seam allowances and some extra to adjust the seam positions so they're hidden under a pleat.

3. Hem the lengths of fabric, but don't sew any side seams—just leave them as lengths.

Pleating at home

You can press in pleats at home on a regular ironing board, but it helps if you have a table to support overhanging fabric. Try setting up your ironing board next to the dining table.

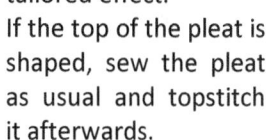

A bigger pressing surface is more efficient and easier, though. You could spread a table top with a blanket covered by a sheet and use that.

Pleating your own fabric at home gives you the advantage of joining two lengths of fabric then pleating around the seams, rather than pleating first then juggling the seams to hide them under a pleat.

If the pleats are going to be stitched down at the top and you're absolutely 100% happy with how they're going to fit, then go ahead and stitch them down *before* pressing the folds in the rest of the pleats (see Unpressed pleats, page 214). It will be much easier.

1. Hem the length of fabric.

2. Mark the top of each pleat with a tiny 3mm (⅛") snip and the bottom with a removable chalk mark. If the pleats are very long, it's helpful to mark intermediate points with either thread, removable chalk or pins. Make a cardboard template with notches in it to accurately and quickly do this.

3. Hand-baste (or I usually pin) the pleat arrangement, using a tape measure, measuring gauge or home-made template to keep them consistent.

4. Carefully and gently press the folds with steam to make preliminary creases, then remove the basting and pins. If you press over them they'll leave an imprint on the fabric.

5. Firmly press each pleat into place. It's important to use an up-and-down motion to press, rather than sliding the iron. To achieve sharp, crisp folds on the pleats use a Rajah cloth OR a wrung-out damp pressing cloth (pressing until the cloth is dry) OR 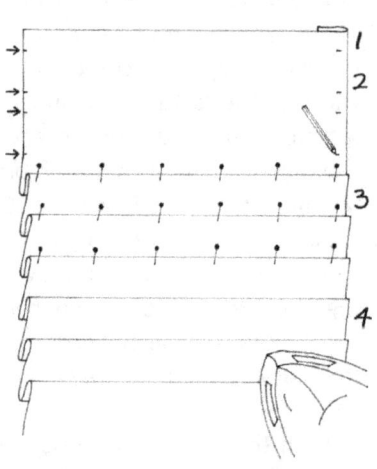 some brown paper wet with water and vinegar (try 3:1 water:vinegar and see page 268) OR put the water and vinegar in a spray bottle and spray it on. Let the fabric cool and dry before moving on to the next lot of pleats. You may also use a clapper to pound the folds of the steamy-warm pleats until cool. If the underfolds of the pleats leave ridges on the right side, slip a strip of heavy brown paper behind to stop the imprint.

Joining pleated pieces

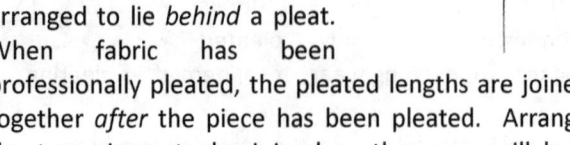

Seams in pleated fabric are arranged to lie *behind* a pleat. When fabric has been professionally pleated, the pleated lengths are joined together *after* the piece has been pleated. Arrange the two pieces to be joined so the seam will land behind a pleat—this usually means trimming off some fabric at the edge of each piece to get them lined up properly.

The seam will run through the already-stitched hem. Match up the ends perfectly so there's no step, and begin sewing the seam at the hem end so the layers don't move as you stitch. If you overlock the seam to 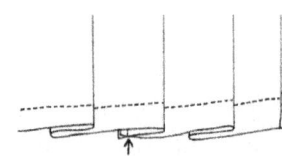 neaten the edge, the tail of the overlocking needs to be finished neatly so it doesn't undo or dangle. See page 190 for options.

Tapering the waist of a skirt

For ladies pleated skirts, the tops of the pleats need to be equally tapered to fit the waist measurement. For women, generally the waist-hip difference is about 20cm-25cm (8"-10"). By the way, for men it's about 0cm-2.5cm (0"-1") and children are basically tube shaped with the same waist and hip measurement (calculate the pleats on their waist measurement).

1. Join all the lengths together to form one long flat length of pleating, leaving one side open (the left hand side or the centre back) to insert the closure.

2. Lay the pleated piece flat on the table and check the finished hip measurement that you calculated earlier (my example was 97cm + 7cm ease = 104cm). The hip measurement is 18cm-20 cm (7"-8") down from the waist.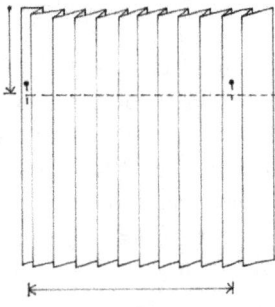

3. The tops of the pleats need to be tapered to your waist measurement. Use the chart on the next page to calculate how much each pleat needs to be tapered. You may find millimetres easier to work with than inches. Lap over each pleat this amount and pin it until the desired waist measurement is reached. You may only be moving each pleat a couple of millimetres depending on how many pleats there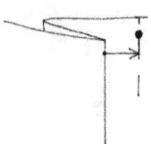

are. Run the amount back to nothing about 10cm-15cm (4"-6") below the waist.

Calculating pleat waist taper		
Calculation	Example	Your measurement
Take the waist measurement and add ease.	74cm waist + 1.5cm ease = 75.5cm	
Subtract this figure from the hip + ease measurement.	104cm hip - 75.5cm waist = 28.5cm	
Divide the amount by the number of pleats.	28.5cm ÷ 26 pleats = 1.09cm Therefore, taper each pleat by about 1cm.	

Note that the top edge is now curved. Each pleat should be tapered the same amount, but if you need more shape in one area than another, you can adjust the shape and taper at the fitting. Check the fit before you press or stitch the lapped over pleats into position. Meanwhile just pin or tack the pleats from the hip to the waist.

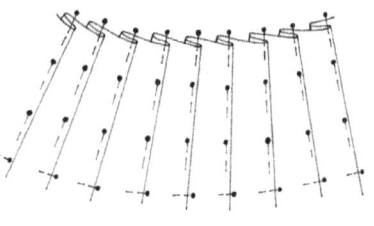

Fitting notes for pleats

✂ Pin or machine baste the waistband on for fitting skirts or trousers.

✂ The pleats should hang straight and closed, not jutting forward or pulling open. There must be enough fabric for the pleats to stay fully pleated and not pull away from each other. If the pleats open out on the body, the garment is too small. Either let out the side seams or reduce the amount of pleating.

✂ Do the pleats need to overlap at the top more in certain spots and less in other? Adjust now.

✂ For skirts and kilts, check the hem is level. Lift it from the waist to level rather than chopping off fabric from the hem (and anyway, you won't be able to adjust it from the bottom because it's already been hemmed).

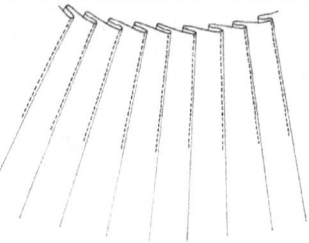

When you're happy with the fit of the pleats, stitch them down from the waist to the end of the shaping to hold the shaped section in place.

You can:

Edgestitch the front folded edge of each lapped pleat from the right side, if you want to see stitching (you may not even notice the stitching if the fabric is, for example, a busy tartan).

OR

Stitch each pleat from behind for a slightly smoother finish. This is more time consuming, but may suit your fabric better. Flip the pleats back one at a time and stitch in the front fold of the pleat, rather like making a tuck or a dart without a point. Flip the pleat back.

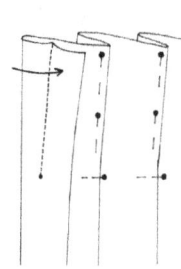

When all the pleats have been stitched, re-press. The skirt will now form an arc if you lay it flat on a table.

Box pleated skirts are a little easier to stitch down at the top than knife pleated ones, because there are usually fewer pleats. We did thousands of these in a factory where I worked in the early 1990's. They were three-quarter length, in navy or black.

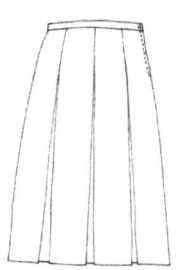

We sent hemmed lengths of fabric to the professional pleaters and when they came back the machinists stitched the folds of the box pleats together tapering the seam in 1cm (⅜") towards the waist (therefore each seam reduced the measurement by 2cm). A cardboard template was made for the machinists to show how much to taper when they stitched the top of the pleat.

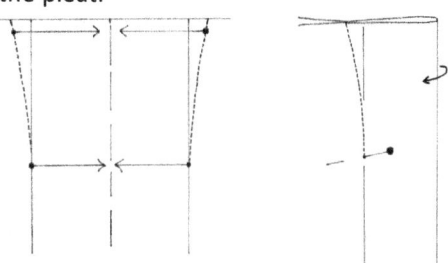

Does all this shaping sound too hard?
An easy and quicker alternative is to find a plain basque/yoke pattern that fits (you could thieve one from another pattern) and stitch the pleated fabric to it.

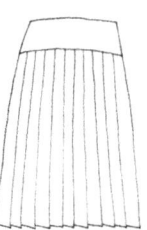

Inverted pleats with an underlay

Inverted pleats with an underlay have a separate piece of fabric for the back of the pleat.
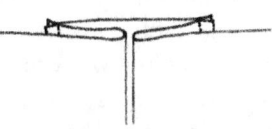
It's not obvious from the right side that it's separate, but the seams form a crisper pleat. Underlays can be a deliberate part of the pleat design, or a solution to a fabric shortage or narrow fabric widths.

The underlay can be a contrasting colour—think of traditional cheerleaders pleated skirts.

The most famous pleat with an underlay is the Dior pleat, used by Christian Dior on the back of skirts instead of a vent or kickpleat.
In this case the pleat only goes a little way up the skirt and so has stitching across the top of it to hold the pleat together. If the pleat was longer, the underlay would continue the length of the skirt.

Making a pleat with an underlay

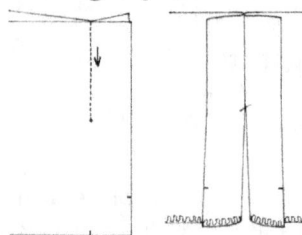
1. If the pleat is be stitched together at the top, do this first. A full-length underlay is shown here.

2. Press the seam open.

3. Hem the pleat and the underlay separately.
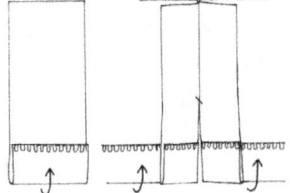

4. Sew the underlay to the edges of the pleat, and overlock the seam allowances. Since you'll be sewing through the pre-sewn hems, make sure the ends match perfectly. Neatly finish the tails of overlocking so they don't undo (see page 190).
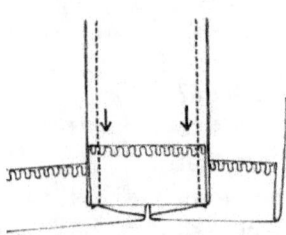

✂ If the top of the inverted pleat is shaped in to fit the waist, stitch a dart in the underlay to correspond. To reduce bulk, you might need to slit the dart and press it open.

✂ If you want to make a Dior pleat for a skirt see pages 359-360 for how.

Installing zips in pleats

If the pleats are **inverted pleats**, position the zip in a seam in the centre of a pleat. Ideally use an invisible zip (page 404) or a regular zip with a centred application (page 410).
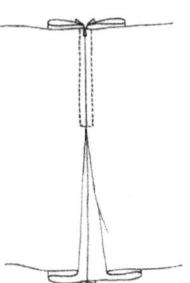

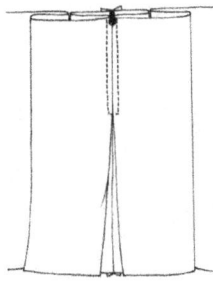
For **box pleats**, position the zip between two box pleats, or use the solution described below for knife pleats.

For **knife pleats**, position a seam behind a pleat and insert the zip into this seam. See page 415 for how-to.
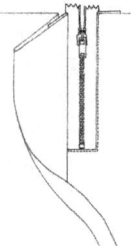

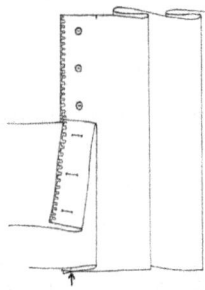
Instead of a zip, you could make a placket closure with (concealed) press studs or (visible) buttons and buttonholes. To form a placket, arrange a seam behind a pleat but don't sew it all the way to the top—stop about 20cm (8") before the waist. Neaten each side separately, OR bind the edges OR organise a fold-back facing when you cut the skirt out. You may need to iron a strip of fusing behind the buttons and buttonholes for strength.

Patterns and calculations for pleats

There are several methods for calculating pleats, depending on the application.

Method 1—pleat a strip of paper

Pleating can easily be calculated using a strip of paper. It's good for free-hanging pleats, or where lengths of fabric needs to be pleated up into a certain

Pleats **219**

measurement. I use this method often as a 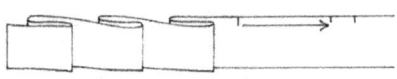 patternmaker when doing sample patterns or one-offs. Cut the length of the paper strip according to your fabric width or the amount of fabric you wish to pleat up. Pleat the strip of paper until it's the correct measurement and you're happy with the arrangement of pleats.

Double-check the pleats are even using a tape measure. The paper strip can then be used as a template for marking the pleat positions straight onto the fabric or pattern.

Method 2—pleat the pattern or fabric

This is good for garments with a single pleat or cluster of pleats, or stitched-down pleats.

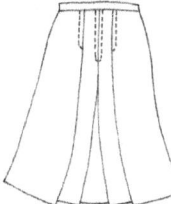

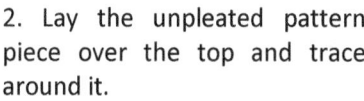

1. Pleat some pattern paper in the arrangement you desire and check that the pleats are even using a tape measure.

2. Lay the unpleated pattern piece over the top and trace around it.

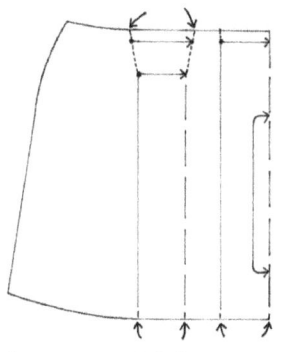

3. Unfold the paper and adjust the tops of the pleats to accommodate any darts. Notch the top and bottom of the pleats and indicate the fold direction. Make sure the new pattern still fits within the width of your fabric.

You can use this method straight onto the fabric by pleating the *fabric* first and then positioning the pattern on top of the pleats. This works well for pleated shirt and dress fronts, however, the left and right fronts need to be cut singly, not paired.

It's a quick and easy way to add pleats to a pattern you already have.

Method 3—pleating according to a plaid or stripe

When it comes to checked or vertically striped fabric, formal pleating calculations, pleating tools or professional pleating will *never* correspond to the fabric pattern. Plaid or striped skirts can be pleated straight onto the fabric. Pleating along different lines of the pattern will emphasize different colours and patterns, and the actual plaid will dictate the depth and frequency of the pleats. The pleats can be pressed or unpressed. After pleating, the tops of the pleats will need to be adjusted to taper in for the waist, if required.

Plaids, checks and tartans can be:

Knife pleated to maintain the original motif.

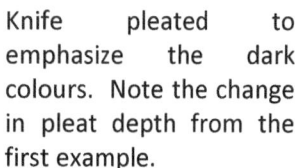

Knife pleated to emphasize the dark colours. Note the change in pleat depth from the first example.

Knife pleated to emphasize the lighter colours. A flash of the opposite colour will appear as the pleats separate while walking, dancing or marching.

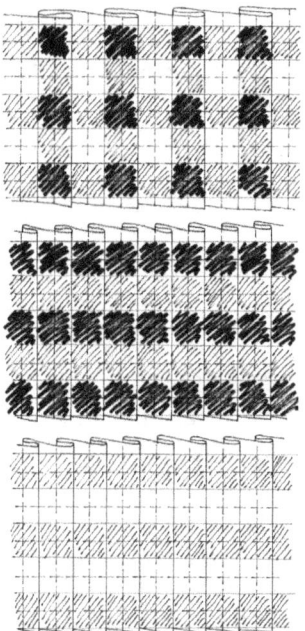

Vertical stripes can be pleated the same way, with either colour emphasized to reveal a flash of the opposite colour when the pleats separate.

You'll need to:

✂ Keep the repeats consistent.

✂ Keep the folds at a satisfactory depth—not too deep and not too shallow.

✂ Choose the fabric carefully; uneven plaids are suitable for knife pleats only, but even plaids can be box, inverted or knife pleated. See page 80 for even and uneven plaids.

✂ Match the pattern when joining fabric, preferably under a pleat.

Method 4—using maths

Don't let the word "maths" turn you off! These are simple calculations of the sort you would have done in primary school. If you're pleating fabric at home you'll need to calculate the fabric and pleat arrangement.

Calculating a **knife pleated skirt** when the pleating is designed to fit a certain width of fabric, for example, two lengths of 148 wide fabric, one for the back and one for the front. For this, the fabric width is pleated into the hip measurement. The folded depth might *not* be the same as the distance between the pleats (it can be more or less).

Calculation	Example	Your measurement
Take the hip measurement loosely and add ease	97cm hip + 7cm ease = 104cm	
Take your given fabric width and deduct seam allowances.	148cm wide fabric, length each for front and back. 1.5cm seam allowances. 148cm - 3cm = 145cm for the front and 145cm for the back = 290cm total.	
Deduct the hip + ease measurement from the fabric measurement. This gives you the amount of fabric to be divided into pleats.	290cm - 104cm = 186cm	
Divide the hip/ease measurement by the distance you want between the pleats. This gives you the number of pleats you will have.	4cm distance. 104cm ÷ 4cm = 26 pleats.	
Divide the amount of pleating fabric by the number of pleats. This gives you the amount of fabric in each pleat.	186cm ÷ 26 pleats = 7.15cm each pleat. (= 3.58cm when each pleat is folded).	

Calculating a **knife pleated skirt** if the pleat depth is to be the *same* as the distance between the pleats. The skirt will be three layers thick when pleated. Therefore, you'll require three times as much fabric as the measurement you're fitting (the hip measurement).

Calculation	Example	Your measurement
Take the hip measurement loosely and add ease.	97cm hip + 7cm ease = 104cm	
Multiply by 3. This gives you the amount (width) of fabric needed for pleating. To see how many lengths of fabric you'll need, divide it by the fabric's width. Allow some extra for seaming the widths together.	104cm x 3 = 312cm Therefore, 3 lengths of 112 wide fabric are required. Or 3 lengths of 150 wide fabric are required, even though not all of the fabric's width will be used.	
Decide on the distance you want between the pleats, and divide the hip + ease measurement by this figure. This gives you the total number of pleats.	4cm distance. 104cm ÷ 4cm = 26 pleats. (Suggest adjusting the pleat distance to arrive at an even number of pleats).	
Deduct the hip/ease measurement from the amount (width) of fabric needed. This gives you the amount of fabric to be divided into pleat depths.	312cm fabric -104cm = 208cm.	
Divide by the number of pleats. This gives you the total depth of each pleat.	208cm ÷ 26 pleats = 8cm pleat value.	

Calculating pleats for a woman's knife pleated **kilt** with an unpleated front panel. The width of the pleat fold is the same as the distance between the pleats.		
Calculation	Example	Your measurement
Take the hip measurement and add ease.	97cm + 7cm ease = 104cm	
Deduct the width of the front panel. This gives you the area to be pleated.	104cm - 20cm panel = 84cm	
Decide on the distance between the pleats and pleat depth. Divide the area to be pleated by the distance between the pleats. This gives you the number of pleats.	3cm pleats folded depth, 3cm apart. 84cm ÷ 3cm pleats = 28 pleats.	
Multiply the area to be pleated by 3. This gives you the fabric needed for pleating.	84cm x 3 = 252cm	
Add twice the panel depth (the kilt has a double wrap over).	(20cm panel) 252cm + 40cm = 292cm	
Finally, add: 2 seam allowances for joining the fabric lengths. 3cm for turn-back facings to neaten each front panel (unless you're having a fringed edge). 1 extra pleat depth for an inverted pleat at the inner edge of the front panel. It enables the panel to lie flat and hang well from the front.	3cm seam allowances + 6cm facings + 6cm extra pleat depth = 15cm 292cm + 15cm = 307cm. Therefore you'll need two lengths of 160 wide fabric. If the fabric is narrower, you'll need another length and extra seam allowances to join them.	
Calculate the pleat taper using the table on page 217. Fasten the waistband with a traditional tab and buckle fastening, a hook and bar or velcro.		

By the way, the front panel of a kilt looks like this: There's an inverted pleat just before the front panel.

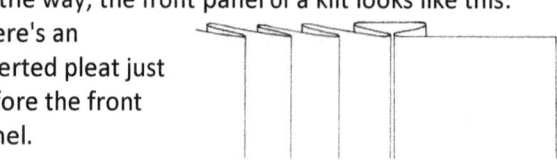

Method 5—using a pleating tool

An all-around knife pleated skirt can be pleated using a pleating tool. A pleating tool is a louvred board folded to resemble corrugations.

It enables pleating to be made without any measuring, and comes in different sizes. The fabric is tucked into each louvre and pressed, forming pleats. It isn't necessary to make a pattern, since all the pieces are rectangles. Individual rectangles of skirt length fabric can be pleated, then joined up to make the desired hip circumference.

Other types of pleating

Sunray pleats are sometimes called sunburst or fan pleating and feature on circular skirts. The pleats are very narrow at the top and widen towards the bottom. They are professionally pleated.

Cartridge pleating is a very old type of pleating done by hand and is sometimes referred to as gauging or gauged plaiting—plaiting meaning pleats and gauged referring to even measurements (cartridge pleating is a modern term). Tight, even gathers are stitched onto a straight edge. Cartridge pleating can be seen on garments circa 1600's such as skirts, neck ruffs and breeches.

Pipe organ pleats, organ pleating or pipe organ folds are so-called because they resemble the large pipes on organs.

Broomstick and contortion pleating are types of wrinkle pleating. They're usually used for skirts.

Sunray pleats

Sunray pleats are professionally pleated and fan out on a circular or flared skirt. Unlike knife or box pleats, the pleats aren't folded on top of each other into a seam; the fabric lays flat. Therefore, the fabric, not the pleating, needs to be shaped to give flare from the waist to the hips.

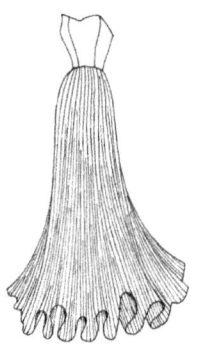

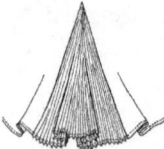 Smaller segments of sunray pleated fabric can be used as godets.

1. Decide if you want a full circle or half circular skirt. Decide on the finished length and add a hem and a waist seam allowance. Cut out the full or half circle. A full circle skirt will have side seams.

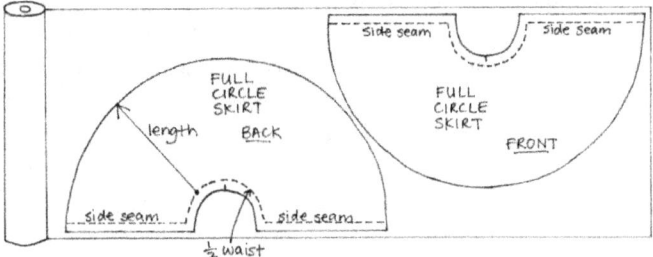

A half circle skirt will be one big piece with only one side seam—position this either at the left side, centre back or centre front, depending on the design.

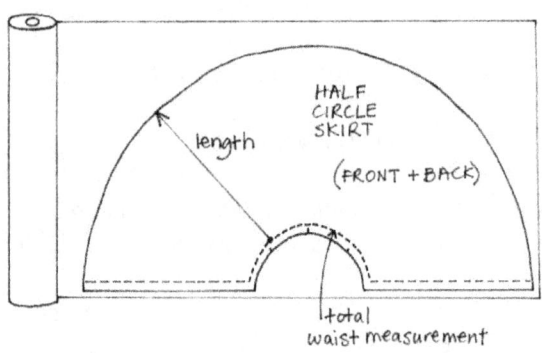

2. Cut out a waistband. If, instead, the skirt is destined to be attached to a strapless top or bodice, you might be able to fit the bodice pieces around the circular skirt when you cut it out. Also, ensure the side seams of the bodice will match the side seams of the skirt when they're sewn together. In other words, the back and front of each must measure the same.

3. A skirt of this type will need the hem levelled. After the fabric comes back from the pleaters, let the pleated panels hang on a dressmakers model to drop. Allow the outfit to hang for as long as possible so the bias parts drop. Have the wearer model it with the correct shoes, measure up from the floor and chop off the excess length. Hem the pleated skirt last of all.

Cartridge pleating

Cartridge pleating is kind of a cross between gathering and pleating. The pleats are formed on evenly-stitched gathering threads, creating a thick mass of folds.  Cartridge pleating can be used for sleeves (notably on academic gowns), capes, caps, bags, period doll costumes, as well as breeches and skirts.

Before pleating, both the edge to be pleated and the edge to attach the pleating to are finished with a hem, facing or lining. Then, two or sometimes three rows of parallel running stitch are made along the top edge and pulled tight. Each pleat formed is evenly hand stitched (right sides together) to the waistband or bodice. Only the peak of each "hill" that touches the band is stitched. This creates a hinge effect that pushes the skirt out and away from the body when worn.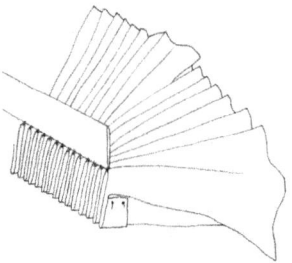

There are two great advantages of cartridge pleating. One is there's no bulk added to the waist—there's no seam allowance or fullness enclosed in the band or bodice as with regular pleating. The other is there's room for a very large volume of fabric to be attached this way. Note that cartridge pleating is stitched entirely by hand.

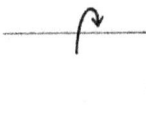 1. Hem the top edge of the fabric to be cartridge pleated.

Alternatively, you could line the fabric, finish the top edge with a facing or simply neaten and fold down the top edge without stitching.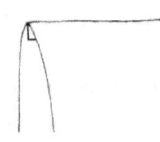

Occasionally the edge to be pleated has a strip of felt sewn inside to give substance to the pleats if the fabric is very thin.

Hem any side edges now, for example the front opening edges of an overskirt or cape, or the edges where the skirt will fasten.

2. On the *wrong* side of the top hemmed edge, mark the spacing for the pleats. Make a cardboard template for the calculated pleat spacing (see advice on pleat depth and fabric needs on page 223-224).

To mark the pleats you can:

✄ Mark a vertical line using a removable fabric marker or a piece of chalk (my preference).

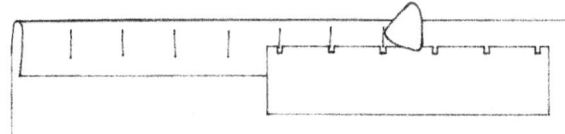

✂ Make a row of dots 6mm (¼") down from the top, using a chalk pencil or removable fabric marker. Then mark a second row of dots at least 6mm (¼") (could be 1cm (⅜") or even 1.2cm (½")) down from the first row. Most often, two rows are made, but three rows will hold the pleats firmer and you may find it easier to work with. It's also good for controlling thick fabrics or if you've used a felt strip. Three rows will make the pleats begin to flare out lower down.

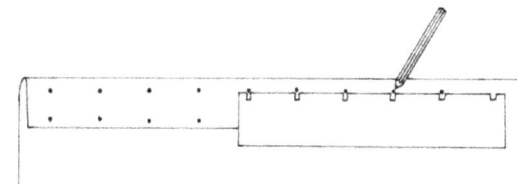

✂ If the fabric is striped or checked, you may like to pleat the fabric according to a stripe or check, in which case you've no need to make a template or mark anything. Experiment with a section first. The pleat depth and position you choose will make a difference to the finished colour of the pleats.

3. Mark the quarter points on the top edge as a guide for when you stitch the pleats to the band. Use a small thread tack on the fold line to mark the spot. This will make it simpler to match up the pleated section to the band or bodice.

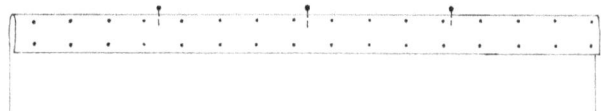

4. Sew the two or three rows of gathering threads using a double strand of very strong thread in a matching colour. Note that these gathering threads will stay in the fabric after the cartridge pleating is finished, although some people take them out. The thread shouldn't be any shorter than the finished length of the pleating, so it can be gathered in one go. However, I suggest sewing both rows of gathering at the same time so you can gather as you stitch and use a shorter thread. Therefore thread two needles (or three if you're doing three rows) and knot the ends.

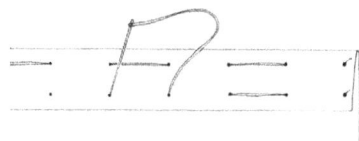

Iron the fabric well first. Begin on the wrong side of the fabric and go down in the first dot and come up in the second. Continue, forming a running stitch. Repeat for the second row of dots.

If you marked the pleats just as a chalk line, stitch the running stitch as just described and eyeball the stitches 6mm (¼") from the top edge. This is quite easy to do and I prefer this method. It's also easy to eyeball a second row 6mm (¼") (or 1cm (⅜") or 1.2cm (½")) away from the first. However, it's **very important** that the two rows of gathering mirror each other—the stitches must be exactly the same.

Gather up both rows when you've gone a little way to give yourself more thread, making the fabric pleat like an accordion. When you reach the end, secure the needles but don't finish off the threads just yet.

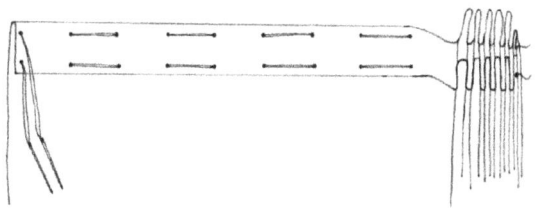

5. Have ready a waistband (or neckband or bodice) ready to sew the pleating to, with all the edges finished. Mark the quarter points to match up with the pleated piece. Place the right sides of the band and pleating together and draw up the gathering threads to fit the band. Match up the quarter points and pin. There should be an identical number of pleats in each section of the band. Distribute the pleats evenly between the quarter points and tie off the ends of the gathering threads.

6. Sew the top of each pleat to the edge of the band, using the same strong thread as before. Stitch each pleat twice for strength, taking a tiny bite of pleat and band with each stitch. *Do* wear a thimble.

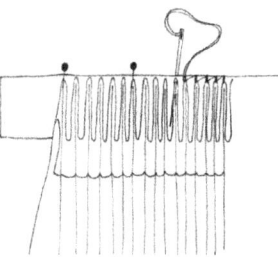

How much fabric do you need? and How far apart do you mark the pleats?
First decide how *deep* you want each finished pleat to be. 6mm (¼") works well, but it could be 1.2cm (½") or even 1.5cm (⅝").
Pleat up a sample in the fabric you'll be using. If you haven't tried cartridge pleating yet this is a valuable exercise and will show how your fabric performs. Cartridge pleating doesn't work as well on bulky fabrics. In my example shown in the table, I counted six pleats per 2.5cm (1"). If I wanted very tight

pleating, I could pull the gathers very close together and fit twelve pleats per 2.5cm (1"). Decide how you want the pleats to look for *your* garment. You can see that by slightly adjusting the depth of the pleats or pulling the gathers tighter (or both), it's possible to pleat a very great amount of fabric.

Calculation	Example	Your example
Decide on the finished pleat depth.	6mm (¼")	
On your sample, count the number of pleats per 2.5cm (1") of pleated fabric.	6 pleats per 2.5cm (1")	
Multiply the pleat depth by 2 to give you the amount of fabric needed for 1 pleat.	1.2cm (½")	
Multiply this number by the number of pleats per 2.5cm (1").	1.2 x 6 = 7.2cm or ½" x 6 = 3"	
Multiply this number by the length of the finished piece of pleating (ie - the length around the waist, neck, etc). For metric, first divide the length by 2.5.	Waistband is 76cm (30"). 30" x 3" = 90" OR 76cm ÷ 2.5 = 30.4 30.4 x 7.2 = 218.8cm	
Move the decimal place to give the number of metres of fabric required OR divide this number by 36" to give the number of yards required.	2.18m OR 2½ yards	

Pipe organ pleating

Pipe organ pleating is sometimes described as large-scale cartridge pleats but the pleats are formed by machine stitching folds of fabric vertically onto a flat backing—quite different from making cartridge pleats. (They don't have to be large-scale either; I've seen small pipe organ pleats around necklines.) The pleats have a three-dimensional form and aren't caught into a seam at the top like flat pleats are. They can look wonderfully dramatic on evening gowns. The stitching can go all the way down between each pleat to form

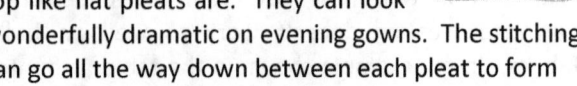

tubes, or only part way down (as illustrated) so the pleats fall clear. The pleats can also be tapered. The best way to determine the size and scale of organ pleats is to pin some pleats in place on a model and see what it looks like.

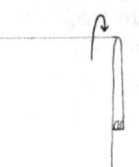

1. Prepare the fabric to be pleated by ensuring it's wrinkle free. You won't be able to easily iron organ pleats, if at all. Neaten the top edge and fold down a wide hem. Depending on the fabric and the look you aim to achieve, you may decide to interface the turned-down part to give stiffness and body.

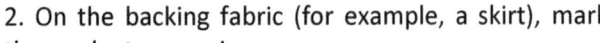

The fabric can also be lined.

2. On the backing fabric (for example, a skirt), mark the pleat spacing using a cardboard template or a tape measure.
You can mark with a chalk line (my preference), hand thread basting, pins or a removable fabric marker.

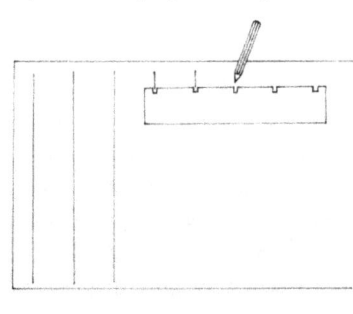

3. Using another template for the pleating, mark the pleat stitching lines on the fabric to be pleated. This part will be visible, so ensure the marking is removable.

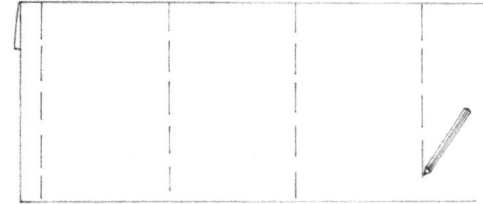

4. Bring together the backing fabric and pleating fabric along the marked stitching lines and pin. The right side of the backing fabric should face the wrong side of the pleating fabric—exactly as the garment will be worn. Machine stitch. Keep this stitching straight! It will be visible.

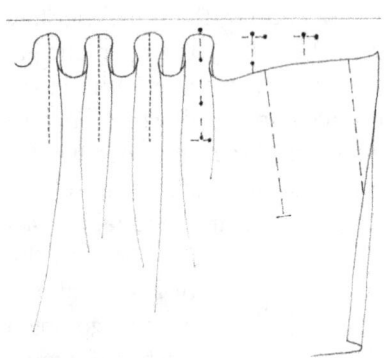

Broomstick pleating

Broomstick pleating has wrinkled folds in one direction with fairly straight sides. Soft, thin lightweight fabrics work well. To broomstick pleat, damp fabric is gathered up, rolled around a cylinder and bound to hold it until it's dry.

1. Hem the fabric first.

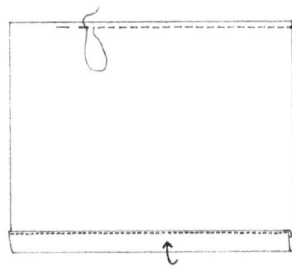

2. Gather the top of the fabric with large running stitches, pushing the gathers together tightly. Very wide, lengthy fabric may need interior rows of gathering as well.

3. Wet the fabric thoroughly, wring, and roll in a towel to absorb excess moisture.

4. Roll the fabric around a broomstick, plastic pipe or other sturdy moisture and rust-proof cylinder. Stretch the fabric so the folds of gathering are parallel to the cylinder.
Tie the fabric to the cylinder at the top, then bind with fabric strips. Wind the strips tightly around and around until the rolled fabric is completely covered. See Contortion pleating, below, for drying.

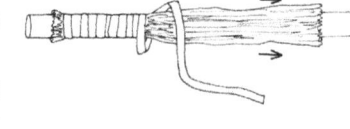

Another method: roll up the damp, gathered fabric and put it into the leg of a nylon stocking. Bind at close intervals with nylon stocking strips or cord.

Contortion pleating

Contortion pleating has multi-directional folds and the sides of the pleating will be uneven and irregular. As with broomstick pleating, fine lightweight fabrics work well. To form contortion pleats, damp fabric is twisted into a rope, coiled and dried.

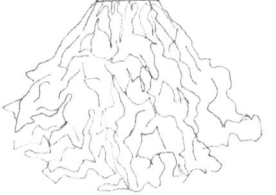

1. Hem the fabric first.

2. Wet the fabric thoroughly, wring, and roll in a towel to absorb excess moisture.

3. Twist the fabric along its length, turning it over repeatedly in one direction so it looks like a rope. Clamp one end of it in a vice or ask a friend to hold it for you. Stretch the fabric taut and twist it so it spirals back on itself when the ends are brought together. Continue twisting so you end up with a tightly twisted knot. Bind the knot with string or tie it inside the toe of a sock.

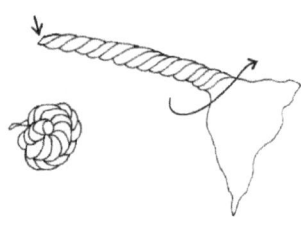

I've successfully contortion pleated bridal tulle for a skirt; I twisted lengths of tulle around the towel rails of a hot sunny bathroom, securing the ends with pins.

To dry broomstick and contortion pleating
The pleating needs to dry thoroughly before it has a chance to mildew. Time your pleating to coincide with the weather. In hot, dry, windy weather both types of pleating will dry in one day if left outside. If broomstick pleating is prepared in a nylon stocking it can by dried in an automatic dryer. Contortion pleating drying can be started in an automatic dryer and finished off in the air.
You could *carefully* dry pleating in a microwave oven, for a minute at a time until the moisture evaporates, but it requires care and attention.
Untie, unwrap, open up and spread the fabric out when it's completely dry. Remove any gathering threads.
To maintain the pleating, gather and twist the pleating into a roll and store it inside a nylon stocking, or coil loosely and keep in a drawer or box. Moisture, heavy pressure or humid weather undoes the wrinkling, but the pleats can be redone.

Pockets

Introduction 226	In-seam pockets sewn to the garment 240
Patch pockets 226	In-seam pockets with welts 241
Unlined patch pockets 227	In-seam pockets as an opening 241
Lined patch pockets 228	Cut away pockets 241
Patch pockets with flaps 229	bottom of diagonal pockets 244
Patch pockets with a self flap 230	pressing notes 244
Patch pockets with pleats or gathers 231	Cut away pocket as an opening 244
pleated safari pockets 231	Slashed pockets 245
pleats on one edge 231	Jet pockets 246
separate band at top 231	Flap jet pockets 248
gathering at the top edge 231	Curved jet pockets 248
gathering at the lower edge 232	Jet pockets with zips 250
Invisibly applied patch pockets 232	False jet pockets with zips 250
Invisibly applied variations 233	Jet pockets—another method 250
easter egg pockets 233	two further notes 252
Patch pockets in stripes or checks 234	for men's trousers 253
Three dimensional patch pockets 234	Welt pockets 253
3-D patch pockets with side gussets 235	Flap pockets 255
3-D pocket in one piece 235	False flap or welt pocket 256
3-D pocket in one piece that sits flat 236	Windowpane welt pocket 257
In-seam pockets 237	Windowpane welt—another method .. 258
In-seam pockets by overlocker 239	Windowpane welt for men's trousers . 260
In-seam pockets with zips 240	Zip pocket 261

Pockets are very personal things—everyone has their own very individual preferences about pockets in their clothes. Some people insist on every pocket being functional, others like the look of pockets but never use them. The great thing about sewing is you can make your pockets exactly how you want them.

There are four main types of pocket:
- Patch pockets
- In seam pockets
- Cutaway pockets
- Slashed pockets

Pocket placement depends on whether the pocket is functional or decorative. Functional pockets should be positioned at a level that's comfortable for the hand to reach. If the pocket is a decorative design feature it should be placed where it looks the most flattering.

Patch pockets

A patch pocket is a piece of fabric which is finished on all sides, then attached to the garment—essentially a patch with one side open. I always thought patch pockets were a bit kindergarten-ish, but in fact they can look extremely smart and sophisticated. They may be unlined or lined.

Patch pockets can make a big area (such as your bottom) look smaller because the pocket visually breaks up the area into smaller area.

Pockets patch

Patch pockets are easiest to sew if they're applied first thing, before the garment is assembled. However, if you don't know where to position them, or decide to add them as an afterthought, sewing them on last or part-way through isn't impossible—just fiddly.

Unlined patch pockets

Unlined patch pockets are most often used on casual clothes such as jeans, shirts and aprons.

Make a pattern

1. The easiest way to make a pattern is to cut a piece of paper the size of the finished pocket and pin it on the garment to check the proportions.
Fold the pattern in half vertically to make sure each side is symmetrical, particularly if the corners are curved.

2. Add seam allowances around the edges and a wider self-facing at the opening edge. The seam allowance around the edges can be 6mm (¼") to 1.5cm (⅝"). I usually make mine 1cm (⅜").
The self facing can be anywhere up to 5cm-6.5cm (2"-2½") wide. When you cut the pocket out, make a tiny 3mm (⅛") snip in the fabric at each end of the self facing so you know where to turn it down.

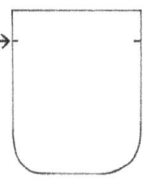

If the pocket is shaped in any way, the self facing at the top will have angled sides. To determine the angle (or jog) at the sides, fold the facing down when you cut out the paper pattern. When the pattern is unfolded, the facing will have the correct jog and you'll know it will fit the pocket perfectly.

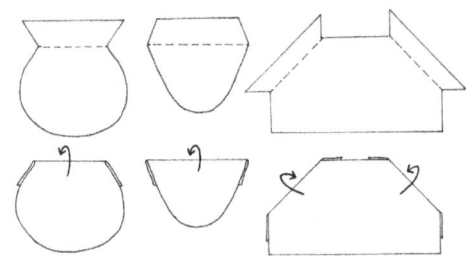

To sew an unlined patch pocket

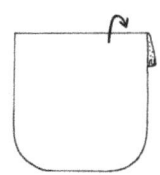

1. Overlock the self facing, fold it to the inside and press. Sometimes the self facing is stitched down, sometimes not.
It can also be turned under twice instead of being overlocked.

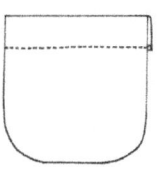

Sometimes the self facing is **interfaced**. I generally only fuse the self facing for knits (where I don't want the top edge to stretch) or if a buttonhole will be made in it (so the buttonhole is supported).

2. Press under the other edges of the pocket.
These edges don't get overlocked or neatened unless the fabric frays badly.

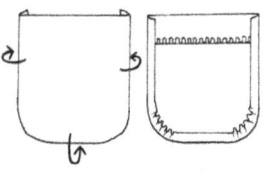

Occasionally the self facing is bagged out first, but you can only do this if you don't plan to topstitch down the self facing, otherwise you'll see the backstitching at each end. Bagging out the self facing makes a neat top, though.

To bag out the facing, fold it back along its fold line so the *right* sides are together and stitch each side taking the correct seam allowance. Turn it through to the right way and carefully poke out the corners.

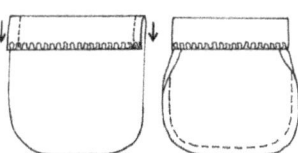

If the pocket has **square corners**, neatly press the seam allowances under along the three sides.

If the pocket has **rounded corners**, you'll find the corners easiest to manage if the seam allowance is no bigger than 1cm (⅜"). You can:

✂ Try just pressing under the rounded corners as they are. I would try this first and see if you can get away with it. Wide curved corners are easier to press under than tight ones.

✂ Ease each corner by stitching a long machine stitch close to the raw edge, then pulling on the stitches to draw in the seam allowance and shape the pocket curve. I think it works better with thicker fabrics. It can be fiddly, but you get a lovely smooth curve.

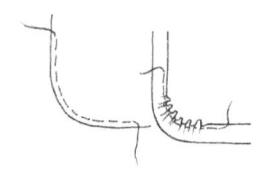

✂ Press the curves over a cardboard template that's the finished size of the pocket. This is convenient if you have a lot of pockets to do, because it makes it worthwhile to create a template. You can also use the template to press the pocket after it has been sewn onto the garment by slipping the template inside the pocket.

✂ Consider a lined pocket (see page 228).

3. Position the prepared patch pocket onto the garment. The location should be marked on the pattern. Transfer the pocket position to the right side of the fabric using pins, tailors tacks or chalk. I usually use pins or chalk pencil dots.

In industry, the location is marked by two small dots, just inside the top two corners. The pocket is sewn on so it *just* covers the dots. Very large pockets may have dots to match the other corners or edges.

4. Begin stitching in one corner, stitching close to the edge of the pocket, removing pins as you go. It doesn't matter whether you start in the left or the right corner. Stitching out a little distance from 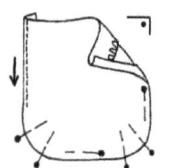 the edge, for example 6mm (¼"), is fine if the pocket is lined or if you're sure the seam allowance is caught in and won't pop out.

To make the corners of the pockets strong, reinforce them at the beginning and end of the seam, tucking the ends in as you do. You could:

✂ Sew a triangle shape to each top corner. It takes a little practice to get the triangles looking the same on both sides.

Start in the top corner and stitch down the vertical edge of the pocket for about 2cm (¾") or to the facing topstitching. Pivot and stitch back up to the top of the pocket, angling the stitching to land two or three stitches away from your starting point. Pivot again to the corner, then stitch over your first row of stitching and onto the rest of the pocket.

✂ Sew a rectangle shape to each top corner, about two or three stitches wide. This is a little easier than a triangle.

Start in the top corner and stitch down the edge of the pocket for about 2cm (¾") or to the facing topstitching if you have it. Pivot 90 degrees and stitch along for two or three stitches. Pivot 90 degrees again and stitch back up to the top of the pocket. Pivot again to the corner, then stitch over your first row of stitching and onto the rest of the pocket.

✂ Bar tack afterwards with a narrow zig zag bar tack. The bar tack can be horizontal, vertical or angled.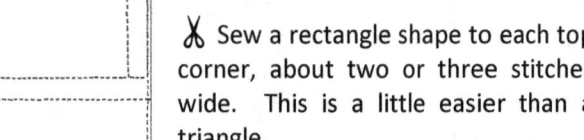

✂ Sew two lines of stitching around the pocket, backstitching at each top corner. This makes a stronger pocket because it's held by two rows of stitching.

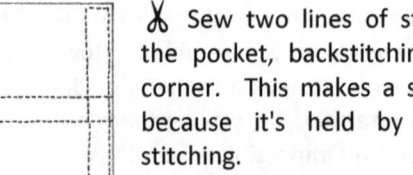

Start in the top corner and stitch around the edge of the pocket. When you reach the other corner, pivot and stitch along the top for two or three stitches. Pivot again and stitch back around the pocket, using the first row as a guide.

A 6mm (¼") distance between the two rows is very easy to do because you can use the edge of the presser foot as a guide. Upon reaching the beginning corner, pivot and stitch the two or three stitches along the top edge. Backstitch to finish.

Also:

✂ On the back pockets of jeans, often the topstitching is wider at the top corners. By the way, if you're making jeans and using copper rivets to reinforce the pocket corners, note that they're usually left off the back 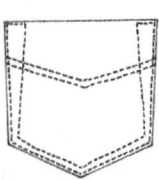 pockets. Rivets can damage furniture when you sit down.

✂ If the pocket is purely decorative, it's OK to simply backstitch at the beginning and end, as you would on a regular seam. If the pocket is going to be used, however, this won't provide enough strength at the stress points of the pocket.

Lined patch pockets

I like to make lined patch pockets on coats and jackets, even if the garment itself is not lined. Lining adds opaqueness to loosely woven or sheer fabrics, and makes them stronger if the pocket is a functional one. If the pocket has rounded corners or is a fancy shape, lining the pocket is an easy and neat way to manage the corners. It's also a good solution if you want wide topstitching around the pocket— there's no chance of the seam allowance not getting caught in.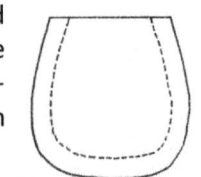

Lined patch pockets are sewn onto the garment the same way as unlined ones (see page 227), but are lined first. The self facing on lined patch pockets is normally interfaced, but sometimes the whole pocket is interfaced if it requires stability (for example, patch pockets cut on the bias or from very loosely woven fabric). Some people like to interface their pockets with white fusing even on dark fabric, so they can see where they've stitched.

Make a pattern

1. If you don't already have one, make a pattern for an unlined patch pocket as described on page 227. A seam allowance of as little as 6mm (¼") around the edge of the pocket is fine, even desirable if the pocket is curved, because it makes it easier to stitch. The raw edge will be easy to line up with the edge of the presser foot as you sew, provided it's a 6mm (¼") foot (check this by measuring the distance from the needle to the right hand side of the presser foot).

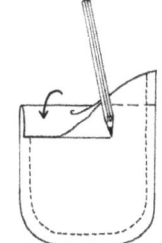

2. On the unlined patch pocket pattern, fold the self facing down and trace the edge.

3. Add two seam allowances above this line to give the cut line for the lining. You can make a new pattern piece, but it's quicker to draw a lining cut line on the old pattern piece.

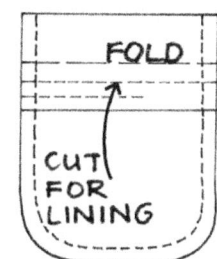

An added refinement is to trim 3mm (⅛") around the edge of the lining, making the lining slightly smaller than the pocket. When the pocket and lining are sewn together the seam will tend towards the inside with no danger of the lining being visible. You can trim this off when you cut out the lining if you don't want to make a separate pattern piece. You'll easily manage to sew them together if you stitch with the lining on top and the main fabric underneath.

To sew a lined pocket

1. Fuse the self facing of the pocket, or all of the pocket if you've decided to stabilize it.

2. With the right sides together, sew the lining and pocket along the top edge, leaving a gap in the centre to turn the pocket through. Press the seam allowance towards the lining.

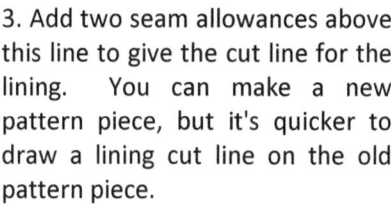

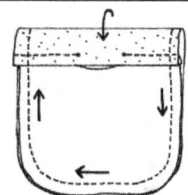

3. Still with the right sides together, fold the pocket along the top edge and match the edges of the lining and pocket. Stitch. This is referred to as bagging out the pocket, because the pocket and lining form a bag. If you trimmed the lining, it's easier to sew with the lining uppermost because it's slightly smaller than the pocket. Trim the corners if necessary.

4. Turn the pocket through to the right side through the gap in the seam. Press, rolling the edges towards the lining so they don't show. Stitch the opening closed.

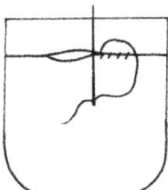

5. Attach to the garment in the same way as an unlined patch pocket (see page 227).

Patch pockets with flaps

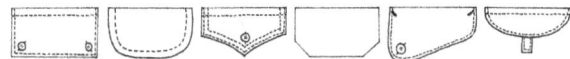

Patch pockets can have a flap added to the top, which may or may not fasten to the pocket. The flap can be any shape, but it looks best if it relates to the pocket shape in some way. It can be topstitched to match the pocket.

I think it looks best if the flap sits 3mm (⅛") over both sides of the patch pocket. It certainly doesn't look good if the flap isn't wide enough to cover the sides of the pocket.

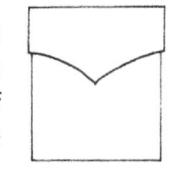

  The pattern will show the position of the flap as well as the patch pocket, so you know how far above the pocket to stitch the flap. Note there's a small gap between the flap and the pocket so you can get your hand in. The flap is never sewn right above the pocket.

If the flap buttons, it's preferable for the button to be sewn on through a double layer of fabric on the patch pocket (in other words, through the facing as well). Otherwise the button will eventually pull through and damage the fabric. Keep this in mind when positioning the pocket and flap together.

Make a pattern

Nothing difficult: draw a shape and add seam allowances. If the flap is rectangular, it may be one piece of fabric with a fold line. Interface the outermost half. 6mm (¼") seam allowances are fine on all edges.

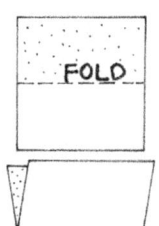

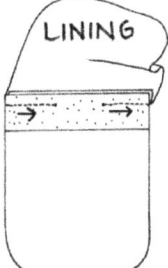

If the flap is shaped, it's made from two pieces of fabric and the outermost one is interfaced. If the fabric is very thick, the underneath can be lining or a thinner fabric or even an interesting contrast fabric. Like lined patch pockets, the lining can be cut 3mm (⅛") smaller around all but the top edge, to ensure it can't be seen when the flap is finished. Sew it with the lining on top and the main fabric underneath.

To sew a patch pocket with a flap
1. Place the flap pieces right sides together and stitch the sides. Leave the top open. Trim any curves and corners and turn to the right side, carefully poking out the corners. Press.
Topstitch the flap now, if desired.

2. Position the flap above the patch pocket and stitch. Flip the flap down over the pocket and press it in place.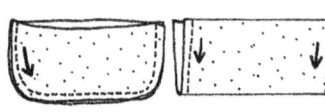

3. You can now either: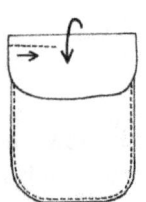
Trim the seam allowance back to 6mm (¼"), then topstitch the flap down, encasing the seam allowance and tucking the ends under. This is a good way for thick fabrics because the flap sits down and is my preferred finish for flap pockets.

OR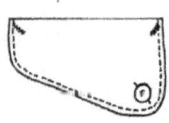
Sew a little bar tack at the top corners of the flap. It looks nice if you have a bar tack theme on the rest of garment. You'll need to overlock the pocket flap before you attach it because the raw edges won't be encased.

If you don't want any visible stitching at the top of the flap, you could: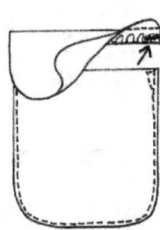
Overlock the top of the flap before stitching it into position. Tuck the corners in and secure with stitching underneath. Give the flap a good solid press. This works well on crisp fabrics that hold a crease.
OR

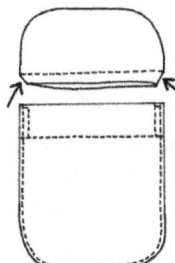
Angle the corners of the flap in on the pattern, then you won't see them peeping out of the sides of the flap. Overlock the raw edge of the flap (not shown in the picture) before stitching it into position. Flip the flap down and press well. This, too, works well on crisp fabrics that hold a crease.

Patch pockets with a self flap
This is a kind of mock flap because the flap is actually part of the patch pocket, so it's purely decorative. It's often seen on coats and jackets. This kind of pocket can be lined in the same way as an ordinary lined patch pocket.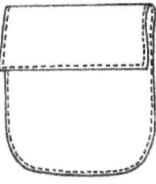

Make a pattern
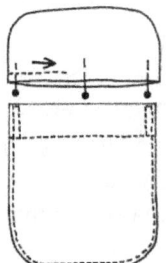
Start with a regular patch pocket pattern (see page 227). Decide on the finished width of the flap. On the pocket pattern, insert twice the finished flap width between the self facing and the pocket.

To sew a patch pocket with a self flap
1. Interface the self facing and half the flap width, as illustrated. Overlock the top straight edge.
With the right sides together, fold along the edge of the flap and stitch the sides.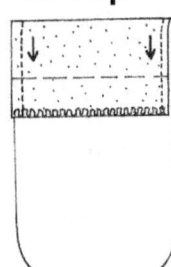

2. Turn through and press. Press under the other edges.

3. Press down the flap. Topstitch the flap part now if you plan to.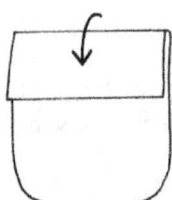

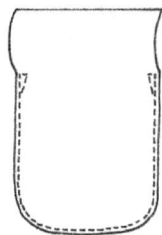

4. To apply the pocket to the garment, stitch it on like a regular patch pocket, keeping the flap up and out of the way. If the fabric is very thick and the flap won't stay down, catch it down in each corner by hand or sew on a decorative button.

Another method:
A simpler, but bulkier, way is to make the pattern with the flap added onto the top of the pocket. The pocket will be a double thickness of fabric.
Cut two. Interface what will be the uppermost flap, if required.
Place the two pieces right sides together and stitch around the edges, leaving a gap to turn through.
Trim the curves and corners, turn to the right side and press.
Press the flap down, and sew it to the garment as above.

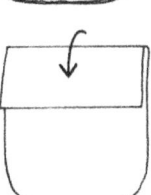

Patch pocket with pleats or gathers
Patch pockets can have pleats or gathers. The easiest way to make a pattern is:
1. Draw the *finished* shape of the pocket.
2. Cut and spread to add the pleats or gathers.
3. Add seam allowances.

It's more accurate to make half the pocket pattern, then fold it when you cut it out to make the other half (leave enough paper for this). This ensures the left and right sides are symmetrical, as well as saving time.

Pleated safari pockets
Pleated pockets will hold the pleats crisply if the pleats are topstitched along the fold lines. Safari pockets can have an inverted pleat (top picture) or box pleat (bottom picture), or more than one of either.

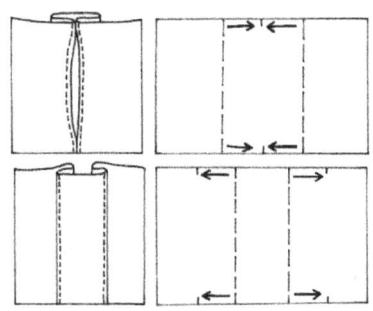

Start with the *finished* size of the pocket, then add in the amount to be pleated. I usually work out the pleats by folding a strip of paper, then I make my final pattern.

A small, 3mm (⅛") snip at the top and bottom of the pocket's fold lines will identify where to fold the fabric. The pocket can have a self-facing that folds over at the top, or, if the fabric is thick, a separate facing.
To sew, edgestitch the pleats in first. To keep the pleats in place while you finish the pocket, stay-stitch across the top and bottom of the pleats. Then sew the pocket on in the usual way.

Pleats on one edge of the pocket
Draw the shape of the *finished* pocket. Cut and spread the pattern where the pleat will be. Stick a piece of paper behind the cut. Fold the pleat into position and trim the excess paper off level with the edge, to create the correct jog for the pleat.
The pocket may look a strange shape after spreading for the pleats, but it will be right when it's made.

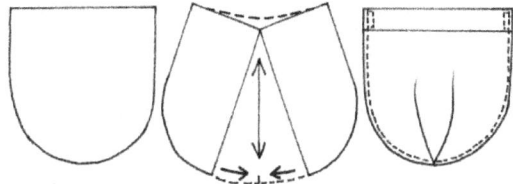

You'll need a separate top band, facing or a binding, since you can't fold under the shaped top edge.

Separate band instead of a self facing
A separate band may be required for a pleated or gathered pocket. It's also quite handy if you've run short of fabric. The separate band can be cut with the opposite grainline, which looks effective in striped fabric.

The separate band is simply a strip of fabric folded lengthwise, with the wrong sides together. It's sewn to the top of the pocket and the seam is pressed towards the pocket. You don't have to interface the band but you could interface all or half of it (the outermost half).

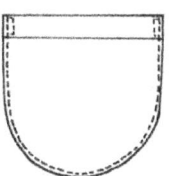

You can also apply the separate band like a binding, which is neat but can be bulky, because all the seam allowance is inside the band (see pages 22-27).

Gathering at the top edge
Draw the shape of the *finished* pocket. Cut and spread the pattern where you'd like the gathers to be. How much to spread? Try doubling the distance. Notch the pattern where the gathering begins and ends and note the measurement that the gathering will be drawn up to (for example "gather to 10cm").

Smooth the cut-and-spread edge of the pattern off into a pleasing curve.

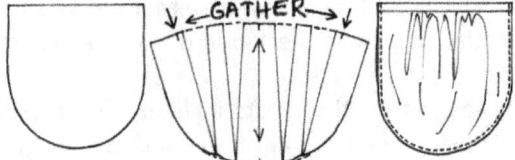

Make a band or binding pattern for the top edge. You could also make a casing and thread ribbon or elastic through, securing it at the corners when you sew the pocket on.

Gathering at the lower edge
Gathering at the lower edge of a patch pocket doesn't work well because you're topstitching over the gathers to attach the pocket. However, it *does* work very well indeed if you're attaching this pocket invisibly from the inside (see this page and next for invisibly applied patch pockets).

Make a pattern by drawing the shape of the *finished* pocket. Cut and spread the pattern where you would like the gathers to be. Not sure how much to spread? Try double the distance. Notch the pattern where the gathering begins and ends, and note the measurement the gathering will be drawn up to (for example "gather to 10cm"). Smooth the cut-and-spread edge of the pattern off into a pleasing curve.

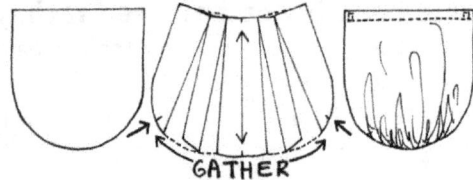

If the top edge is very curved you'll need a band or binding instead of a self-facing.

Invisibly applied patch pockets
Most patch pockets are attached with topstitching, but there are two ways to attach a patch pocket with no visible stitching.

The first way is to **handsew** the pocket on using hidden slip stitch (page 149). The pocket may be lined or unlined, and any shape. Make the stitches small so the pocket is strong, particularly at the top corners.

The second way is done **by machine** on pockets with rounded bottom corners. The corners *must* be curved, not square. The pocket can be lined or unlined. This method is sometimes used for blazer pockets.

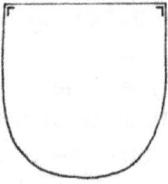

Big shallow pockets with large curved corners are easier to sew than small deep pockets with tight curved corners, but it isn't really hard—the key is in accurate pre-sewing preparation.

Make a pattern
1. Trim the seam allowances of the patch pocket to 6mm (¼"). 1cm (⅜") or 1.5cm (⅝") is too much.

2. Fold the pocket pattern in half vertically and mark (with tiny 3mm (⅛") notches) the centre bottom point and several other points around the curved corners, about 2cm-3cm (¾"-1¼") apart. These will help you position the pocket as you sew it. Note: they need to be symmetrical on the pocket.

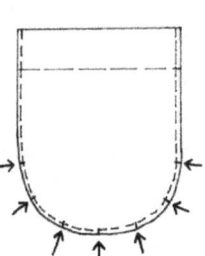

3. Make a cardboard template using the pocket pattern piece. Trace around the pocket, remove the top facing and *twice* the seam allowance (that's 1.2cm or ½") around the sides and bottom edge. Accurately transfer the pocket positioning marks onto the template, so they correspond.

To sew an invisibly applied patch pocket
1. Depending on the stability of your fabric, interface either none of the pocket, the self facing or the entire pocket with a fusible interfacing.

2. Overlock, press and stitch down the top facing of the pocket. If you don't want to see stitching, you can leave it unstitched or sew it by hand.
Alternatively, attach a lining to the facing, in the same way as you would for a regular lined patch pocket (page 228). Don't bag out the pocket, however. Instead, baste the lining to the pocket around the edges using a long machine stitch, and then overlock if the fabric is liable to fray.

3. On the garment, position the top of the template level with the pocket marks. Mark around the template using tailors chalk or a pencil. It doesn't have to be removable because the line will be hidden by the pocket. Don't forget to put in the positioning marks.

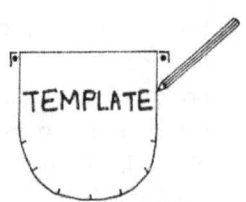

4. Fit the regular foot to your sewing machine, ideally one where the edge of the foot is 6mm (¼") from the needle. Lay one side of the pocket right side down on

the garment, matching the raw edge of the top corner with the chalk line.

Stitch 6mm (¼") from the edge, starting at the top corner and sewing around to the other corner, matching the raw edge with the chalk line as you sew. 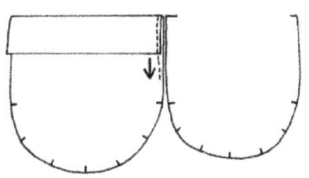 Make sure each point matches before you continue to sew on to the next one.

You'll only be able to sew a few stitches at a time in some places. If you err away from the edge, it's better that the stitching goes towards the raw edge rather than the pocket, because the pocket can be pressed over the stitching if it's slightly too big.

If you find it helps, you can pin the whole pocket in place on the inside first, but I find it easiest to leave it unpinned but to pin the next immediate point as I'm sewing. I use a stiletto, unpicker or pin to help move the fabric under the presser foot at the curves.

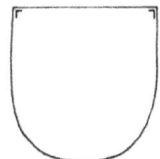 5. Using a press cloth over the pocket, give it a good solid press. Bar tack the top corners of the pocket for strength and to hide the raw edge corner of the pocket.

Invisibly applied variations

Invisibly applied patch pockets lend themselves well to pleated and gathered pockets, where regular edgestitching wouldn't work over the pleats or gathers.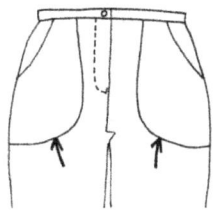

 These pockets aren't limited to just this shape, however. The technique can be used for the long edge of cut-away style patch pockets, as shown.

Easter egg pockets

Circles or ovals are also possible. I call them Easter egg pockets. The hand opening can be any shape.

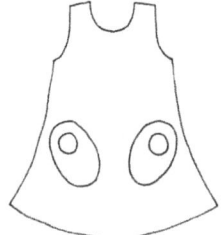

1. Draw the *finished* oval or circle shape, with any shaped opening to put your hand in (mine is circular).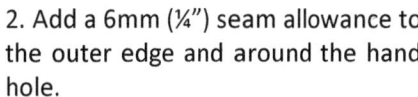

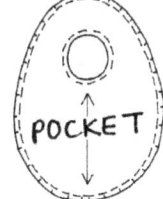

2. Add a 6mm (¼") seam allowance to the outer edge and around the hand hole.

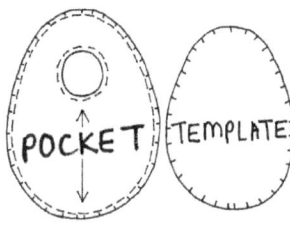 3. Make a template in the same way as described on page 232. That is, remove double the seam allowance (that's 1.2cm or ½") from the outside edge of the pocket. Leave the hand hole as it is. Mark matching notches on both the pocket pattern and the template about 2.5cm (1") apart. There'll be a lot of notches but you'll need them all.

4. Cut from fabric a pair of the pocket—one for the inside and one for the outside. Carefully snip all the notches with tiny 3mm (⅛") snips.

5. With the right sides together, stitch around the hand opening. Clip the curves or corners, turn through and understitch (or topstitch) around the edge. Press the pocket. Stay-stitch the raw outside edges together, so you have one unit. Overlock the edge if the fabric is a very loose weave or frays badly.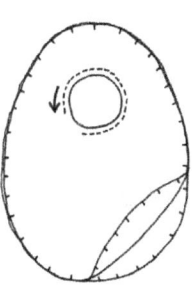

6. On the garment, trace around the template to give you the guide line. Place the right side of the prepared pocket face down on the garment next to the guide line, matching the correct notches. Begin stitching and sew around as far as you can—you'll be able to get at least three quarters of the way. Access the final section through the hand hole. Press.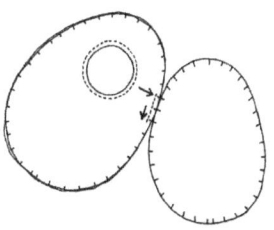

Patch pockets in stripes and checks

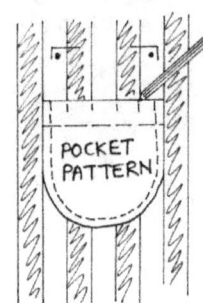

To match **stripes** on a patch pocket, cut out the garment first, marking the pocket position on the fabric. Lay the pocket pattern onto the garment in the correct position. Mark on the pattern with a pencil where the stripes land, then use the marks as a guide when you cut out the pocket.

For **checks,** mark the check position on the top *and* the side, so the vertical and horizontal lines will match. Note that for some checks, the left and right pockets will be different.

In industry, pocket positions for checks are marked with only one dot (the "dot" is a hole drilled into the fabric that's covered by the corner of the pocket), so that the machinist can shift the pocket if needed to make the checks match *and* cover the dot hole.

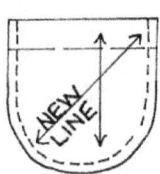

Consider cutting patch pockets on the bias to avoid matching difficulties. It also looks more interesting, too. To do this, simply draw in a new grainline at 45 degrees to the old one. Interface the whole pocket for stability, if required.

Three dimensional patch pockets

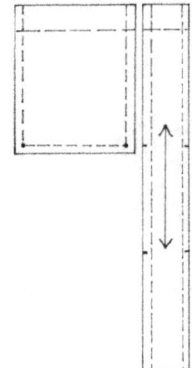

Sometimes called cargo pockets, poacher's pockets or bellows pockets, 3-D patch pockets lie flat against the garment but can expand because of pleats or gussets on the sides or bottom.

The gusset may be cut in a matching or contrasting fabric. 3-D pocket are always unlined and often, but not always, have a flap over the top.

A primary consideration is the thickness of the fabric. It's best to use a lightweight to medium fabric or the pocket will be too bulky.

Make a pattern

One way to make a pattern is to add a gusset to a regular patch pocket. The seam allowance can be 6mm (¼") or 1cm (⅜").

Measure the *stitching* line of the patch pocket to get the required gusset length.

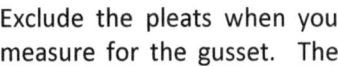

Place notches on the sides of the gusset to match the corners of the patch pocket. Be accurate! Otherwise the gusset won't fit on when you sew it.

The self facing at the top of the pocket and gusset are folded down separately before sewing the gusset to the pocket. The facing can be stitched down or just folded.

✂ For extra expansion, sometimes the patch pocket also has pleats (or it could have gathers).

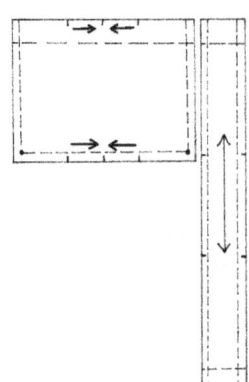

Exclude the pleats when you measure for the gusset. The pleats get sewn first and then the gusset is applied.

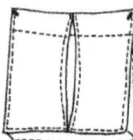

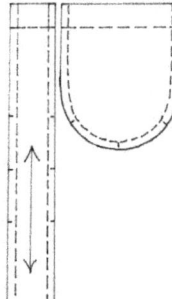

✂ The patch pocket can have rounded corners. Place notches on the curve and corresponding ones on the gusset.

Measure the length of the curved seam line by placing a tape measure on its side.

✂ The gusset doesn't have to be a long rectangle. It could be wider in the middle for the bottom of the pocket, however, the left and the right sides should be symmetrical.

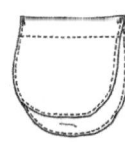
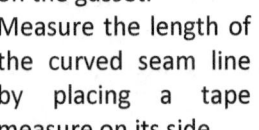

To sew a 3-D patch pocket

1. On the garment, you'll need points to align the top edge of the patch pocket and also points for aligning the bottom corners. Mark these as dots *just* inside the stitching line using a chalk pencil,

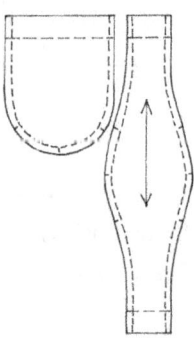
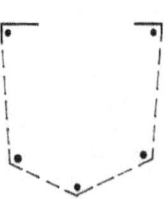

water soluble texta, chinagraph pencil or a pin. The dots will be covered with the stitching when you sew the pocket on. If the pocket is very large, some intermediate points may be required.

2. Apply interfacing to the pocket self-facing if you need to. Leave the gusset facing un-interfaced. Overlock the top edge of the pocket and gusset.
Fold down the self facing on the pocket and the gusset and stitch the pocket's facing down if desired.

3. With the right sides together and the gusset uppermost, sew the gusset to the pocket. When you reach the corners, stop with the needle down exactly in the corner. Lift the foot, pivot 90 degrees, snip the seam allowance in the gusset half way, and reposition the gusset along the lower edge (the snip will sit closed when the pocket is finished).

If the pocket is curved, you may need to strategically snip the gusset to get it to curve around the edge. The sharper the curve and the deeper the seam allowance, the more snips you'll need. Snip only half way into the seam allowance. A 6mm (¼") seam allowance shouldn't need any snips.

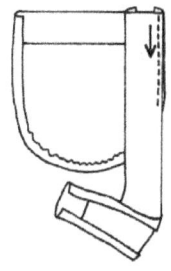

Optional: if you're planning to edgestitch the pocket seams, you can save time by skipping the initial seam. Fold down the self-facing, fold in the edges, place the wrong sides together and edgestitch the two pieces together.

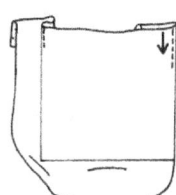

4. Press the pocket along the seams to define the fold.
Topstitch around the whole pocket, just for a centimetre or two at the top, or not at all.

5. Press under the edges of the gusset and pin the pocket into position on the garment, matching your previously marked points. Stitch close to the edge, just like an ordinary patch pocket.

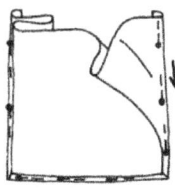

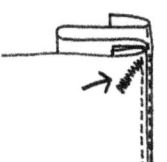

6. Pleat the top corners of the pocket into position and bar tack through all the layers to hold the pleats in place.

3-D patch pocket with gussets at the sides only

This is a very easy pocket to construct, with only one pattern piece. Make a pattern by adding a gusset width to each side of a regular square patch pocket pattern.

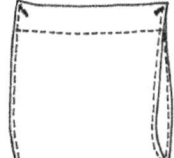

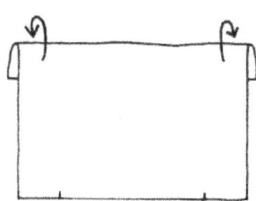

1. Overlock the top facing (not shown for clarity). Fold the top facing to the inside and press.

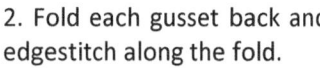 

2. Fold each gusset back and edgestitch along the fold.

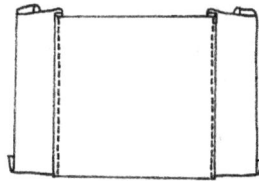

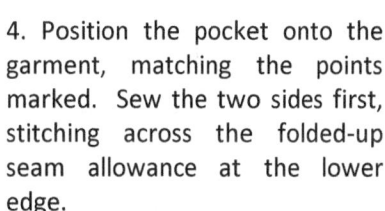 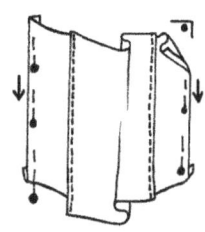

3. Press under the seam allowance on the sides, then press under the seam allowance on the lower edge.

4. Position the pocket onto the garment, matching the points marked. Sew the two sides first, stitching across the folded-up seam allowance at the lower edge.
Pleat the side gussets of the pocket into position and stitch across the lower edge.

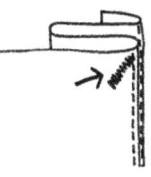

5. Pleat the top corners of the pocket into position. Bar tack through all of the layers to hold the pleats in place.

3-D pocket in one piece

This is a little easier to sew than a pocket with a separate gusset because you don't have the corners to contend with. It's also less bulky because there are fewer seams.

Make a pattern
1. Draw the shape of the *finished* pocket, then add the gussets on the sides, excluding the lower two corners.

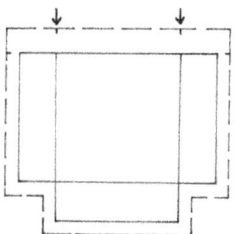

The gusset needs to be the same width at each corner.

2. Add a seam allowance all the way around and a self-facing along the top. Notch the top edge to indicate the gusset fold lines, as illustrated.

3. On the garment, mark the positions of all four corners of the pocket.

To sew a one piece 3-D pocket
1. Interface the self facing if necessary, overlock, and press under.

2. Place the two sides of each corner right sides together and sew across.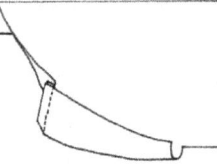

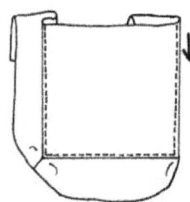
3. Press the fold lines of the gusset. **Optional:** stitch along the edges of the folds to keep the pocket defined.

4. Press under the seam allowances all the way around the pocket. Position it on the garment and sew closely around the edges.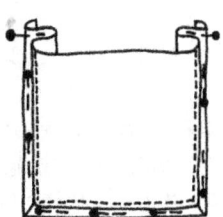

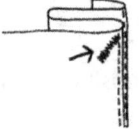
5. Stitch a bar tack at the top corners of the pleated pocket to hold the pleats in position.

3-D pocket in one piece that sits very flat against the garment
This pocket sits flatter and is less pouchy. It's fairly easy to sew but the pattern looks a strange shape!

Make a pattern
You'll need a ruler with a 45 degree line marked on it.

1. Draw the *finished* pocket size.

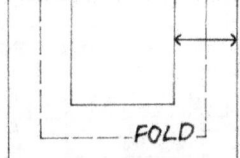
2. Decide on the gusset width the pocket will have when it's folded flat against the garment, for example 4cm (1½"). Add twice this amount to the sides and bottom edge. The lines must be parallel.

3. Draw a 45 degree line across the lower pocket corners, to form an isosceles triangle in each corner.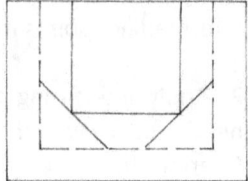

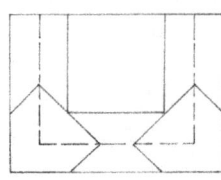
4. Draw two lines at right angles to them, connecting the gusset lines.

5. Rub out the corner lines.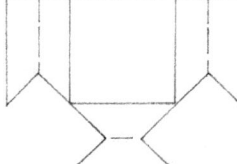

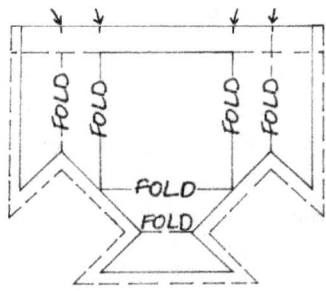
6. Add a seam allowance all the way around and a self-facing on the top edge. Notch the top edge to indicate where the gussets will be folded.

To sew a 3-D pocket that sits flat
1. Apply interfacing to the top self-facing of the pocket, if required.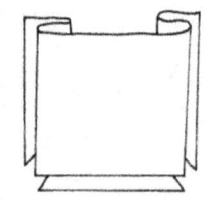
Press in the fold lines of the gusset so they fold in the correct direction.
Press under the self facing at the top, overlock the edge and stitch it down.

2. Sew the two lower corners with right sides together, using a small stitch for added strength. 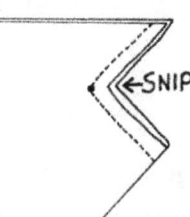 Pivot at the angles, leaving the needle in the fabric as you turn the work. Snip to the pivot point. You can overlock the mitred corners if you wish, but they shouldn't fray since they're cut on the bias.

3. Turn the pocket carefully to the right side and poke out the corners. **Optional:** edgestitch along the fold lines of the gusset to define the edge.

4. Press under the seam allowance on the sides and bottom edge. Fold the pocket into shape along the pre-pressed fold lines, matching the folds to the outside edges. Press.

5. Position the pocket on the garment and sew closely around the edges.

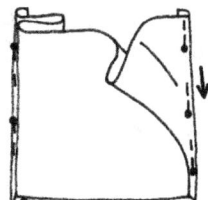

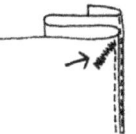

6. Pleat the top two corners of the pocket into position and bar tack through all of the layers to hold the pleats in place.

In-seam pockets

Invisible from the outside, in-seam pockets are also called secret pockets or hidden pockets. They're suitable for tops, jackets, skirts or trousers. Pre-schoolers and young children like the idea of a secret pocket. In most cases, with a little unpicking, it's possible to retrofit in-seam pockets to finished garments.

In-seam pockets don't work well on tight or fitted clothes such as pencil skirts or slim trousers, because the pocket opening will pull open when you sit down (or eat too much dessert) and there's no room to fit your hand in due to the fitted nature of the garment.

Inconveniently, alterations to seams with in-seam pockets require unpicking the pocket as well.

The pattern pieces can be designed several different ways, depending on the thickness of the fabric, the style of the garment and your own personal preference.

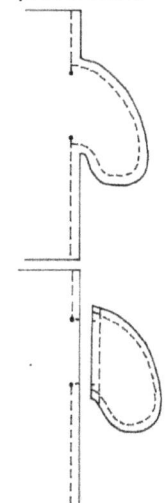

All-in-one
Sometimes the pocket bag is cut as an extension of the garment, so there's no seam at the opening of the pocket. It's very simple to sew, but it may not be an economical use of fabric.

Separate
More often, the pocket bag is cut separately. I prefer this to the bag being cut all-in-one, because it uses less fabric, it's easier to position the pieces on the fabric when cutting out and you can use a different fabric (lining, for example) for the pocket bag if you want to.

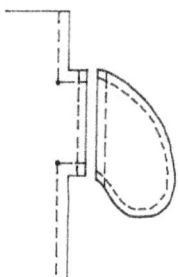

Separate-with-extension
Occasionally, there's a small extension added onto the garment, which the pocket bag is sewn to. It's often seen in coats and jackets, especially if the pocket is in a front seam. If the fabric is thick, all the pocket pieces can be cut from thinner lining and they won't be easily seen.

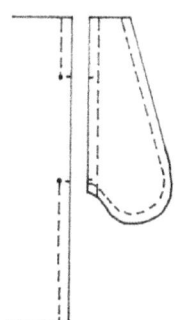

Separate-sewn-into-a-waist-seam
For skirts or garments with a waist seam, the top of this pocket bag extends and is stitched into the waist seam. If there's an available waist seam, I always make my patterns this way because when the garment is put on the pocket faces the correct way.

Jackets and tops can have this type of pocket but the pattern looks a little different—see page 240.

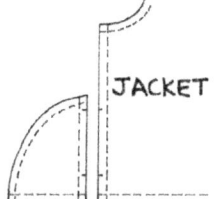

Make a pattern
1. Draw a straight line, then place your hand over the line as if putting your hand in your pocket. Use your hand as a guide to draw the pocket bag. The opening needs to be at least 14cm-15cm (5½"-6" wide) to get your hand in. Make it at least 18cm (7") for a man's hand. For children's pockets it depends on the age of the child, but 10cm (4") would be a good size for young children. Extend the line 2.5cm (1") either side of the opening.

2. Add seam allowances. The seam allowance on the straight edge needs to be the same as the garment's. The seam allowance on the actual pocket bag can be whatever you like, for example 1cm (⅜"), 1.5cm (⅝") or make it the same as the straight edge if you want to keep it simple.

3. On the garment, decide where you want the pocket opening to be. About 5cm-7cm (2"-3") below the waist is a good place. Mark the pocket opening on the seam

allowance—obviously the same size as the pocket's opening.

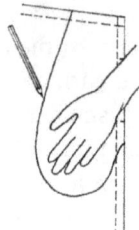
For a pocket bag that extends into a waist seam, you may like to draw the pocket onto the pattern piece, then trace it off. That way, the angle at the top of the pocket bag will be correct and the pocket pattern will fit the garment pattern.

On separate pocket bags, the front is 1cm (⅜") smaller than the back; trim this amount off as illustrated.

If you neglect to trim, the pocket bags won't match up when they're sewn.

(What if you *did* forget? If the garment has a closed lining, or if you don't care about the mis-match, you could just stitch them together then trim BUT be sure to catch both bags in the stitching or the pocket will have a hole.)

✂ The grainline of the pocket bag is drawn parallel to the opening. The opening is usually straight, but if the garment has a curved edge, the curve on the pocket bag is the same.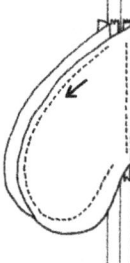

✂ If the top of the pocket bag will be caught in the waist seam, you could have a one-piece pocket bag that's a rectangle. After sewing each side onto the edges of seam, all that's required is to stitch it across the bottom.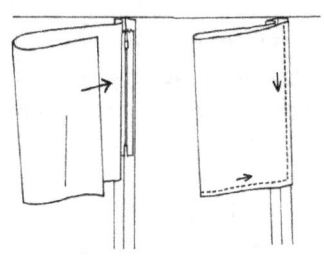

✂ If the waist is pleated or gathered, make sure the pocket bag is not included in the pleats or gathers when you sew it—it should sit flat behind.

✂ Often a fashion business will have a standard pocket pattern that fits all of their styles. You could do this too: create a preferred pocket pattern and use it in many garments rather than creating a new pattern every time you want to add a pocket.

✂ When cutting out, mark the notches as small 3mm (⅛") snips in the seam allowance. For all-in-one pockets there may be dots for the opening; mark on the wrong side with a chalk pencil. If the garment's pocket opening is on the bias or unstable in any way, iron a strip of interfacing onto it for reinforcement.

To sew an all-in-one in-seam pocket

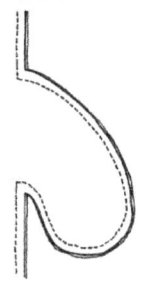
Place the right sides together and stitch the seam, pivoting at the corners of the opening and sewing around the pocket bag in one continuous seam.

Note that sometimes the pocket bag is longer than the actual opening. In this case, the size of the opening should be marked on the pattern with dots and transferred by you to the wrong side of the fabric. Sew the garment's seam, back stitching at the top and bottom of the opening for strength, then separately sew around the pocket bag.

To neaten and press, you can:

Overlock around the entire edge, overlocking the edges together to make a closed seam. Press the seam allowance and pocket bag to the front of the garment.

OR

For thick fabrics, it's preferable to press the seams open to reduce bulk, so press the pocket towards the front and press the garment's seams open. In this case it's easier to overlock the edges separately first, before sewing the pocket.

OR

As above, but the clip the seam allowance at the pocket corners to allow it to sit flat. I would only do this for very bulky fabrics because the clipping weakens the pocket at the stress points.

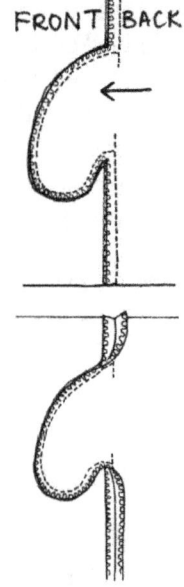
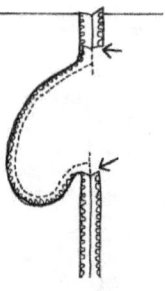

To sew a separate in-seam pocket
(that may or may not be stitched in a waist seam)
In this type of pocket, sometimes the back pocket bag is cut in fashion fabric and the front one in lining, but sometimes both are cut in lining or both in main fabric—it depends on how thick the fabric is.

Check that the front is 1cm (⅜") smaller than the back. If not, trim it off now.

1. Overlock the straight edge of the pocket bags and the garment's seams. Don't trim anything off with the overlocker—just graze the edge. You should still see the pocket opening snips through the overlocking. The overlocking isn't shown on the following pictures for clarity.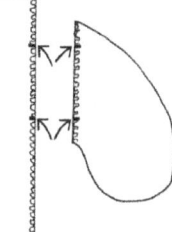

2. With the right sides together, sew each pocket bag to the front and back garment, taking 5mm (scant ¼") *less* than the garment's seam allowance (so, if the seam allowance is 1.5cm, you'll make a 1cm seam).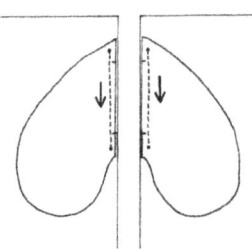
Sew along the length of the pocket bag, but don't stitch into the seam allowance of the pocket bag at each end.

3. On the *front only*, understitch the pocket bag, once again not stitching into the seam allowance of the pocket bag at each end.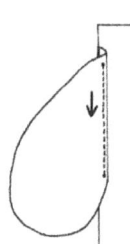

4. Place the front and back right sides together, matching the pocket bag, and stitch the seam leaving a gap for the pocket opening.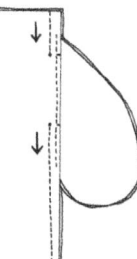
Take the correct seam allowance this time and be sure to backstitch securely at each end of the opening.

5. Sew around the pocket bag, stitching across the folded seam allowance at the bottom as shown.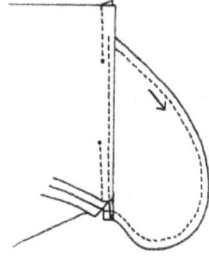
Overlock the pocket bag seams together.

6. Press the garment seams open and press the pocket bag to the front.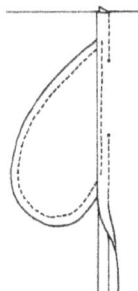
If the fabric is very thick, you could snip the seam allowance just below the pocket so it lies flat. Obviously this makes a weak point, so don't do it unless you have to and reinforce it with an additional row of stitching a few centimetres either side of the snip.

To sew an in-seam pocket with extension
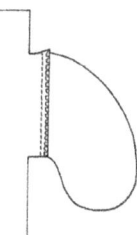
It's sewn in exactly the same way as an all-in-one pocket (page 238), except that first the pocket bags are sewn onto the extensions and overlocked first. The seam is pressed towards the pocket. The pocket bags are usually both cut in lining fabric.

In-seam pockets by overlocker
In-seam pockets can be sewn entirely on an overlocker, if you're making, for example, sports shorts. Ensure the overlocker is suitable to sew a four thread seam, not just finish the edge. You'll need 6mm (¼") seam allowances and the pocket bags can be any of the types shown on page 237.

1. Overlock the pocket bags on, stitching the entire length of the straight side.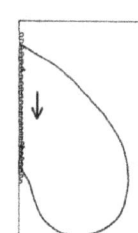

2. With the right sides together, overlock the garment's seam and pocket bag in one operation.

3. You may need to follow up with straight stitching at the top and bottom of the opening (to reinforce), however, sometimes the top and bottom points are simply bartacked on the outside.

In-seam pockets with zips

This type of pocket is frequently used on tracksuit pants and exercise clothes. My school uniform dress had a pocket like this.

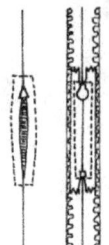

1. Install a centred or lapped zip into the (already overlocked) side seam of the garment. See pages 409 and 410, or page 404 for an invisible zip.
Make sure the zipper zips *upwards*, so that if it's only half zipped up you won't lose things out of the pocket.

2. Check that the front is 1cm (⅜") smaller than the back. If not, trim it off now.

Overlock the straight edges of both pocket bags.
If the bags will be enclosed in the garment's lining, you won't need to overlock.

3. Stitch each pocket bag to the side of the zip, right sides together. Sew the shorter one on the *front* and the larger one on the *back*. Leave 1.5cm (⅝") unstitched at each end so you can overlock afterwards.

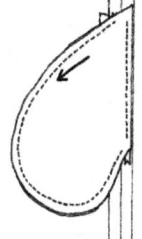

4. Lay the pocket in the direction it will sit (to the front) and stitch the pocket bags together, forming the pocket. Overlock around the edges of the bags.

✂ If you have insufficient seam allowance on the garment to easily sew a lapped zipper in, try stitching the front pocket bag onto the front of the garment (the overlap side of the zip) *before* sewing the zip in. After the zip is in, sew the other pocket bag to the back as usual. Alternatively, install an invisible zip because only a 1cm (⅜") seam allowance is required.

In-seam pockets sewn to the garment

For these pockets, only one pocket bag is required, because the garment forms the front of the pocket. The pocket bag is cut in the same fabric as the garment. They're most often used on jackets, with a feature made of the stitching. They're also good for unlined garments when you don't want to have flappy, visible pocket linings. Breast pockets in denim jackets are made in the same way and a flap is added to the top.

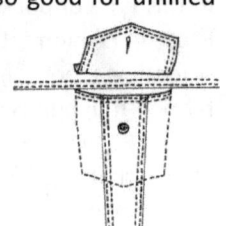

Make a pattern

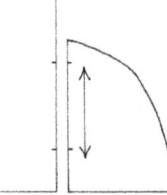

Make a pattern following the same guidelines as other in-seam pockets, but note the different shape. Make sure the pocket opening is high enough so things don't fall out, but not too high to put your hand in.

If you'll be turning up a hem, cut the bottom edge of the pocket bag *on* the hem fold line. That way the pocket will sit flat inside the hem, reducing bulk.
To further reduce bulk at the side seam/hem junction, cut the lower corner off the pocket and overlock across it.

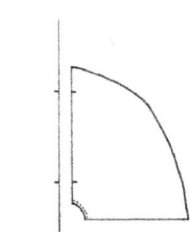

To sew an in-seam pocket to the garment

1. Overlock the long rounded edge of the pocket bag.

2. On the garment front, if you think the opening will stretch, reinforce it with a strip of fusible interfacing.
At the two notches, snip into the garment to the depth of the seam allowance.

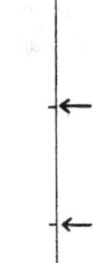

3. Hem the opening in between the snips. Either turn it under twice and stitch to make a double folded hem, or overlock, turn under once and stitch.

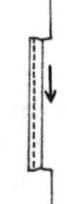

4. Lay the pocket bag behind the opening on the garment and stitch it in position. Use the edge of the pocket bag as a guide—you should be able to feel it through the fabric as you stitch.

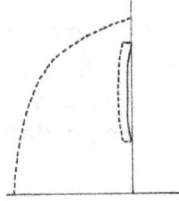

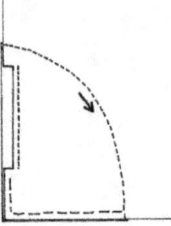

Match the edges and tack them together. You can now treat the front as one piece and sew the rest of the garment.

When you sew the side seam, be very careful to catch the corners of the pocket opening so no raw edges are visible. Take care also not to catch the pocket opening.

In seam pockets with welts

Sometimes a welt or flap is incorporated into the pocket.

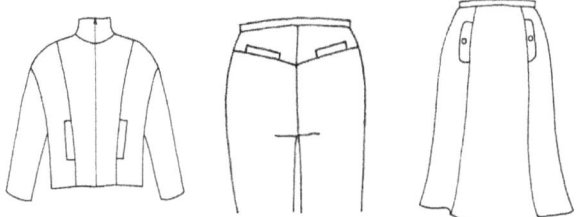

To sew an in-seam pocket with a welt

1. Make the welt first. Cut it twice the finished size with seam allowances added. Interface half. Fold the right sides together and sew across the ends. Trim the corners and turn to the right side. Press. Topstitch the welt now if you plan to. The outermost side of the welt is the one with fusing on it.

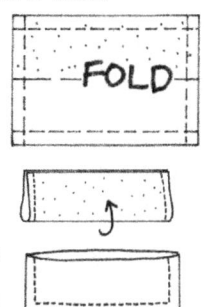

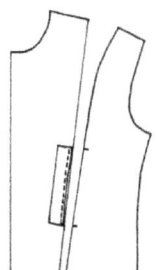

2. Position the welt right sides together on the garment and tack it in place. Note which side it's positioned on—it's the side that the pocket *bag* will be pressed to. Now sew the in-seam pocket as normal, sewing the pocket bags over the top of the welt.

3. After the pocket is sewn and pushed to the inside, stitch down the short ends of the welt.

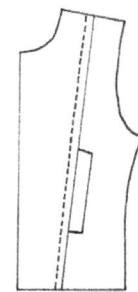

If you want to topstitch the length of the seam, do this *before* you sew the pocket bags together (otherwise you'll sew the pocket opening shut).

Pockets cut away **241**

In-seam pockets incorporated into the garment's opening

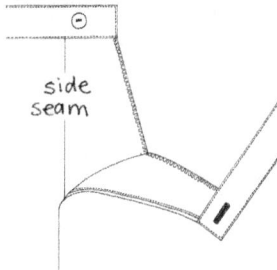

An in-seam pocket that's sewn into a waist seam can also conceal the opening of a garment on one or both sides. It can be a feature of skirts, trousers or bib overalls.

1. Make the pocket pattern in the usual way for a pocket sewn into a waist seam (pages 237-238).

2. Make the underlap/extension on the waistband pattern long enough to sew onto the top edge of the pocket bag.

3. Overlock (or bind) around the long curved edges of the pocket bags separately first.

4. Leave the top of the pocket bag unstitched as shown.

If both sides of the garment will open, then make each side of the pocket open 10cm (4") at the top. If only one side will be the garment's opening and the other will be just a pocket (or entirely absent), make the opening 20cm (8").

The pocket could have buttons and buttonholes along the opening.

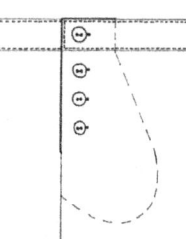
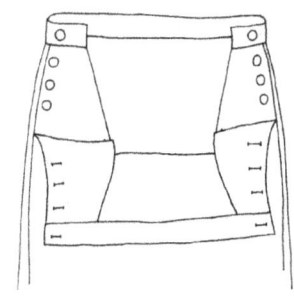

Cut away pockets

Although cut away pockets can vary in shape, from almost a straight vertical line to rounded shapes, shallow or deep, they're all constructed in the same way. Mostly, cut away pockets use two pattern pieces: a pocket facing and a pocket back. The pocket facing is used to neatly finish the cut-away edge, and the pocket back is placed behind this. Then, the pocket facing and pocket back are stitched together inside the garment to form the pocket bag.

A drawback of cut away pockets is if the garment needs to be altered. Taking the garment in at the sides means that the pocket opening will get smaller and/or shorter, but a solution is to take the garment in on the back only.

The shape of the pocket pieces depends on the style of the pocket. The opening can be an angled line, a mainly horizontal line or curved:

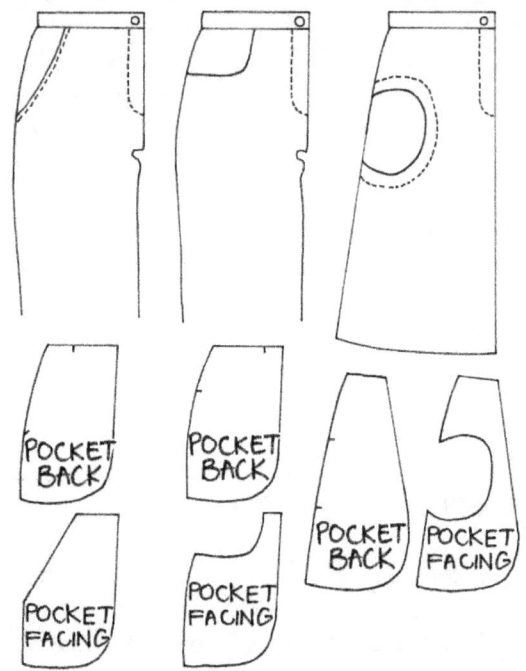

The **pocket back** needs to be cut in the same fashion fabric as the garment, but if the fabric is very thick the back can be cut in pocket lining and a piece of fashion fabric sewn on top where it will show.

The **pocket facing** can be any fabric. It's usually a lighter weight fabric, such as lining. If the pocket is to withstand keys etc being put into it, regular polyester or acetate lining won't be strong enough—use cotton pocket lining. I like to look through my scrap bag and choose something interesting for the facing.

✂ Sometimes the pocket facing and pocket back are cut in one piece, in a lining fabric. In this situation, a small piece of the fashion fabric is stitched onto the pocket back so the lining won't show. A one piece pocket bag is faster to sew because there's one less seam and it uses less of the fashion fabric.

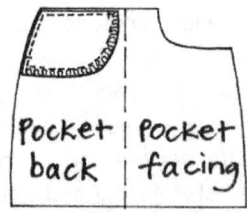

Make a pattern

1. Draw the shape and depth of the finished pocket onto the front pattern piece. I like to lay my hand on the pattern to make sure the pocket will be big and deep enough to get my hand in.

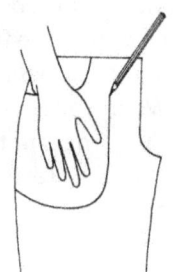

2. Trace off the pattern pieces for the pocket back and the pocket facing and trim down the garment front, adding seam allowances.

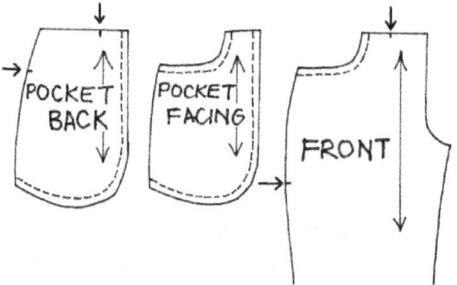

Make the grainlines the same as the garment's. The **pocket back** needs two notches to match the *finished* pocket opening to. The **garment front** needs two notches to match the edges of the pocket bag to. The **pocket facing** needs no notches.

✂ On pockets that are mainly horizontal (such as classic jeans pockets), you'll need to add up to 5mm (scant ¼") to each end of the pocket opening to give it some play so you can get your hand in.

Add the same amount to the garment and the pocket facing. Don't be tempted to add only onto one end (for example the waist)—it needs to be added at *both* ends of the pocket opening.

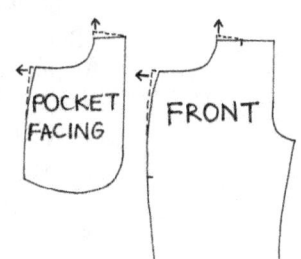

It's generally not necessary on mainly vertical pockets or pockets with a very big or deep opening.

✂ If you're planning a one piece bag, join the pocket back and facing together at the stitching line and draw in a new lower edge. You won't need to mark the foldline on the fabric when you cut it out—it will just fold back to where it fits.

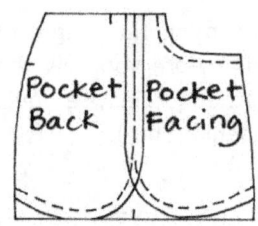
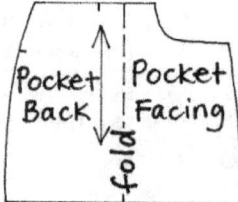

✂ On some trousers, the pocket bag is connected to the centre front. This not only holds the pocket in place, but acts as a stay for any front pleats in the garment. If there *are* front pleats, fold the pleats into place on the front pattern before drawing the pocket in, so the pocket pattern is correct.

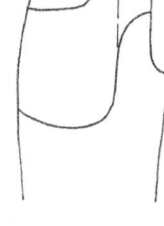

This pocket needs to be sewn before the centre front seam and front zip.

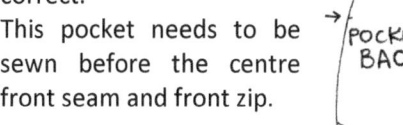

Some trousers have a separate stay in a firm stretch fabric to give a comfortable fit.

✂ If the pocket back will be cut in lining, make a pattern for the top part to be cut in fashion fabric. It should be about 2.5cm (1") deeper all round than the faced edge, so the lining doesn't show and the overlocked edges are hidden inside the pocket.

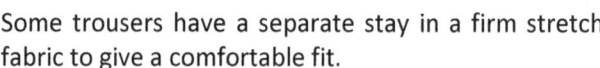

This part is overlocked, then stitched *on top* of the pocket bag.

If you're adding a coin/fob pocket, this gets stitched on top, *before* it's applied to the pocket back; that way the lower edges of both get overlocked together. These little pockets are generally on the right hand side only.

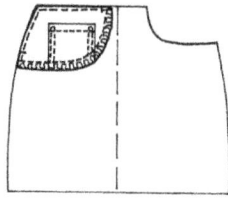

✂ Sometimes the opening edge of the pocket facing has a strip of the fashion fabric sewn onto the lining. It's to make the opening more durable without adding bulk.

The grainline of the strip is parallel to the pocket opening to stop the edge stretching and often the strip is interfaced to give support.

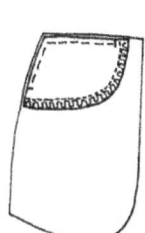

The strip is overlocked on the long edge, then stitched flat on top of the pocket facing.

✂ On light coloured garments, you can cut the hidden parts of the pocket in a fabric that matches your skin tone, to avoid seeing the outline of the pocket bags through the fabric. Then you'll only need a

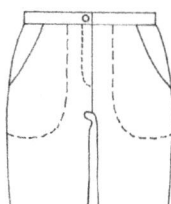

piece of the fashion fabric stitched to the visible part of the pocket back.

To sew a cut away pocket

1. If the pocket is a diagonal shape, and therefore likely to stretch, apply a strip of interfacing either to the garment or the pocket facing. It only needs to be about 2cm (¾") wide, but make sure you cut it in the firmest direction so it doesn't stretch. I sometimes use 6mm (¼") cotton tape instead, and stitch it just inside the seam line of the garment.

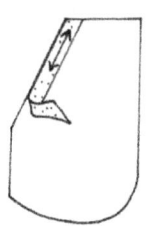

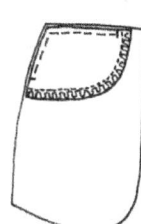

2. Overlock and apply any fashion fabric pieces to the pocket bag or facing.

3. With the right sides together, sew the pocket facing to the garment. Trim the seam (unless you've made your pattern with a "pre-trimmed" 6mm (¼") seam allowance) and clip any curves so it sits flat when turned through.

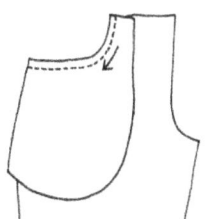

4. Press the seam allowance towards the pocket facing and understitch the seam on the facing side. This keeps the pocket facing hidden and stops it rolling to the outside.

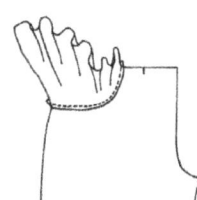

I often understitch even if I plan to topstitch later, because it makes pressing and topstitching easier.

5. Turn the facing to the inside and press. If you plan to topstitch the pocket opening, do so now.

Stitch from the *bottom up* for both left and right pockets to reduce rippling, particularly on diagonally shaped pockets as shown here.

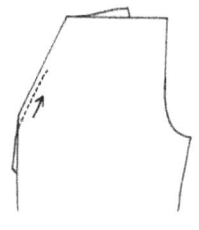

6. If the pocket is the type that's extended all the way to the centre front, stitch the facing to the pocket back now. Turn back the seam allowance on the straight edge of the pocket facing and align it with the placement line on the pocket back. Edgestitch it into position.

7. Place the pocket back and facing right sides together and stitch around the edge, forming the pocket bag. Overlock the seam.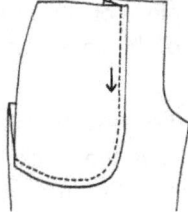

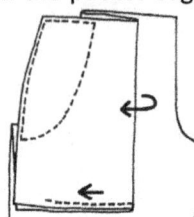 If the pocket bag is one piece, all you'll need to do is fold it into position and stitch across the lower edge. Note that this seam can be sewn as a French seam, which gives a very strong and neat-looking pocket bag (and great news if you don't have an overlocker).

To sew a French seam:
Place the *wrong* sides together and sew the seam taking half the seam allowance. Trim, press, then place the *right* sides together and sew the seam taking the rest of the seam allowance, encasing the raw edges (see pages 293 and 294). Don't aim for a superfine, narrow French seam—you want a substantial, strong seam able to take weight and strain.

A French seam will add a little bulky ridge to the edge, so take care when pressing the garment that it doesn't imprint a line on the outside.

8. Using a long machine stitch, tack the side edges of the pocket to the side edges of the garment, and the top edge of the pocket to the waistline (and the centre front edges together if you have that type of pocket). You can now treat the garment front as one unit and get on with sewing the rest of the garment.

Not sure about what to do with the area at the bottom of diagonal pockets?
This area, if not sewn accurately, will result in an inconsistently sized pocket opening. It can be sewn in either of two ways:

✂ Attach the facing to the garment only as far as the side seam allowance on the garment. Snip the fabric to the point.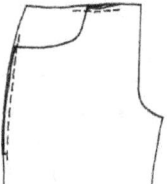

When you sew the garment's side seam you *must* catch in the raw edge at the bottom of the pocket.

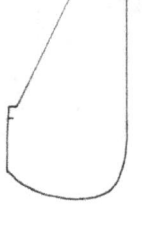 Sometimes the pattern is made this way so you know where to sew and to snip. I usually do mine this way.

✂ Sew the pocket facing to the garment all the way through.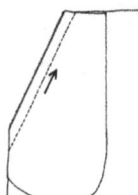

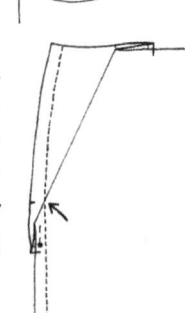 When the pocket is tacked to the sides of the garment, the point of the finished opening must align with the notch on the pocket back. This, and taking the correct seam allowance for the side seam, will ensure consistent pocket opening size.

Pressing notes
The bottom of the pocket opening can be bulky. If you're pressing the seams open, you may find it hard to press this back on itself. On some garments, jeans for example, the seam allowance is pressed towards the back for the length of the pocket bag and edgestitched to hold it flat. The rest of the seam is pressed either open or to the back.

Sometimes a bar tack is sewn across to strengthen and flatten this point.

Cutaway pockets as a garment's opening

Cutaway pockets can conceal the opening of a garment. One or both pockets can be used for the opening. It can be a feature of skirts, trousers or bib overalls.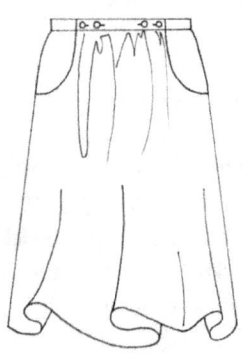

If the pockets are large and the garment is roomy, some allowance for waist adjustment can be incorporated into the design.

My mum once had some loose maternity trousers with cutaway pockets that velcroed onto the waistband (although she said the pockets were fake).

Make a pattern

1. Make the cut away pocket pattern in the usual way.

2. Make the waistband pattern in two parts—a short waistband for the front and a longer one for the rest of the waist. Ensure that the underlap/extension section is long enough to sew to the top edge of the pocket back.

To sew a pocket as a garment's opening

1. Overlock around the curved edges of the pocket facing and pocket back separately first.

2. Leave the top 10cm (4") of the pocket bags open as shown if both pockets will undo. If only one pocket will be the opening and the other pocket will just be a pocket, then leave a 20cm (8") opening.

3. The waistband can be fastened by buttons and buttonholes, hooks and bars or velcro. When sewing on the fastenings, refer to the pattern to make sure you have the correct waist measurement, since you won't be able to see where to place the top of the pocket (because the waistband has been sewn over the top of the pocket notches). Extra buttons, hooks, or velcro can be sewn on to allow the waist to be adjusted, if that is what you plan to do.

Slashed pockets

Slashed pockets are essentially a cut or slit in the fabric that's finished with strips of fabric. They're thought to be the most difficult type of pocket to construct, perhaps because of the commitment required to cut into the actual garment. Success depends on accurate and careful marking, cutting and sewing. Some practice helps, too.
There are several different types of slashed pockets:

Jet pockets, sometimes called bound, double welt or Besom pockets, look like big bound buttonholes.

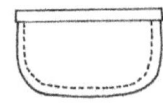 A flap can be inserted between the lips during construction. The flap can be tucked in or out when the garment is worn.
Jet pockets can also be angled, curved or buttoned:

Welt pockets, sometimes called a single welt pocket, can be plain, angled or buttonholed. I think they're the easiest to make of all the slashed pockets.

Flap pockets have, as the name says, a flap.

A variation of a flap pocket is what I call a men's welt pocket. It's constructed as a flap pocket but without the flap. It looks similar to a regular welt pocket. The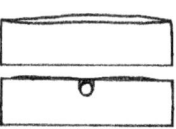
advantage is you can insert a loop into the top seam for a button and loop closure.

For all slashed pockets

✂ Iron a strip of fusible interfacing on the wrong side of where the pocket will be slashed, for reinforcing. Make sure it's bonded very well.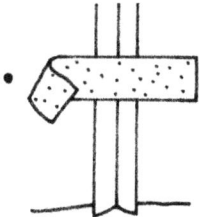
If the pocket goes through a seam, it's fine to sew the seam first then iron the fusing over the top, or else you can fuse each side separately then sew the seam.

✂ Mark the pocket positions on the right side with
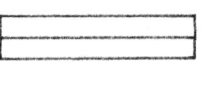 dots to indicate the length. You can join the dots with a ruled chalk or pencil line if you need a straight edge to align the pocket pieces.

✂ The pocket bag pieces should extend about 2.5cm (1") beyond each end of the slash.
In other words, the pocket bag should be 5cm (2") wider than the finished pocket.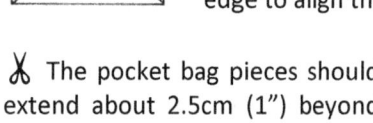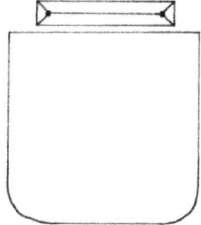

✂ Pocket bags are usually around 15-20cm (6-8") deep, or about 10cm (4") deep for breast pockets.
It's OK to cut the pocket bags deeper than required, then trim off any excess.
Some people like the bottom corners of the pocket bag to be rounded, to avoid pocket lint in the corners. Rounded corners also look neater when overlocked, if the garment is unlined.

✂ When stitching around the slash line, use a shorter machine stitch for extra strength (for example 1.5 or 2, instead of the usual 2.5).

✂ Regarding pressing, take care if the fabric you're using bruises or shines when you press it with an iron. The thickness of the pocket seam allowance may go shiny on the right side if you're heavy handed with the iron. Experiment first before you press the garment. You might need to press the pocket from the wrong side only and/or use a press cloth.

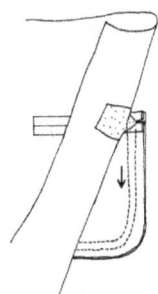

✂ Stitch two parallel rows of stitching about 6mm (¼") apart around the pocket bag for strength, especially in lined garments where repairing pocket bags is fiddly.
The pocket bag is normally left with raw edges, unless the garment is unlined or the fabric is liable to fray badly.

An overlocker can be used to neaten the edges, but for an ultra-neat and strong finish (for example, for men's trousers), the edges can be bound in bias binding. The lower corners are always curved to make binding easier.

Jet pockets

The lips of a jet pocket are usually 6mm (¼") wide each finished, but can be any width you like. These instructions are written for 6mm wide lips. For wider ones, simply cut the strips four times as wide as your finished width.

Make a pattern

1. For the lips of the jet pockets, cut two strips of main fabric 2.5cm (1") deep by 5cm (2") wider than the finished pocket size. Interface both.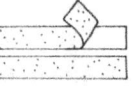
The grainline is usually parallel to the long edge, but can be cut in the other direction too.

On checked or striped fabric the strips are often cut on the bias, or longways along a prominent stripe.

2. For the pocket bags, cut one of main fabric and one of lining. The width of both should be 5cm (2") wider than the finished pocket size. The depth is up to you, but the one in main fabric should be 1.2cm 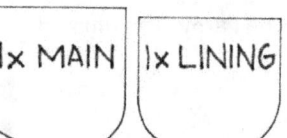 (½") deeper than the lining one.
You can curve the bottom corners of the pocket bags if you want to, or leave them square.

3. Cut a strip of fusing approximately 2.5cm (1") wide to iron on behind where the pocket will be, to reinforce it.

To sew a jet pocket

1. On the garment, iron the strip of fusing behind where the pocket will be slashed. Make sure it's bonded very well.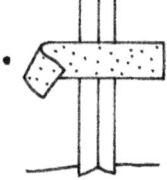

If the pocket goes through a seam, it's fine to sew the seam first then stick the fusing over the top, or else you can fuse each side separately and then sew the seam.

2. While you're at the ironing board, iron the interfacing onto the narrow strips if you haven't already and iron them in half longways with the wrong sides together.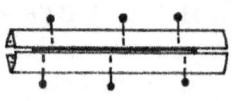

3. On the garment, mark the pocket position on the right side with two dots to indicate each end. You may join the dots with a ruled chalk line so you have a straight line to help position the pocket pieces.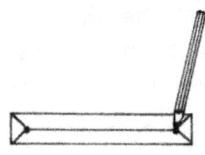

4. On the right side of the garment, position the lips either side of the marked slash, raw edges touching.
For stability, you can hand or machine tack them in place, close to the raw edges. I usually just pin them, unless the fabric is hard to handle.

5. Lay the pocket bags over the top, right sides down. Place the main fabric one above the pocket opening and the lining one below.

6. Feeling through the layers, machine stitch along the centre of each lip, which will be 6mm (¼") away from the raw edge. (If you have decided to have wider lips, still sew them down the centre).

Pockets slashed **247**

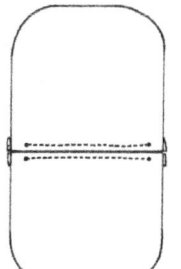 Use a 6mm (¼") machine foot if you have one, or move the needle position so that you can line up the edge of the machine's foot 6mm (¼") away from the edge. Use a shorter machine stitch for extra strength, for example 1.5 or 2 instead of the usual 2.5.

Finish each side *exactly* level with the other, backstitching securely at beginning and end. The stitching needs to be the length of the finished pocket and the two rows should be perfectly parallel.

Quality check: use a ruler to measure the distance between the two rows of stitching to make sure they really are parallel, and correct if need be. If you're sewing wider pocket lips, I recommend doing this before you go any further.

7. With sharp scissors, accurately cut a slit in the garment between the two lips, 1.5cm (⅝") short of each end. Cut diagonally into each corner forming a triangle at each end. Be sure to cut *exactly* to each corner of the stitching. Cut *only* through the garment *not* the lips or pocket bags.

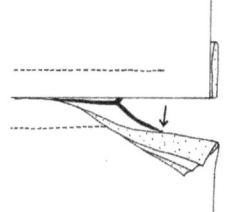

8. Gently push the lips and pocket bags through the slash to the wrong sides. Push the triangular ends through to the wrong side as well. Press the seam allowances and triangular ends *away* from the opening.

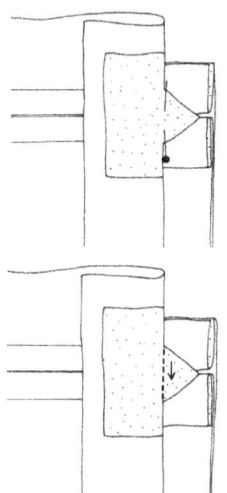

9. Still with the garment right side up, flip up the garment at one end of the slash. Position and stitch over the triangle and the lips at one end. I like to pin the triangle before stitching and check it on the right side to make sure it's squarely positioned.

Stitch using a zipper foot to get in nice and close to the edge. Repeat with the other end.

10. Sew the pocket bags together to form the pocket, stitching two parallel rows about 6mm (¼" or a footwidth) apart for strength. Overlock around the pocket bag if the garment is unlined or if the fabric will fray badly.

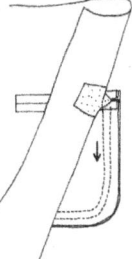

On unlined garments sometimes the edges are neatened with binding for a very smart finish.

✂ In manufacturing, the lower lip of the jet pocket is often tacked to the pocket bag with a long machine stitch. This allows the pocket to sit smoothly and the tacking is undone by the customer after purchase.

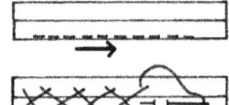

The lips can also be sewn together by hand using herringbone stitch (see page 149).

✂ On pockets that see heavy wear, the corners are sometimes bar tacked.

You may also see jet pockets that are edgestitched all the way around the lips. If you want to do this on your pockets, edgestitch *before* sewing the pocket bags together, but *after* sewing down the end triangles. You'll need to edgestitch in two stages, as illustrated, to avoid catching the pocket bags.

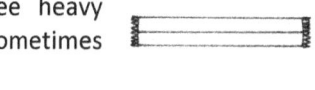

Jet pockets can be, and often are, bartacked *and* edgestitched.

✂ For jet pocket fastened with a button and loop, slip the loop in between the top lip and the pocket bag, before stitching the pocket bags on.

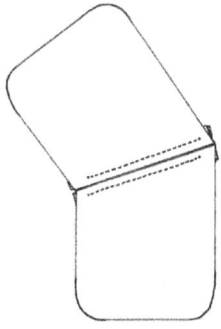

✂ **Diagonal jet pockets** have pocket bags with a diagonal top edge. For neat vertical ends, note that the stitching lines begin and end in a vertical line, not level with each other. Note also that the triangles will be stitched down at an angle.

✂ **False jet pockets** are made like real jet pockets, except with no pocket bags.

They can be used on tight trousers, for example, where real jet pockets would gape.

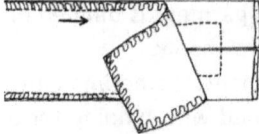

After the opening is slashed, turn the lips through and sew the triangular ends down. Sew a pre-overlocked backing of main fabric to the back of the pocket around the edges.

It's easiest to sew this on using a zipper foot, with the backing underneath (it's illustrated here with the backing on top, for clarity).

Flap jet pockets

Jet pockets can have a flap inserted during construction. The flap can be tucked in or out when the garment is worn. The flap is made first, then the rest of the pocket is sewn as a regular jet pocket. The finished flap needs to be the same width as the pocket opening.

Make a pattern

Draw the desired flap shape, making it the same width as the finished pocket opening, and add a 6mm (¼") seam allowance all the way around.

Curved flaps are made from two pieces of fabric. The outermost one is interfaced. If the fabric is very thick, cut the underneath one of lining.

The lining can be trimmed by 3mm (⅛") around all but the top edge, to ensure it can't be seen when the flap is finished. Sew it with the lining on top and the main fabric underneath.

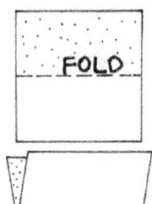

Rectangular flaps are made with one piece of fabric with a fold line. Interface (what will be the outermost) half of it.

To sew a flap jet pocket

1. Make the flap: place the flap pieces right sides together and stitch the sides, leaving the top open. Trim any curves and corners then turn to the right side. Press. Topstitch now if desired.

2. Sandwich the flap between the top lip and the pocket bag (see Step 5 of making a jet pocket, on page 246). Lay the flap *right side down* on top of the upper lip, matching the raw edges, and lay the pocket bag on top.

3. Stitch the rest of the jet pocket as normal, but sew the side with the flap first. Make sure both rows of stitching start and finish exactly in line with the edges of the flap.

Curved jet pockets

Curved jet pockets are traditionally worn on cowboy and rodeo shirts. The lips of the jet pocket and the end triangles can be cut in a contrasting colour. The pattern pieces are essentially the same as a regular jet pocket, but with a few important differences. The pocket lips are cut on the bias to allow them to follow the curved shape and the pocket bags are curved at the tops.

The width of each pocket lip must be no more than 6mm (¼") finished—don't try and get creative with wider pocket lips, because they won't work on the curve. These instructions are written for 6mm lips but to make narrower ones simply cut the strips four times as wide as your finished width.

Curved jet pockets can also be made with piping (either your own or ready-made) instead of strips. You can achieve very narrow lips using a fine sized piping cord (for example 0000). The pocket is sewn in exactly the same way, except that you'll need to use a zipper foot when attaching the piping lips.

Make a pattern

1. On the garment pattern, draw the curve required for the pocket in the desired place. Use a saucer or similar shape to trace around to get a good curve. Using a tape measure held standing on its side, measure the length of the curve. Mark the exact centre point of the curve.

2. Cut two strips 5cm (2") longer than the curve and 2.5cm (1") wide, on the bias (or narrower if that's what you've decided to do).

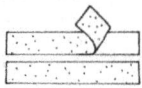

Interface both with a lightweight woven or knitted interfacing, also cut on the bias.

3. Cut two triangles for the ends in soft leather, suede, ultrasuede or something similar that doesn't fray. The size of the triangles depends on the finished width of the pocket lips—the corners of the triangles should extend past the width of the finished pocket. Since the end triangles are sewn on last, cut

one in paper when the pocket is finished and judge whether it looks the right size.

4. Cut a curved piece of fusing for behind the pocket opening, 2.5cm (1") wide, to match the curve.

5. Cut the pocket bags with the same curve as the pocket. Cut both of them the same width as the pocket lips, that is,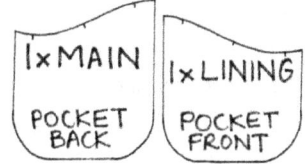
5cm (2") wider than the finished pocket curve.
Cut the pocket bag back out of main fabric with the curve exactly matching the one on the garment. Cut the pocket bag front out of of lining with a mirror-imaged curve. Make it 1.2cm (½") shorter. On the top edge of both pocket bags, make a small 3mm (⅛") notch 2.5cm (1") in from each end and also at the exact centre of each, as illustrated. The notches will help you position the pocket bags correctly when you sew. You can round the bottom corners of the pocket bags if you want to, or leave them square. If you make the pocket bag patterns in cardboard (cereal box weight), you can also use them as a template to mark the curve on the garment.

To sew curved jet pockets

1. On the garment, iron a strip of fusing behind where the pocket will be slashed, to reinforce it. Make sure it's bonded very well.
While still at the ironing board, fuse the interfacing
onto the bias strips if you haven't already done so. Press the strips in half longways.

2. Mark the pocket position on the right side of the garment. The way I do this is to mark each end of the pocket on the garment with a dot, as you would for a regular jet pocket. Then I use a pocket bag pattern, which I have cut out of cardboard, to trace the correct curve onto the fabric using tailors chalk. Don't forget to mark the centre of the curve and the two end points.

3. On the right side of the garment, position the bias lips either side of the marked slash, raw edges
touching. Set the machine to a long stitch and machine tack them in place, stitching about 3mm (⅛") away from the raw edge.
You don't need to pin them first—it's quite easy to just stitch along and curve the strips to fit. Don't sew them all the way to the end of the strip; only to the end of the pocket position.
If you're using piping, sew it on with a zipper foot. Ensure that the cord is the correct distance away from the marked line (the correct distance is the width of the piping cord).

4. Lay the pocket bags over the top, right sides down. Place the main fabric bag above the pocket opening and the lining one below. Be *extremely careful* that the lining piece gets sewn on around the right way—it's very easy to accidentally flip it when there's no right or wrong side to the fabric. Pin the pocket bags in place, first matching the notches at each end and in the centre.

5. Feeling through the layers, stitch down the centre of each lip (which will be 6mm (¼") away from the folded edge if you're having 6mm finished lips). Use a 6mm (¼") machine foot if you have one, or move the needle
position so you can line up the edge of the machine's foot 6mm (¼") away from the edge. If you're using piping, stitch next to the piping cord, using a zipper foot. Use a shorter machine stitch for extra strength (1.5 or 2, instead of the usual 2.5). Finish each side exactly level with the other, backstitching securely at beginning and end. The stitching should be the length of the finished pocket.

6. With sharp scissors, accurately cut a slit in the garment between the two lips. At 1.5cm (⅝") short of each end, cut diagonally into each corner forming a triangle at each end, being sure to cut *exactly* to each corner of the stitching. Cut *only* through the garment, *not* the lips or pocket bags.

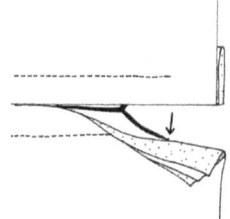

7. Carefully push the lips and pocket bags through the slash to the wrong side. Push the triangular ends through to the wrong side as well.
Press the seam allowances and triangular ends away from the opening.

8. Still with the garment right side up, flip up the garment at one end of the slash. Position and stitch over the triangle and the lips at one end. If the fabric is very thick, use a zipper foot to

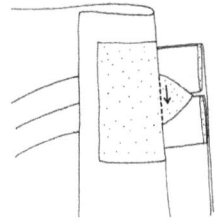

get in nice and close to the edge. Repeat with the other end.

9. Edgestitch either side of the lips to help make them lie flat. This looks effective if you use a contrasting thread that matches  the colour of the lips and leather end triangles.
Don't catch the *lining* pocket bag in the edgestitching—flip the lining up so you're only stitching through the garment and the pocket lips. Extend the edgestitching a couple of stitches past the end so the backstitch is hidden under the leather end triangles.

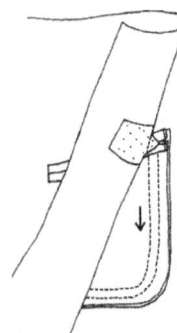 10. Sew the pocket bags together to form the pocket, stitching two parallel rows about 6mm (¼" or a footwidth) apart for strength. Overlock around the pocket bag if the garment is unlined or if the fabric will fray badly.

11. Position the leather end triangles at each end of the pocket and edgestitch in position.

Jet pockets with zips
A zip is fairly easy to add to a jet pocket (page 246). The pattern pieces are the same as a regular jet pocket. If the jet pocket is positioned diagonally or vertically, ensure the zip zips *upwards* so the contents won't be lost if the pocket is only half done up.

To sew a jet pocket with a zip
1. Make a jet pocket without the pocket bags. That is, fuse behind the slash line, sew the lips on, slash the opening, turn through and sew the triangular ends down. Tack the lips of the pocket together by hand using 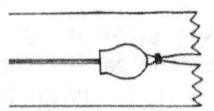 herringbone stitch (page 149).

2. Choose a zip that's the correct length for the jet pocket. Stitch together the zipper tape just above the zip slide using a zipper foot on your machine or sewing by hand.

3. Slip the zipper underneath the lips, centre it, and pin in position. With the zipper underneath, sew each

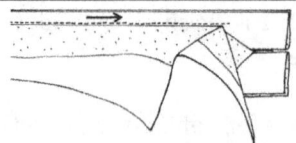 long side of the zip to the edge of the lips using a zipper foot.

You might need to unzip the zip part way through sewing, to get past the zipper slide.

4. Take the pocket bags and overlock the top edge of each. Sew each pocket bag to the long edges, so the zipper tape is sandwiched between the lip and the 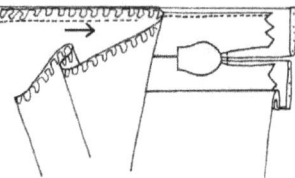 pocket bag. It's easier to do this with the zipper and pocket bag face up (not face down, as illustrated here for clarity).

5. Stitch together the pocket bags around the edges, stitching two parallel rows about 6mm (¼" or a footwidth) apart for strength. Overlock around the pocket bag if the garment is unlined or the fabric frays badly.

False jet pockets with zips
False jet pockets with zips are made in the same way as real jet pockets with zips, just without pocket bags. 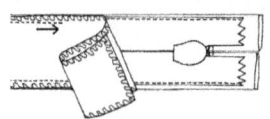 A backing of (overlocked) main fabric is stitched to the back of the pocket.

Jet pockets—another method
In this method, the pocket bags themselves form the lips that bind the edges of the slash, rather than separate strips. An attractive feature of making a pocket this way is that there's only one pattern piece. This type of jet pocket is used as an interior pocket in men's jackets, where it's made entirely of lining fabric and possibly in a contrasting colour.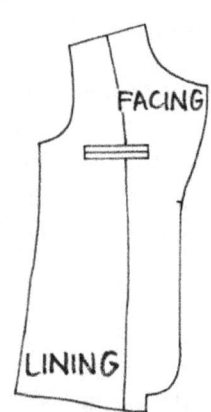
It's also sometimes used for men's back trouser pockets (see page 253).
As with the other method of making a jet pocket, the finished width of the lips can be any measurement you like, from fine narrow lines to wide and chunky.

Pockets slashed **251**

Make a pattern
1. Cut a piece of fabric 5cm (2") wider than the finished pocket opening and twice the pocket depth plus 4cm (1½"). You can curve the corners if you like, or leave them square.

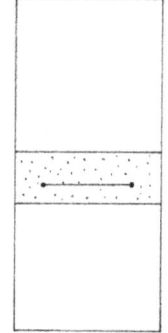

2. Fuse a strip of interfacing 5cm (2") wide in the centre. Make sure it's bonded well.

3. Mark the slash position 1.2cm (½") below the half way point, on top of the fusing.

4. Cut a strip of fusing approximately 2.5cm (1") wide to iron on the garment behind where the pocket will be, to reinforce it.

To sew another method of a jet pocket
1. Mark the slash position on the right side of the garment with dots.

Interior pockets in **jackets** are made across the facing and front lining before the lining is sewn into the jacket. The jet pocket usually sits mostly on the lining side, and juts into the facing by about 2.5cm (1"). On an unlined jacket it's placed completely on an extra-wide facing. Interior jacket pockets can be positioned on both sides or just on one side.

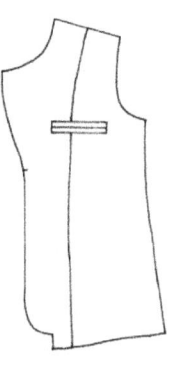

2. On the garment, iron the strip of fusing behind where the pocket will be slashed, to reinforce it. If the pocket goes through a seam, it's fine to sew the seam first then iron the fusing over the top, or else you can fuse each side separately and then sew the seam.

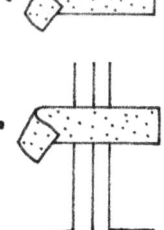

3. Position the pocket bag right side down over the right side of the garment, matching the opening position. I like to push pins through to match it.

4. Sew 6mm (¼") away from the slash line, forming a rectangle. Use a smaller stitch, such as 1.5 or 2 instead of the usual 2.5, for strength. Draw in the stitching line using a pencil and ruler before you start sewing if you need a guide.

The corners need to be exactly square and the lines need to be perfectly parallel, because this rectangle will be the finished shape of the pocket. If you'd like the pocket lips to be narrower, stitch closer to the slash line. For wider lips, stitch further away.

5. With sharp scissors, cut exactly in the centre of the stitching, stopping 1.5cm (⅝") before each end. Cut diagonally into the four corners, forming triangles.

6. Gently push the pocket and triangular ends to the wrong side of the garment. Pull on the triangles to help make the corners of the opening square.

7. There are two ways in which this next part can be made. I think this first way is a bit quicker. Try it if:
✂ The fabric is fairly thin
✂ You aren't having a button and loop closure
✂ You aren't edgestitching around the edge of the pocket
✂ You're confident with your stitching-in-the-ditch
✂ You aren't using making one of the two pattern variations at the end of this section or men's trousers

Press the long slashed edges *towards* the opening and the triangular ends *away* from the opening.

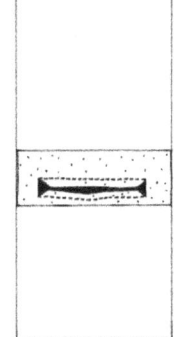

Form the lips by surrounding the long slashed edges with the pocket fabric. Follow the folds through all the way to the ends. Press in place. Stitch-in-the-ditch by stitching exactly in the grooves formed by the seams of the lips. Stitch only on the horizontals, *not* the ends.

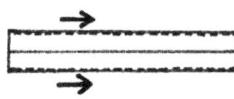

252 The Dressmaker's Companion

On the reverse side, bring the top pocket bag down over the pocket opening. Proceed to Step 8.

OR
Press both the triangles and the long slashed edges *away* from the opening. Press a horizontal fold in each pocket bag 6mm (¼") away from the seam, to form the pocket lips.

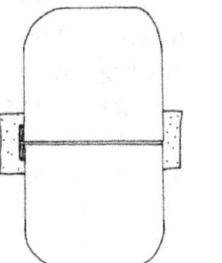

Check the right side to make sure the pocket lips are an equal depth the entire width along and make sure the corners are neat and square.

Tack through the folded edges to hold the lips in place and stitch the lips together with herringbone stitch.

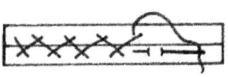

With the right side of the garment facing you, flip up the fabric below the pocket. Stitch through the lower seam allowance over the first line of stitching.

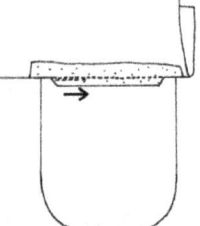

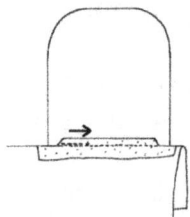

Repeat for the seam above the pocket.

If you desire a button and loop closure on the jet pocket, insert the loop into this seam as you sew it. The two ends of the loop should sit against the fold.

Bring the top pocket bag down over the pocket opening.

For both methods:

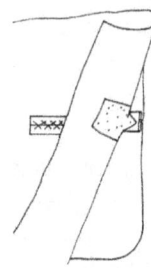

8. Stitch the triangles at each end. You can pin the triangle before stitching and check it on the right side to make sure it's squarely positioned (I do). If the fabric is very thick, use a zipper foot to get in nice and close to the edge. Repeat with the other end.

9. Trim the lower raw edges of the pocket bags to make them the same length if they aren't already.

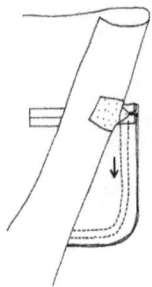

Stitch around the edges of the pocket bag starting at the top where the triangles are. Stitch two parallel rows about 6mm (¼" or a footwidth) apart for strength. Overlock the pocket bags if the garment is unlined or if the fabric will fray badly.
Remove the tacking.

Two further notes on this method

You may prefer this alternative method of making jet pockets and decide to forever make them this way.
If the main fabric is lightweight enough, this pocket can be made all in main fabric, which looks good if the garment is unlined.

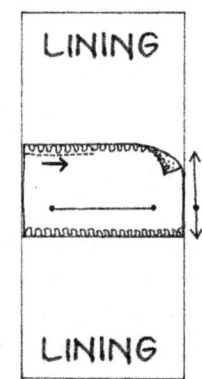

If you want the pocket to be in main fabric, you can reduce bulk in the pocket bag by cutting it in lining with a 10cm (4") deep rectangle of main fabric stitched on top. Overlock the long edges of the main fabric before attaching it.
To position the rectangle of main fabric, first establish where the slash line will be, 1.2cm (½") below the half way point. Then position the rectangle 7.5cm (3") above the slash line and 2.5cm (1") below it. Proceed to sew the pocket as normal.

Alternatively, the pocket bag can be cut in two pieces. The upper one in main fabric will make the lips and the lower one is cut in lining.
On the wrong side, iron a 7.5cm (3") wide strip of fusing over the slash position as illustrated, then mark the slash position over the fusing, 2.5cm (1") up from the raw edge.

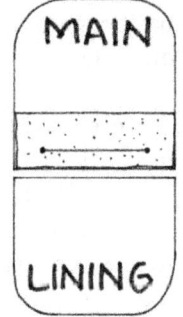

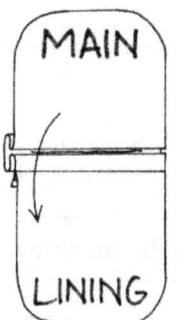

After forming the lips of the pocket, sew the lining onto the slashed edge and the main pocket bag with one row of stitching.

Men's trouser back jet pockets

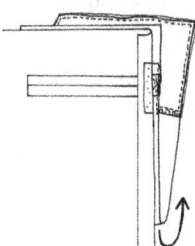
These have the pocket bag extended up into the waist to give support to the pocket and all the stuff that gets put into it. The pocket is cut in thin cotton pocket lining with two pieces of main fabric sewn on in strategic places—one for the lips and the other for the backing. The pocket is typically 14cm (5½") across finished and can be positioned on both backs or just the right hand one.

1. On the trousers, mark the position of the pocket slash 6.3cm (2½") below the waist seam. The pocket is usually centred between the side seam of the trousers and the centre back seam. If there's a dart, it looks best to have the dart in the centre of the jet pocket. Sew the dart before making the pocket.

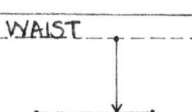

2. For the pocket lining, make the **width** of the pocket bag 5cm (2") wider than the finished pocket opening. Make the **length** 53.5cm (21").

3. Measure down 9cm (3⅝") from the the top and, on the wrong side of the pocket bag, draw in the slash line.

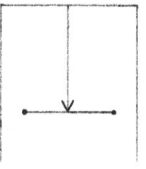

4. Over the slash line, on the right side, position a rectangle of main fabric, 7.5cm (3") deep. 5cm (2") goes above the slash line, and 2.5cm (1") below (the slash line is shown here but it's actually underneath). Overlock the long sides of the rectangle before you sew it on top of the pocket lining.

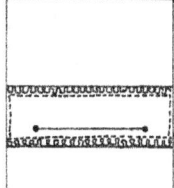

5. At the other end of the pocket, position a rectangle of main fabric 10cm (4") deep. This will sit behind the jet pocket when it's finished. Once again, overlock the long side before you sew it on top.

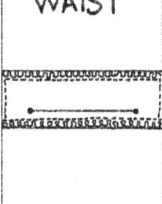

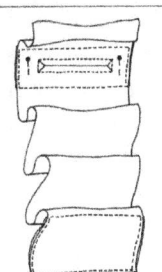
6. Sew the jet pocket in the alternative method described on page 250. That is, place the prepared pocket piece right sides together with the garment and stitch the window. Slash, turn, press, and stitch the lower lip and the end triangles.

Bring the back of the pocket into position, and stitch the top lip seam allowance through both pocket pieces. Sew around the pocket bags.

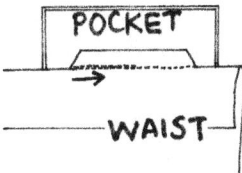

Welt pockets

I think welt pockets are the easiest to make of all the slashed pockets. The welt is made first, then it's attached it to the garment with the pocket bags. The depth of the welt can be anywhere from 1.2cm (½") to 6.5cm (2½") but around 2.5cm (1") is the most usual size.

Make a pattern

1. Make the welt twice the finished size plus a 6mm (¼") seam allowances all the way around. Interface half (on the side that will be uppermost).

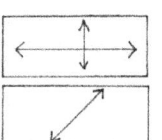
The grainline can go in either direction. For napped fabrics, it should go in the same direction as the garment. For checks and plaids, the welt can look good cut on the bias. In this case interface the whole welt for stability.

An angled welt will look like this:

2. You'll also need two pocket bags which will both be cut in lining. Make them 5cm (2") wider than the finished welt and make one 1.2cm (½") deeper than the other. 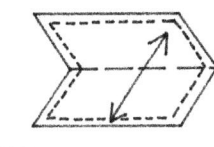 The deeper one will be used for the pocket's back.

An angled welt pocket will have pocket bags with angled tops.

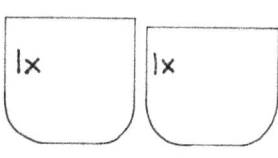

Try to find a lining that's a perfect colour match to the fashion fabric, so the lining will be invisible when you stitch the sides of the welt down at the ends.

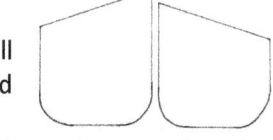

However, if you're making a welt pocket as a breast pocket on a jacket, you could use a contrast lining. When you pull the pocket lining half out of the welt pocket it will look like a coloured handkerchief.

3. Cut a strip of fusing to iron onto the garment behind where the pocket will be, to reinforce it. Make the strip deep enough to accommodate the depth of the welt.

To sew a welt pocket

1. On the garment, iron the strip of fusing behind where the pocket will be slashed, to reinforce it. Make sure it's bonded very well.
If the pocket goes through a seam, it's fine to sew the seam first then stick the fusing over the top, or else you can fuse each side separately and then sew the seam.

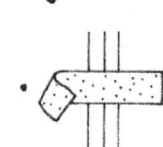

2. On the right side of the garment, mark the pocket slash line with two dots. The slash line is marked 6mm (¼") up from the lower edge of the finished welt position. I mark the dots 6mm (¼") in from each side so there's no chance of them showing when the pocket is finished. Join the dots with a ruled chalk line so you have a straight line to help position the pocket pieces.

3. Make the welt: fold the welt right sides together and sew the sides. Trim the corners and turn to the right side. Press. Topstitch and/or buttonhole the welt now if you plan to.

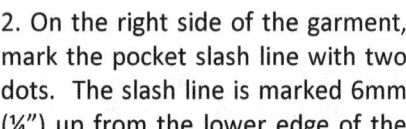

4. Place the welt right side down onto the garment below the slash line, matching the raw edge of the welt to the slash line. Pin into position. If you prefer, you can machine or hand baste the welt into position, about 3mm (⅛") from the raw edge. I usually just leave it pinned.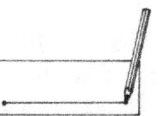

5. Place the two pocket bags right side down over the top, so the straight sides meet at the slash line. The longer pocket bag goes above the slash line and the shorter one goes below it (over the welt). Pin in place.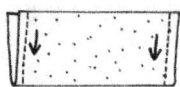

6. Sew the lower pocket bag first (the one with the welt under it), 6mm (¼") away from the edge. For easier sewing, fit a 6mm (¼") foot, if you have one, to your machine and use the edge of the foot as a guide. Use a shorter machine stitch for extra strength, such as 1.5 or 2 instead of the usual 2.5. Sew *exactly* from one end of the welt to the other, not over. Begin the seam by plunging the needle into the exact spot before lowering the presser foot. Backstitch securely at both ends.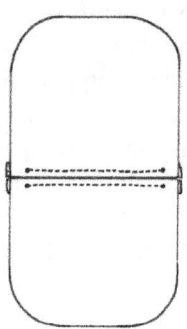

Quality check: flip back the pocket bag and measure the width of the welt. Sometimes the ends end up wider than the middle. If it isn't the same width all the way along, unpick and re-stitch to correct.

Then sew the top row parallel to the bottom one, beginning and ending exactly in line.

Note that if the welt pocket is on an angle, the beginning and end points of each row of stitching should not be adjacent. Rather, they should be directly above each other when the garment is being worn, otherwise the welt won't cover the corner.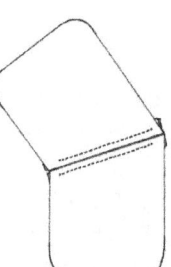

7. Cut carefully through the centre with sharp scissors. Stop 1.5cm (⅝") before the ends and cut diagonally into the four corners, exactly to the stitching, forming a triangle at each end. Cut *only* through the garment, *not* the welt or pocket bags.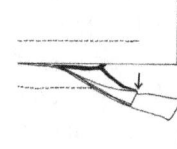

8. Gently push the pocket bags and the triangular ends through to  the wrong side. Press the lower seam allowance and the triangular ends away from the opening. Press the welt up and pin into position.

9. With the right side of the garment facing you, flip up the sides and stitch across the triangle using a zipper foot, to form neat rectangles at the ends. I like to pin the triangles first, check what the right side looks like, then sew.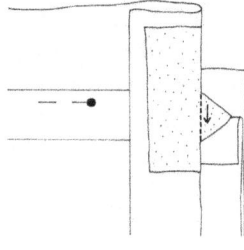

✂ Some people like to sew the *top* pocket bag a few stitches shorter (at both ends) than the lower one, so that the welt will definitely cover the ends. If you want to try this, you'll find that the triangular ends will be stitched at an angle to the pocket welt. I've tried it but decided I didn't like it.

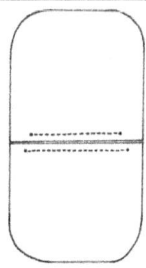

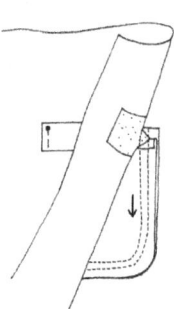

10. With the welt facing up, flip the garment back so the pocket bags are exposed. Stitch them together around the edges starting at one of the triangular ends. Stitch two parallel rows about 6mm (¼" or a footwidth) apart for strength. If the garment is unlined or the fabric frays badly, overlock around the edges of the pocket bag.

11. Sew the ends of the welt to the garment, either by machine or invisibly by hand.

Flap pockets

A flap pocket is constructed in the same manner as a jet pocket (page 246), but using an already-made flap instead of the top lip and a slightly wider lower lip. The lower lip is generally 1.2cm (½") wide when finished.

Make a pattern

1. For the flap, draw the desired shape and add a 6mm (¼") seam allowance around all the edges. The finished flap should be the same width as the pocket opening. The grainline of the flap should run in the same direction as the garment.

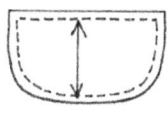

If the fabric is striped or checked, consider cutting the flap on the bias (highly recommended), or else match the check or stripe perfectly.

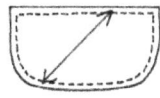

Cut two flaps in main fabric, or if the main fabric is thick, cut one of main fabric and one of lining. Interface what will be the uppermost flap.

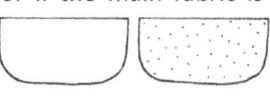

As an added refinement, the lining can be trimmed by 3mm (⅛") around all but the top edge, to ensure it

can't be seen when the flap is finished. When you sew the flap, have the lining on top and the main fabric underneath.

If the flap is rectangular, you can cut it in one piece. Interface half of it (the outermost side).

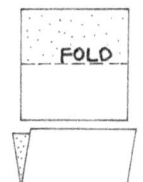

2. For the lower lip, cut a strip of main fabric 5cm (2") wider than the pocket opening and 4cm (1½") deep. Interface the strip with iron-on interfacing. The grainline of this piece can run either way.

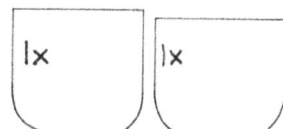

3. Cut two pocket bags both in lining, 5cm (2") wider than the pocket opening. Make one 1.2cm (½") deeper than the other. The deeper one will become the pocket back.

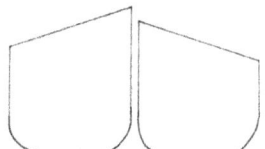

If the flap pocket is angled, then the tops of the pocket bags will also be angled to match.

4. Cut a strip of fusing to iron onto the garment behind where the pocket will be, to reinforce it. Make the strip about 4cm (1½") wide to accommodate the depth of the lower lip.

To sew a flap pocket

1. On the garment, iron the strip of fusing behind where the pocket will be slashed, to reinforce it. Make sure it's bonded very well.

If the pocket goes through a seam, it's fine to sew the seam first then stick the fusing over the top, or else you can fuse each side separately and then sew the seam.

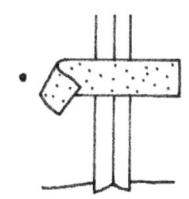

2. While you're at the ironing board, interface the flap if you haven't already. Interface the lower lip of the pocket and press it in half longways.

3. On the right side of the garment, mark the pocket slash line with two dots, one at each end of the slash line. The slash line is located 6mm (¼") from the top of the finished flap.

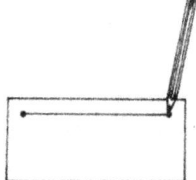

4. Make the flap: sew the two flap pieces with right sides together around the edges, leaving the top edge open. Trim any curves and corners and turn to the right side. Press. Topstitch now if desired, otherwise you may understitch the flap (if you can) to stop the underneath rolling to the front.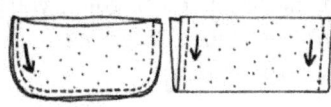

5. On the garment, place the flap above the slash position and the lower lip below it, both with right sides to the garment and raw edges touching. Pin into position.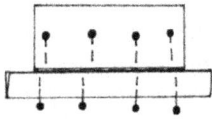

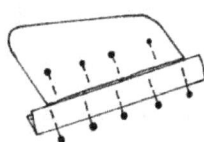 An angled flap pocket is positioned in the same way. Make sure the flap is not upside down.

6. Lay the pocket bags on top, right sides down. Place the deeper pocket bag over the flap. Stitch the flap side first, 6mm (¼") away from the edge. Sew *exactly* to and from each edge of the flap and not over. Begin the seam by plunging the needle into the exact spot before lowering the presser foot. Use a shorter machine stitch for extra strength, such as 1.5 or 2 instead of the usual 2.5. Backstitch at both ends securely.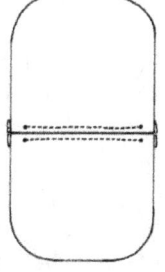
Quality check: flip back the pocket bag and measure the width of the flap. If it isn't the correct width all the way along, unpick and re-stitch to correct.

Next sew the side with the lower lip 6mm (¼") away from the edge, so the two lines of stitching are 1.2cm (½") apart. Make sure both lines of stitching are parallel and the same length. The beginning and end points should be level with each other.

Note that for an angled flap pocket, the beginning and end points of each row of stitching will not be level— they'll be directly in line with each other vertically, one point above the other.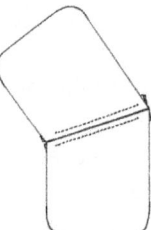

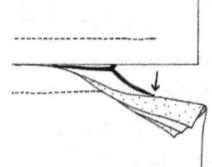 7. Cut carefully through the centre with sharp scissors. Stop 1.5cm (⅝") before the ends and cut diagonally into the four corners, exactly to the stitching, forming a triangle at each end. Cut *only* through the garment, *not* the flap, lower lip or pocket bags.

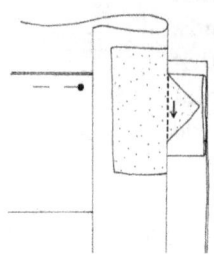 8. Gently push the pocket bags and the triangular ends through to the wrong side. Press the seam allowance and the triangular ends away from the opening. Press the lower lip up and pin it into position. With the right side of the garment facing you, flip up the sides and stitch across the triangle using a zipper foot, to form neat rectangles at the ends. Ensure the flap covers the ends of the pocket when viewed from the right side. I like to pin the triangles first, check, then sew.

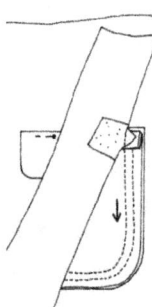 9. Flip the garment back so the pocket bag is exposed and stitch around the edges of it starting at one of the triangular ends. Stitch two parallel rows about 6mm (¼" or a footwidth) apart for strength. If the garment is unlined or the fabric frays badly, overlock around the edges of the pocket bag.

In industry, the lower lip is tacked in place with a long stitch by machine to hold the pocket smoothly to the garment. The customer undoes the stitching after purchase (if they know about it; some men complain to me that the pockets on their jacket are fake).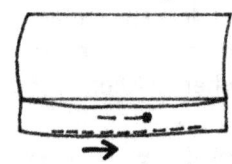

False flap or welt pocket

Sometimes a false flap or welt pocket is desirable. It's much quicker to make (= cheaper to manufacture), there's less wear and tear on the garment because the pockets aren't being used and therefore it stays looking smarter for longer.

1. Make the flap or welt in the same way as you would for a flap pocket (page 255) or a welt pocket (page 253).
For diagonal welts and flaps, make them with the end corners angled in, so when they're stitched onto the garment and folded into position the corners won't show.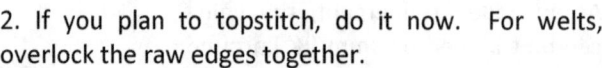

2. If you plan to topstitch, do it now. For welts, overlock the raw edges together.

3. Lay the flap or welt on the garment, right side down. Pin.
Position **flap**s with the raw edge pointing down.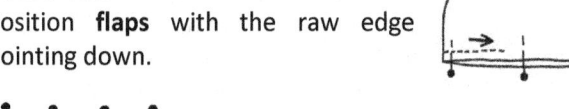

 Position **welt**s with the raw edge pointing up.

4. Sew the welt or flap in place, 6mm (¼") from the raw edge. Press flaps *down* and welts *up*.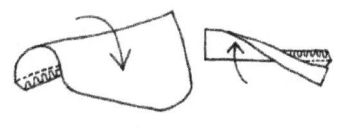

5. For **flap**s, stitch across the top to help them stay down. Trim the seam allowance before sewing this line of stitching so the raw edge is completely enclosed in the top of the flap.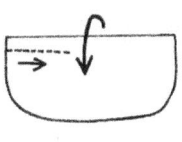

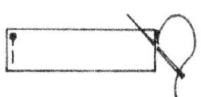 For **welt**s, stitch across each end, either by hand or by machine, just as you would for a regular welt pocket.

Windowpane welt pocket

or what I call a men's welt pocket, because it often features on the back of men's trousers (see page 260). An advantage of this kind of welt pocket is you can slip a loop or tab into the top seam for a button and loop closure. Read through the instructions first; there's an alternative method described afterwards (which I think is easier).

Make a pattern

1. On the garment pattern, draw in the finished size of the pocket in the correct position. It's typically 14cm (5½") across for men's back pockets and 1.2cm-2.5cm (½"-1") deep. Draw two lines parallel to the long sides of the welt and 6mm (¼") in. Transfer these two lines to the fabric when you cut the garment out. The two lines will help you position the pocket pieces (they *aren't* the slash lines).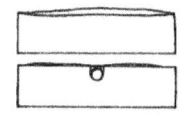

2. Make a welt pattern twice the finished depth plus two 6mm (¼") seam allowances. It should be 5cm (2") wider than the finished pocket opening. Cut one in main fabric and fuse half. The fused side will be outermost.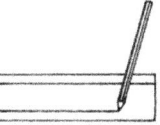

3. You'll also need two pocket bags, one in main fabric and one in lining.
Cut them 5cm (2") wider than the finished welt. The fabric one should be deeper than the lining by the depth of the finished welt.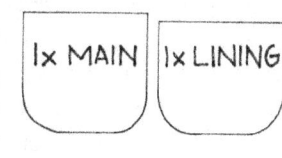

4. Cut a piece of fusing to apply behind the welt pocket on the garment, to reinforce it. Make the strip deep enough to accommodate the depth of the welt.

To sew a windowpane welt pocket

1. On the garment, iron the strip of fusing behind where the pocket will be slashed, to reinforce it. Make sure it's bonded very well.
If the pocket goes through a seam, it's fine to sew the seam first then stick the fusing over the top, or else you can fuse each side separately and then sew the seam.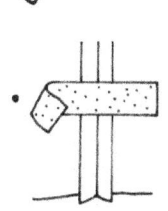

2. While you're at the ironing board, fuse the interfacing onto half the welt if you haven't already. Iron the welt in half longways, wrong sides together.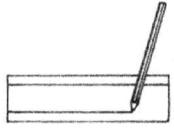

3. On the garment, ensure the pocket position is accurately marked on the right side of the fabric as described above.

4. Pin the pressed-in-half welt to the garment, right sides together, so the raw edge is matched to the lower line marked on the garment.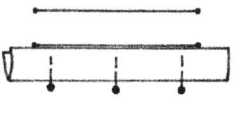

5. Lay the lining pocket bag face down over the top of it, matching the straight raw edges. Stitch 6mm (¼") away from the raw edge, backstitching securely at both ends. Use a shorter machine stitch for extra strength, such as 1.5 or 2 instead of the usual 2.5.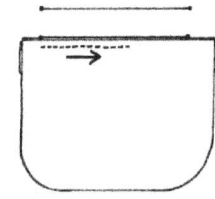

Quality check: lift the lining and measure the depth of the welt. Ensure it's the same all the way along. It's fine if it's a different width than you intended and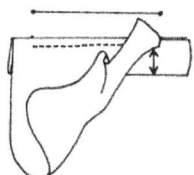

you're happy with that, but it has to be consistent the whole way along, not different at one end.

6. Lay the main fabric pocket bag right side down above the lining so the distance between the two *stitching* lines will be exactly the width of the finished welt (as measured in Step 5). Stitch with a 6mm (¼") seam, making sure the beginning and end points are exactly above the first line of stitching.

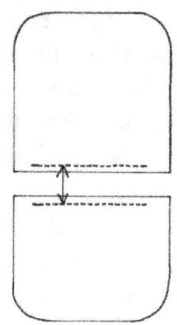

If you intend this pocket to have a button and loop closure, slip the loop into the centre of this seam before you sew it, matching the ends of the loop with the raw edge of the pocket bag.

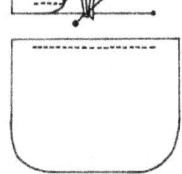

Another quality check: measure the space between the two rows of stitching with a ruler, just to make sure they're the correct distance apart before you cut.

7. Cut through the garment between the two rows of stitching to 1.5cm (⅝") short of each end. Cut diagonally into each corner, exactly to the stitching, to form a triangle at each end. Only cut the garment, *not* the pocket bags or welt.

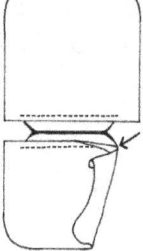

8. Push the pocket pieces and triangular ends through to the wrong side and flip the welt into position. Tuck the ends of the welt in so they're on the wrong side. The welt should sit neatly in a rectangle, with square corners and the top edge level with the seam. Press.

9. Flip up each end of the welt pocket and sew the triangle close to the edge, forming a neat rectangular end on the right side. Use a zipper foot to get in close. I like to pin the triangles in position first, check on the right side to see I've positioned them straight, then sew.

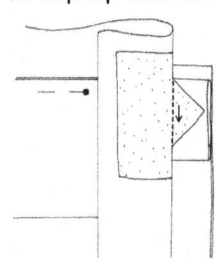

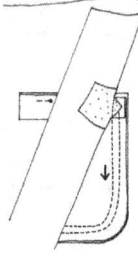

10. Lay the pocket bags together and stitch around the edges. Stitch two parallel rows about 6mm (¼" or a footwidth) apart for strength. If the garment is unlined or the fabric frays badly, overlock around the edges of the pocket bag.

Alternative method of making a windowpane welt pocket

In my opinion, this is a much easier method of making this type of pocket. There is only one pattern piece. This is very suitable for unlined garments because the pocket bag is all in main fabric.

Make a pattern

1. Decide on the finished dimensions of the welt and the depth of the pocket bag. Make a cardboard template the finished size of the welt, to use as a stitching guide.

2. The pocket bag is one rectangle, cut in main fabric. It should be 5cm (2") wider than the finished welt.
The length should be twice the intended depth of the pocket bag plus four times the finished welt depth. You can curve the corners if desired, or leave them square.

✂ If you want to reduce bulk, the pocket bag can be cut in two pieces—one in main fabric and the other lining. The depth of the lining piece should be the depth of the pocket bag + half the welt depth. The depth of the fabric piece should be the depth of the pocket bag plus 4½ times the welt depth. If the garment will be unlined, overlock the short straight edge of each first.

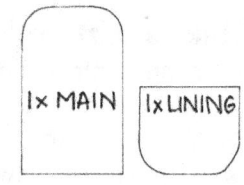

3. Cut a piece of fusing for the pocket measuring the width of the pocket bag and 2½ times the finished welt depth. This gets ironed onto the pocket bag.

4. Cut another piece of fusing to iron on the garment behind the welt to reinforce it. Make the strip deep enough to accommodate the depth of the welt.

Pockets slashed **259**

To sew a windowpane welt pocket (alternative method)

1. On the garment, iron the strip of fusing behind where the pocket will be slashed, to reinforce it. Make sure it's bonded very well.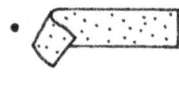
If the pocket goes through a seam, it's fine to sew the seam first then iron the fusing over the top, or else you can fuse each side separately and then sew the seam.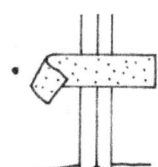

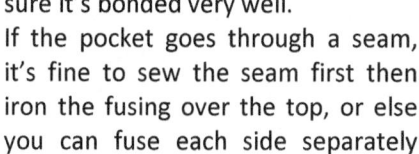

2. On the pocket piece, iron the fusing onto the wrong side.
If you're making the pocket with a one piece pocket bag, fuse it in exactly the centre.

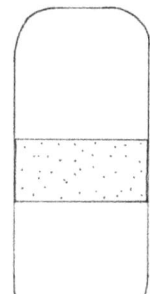

For a two piece pocket bag, iron it onto the wrong side of the main fabric piece, 1½ times the depth of the welt up from the lower edge. Set the lining pocket bag aside for the moment.

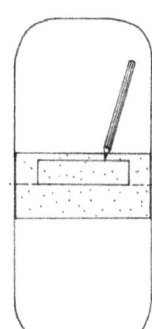

3. Using the cardboard template, mark the stitching position of the welt on the wrong side of the pocket bag. It will be marked over the fusing. Use a pencil, sharpened chalk or something to give you a narrow, defined line.
On a one piece pocket bag, mark it so the lower edge of the template sits on the half way line of the pocket bag.

On a two piece pocket bag, mark it 2½ times the depth of the welt up from the lower edge.

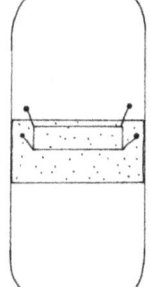

4. Place the pocket bag on the garment, right sides together, aligning the window you've just marked to the designated pocket position. I like to push pins through the corners to match them to the garment. Pin in place. (Only the one piece pocket bag is illustrated here, but the two piece is done the same way).

5. Stitch around the window, pivoting at the corners, to form a perfect rectangle the exact size of the finished welt. Use a shorter machine stitch for extra strength, such as 1.5 or 2 instead of the usual 2.5.

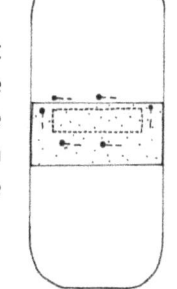

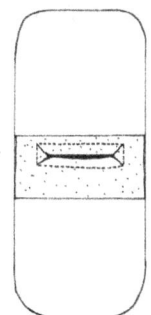

6. Carefully slash through the centre of the rectangle, stopping 1.5cm (⅝") short of the ends. Cut diagonally into each corner *exactly* to the stitching, forming triangles at the ends.
Push the pocket bag through to the wrong side. Press the triangular ends and seam allowances *away* from the opening.

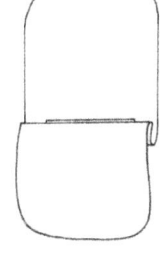

7. Fold the lower half of the pocket bag to form the welt. Press.
On a two piece pocket bag, the lower edge of the pocket bag should match the lower edge of the slash you've just made.

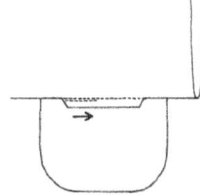

8. With the garment right side up, flip up the lower part to expose the pocket edge. Fit a zipper foot to your machine.
For a one piece pocket bag, stitch the lower seam allowance to the lower pocket bag, stitching on top of the first (windowpane) line of stitching.
On a two piece pocket bag, slip the lining pocket bag underneath the lower seam allowance, right sides together, matching the raw edges. Stitch close to the first (windowpane) line of stitching.

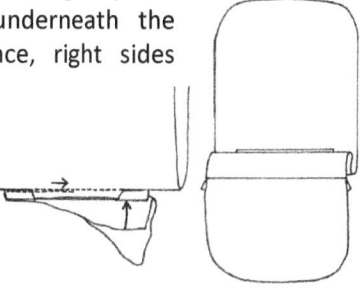

9. On the reverse side of the pocket, bring the upper pocket bag down over the welt. Pin the pocket bags together, taking care not to catch the garment.

A one piece pocket bag will look like this:

A two piece pocket bag will look like this:

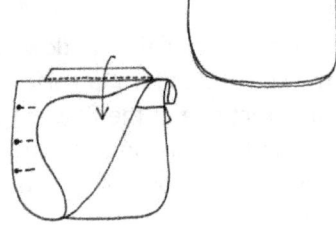

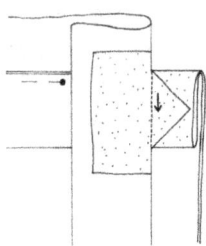

10. Turn the garment face up. Flip each side back and pin each triangular end neatly in place. Check how it looks on the right side to make sure the ends are neat and square. Stitch across the triangular ends using a zipper foot to get in close.

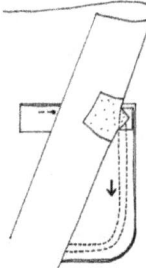

11. Stitch around the edges of the pocket bags, starting at one of the triangular ends.
Stitch two parallel rows about 6mm (¼" or a footwidth) apart, for strength. If the garment is unlined or the fabric frays badly, overlock around the edges of the pocket bag.

Men's trouser windowpane welt pocket

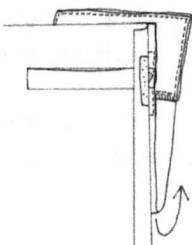

A back welt pocket on trousers generally sees hard wear and needs to be very strong. This pocket has the pocket bag extended up into the waist to give support to the welt and pocket bag.

Make a pattern
and assemble the pocket pieces

This pocket is cut in one piece in cotton pocket lining with two pieces of main fabric sewn on in strategic places—one for the welt and the other for behind the welt.

1. Decide on the finished welt dimensions. The welt can be 1.2cm-2.5cm (½"-1") deep and is typically 14cm (5½") across. On the garment, mark the position of the welt 6.3cm (2½") below the waist seam.

The welt is usually centred between the side seam of the trousers and the centre back seam. If there's a dart, it looks best to have the dart in the centre of the welt pocket. Sew the dart before making the pocket.

2. Make the cotton pocket lining 5cm (2") wider than the finished pocket width and 58cm (23") long. On the *wrong* side of the lining, mark the position of the welt. The welt should be the same distance from the top as it is on the garment. Accurately draw it in using a pencil and ruler, or trace around a cardboard template. You'll be stitching on this line for the welt.

3. Cut two rectangles of fabric 10cm (4") deep and the same width as the lining. On one, overlock both long edges and stitch it face up on the right side of the lining. Position the top edge 1cm (⅜") above the top of the welt.
(The rectangle you drew is shown but is behind this.)

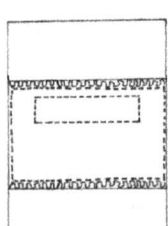

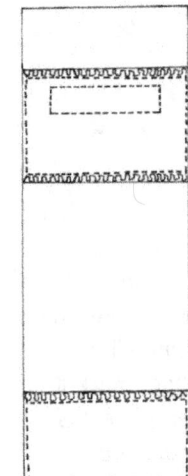

4. Overlock one long edge of the other rectangle and stitch it at the opposite end of the lining.
This part will sit behind the welt when the pocket is finished.
The pocket bag is now ready to sew.

To sew a men's windowpane welt pocket

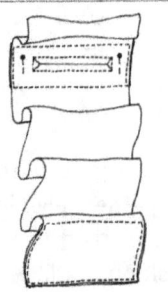

1. Make the welt in the alternate way as described on page 259. That is, place the prepared pocket piece right sides together with the garment and stitch around the window. Slash, turn, press, form the welt and stitch the lower edge of the welt and the end triangles.

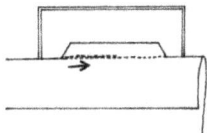
2. Position the back of the pocket behind the welt and stitch the top seam allowance of the welt through both pocket pieces.

Sew around the pocket bags and overlock or bind the edge. Sometimes the pocket bags are topstitched to the garment.

Zip pocket

This method uses two pocket pieces. One is used as a facing around the edges of a "window",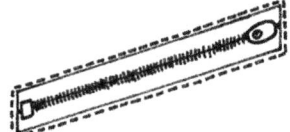
framing the zip. The other acts as a backing. Choose a zip the finished length of the pocket opening, anywhere from 10cm (4") to 18cm (7") long. If you want the zip pocket to be a **false zip pocket**, simply cut very short pocket bags, to cover the zip but not big enough to put your hand in.

Make a pattern
1. Cut a cardboard template the size of the zipper window box. Measure the zip to check exactly how long it is to make sure it will fit. Check also the *width* of the box. I suggest making it between 1cm (⅜") and 1.5cm (⅝") wide, depending on how chunky the zip is.

2. Make a pocket bag pattern, 5cm (2") wider than the pocket opening. You'll need a pair—they can be both cut in main fabric, both in lining or one of each.

If the zip pocket is going to be on an angle, the top of the pocket bags will be angled.

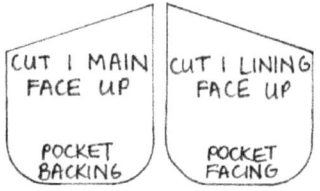

For angled-top pocket bags, it's important to note which pocket bag will be the facing and which will be the backing and to cut them with the correct side of the fabric up. The pocket bags illustrated above are correct for a pocket sloping like this:

3. Cut two strips of fusing, paired, the same width as the pocket bags and about 5cm (2") deep. One of them will go on the garment behind where the pocket will be slashed. The other will be ironed onto one of the pocket bags (the one that acts as a facing).

To sew a zip pocket
1. On the garment, iron the strip of fusing behind where the pocket will be slashed, to reinforce it. Make sure it's bonded very well. If the pocket goes through a seam, it's fine to sew the seam first then stick the fusing over the top, or else you can fuse each side separately and then sew the seam.

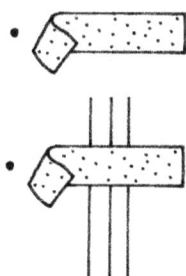

2. Mark the pocket position on the right side of the garment with dots.

3. Iron the remaining strip of fusing to the wrong side of the *facing* pocket bag, at the top. (If you're using one of fabric and one of lining, this should be the *lining* one.) Using the cardboard template, mark the zipper opening box on top of the fusing, 2.5cm (1") down from the top edge and centred.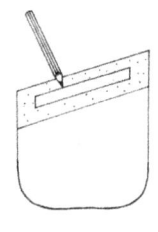

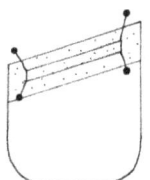
4. Place the pocket piece and garment right sides together, matching the pocket opening positions.
Push pins through the corners to help match them up.

5. Using a small stitch for extra strength, such as 1.5 or 2 instead of the usual 2.5, stitch around the box, pivoting at the corners and ensuring the long lines are parallel.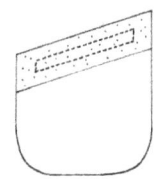

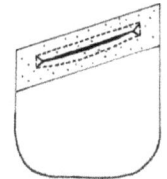
6. Cut between the rows of stitching, stopping 1.5cm (⅝") short of the ends. Cut diagonally into each corner, forming triangles at each end.

7. Turn the pocket bag through to the wrong side of the garment and press so you can't see any of the pocket bag from the right side. This forms the facing that will frame the zip.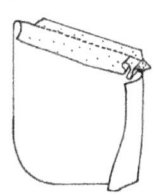

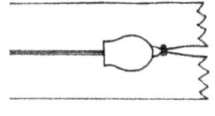
8. Stitch the ends of the zipper tape together above the zip pull.

9. Place the zipper under the opening and pin it in place. It should neatly fit in the window you've made.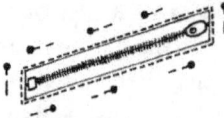
If the opening is angled, position the zipper pull at the higher end of the opening, so the pocket contents won't fall out if the zip is only half closed.
Using a zipper foot to get close to the edge, edgestitch around the edges of the zipper opening.

✂ For non-visible stitching, stitch the zip onto the seam allowances of the slash only. To do this, lay the garment right side up and flip back each side in turn, exposing the seam allowance. Pin each seam allowance to the zipper tape. Using a zipper foot, sew each seam allowance to the zipper, stitching on top of the first (windowpane) row of stitching. Make sure the zip sits flat after sewing each side.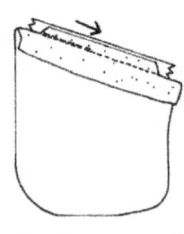

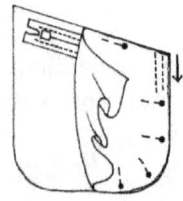 10. With the right sides together, lay the second pocket piece over the back of the pocket behind the zip, pin then stitch around the edges.

Stitch two parallel rows about 6mm (¼" or a footwidth) apart for strength. Overlock around the edge.

Pressing

Introduction... 263	pressing gathers........................... 267
Some pressing equipment................ 263	shrinking and stretching........... 267
Heat, moisture and pressure............ 265	precision-pressing...................... 268
Test pressing 265	pressing permanent creases ... 268
Some pressing techniques................ 266	*when* to press 268
ironing and pressing 266	Miscellaneous pressing notes 268
pressing seams 266	Troubleshooting pressing...................... 269
pressing direction of seams 266	Making pressing tools........................... 270
pressing darts 266	requirements................................ 270
"the coat hanger stage" 267	pressing mitt 270
pressing hems............................... 267	seam roll 271
finger and table pressing 267	tailors ham 271

Pressing helps to give a garment shape and form, assisting the transformation of a flat piece of fabric into a three dimensional garment. The combination of heat, steam and pressure encourages each garment section to fit together correctly and conform to the curves and angles of your body. Pressing is the easiest way to improve the look of your sewing without actually changing the way you sew.

Pressing is very important at every stage of sewing. Thorough, careful pressing makes a tremendous difference to the finished look of your garment. Be patient and don't rush it—on some fabrics and garments your pressing time will take as long as your sewing time. Pressing requires a certain care, gentleness and empathy, which you'll notice when watching someone who's really good at pressing.

Some pressing equipment

Don't feel that you need lots of fancy equipment to be good at pressing—they're simply tools for making the job easier. I don't own all of these tools. I get along well with a regular iron, an ironing board, a few pressing cloths, spray bottle, a homemade pressing mitt and a sleeve board (second-hand, re-covered).

Iron. The "shot of extra steam" type is recommended. Some irons have an attachable teflon soleplate to protect the iron and give a non-stick surface.

Ironing board. Make sure it's firm, well-padded and covered with a cotton ironing board cover. Replace the cover if it's stained or torn.

Pressing cloth. A pressing cloth is used to prevent shine or iron marks on the fabric. It also protects the iron soleplate from interfacing glue and scratches caused by accidentally pressing over hooks, zips and buttons. The cloth can be used wet or dry. A pressing cloth can be a large handkerchief or a piece of lint-free cotton fabric. A piece of silk organza can be used to press silk and lace.

A **Rajah cloth** will press a permanent crease in fabric. The cloth has to be used a certain way up.

Spray bottle. Essential! You can mist water onto a pressing cloth or squirt or mist water directly onto the fabric.

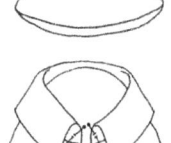

Tailor's ham. A tailor's ham is a firm cushion with rounded surfaces for pressing shaped areas such as bust seams or curved seams.

It's also used for moulding collars. You can buy them or make them.

Sleeve board. A covered strip of wood that clips or sits onto the ironing board, providing a small flat surface for pressing.

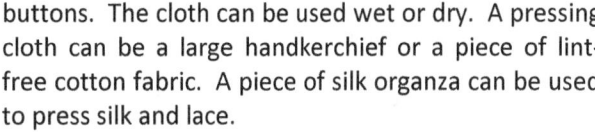

263

It's very helpful for pressing sleeve seams or trouser legs and also hard-to-reach areas like necklines. As well as pressing, it's also useful for general everyday ironing.

Clapper. Sometimes called a pounding block. A clapper is a heavy, smooth piece of wood about as big as your hand and 5cm (2") wide. It's used to reduce bulk by making seams and edges *really* flat. After removing the iron, press the clapper onto the seam and hold it there with pressure until the seam has cooled.

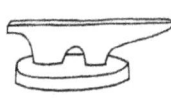 It's also available as a clapper/point presser. The point is used to press seams and corners open, and the clapper is on the bottom.

Seam roll. A firmly packed cylindrical cushion used for pressing seams in very narrow areas. It can be used in the same way as a sleeve board. If you have neither a sleeve board nor a seam roll, a tightly rolled hand towel or rolled up magazine can be used.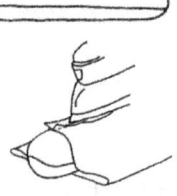

Press mitt. A padded cushion used as a pressing area for small, curved garment areas.
It has a pocket to slip your hand into. They're especially good for pressing rounded sleeve caps. You can also put them over the end of a sleeve board. Some people prefer these to tailor's hams.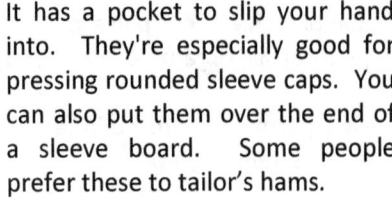

Appliqué sheet. A sheet of non-stick material. Quilters use it when preparing appliqué and you can buy it at quilting supply shops. Put it on your ironing board when ironing on interfacing to stop glue ending up on your ironing board cover and subsequently your garment. Baking paper is a good substitute.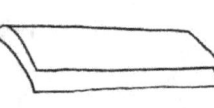

Needleboard or Velvaboard. These are used to safely press napped or embellished fabrics, such as velvet, synthetic suede, corduroy, silk ribbon embroidery and beadwork. A needleboard is a flat board with a raised prickly surface. It's also called a bristle board. The fabric is placed right side down onto the raised surface and gently pressed with steam. If you press too hard, however, the needles will puncture the fabric.

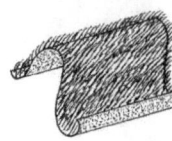 A Velvaboard (pictured) is a fabric mat with a deep, flexible pile on one side and is used in the same way: velvets are laid face down on the surface and pressed, using steam and minimal pressure from the iron.
A large scrap of velvet can be used in the same way.

Tailor board. A very versatile pressing tool, it has multiple pressing surfaces including large and small curves, as well as points for pressing inside collars and mitres. Made of wood, it has a removable padded cover. They are expensive.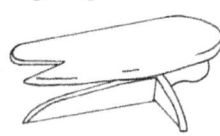

Ham holder. A moulded plastic container that holds the tailors ham in any position when you are moulding fabric around it, for example a collar.
 A hole in the outer rim allows you to pin it securely onto an ironing board. You could improvise with a small biscuit tin or an ice cream container.

Steam stick. A steam stick is a length of dowel cut in half 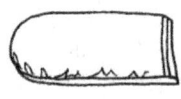 longways, resulting in a rounded edge and a flat edge. It's used to press seams without affecting other areas and can also be inserted into a tube to press the seam open before turning it through to the right side. You could also use a wooden chopstick.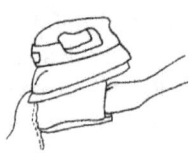

Pressing tools can be divided into three groups.

Wooden:	Clapper
	Point presser/clapper
	Tailor board
	Steam stick/dowel
Padded:	Ironing board
	Sleeve board
	Seam roll
	Tailors ham and ham holder
	Pressing mitt
	Velvaboard/needleboard
Moisture producing:	Steam iron
	Steamer
	Pressing cloths
	Spray bottle/wet sponge

Heat, moisture and pressure

It's important to understand how the three essential elements of pressing—heat, moisture and pressure—work together and affect the fabric. The amount of heat, moisture and pressure needed for successful pressing depends on the fibre content, weight, thickness and texture of the fabric.

Heat

✂ Cotton and linen need more heat than wool, silk or synthetics. If the fabric is made from a blend of fibres, set the heat for the most sensitive one.

✂ Thin fabrics may require less heat than thick fabrics even when they're the same fibre content.

✂ Pressing *with* a pressing cloth requires a hotter iron than pressing without one, because the heat has to get through the press cloth.

Moisture

Moisture helps the fabric become more malleable and removes creases, and this is the key to shaping fabrics. You can apply moisture with a steam iron, damp pressing cloth, spray bottle, sponge or dauber (see top of next column) or wet fingers. After pressing with moisture, don't move the fabric until it's dry. Either iron it dry or press with a dry press cloth. Be careful: too much moisture and heat will shrink some fabrics such as wool.

✂ A **steam iron** is the easiest way to deliver moisture. Set the iron to steam and let it heat up fully before pressing. Test the steam function first to be sure the iron isn't dripping. Also check: some irons drip if they are full of water but switched to dry.

✂ My iron doesn't do steam very well, so I use a **spray bottle** to mist water either directly onto the fabric or onto a pressing cloth.

✂ Some people prefer a **damp pressing cloth with a dry iron** rather than a steam iron. This combination controls the amount of moisture, avoids water spotting or minerals from the iron on the fabric and protects delicate fabrics from excessive heat. To dampen a press cloth, either wet it and wring it out tightly, or spray it with a spray bottle. You can remove moisture by pressing with a dry press cloth.

✂ Water can also be dabbed onto small areas, using your **fingers dipped in water, a wet sponge or a dauber**. It's an excellent way to precisely apply moisture just where you need it. **To make a dauber**, tightly roll up a length of woollen fabric and secure with an elastic band, string or thread. Dip the dauber into water and dab along the seam lines.

Pressure

You can apply pressure just by pressing harder with the iron, using a clapper or pressing with your fingers. The amount of pressure required varies with the fabric and pressing task. For example, thick fabrics require more pressure to flatten the seams and edges than lightweight fabrics or napped fabrics.

✂ A softer ironing board surface is needed for pressing textured fabrics, embroidery, buttonholes and details to avoid flattening or causing imprints. Place the fabric right side down onto a soft surface such as a folded towel, soft padding or some soft flannelette.

✂ For sharp, crisp creases and edges, press against an unpadded wooden surface, such as a clapper or a sleeve board with the cover taken off.

Test pressing

Test-press seams and darts on fabric scraps first and experiment with various heat settings, damp and dry press cloths, steam or dry and clappers. The fabric must look pressed, but not be altered in size or texture. Things to note:

✂ What iron temperature?
✂ Do you need steam or a dry iron?
✂ Is the fabric affected by spots of water?
✂ Can you only press this fabric on the wrong side?
✂ Do you need to use a press cloth? Dry or wet?
✂ Do you need more pressure than just pressing hard on the iron to make the seams flat? If so, try using a clapper.
✂ Do seams and darts imprint through and become shiny on the right side?
✂ What pressing tools will help you?
✂ Are the seams going to be pressed open or closed?
✂ Which seams will you press open or closed?
✂ Do you need to press the seams before neatening them? In other words, does the overlocking outline imprint through to the right side when you press?
✂ Does the fabric shrink with steam? A lot? Do you need to steam the fabric before cutting it out?

Some pressing techniques
Ironing and pressing
Ironing is a back and forth motion, sliding the iron over the fabric when you move it. Ironing smooths and stretches the fabric slightly, encouraging each garment section to lie flat. It's ideal for broad expanses of fabric in finished garments, as well as uncut fabric.

For greater accuracy of fit, iron creased fabric flat before cutting out, particularly if you have prewashed it. You can also iron tissue pattern pieces flat, provided you don't get any water on them and avoid any areas with sticky tape.

Pressing is a lifting up and down motion with the weight of the iron (along with the weight of your arm) creating sharp folds, soft curves or smooth seams. The goal of pressing is to shape fabric the way you want it. The up and down motion prevents distortion of the fabric's grain and shape.

When pressing garments, press flat areas on flat surfaces and shaped sections over pads or hams that match the shape of the garment.

Pressing seams
After stitching a straight seam, first press it flat to help marry or integrate the stitches with the fabric.

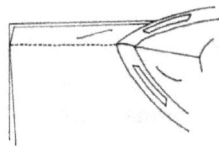

Then press the seam either open or closed.
Open seams are easier to press on the *wrong* side, and **closed seams** (to one side) on the *right* side.

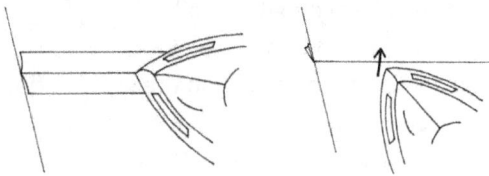

In some cases it helps to finger-press the seam allowances first, to create a clear path for the tip of the iron.

After pressing seams open (on the wrong side), I sometimes press them again on the right side.

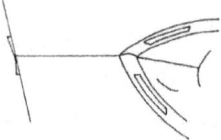

Curved seams receive much the same treatment as straight seams. Start by pressing the seam together as it was sewn, then press the seam allowances in the desired direction. Snip the seam allowances as needed to make them lie flat. The sharper the curve, the more snips you'll need. On open seams, the snips should be staggered to avoid weakening the seam.

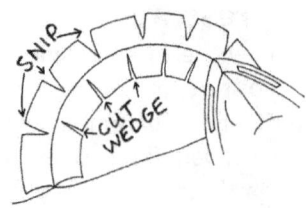

On inside curves, you might need to cut little wedges out of the seam allowance to help inside curves sit flat (as illustrated above). Otherwise try shrinking the excess in with steam (see page 267). Press curved seams over a ham to accommodate the curves.

Pressing direction of seam allowances
✂ Curved seams are often pressed together (as closed seams) in a particular direction because of the curves. Princess line seams are pressed towards the *centre* of the garment.

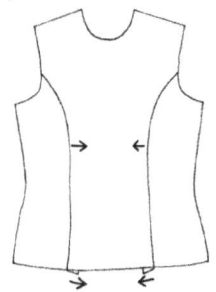

✂ Shoulder and side seams are pressed towards the *back*.

✂ Armhole seams of set-in sleeves are pressed towards the sleeve.

✂ Seams that are plain on one side and gathered or pleated on the other are pressed towards the plain side to avoid turning the bulky edge back on itself.

✂ Waistline seams are pressed *up*.

✂ Seams joining a yoke to a blouse or a skirt are pressed towards the yoke.

✂ Transparent fabrics joined to non-transparent fabrics are pressed towards the solid side so they're hidden.

Pressing darts
Darts turn flat garments into shaped ones and good pressing will mould the darts to shape almost invisibly.

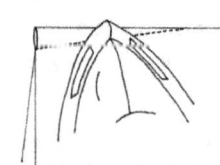

Begin by pressing the dart flat as it was sewn, to smooth the stitching and work it into the cloth.

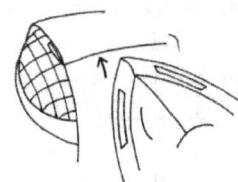

Then on the right side, press the wide part of the dart to one side.

Vertical darts are pressed either towards the centre or the sides (but not one one way and one the other).

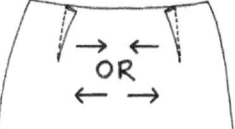

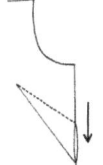

Horizontal darts are pressed down.

Mould the point of the dart over a ham, using the tip of the iron to press the point. Be careful not to steam out all the shaping you've just sewn in, especially if the fabric is wool and can be shrunk or moulded easily.

I like to press darts on the right side if I can, so I can see what they look like. Sometimes an extra mist of water and press on the point can make all the difference between a pointy dart and a smooth moulded one.

If necessary, tuck a strip of heavy paper under the fold to prevent the dart imprinting through to the right side.

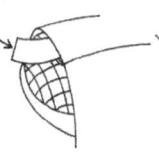

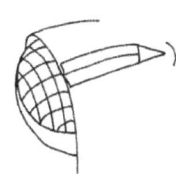

If the dart has been slashed open and trimmed, for example for heavier fabrics or extra-big darts, press the seam open on the wrong side over a ham. I still like to press the actual point on the right side.

The Coat Hanger Stage

At some point in your garment's construction, you'll reach what I call The Coat Hanger Stage. It's when there are enough sections seamed together to be able to hang the garment on a hanger without it stretching out of shape. Storing partly finished garments on a hanger helps prevent crushing or creasing the fabric you've already pressed. You can use a dressmakers model instead of a hanger, if you have one.

Pressing hems

There are two schools of thought when it comes to pressing hems. Some say you shouldn't press the hem until it's been sewn (in case the position changes and you end up with train track-like folds), however I like to press up all the hems and vents before sewing them. Either way, press only the *fold* of the hem, not over the top edge, otherwise a ridge will show through on the right side, very noticeably on thick fabrics.

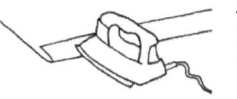

Finger pressing and table pressing

Finger pressing is simply pressing the fabric with your fingers. Use your fingers to pre-press seams before pressing them with an iron, to create a clear pathway for the tip of the iron.

Table pressing is useful to use while you're sewing. It doesn't replace pressing with an iron, but it can save you time.

Hold the fabric taut and scrape the seam or fold along the edge of the table. It works best on crisp fabrics that hold a crease well.

Pressing gathers

Gathered seams are closed seams, that is, folded to one side, not opened out. The seam is pressed *away* from the gathering.

Slide the tip of the iron into the gathers and then lift it or move it straight back. Be careful not to press beyond the seam line onto the plain side.

Shrinking and stretching

Fabric can be shrunk or stretched by pressing. The degree depends on the fibre content, the weave, the grain of the garment section and the edge to be shaped.

Note that:

✂ Wools, wool blends and loosely woven fabrics are more malleable and can be shrunk or stretched more easily.

✂ Bias sections and edges are easier to shape, while sections on the straight grain are more difficult.

✂ Tightly woven fabrics, silk, cotton, linen and synthetic fabrics are harder to shrink or stretch.

✂ It's best to avoid pressing circular sections (such as wristlines of sleeves) or rolled sections (such as lapels) inside out, since this will stretch the inner layer and shrink the outer one.

Shrinking is used for:

✂ Shaping sleeve heads

✂ Removing fullness at points of darts (particularly bust darts, for a smooth shape)

✂ Shrinking in a curved hemline

✂ Easing sections to be eased

✂ Restoring sections that have been stretched (for example necklines and armholes)

To shrink an edge, moisten or steam the garment section and apply heat. As the fabric shrinks, apply pressure with the iron or your fingers.

Depending on the application you might need to run a line of ease stitching and pull up the threads until the edge is the desired length. When the surplus fabric has been shrunken in, press with a dry press cloth to press the fabric dry.

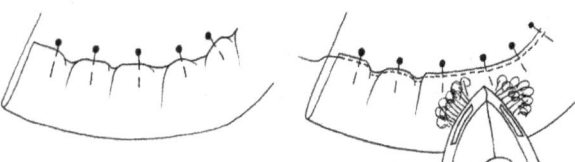

Stretching is used for:
- Frilling flared hems and frill edges
- Stretching a hemline that is smaller
- Transforming straight bias strips into curved shapes

To stretch an edge, dampen it with steam, a spray bottle or a damp press cloth. Press one end under the iron and hold the other end in your hand. As you press, use the iron as a weight and use your hand to stretch the edge in the desired shape. Be sure not to overstretch

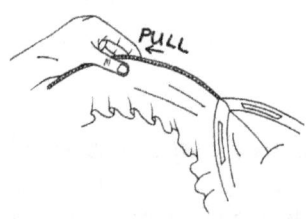

it. Stretching is often used in tandem with shrinking. I have unfortunately known it to be used in clothing factories to stretch waistbands to the right size when they come up smaller than spec (knowing that the waistbands will shrink back after washing).

Precision-press with the iron's point
For pressing sharp curves or tight spots, use just the tip of the iron to press, holding the rest of the soleplate away from the garment.

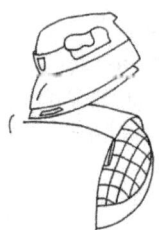

Use the end or edge of a sleeve board to isolate the area and stop you from pressing creases into other areas by mistake. Press small components like collars or pocket flaps separately before joining them to other sections.

Pressing in permanent creases
Some garments require permanent creases pressed in, for example pleats or front creases on trousers. You'll find that certain fabrics hold a crease better and longer than others. There are several ways to press permanent folds.

✂ Try using a **Rajah cloth** instead of a regular pressing cloth. It has to be used a certain way up.

✂ **Pressure and steam** help. Try a damp (wrung out) press cloth over the fabric and press until the cloth is dry. Use a clapper to provide extra pressure. Don't move the fabric until it's cool and dry.

✂ An old but effective method is pressing with **vinegar**. The vinegar smell doesn't linger, so your fabric won't smell like a pickle! Dilute the vinegar with water. How much to dilute? You need more water than vinegar but you can add any amount of vinegar up to 50%. Try three parts water to one part vinegar. Wet brown paper with it and use the paper as a press cloth. You could also mix it in a spray bottle and spray it on, or dampen a press cloth with the mixture and use that. Don't move the fabric until it's cool and dry. **Interesting tip:** some people add 1-2 tablespoons of vinegar to the water chamber of their steam iron for regular ironing, to help remove creases.

When to press?
Pressing-as-you-go makes sewing easier and more accurate, it's easier to press smaller sections and there's less to do at the end. I highly recommend it. Save time by sewing as much of the garment as you can before pressing is required.

Factories press garments only once, at the end (except for jackets; the main and lining are pressed separately before being sewn together). However, factory irons have considerably more grunt than domestic ones.

Miscellaneous pressing notes
✂ Press **seams** and **darts** before crossing them with another line of stitching.

✂ Check the **fit** before pressing seams and darts.

✂ Don't press over **pins or basting threads** because the marks will show.

✂ For **edges and enclosed seams**, such as faced edges or collars, press the seam open and flat before pressing the edge folded.

✂ Don't allow **knits** or unstable garment sections to hang off the ironing board unsupported or they'll stretch out of shape. Either make sure all of the garment is on the ironing board, or support the excess with a nearby table.

Pressing

✂ Before turning through **tubes** of fabric, for example fabric belts and sashes, press the seam allowance open. Use just the tip of the iron to avoid pressing creases in the rest of the tube. A steam stick or chopstick inserted into the tube will raise the area to be pressed. It will then be much easier to press the edge after the tube has been turned through to the right side.

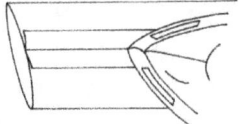

✂ Press **seams** flat before topstitching.

✂ When making **jackets**, both the main and lining seams must be thoroughly pressed *before* the lining is sewn in and closed up, otherwise there's no way to press them.

✂ For **wool and wool blends**, dampen the seam with water before pressing with a steam iron. Allow to dry before moving.

✂ When one edge is **eased** to another, avoid heavy pressing on the eased part just next to the seam, otherwise you'll shrink out all the ease you've just created.

✂ For **leather**, use a piece of cardboard as a pressing cloth to avoid iron marks. Use a dry iron.

✂ For **princess line** tops and jackets, I like to sew and press the princess lines before sewing the shoulder and side seams, so I can concentrate on getting really good seams. Use a tailors ham to press the princess lines into a curve, paying particular attention to the front ones.

✂ For **two piece sleeves**, sew and press the longest seam first (that's the back one), then sew the second seam and press using a sleeve board or seam roll.

✂ When pressing **fabrics with a pile** (such as velvet) avoid flattening or crushing the pile. Place the garment face down onto a needleboard, Velvaboard or a piece of the same fabric. Hold the iron above the seam to steam it, then finger-press flat or press with minimal pressure from the iron. Don't allow the iron to rest on the fabric. To press curved seams, put a Velvaboard or piece of the same fabric over a ham. If the garment has a facing of the (same) pile fabric, press between two pieces of fabric, or a Velvaboard folded in half over the facing. Use steam.

After pressing, while the fabric is still steaming, brush with a clothes brush in the direction of the pile.

Troubleshooting pressing

The seam bruises or imprints through

✂ Try using a pressing cloth.

✂ If this makes no difference, cut two strips of cardboard 2.5cm (1") wide, either patternmaking cardboard or from a cereal box. With the wrong side of fabric up, insert each strip under the seam allowances, then press the seam open with steam. Use a damp pressing cloth (not shown in illustration). Sometimes it helps to dampen the seam as well.

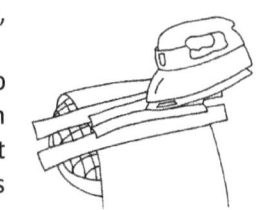

It's a time-consuming method, but it does work. I use it for wool coating. It's helpful to cut some curved strips of cardboard if doing curved or princess line seams.

✂ Another idea is to use a seam stick—a length of wooden dowel cut in half so there's a long flat side. Press the seam open along the dowel, but be careful—you may end up with a shiny line along the length of the seam.

To remove shine caused by pressing

✂ Hold a steam iron just above the seam and allow the steam to penetrate. It helps if you have a "shot of steam" iron to pump extra steam. It also helps to slightly dampen the seam first. A very gentle brush with a clothes brush may also help restore the surface.

✂ Another way to remove seam imprints is to slip the point of the iron under the seam allowance and press away any imprints.

✂ An untried remedy I have heard of is to rub a penny along the surface.

To restore squashed pile

Steaming by holding the iron just over the surface will help restore squashed pile. A light brush with a clothes brush will also help.

Removing holes from unpicking

Here's a tip from the workrooms of Caroline Charles. You'll need some water and a steam iron.

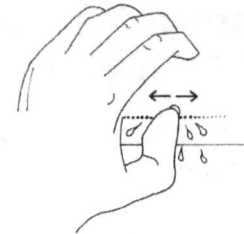

Dip your thumb into the water and rub the line of holes with your thumbnail. Press the fabric with steam until it dries.

The holes won't come out as well if you've pressed with steam first.

Check before using this method that it doesn't watermark the fabric, particularly on silk (see below).

To minimise water damage

Be very careful with moisture if your fabric is liable to watermark or waterspot, that is, leave a tide line where spots of water have landed.

Silk is particularly prone to watermarking. Check before you begin. If it does watermark,

✂ You can usually use a steam iron, provided that your iron doesn't spit water or leak onto the fabric. It may give more control to use a dry iron and a damp press cloth.

✂ Wet an area with a spray bottle, then press. The mist of a spray bottle produces a less definite watermark line—but please check first.

✂ And if you need to remove unpicking holes, use a *very* sparing amount of water *only* where you need it (or mist with a spray bottle—but check first).

Over-pressing: A Warning

Be careful not to over-press! An over pressed, over-steamed garment hangs limply and has no shape and cannot be brought back. Admittedly, this is easier to do with an industrial high-powered steam iron rather than a domestic iron. Synthetic fabrics are more prone to over-pressing than natural fibres.

I've only ever once over-pressed a garment and my workmate said to me: "You've pressed the guts out of it!"

Making pressing tools

Padded pressing tools such as tailors hams, pressing mitts and sleeve rolls aren't expensive to buy, but you may enjoy making your own. They're nothing more than cushions. They last for years and re-covering an old one will give it more years of use.

The following patterns are also available as PDFs at www.thedressmakerscompanion.com if you prefer to print one out rather than trace from the book. Feel free to customize these to suit yourself—you may like to have them larger, smaller or a different shape.

Requirements

✂ Cotton drill and wool fabric. All of these pressing tools have wool on one side (for pressing wool fabrics) and cotton drill on the other (for pressing everything else).

✂ Calico fabric if you plan to stuff with sawdust. Back the cotton drill and wool with a layer of calico and treat it as one unit, to make it stronger.

✂ Stuffing. The pressing mitt is stuffed with wool. Wool batting used for felt making is ideal. The seam roll can be stuffed with wool or sawdust. My own seam roll is stuffed firmly with wool, but sawdust will give a firmer, harder surface. Tailors hams are traditionally stuffed with sawdust, although you could use fine birdseed. Pet shops are a useful place to buy sawdust.

To stuff with sawdust, leave a gap at the *top* to stuff into. Stand the tailors ham in a bowl and fill using a spoon and funnel. Push the sawdust down firmly as you go. Top up with sawdust as you sew the gap shut by hand.

Pressing mitt

The pattern is on page 272. Mirror the pattern along the broken line to make a complete pattern piece.

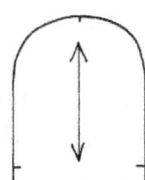

1. Cut one of wool and two of cotton drill.

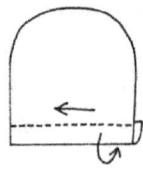

2. Hem one of the cotton drill pieces, using the notches as a guide for turning up the hem.

3. Lay the hemmed cotton piece onto the second cotton piece, both with the right side facing up. Treat as one unit. This makes the pocket.

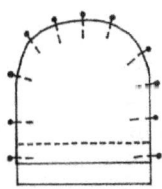

4. Lay the cotton and wool pieces together with the right sides together and sew around the outside leaving a gap to turn through.

5. Turn through, stuff with wool and hand sew the gap shut.

Seam roll

The pattern pieces are on pages 273 and 274.
Are you going to have squared or rounded ends or one of each?
Join the paper patterns together to have one of each

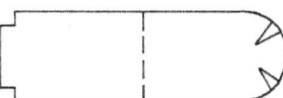

OR

Place the pattern on the fold of the fabric to make both ends the same.

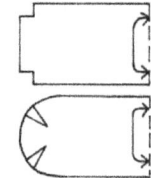

1. Cut one of wool and one of cotton drill.
If you're stuffing with sawdust, also cut two of calico. Back the cotton drill and wool with a layer of calico and treat it as one unit.

2. For a **rounded end,** sew the darts first.
Press the wool darts in one direction and the cotton drill darts in the opposite. Place the right sides together and sew around the edges leaving a gap to turn through.

For a **squared end**, sew the squared part last. Place the right sides together and sew the sides and ends, leaving a gap at one end to turn through.

Press the seams open and stitch across each corner to create 3-dimensional ends.

3. Turn through to the right side and stuff with wool or sawdust.

Tailors ham

The pattern is on page 275. Join the two pieces together along the broken line to make one pattern piece.

1. Cut one of wool, one of cotton drill and two of calico.

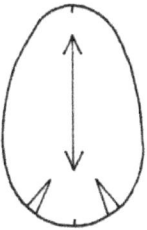

2. Match a calico piece to each wool and cotton drill piece and treat as one layer.

3. Make the darts. Press the wool darts in one direction and the cotton drill darts in the opposite.

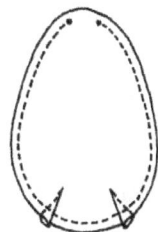

4. Place the right sides together and sew around the edges, leaving a gap at the top to turn through. You may like to sew a double row of stitching for strength.

5. Turn through and stuff very firmly with sawdust as described on page 270.

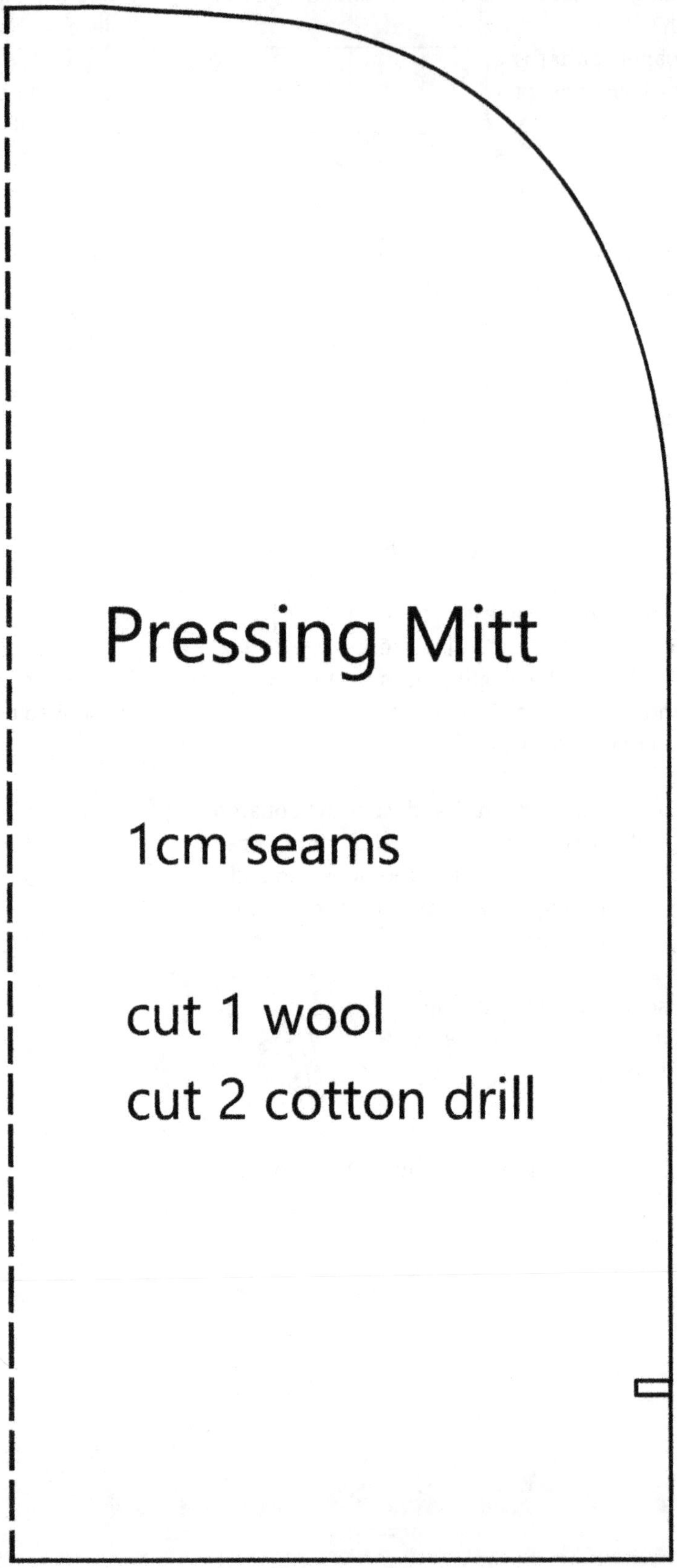

Pressing Mitt

1cm seams

cut 1 wool
cut 2 cotton drill

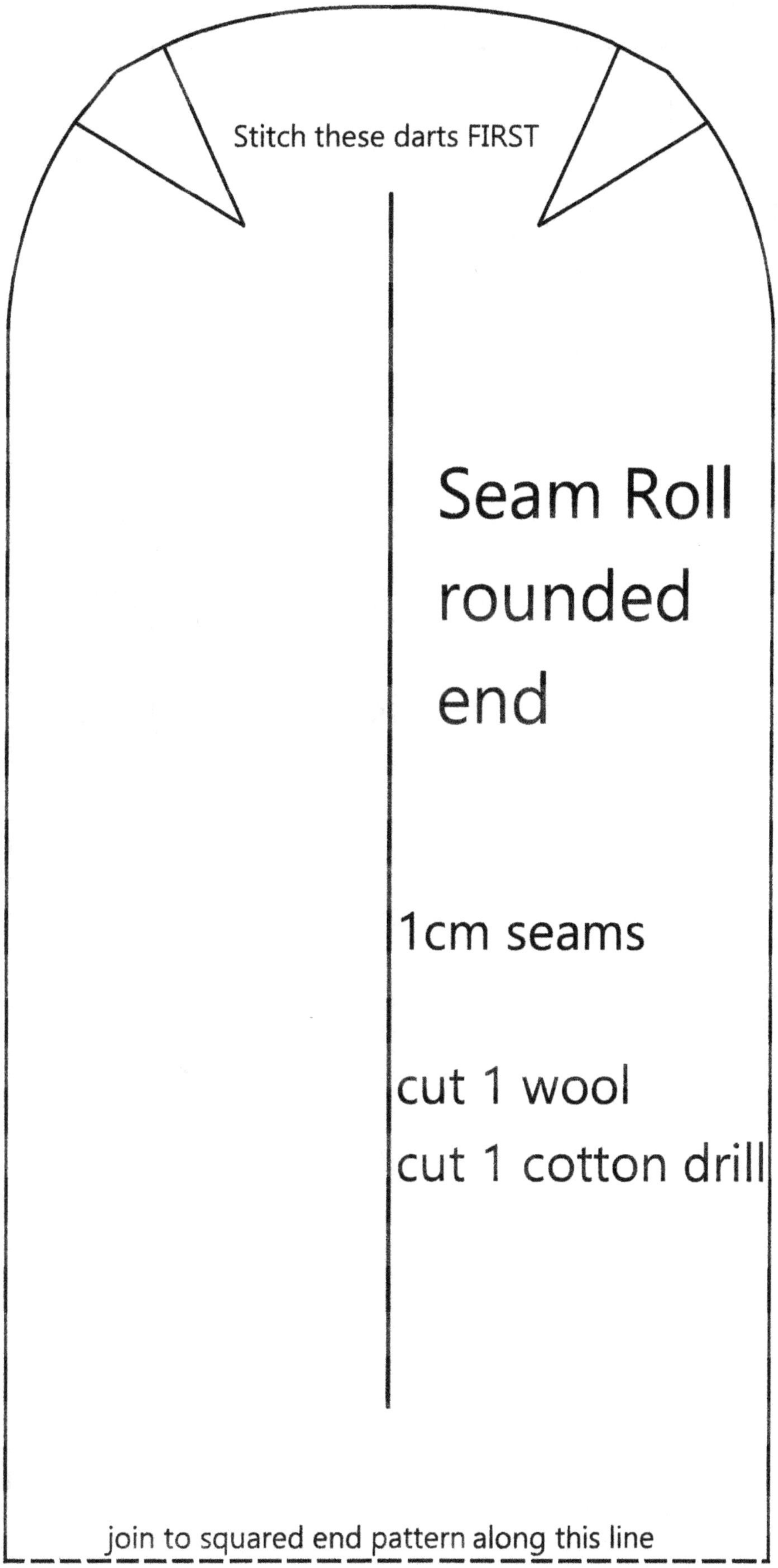

Stitch these darts FIRST

Seam Roll rounded end

1cm seams

cut 1 wool
cut 1 cotton drill

join to squared end pattern along this line

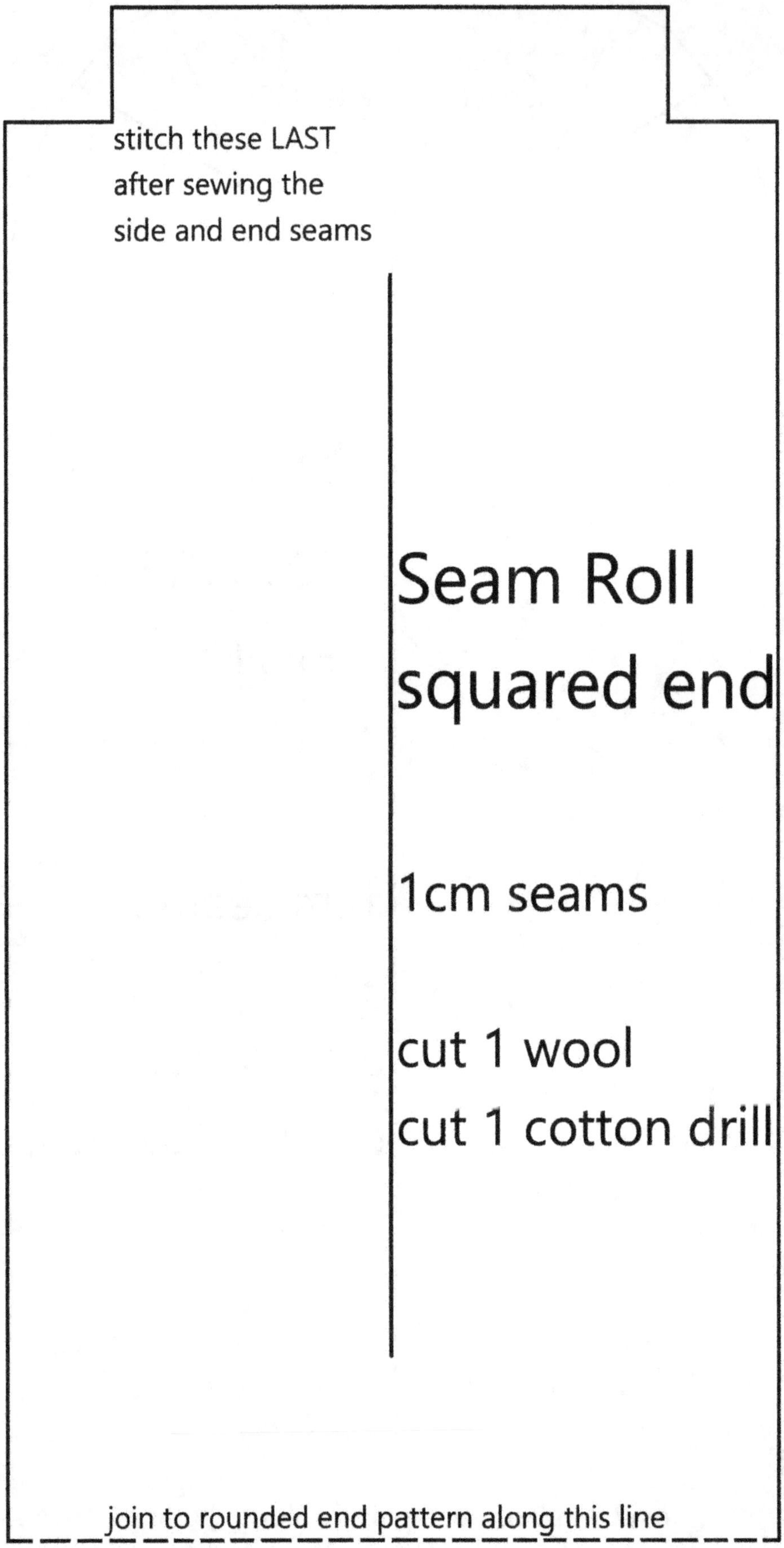

stitch these LAST
after sewing the
side and end seams

Seam Roll
squared end

1cm seams

cut 1 wool
cut 1 cotton drill

join to rounded end pattern along this line

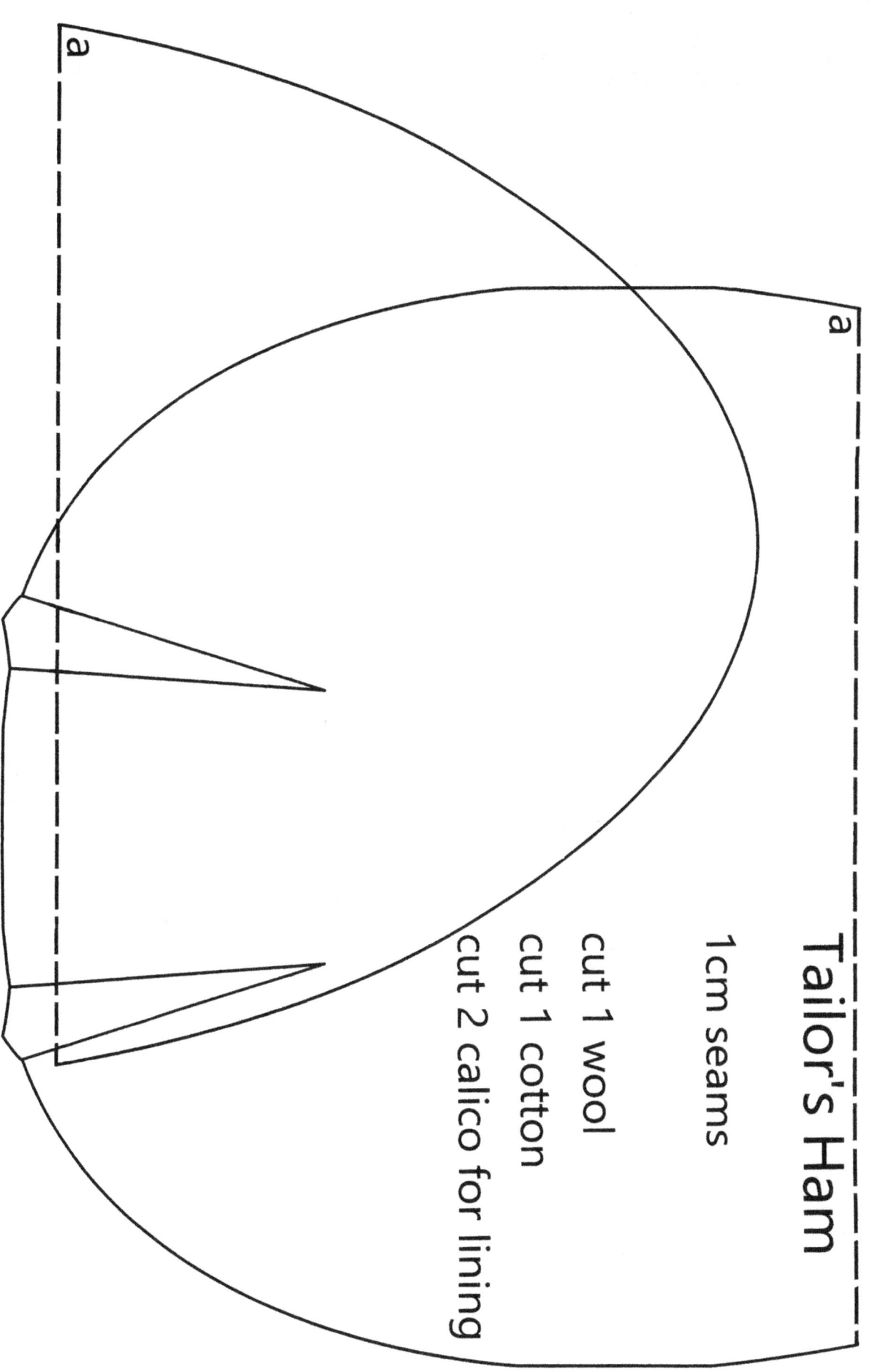

Rouleau

Introduction/uses 276	Finishing two cord ends........................... 280
Fabric for rouleau 276	Frog loops 280
Making rouleau 276	a fancier frog 281
Rouleau with stretch fabrics 277	Five petal flower ornament..................... 281
Leather "rouleau".................................... 278	Figure 8 ornament 281
Rouleau filled with cord 278	Woven ornament..................................... 281
Chinese ball buttons and loops 278	Circular ornament 282
a simple ball button 279	Three-circle ornament............................. 282
another ball button (and knot ornament) 279	Celtic ornament.. 283
Finishing the cord ends........................... 280	Regency ornament................................... 283

A rouleau is a narrow tube sewn of fabric, using a strip of fabric cut on the true bias.

Rouleau are used to make:

✂ Loops for button and loop closures

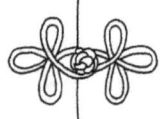

✂ Frog closures, also called frogs or Chinese ball buttons and loops

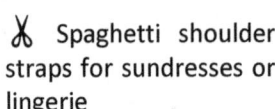

✂ Ties or drawcords

✂ Spaghetti shoulder straps for sundresses or lingerie

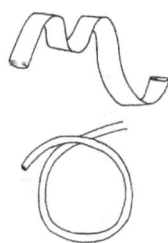

Rouleau can be made flat like ribbon or fettucine (for shoulder straps), or round, tight and tubular (for button loops and frogs). Round rouleau can be filled with a cord or its own seam allowance.

Fabric for rouleau

Smooth, fine fabrics work best for making rouleau. Soft floppy satin is excellent because the slippery surface makes turning the tubes through easy. Cotton voile, cheesecloth and organza are all suitable too. You could also use ready-made bias binding.

Making rouleau

Always make a test to see how the fabric performs when it's made into rouleau. You'll have to experiment to achieve the rouleau you want.

To cut rouleau

1. Cut some bias strips about 3cm-5cm (1¼"-2") wide (see pages 20-21 for how). A filled rouleau will need a wider strip than a flat one, but you can trim off any excess as needed. Cut the strips 5cm (2") wide for filled rouleau and at least 3cm (1¼") otherwise.

✂ If you're cutting out just a few bias strips at the same time as a garment, position the strips on the fabric *first* then place the garment pieces.

✂ If you're cutting *only* bias strips on their own, the amount of fabric required can be deceptive—the more strips you cut, the lower becomes the average amount of fabric per strip, because there are two triangular waste sections at both ends.

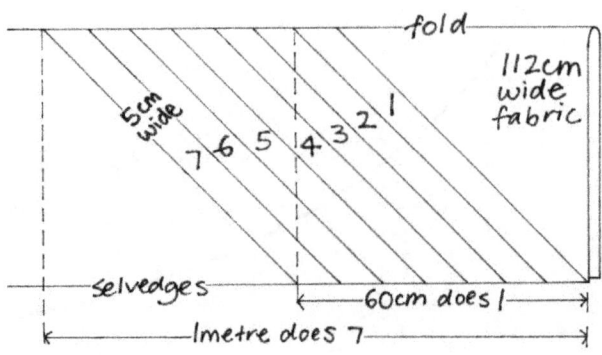

On a one metre (39½") length of 112cm (45") wide fabric, it's possible to cut seven (paired) strips 5cm (2") wide (the fabric is cut doubled, as illustrated above—slit the top fold). 60cm is needed for just one (paired) strip yet 80cm yields four—see what I mean about the average?

Each strip cut 75cm long will grow to about 85cm when sewn into a rouleau (the bias will stretch). You *could* cut the fabric in a single layer and achieve 1.5m long strips, but these become too long to easily work with and you'll need more fabric to accommodate the length of the strips.

✂ I always cut extra (shorter) strips from the waste triangles at the ends to practise on before using my long strips. I also cut a couple more full-length strips as spares.

✂ Ensure the strips are cut at *exactly* 45 degrees to the selvedge (that is, on the true bias). If a bias strip isn't cut on the true bias, the seam will twist around and around the rouleau.

✂ Rouleau made from **stretch fabrics** do not need to be cut on the bias, unless the fabric is striped and you want the effect. Cut the strips across the stretchiest part of the fabric.

To sew rouleau

1. Fold the bias strip in half longways with the right side inside. Place the fold of the strip on the right hand side and the raw edges on the left hand side and stitch about 3mm-6mm (⅛"-¼") from the fold.

A test rouleau will show you exactly where you need to stitch. Watch carefully when you sew and line up the folded edge with some part of your sewing machine, for example the edge of the presser foot. Millimetres count here, so if the finished practise rouleau isn't filled out enough, stitch another 1mm in (= making the tube 2mm smaller) and see what it looks like.

The fabric will gently stretch as you sew it—don't pull it tight but let it pull a little as it feeds through. The important thing is to be consistent and use the same tension on all the rouleau. Try to sew them all in one sitting if possible.

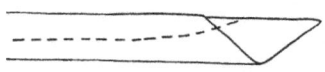

To make turning the rouleau through easier, splay the stitching out at the end. It makes it easier to get the loop turner started. You can also trim off excess fabric at the end to make it finer.

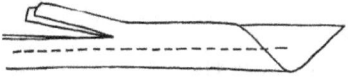

For flat rouleau, trim the seam allowance back to 3mm (⅛"). Once again, a test will show you how much you need to trim back, if at all.

2. Turn the tube through to the right side using a loop turner.

To use a loop turner, slide it through the tube and push the moveable arm of the turner 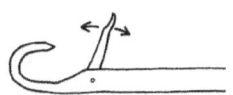 through the fabric when you reach the end. You're actually making a little hole in the fabric.

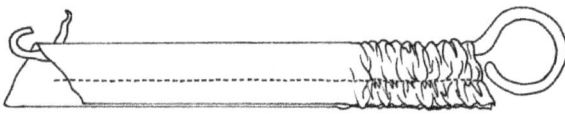

Slowly pull the tube through to the right side, maintaining tension on the hook as you do.

Be *extremely* careful not to lose the fabric off the end of the loop turner. If this happens you'll probably have to kiss it goodbye and start again (although you might be able to push the loop turner back in and hook the end of it, or if you've only just started to pull it through, you could cut off the turned part and still use the rest).

Filled rouleau shouldn't be *too* easy to turn through to the right side; there should be a firmness as you slide it through the loop turner. If it turns through too easily, you can tell the rouleau won't be tightly filled enough.

The bias allows the fabric to stretch slightly as you pull it through.

If you don't have a loop turner, leave long threads at the end of the seam, knot them onto a blunt darning needle, then drop it down the tube to turn it inside out.

Rouleau with stretch fabrics

Rouleau can also be made on your overlocker if you're sewing stretch fabrics, for example straps for a stretch camisole. Use all four threads on the overlocker and check the stitching doesn't pop undone when stretched.

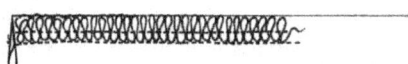

If you don't have an overlocker, try using a small zig zag stitch to sew stretch knits. As with overlocking, stretch the stitching to make sure it doesn't pop.

Leather "rouleau"

Cut a 2.5cm (1") wide strip of leather the desired length. Fold it in half longways, right side facing out, and edgestitch next to the *fold line*. Trim close to the stitched line.

Rouleau filled with cord

1. Cut the cord twice as long as the bias strip.

2. Fold the fabric over half of the length of the cord, right sides together.
Using a zipper foot, stitch across the end of the bias strip that's at the centre of the cord, then down the long edge, enclosing the cord.
Trim the seam allowances back to 3mm (⅛").

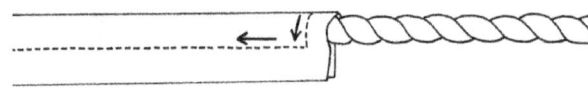

3. Turn the right way by drawing the fabric over the cord, which will automatically fill the tube. Trim off the excess cord.

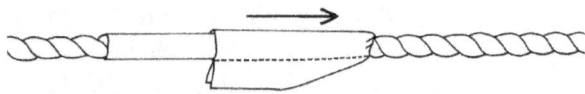

Chinese ball buttons and loops

Also known as frog closures, frogs, or just rouleau buttons and loops. You can make these with cord, tubular braid or your own rouleau.
If you use rouleau, it needs to be 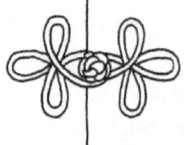 round, tight and filled. If the tube turns through too easily, it's probably too wide or doesn't have enough filling. It should turn through firmly.
Keep the size of the cord proportionate to the button size; a fatter rouleau will make a bigger button and a bigger loop. If the rouleau is too thin, try using a double strand.

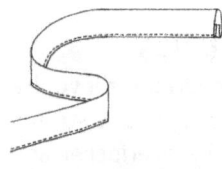 Sometimes Chinese ball buttons and frog closures are made from **a flat rouleau**. It yields a totally legitimate yet different looking type of button and frog. Flat rouleau can be made from ready-made bias binding. Either invisibly hand sew the edges together or machine edgestitch them *flat* on the *outside* as shown. If you own a binding attachment for your sewing machine it's very quick to make—just run it through the binder.

✂ Frog closures fall into two types: looped and knotted. The knotted type require little if any sewing to keep everything in place, while the looped type are stitched at the back every time the cord crosses over itself.

✂ Frog closures aren't hard to make but can be fiddly and do require practise to make a matching set.
After you've made a few different types, try making up your own. Look at books on knot work or Celtic/Viking knot designs for inspiration.

Frogs are used in pairs: one side has the button loop and the other side has the button. Ideally they should be a mirror image.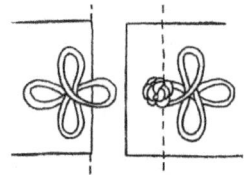

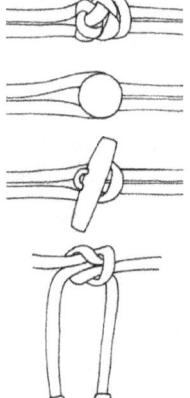 The button is usually a ball button made from the same cord, but it could also be a regular button (either a round button with a shank or a flat button with holes depending on the look you're after) or a toggle. You may be able to thread the rouleau through the toggle holes before you start if the holes are large enough and the rouleau fine enough. Sometimes the button or toggle needs to be in place before the frog closure is made and other times it can be made last.

You can also simply leave ends to tie together. The ends of the ties can be knotted or finished in a fancy way (see page 280 for finishing the ends of the cords).

✂ Frog loops can also be fashioned from cord for double breasted jackets with a military look.

✂ Keep the seam in the rouleau facing down at all times, so only the smooth unseamed side will be visible on the finished frog.

✂ Before you begin, be prepared with an already threaded and knotted needle stuck in your pincushion. Use a double strand of a perfectly matching colour thread. Also have handy a thimble for pushing the needle through and a small pair of pliers to pull the needle through if required.

A simple ball button

1. Loop the cord over once.

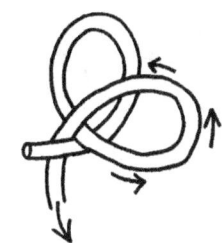

2. Loop the cord over the first loop. Keep the seam in the rouleau facing down.

3. Loop the cord a third time, weaving through the previous two loops. Make sure you don't twist the cord.

4. Ease the loop to a tight ball shape. Leave the ends long in order to make the rest of the frog.

Ball buttons can be used on their own without loops or frogs—just with regular button holes. Cut the ends 6mm (¼") from the button and sew them neatly down underneath. Keep this part underneath when you sew the button to the garment. Create a thread shank as you sew the button on.

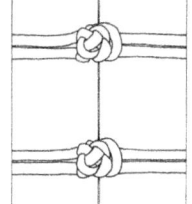

The ends of ball buttons and loops can be inserted into vertical seams down the front of the garment, if you plan ahead.

Alternatively, the ends can be simply tucked under and stitched into position.

Another ball button (and knot ornament)

This forms a slightly bigger knot when drawn up than the simple ball button described above. The two ends of the rouleau will emerge together from the button. This button doesn't take much rouleau, but you'll need extra length to make it to form all the loops.

Rouleau 279

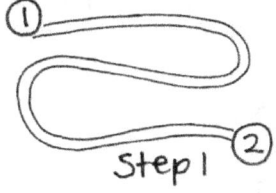

Keep the seam in the rouleau facing down as you loop the loops.

Draw up the ball button by cupping the knot over the end of your finger and pulling the loops to tighten.

For a larger button, hold two rouleau together.

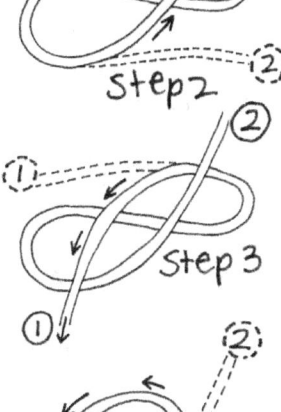

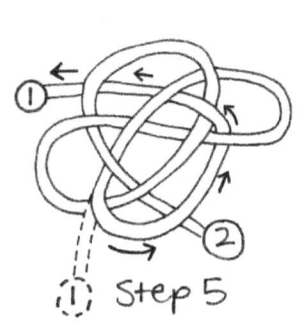

Instead of drawing the loops up into a button, they can be arranged flat to form a **Chinese Knot ornament**. It looks very effective when made with two strands of rouleau.

Don't be tempted to tack the two strands together beforehand to make it easier to form the shape—you'll need to be able to adjust each rouleau around the curves.

Take a long 85cm (33½") rouleau and fold it in half. You'll begin making the design from this fold which will become the button loop (Strand 2 in the ball button illustration). When you ease up all the loops at the end to form the ornament, adjust the loop (Strand 2) to be the required length.

When you're making the button side of the frog, make the button first. The Chinese Knot ornament will hold together without any stitching but the ends (Strand 1) will need to be cut and stitched underneath to hide them.

Finishing the cord ends

If you're closing the frogs with ties, you can neatly finish off the ends of the dangling ties. The method is similar to whipping the ends of rope to stop them fraying. Have ready a needle threaded with double thread in a perfectly matching colour, end knotted.

Form a loop of rouleau (Step 1, below), then begin winding at the top of the loop (Steps 2 and 3). When you've wound the desired length, slip the end of the rouleau through the remaining loop at the bottom (Step 4). Pull the opposite end firmly until you can't see the loop anymore (Step 5). Take the needle and thread and secure the rouleau in the loop with invisible stitches. Don't cut the thread yet. Cut off the excess rouleau close to the loop and push the cut edges into the tube of wound rouleau. Finish with a few stitches in the end to secure.

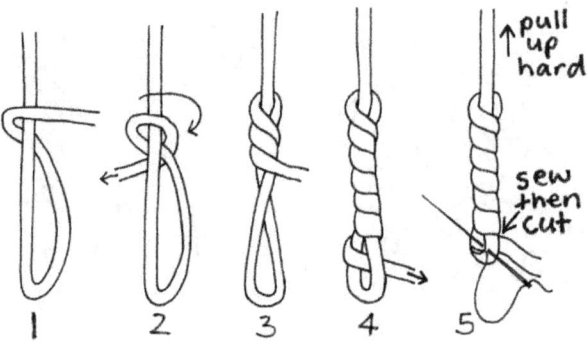

Finishing the cord ends—two ends

Use this if you've made the ornament by holding two rouleau together. This doesn't take much cord when finished, but you'll need a long piece for all the looping. Have ready a needle threaded with double thread in a perfectly matching colour, end knotted.

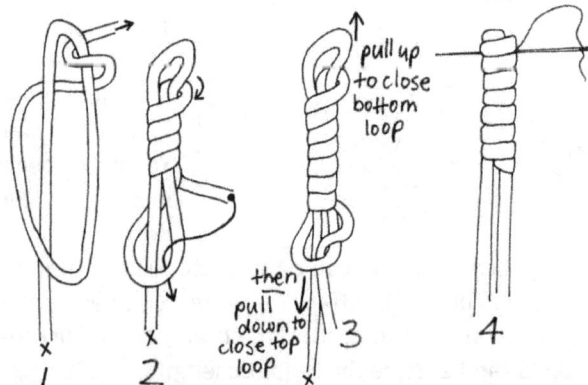

Loop the cord as shown in Step 1. Begin winding very firmly to the required length, finishing by slipping the working end through the bottom loop (Step 2). Pull one side of the top loop, closing up the bottom loop, then pull down the long end at the bottom to close up the top loop (Step 3).

Take the needle and thread and invisibly stab stitch through the top to hold the coil in place, otherwise it will undo from the top.

Frog loops

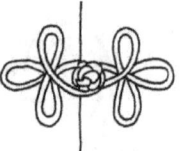

Funnily, the simple loop type of frog closure seems to be the hardest to make. Forming perfectly shaped freehand loops that all match each other isn't that easy. Have ready a needle threaded with double thread in a perfectly matching colour, end knotted.

Loop the cord as illustrated, keeping the seam in the rouleau facing *down* all the time. As you form each loop, secure it in place at the back with a few stitches. You may need to wear a thimble and use a small pair of pliers to pull the needle through. When the frog is finished, trim the ends and sew them in place.

Button side:

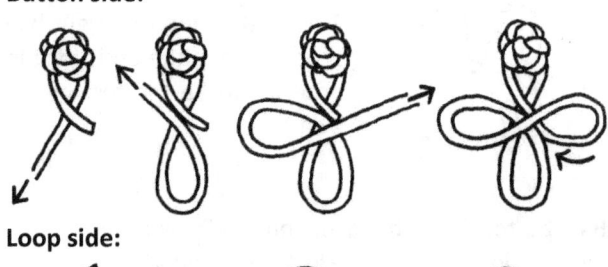

Loop side:

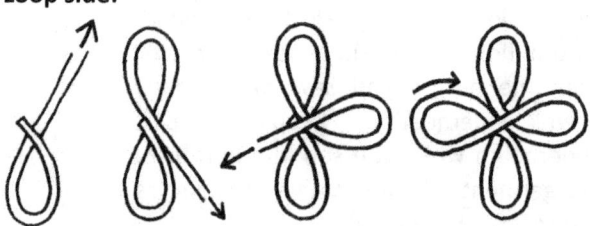

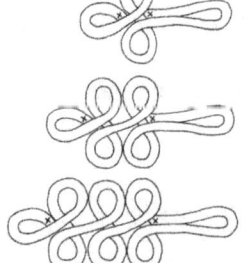

Ensure the button and loop sides mirror each other when in position.

You can increase the number of loops to make a bigger ornament. Note that odd numbers of loops look better than even numbers.

The loops can be made alternating from top to bottom (as above), or all the top loops can be made then all the bottom loops (shown at left).

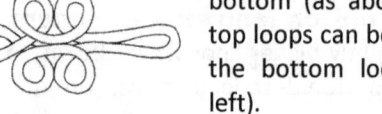

A fancier frog

A fancier frog can be made just by varying some of the loops. Have ready a needle threaded with double thread in a perfectly matching colour, end knotted.
Loop the rouleau around as illustrated, starting and finishing where indicated. When all the loops are made, join them together at the sides to hold the piece together.

Five petal flower ornament

Have ready a needle threaded with double thread in a perfectly matching colour, end knotted. Make a ball button for the centre, then loop the petals one at a time underneath and stitch in place. Make another longer loop for the button closure. When all the petals are sewn, stab the needle through all layers in several places to secure together.

You could also use a regular shank or hole button for the centre—in this case sew the button on last.
Try it with doubled rouleau for the petals.

Figure eight ornament

This is made by winding the cord like a figure 8. It's fairly easy but it looks much more complicated to make than it is. Have ready a needle threaded with double thread in a perfectly matching colour, end knotted. Make the figure eight totally (as illustrated) then hold it carefully to sew together.
Illustrated here are two similar methods of making a figure eight—they vary at the beginning and ending points.
Four passes around the figure eight can look better than the three illustrated, but it depends on the width of the cord and how big you want the closure to be. To accommodate four passes around, make the initial loop a little bigger.

Figure eight method 1

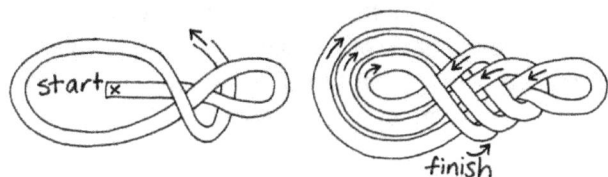

Figure eight method 2

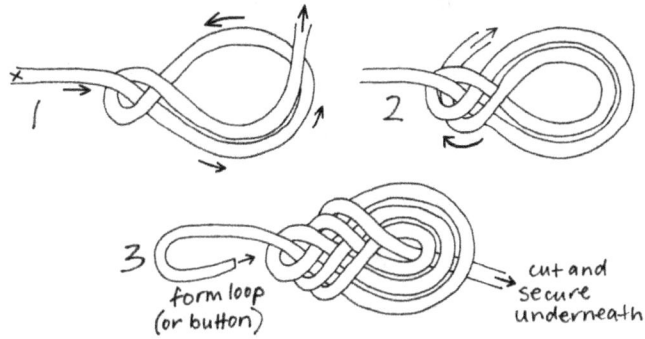

Woven ornament

This looks GREAT using a chunky cord or two strands of rouleau held together. If you're using two strands, one 85cm (33½") rouleau folded in half won't be long enough (inconveniently)—you'll need two separate strands. Make the ball button first, then lay the cord on the table to begin weaving, following the diagram. Towards the end you'll be able to pick it up and finish weaving in your hands. Work the cords tighter until all the gaps are closed up. It won't need any stitching to hold it together, but sew the ends underneath at the finish.

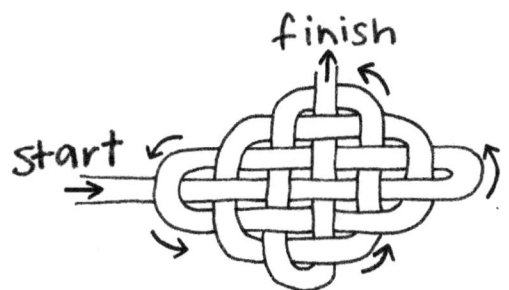

Weave the opposite side in a clockwise direction for mirrored closures:

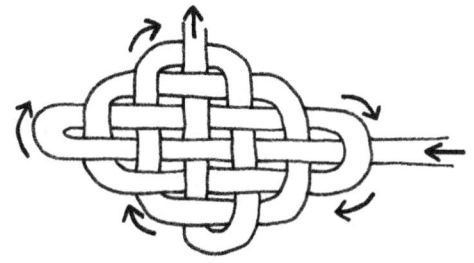

Circular ornament

1. Make a ball button and cut both ends leaving several centimetres of rouleau. Have ready a needle threaded with double thread in a perfectly matching colour, end knotted. You'll need a thimble, too.

2. Take another length of rouleau and begin winding it around the held-together rouleau of the ball button. Tuck the end in as you begin to wind so it's on the inside. Hold the rounds flat between your finger and thumb as you wind, and keep the rouleau seam underneath. You *could* stitch the rounds in place as you make them, but I think it's easier to sew them all together at the end.

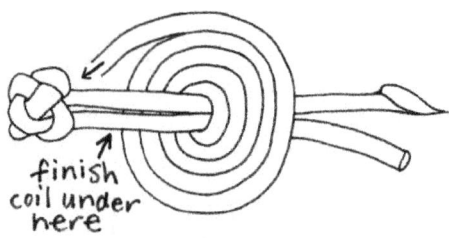

3. When the circle is the desired size, turn it over and stitch across the rounds from the middle to the outside to secure the circles. The stitching will form sort of a star shape. Don't actually catch the ball button rouleau yet—you might want to adjust its position when you attach it to the garment. Cut the end of the rouleau and tuck it behind, where it will be covered by the ball button rouleau, and sew it in place.

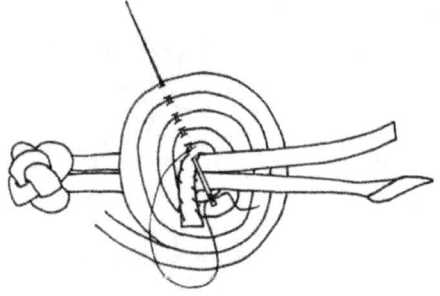

For the opposite side, simply make a loop of rouleau instead of a ball button.

Three-circle ornament

1. Have ready a needle threaded with double thread in a perfectly matching colour, end knotted. You'll need a thimble, too. You'll need a rouleau measuring at least 1 metre (39½")—85cm (33½") won't be quite long enough. Fold the rouleau in half.

2. Beginning at the fold, coil a circle holding the two ends together, keeping the seam in the rouleau facing down.

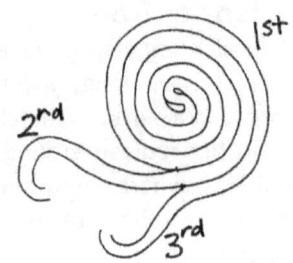

3. When it's the desired circumference (say, about 2.5cm-3cm (1"-1¼") in diameter), carefully turn it over and secure all the rounds at the back. Stitch across the circle taking a small stitch in every round. It's helpful to use a thimble and/or small pliers to pull the needle through. Secure strongly at the end of the circle and cut the thread (it isn't helpful to leave the needle dangling; it's easier to sew each circle separately).

4. Separate the two rouleau and begin the second circle. When it looks the same as the first, secure it at the back with stitches as before. You can estimate the length of cord required by curling it into a circle and checking the size first.

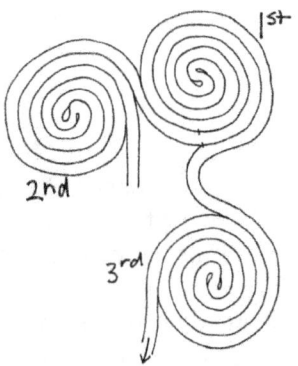

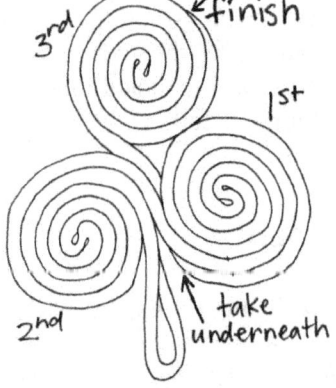

5. For the third circle, estimate and coil it as for the other two. Before attaching it to the others, slip it underneath between the first and second circles and bring it out on the other side. Attach all three circles together.

Make the ball button or loop last, using the end from the second circle.

You could also combine this with the design of the single circle ornament and bring the ball button out from the centre, but you'll need to do this at the start.

Celtic ornament

1. Begin forming this ornament at the top loop, rather than the button and loop end (the ball button or loop is made last).

2. Lay the cord flat on the table on top of the diagram and follow the drawing. Lay the cord down on the black shaded area first then loop the other end around it. Note that you'll be looping the cord around loops you haven't made yet, so pay close attention to the under-over sequence.

For a mirrored pair of ornaments, make one using each illustration:

3. Draw up the cord to close the gaps. No stitching is needed to hold this part together.

4. Form the two coils, stitching them in place.

Regency ornament

Here's a fashion detail from a dress circa 1821 at the Albany Institute of History and Art, NY, USA.

1. Start at the top and cross the cords over each other.

2. Bring the cords around to form side loops, weaving the ends through the loops.

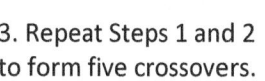

3. Repeat Steps 1 and 2 to form five crossovers.

Seams

Introduction 284
Forming a plain seam 101 284
    pins 284
    sewing 285
    sew with which side on top? 285
Seam allowance 285
Open and closed seam allowaces 286
Neatening seams 286
    ways of neatening seams 287
Some sewing techniques 288
    sewing corners 288
    sewing pointy corners 288
    pivoting inward corners 288
    sewing curves 289
    sewing opposite curves 289
    trimming and grading 289
    clipping and notching 289
    understitching 290
    trimming and turning corners 290
    matching seam junctions 290
    easing 291
    stitching-in-the-ditch 291
    taut sewing 291
    sewing down a folded edge 292
    tacking 292
    stay stitching and
    stabilizing seams 292
Two techniques for faster sewing 293
    sewing without pins 293
    chain piecing 293
Some other types of seams 293
    french seam 293
    mock french seam 294
    flat felled seam 294
    lapped seam 296
    butted seam 296
    slot seam 296
Troubleshooting seams 297
Changing the seam after a fitting 298
How to unpick 298
    straight stitching 298
    overlocking 299
    chainstitching 299
    factory twinneedling 299
    to remove holes afterwards 299

The importance of seam allowances was shown to me early on in life, as I watched my younger brother make some blue felt trousers for his teddy. He placed teddy on the felt and drew around the bear's legs. He cut out the trousers and carefully sewed up the sides with running stitch. When they were finished, they were far too small for teddy, because he had forgotten to add seam allowances.

A **seam** is made when two or more pieces of fabric are joined together. A seam is the basic structural element of a garment.

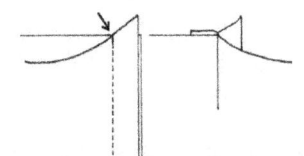

The **seam allowance** is the distance a seam is sewn from the raw edge. Naturally, the two edges being seamed together must have the *same* seam allowance, so that the raw edges can be matched for an accurate seam.

At the top, match the *stitching line*, not the cut edge.

If the *stitching lines* aren't matched properly you'll end up with a step at the ends of the seam.

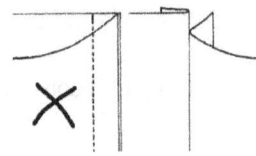

Forming a plain seam 101

A plain seam is the type you'll make most of the time. Place together the right sides of the fabric, matching the raw edges.

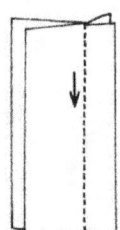

Pins

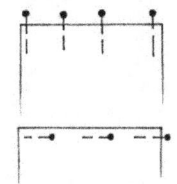

You may pin the seam to hold it. Pins can be inserted perpendicular to the edge or parallel to the edge. Pins inserted perpendicularly can be sewn over if you're careful.

If you place parallel pins in *this* direction, they won't be easy to pull out when you sew, because the heads are facing the wrong way.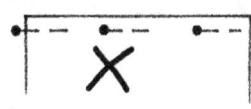

To pin a seam, place a pin at each end of the seam and at any matched notches or seam junctions. Pin the centre between the pins.

Pin the centres of the centres and so on.

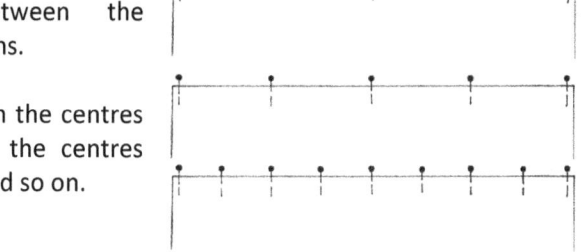

In this way you can evenly distribute any fullness, ease or stretched sections so it matches the other side.

Sewing

Prepare your machine:
- ✂ Have the machine set at the correct tension
- ✂ Set the stitch length to 2.5
- ✂ Install a correct and sharp needle

Place the beginning of the seam under the machine foot with the bulk of the garment to the left.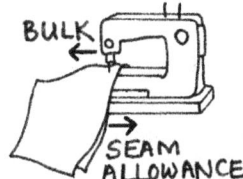

Keep the seam straight by following the seam guidelines on the needle plate, to the right of the needle. The guidelines indicate the amount of seam allowance in millimetres or eighths of an inch. You can also use a magnetic seam guide, sticky tape or a screw-in quilters bar. For narrow 6mm (¼") seams you can use the edge of the presser foot if it's the correct width.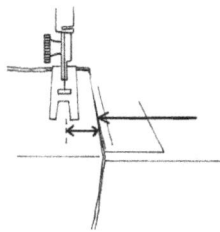

Watch others and experiment yourself for the best position to place your hands. I sew with my right hand in front of the presser foot and my left hand to the side.

 Seams need **backstitching** at each end to stop them coming undone—about 1cm (⅜") of backstitching is enough. I like to begin seams 1cm *in* from the beginning, backstitching first, then sewing forward to sew the seam.

There needs to be enough fabric under the presser foot for the machine to start off, otherwise it will jam. If, by any chance, your machine won't stitch backwards (very old machines didn't) then stitch forwards for 1cm (⅜"), lift the needle and presser foot and go back to the beginning and sew the seam. In this way you'll have double stitching at the beginning. Do the same when you get to the end.

After sewing the seam, cut the threads close to the edge. A good habit is to cut all the threads immediately after sewing each seam. They're going to have to be cut off at some stage, so do it now and keep your work neat.

Sew with which side on top?

✂ Sew with the *most stable* side on top, for example the side with the stay tape, interfacing or stay-stitching.

✂ Sew with the side *to be eased* on the bottom next to the feed dogs on your machine, which will help feed the bottom layer through. The exception is when you've sewn an ease stitch—in that case, sew with the ease stitching on top. See page 291 for more on ease.

Seam allowance

A seam allowance can be as small as 6mm (¼") or as large as 2.5cm (1"). I've seen 3mm (⅛") seams (on doll's clothes) and 5cm (2") seams (for costumes).

Commercial paper sewing patterns allow 1.5cm (⅝") for every seam. Kwik Sew patterns for stretch knits allow 6mm (¼") seams so the garment can be overlocked together without trimming off excess seam allowance. Burda magazine patterns require you to add your own seam allowance. The amount of seam allowance is written on the instruction sheet and sometimes on the pattern pieces as well, so check to confirm.

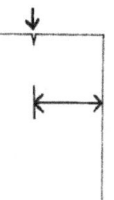 **Clothing factories** decide their own seam allowances and their patterns are consistent so every machinist knows how much seam allowance to take. Sometimes the amount of seam allowance is indicated by a tiny snip at the beginning of the seam.

My own personal preference is for 1cm (⅜") or 1.5cm (⅝") seam allowances and 6mm (¼") for any seams that are bagged out or enclosed, for example pocket flaps, welts, lined patch pockets, edges of collars and front edges. It saves trimming the seam allowance back after sewing and it makes it easier to negotiate small curved edges accurately. A 6mm (¼") machine foot can be used as a guide when sewing these.

Large seam allowances of 1.5cm or 2cm (⅝" or ¾") are required for thick fabrics to give a more substantial seam that stays flatter after pressing. Sometimes side seams are made 2cm (¾") or even 2.5cm (1") to allow for adjustments at fittings, or for weight change later. Costumes can have very big side seam allowances, up to 5cm (2"), for later alterations. Larger seam allowances are also required if you're having very wide topstitching.

Linings are cut with the same seam allowances as the main fabric, but often slightly less is taken when sewing, for example if the seam is 1.2cm (½"), the lining is sewn with 1cm (⅜"). It's OK if the lining is a little bigger than the garment, but not if it's smaller.

It's ***very important*** to take consistent, correct seam allowances so the garment will end up the right size. For example, if you were making a skirt with eight panels and took 2mm bigger seam allowances, that would be 4mm per seam. 4mm times eight panels equals 3.2cm, therefore making the skirt more than half a size too small.

Open and closed seam allowances

After sewing, the seam allowance can be pressed closed (to one side), or open.

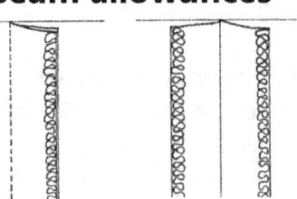

Open seams look smoother from the right side and are flatter and more flexible because there's only two layers of fabric.
Closed seams look neater on the inside, particularly on fine fabrics, because all the raw edges are held together. The seam allowances tend not to flip around as much after washing. Closed seams can show as a ridge on the right side, because there are three thicknesses of fabric on one side of the seam and only one on the other. A closed seam is called for if the seam will be topstitched on one side.

✂ If seams are pressed to one side, which way should you press them? Generally, towards the *back* of the garment (for side seams), or *up* (for waist seams), or towards the *centre front or centre back* (for princess line seams). For shoulder seams, I favour pressing towards the back unless I'm topstitching. Other people prefer the front because the seam is less visible. The important thing is to be consistent—don't press the seams on the left of the garment one way and the seams on the right the other.

✂ A garment doesn't have to have all closed seams or all open seams. For example, when I sew trousers, I like to make the outside leg seam an open seam and the inside leg a closed seam. I tend to make all shoulder seams closed, unless the fabric is very thick. On blouses with side splits at the hem, I make part of the seam open to accommodate the splits, then blend back to a closed seam higher up.
Examples of when to use open seams:
✂ Thick fabrics
✂ Zips
✂ Splits
✂ Fully lined jackets
Examples of when to use closed seams:
✂ Armholes
✂ Sheer, fine and transparent fabrics
✂ Seams topstitched on one side
✂ Gathered or pleated fabric
✂ Linings

Neatening seams

The edges of the seam allowance are neatened primarily to stop the fabric from fraying. Sometimes it's referred to as a "seam finish". Neatening can serve other purposes too. It can improve the inside appearance of unlined jackets, coats and capes. It can cover the raw edges of rough or hairy fabrics so they're comfortable next to the skin and it can make the seam allowances on transparent fabrics less noticeable on the right side. Seams and seam finishes should be flat and inconspicuous on the right side of the garment, unless they're decorative.
Sometimes a seam is pressed *before* neatening in case the overlocking (or other seam finish) imprints through to the right side.

Open seams are neatened each side. The edges can be neatened before or after sewing the seam.
If you're overlocking the edges *before* sewing the seam, you must not trim any fabric off with the overlocker, otherwise you won't know where your stitching line is. If the fabric is very thick and you've already sewn the seam, your overlocker might not be able to get past the thick ridge of fabric next to the stitching line, unless the seam allowance is at least 2cm (¾"). Check before seaming.

Closed seams are neatened together, through both layers of the fabric.

Ways of neatening seams
(and how to decide which one to use)

Overlocking has superseded most of these types of seam finishes, but different methods are useful to know if you don't have an overlocker or want to try something different.

None. If the fabric doesn't fray and looks fine as it is, you can just leave it. Fully lined garments require no neatening unless the fabric frays a lot, because all the seam allowances are enclosed in the lining (why add extra bulk to the seam allowance by neatening it with stitching?). For open or closed seams.

Overlocking. Overlocking (or serging) is fast, neat and durable. If you have an overlocker you can use it for almost everything. I highly recommend spending some time getting to know your machine. For open or closed seams.

Zig zag on sewing machine. Set the zig zag to a wide width and medium length and let one edge of the zig zag sit along the raw edge of the seam allowance. If the fabric is very fine and frays easily, the raw edge can be turned under before zig zagging. I used zig zag before I had an overlocker. It's reasonably durable and quick to do. Note that you may need to buy an extra reel of thread to make the garment. For open or closed seams.

Overlocking stitch on sewing machine. Some newer machines have an overlocker facsimile stitch. It's usually a little slow, but sits flatter than zig zag stitch. For open or closed seams.

Turn under edge of seam allowance 5mm and straight stitch. Also called turned-and-stitched. A vintage method of neatening the edges, seen on  old clothes pre-zig zag era. It's effective, but tends to leave a ridge where the edge is folded under. For open seams only.

Pinking shears. Sometimes used for linings. Not used in factories because it's too slow and labour intensive. An advantage is that it doesn't add any extra (stitching) bulk to the seam allowances, so it's very flat. I would hesitate to use it on garments that need frequent washing because it's not very durable. However, sometimes a line of straight stitching is sewn 6mm (¼") from the edge before pinking, to minimise fraying. For open or closed seams.

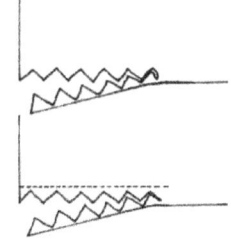

Overcast by hand. The edge is whipstitched (page 150) using a single strand of thread, yielding a flat, flexible finish. This is a seriously Old School method, used when clothes were sewn by hand or with early pre-zig zag sewing machines. It's also used on couture clothes. Space the stitches about 6mm (¼") apart, and make them 3mm-4mm (⅛" or slightly more) deep. You may find it easier to work from left to right as illustrated, so your hand doesn't hide the stitches you've already done. Don't pull the stitches too tight or you'll get a hard ridge.

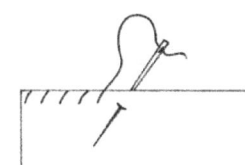

You can make one stitch at a time or try winding the needle around the edge to form several stitches at once, though you'll need to work from right to left to do this.

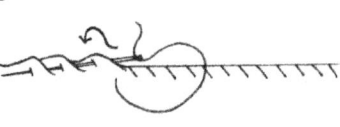

For open or closed seams (but open seams are double the work and time).

Herringbone stitch. Use this for thick fabrics only, to both neaten and hold flat the seam allowance at the same time. If the seam is closed, trim off the underneath seam allowance before neatening. See page 149 for herringbone stitch.

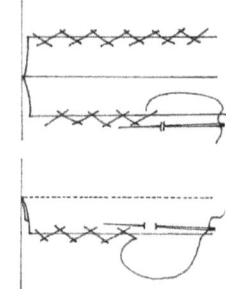

Bind the edges. A classy finish for unlined jackets, coats and capes, or anywhere where a flash of the inside might be seen. It *does* add bulk and rigidity to the seam allowance, and will imprint through to the right side if you're heavy with the iron. The edges can be bound with a matching or contrasting-colour binding. You can use ready-made bias binding, self-made bias binding made from strips of lining cut on the bias, nylon net (the type used for knitted coat hangers) or thin 1cm (⅜") wide herringbone twill tape.

For a Hong Kong finish, bias binding is stitched to the front of the seam allowance, then brought around underneath and stitched-in-the-ditch to hold it in place. 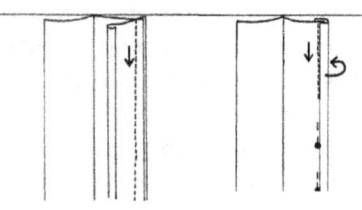 Bias binding can also be applied by a binding foot attachment on a sewing machine, if you have lots to do.

Nylon net or herringbone twill tape can simply be folded in half longways (iron the twill tape to hold the fold) and sewn on in one operation using straight stitch or zig zag. The net adds virtually no bulk at all to the seam allowance.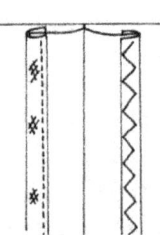

Seam allowances can also be self-bound, by trimming one side and using the long side as a binding. The seam is then pressed to one side. It's called a standing fell. 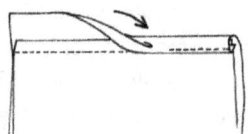 I've used this around the armholes of transparent shirts, where French seams are impractical. Stitch a plain seam and trim one edge back to 3mm-6mm (⅛"-¼"). Leave whichever side is fuller or has more bias, and trim the other one. For armhole/sleeve seams, trim the body and use the sleeve as a binding. Turn under the untrimmed edge and sew by hand or machine to the first line of stitching. Machine sewing is stronger, quicker and hard wearing. By hand is more flexible, softer and can be used on sheer fabrics.

Some sewing techniques

Sewing corners

As you approach the corner, slow down and if necessary turn the machine using the handwheel. Your aim is to plunge the needle exactly down into the point of the corner, but it can be a matter of trial and error. When you think the needle's in the right spot, raise the presser foot and pivot 90 degrees. Check the seam allowance on the second side according to the guidelines on the needle plate. If it  isn't correct, pivot back and reposition the needle using the hand wheel. Check again. When it's correct, lower the presser foot and stitch in the new direction.

Sewing pointy corners on enclosed seams

Take one stitch diagonally across the corner. If the fabric is very thick and bulky, take two diagonal stitches. It's a good idea to reduce the stitch length to 2 instead of the usual 2.5 since you'll be trimming away the corner and a shorter stitch will be stronger.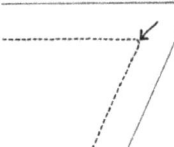
This technique is the best way to achieve a well-formed, acute-angled point on an enclosed seam. Typical examples are the points of collars (see page 46) and lapels.

Pivoting inward corners

1. Reinforce the inward corner by stay stitching on the stitching line, a few centimetres either side of the corner. I like to use a small stitch (1 or 1.5) for strength.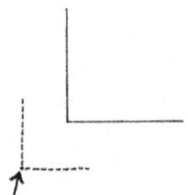
Ensure that you've pivoted *exactly* on the pivot point. Some people like to mark the point with a dot on the wrong side before they stay-stitch, either with a pencil or water-soluble texta. I don't—I stitch to where I estimate the pivot point is, then, with the needle down I lift the presser foot and turn the fabric. I check the seam allowance on the second side according to the guidelines on the needle plate. If it isn't correct I pivot back and reposition the needle using the handwheel.
Factory machinists may or may not stitch the reinforcing stitching—it depends on the fabric and situation. If they don't reinforce, they'll snip in *almost* to the point as they reach the pivot point when they sew the seam.

2. Snip exactly to, but not on, the stitching. If you don't snip in far enough the corner won't sit flat.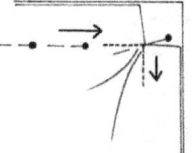

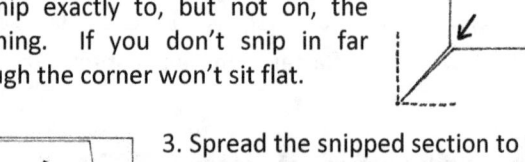
3. Spread the snipped section to fit the other edge. Push a pin exactly through the pivot point and match it to the corresponding point on the other side. You'll only be able to pin the seam up to the pivot point, but don't worry, you can pin the second part

after pivoting while it's still in the machine. Sew the seam with the snipped edge facing up, stitching *just* inside the stay stitching so it doesn't show on the right side. When you reach the snipped corner, plunge the needle into the point where the pin is, pull out the pin, pivot, and then re-arrange the folds of the fabric to sew in the new direction. A small tug on the fabric will pull the corner smooth.

I like to make my machine stitch smaller (1 or 1.5 instead of the usual 2.5) at the corner section for strength, particularly on loosely woven fabrics or fabrics that fray badly. If the fabric is ultra fray-ey, iron a small piece of sheer fusible interfacing onto the corner before stay stitching and snipping.

If you have to *begin* a seam at a pivot point or dot, for example on a rever collar, push a pin exactly through the point and the corresponding point on the other side. Begin the seam by plunging the machine's needle in exactly where the pin is, then whipping out the pin so you're starting seam in precisely the right place. It's easier to begin *at* the pivot point/dot and stitch out from there, rather than try to stitch *to* it, because the layers will move slightly while sewing, making it hard to line up the points.

Sewing curves

Guide the fabric carefully so the seam allowance is correct at the point it passes under the needle. Sew slowly. A shorter machine stitch, such as 2 instead of the usual 2.5, may give you better control.

Sewing opposite curves

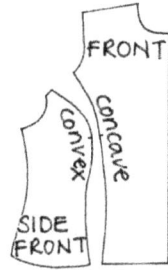

Opposite curves are encountered when you sew a princess line seam or sew a yoke onto a skirt.
The *cut edges* will be different measurements, but the *stitching lines* will be the same.

One side of the seam is an inward (concave) curve and the other is an outward (convex) curve. The inward (concave) curve is more flexible, so sew with that side on top.

With the right sides together, match and pin the beginning and end of the seam, and any notches. Pin centrally between the two pins, dividing any fullness in half, either side of the pin. Continue in this way, placing a pin centrally between two existing pins so the entire curve is evenly matched.

If the two curves are *very* curvy, you might need to strategically clip the inside curve and let the edge spread to make it fit around. Snip in to about half the depth of the seam allowance. The tighter the curve, the more snips you'll need.

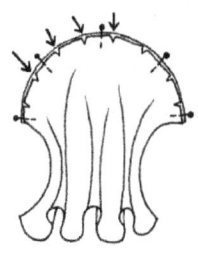

Trimming and grading

Trimming means cutting away some of the seam allowance after the seam has been sewn. It's done when the full amount of seam allowance, if left, would be too bulky, or is not required for further construction, for example French seams.

Grading, also called blending, bevelling or layering, is trimming the seam allowances to different widths so the seam lies flat without causing a bulky ridge. Grading is done on seams that will form an edge or be enclosed, such as the inside of a collar or a faced edge. The seam allowance that will fall nearest to the garment side is cut the widest. Duck billed/appliqué scissors are designed to easily trim one layer at a time, but normal scissors will do fine.

I confess that I rarely trim or grade my seams but some people do it often. I cut my patterns with 6mm (¼") seam allowances on the enclosed seams, so they're "pre-trimmed".

Clipping and notching

Snipping (or clipping) and notching are used on curved seams to allow them to lie flat and smooth.
The distance between the snips is determined by the sharpness of the curves.

Inward curves are snipped to permit the edges to spread. The pattern instructions will typically say: "clip the curves".

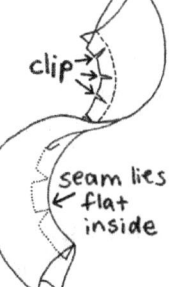

Outward curves have notches (really wedges) cut out of the seam allowance, like little pieces of pie. The

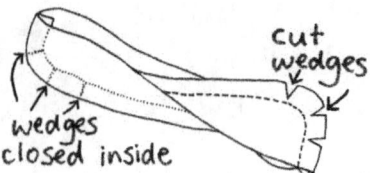

space opened by the removal of a wedge of fabric lets the edge sit flat with no folds.

Clips and notches do weaken the seam, so ideally they should be staggered each side of the seam to minimize this.

If you've allowed 6mm (¼") seam allowances for enclosed seams like collars and cuffs (like I like to do), there's hardly any need to clip the curves—the narrow seam will permit the curve to lie flat. Having said that, if the curve is really tight, you might still need to snip.

If you have to snip or notch a seam that will be overlocked, snip or notch the seam first, press it, then overlock allowing for any spread.

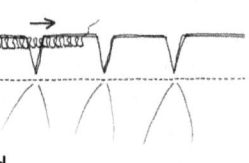

Understitching

Understitching keeps a facing or undercollar and their seam lines from rolling to the right side of the garment. It's an

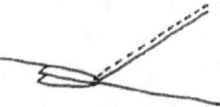

excellent technique for neat, controlled collars and facings. It makes it easier to iron a garment too, especially on fabrics that don't press into crisp folds. I would probably use understitching on almost every garment I sew.

Understitching is done after the seam has been sewn, neatened if necessary and any trimming or snipping has been done to the seam allowance. The seam allowance is pressed towards the facing or underneath side, either with an iron or with your fingers as you sew. Hold the fabric with your thumbs underneath to feel where the seam allowance is and put your fingers on top to pull the fabric flat either side. With the right side facing up, stitch through the facing and seam allowance, staying close to the seam line (between 1mm-3mm). If you've snipped any curves, make sure all the little sections between the snips are pushed to the same side.

You can also do understitching by hand, using backstitch, although I never have.

Trimming and turning corners

Corners of enclosed seams, for example the points of a collar, are trimmed *after* sewing the seam, but *before* they are turned the right way. Take care not to trim too finely otherwise the corner may fray out, either while you're still sewing or after laundering (taking a shorter stitch length will help prevent this). **Trim no closer than 3mm (⅛").**

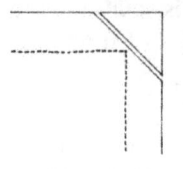

90 degree corners are trimmed diagonally across.

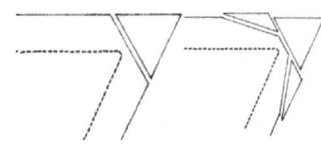

Acute angles are trimmed across the point, then tapered on each side.

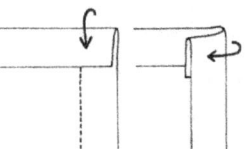

To turn the corner, you'll get a flatter result if you *fold* the seam allowance into the corner, holding it with your thumb as you turn it through. Be quite deliberate with the folding so the seam allowances will be folded on top of each other, not stuffed into the corner.

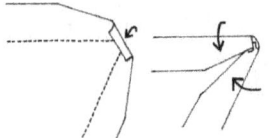

Even if I've trimmed, I still fold what's left of the seam allowance before turning the corner through.

Matching seam junctions

The flattest type of seam junction has both seams pressed open.

If the seams are closed seams, they can be pressed in opposite directions to reduce bulk. This works well not only for thick fabrics but also on seams sewn by overlocker.

Fine fabrics can have both seams facing the same way.

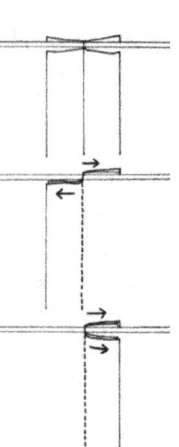

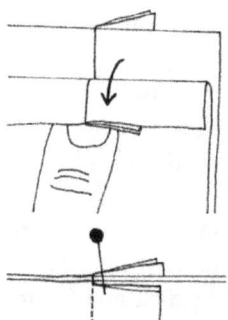

To match a seam junction, for example at an underarm seam, place your thumb on the intended stitching line then flip back the seam allowance.

Match the two seams, flip the seam allowance back again and put a pin through all layers right next to the junction or across it if the seam is open. Sew the seam very carefully over the pin, then take it out.

You can also use this method for reliably matching **stripes or checks**.

Matching seams, stripes or checks on an **overlocker** can be difficult because you can't use pins. For sure-fire results, stitch the seam first on a regular machine using a long stitch, taking the correct 6mm (¼") seam allowance. Check that the stripes match perfectly, then overlock over the top. You don't have to undo the straight stitching—pull gently on the seam to crack the stitching if the fabric is stretchy.

Easing

Ease refers to how a seam is sewn when one side is longer than the other. The longer side of the seam is "eased" onto the shorter side.

The area to be eased is indicated on the pattern between two notches.

Generally, to sew ease, the side that is longer (to be eased) is placed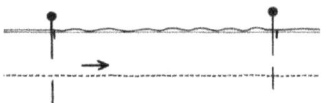
underneath. Pin the seam together at each end of the eased section. When you arrive at the section to be eased, place your left hand between the two layers of fabric and push the underneath layer through. You should see even ripples, but *not* pleats, along the raw edge of the fabric underneath. The machine's feed dogs will feed the underneath in and help it to ease.

I use this method for all easing except setting sleeves into armholes.

Another method to sew ease, one that I always use for setting sleeves into armholes, is to sew a row of long stitches *on* the seam between the ease notches.

Leave long threads at both ends. These are the ease stitches.

Pin the seams together and pull up the ease thread. Distribute the fullness evenly without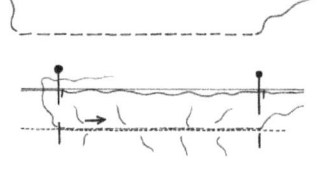
any gathers—the fabric should ripple but *not* gather. Secure with pins parallel to the raw edge. Sew with the ease stitches on top, stitching exactly on or just outside so the ease stitches won't show. Don't unpick the ease stitches (they stay there forever), but do trim their long ends.

Some people like to sew two rows of ease stitches, the second row in between the first and the raw edge, in the same way as gathering stitches, but I never do.

Stitching-in-the-ditch

Stitching-in-the-ditch is a line of stitching used to hold down a seam line onto the fabric behind it. The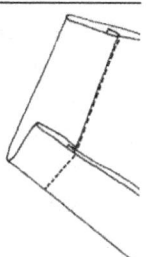
stitching is done on the right side of the garment and doesn't show because it's hidden in the ditch of the seam line. It's used to sew binding down, stitch waistbands flat and quilters use it as well—they quilt in-the-ditch along the seam lines of the patchwork.

Stitching-in-the-ditch is something that many people find difficult because it can be hard to keep the needle *in* the seam line. It's harder to do on fine, smooth, plain-coloured fabrics because inaccuracies show more clearly. Old-fashioned practise and confidence with your machine will help. Some tips:

✂ Use perfectly matching thread so the stitches will blend in. If you have to choose between a slightly darker or slightly lighter shade, pick the darker because it will be less visible.

✂ If the machine has variable speeds, use a slow one.

✂ Press and pin along the seam line so everything lies flat before you begin. I get it all pressed and pinned at the ironing board, then take it to the machine.

✂ Start with the needle *down* in the ditch, lower the presser foot, then start sewing. That way, you're already in the ditch when you start.

✂ As you sew, place one hand each side of the presser foot to pull the ditch flat as you sew in it. To prevent the fabric from rippling, use both of your hands to push the top layers backwards as the presser foot pushes it forwards.

✂ Remember that stitching-in-the-ditch is more noticeable when you're looking at it up close under a bright machine light—when the garment is being worn you'll hardly see it.

Taut sewing

Any line of machine stitching will cause the fabric to be brought-in and made smaller. Most of the time this is unnoticeable, but sometimes it results in a puckered seam. It's most liable to happen on floppy, fine, synthetic fabrics, single layers and on the straight rather than bias grain. No amount of pressing will make the seam smooth.

If the seam puckers along the stitching line, hold it taut while sewing. To do this, hold the fabric in front of and behind the needle as the seam is sewn. Hold the fabric firmly without stretching it and just let it feed through the machine on its own. Keep repositioning your hands as you sew each section.

You can also taut sew overlocking using the same technique, particularly on linings.

Sewing down a folded edge

In industry more than in home sewing pattern instructions, folded edges are edgestitched into place along the edge of the fold. Cuffs, cuff plackets, front button stands, tab fronts, waistbands and shirt collars all employ this technique. It's a fast and neat way to sew. It takes a little practise, but experienced machinists can make the back of the work look identical to the front.

Instead of pressing the edge to be sewn down with an iron, the fold can be drawn sharply down the edge of the table to crease it before sewing.

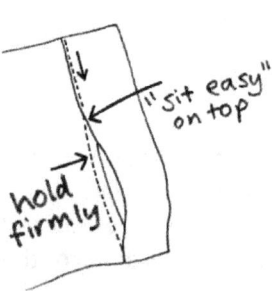

To sew, firmly hold the underneath section with your left hand. Let the top folded edge "sit easy" on top, guiding it with your right hand, and just covering the first line of stitching with the folded edge.

If the top layer should start to ripple, stop sewing and undo the stitching you've just done. Sorry to say, the rippling won't press out and won't improve further along if you keep sewing.

Tacking

Should you tack (or baste) a seam before sewing it? Old sewing books encourage hand tacking the seams together before sewing them by machine, but you don't need to—you have pins to hold the fabric in place and a guide on the machine needle plate to take the correct seam allowance. I would go so far as to say that hand tacking seams before sewing them is a pure waste of time. However, it *is* worthwhile when preparing velvet and velveteen for a fitting, because machine stitches will show if you have to unpick them. Heavily beaded lace is also easier to tack by hand for a fitting.

Stay stitching and stabilizing seams

Stay stitching is a line of machine stitching sewn to prevent the fabric from stretching and to reinforce it, sewn before the seam. It's typically sewn around necklines and sometimes waists, within the seam allowance. It isn't removed later. I use a long stitch but some people use a regular length or short stitch.

I rarely stay stitch unless I need to do a fitting. Instead I handle the garment pieces very gently and support them so they don't stretch from their own weight until they're stabilized by a seam.

If a neckline, waist, or any edge *has* stretched, it's possible to bring it back to the correct length. Sew a line of stitching using a long stitch along the garment edge, with your middle finger held firmly behind the presser foot. 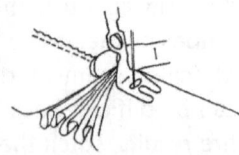 It doesn't have to be *on* the stitching line; it can be anywhere within the seam allowance. When the fabric has bunched up, take your finger away and release the built up fabric, then put your finger back. The fabric should have mini concertina folds in it. This should pull in the garment's edge enough for you to attach it to the facing, collar, waistband or whatever. I find I often need to do this when sewing stretch corduroy or other stretch wovens.

Tape is used around faced waists, edges of cut-away pockets, plunging necklines, parts of bias cut garments or on any edge to give strength and stability. It's stronger than stay stitching. Even if the piece has interfacing on it, taping the edge will stop it from stretching while it's being worn.

I favour 6mm (¼") cotton tape in black or white, but you can also use a 6mm strip cut from the fabric's selvedge if it's smooth and even, or the selvedge from some silk organza. Tape is generally not pre-shrunk before using it. Tape needs to be applied *before you do a fitting*—otherwise you won't know what size the edge should be and it will stretch more when it's being tried on.

Using the pattern as a guide, rather than the garment that may have already stretched, place the tape along the stitching line and cut it to the correct length.

Include the side seam allowance. Mark the centre front or centre back with a pencil dot. Be exact.

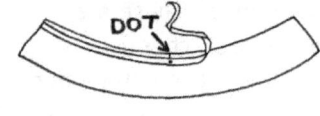

Sew any darts in the garment first. Pin the tape around the edge on the stitching line and sew it on with a long stitch. It's easier to apply tape when the seam allowance is only 6mm (¼").

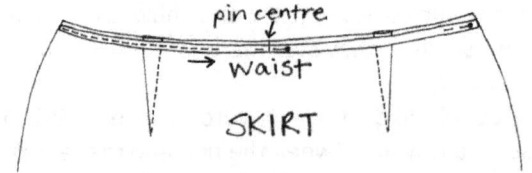

When you sew this edge in a seam (to attach the facing), stitch *on* or just outside the tape stitching, so it won't show on the outside

Seams 293

Tear-away stabilizer is applied a little differently from tape.

1. Cut a strip about 2.5cm (1") wide in the same shape as the edge. Tear-away tears in only one direction, so orientate the strip when you cut it out to tear parallel with the seam.

2. Sew the strip onto the edges of the wrong side of the fabric using a long stitch within the seam allowance. Treat this as one layer when you sew this edge in a seam (to attach the facing) and understitch (***important***).

3. At the end, tear away the excess that you can see. A narrow strip of tear-away will remain held by the seam and understitching.

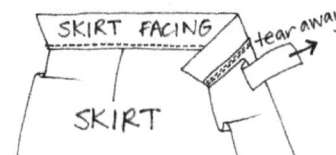

Two techniques for faster sewing
Sewing a seam without pins
The more pins you use, the longer things will take. We do need pins, but, with practise, many seams can be sewn by holding the fabric with your fingers instead of pins.

Here's a technique to try when seaming long lengths together:

1. Begin by sewing the first few centimetres of the seam, to hold it.

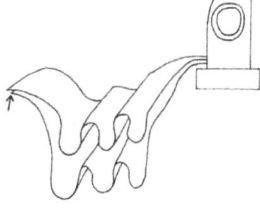

2. Stop sewing and run the two edges together through your hand until you reach the end. Hold the ends together with your thumb and first finger of your right hand. Find the halfway point between the ends and the bit you've started sewing, and hold it between your first and second fingers.

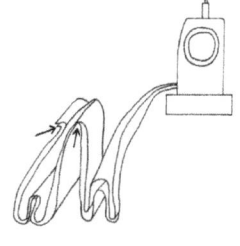

3. Find the halfway point again, working your way towards the machine. Do this until you've run out of fingers to hold the cloth; your right hand will now have cloth inserted between all the fingers.

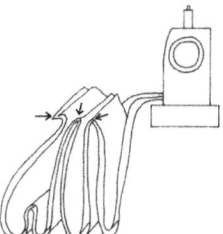

4. Begin sewing again, using your left hand to guide the fabric and your right hand holding the layers away from the machine. As you reach each point held in your right hand, drop it and keep sewing. When you reach (what was) the halfway point, re-arrange the cloth in your fingers again as described above.

Chain piecing
Chain piecing, as it's known in the quilting world, is simply running from one seam straight onto the next, saving time and thread. The small links of thread are cut to separate the seams. Remember you still need to backstitch at the beginning and end of each seam (although quilters don't because the seam is pressed to one side and is always intersected by another seam).

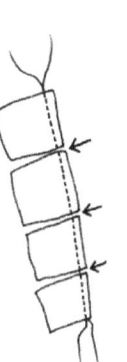

Some other types of seams
While most of the seams you'll ever sew are plain seams, occasionally something different is called for depending on the fabric, the garment, or machines you have. For example, if you were sewing lingerie, you could use French seams for a high quality finish. You could also use French seams when sewing a shopping or library bag for a strong, neat finish. Classic men's dress shirts use flat felled seams, or you could design a garment using a particular decorative seam as a feature.

French seam
French seams look like a plain seam on the right side, and a small neat tuck on the wrong side.

French seams are excellent on fine fabrics and garments when the wrong side might be seen, for example a transparent blouse. They could be your choice if you can't get matching overlocker thread or don't have a overlocker. They can be used on bias-cut seams or seams on the straight grain and for curved seams as well as straight seams.

French seams are not suitable for side seams that end in splits, where alterations are likely, where one side is eased onto the other or for thick fabrics. French seams are strong but not as flexible as plain seams.

Although French seams can be trimmed and sewn very finely, finer seams are not as strong or as hard wearing.

The two keys to really good French seams are trimming and pressing.

1. Place the *wrong* sides of the fabric together. Stitch the seam, taking just under half of the seam allowance. For example if the seam allowance is 1cm, take a 4mm seam.

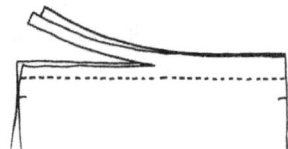

2. After sewing, trim the seam back to 3-4mm (a generous ⅛"). Press the seam flat, then press it folded with the right sides on the inside. Don't be tempted to omit the pressing. It ensures a really neat, flat seam.

3. Stitch the seam again, this time with the *right* sides together as you've pressed it. This second stitching line should fall on the actual seam line. The raw edges will now be neatly encased in the seam.

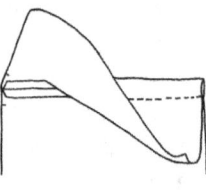

Troubleshooting French seams

A common problem you may have is ending up with "hairy" seams. You've either not taken enough seam allowance

for the second row of stitching, or haven't trimmed sufficiently (or at all). It can happen when you're striving to produce a really fine French seam.

The best remedy is to unpick the second row of stitching and re-do it. If you don't want to unpick, trim the offending threads of fabric and either re-sew the second row of stitching further out or leave it if it looks OK now.

Mock French Seam

Mock French seams employ the same idea of enclosing the raw edge as real French seams do, but they're made in

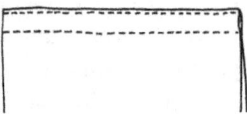

a different way and have two visible rows of stitching inside.

I've used mock French seams when I've made a regular seam and then as an afterthought decided to turn the raw edges in to finish them off. It makes a strong finish. I've also used them when I meant to make a French seam but accidentally stitched the first row with the right sides together!

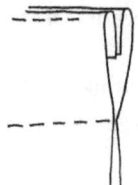

Sew the seam normally, that is with the right sides together with the correct seam allowance, and afterwards turn in and stitch the edges together.

Actually, mock French seams can be sewn more easily in the reverse order. First, press under a small amount along each raw edge, for example 6mm (¼"). Sew the edges together next to the fold, then sew the actual seam, being sure it's on the correct stitching line.

Flat felled seam

A flat felled seam is a strong seam and the classic choice for men's shirts. This seam can be easily sewn on gently curved seams, but not sharp curves. It can't be used when one side has to be eased onto the other, so both sides need to be the same length. There are several ways of forming a flat felled seam, but they're all a two-stage operation. The first row of stitching joins the two pieces of fabric, then the second row stitches them down flat, hiding the raw edges. Here are three methods.

Using a felling foot. The very neatest way to make a flat felled seam is with a felling foot on your sewing machine, and is a worthwhile consideration if you plan to use this type of seam often. It produces uniform, narrow felled seams far more neatly than you can produce by the next two (manual) methods. Note that a felling foot can only make felled seams of one particular width; for a different width seam you'll need a different size foot.

Either side of the flat felled seam can be used on the outside. It just depends which sides you put together first. Putting the *wrong* sides together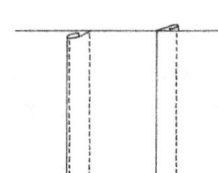
produces two parallel rows of stitching. Putting the *right* sides together yields a seam with one parallel line of stitching.

If you're using a 6mm (¼") felling foot, you'll need a 6mm (¼") seam allowance on each edge.

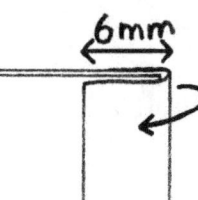

1. The first row of stitching encases one of the raw edges. Fold the edge first by hand to get started, as shown. Wrap the seam allowance (in this case 6mm) around the raw edge.

Seams

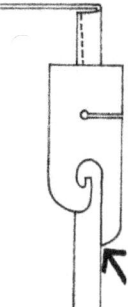
Begin sewing with the foot on top of the folded edge for a couple of centimetres.

2. Stop sewing with the needle down and lift the presser foot. Lift the top layer of fabric over the lip in the centre of the foot. Continue sewing with the folded edge up against the inside edge of the foot. If the fabric starts to go off the rails, a pin is useful to guide it back into position.

3. The second row of stitching is easier to do than the first. Open out the fabric so it's flat. Go back to the beginning of the seam, but this time line up the inside edge of the foot with the previous row of stitching.

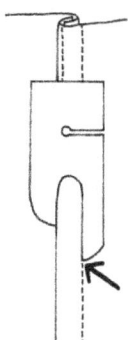

✄ Stitching a felled seam in a tube, for example a sleeve underarm seam, *is* possible, provided the tube isn't too small. The first row of stitching is easy. The second row needs to be done a little bit at a time with the fabric bunched up. It's much easier if you turn the tube through so you're sewing *inside* the tube.
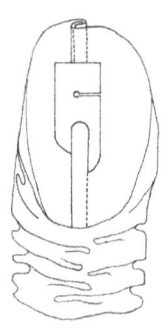
Make sure you sew each sleeve in opposite directions so you have a pair.

✄ The felling foot doesn't cope too well when encountering bulk such as crossing other seams. You might have to stop just short of the intersecting seam and begin sewing again on the other side of it. When you've finished the seam, go back to the skipped part and hand-form that part of the seam, topstitching it down to match the rest of the seam.

✄ Slight curves work OK with a felling foot, as long as you take it a little bit at a time, and maybe use a pin to help guide the fabric through. The bias areas may stretch a little, but you might be able to shrink them back to shape with the iron later on.
For princess line seams, have the curved side panel on top. The shallower the curve the easier it will be.

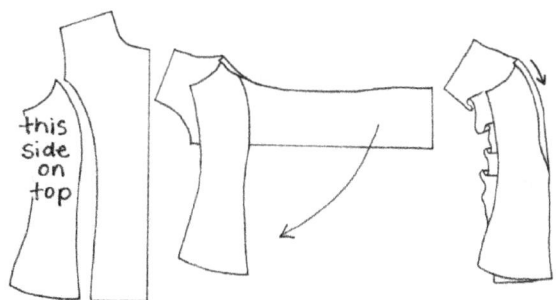

For armhole seams, make sure the curve is gentle. Only flat fell drop-shoulder sleeves, not set-in sleeves. Have the body on top and the sleeve underneath.

✄ Bias edges will stretch but *do* work with a felling foot.

Manual flat felled seams. There are two ways to make a flat felled seam manually, giving you control over the finished width.
Either side of the flat felled seam can be used on the outside, depending which sides you put together first. If you place the *wrong* sides of the fabric together first, you'll finish with two parallel rows of stitching. With the *right* sides together, you'll have a seam with a parallel line of stitching.

Method 1
1. Allow 1.5cm (⅝") seam allowances. Sew the seam with the wrong or right sides together (depending on the finished look you want).

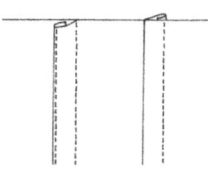
2. Trim the inner seam allowance to 3mm-4mm (generous ⅛"). Press under 6mm (¼") on the edge of the outer seam allowance. It doesn't matter which side you decide to trim, but for shirt armholes, trim the body.

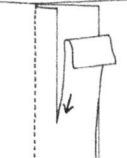
3. Stitch this folded edge onto the garment, encasing the raw edge.
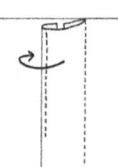

Method 2
This is a bit quicker because there's no trimming.

1. Allow 1cm (⅜") seam allowances. Sew the seam with either the wrong or right sides together, taking 1.5cm (⅝") on one side and 5mm (a scant ¼") on the other side. For shirt armholes, have the 5mm on the body and 1.5cm on the sleeve.

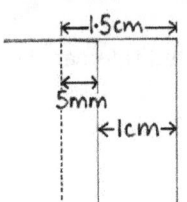

2. Fold under 6mm (¼") on the wider seam allowance, lap it over the narrower one and stitch along the fold.

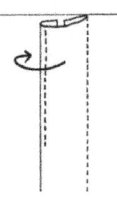

This method displaces the seam line so the *centre* of the felled seam is where the regular stitching line *would* be.

Lapped seam
Lapped seams are as their title describes them—the two edges are lapped over each other and stitched from the right side. Sometimes the two raw edges are simply lapped over each other without any type of neatening for the raw edge. This can be used for leather or any fabric that doesn't fray. It's often used for seams in interfacing to reduce bulk.

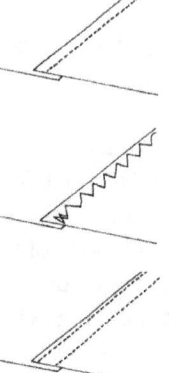

The seam allowance can be as small as 3mm (⅛") on each side, which will result in a 6mm (¼") lap. Sometimes both seam allowances are trimmed close to the stitching after the seam is made. The stitching can be regular straight stitching, zig zag or two or more rows of straight stitching.

If there are notches on the pattern to match the seam, you won't be able to snip them because the snips will be visible when the seam is sewn. Mark with a pin or a water soluble texta instead.

Mark a guide line for the top raw edge with a removable pencil or chalk line, OR notch the seam allowances at the top and match them (my preference). Check the layers as you sew to ensure an even lap.

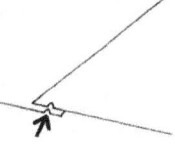

A lapped seam can also be made with the top edge folded under. It looks like a plain seam that's been pressed to one side and edgestitched. The side that will be on top has the seam allowance pressed under, then it's laid over the other side so the raw edges sit on top of one another underneath. The seam is sewn next to the folded edge, using one or more rows of straight stitch, or zig zag.

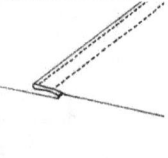

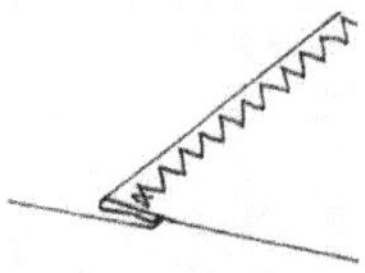

A **tucked seam** is similar to a lapped seam but the stitching is 6mm (¼") or more away from the folded edge, which is the true seam line. It looks like a tuck.

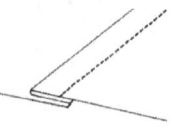

You may need extra seam allowance, so decide if you're going to use this type of seam before cutting the garment out.

A **curved tucked seam** is also possible for shaped edges. You'll need to make a narrow facing for the curved edge. Allow a 6mm (¼") seam allowance on the curved edge. If the edge is thin, unstable or stretchy, interface the facing with a light fusing. Stitch the facing on right sides together, snip the curves, turn through, press, then lap the faced edge onto the other side to stitch into position.

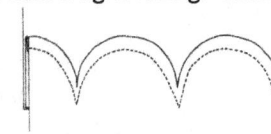

Butted seam
A butted seam is the flattest seam you can make. A butted seam has no seam allowances. The edges are cut along the stitching line and butted together, then stitched. I sometimes use a butted seam when seaming heavy interfacing to reduce bulk. It's also used on neoprene (for wetsuits and stubby holders), leather or on sheepskin to make a flat, interesting seam.

Sew the butted seam with zig zag stitch, aligning the centre of the presser foot with the butted edges so the stitches catch both sides equally. Sometimes an underlay of cotton tape or seam binding is placed under the butted edges, for strength. If an underlay is used, straight stitching may be sewn either side of the butted edge instead of zig zag.

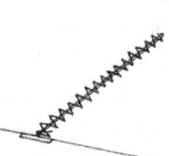

Slot seam
A slot seam, also called a channel seam, is a decorative seam that's most easily done on straight seams, but can be adapted for curved seams.

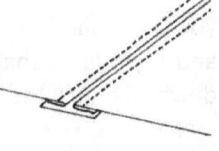

Decide how far away you want the topstitching from the edges, because this affects the amount of seam allowance you'll need. If 6mm (¼") topstitching is planned, I suggest 1cm (⅜") seam allowances.

1. Neaten the raw edges first unless the garment has a closed lining, because there won't be an opportunity to later. Press under the seam allowance on both edges. Place the folded edges side by side, touching. Position an underlay cut from a strip of fabric centrally underneath. The underlap could be a contrasting fabric for a flash of colour. Overlock it, if required, before positioning it.

2. Topstitch an equal distance from the centre on each side. Since you won't be able to use the stitch guide on the throat plate, use the edge of the presser foot as a guide. If you can move the needle position you'll easily be able to vary the width if desired.

For a **curved slot seam**, clipping the inward (concave) edge is necessary. Snip to a depth of about half the seam allowance when you press the edges under. Cut the underlay strip on the bias and steam it to the curved shape required.

Troubleshooting seams

Puckered stitching
Sometimes ordinary straight stitching can make a seam bunch up or pucker slightly and no amount of pressing can make it flat. It tends to happen more with polyesters, cheap smooth fabrics, thin fabrics and fabrics sewn in a single layer. Have you changed the needle lately? Check the tension too. If changing the tension doesn't make a difference, try holding the seam taut as you sew it (see page 291). Hold the back of the seam with your left hand and the front with your right, and let the machine feed the fabric at its own rate. If you pull too tightly with either hand the stitches will be different lengths.

Machine jams up at the beginning of a seam
You probably don't have enough fabric under the presser foot for the machine to start feeding it in. Try starting 1cm (⅜") in, sewing backwards to the edge, then sewing forwards.
Another reason might be that the threads aren't lying under the foot and towards the back. Begin sewing by holding taut the two threads with your left hand until the seam is under way.

Machine skips stitches
Change the needle. If that doesn't solve it, try a different size or type of needle.

Machine sews horribly, for example with big loopy stitches underneath
Re-thread the top and bobbin threads.

No backstitch facility on sewing machine
I've only ever met a couple of machines that couldn't do backstitch. Possible solutions:
- Sew forwards for the first 1cm (⅜") of the seam, lift the foot and reposition it at the beginning of seam again and then sew the seam.
- Sew the first few centimetres using a very small stitch length.
- Tie off the ends in a knot instead.

One side longer by the time the end of the seam is sewn
It helps to understand how the fabric feeds in as the machine sews: the top layer is pushed forwards by the presser foot and the underneath layer is pushed backwards by the feed dogs. Therefore, if you allow the machine to feed naturally, the top layer will end up longer. It can happen on some fabrics more than others. You can use this to your advantage if you're easing a longer length into a shorter one—put the longer side underneath and the machine will help you ease it. Possible solutions:
- Use your hands to encourage the top layer backwards as you sew.
- Use a walking foot, if you have one.
- Slacken off the foot pressure. The machine should have a knob, lever or dial on top to adjust this.
- Put pins in both directions (parallel and perpendicular) and use lots of them to hold the layers in place. Sew carefully and slowly over the pins, or whip them out at the last moment.
- Hand baste the seam before sewing it.

Seam won't sew straight easily and the fabric is hard to control
AND/OR
It's really hard to pivot corners, too.
- Do you have a large amount of heavy fabric to the left of the needle, that might be pulling the fabric away as you stitch? Support the bulk with a chair, table or lowered ironing board.
- Is the presser foot pressure correct? There should be a dial, screw or lever at the top of the machine to adjust it. If it's too loose, the presser foot won't clamp down firmly enough on the fabric to sew properly.
- Are the presser foot and needle screwed in tightly enough and not wobbly?

Changing the seam after a fitting

Fittings should be done with the right side of the fabric facing out, just the same as wearing the garment. After the fitting, you'll need to move the pins (without loosing their place) so you can accurately sew the adjusted seams.

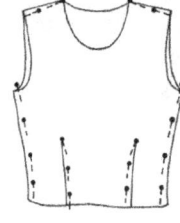

Sometimes it seems like you're going backwards and not achieving much, but after the adjustments are done you can really get on with the sewing.

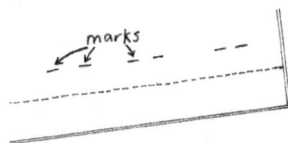

Turn the garment inside out and rub a piece of chalk along the side of each pin.

Remove the pins. You should see a line of chalk dashes where the pins were, indicating your new stitching line.

If the fabric shows the pin holes, you can whip out the pins, turn the garment inside out and re-pin the seam ready to sew on the inside following the pin holes.

Using a pencil, chalk, water soluble texta or more pins, join the marks so they blend into a smooth line.

Then you can either:

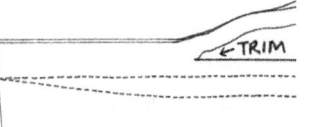

Stitch along this line *then* trim off the excess to make a uniform seam allowance (or don't trim if it isn't much). It's much simpler to sew a new seam *before* unpicking the old one, because the old row of stitching holds things in place. You'll need to unpick the old row of stitching if the seam is to be pressed open, but you can leave it if pressing to one side.

OR

Trim off the excess *first* and then sew the seam as normal. It's easier and more accurate to trim off both sides together.

For **darts**, remember that you only need the end point/s and the widest part marked, so mark these on the wrong side with a pin or chalk dot and remove all the other pins so it lies flat. You'll never be able to pin the left and right sides exactly the same on the body, so compare the left and right sides by folding the piece in half, and make any minor adjustments.

After pinning up **hems**, shift the pins to the folded edge—insert the pin along through the fold. You can then unfold the edge and lay the garment flat to trim.

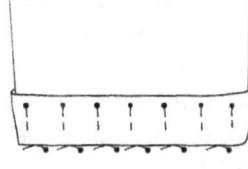

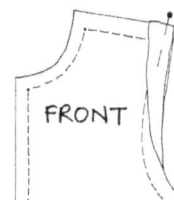

It's wise to mark the alterations you've made on the pattern in case you want to make it again. If I'm not sure whether I'll use a pattern again and don't want to spend a lot of time on it, I simply pin the fabric trimmings to the appropriate part of the pattern when I put it away. Sometimes I slip a short, dated, note in with the pattern, for example: shortened 5cm, lowered front neck 2cm, took sides in 1cm on the double = 4cm.

How to unpick

Unpicking for machinists was one of my many jobs as a factory junior. I got quite good at it! The best tools for unpicking are either an unpicker or a pair of thread snips.

If you're unpicking because the stitching is in the wrong place, it's easier to re-sew the seam *before* unpicking the old one.

Unpicking straight stitching

✂ For **linings and fine fabrics**, pull one thread out. Or, snip the threads at intervals and pull. If you do the latter, you'll have to go back afterwards and remove the short bits of thread.

✂ Pull the edges of the seam apart and snip (with fine scissors or snips) or cut (with an unpicker) one stitch, then pull gently until you feel resistance, then repeat.

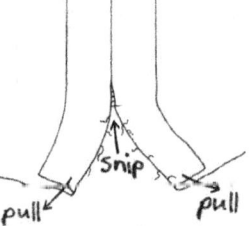

✂ On **stiff, firm fabrics**, such as denim, slide the blade of a sharp, good quality unpicker along the length of the seam. Have the longer side of the unpicker on top and the shorter side with the ball underneath. *At the same time* hold both the ends firmly with your other hand to keep the seam taut. Pull out the bits of thread afterwards.

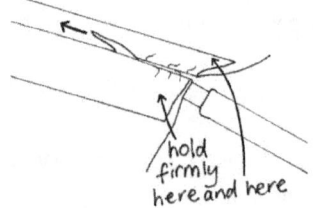

Seams

✂ On **strong fabrics**, you might be able to pull the fabric firmly each side of the seam and literally rip the stitching. Wrap the fabric firmly around your fingers and pull hard. You may need to snip the stitching to get started. Don't try this on delicate fabrics! This method is most effective on straight seams—it might cause curved seams to stretch out of shape.

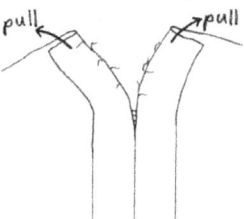

✂ Hold one thread and quickly pull it back on it until the stitching breaks. Turn the seam over, find the end of the thread, and quickly pull it back on the stitching until it breaks. Repeat, alternating each side. Once you get going you won't need an unpicker. The advantage of this method is not having bits of thread to remove afterwards.

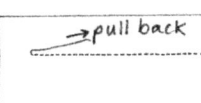

Unpicking overlocking

✂ On fine fabrics, locate and pull out the needle thread (or both threads, if it's a four-thread overlocker). The other two (looper) threads will then just pull off, like undoing knitting. On fine fabrics the needle threads should pull out very easily.

✂ Using a very sharp, long bladed pair of scissors, trim off the threads on the very edge where the looper threads meet each other (hopefully the overlocking has perfect tension).

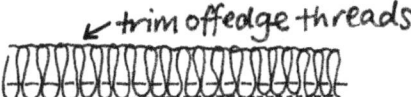

Pull the overlocking apart and remove all the bits of thread. Sometimes you can brush the threads out with a clothes brush if the fabric won't fray too much.

✂ Cut off the overlocking completely, if it won't matter.

Unpicking chainstitching

Chainstitching is sewn using one or two threads depending on the machine. The trick with unpicking it is finding which end to pull. Find the end where the stitching *finished* (picture the seam being sewn, with the chain underneath and the straight stitch on top and the bulk of the garment to the left hand side). Cut the threads off next to this end and pull. If the chainstitch has been made with two threads, pull on both evenly.

Unpicking factory twin needling

Twin needling looks like two parallel lines of straight stitching on the right side and overlocking on the wrong side. To unpick, find where the stitching *finished* (picture the straight stitching on top and the overlocking underneath and the bulk of the garment to the left hand side) and start unpicking from that end.

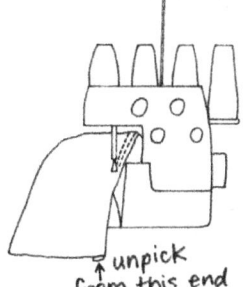

Pull at the same time: the two top threads and the underneath overlocking thread. (Hopefully) the twin needling should undo like undoing knitting. It will be harder to undo if the garment has been washed and the stitches have become embedded.

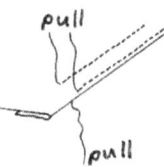

To remove holes from fabric after unpicking

A technique from the workrooms of Caroline Charles. You'll need some water and a steam iron. Dip your thumb into the water and rub the line of holes with the back of your thumbnail. Press with steam until it dries.

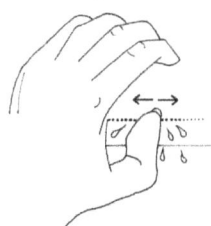

The holes won't come out as well if you press with steam first.

Check before using this method that it doesn't watermark the fabric, particularly on silk. If it does, either use a very sparing amount of water only where you need it, or wet the holes with a spray bottle set to mist, quickly rub with your thumbnail, then press. The spray bottle produces a less definite watermark line, but check first.

Shirt cuffs and plackets

Introduction 300	shirt cuff placket with 2 strips . 304
Plackets 300	simple shirt cuff placket 306
Seven types of plackets 301	Cuffs 306
rolled edge placket 301	sewing a cuff 308
"no placket" placket 301	another way to sew a cuff 309
faced placket 301	men's shirt variation 309
continuous bound placket 302	french cuffs 310
shirt cuff placket (intro) 303	foldback cuffs 310
my fav shirt cuff placket 303	Troubleshooting cuffs and plackets 310

A **cuff** is a fabric band at the bottom of a straight, gathered or pleated sleeve edge. A **placket** is a strip of fabric that finishes an opening or slit in a garment. Shirt cuffs fit around the wrist and require a placket to make the opening big enough to slip the hand in and out easily.

The cuff is applied to the sleeve *after* the placket has been made and *after* the sleeve's underarm seam has been sewn.
The sewing order is therefore:
1. placket
2. sleeve underarm seam
3. cuff

The sleeve length of a cuffed shirt is the length of your arm measured from shoulder seam to wrist, with your arm straight. Add approximately 2cm (¾") for ease then subtract the cuff width.

A slight curving of the wrist line is helpful for shirt sleeves, giving extra length over the elbow to ease any strain on the fabric. I usually make it 1cm (⅜") lower at the back and 1cm higher at the front, but this can be exaggerated for very full sleeves.

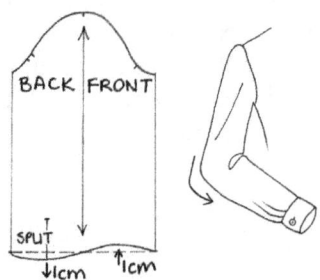

If the sleeve is gathered and full, the sleeve needs to be slightly longer to allow the gathering to be "boofy". The fuller and more blousey the sleeve, the longer it needs to be. In the drawing shown here, probably 5cm-6cm (2"-2⅜") would have been added.

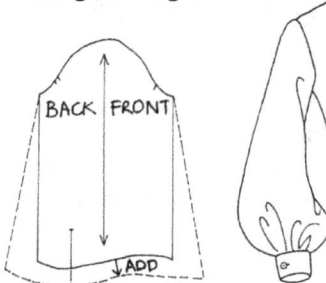

Plackets

✂ Plackets are made *before* the underarm seams are stitched so the placket can be easily constructed on a flat sleeve.

✂ The slit for the placket is on the *back* of the sleeve, half way between the underarm seam and the centre of the sleeve. Cut the slit when you cut out the garment (unless you're sewing the "no-placket" placket, as described on page 301). The slit for the placket is usually about 10cm (4") long for ladies shirts and about 13cm (5") for mens.

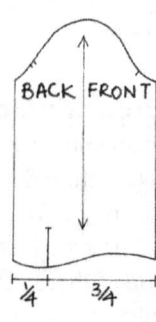

✂ Make sure the right and wrong sides of the fabric don't get confused, of both placket and sleeve.

✂ Sometimes the slit is formed simply by leaving open the end of the underarm seam. While this sounds convenient, it positions the cuff fastening underneath the wrist instead of to one side.

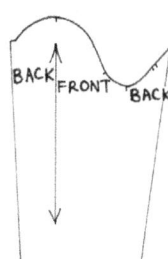

A solution is to move or add a seam to the back of the sleeve, as seen in denim jackets for example. The placket can be made by leaving the last part of the seam unstitched, then folding the seam allowance under and hemming it.

✂ Note that different types of plackets will slightly change the amount of pleating or gathering required to attach the cuff, so you'll need to take bigger or smaller pleats, or more or less gathering to make the cuff fit.

✂ Pressing as you go will make plackets easier to sew, but if you can't get to an iron, table pressing can be very useful and quick. Hold the fabric taut and scrape the seam or fold along the edge of the table. It works best on crisp fabrics that hold a crease well.

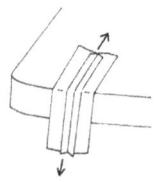

Seven types of placket
1. Rolled edge placket (page 301)
2. The "no placket" placket (page 301)
3. Faced placket (pages 301-302)
4. Continuous bound placket (pages 302-303)
5-7. Shirt cuff placket (three types on pages 303-306)

The style of placket you decide to make will depend on the style of shirt or blouse, your skill level, the amount of time you want to spend, (possibly) the fabric and how visible you want the placket to be.

Rolled edge placket
This method is often seen on school shirts and budget clothing. It has two advantages: it's fast to do and it doesn't require any extra pieces of fabric.

1. Cut the slit in the sleeve.

2. With the wrong side facing up, sew a double rolled hem along each side of the slit, starting at the top. Sew as far as you can towards the point of the slit.

3. Place the right sides together and match up the edges of the rolled hems. Sew a small dart at the bottom to cover the raw edges.

The "no placket" placket
This placket doesn't require any extra fabric to make and suits sleeves that are gathered into a cuff. It would be a good method for nightdresses or nightshirts.

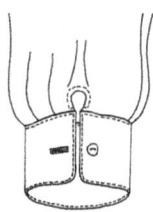

1. Don't cut the slit. Instead, make two snips the same depth as the seam allowance, 2cm (¾") either side of the slit position.

2. Either: overlock this short length and turn it to the wrong side and stitch
Or: make a neat double rolled hem.

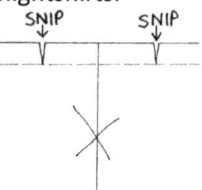

This makes a gap that replaces the slit opening. It forms a pleat when the cuff is fastened.

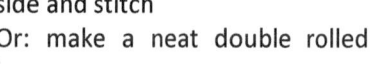

Another kind of "no placket" sleeve finish can be made with no cuff either. Simply hem the sleeve to the correct length, sew a buttonhole through a double layer of fabric as illustrated, and attach a corresponding button.

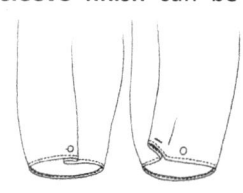

Faced placket
This can be a non-conventional/creative type of placket, in any shape you choose. It could be embellished with extra stitching or fancy stitches. You could also cut the facing in a contrasting fabric or perhaps sew it on the exterior of the sleeve.

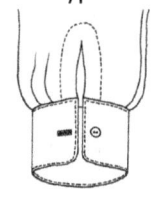

1. Cut the slit in the sleeve.

2. Cut a shape of fabric with a slit as long as the garment's slit. It can be any shape—triangular, rectangular, whatever. The example here is U shaped. Fuse it with light weight interfacing.

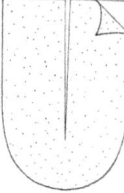

3. Place the facing on the garment, right sides together, matching the slits. Using a short machine stitch for strength, such as 1.5 or 2 instead of the usual 2.5, stitch around the slit, pivoting at the point. Take a minimal seam allowance, 6mm (¼") or less. After sewing, take a very sharp pair of scissors and snip exactly to the pivot point. If you don't cut exactly to the point, you won't be able to turn it through neatly—it will pull and crease.

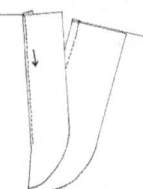

4. Press the seam allowance towards the facing and understitch each side, to as far as you can. Press.

Alternatively, press and edgestitch all around the slit; that way the facing will look good on both sides if you decide to roll your sleeves up.

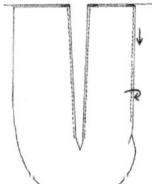

5. Press under 6mm (¼") around the edge of the facing and stitch into position.

On the right side you'll see a slit with a single line of stitching outlining the shape of the facing.

Continuous bound placket

This is sometimes called a continuous lap and it's like a binding. It's an easy way to make a smart, discreet placket on women's shirts and blouses. It's sometimes used for men's work shirts, because it's quicker to make than a

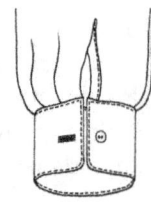

traditional shirt cuff placket. It can also be used for casual jackets. I like to use this for my own blouses.

1. Cut a strip of fabric 4cm (1½") **wide** and twice as **long** as the slit plus 5mm (a scant ¼"). The 5mm is taken up when sewing the point. Sometimes the strip is just cut longer and the excess length is trimmed off afterwards.

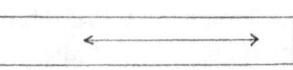

2. Cut the slit in the sleeve.

3. Lay the placket underneath one side of the slit, matching the edges. Have the right side facing up for both.
Begin sewing, taking a 6mm (¼") seam allowance.

4. As you approach the point of the slit, spread the slit so it's straight.
Continue sewing with a 6mm (¼") seam allowance on the placket, but just catch the point of the slit.

5. Press the seam towards the placket and press under 6mm (¼") along the other long edge of the placket. Often I just scrape the folded edge on the table to create the fold.

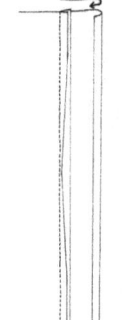

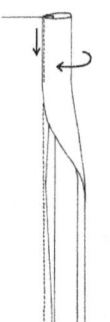

6. Fold the pressed edge of the placket over to encase the raw edge. Edgestitch in place, just covering the previous stitching line with the folded edge. In a perfect world, the back and the front of the finished placket will look the same.
To prevent the placket from rippling or twisting as you sew it, hold the bottom layer firmly towards you and let the placket "sit easy" on top. It's easier to sew if you press it first.

7. *Before* sewing the cuff on, fold the end of the placket under on the front of the sleeve.

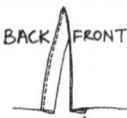

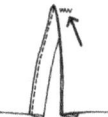
After sewing the cuff on, match the right sides of the placket together and stitch diagonally across the bottom of the placket, from the fold to the stitching (but don't go beyond the stitching). It will form a V shape when opened out.

Sometimes the front of the placket is bartacked to the shirt, as a feature.

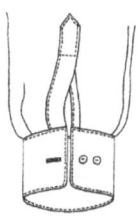

Shirt cuff placket

THE classic choice for men's shirts and sometimes for women's. It can also be used on casual jackets. I always use it for men's shirts, and on my own shirts if I want a sportier look. In essence, the shirt cuff placket is made by sewing a binding onto each side of the slit, which are then overlapped at the end. It appears tricky to make but isn't really—it just has a few more steps than the other plackets.

Shirt cuff plackets have the same grainline as the shirt sleeve. On men's shirts, the placket is typically 2.5cm (1") wide finished and the slash length is about 13cm (5") long. The placket may have a button, called a gauntlet button here, half way up to allow the sleeves to be rolled up neatly (also a sign of a higher quality shirt). Women's plackets may or may not be a little narrower, for example 2cm (¾") with a slash length about 10cm (4") long.

The top of the placket can be either square or pointed. You might like to vary the stitching around the top.

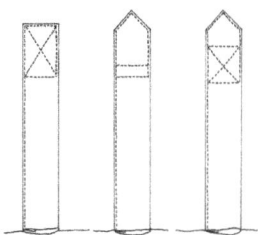

My favourite shirt cuff placket

This is my all-time favourite method for men's shirts. The pattern looks like a house with a chimney; the same pattern is used for either a square or pointy top. I have this pattern piece in cardboard and keep it handy to use it on any of my shirt patterns.

Lengthen or shorten the placket pattern at the bottom according to the length of the slit on the sleeve.

The overlap of the placket will be 2.5cm (1") finished and the underlap will be 1.2cm (½") finished.

Cut out two plackets as a pair, cutting the slit.

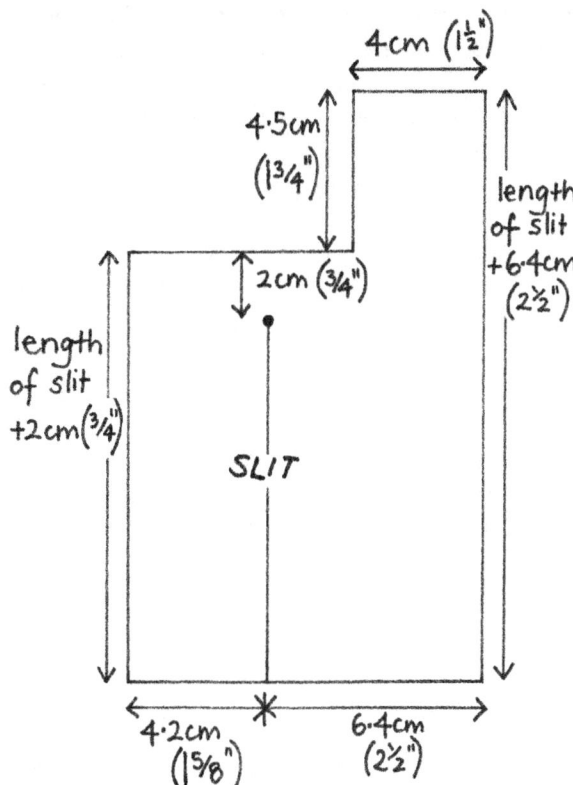

If the fabric is **striped or checked**, it looks good if you can match the pattern to the sleeve.

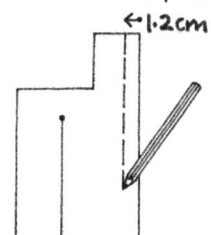
To do this, draw a line on the placket pattern 1.2cm (½") in from the long edge.

Match this line to whatever stripe lands on the slit line of the pattern, as illustrated. Notice on the illustration that whatever is to the left of the line matches whatever is to the left of the slit on the sleeve. For checked fabrics, place the placket on the same horizontal stripe as the bottom of the sleeve (as well as matching the vertical stripe).

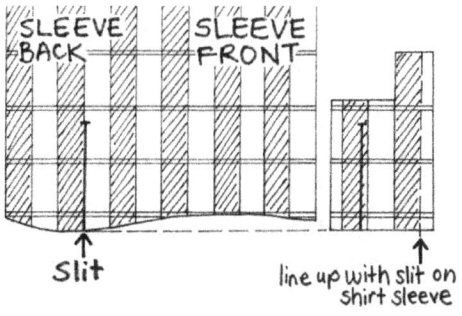

1. Lay the right side of the placket onto the wrong side of the sleeve, matching the (already cut) slits. In other

words, the wrong sides of both sleeve and placket will be facing up. The tall chimney side of the placket goes to the front. Stitch *exactly* 6mm (¼") around the edge of the slit, pivoting 90 degrees at the top two corners.

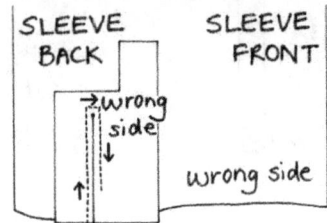

You may like to use a slightly smaller stitch at the top corners, such as 1.5 or 2 instead of the usual 2.5, for added strength.

2. Snip diagonally exactly into each corner and turn the placket through to the right side of the sleeve.

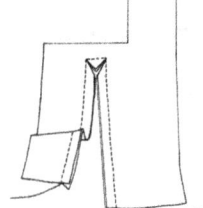

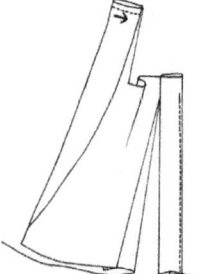

3. Sew the underlap first, that is, not the tall chimney side. Fold under 1cm (⅜") along the edge and stitch it down over the previous line of stitching, just covering the stitching with the folded edge.

The band should measure 1.2cm (½") wide and fit neatly in the square at the top of the slit.
To prevent it from rippling or twisting as you sew, hold the bottom layer firmly towards you, and let the placket "sit easy" on top.

4. Now for the overlap, the side shaped like a chimney. If you're having a placket with a pointed top, fold the top of the chimney in half longways and stitch across the top. Turn through, and position the seam in the centre underneath.

5. Fold under 6mm (¼") on the long side of the placket and position it over the first line of stitching. At this stage I like to press the placket to make sure everything is flat and in order for the final row of stitching.

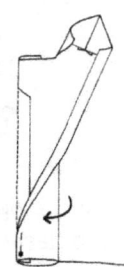

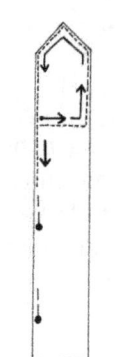

6. Begin sewing as illustrated, making the first part of the stitching come just above the square at the top of the slit, which will hold the underlap in place. Make sure the underlap is sitting straight beneath the overlap and not kicking out to the side. Continue around the top of the placket, finishing down the long side, so the folded edge just covers the first line of stitching. Be careful not to catch the underlap when you stitch.

The back of the placket will look like this:

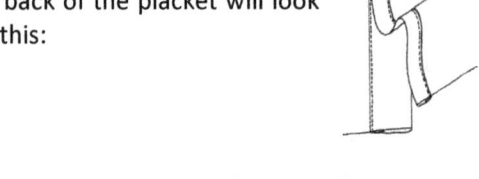

For a different look, this placket (or, actually, any of the others) can be extended to the end of the cuff. Make the placket pattern long enough to reach to the end of the cuff plus a seam allowance.

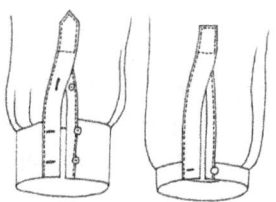

1. Sew the cuff on first.

2. Sew the placket on, leaving the seam allowance hanging over the lower edge of the cuff.

3. Before sewing each side down, bag out the end of the placket as shown by folding it back on itself and stitching across the bottom.

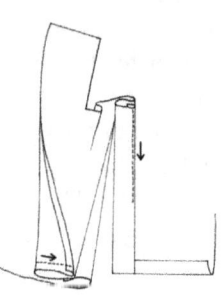

4. Fold it through to the right side and continue sewing the placket.

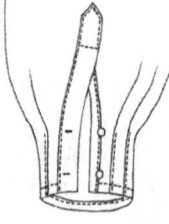

A cuff isn't always necessary. The extended placket can be sewn onto a sleeve with just a hemmed edge at the wrist.

Shirt cuff placket made with two strips

This method is essentially the same as my all-time favourite method described above, but made with two strips of fabric. The underlap can be a contrasting fabric. The overlap strip can be varied in size. The top

Shirt cuffs and plackets

of the placket can be pointed or square, but it's easier to sew if you have it square. The two strip method seems to be (in my experience) the most common one encountered in factory production.

Cut the strip for the placket's underlap at 4cm (1½") **wide**; it will be 1.2cm (½") finished. Make the **length** the same as the length of the slit plus 2cm (¾").

The strip for the overlap can be cut at any **width** from 5cm (2") to 6.2cm (2½"). A wider overlap cut at 6.2cm (2½") wide will result in the classic 2.5cm (1") placket for men's shirts. 5cm (2") will yield a slim, 2cm (¾") finished placket. Make the **length** the same as the length of the slit plus 4cm (1½").

Cut a pair of both strips—one set for each sleeve.

If the fabric is **checked or striped**, it looks smart if the pattern matches the sleeve. On the strip patterns, draw a line 1.2cm (½") in from the long edge of the plackets as illustrated. Usually no-one bothers to match the underlap strip, but you might want to depending on the fabric.

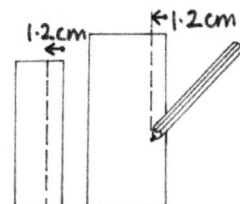

Match this line to whatever stripe lands on the slit line of the pattern, as illustrated. Notice that whatever is to the left of the line matches whatever is to the left of the slit on the sleeve.

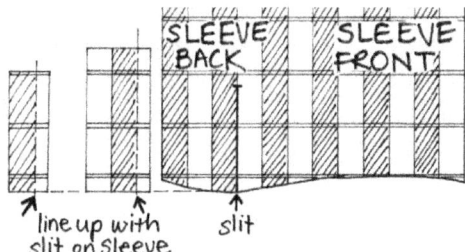

For checked fabrics, place the placket on the same horizontal stripe as the bottom of the sleeve (as well as matching the vertical stripe).

1. Lay the right sides of the strips onto the wrong side of the sleeve, with one edge of each strip on the slit. In other words, the wrong side of both sleeve and strips will be facing up.

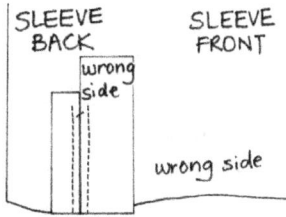

The wider strip goes to the front of the sleeve.
Note: if you're matching checks or stripes, the edge that you need to lay next to the slit is *not* the one that you drew a 1.2cm (½") line in from.
Machine sew 6mm (¼") from the raw edge on each side, stopping 6mm (¼") above the top of the slit. Be sure to backstitch securely at the ends.

2. Cut the *sleeve only* diagonally from the top of the slit to each end of the stitching, forming a triangular flap at the top of the slit. Bring both strips to the right side of the sleeve.

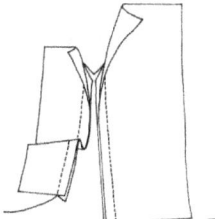

3. Stitch down the underlap first (the narrower strip): press under 6mm (¼") on the remaining long edge and stitch it down over the previous line of stitching, just covering the stitching with the folded edge. The underlap should measure 1.2cm (½") wide and fit neatly over the horizontal base of the triangle.

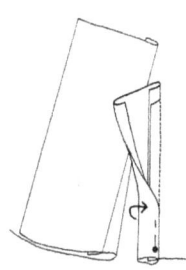

To prevent the strip from rippling or twisting as you sew, hold the bottom layer firmly towards you, and let the folded edge "sit easy" on top.

4. Prepare the overlap next (the wider strip): fold under 6mm (¼") on the remaining long edge and lay it so the fold just covers the previous line of stitching. Pin. Lap the overlap over the underlap, flipping the triangular piece upwards.
Make sure the underlap and overlap are in line and the underlap doesn't kick out at the wrong angle.

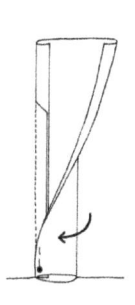

5. For a square-ended placket, press down 6mm (¼") at the top of the overlap.
For a pointy end, press the two sides into a point.
If the fabric is very thick you might need to trim away a bit of the underneath layer to reduce the bulk.

6. Following the illustration, begin stitching the overlap. The first part of the stitching needs to catch the base of the triangle at the top of the slit, to hold everything in place. Continue around the top of the placket, then finally down the long side. Be sure not to catch the underlap as you stitch.

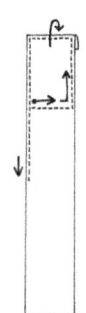

The back of the placket will look like this:

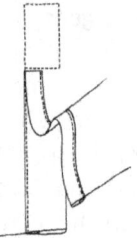

A simple shirt cuff placket with one strip

This method came from my teacher when I was a fashion student. It's a bit quicker than the other two methods described and it takes the bare minimum of fabric. However, the result isn't quite as high quality—the back doesn't look as neat. The top can be pointed or square, but it's easier to sew if you have it square.

The finished **width** of the placket can be anywhere from  a slim 2cm (¾") to a classic men's shirt width of 2.5cm (1"). For a 2cm (¾") wide placket, cut the strip at 5cm (2") wide. For a 2.5cm (1") wide placket, cut the strip at 6.2cm (2½") wide. Cut the **length** of the strip 4cm (1½") longer than the slit.

Cut two strips in fabric, one for each sleeve.

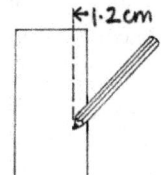 If the fabric is **striped or checked**, it's desirable to match the pattern. To do this, draw a line on the pattern 1.2cm (½") in from the long edge of the strip as illustrated.

Match this line to whatever stripe lands on the slit line of the pattern, as illustrated. Notice on the illustration that whatever's to the left of the line matches whatever's to the left of the slit on the sleeve.

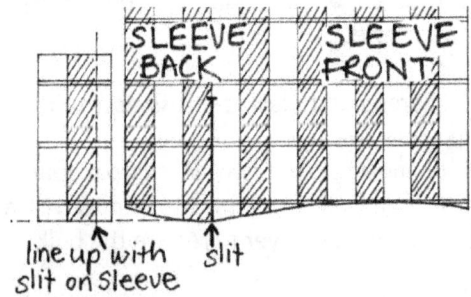

For checked fabrics, place the placket on the same horizontal stripe as the bottom of the sleeve (as well as matching the vertical stripe).

1. Lay the sleeve in front of you with the wrong side facing up. On the edge of the slit that is towards the 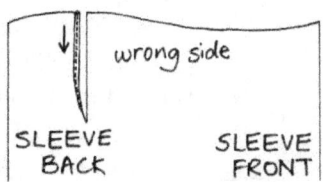 back, roll under the edge twice and stitch, tapering to nothing at the point of the slit.

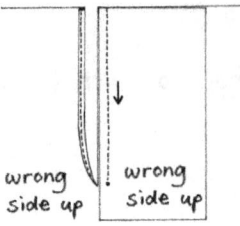

2. Lay the right side of the placket strip down onto the wrong side of the sleeve (so the wrong side of both are facing up), matching the slit and raw edge.

Note: if you're matching checks or stripes, the edge that you need to lay next to the slit is *not* the one that you drew a 1.2cm (½") line in from.

Stitch 6mm (¼") from the edge, finishing level with the top of the slit.

3. Snip the *sleeve only* from the point of the slit to the end of the stitching.

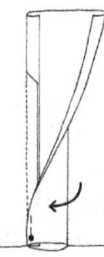

4. Turn the sleeve over to the right side and bring the strip through. Press 6mm (¼") under on the remaining long side of the strip and lay it so the folded edge just covers the previous line of stitching. Pin.

For a square-ended placket, press down 6mm (¼") at the top of the strip.

For a pointy end, press the two sides into a point. If the fabric is very thick you might need to trim away a bit of the underneath layer to reduce the bulk.

5. Ensure the strip is sitting correctly over the top of the rolled edge and the rolled edge isn't kicking out to one side. Stitch the strip as illustrated. Begin just *below* where you snipped in at the point of the slit. Stitch around the top of the placket then down the long side. To stop the strip from rippling or twisting as you sew the folded edge over the stitching, hold the bottom layer firmly towards you, and let the folded edge "sit easy" on top.

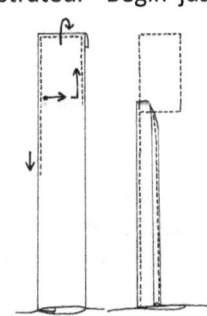

Cuffs

Before applying cuffs:
1. Sew the placket
2. Sew the underarm seam of the sleeve
3. Prepare any pleats or gathers at the sleeve edge

Shirt cuffs and plackets

✂ The simplest (and fastest to make) cuffs are cut in one piece with a fold line through the centre.

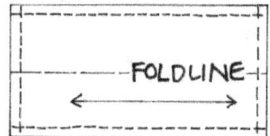

The grainline runs longways, along the length of the cuff. The grain is stronger in that direction and the cuff is less likely to stretch when you stitch it onto the sleeve and when you wear it. It also looks good for striped shirts.

The corners of the cuff can be square (as above), curved or angled (with the corner cut off). If the cuff has curved or angled corners, it needs to be cut in two pieces—one for the outside and one for the inside, with a seam allowance added.

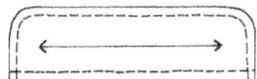

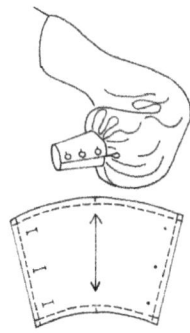

Cuffs that are wider than 15cm (6") will need to be shaped to fit the widening curves of the arm. They're therefore cut in two pieces—an outside and inside. This type of cuff has the grainline running in the same direction as the sleeve, rather than perpendicular to.

✂ To calculate the **length** of a cuff:
(useful to check if you have big or thin wrists)

	Example
1. Measure around the wrist	16cm (6¼")
2. Add ease (so the cuff isn't skin tight)	3cm or 4cm (1¼"-1½") I prefer 4cm
3. Add a button stand	1.5cm (⅝")
4. Add a buttonhole stand	1.5cm (⅝")
Finished length	23cm (9")

The **width** of the cuff is a design feature. If you want to change the cuff width, you'll need to lengthen or shorten the sleeve to correspond, to make the total length correct.

Average sized men's shirt cuffs are typically 24cm-25.5cm long (9½"-10") and 6.5cm-7cm wide (2½"-2¾").

✂ I like to have 1cm (⅜") **seam allowances** on my cuff patterns, but if you're using a commercial paper pattern with 1.5cm (⅝") seams, that's OK too.
On two piece cuffs with curved corners I make the seam allowance 6mm (¼") on the outside edge. It makes the curves easier and more accurate to sew, however, I still use 1cm (⅜") seams to attach the cuff to the sleeves.

✂ Cuffs need **interfacing** to provide support, strength and to stop the buttonholes from ripping out. The whole cuff can be interfaced or, more often, just half of the cuff. If half of the cuff is interfaced, the interfaced side goes on the outermost layer.
Shirt cuffs cut on the bias will need to be totally interfaced to stop the fabric stretching and distorting. Cut the interfacing on the straight grain, not the bias.
On men's shirts, a very firm interfacing is used on half the cuff (the outermost half).
Try out your fabric and interfacing and see if you need to apply interfacing to all or only half the cuff.

✂ The ends of cuffs can finish flush with the edges of the placket (left picture), or there can be a small extension underneath like a waistband (right picture). The extension is always on the back (button) side.

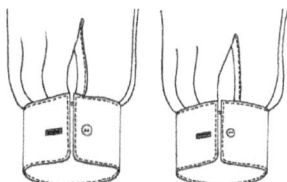

I think that flush-with-the-edges makes a far neater cuff and I never do mine with an extension. If yours has an extension, you can adjust the pleats or gathers to make the edge of the placket flush with the edge of the cuff, if you want to.

✂ **Pleats and gathers** are necessary to provide movement for the arm. A shirt sleeve with no pleats or gathers *is* possible, but tends to be tight around the elbow. Pleats and gathers can be easily adjusted to fit the cuff. Their purpose for existing is to make the sleeve fit into the cuff, so don't be afraid to change them! Different plackets will change the amount of pleating or gathering required, so be prepared to take bigger or smaller pleats, or more or less gathering to make the cuff fit.

Pleats are usually, but not always, folded towards the placket. Pleats can be on one or both sides of the placket. If they're only on one side, it's the front. If they're on both sides, there are usually more pleats on the front than the back. The pleats don't have to be all the same size (or the same *pleat value*, as patternmakers say).

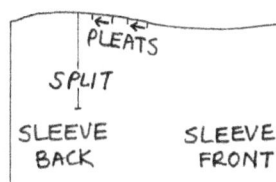

Gathers are usually around the whole wrist, which means the underarm seam needs to be sewn and neatened before you can sew the gathering threads.

308 The Dressmaker's Companion

Sewing a cuff

A cuff is applied like a mini waistband. There are three steps:
1. Sew the cuff to the wrong side of the sleeve
2. Finish the ends
3. Bring cuff over to the right side and topstitch into position

Before you sew the cuff on: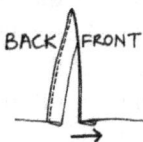

✂ If you've made a continuous bound placket, remember to fold the front of it underneath.

✂ Sew the underarm seam of the sleeve, neaten the seam allowance and turn the sleeve right side out.

✂ Stay-stitch the pleats into position before applying the cuff (using a long stitch on your machine) if you like, but I always pin mine in case I want to change them. Factory machinists form the pleats as they sew the cuff on, without pins.

1. Iron the interfacing onto the cuff, then iron the cuff in half longways.

2. With the *right* side of the cuff on the *wrong* side of the sleeve, sew the sleeve to the cuff. If you've only interfaced half of the cuff, sew the un-interfaced side on (this is the side that will be next to your skin when the shirt is worn).

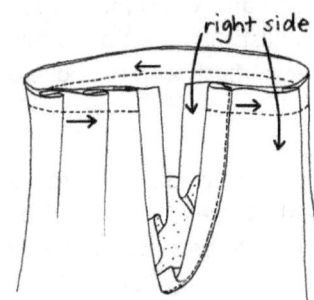

Important: make sure the end seam allowances of the cuff extend beyond the edges, otherwise you won't be able to stitch across the ends of the cuffs because you won't have any seam allowance to do it with.

I like to sit the cuff inside the sleeve, as shown. If you have a free-arm option on your sewing machine, this will make it easier to sew around. I also like to sew it with the sleeve uppermost so I can adjust the pleats if needed. If the sleeve is too big or small for the cuff, adjust the pleats to make it fit.

3. Flip the cuff up and hold the placket closed to check for a good flow-through line where the ends of the cuff meet each other (if you've made a continuous bound placket, you don't need to do this). If there's a difference, fix it now.

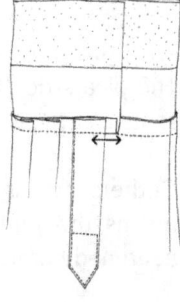

Don't try to fix it by stitching another row higher or lower—the cuff will end up the wrong width. Instead, note the amount to correct, unpick the section and re-sew it.

4. Finish the ends: fold the cuff in half longways, right sides together as illustrated. Measure the width of the cuff to make sure both ends are the same. Stitch across the ends.
Make sure you stitch *exactly* in line with the edge of the placket.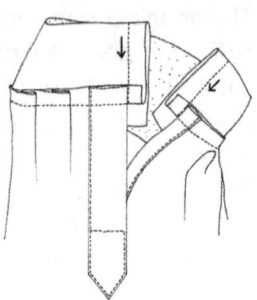

 If you stitch too far away there'll be a step

If you stitch too close it will make a pucker.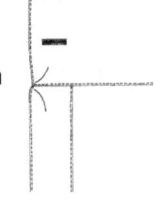

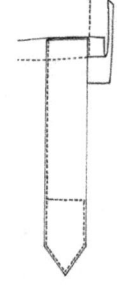

5. Trim off the seam allowance in the corner (or not, for light fabrics) and turn the ends through to the right side.
Hold the ends of the cuffs together and double-check the cuff is the same width both sides (which they should be, since you measured them when you finished the ends).

6. Fold in the ends of the cuff neatly as illustrated. Try to keep the corners really square as you fold. Secure with a pin.

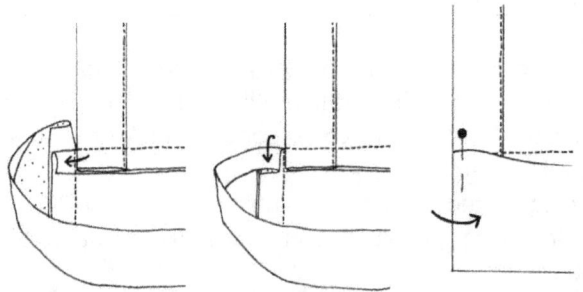

7. Fold the cuff over to the right side and edgestitch it into position, just covering the previous line of stitching with the folded edge. To prevent the top layer of the cuff from rippling or twisting as you sew it,

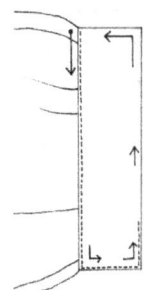

hold the bottom layer firmly towards you, and let the cuff "sit easy" on top. You can continue topstitching around the edge of the cuff (I like to), either with an edgestitch, or a wider topstitching like 6mm (¼"). It helps keep the cuff neat after laundering and keeps the fusing from coming unstuck after repeated washes.

8. Sew a buttonhole and button to the cuff. The buttonhole goes on the front (top layer) of the cuff, and the button underneath. The cuff can be made adjustable with the addition of a second button.

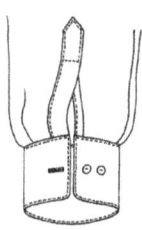

Another way to sew a cuff

This nifty idea comes from *Sewing Magic* by Barbara Hellyer. It's a way to stitch the ends of the cuffs with very neat corners at the sleeve edge. You might like to try it if you've struggled with finishing the ends as described above.

1. Sew the *right* side of the innermost cuff onto the *wrong* side of the sleeve, as usual.

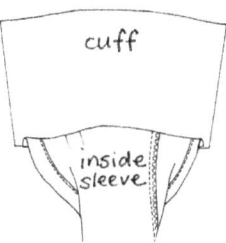

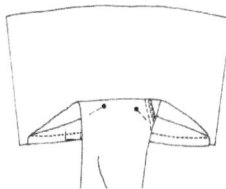

2. Fold the sleeve into the cuff at both ends and pin in place. You'll need about 3cm-5cm (1¼"-2") of stitching clear at each end.

3. Bring the cuff over so the right sides are together, matching the ends. Have the *underneath* cuff facing *up* so you can see the previous stitching line. Begin sewing 3cm-5cm (1¼"-2") in from the cuff edge and stitch exactly on the seam, before turning at the corner and stitching the end of the cuff. Sew both ends in the same way.

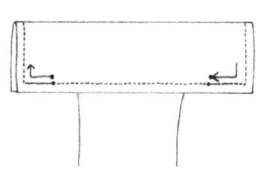

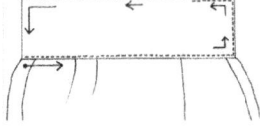

4. Trim the corners, turn through and edgestitch the cuff to hold it in place as usual.

Shirt cuffs and plackets

Men's shirt variation

Men's shirts usually have a two piece cuff, to allow rounded corners, and this method is fine for one or two piece cuffs (two piece is illustrated here).

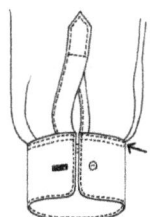

This method results in two visible rows of stitching on the sleeve side of the cuff—it looks smart and neat. You might prefer this way, and forever attach all your cuffs like this.

This method requires a 1cm (⅜") seam allowance on the cuff/wrist seam.

1. On the outermost (interfaced) side, fold under 8mm on the long edge and stitch close to the *raw* edge, not the folded edge. Put this piece aside for the moment.

2. Sew the *right* side of the underneath cuff to the *wrong* side of the shirt sleeve.

It's important that the correct cuff seam allowances stick out over the ends, otherwise you won't be able to sew the ends of the cuffs.

Flip the cuff up and press the cuff and seam allowance away from the sleeve.

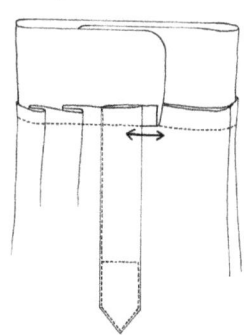

Hold the placket closed to check for a good flow-through line where the ends of the cuff meet each other (if you've made a continuous bound placket, you don't need to do this). If there's a difference, fix it now. Don't try to fix it by stitching another row higher or lower—the cuff will end up the wrong width. Note the amount to correct, unpick the section and re-sew it.

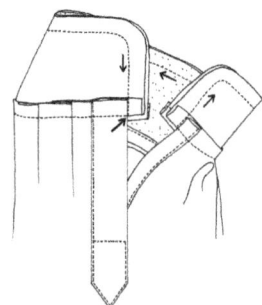

3. Attach the outside cuff to the inside one around the edges. Remember that you folded up the long edge only 8mm, not 1cm, so it will extend 2mm over the edge.

When you stitch the ends, make sure you stitch *exactly* in line with the edge of the placket. If you stitch too far away there will be a step.

310 The Dressmaker's Companion

Stitching too close will make a pucker.

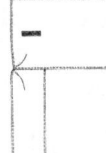

After sewing, hold both sides of the cuff together to check they're the same shape and width. Trim any curves or corners before turning the cuff the right way.

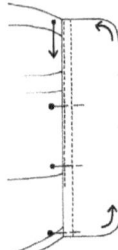

4. Fold the cuff to the right side. The 2mm extension should neatly cover the first line of stitching, ready to sew the final row. Edgestitch the long edge of the cuff into position, just covering the first row of stitching with the folded edge that you previously stitched down.

To prevent the top layer of the cuff from rippling or twisting as you sew it, hold the bottom layer firmly towards you and let the cuff "sit easy" on top.

Continue stitching around the whole cuff either with an edgestitch, or a wider topstitching such as 6mm (¼"). It helps keep the cuff neat after laundering and keeps the fusing in position if it comes unstuck after repeated washes.

5. Sew a buttonhole and button to the cuff. The buttonhole goes on the front (top layer) of the cuff, and the button underneath. The cuff can be made adjustable with the addition of a second button.

French cuffs

Mickey Mouse wore them and so did the girl in *Flashdance*. French cuffs, also called double cuffs, are much dressier and more formal than regular cuffs, but are sewn in exactly the same way. French cuffs are designed to be worn with cufflinks instead of buttons. The cuff is folded up and both sides of the cuff are pressed together like they're kissing, pointing away from the wrist. As with regular cuffs, the corners can be square, angled or curved.

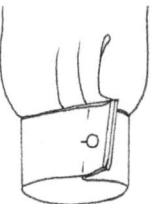

French cuffs generally *aren't* worn lapped over like a regular cuff.

✂ If you don't own cufflinks, you could make some by sewing two buttons together with a shank in the middle. Speciality button shops are sometimes able to convert buttons to cufflinks for you.

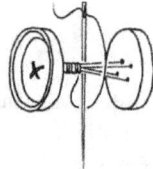

✂ Both sides of a French cuff can be **interfaced**, or the interfacing can be applied to the inside cuff only. When the cuff is folded up, it will be outermost.

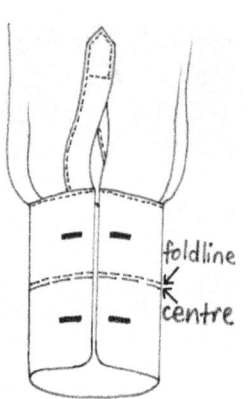

✂ A men's shirt cuff placket (as shown at left) is the classic placket choice for French cuffs, but the underlap of the placket must be folded towards the inside of the sleeve, so the placket will close without overlapping. You'll therefore need extra width around the sleeve end to compensate for this, but this simply might mean taking smaller pleats.

✂ The fold in a French cuff isn't at the halfway point but slightly above it towards the sleeve, so the folded-up part covers the seam where the sleeve and cuff join. The placement of the buttonholes determines the fold line, so position the buttonholes carefully to match when the fold is in the correct position.

Foldback cuffs

While these aren't the classic French cuff, they look very smart for women's blouses. No button is visible when it's done up. Sometimes the underneath cuff is cut in a contrasting fabric that shows when the cuff is folded back.

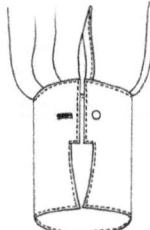

A foldback cuff is sewn in the same way as an ordinary cuff and interfaced like a French cuff.

Troubleshooting cuffs and plackets

Cuffed sleeves too short and cuff is already sewn on
Possible solutions:

✂ Remove the cuff and replace it with a wider one. If you have no more fabric and the cuff is one piece, unpick the cuff and open it out. Use the old cuff for the top layer and a different fabric for the underneath one.

✂ Sew a frill or ruffle onto the edge of the cuff to make it look longer.

✂ Cut the cuff off and turn the sleeves into short or three-quarter length.

✂ Always wear the sleeves rolled up.

Shirt cuffs and plackets **311**

Cuffed sleeves too long and cuff is already sewn on
Possible solutions:
- Can the cuffs be folded back, French cuff style?
- Remove the cuffs and shorten the sleeve.
- Shorten the sleeve at the top.
- Always wear the shirt with the sleeves rolled up.

Point of continuous placket fraying
Possible solutions:
- Repair by hand.
- Sew a patch over the top and call it a feature.

Cuff too tight around wrist and already sewn on
Possible solutions:
- Sew the button right on the edge of the cuff and remember to cut bigger cuffs next time.
- Sew a button and loop right on the edges of the cuff, instead of a buttonhole. Or sew a row of loops.

Cuff rippling when being topstitched

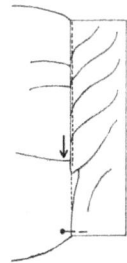

The last step where the cuff is stitched down can cause the cuff to ripple and twist if it isn't handled correctly.

It's important to hold the underneath layer firmly with your left hand, pulling it forward and let the cuff "sit easy" on top with your right hand.

If you begin sewing and the cuff begins to ripple, stop sewing and unpick what you've done. The ripples will never go away as you sew—they will get worse.

Although rippling can happen if the fabric isn't cut on grain, your sewing technique is a major factor.

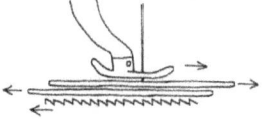

Why does it do it? As a sewing machine sews, the presser foot pushes the top layer of fabric forward, with the feed dogs feeding the underneath layer backwards. Thus, if you let a machine just sew naturally, the top layer will be longer by the time you get to the end. When topstitching down a cuff, this is what causes the rippling effect.

Although your sewing technique is what will make the biggest difference, some other things will help reduce rippling:
- Ease off the pressure on the presser foot (there should be a knob to adjust the pressure on the top of the machine—consult your manual). The thicker the fabric, the less pressure needed, so the fabric will fit under the foot.
- Try using a walking foot, if you have one.
- Ironing a one piece cuff in half lengthways before you start sewing helps to reduce rippling.

Shirt yokes

Introduction 312	To sew a shirt yoke 314
Make a pattern 312	with front facings 314
back pleats and gathers 313	Western shirt yokes 315
Fitting note: rounded shoulders 314	

A shirt yoke is a fitted section across the shoulders and around the back neck. It's an important design element of a shirt. A yoke supports and gives extra strength to this area of the shirt, from which the rest of the shirt hangs.
The shoulder seams are concealed within the yoke, making the shirt more comfortable. A shirt yoke is always two thicknesses of material.

✂ Narrow yokes are considered classic and dressy.

✂ Deeper yokes are sportier and more casual.

✂ Deep yokes that go through the centre front band are seen on traditional smocks and children's and women's clothes.
Ensure the yokes meet up in the centre.

✂ Yokes can also be curved, but the curves need to be very gentle so they're easy to sew.

✂ Occasionally the yoke is on the back of the shirt only (but rarely on men's shirts).

✂ The design of the back yoke should relate to the front yoke.

✂ The **grainline** on a yoke is almost always perpendicular to the grainline on the rest of the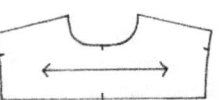
shirt because the grain is stronger in this direction, it provides shoulder emphasis on men's shirts and it looks visually pleasing in stripes. It also saves having to match the stripes to the back of striped or checked shirts.

The exception to the grainline rule is corduroy and other napped fabrics, where the colour would look different. In this case, the yoke is cut with the same vertical grainline as the rest of the shirt.

Don't be tempted to have different grainlines on the outermost and innermost yokes. It's better to have both grainlines vertical than have one run one way and one the other, in case the fabric performs differently or shrinks only in one direction.

Plaid shirts often, but not always, have the yoke cut on the bias. To do this, draw in a new grainline at 45 degrees to the old one.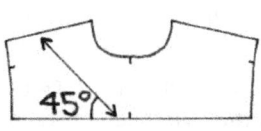
Cut both inner and outer yokes on the bias. If the fabric is very unstable, consider fusing both yokes with a very light weight interfacing.

✂ Occasionally, one or both of the yokes are **interfaced** with a light interfacing, to give them body. I would recommended it on floppy or fine fabrics. On fine, patterned fabrics it prevents the pattern of the underneath yoke showing through.
On some men's shirts, the yoke is made of a triple thickness of fabric.

Make a pattern
Making a pattern for a shirt yoke fairly easy. It's also quite simple to un-make a pattern if you want a shirt without a yoke, or to change the shape of a yoke.

Shirt yokes

A yoke pattern has notches at the sides for matching the top of the sleeve, and centre notches for attaching the collar and back accurately.

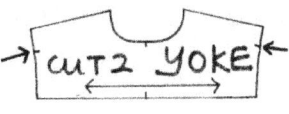

1. Draw on the front and back shirt pattern where you'd like the yoke to be. The line for the front yoke is usually parallel to the shoulder seam. If you want the yoke to be curved, a French curve is a handy tool for drawing in a smooth curved line.

2. Trace off the yoke and join the shoulders together on the shoulder *stitching* line. Mark a notch at the ends for matching the top of the sleeve, where the shoulder seam would have been.

Add seam allowances to the yoke for the front and back. For curved yokes, a small seam allowance of 6mm (¼") or 1cm (⅜") will make the curves easier to sew.

3. On the front and back, add a seam allowance (the same as the yoke's) to the line you drew in Step 1. Trim off the excess.

On patterns for myself, I just fold under the tops of the front and back instead of trimming off. Then if I decide to make a shirt without a yoke, I still have an intact shirt pattern.

A rather English variation is to cut the yoke in two pieces with a centre back seam. This gives an interesting effect for stripes. The stripes meet in a shallow chevron at the back.
The grainline is parallel to the front yoke seam.

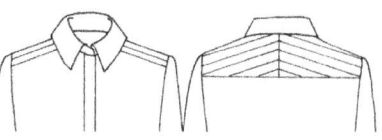
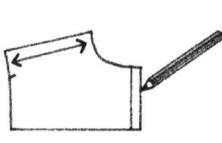

Back pleats and gathers

If you'd like the shirt to have a back pleat falling from the yoke, simply add the amount of the pleat along the entire centre back and mark a notch at the top to show where to fold the pleat to.

How much to add?
I usually add about 3cm (1¼"), which will be 1.5cm (⅝") when the pleat is folded, yielding 6cm (2½") extra in total width across the back.

The pleat can be stitched as a classic box pleat.

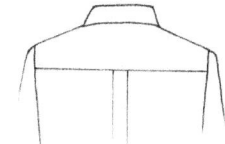

Sometimes a loop is sewn above the box pleat for casual shirts. It's either inserted into the seam or stitched on top of the yoke.

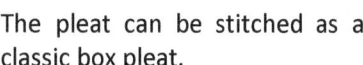

Alternatively, the pleat can be folded in the opposite direction to become an inverted pleat. The inverted pleat could fall straight from the yoke seam, or be stitched down for a few centimetres. It could also be topstitched for a casual look.

The pleat value can be divided into two side pleats.
Position them no closer than 5cm (2") to the sleeve seams. Sew them so they point towards the sleeve.

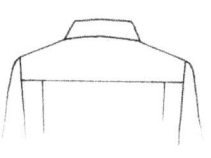

Gathers can also be added to a shirt in the same way. The amount to add will vary according to the style and fabric. For example, fine fabrics require denser gathering to look substantial. Generous, voluminous gathers are a feature of pirate/buccaneer shirts.

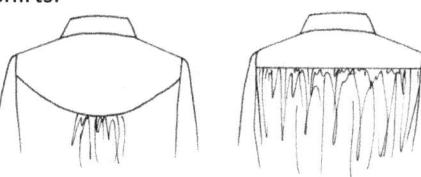

Fitting note: rounded shoulders

To accommodate rounded shoulders or a dowager's hump in a yoke, where a shoulder or neck dart can't be used, a wedge can be taken below the yoke into the armhole (like taking a dart).

How much should the wedge be? 2cm-2.5cm (¾"-1") seems to be about right for most people, but obviously the more curved the back the greater the amount.

To compensate for the armhole now being smaller and also the extra length required over the rounded shoulders, add the same amount through the back that you removed for the wedge.

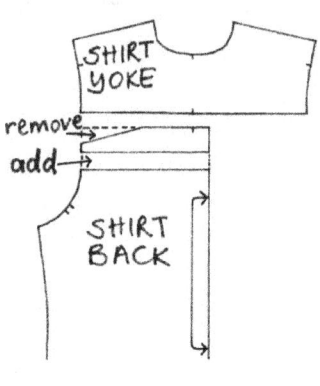

If you've already cut out the shirt and realized this alteration is called for, remove the wedge below the yoke then lower the back armhole the same amount.

The back will now be shorter than the front, so trim the extra length off the bottom of the front. Hopefully you can afford to lose the length.

To sew a shirt yoke

The yoke is one of the first things to sew when making a shirt. It's made before the collar and the sleeves are sewn on. The only things sewn before a yoke are the front pockets, if the shirt has any, and the front stand.

It the shirt is striped, match the yoke to the sleeve stripes when you cut it out.

1. Form the pleat at the back of the shirt, if it has one.

2. Sandwich the back of the shirt between the right sides of the two yokes, and sew the seam.

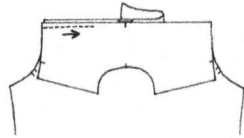

3. Press both yokes up and away from the shirt's back.

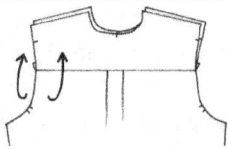

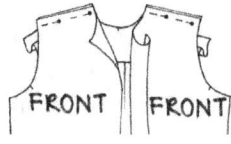

4. Lay the yokes and back out flat on the table, right side up. Pin the shirt fronts to the top yoke at the shoulders, right sides together.

5. Roll the fronts and backs together, starting from the lower edge, until you reach the yokes.

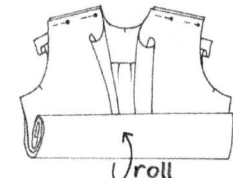

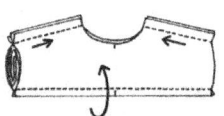

6. Flip the underneath yoke so the right sides of the yoke are together, encasing the rolled up shirt between them.

Sew the shoulder seams of the yoke, sandwiching the fronts between the yokes.

7. Turn the shirt to the right way. If you're planning to topstitch the yoke, do so now before applying the collar and sleeves.

To avoid ripples when topstitching, stitch the front yoke from neck to armhole.

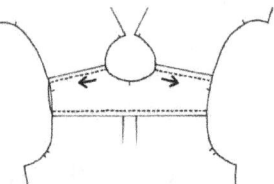

Sewing a shirt yoke with front facings

While a yoke is easy to attach when the collar and front button stand are sewn separately, it's a little trickier when you have a collar that's attached by sandwiching it between facings, using the underneath yoke as a substitute back neck facing.

The yoke pattern is the same, but the order of sewing is a little different from a regular shirt yoke.

1. Put the back of the shirt aside for the moment. Prepare the front facings: apply interfacing and overlock the long outer edge.

2. Sew the top yoke to the fronts at the shoulder seams. Sew the underneath yoke to the prepared front facings. Take the regular seam allowance for both, and press the seams towards the yokes.

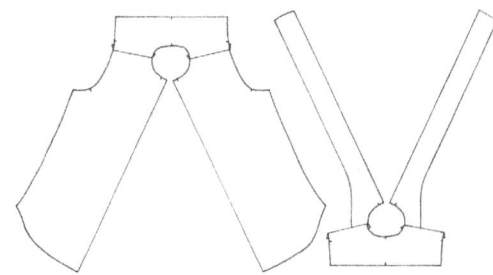

3. Make the collar up. If you're planning to topstitch the collar and front edges, don't topstitch the collar now–do it all at the end.

4. Sandwich the collar between the right sides of the two yokes and stitch around the neck and fronts. Ensure that the yoke seams are pressed towards the yoke and the seams line up on top of each other. Trim the corners, clip the curves and turn the yokes and facings to the right side.

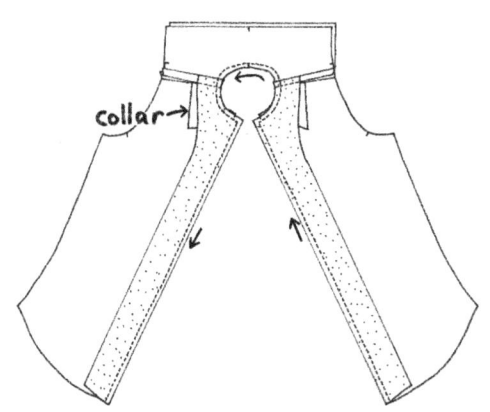

5. With the right sides of the yokes together, sew the front yoke seams together.

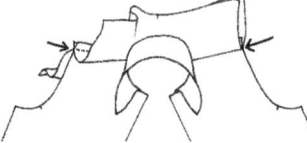

Start at the armhole end and sew as far as you can towards the collar, sewing exactly over the first line of stitching made in Step 2. There'll be a short gap next to the neckline where you won't be able to sew.

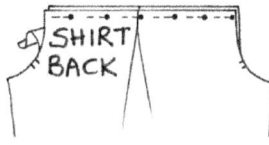

6. Attach the back: pin the back to the *top* yoke, right sides together.

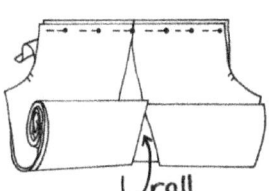

7. Roll up the back and fronts together.

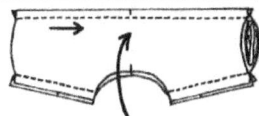

8. Flip the underneath yoke around and sew the back yoke seam.

9. Topstitch the yoke now if you want to. The backstitching next to the neck will be hidden by the collar, but for a perfect finish with no backstitching you can pull the threads through to the wrong side and tie them off.

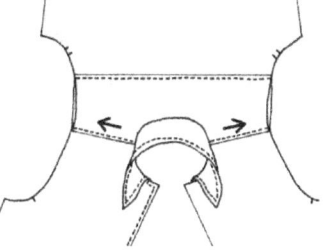

To avoid ripples when topstitching, stitch the front yoke from neck to armhole.

You can now topstitch the collar and front edges in one operation.

Western shirt yokes

The shaped yokes of western (or cowboy) shirts are simply stitched *on top* of the shirt, like a giant appliqué. 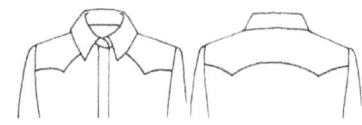 Unlike regular yokes, western shirt yokes are usually in two parts—a front and a back joined with a shoulder seam.

✂ Western shirts don't have a back pleat.

✂ Western shirts can have curved or pointy yokes. Sometimes they're very elaborate with embroidery, fringing or piping. Have a look on the Internet for some ideas.

✂ The shape of the front yoke should relate to the back yoke.

Make a pattern

1. Draw the shape of the yoke on the shirt pattern. Use a French curve to create smooth, pleasing curves.

2. Trace off the front and back yoke and add a seam allowance on the lower edge.

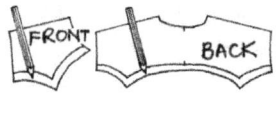

3. Add a grainline, the same as the shirt's grainline.

For **plain** coloured western shirts, the grainline runs in the same direction as the rest of the shirt.

For **striped or plaid** western shirts, the yokes are cut on the bias. To do this, draw in a new grainline at 45 degrees to the old one.

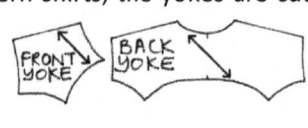

To sew a western shirt yoke

If the fabric is light, unstable or cut on the bias, I suggest interfacing the yokes with a light weight fusible jersey interfacing to help them sit smoothly and make sewing easier.

1. Sew the shoulder seams on the shirt with the *wrong* sides together. Press the seams open. No need to overlock.
Sew the shoulder seams of the yoke with the *right* sides together and press the seams open. Again, no need to overlock.
Important: make sure the front yokes are sewn on around the right way. The pieces can easily be confused once the pattern is removed.

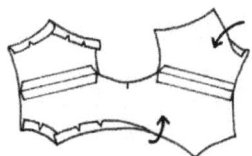

2. Press under the front and back seam allowances of the yoke. Clip the curves to make the edges sit flat.

Optional: piping or fringing

If you plan to have piping or fringing on the edges of the yoke, attach it *before* pressing under the edge.
Stitch the piping or fringing onto the edge of the yoke, along the stitching line, clipping the curves and corners, then press under the edge ready to topstitch the yoke on in the next step.

3. Pin the wrong side of the yoke to the right side of the shirt, matching the shoulder seams, neck and armhole edges. Edgestitch the front and back of the yoke into position, around the shaped edges of the yoke.

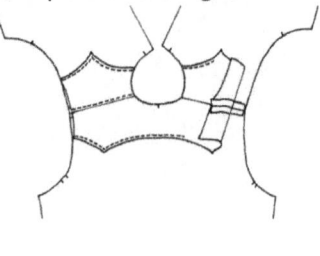

Optional: with the yoke uppermost, edgestitch the shoulder seams together, stitching on the front yoke.

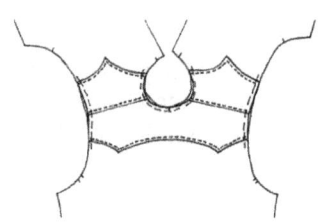

4. Machine baste the neck and armhole edges together, in preparation for attaching the collar and sleeves.

Shoulder pads

Introduction.................................. 317	raglan pads................................... 319
Do you *need* shoulder pads?........... 317	Adjusting a pattern for pads 319
shoulder darts........................ 318	Making shoulder pads 320
Positioning shoulder pads............... 318	materials................................ 320
To sew pads in jackets.................... 318	patterns................................. 320
square pad.............................. 318	general instructions................. 320
raglan pad 318	square shoulder pads.............. 320
To sew pads in tops........................ 318	raglan shoulder pads............... 321
Pads in reversible garments............ 319	Sleeve header................................... 321
Covering shoulder pads.................. 319	to sew sleeve header in 321
square pads............................. 319	another method...................... 321

As a fashion student in the early 1990's, I visited a fashion designer's workroom. In the patternmaking room, there was an pinboard office partition completely covered with different shoulder pads, all numbered for the patternmaker's reference. Thirteen years later, I became the patternmaker there. By then shoulder pads had gone out of fashion and there was only one type, which we used for coats.

There are two types of shoulder pads: square and raglan. Square pads produce a squarer shoulder, however, they aren't restricted to set-in sleeves, nor are raglan pads used only on raglan sleeves.

Square pads finish at the armhole, extending just past the shoulder seam.
When flat, they're roughly semi-circular in shape.

Raglan pads extend over the shoulder to the top of the arm. They're a rounded, three-dimensional shape.
My dad always thought they looked like cricketer's groin protectors.

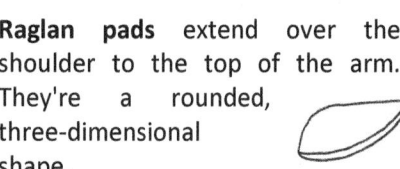

✂ Shoulder pads are made out of layers of batting (wool, cotton or polyester) or moulded foam. The advantage of the layered type is that layers can be removed if you want a thinner pad. You can add layers to any type to make a thicker pad.
Felt shoulder pads used in lined jackets should be dry cleaned, but since the rest of the jacket usually requires dry cleaning, this presents no problems. If you plan to hand wash the jacket, use a shoulder pad that can be washed, for example one made of polyester.

✂ If you're using shoulder pads, include them in your fittings from the beginning, otherwise the garment's sleeves will end up too short.

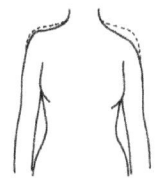

✂ Shoulder pads can be used on uneven shoulders to even them up. Use a thicker pad on the low side, or add a few extra layers to the existing pad.

✂ Shoulder pads can be used to build up sloping shoulders.

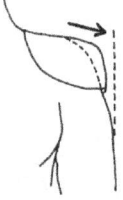

✂ They can also be used to disguise full upper arms. Use a raglan pad and move the pad out until the edge lines up with the fullest part of the arm.

Do you *need* shoulder pads?
I think shoulder pads are essential...
✂ in coats
✂ in any garment for larger figures
✂ for uneven or very sloping shoulders

You don't always need shoulder pads in tailored jackets. I don't use them in mine. Try using just sleeve header (page 321) and see if you like the look.

Shoulder darts

If you *aren't* using shoulder pads in a jacket, you may require a shoulder dart for a smooth fit. Very rounded people may require shoulder darts *and* shoulder pads.

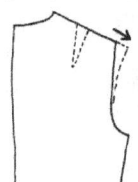

To add a shoulder dart, add 1cm-1.5cm (⅜"-⅝") onto the edge of the back shoulder, then take a 1cm-1.5cm (⅜"-⅝") dart. Make the dart about 6cm (2⅜") long.

A neck dart will also give a smoother fit, particularly on elderly figures. See page 2 for more on neck or shoulder darts for older people.

Positioning shoulder pads

Square shoulder pads usually have a front and a back. Put the longer, pointier end at the front so it fills in the hollow in front of the shoulder. Raglan shoulder pads are the same front and back and can be used on either shoulder.

Try the garment on with the shoulder pads on your shoulders, then pin the pads in place through the garment. Square shoulder pads should extend 1cm (⅜") beyond the shoulder seam into the armhole.

Raglan pads can fit on your shoulders or can extend as much as 2cm (¾") beyond your natural shoulder line. Move the pads in or out depending how much wider you want your shoulders.

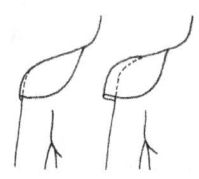

If the shoulder pad is too big and it shows in the neckline, the edges can be trimmed.

To sew shoulder pads in jackets

Insert the shoulder pad *after* you've sewn the sleeve and sleeve header in, but *before* the lining.

Square pads

1. Stitch square shoulder pads in by hand along the armhole edge using double thread and an overcast stitch (page 150). Some people prefer to sew backstitch (page 148) on the armhole seam.

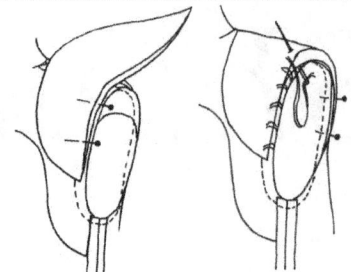

Make sure you don't sew the pad in upside down. If it's in correctly it will want to curl up when you're positioning it in an inside-out jacket.

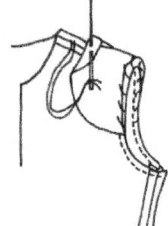

2. Make a 2cm (¾") long loose thread shank to secure the pad to the shoulder seam.

✂ When I was a fashion student, my sewing teacher demonstrated sewing them in by machine.

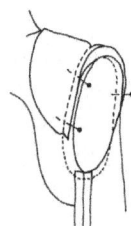

She sewed the pad straight onto the armhole edge, stitching on top of the armhole stitching. She was using an industrial machine, so she managed the thickness. She sewed with the pad underneath, exactly on the previous row of stitching.

It gave a very pronounced groove around the top of the armhole.

Raglan pads

Attach raglan shoulder pads by hand to the jacket's shoulder seam.

For very rounded shoulders in set-in sleeves (as in Armani shoulders) use a raglan pad. Press the armhole seam allowance *open* at the top, 5cm (2") either side of the shoulder seam. Sew the raglan pad in by hand.

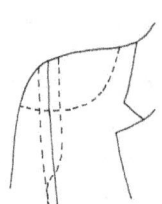

To sew shoulder pads in tops

Removable pads are best for tops because they can be taken out before washing the garment.

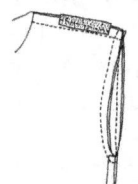

Removable pads are attached with velcro. The soft side of the velcro is sewn to the shoulder seam allowance and the rough side is sewn on the pad.

Some budget ready-to-wear garments have non-removable shoulder pads sewn by machine to the shoulder seam.

Shoulder pads in reversible garments

Shoulder pads in reversible garments are always a problem, since the shoulder pad isn't reversible. You could make covered shoulder pads that can be pinned in place if required.

If there's no shoulder or sleeve seam to attach a pad to, place a lingerie strap guard underneath the shoulder pad and attach it to your bra instead of the garment.

Covering shoulder pads

Shoulder pads should be covered unless they're in a lined garment. Shoulder pads are covered with the same fabric as the garment or a plain fabric. To avoid seeing shoulder pads through fine or light coloured garments, cover the pad with a fabric to match the skin tone of the wearer.

Square pads

If the pad is to be removable, sew a piece of velcro to the cover before the pad is covered. Cut a strip 8cm (3⅛") long. Cut it in half down the middle so you have two skinny strips—one for the left pad and one for the right. The rough side gets sewn to the shoulder pad cover.

1. Cut a square of fabric big enough to cover the shoulder pad with the straight edge of the pad on a diagonal.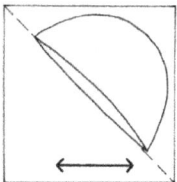

2. Sew the rough piece of velcro along a diagonal as illustrated.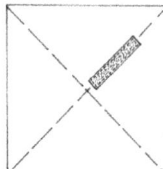

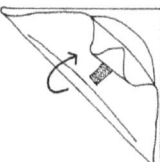
3. Lay the pad on the square with a long edge on the other diagonal. Fold over the fabric, encasing the shoulder pad.

4. Stitch around the edge of the pad.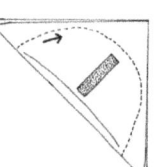

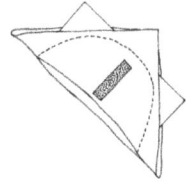
If the pad is rectangular, stitch in a semi-circular shape through all the layers.

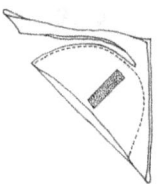
5. Trim the excess off the edges, then overlock.

Raglan pads

Raglan shoulder pads are best covered with some sort of knit that will stretch over the curved shape. Try swimsuit lining or some other sort of non-slippery knit. You could also fuse stretch interfacing to the top and bottom sides and overlock the edges. Stretch the interfacing to fit.

1. Cut two pieces, one for the top and one for the bottom. For very curved, rounded shoulder pads, you might need to seam the top layer to get a smooth fit.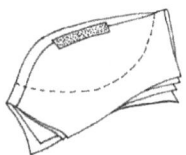

If the pad is to be removable, sew the rough side of a piece of velcro to the top.

2. Sandwich the shoulder pad between the two pieces, stretching the knit to fit, and stitch around the edge. Trim off the excess and overlock the edge.

Adjusting a pattern for shoulder pads

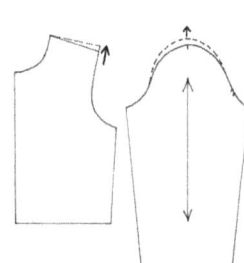
Measure the height of the pad at its highest point. If the pad is very soft, compress it gently with your fingers while you measure it. Add this amount to the top of the sleeve head and raise the shoulder seam by this amount at the sleeve end of the shoulder.

For raglan shapes, add the height of the pad to the shoulder point and blend back to the neck and wrist points.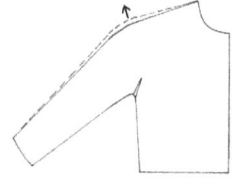

The reverse alterations can be done if you *don't* want shoulder pads.

Making your own shoulder pads—raglan and square

Shoulder pads are actually very quick to make once all the pieces have been cut out.

Materials

You'll need some cotton, wool or polyester batting, available where quilting supplies are sold. You can also use fusible fleece (polyester). I like to use cotton batting because I think it makes a more substantial pad, however, polyester batting has some advantages: it tends to be loftier than cotton, so you might need less layers, and a polyester pad will dry much quicker when the garment is washed.

Patterns

There are four patterns for shoulder pads in this book: two square pads and two raglans. Make the pattern pieces by tracing each layer off separately. You can use pattern tracing paper, or make cardboard templates by using a tracing wheel to transfer them to cardboard. Cardboard patterns are quicker to use because you can draw around them directly onto the batting. These patterns are all available as PDFs at www.thedressmakerscompanion.com.

General instructions

The largest layer of a shoulder pad is always the top layer and the second largest is always the bottom. The other pieces stack in size order between them like a topographical map.

If you're using **fusible fleece**, curve the shoulder pad into shape before fusing. Curve it over a tailor's ham or towel, or even a bottle. Cover it with a light press cloth and steam press with the iron set at "wool". Press for about ten seconds. Don't glide the iron back and forth—move it around in an up-and-down motion. Allow the shoulder pad to cool, then check the adhesion. You might need to turn the shoulder pad over and press it from the other side as well.

With **cotton, wool or polyester batting**, the layers are sewn together but you won't need lots of stitching. Pin the pad together first, curving it around your hand as you do. Long quilting pins are excellent to use.

Hold the shoulder pad in the curved shape as you sew. Use two strands of thread and take large tacking stitches, but instead of using ordinary running stitch, use pad stitch like tailors use. It holds the layers in two directions instead of one.

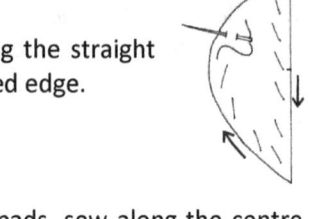

For square pads, sew along the straight side, then around the curved edge.

For raglan pads, sew along the centre (from shoulder to neck), then around the whole edge.

You could also join the layers together by...

✄ Gluing them, being very sparing with the glue. Keep the pad in a curved shape while the glue dries. Use a glue that's flexible when dry.

✄ Needle felting, although you might have problems with thick shoulder pads.

Square shoulder pads

1. Cut out all the pieces:

✄ For each **small** shoulder pad (pattern on page 322), cut one of every layer in batting.

✄ For each **large (jacket)** pad (pattern on page 323), cut one each of the top and bottom layers and two of the other layers. If you're using polyester batting or fusible fleece you might only need one of each layer. For bigger pads, suitable for men's jackets, note the different cutting lines.

2. Assemble the layers. Start with the bottom layer (the second largest piece), then stack the layers in order so it looks like a topographical map, matching the shoulder point. Finish with the top layer (the largest piece). Pin the pad together, curving it in your hand. Check that it's the right size and height. If not, remove or add layers until you're happy with it.

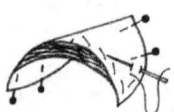

3. Sew the pad together as described above on this page.

Raglan shoulder pads

1. Cut out all the pieces: for each pad cut one of the top and bottom layer and two of all the other layers.

✂ There are two versions of the **small raglan pad** (patterns on page 325) but the only difference is how the top layer is constructed. The other layers are the same. One has the top layer shaped by darts, and the other is shaped by a seam.

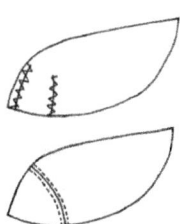

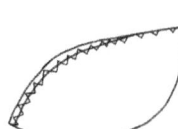 ✂ For the **large (coat) pad** (pattern on page 324) you'll need a *pair* of the top layer to seam together.

2. Machine sew any seams or darts in the top layer to shape it:

✂ For the **darted shoulder pad**, sew the darts by butting the edges together and joining with a zig zag stitch.

✂ For the **seamed shoulder pad**, sew the curved seam with a 6mm (¼") seam allowance, press the seam open and topstitch each side to make it flat.

✂ For the **large coat pad**, sew the central seam in the top layer by butting the edges together and zig zagging.

3. Assemble the layers: start with the top layer that you've sewn by machine, then stack the layers inside starting with the smallest. Finish with the bottom layer.

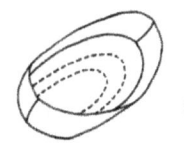 

4. Pin the pad together and sew through all the layers as described on page 320.

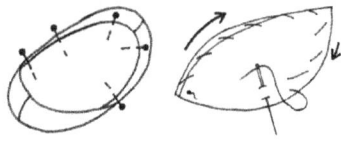

Sleeve Header

Sleeve header is used in jackets that have set-in sleeves. It's a strip of fabric sewn into the sleeve head of a jacket *after* the sleeves have been set in, but *before* the shoulder pads are attached. Its purpose is to fill out the ease area of the sleeve head so it doesn't cave in. Sew sleeve header in even if you aren't using shoulder pads. Unlined jackets don't have header in them.

You'll need 25cm (10") of header per sleeve, or 30cm (12") for large sizes or men's jackets.

You can use:

✂ A strip of felt 5cm (2") wide.

✂ A pre-cut felt boomerang. There's a pattern for one on page 326.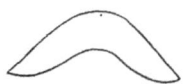

✂ A purchased length of sleeve header. It's a strip of felt with a strip of bias-cut hair canvas on top. The felt is folded and stitched on one long edge and the *other* edge is the one that gets sewn in the armhole. I undo the stitching and cut along the folded line because the fold tends to be visible through the sleeve.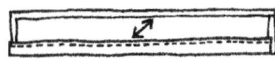

✂ A 5cm (2") wide bias-cut strip of thick wool. You could use the same fabric as your jacket if it's suitable.

✂ A 10cm (4") wide bias strip of linen folded in half lengthwise.

✂ A 5cm (2") wide strip of polyester wadding, split in half to make it thinner. Use one half for each sleeve. If you've got some thin batting handy after making shoulder pads, you could use that.

To sew sleeve header in

1. Arrange the garment so you're looking down into the inside of the sleeve. Sit the header in the sleeve head with the middle matched to the shoulder seam. Smooth it to fit in the sleeve head and pin it perpendicular to the seam. Let the ends run off to nothing.

2. Sew the header in from the body side, not the sleeve side, stitching *exactly* on top of the sleeve seam. You can use a slightly longer stitch, such as 3 instead of the usual 2.5.

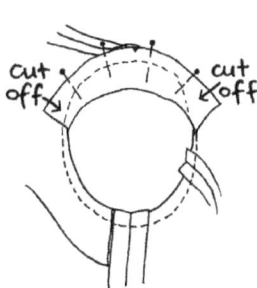

3. Trim off the excess at the ends.

Another method

Some people stitch on the header without running it off at the ends.

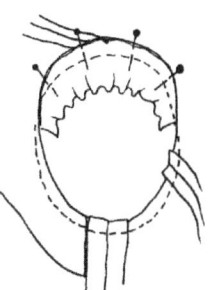

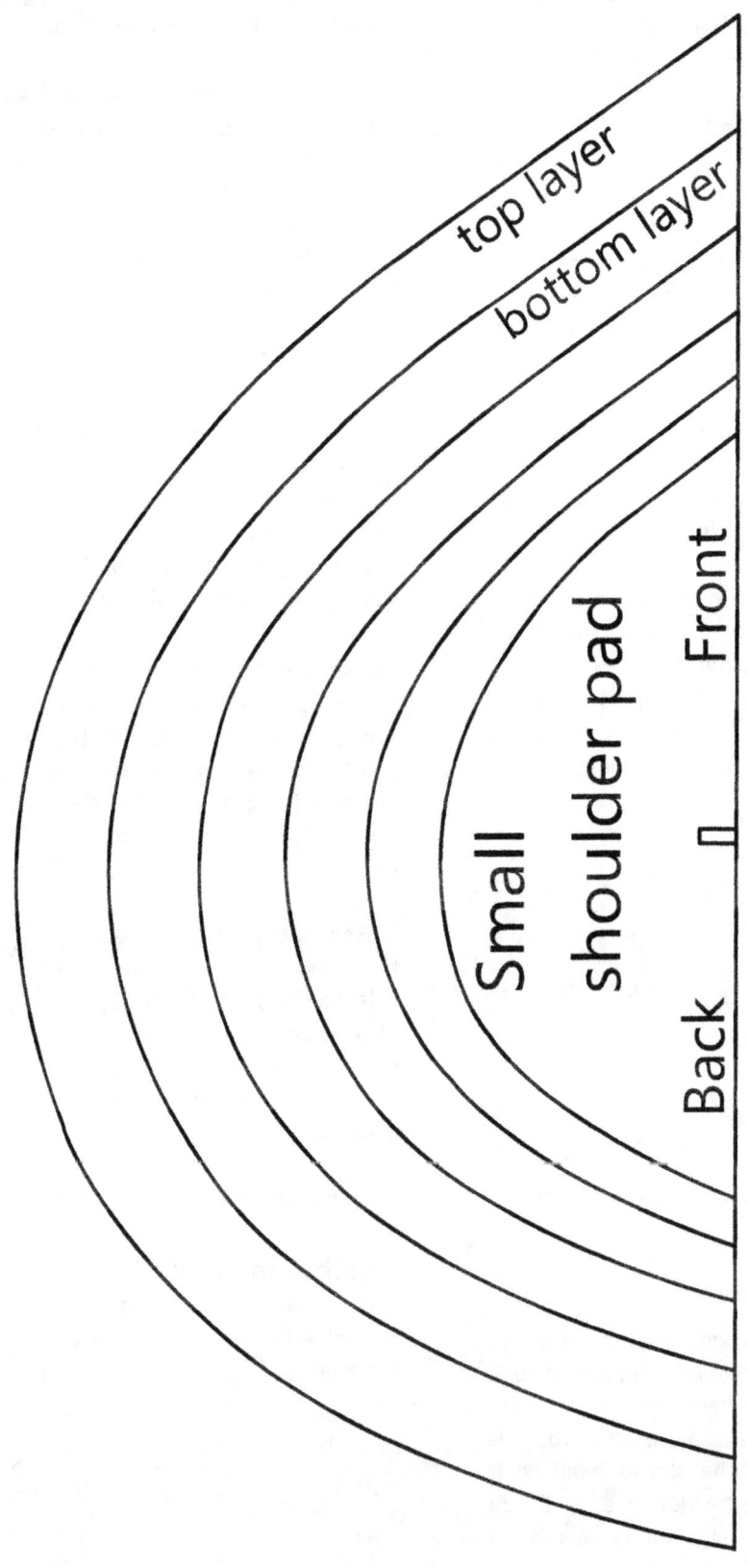

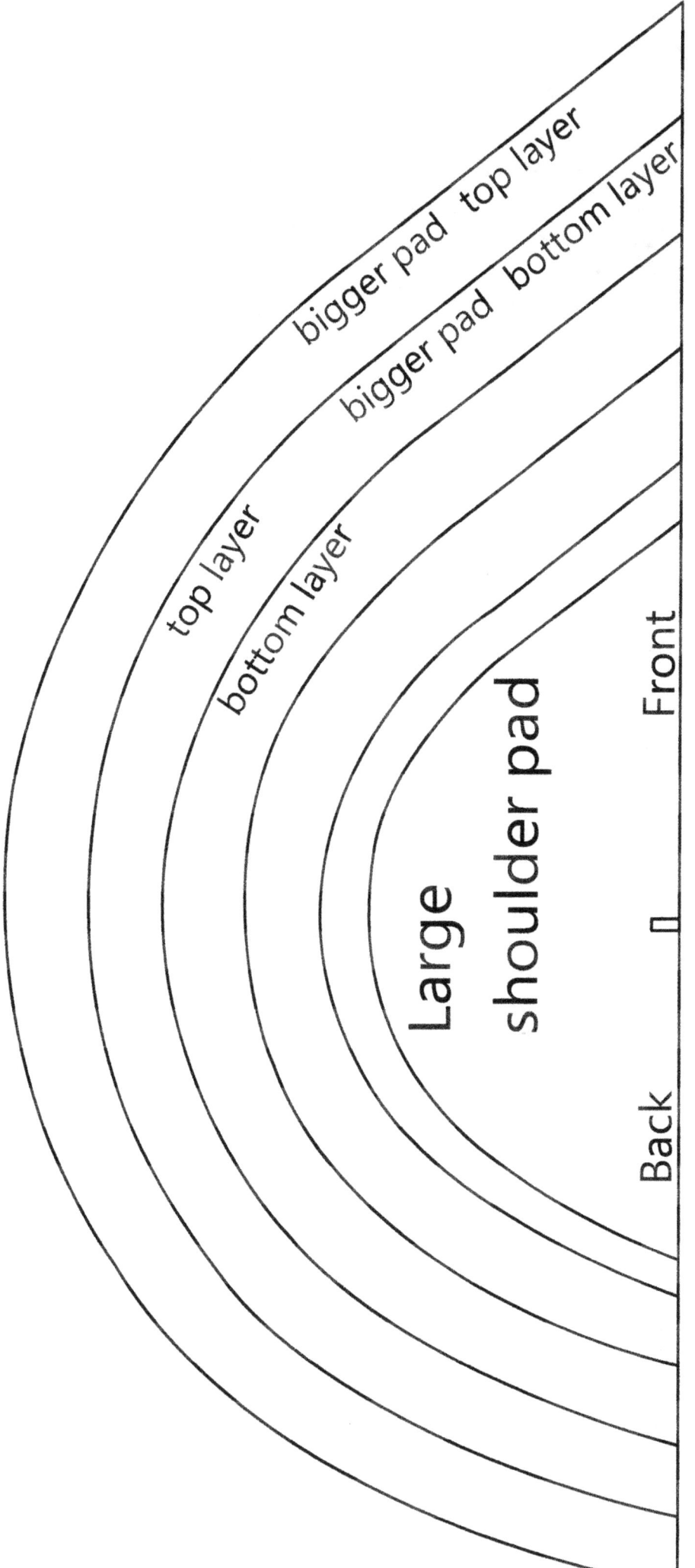

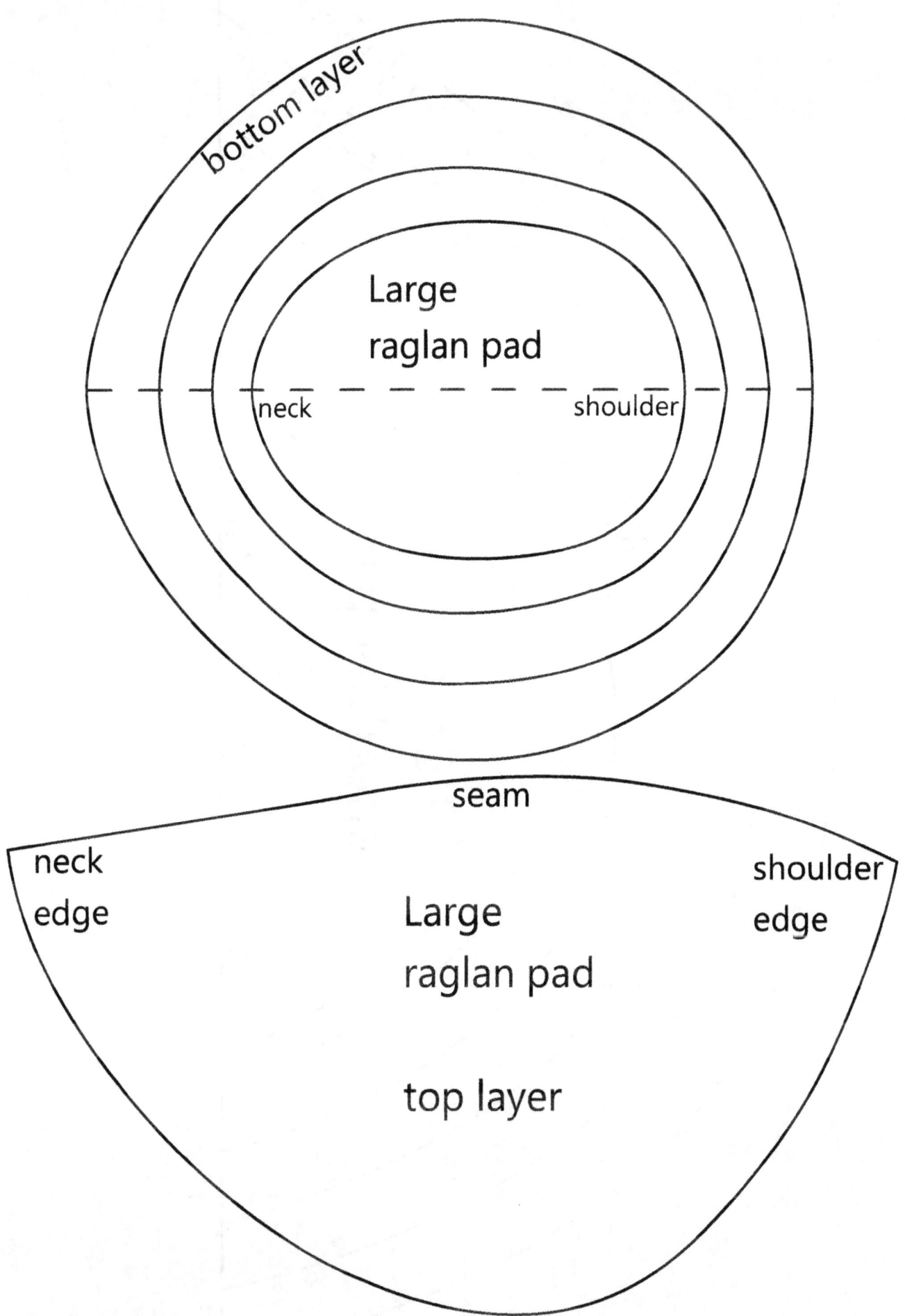

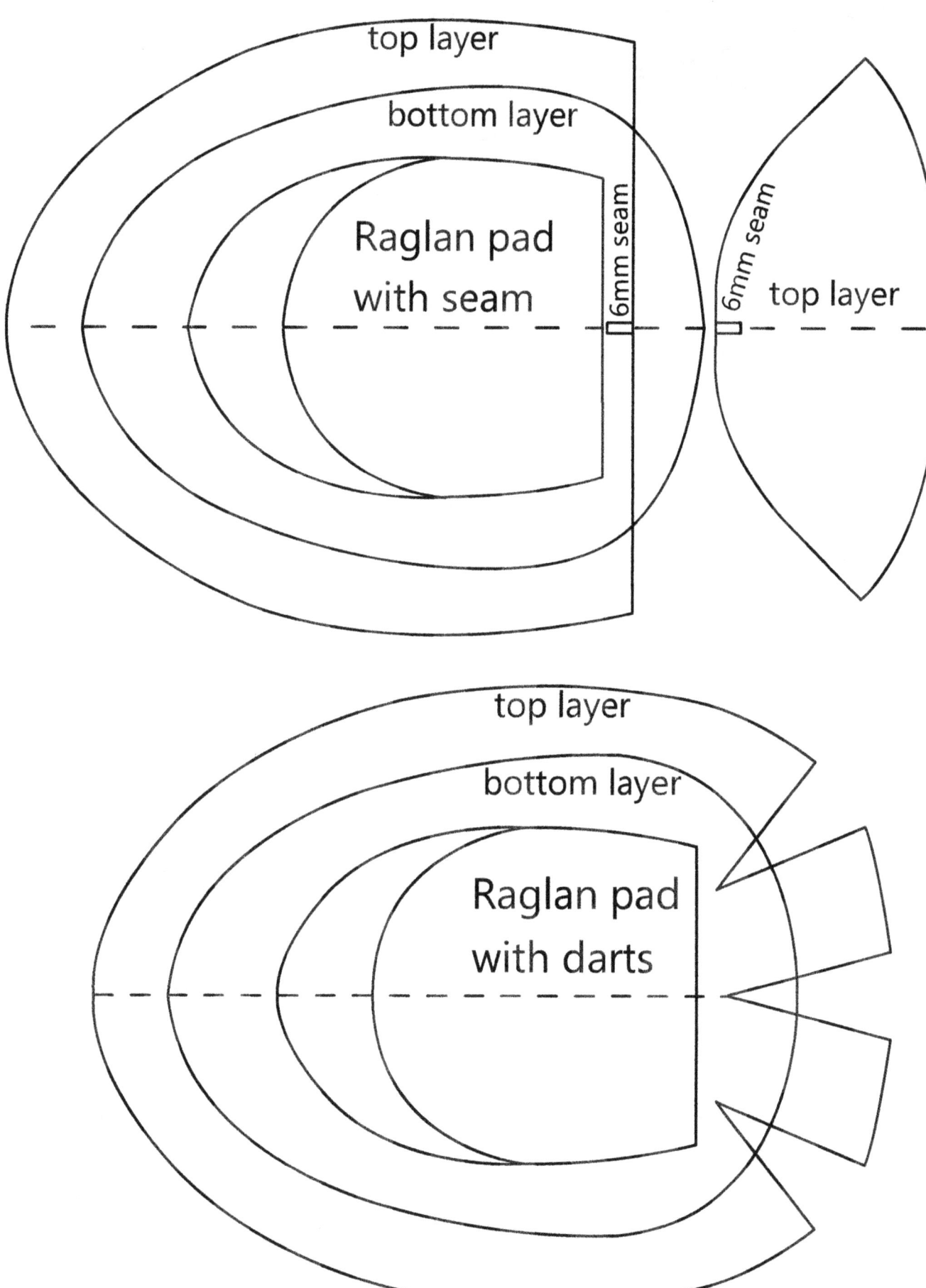

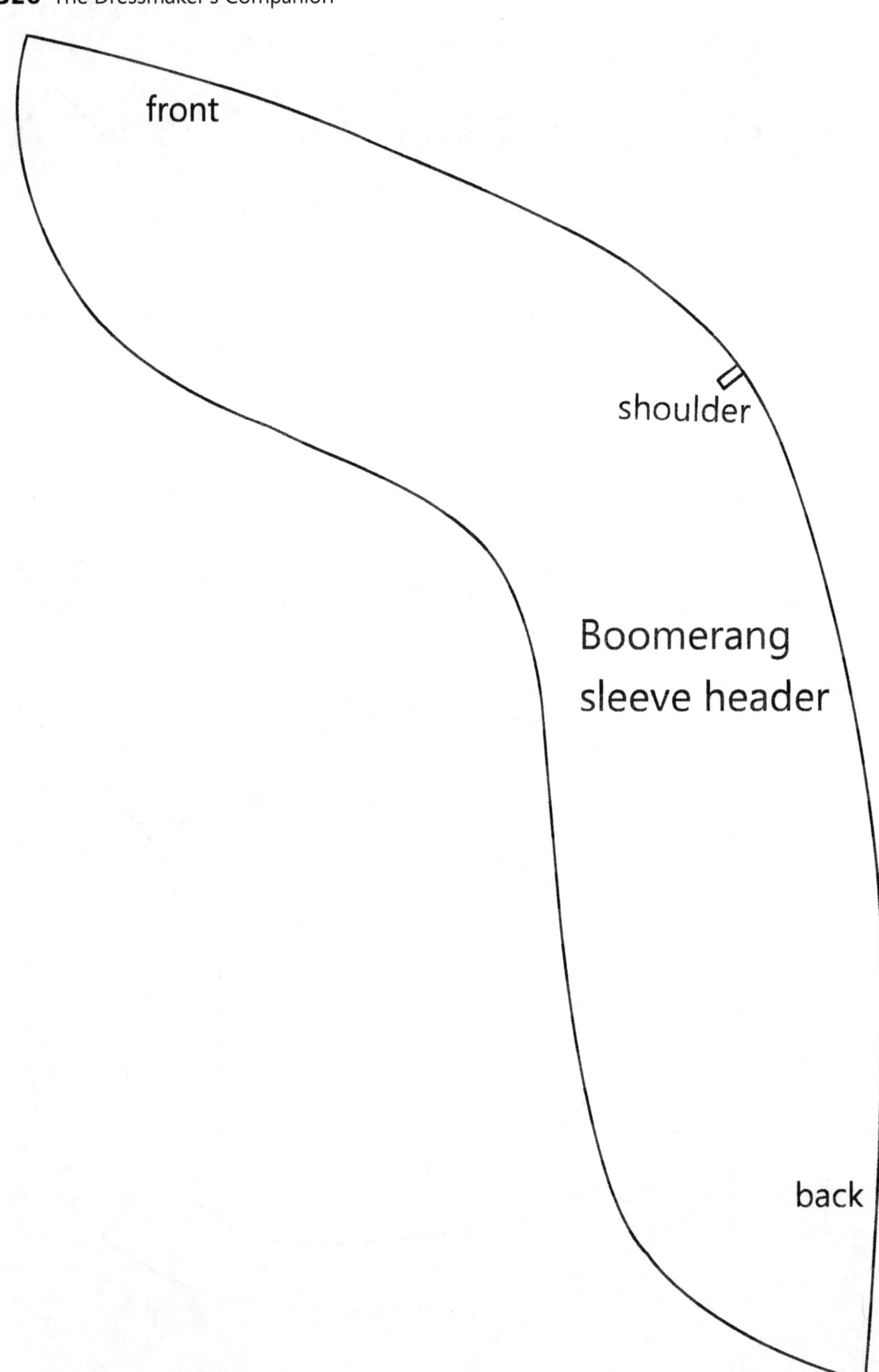

Sleeves

Introduction 327	elbow darts and ease 332
Kimono sleeves 327	sleeve notches 333
to sew 327	to sew a set-in sleeve 333
kimono sleeve with gusset 328	fitting notes 334
to sew a gusseted sleeve 328	set-in sleeve variations 336
fitting notes 329	Large upper arms 337
Raglan sleeves 329	Two ways to measure an armhole 338
to sew 330	Sewing sleeves in sheer fabric 338
fitting notes 330	2 piece jacket sleeve with a vent 338
Set-in sleeves 331	Sleeveless garments 340
one and two piece sleeves 332	

Sleeves fall into three general categories:

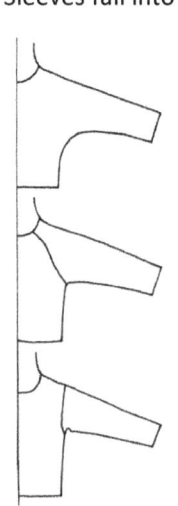

A **kimono** sleeve is an extension of the body of the blouse, jacket or dress.

A **raglan** sleeve has a diagonal seam from the neckline to the underarm.

Set-in sleeves have a seam around the armhole. They're the most widely used type of sleeve, with numerous variations.

✂ The amount of ease around the upper arm needs to be a minimum of 5cm (2"). That is, 2.5cm (1") pinched when the sleeve is being worn. For close fitting knits, the amount could be 2.5cm (1") total.

✂ Shoulder pads may be sewn into any of these types of sleeves.

✂ Wherever possible when sewing a sleeve, finish off the lower edge of the sleeve before attaching it to the garment.

Kimono Sleeves

These are the easiest type of sleeve to construct because the sleeve is just an extension of the body. Kimono sleeves have a deep armhole  with soft drapes under the arm. They're also called a batwing or magyar sleeve.

 If it's a short sleeve it may be called an extended or cap sleeve.

When a more fitted shape is required, a gusset is sewn under the arm for comfort and ease of movement.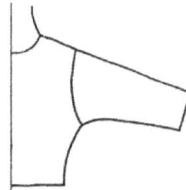

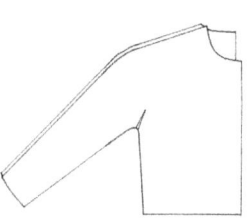 A dolman sleeve is similar in appearance to a kimono sleeve, but it has a seam over the arm.

On all kimono sleeves, the front and back arms should be the same *shape* and at the same *angle* as each other when the centre front and back are parallel.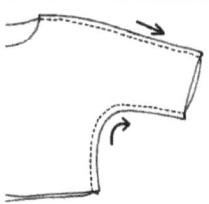

To sew a kimono sleeve

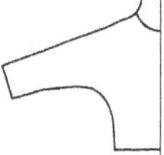 1. Sew the underarm seam and the shoulder seam. Press the seam either open, or closed towards the back. Press it over a seam roll or ham to press the curve.

327

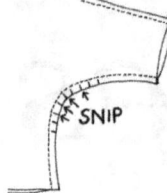

2. If the underarm seam is very curved and/or has a wide seam allowance, you'll need to either snip the seam allowance to make it sit flat or trim the seam allowance to make it narrower.

3. Overlock the seam to neaten it. If you've snipped the seam allowance, overlock with the snipped edges pulled flat to make V shapes.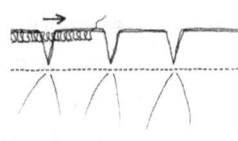

Sometimes the curved part of the underarm seam is taped to **reinforce** it. I rarely do this; kimono sleeves are usually loose and flowing and not subject to stress. However, if you think it will require reinforcement, there are a couple of ways to do it:

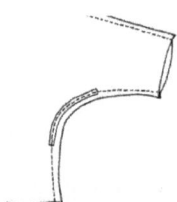 ✂ For closed seams, catch a bias cut strip (perhaps cut from the same fabric as the garment) in the stitching as you sew the seam.

✂ For open seams, 6mm (¼") tape can be stitched on. Centre a length of tape over the (stitched, pressed open, snipped and overlocked) seam. Stitch the tape 3mm (⅛") either side of the seam, through all layers. On the right side you'll see a long skinny rectangle of stitching around the seam.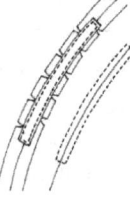

✂ Another way to reinforce the seam (with less strength but less bulk than tape) is to simply sew two rows of stitching, one on top of the other.

Kimono sleeves with a gusset
The more closely a kimono sleeve is fitted, and the smaller the armhole, the more movement is restricted. A gusset can be added to the underarm seam to increase flexibility and comfort. A gusset makes it possible to have longer, slimmer kimono sleeves with the armhole fitting closely to the body.
An underarm gusset is a diamond shaped piece of fabric set into a slash in the garment.
Gussets can be one-piece (diamond shaped):

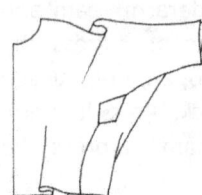 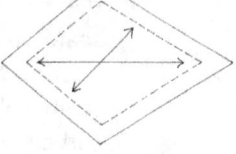

OR two-piece (two triangles):

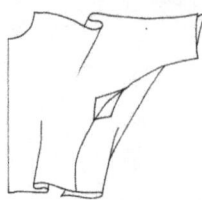 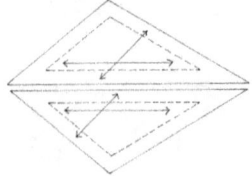

✂ Two-piece gussets are easier to sew because each gusset can be separately sewn in, then the underarm seam can be sewn in one operation. However, one-piece gussets are less bulky because there are fewer seams and are my preferred choice.

✂ You can easily convert a one-piece gusset to a two-piece gusset by cutting it through the centre and adding a seam allowance to each edge. Conversely, you can join the edges of a two-piece gusset together to make a one-piece gusset.

✂ Note that the pointier end of the gusset goes towards the sleeve.

✂ The grain line of a gusset can be along its length or on the bias. Bias-cut gussets give maximum comfort and ease of movement.

✂ Gussets can be topstitched on the garment side for greater strength and to keep the seams lying flat.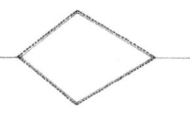

To sew a gusseted kimono sleeve
(Illustrated is a one-piece gusset.)
1. Because the point of the slash opening on the garment is a stress point, it needs to be reinforced before the gusset is sewn in. Cut a circle of interfacing and iron it onto the point of the slash opening. A circular patch is less liable to pick off at the edges than a square one.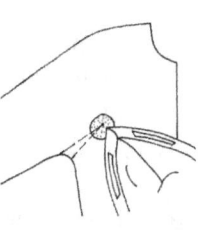

2. Stay-stitch along the marked line. Start at the wide end, stitch up one side, pivot at the point and stitch down the other side. Use a small stitch length around the point, such as 1.5 instead of the usual 2.5.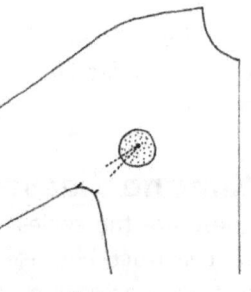

3. Carefully cut through the centre of the opening to the point.

4. **For a one piece gusset,** sew the underarm seams, press them open and overlock.
Important: don't sew across the seam allowance for the slit.

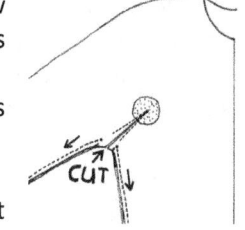

For a two piece gusset, don't sew the underarm seam yet.

5. Spread open the slit and position it over the gusset.

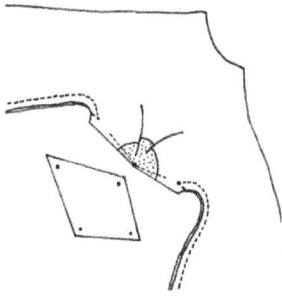

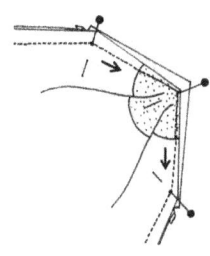

6. With the right sides together, pin the gusset into the slashed opening, matching the points and aligning the seamlines. Sew the gusset with the garment side up, pivoting at the point. Be sure to back stitch securely and accurately at each end.

Stitch the other side of the gusset the same way.

7. Press the seam allowance away from the gusset; the finished gusset should sit flat. Overlock all four sides. Turn the garment over so the right side is facing up and edgestitch around the gusset on the garment side.

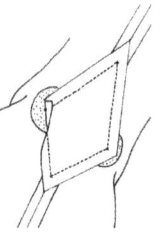

For a two piece gusset, sew the underarm seam now, press open or closed, and overlock.

Kimono sleeve fitting notes
A loose kimono sleeve is a lot easier to fit than a tight one. A fitted, gusseted kimono sleeve will need very careful fitting.

Drag lines between shoulder and underarm
✂ If the drag lines come from the underarm and the underarm feels tight, lower the underarm to make it deeper.
✂ If the drag lines come from the shoulder, it means there's not enough shoulder height. Add onto the shoulder then taper back to nothing at the wrist and neck. If you decide to add **shoulder pads** to your garment, you'll have to do this alteration to accommodate the extra height.

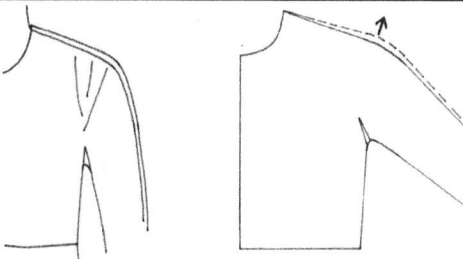

Occasionally this adjustment will need to be done on the front sleeve only to accommodate a protruding front shoulder bone.

Raglan sleeves
A raglan sleeve is a looser, easier fitting sleeve than a regular set-in sleeve. They were named after Lord Raglan (1788-1855), a British commander in the Crimean War. He lost an arm at Waterloo and his tailor devised this sleeve (it should have been named after the tailor).

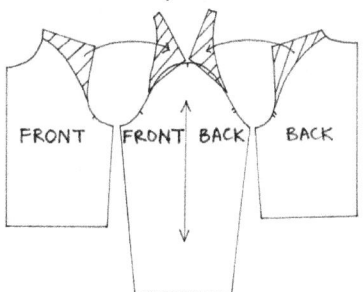

Raglan sleeve patterns look strange because part of the body's neck and shoulder has become part of the sleeve.

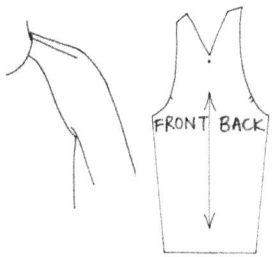

Raglan sleeves may be cut in one piece. The shoulder shaping is achieved by a dart along the shoulder line.

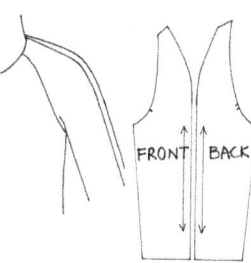

Raglan sleeves may also be two pattern pieces—a back and front sleeve. The shoulder shaping is achieved via a seam down the middle. The dart has been converted to a seam.

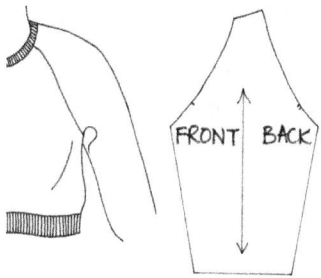

On very easy fitting knitwear garments such as windcheaters, there's no dart or seam.

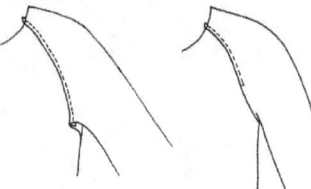

✂ The diagonal raglan seam can be curved or straight. If it's pressed to one side it's usually towards the sleeve because of the shape. Sometimes the seam is topstitched or topstitched only part of the way.

✂ It can be difficult to tell the back sleeve from the front, but you can see by looking at the length of the raglan seam. As part of the garment's neckline is at the top of the raglan sleeve, the back armhole is always longer than the front, because the back neck is higher than the front neck.

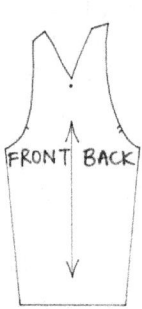

There should also be two notches to match the back armhole and one to match the front, as with regular sleeve patterns.

✂ To find the grainline, fold the pattern in half longways, matching the underarm seam. On two piece raglan sleeves, the grainline is parallel to the central seam.

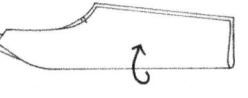

To sew a raglan sleeve

Unlike a set-in sleeve, there shouldn't be any ease in the seams of a raglan sleeve. All the seams should be the same length. There are two ways to sew a raglan:

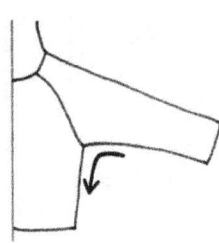

Method 1 is an easy method and is good for casual clothes, windcheaters, children's clothes and other easy-fitting garments. The diagonal raglan seams are sewn first attaching the sleeve to the body, then the underarm/side seam is sewn.

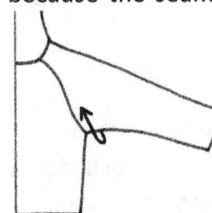

Method 2 is considered a better quality method because the seam curves around the underarm. It's used on coats, jackets and blouses. The side seams and underarm seams are sewn first, then the raglan seam is sewn in one operation from front neck to back neck.

Methods 1 and 2

1. Sew the shoulder darts or shoulder-to-wrist seam, depending on your type of raglan. Neaten the seam and press. The dart or seam may be pressed open or to one side (usually the back). If you plan to topstitch this seam, do so now.

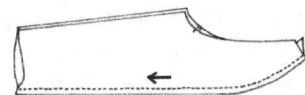

Method 1

2. Sew the raglan seams to their respective back or fronts.
Neaten the seams and press towards the sleeve.
If you plan to topstitch the these seams, do so now.

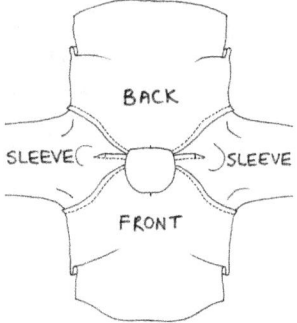

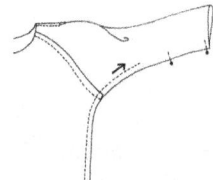

3. Sew the underarm-side seam, matching the raglan seams at the underarm junction. Neaten and press.

Method 2

2. Sew the side seams of the garment and the underarm seams of the sleeves.

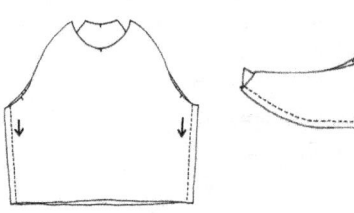

3. Pin the sleeves to the armhole, aligning the underarm seams. Sew the seam with the sleeve side up. Neaten the seam and press it towards the sleeve. Topstitch the seam if desired.

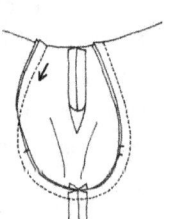

Raglan sleeves fitting notes

Drag lines from under arm

If drag lines come from the underarm and the underarm feels tight, lower the underarm to make it deeper. Draw in a new armhole on the pattern. Lower the armhole the same amount on the body and sleeve.

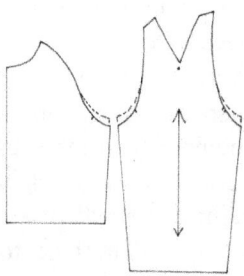

Sleeves **331**

Drag lines from shoulder

If the underarm is the correct height, drag lines indicate there isn't enough height on the shoulder.

For one-pieces sleeves with a dart, split the sleeve along the centre, add more room in, then take it in on both sides of the wrist to keep the wrist measurement the same. Taper to nothing at the neck.

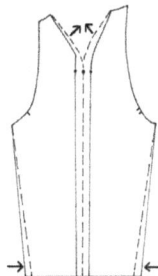

For two piece sleeves, add at the shoulder and all the way along the centre seam. Taper to nothing at the neck. Take in at the wrist to keep the wrist measurement the same. Do the same alteration to the back and front sleeves.

If you plan to add **shoulder pads**, you'll need to do this adjustment.

Set-in sleeves

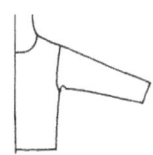

There are an enormous number of variations of set-in sleeves. Different sleeves often have different armhole shapes to accommodate the sleeve. If you're designing a clothing range, one way to keep costs down is to use the same sleeve pattern for several styles. It will ensure consistent sizing, too.

✂ The rounded part at the top of the sleeve is called the sleeve head or sleeve cap. Most set-in sleeves have a sleeve head that's slightly bigger than the corresponding part of the armhole and must be eased into the armhole. Only the top part of the sleeve is eased, never the underarm, otherwise you'll have excess fabric under the arm that won't sit smoothly. The more ease in the top of the sleeve, the more the sleeve head will "roll" over. There can be 2.5cm-4.5cm (1"-1¾") ease in a fitted sleeve. The back of the sleeve has slightly more ease than the front.

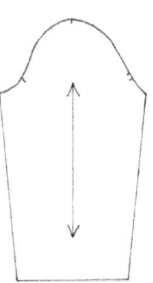

✂ The more fitted the sleeve, the higher the armhole needs to be so you can move your arm comfortably.

A low armhole in a fitted garment will restrict your movement.

The higher the armhole, the longer the body will look.

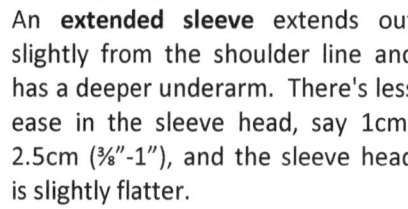

Fitted sleeves have a high armhole, and the armhole seam should sit *on* the shoulder. There's 2.5cm-4.5cm (1" to 1¾") ease in the sleeve head. A wool tailored jacket may have up to 6cm (2⅜") ease.

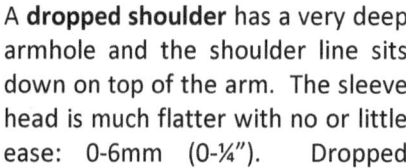

An **extended sleeve** extends out slightly from the shoulder line and has a deeper underarm. There's less ease in the sleeve head, say 1cm-2.5cm (⅜"-1"), and the sleeve head is slightly flatter.

A **dropped shoulder** has a very deep armhole and the shoulder line sits down on top of the arm. The sleeve head is much flatter with no or little ease: 0-6mm (0-¼"). Dropped shoulders are a feature of oversized garments. There will always be drag lines/drape in the sleeve.

If we stacked the pattern pieces on top of each other they might look like this:

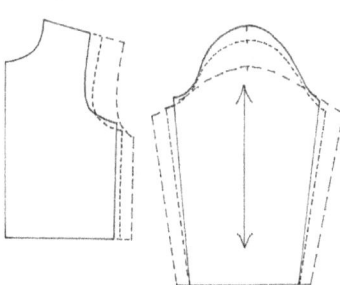

✂ Sleeve heads can be **gathered** into the armhole. To add gathers, raise the sleeve head. By how much?

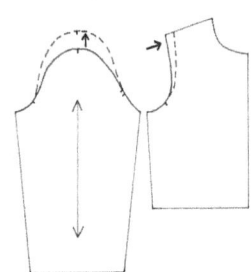

At least 2cm (¾") for small gathers; the more you raise it the more voluminous the gathers. Whatever you add, cut away the armhole at the shoulder by about 2cm (¾") so the shoulder sits inside the gathers when it's worn.

Press the seam allowances *towards* the sleeve and away from the body for perky, puffed gathers

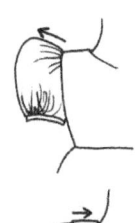

Press *away* from the sleeve and towards the body for flat gathers. You'll have to topstitch the armhole to make the gathers stay put.

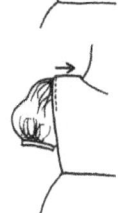

The sleeve head may also be darted or pleated.

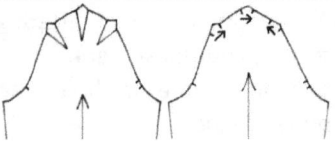

✂ Sleeve **length** is best determined at a fitting, especially if you know you have particularly short or long arms, or one arm longer than the other. An "average" sleeve length for women's sleeves is 60cm (23⅜") from shoulder to wrist for long sleeves (measured with the arm straight), about 18cm (7") for a short sleeve, about 27cm (10⅝") for an above elbow sleeve, and about 40cm-45cm (15¾"-17¾") for a three-quarter sleeve. A seven-eighths or bracelet length sleeve is about 4cm-5cm (1½"-2") shorter than a long sleeve.

On men's blazers and suit jackets, the sleeve length should leave room for about 6mm-1.2cm (¼"-½") of shirt cuff to show.

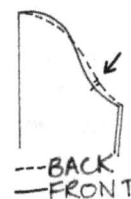

✂ **To tell the back of a sleeve from the front**, fold the sleeve in half and match the underarm seam. The front should scoop out more at the underarm. The front may be the same or bigger than the back at the very top of the head.

There should be two notches to match the back of the sleeve to the back armhole on the body, and one to match the front. Sometimes there are only the two back notches. Burda patterns have one notch to match the front and none on the back.

✂ To find the **grainline**, fold the sleeve in half longways and match the underarm seam. The grainline will be parallel with the fold. If the sleeve isn't cut on grain, it will twist around the arm.

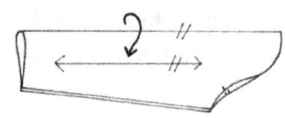

✂ **To raise or lower the armhole**, simply draw in the new higher or lower armhole on the sleeve and the same amount on the body.

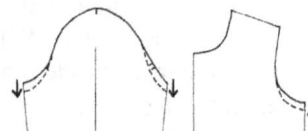

One and two piece sleeves

Set-in sleeves are often one piece, but a two piece sleeve is the traditional choice for a tailored jacket. A two piece sleeve follows the natural bend of the arm. I always prefer a two piece sleeve for jackets because I think they hang better, and they aren't any harder to sew. A two piece jacket sleeve may incorporate a vent at the hem.

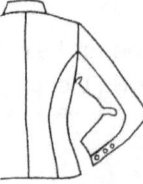

In princess line jackets with two piece sleeves, the back body seams should ideally match the sleeve seam.

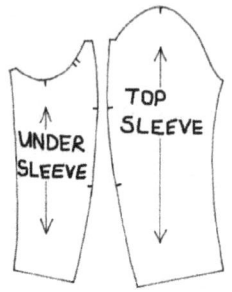

Often, ease is incorporated into the back vertical seam at the elbow. The area to be eased is indicated by a set of notches. The top sleeve's seam is longer and is eased onto the under sleeve. The amount is up to 5mm (scant ¼"). Sew this seam by matching the notches to isolate the eased section, then sew with the under sleeve on top and the top sleeve underneath.

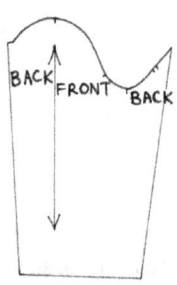

Another type of one piece sleeve looks like a two piece sleeve but really the underarm seam has been positioned at the back of the sleeve instead of the underarm. It's used on blouses, shirts and casual jackets. An advantage is the bottom of the seam can be left open to make a placket for a cuff.

Elbow darts and ease

Very close fitting one piece sleeves usually need darts or ease at the elbow to give the sleeve the shaping and room necessary for the elbow to bend completely. The darts or ease are always at the back. To convert darts to ease, simply ignore the darts and ease the amount in (see page 95).

There can be one, two or three **elbow darts**. Sew them before you sew the underarm seam. Press the darts towards the bottom of the sleeve.

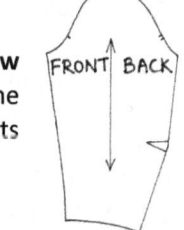

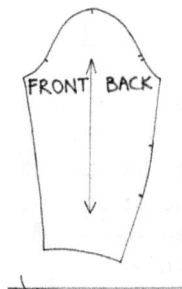

Elbow ease is denoted by two notches on the back to let you know where the eased section is.

One method to sew ease is to sew a row of long stitches within the notches, **on** the stitching line. Pin the seams together and pull up the ease threads. Distribute the fullness evenly without any gathers. Sew with the ease stitches on top, exactly on or just outside.

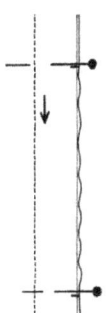A quicker method, which I prefer for elbow ease, is to omit the row of ease stitching. Pin the seam together at either end of the eased section to isolate the area. Sew the seam with the eased side underneath. When you arrive at the section to be eased, place your left hand between the two layers of fabric and push the underneath layer through; you should see ripples but not gathers. The feed dogs on the machine will feed the underneath layer through and help it ease.

Sleeve notches

The notches help to line up the pieces correctly when you sew them together and without them your sleeve may twist or not sit correctly. Even if you had to make changes to the pattern, the existing notches will give you a reference point. Take the extra minute or so to snip the notches and check before you remove the pattern that *all* the notches have been snipped. Snip them only about 3mm (⅛").

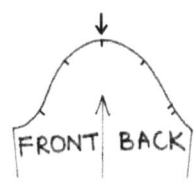✄ The most important notch is at the top of the sleeve head to match it to the shoulder seam. If you fold the sleeve in half, the notch may be in the centre or it may be slightly towards the front.

✄ There should also be notches to indicate the front and the back near the armhole curves. There's one for the front and two for the back. Their main purpose is to 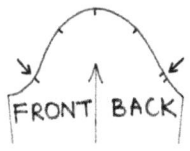indicate the front and the back of the sleeve. They may not necessarily match the body (you might have done an alteration on the pattern and now they don't match) but it doesn't matter. There's never any ease under the arm—only over the top—so just sew this section flat to the garment.

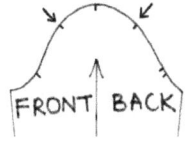✄ There may also be another set of notches on the sleeve head, depending on the style of sleeve. They might mean "gather between these notches" if the sleeve head is gathered, or they might be there to just to help distribute ease more evenly. Sleeve heads may also have notches for darts or pleats.

✄ A two piece sleeve has an underarm notch to match to the side seam of the body. If the body has no side seam, say, a side panel instead, then the side panel will also have a notch.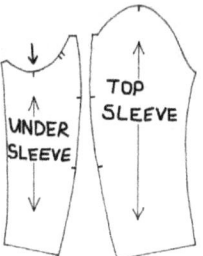

To sew a set-in sleeve

There are two ways to sew a set-in sleeve:

Method 1 is the quicker and easier method. The sleeve is sewn in flat first, then the underarm/side is sewn in one seam. This method is used where the sleeve head is flatter and there's little or no ease, for example men's shirts, drop shoulders, children's sleeves and doll's clothes. An advantage with this method is that it's easier to fit.

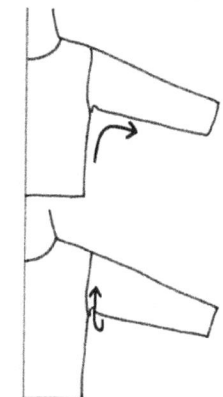**Method 2** is considered a better quality method because the seam is sewn in a continuous curve around the armhole. The side seam of the garment and the underarm seam of the sleeve are sewn first, then the sleeve is "set in" (sewn) to the armhole. This method is always used for coats and jackets, and also for blouses and dresses. You'll *have* to use this method for two piece sleeves or garments with a side panel instead of a side seam, because there's no underarm seam.

Method 1 can be sewn with few or no pins.

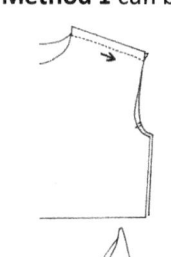1. Sew the shoulder seam of the garment, neaten and press. Press the seam open if the fabric is very thick or if the garment is fully lined (to reduce bulk and make a flatter shoulder). Otherwise press it towards the back.

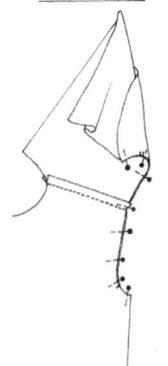2. With the right sides together, match the sleeve to the armhole. Sew with the sleeve underneath. I place my left hand between the two layers to help the machine sew any ease on the sleeve head. Neaten the seam and press it towards the sleeve. If you're making a man's shirt, you could sew this seam as a flat-felled seam (see page 294).

Sometimes the armhole seam is topstitched—if so, do it now. If you wish the topstitching to be on the body side of the seam, rather than the sleeve, you might need to snip the curved underarm section to get it to sit flat.

Snip before overlocking, and as you overlock pull the snips straight so they look like Vs.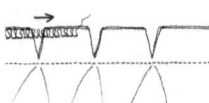

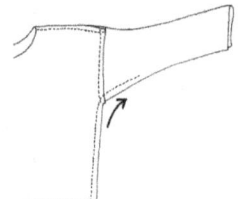

3. Press the armhole seam towards the sleeve and sew the underarm and side seam in one continuous seam.

Method 2

1. As mentioned on page 331, the sleeve head on most set-in sleeves measures *more* than the armhole and will need to be eased in. Sew a row of ease stitches (that is, long machine stitches) over the sleeve head, leaving long thread tails at the end.

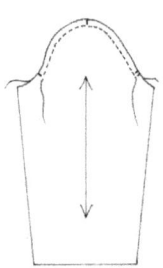

There are a few different ways of sewing an ease stitch:

✂ I like to sew one row *on* the stitching line. When I sew the sleeve in I stitch exactly *on* this line.

✂ Some people like to sew one row inside the stitching line, say, half way between the stitching line and the raw edge.

✂ Others like to do two rows, like gathering. One row is *on* the stitching line and the other row is halfway between the stitching line and the raw edge.

You can gently pull up the ease stitching now, or do it when you're pinning the sleeve in.

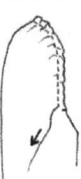

Sometimes when you're pulling up the ease stitches 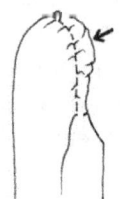 the seam allowance at the sides increases. It often happens on light or loosely woven fabrics. It happens because this part of the sleeve head is on the bias. Ignore it, but make sure you match up the *stitching* lines when you sew it.

2. Sew the shoulder and side seam of the garment. Sew the underarm seam of the sleeve. Neaten and press all the seams.

3. Turn both the sleeve and the garment right side out. **Check** that the correct sleeve is going into the correct armhole (I speak from experience).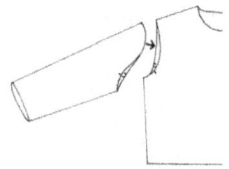

4. Pin the sleeve in. If you aren't sure if the sleeve will fit properly and you're planning to do a fitting, place the pins on the *sleeve's* stitching line, parallel to the seam. Ideally use pins without heads.

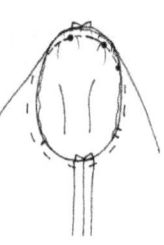

From inside the body, hold the sleeve and the armhole right sides together so you're looking down into the sleeve. Start by matching and pinning the underarm and shoulder points. Then pin 5cm (2") either side of the underarm. There shouldn't be any ease in this area, so sit the sleeve in flat. The notches indicating back and front (one notch for the front, two notches for the back) may not match.

Gently pull up the easing stitch if you haven't already. You don't want gathers or pleats, just ripply fabric. Pull up the ease stitches until the sleeve matches the armhole and distribute the ease evenly. There should be more ease in the back than the front. If there's too much ease and you can't get the sleeve head in without gathers, I sometimes sneak 6mm (¼") ease in under the arms, each side of the underarm seam. Sometimes it's *just* enough to ease the sleeve head in.

With the sleeve pinned in, prepare to fit the garment by pushing the seam allowance towards the sleeve so it covers the pins. Try the garment on carefully. If you're allergic to pins, sew the sleeve on in a big stitch.

5. When and if you're sure the sleeve is going to fit properly, go ahead and sew it: sew it with the sleeve facing up and the armhole underneath, stitching exactly on your ease stitching. I start sewing at the underarm or just to one side.

6. Neaten the seam, unless the garment has a closed lining, for example a jacket. Press the seam allowance towards the sleeve. If you're making a jacket, apply sleeve header (page 321) and/or shoulder pads (page 317) if required.

Set-in sleeve fitting notes

Remember, there's *always* a solution to a fitting problem. Of the many, many bodies I've fitted, there's *never* been an impossible case.

✂ Sew the collar or neck *before* fitting the sleeves, to stabilize the neck and shoulders. If you don't want to sew the collar yet, pin it on or stabilize the neck in some other way, for example tack cotton tape on.

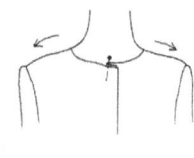

✂ Fit with shoulder pads if the garment will have them.

✂ I highly recommend *first* fitting the armhole, *then* fitting the sleeve. First fit the body and armhole without the sleeve, then pin the sleeves in and fit the sleeves. Actually, you *can* fit body and sleeve together, but doing one after the other saves undoing the sleeves to make any changes.

Armholes

✂ Does the underarm need raising or lowering? You can check again once the sleeve is in.

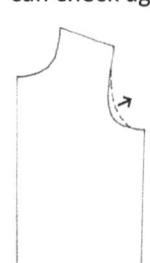

✂ Does the armhole need to be filled in anywhere? I mean, is it too "cut-away", especially at the front armhole of big people. Is there enough seam allowance to accommodate a new stitching line?
Alternatively, does the armhole need trimming off anywhere?

✂ For some people, 1.2cm (½") needs removing from the back side seam *only*, tapering to nothing at the waist. I don't know why, but it does sometimes.

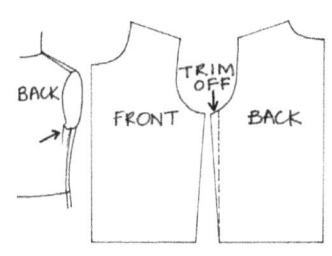

Shoulder too wide

Stand in front of the mirror and decide where the new shoulder line needs to be. You can re-check this once the sleeves are in.

Draw a new shoulder line with pins (my preference)

OR

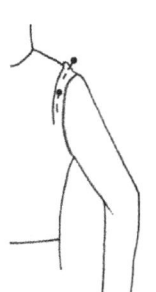

Pinch the amount in and pin.

Draw in the new shoulder line on the pattern, blending it into the underarm.
Trim the fabric before sewing the sleeve in.

Drag lines from the underarm to neck

This indicates sloping shoulders. It could also indicate a pattern adjusted to allow for a shoulder pad.
If you have uneven shoulders, the drag lines will only be on one side, or more pronounced on one side than the other.

Possible solutions:

✂ Try adding a shoulder pad, or increasing the size of the existing shoulder pad.

✂ Take in the shoulder seam at the sleeve end, blending to nothing at the neck. Lower the stitching line on the pattern. Try the garment on and see if you need to lower the armhole the same amount.

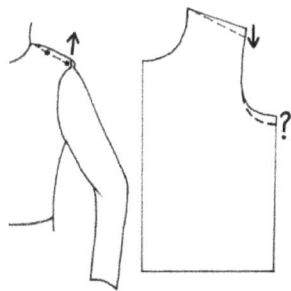

Drag lines towards the shoulder

This indicates square shoulders.
If you have uneven shoulders, the drag lines will only be on one side, or more pronounced on one side than the other.

Possible solutions:

✂ If you've put shoulder pads in, take them out or put in smaller ones.

✂ Undo the shoulder seam and re-pin it, releasing it at the sleeve end. Raise the stitching line on the pattern. Try the garment on and check the position of the armhole to see if it needs to be made correspondingly higher.

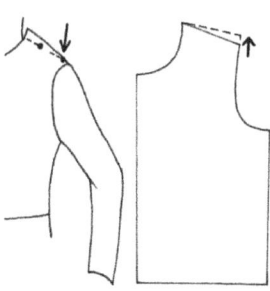

Too much ease in sleeve

In other words, the sleeve is too big for the armhole.
Possible solutions:

✂ Try the garment on and see if the body underarm needs lowering, thus making the armhole bigger.

✂ Take in the sleeve's underarm seam to make the sleeve smaller, if the sleeve is too big on the arm.

✂ Let out the side seams on the body, if it needs it, making the armhole bigger.

✂ The sleeve head might be too high, but before you trim off the top of the sleeve, try the garment on with the estimated amount pinned in and see what it's like.

Not enough ease in sleeve
The sleeve is too small for the armhole.
Possible solutions:

✂ Cut new, bigger sleeves if they are too tight on the arm.

✂ Lower the underarm on the sleeve.

✂ Try the garment on and see if the body armhole is too big. Is the underarm too low? If appropriate, you could take a bigger shoulder seam to lift the underarm. Re-cut the neckline if it's now too high.

Too much fullness in the sleeve at the front or back

The notch at the top of the sleeve is in the wrong place. The sleeve needs to be turned either to the front or the back. Unpin the sleeve at the fitting and re-pin it on the person—you'll see where it needs to go.

In this illustration, there's too much ease at the back, so the sleeve needs to be turned towards the front. The top centre notch will therefore be shifted towards the back.

Drag lines on sleeve
This indicates there's not enough height on the sleeve head. The remedy is to re-cut the sleeves with a higher sleeve head, but if you've already cut the sleeves, simply lower the armhole. Also, this way will not affect the total length of the sleeve.

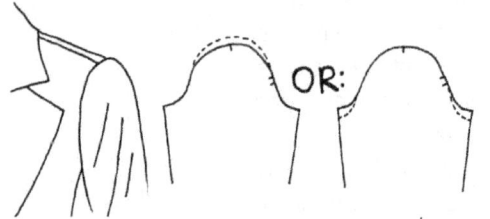

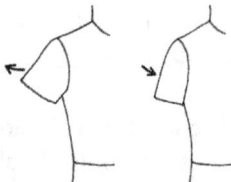

Short sleeves will kick out if the sleeve head needs to be higher. Sometimes this looks OK, especially on casual shirts.

Regarding underarms, note that:

✂ A higher underarm on a garment will make the body look longer.

✂ The shallower the sleeve head and the higher the underarm, the more movement. Ballet costumes typically have high armholes and sometimes the sleeves are not even sewn in under the arms.

Sleeve is too tight around the top when arm is raised
The sleeve head is too narrow and possibly the rest of the sleeve is too narrow. Try the garment on and note

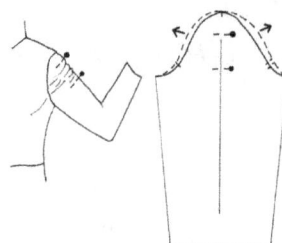

where the strain is when the arm is raised. Release the pinned-in sleeve at the edges of the strained area and try the garment on again. On the pattern, make the sleeve wider at the area of strain.

Sleeve is too tight around the upper arm.
Possible solutions:

✂ If you have more fabric, cut new, bigger sleeves.

✂ If you have adequate seam allowances, let out the underarm seam.

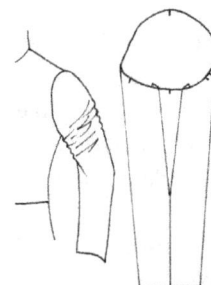

✂ Insert a gusset under the arm to give more room, as illustrated.

✂ Make a note to check the upper arm measurement each time you use a new pattern. There should be at least 5cm (2") ease around the upper arm.

Set-in sleeve variations
There are loads of variations of set-in sleeves. Here are just a few.

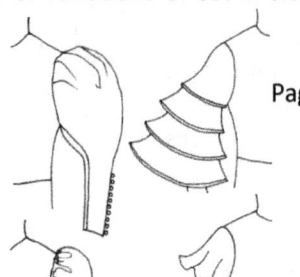

Leg of mutton or Gigot sleeve

Pagoda sleeve

Puffed sleeve

Fluted sleeve

Cap sleeve

Bishop sleeve

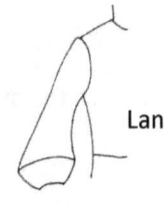

Juliet sleeve

Lantern sleeve

Sleeves **337**

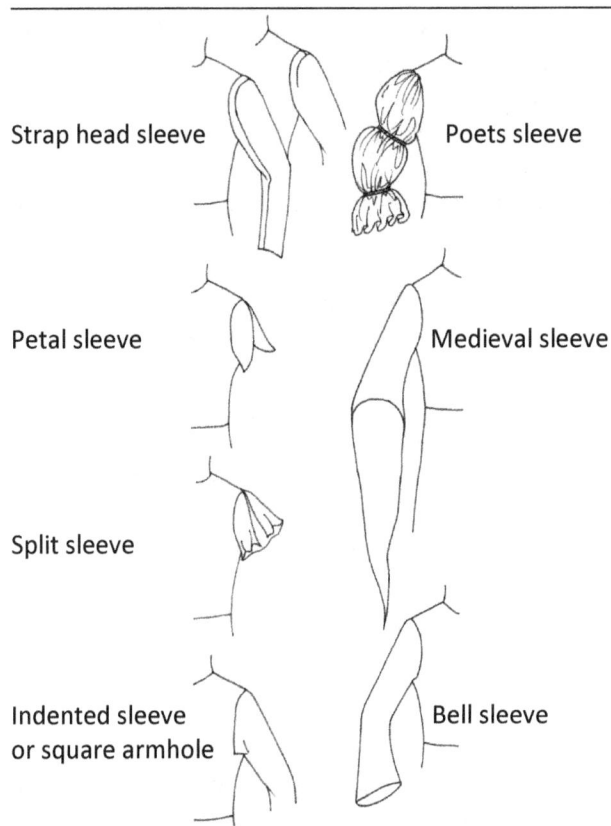

Strap head sleeve
Poets sleeve
Petal sleeve
Medieval sleeve
Split sleeve
Indented sleeve or square armhole
Bell sleeve

Large upper arms
People with large upper arms fall into two groups:
✂ An average sized torso with large upper arms
✂ Large torso and large upper arms

For both groups, check the upper arm measurement against the pattern. There should be at least 2" (5cm) ease. Extend the width of the sleeve to fit if necessary, then check the armhole and sleeve measurements to see how much ease there now is in the sleeve head (see page 338 for measuring an armhole). If there's too much ease and you predict problems in setting the sleeve in, add a little to the side seams of the body. You might not need to add as much as you did to the sleeves.

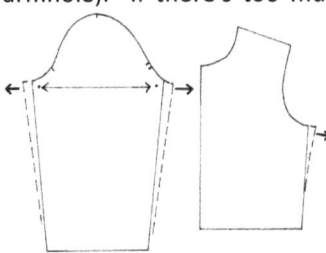

If the sleeve is two piece, split the under sleeve either side of the underarm notch, and spread the pattern as shown. Smooth off the underarm in a curve. For large upper arms, I also like to add some extra curve onto the back vertical seam, as illustrated.

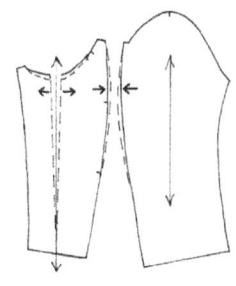

Still got too much ease in the sleeve? Does the armhole need to be lowered in the body only?

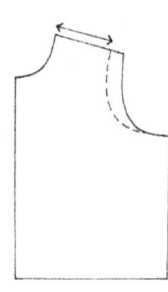

For large people with large upper arms, check the shoulder length. Generally, shoulders don't become any wider beyond an Aussie size 16. A size 20 body with a size 14 shoulder, for example, is quite common. Narrowing the shoulder will make the armhole bigger thus making it easier to set the sleeve in.

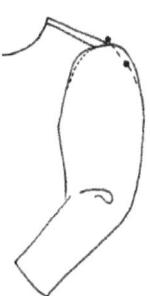

On *very* large sleeves there'll be an excess of fabric at the back of the sleeve and the front might need more fabric at the sleeve head.

If you translate these adjustments to the pattern, the front of the sleeve head tends to get steeper and the back tends to slope more.

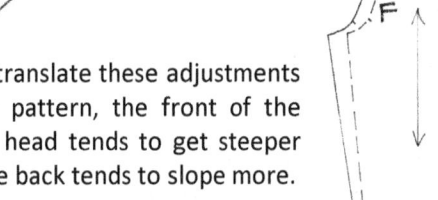

Other ideas for large torsos and large upper arms
✂ Try not to choose puffy or gathered sleeves, which will make the arms look bigger.

✂ Make an inverted pleat down the centre of the sleeve.

✂ Cut the sleeve with a central seam and add curve to the seam to accommodate arm fullness where it's needed.

✂ Split the centre of the sleeve and join the two edges together at intervals. You could place a bead at the joins.

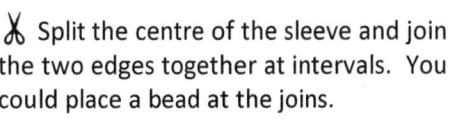
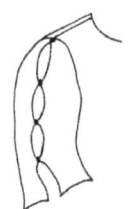

Two ways to measure an armhole

If you've made alterations to the sleeve or armhole, or if you want to know how much ease a sleeve has, you'll need to measure the sleeve and armhole.

Here are two methods, the direct method and the tape measure method; I use both. The direct method is good for a quick check.

The tape measure method

Holding the tape measure on its edge, place it on the stitching line and measure. Omit the seam allowance at each end as you measure. You'll find it easier if you draw in the stitching line first.

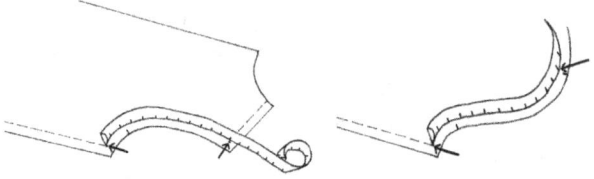

Note the measurements, for example:
Front armhole   20.5cm
Front sleeve   22cm
Back armhole   22cm
Back sleeve   24cm

Therefore there's 1.5cm ease in the front of the sleeve and 2cm ease in the back, totaling 3.5cm ease.

The direct method

Place the sleeve pattern on top of the corresponding front or back body, matching the stitching line at the underarm point. Place a pencil *on* the stitching line and "walk" the sleeve around the armhole at the stitching line, moving the pencil point to pivot.

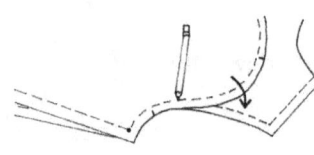

When you reach the shoulder point, note how far away the centre sleeve notch is; the distance equals the amount of ease for that side of the sleeve. Repeat for the other side.

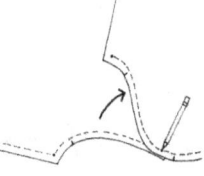

Sewing sleeves in sheer fabric

What if you're sewing a garment in sheer fabric? How do you sew the armholes?

✂ If you're overlocking all the garment seams, sew the sleeve in as usual and overlock the armhole.

✂ If you've used French seams throughout you'll want a matching armhole seam. However, if the seam is too curved to use French seams, the (high end) answer is to bind them in the same fabric, so the bound seam will match.

Cut two bias strips about 3cm-3.5cm (1⅛"-1⅜") wide and long enough to reach around the armhole.

You *could* sew the sleeve into the armhole and then trim and bind the seam, but if you sew the binding strips on at the same time as the sleeve you'll have one less line of stitching. One less line of machine stitching on such fine fabric will make a noticeable difference to the softness and flexibility of the seam.

To sew, place the right sides of the sleeve and body together as usual. Have the sleeve uppermost and the body underneath. Place a bias strip right side up underneath this layer. Begin sewing at the underarm point. Fold under the end of the bias strip and position it at the underarm, to make a neat beginning. Sew all three layers together as you sew the sleeve in. Trim the seam back to 6mm (¼"), fold over the binding and hand sew it in place. Alternatively, machine sew it in place, but it will make the seam slightly stiffer.

✂ If you happen to have 1.5cm (⅝") seam allowances, you can bind the armhole with its own seam allowance. It's called a **standing fell**. Sew the sleeve in as usual, then trim back the *body* seam allowance to 6mm (¼"). Use the sleeve seam allowance as a binding. Turn under the untrimmed edge and sew it by hand or machine to the first line of stitching. I recommend sewing it by hand—it's more flexible, softer and the line of machine stitches won't show.

2 piece jacket sleeve with a vent

Adding a vent to a two piece jacket sleeve pattern is quite simple. Actually, it's really a mock vent because it doesn't open.

Make a pattern

Add a vent extension onto the *back* seam of both top sleeve and under sleeve.

The **width** (measured from the seam line, not the cutting line) should be the same as the hem depth—usually about 4cm (1½").

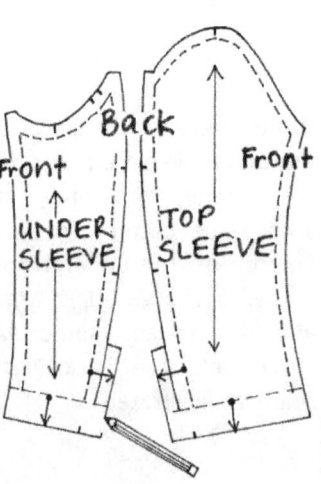

Sleeves **339**

Make the **length** about 8cm-10cm (3"-4") long from the finished sleeve length.

The top sleeve has the corner mitred. Be absolutely sure of your sleeve length before planning the mitre and vent, because the sleeve cannot be lengthened later.

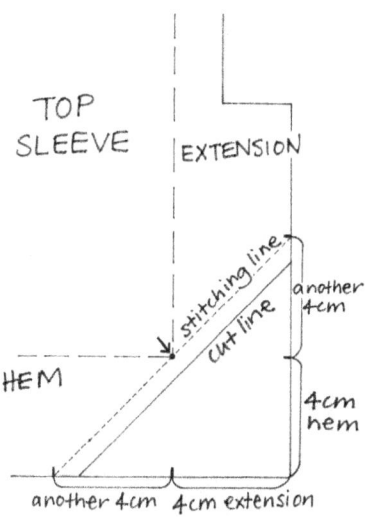

To find the stitching line for the mitre, double the hem/extension width (for example 4cm + 4cm) and measure this amount in both directions from the corner. Join the two points. Add a 6mm (¼") seam allowance, then cut off the triangle.

On an unlined jacket, you may wish to mitre the corners of both top and under sleeve.

On the under sleeve, notch the hem fold line and the extension fold/stitching line. Note the notches on the rest of the sleeve.

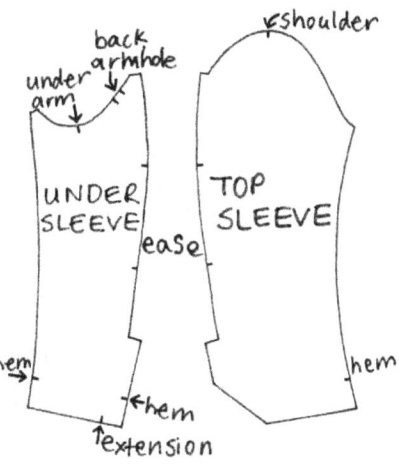

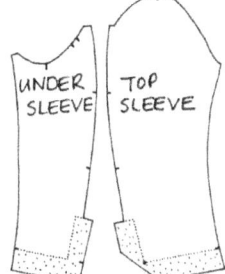
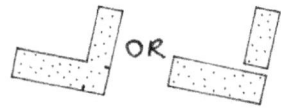

Interface both hem and extension. The interfacing can be cut in one piece or as separate strips.

When you've ironed the interfacing on and you're still at the ironing board, press up the hem allowances.

Cut the jacket sleeve **lining** (see page 178) without the hem or vent extension. I don't make separate patterns for the sleeve lining—I just fold the hem and extension up and use the same pattern. In some situations it might be possible to save time by cutting the fabric and lining together, then just trimming the lining pieces down.

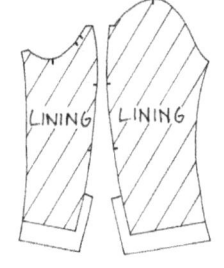

To sew a 2pce jacket sleeve with a vent

1. Make the mitre first by folding the diagonal edge back on itself, right sides together, and stitching the 6mm (¼") seam.
Press the seam open and turn it through to the right side.

2. On the under sleeve, fold up the sleeve hem and stitch along the edge of the extension, taking a 6mm (¼") seam. Trim the corner, turn and press.

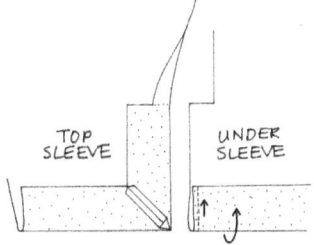

Some jackets have **non-functional buttonholes** under the buttons on the vent. The buttonholes don't have the slit cut—the buttons are sewn on over the top of them. If you're having buttonholes, make them on the top sleeve now.

3. Place the top sleeve and under sleeve right sides together and stitch the back seam. When you reach the extension, pivot and sew along the top then a short way down the extension. Some people stop sewing at the top of the extension—the buttons hold the layers in place anyway.

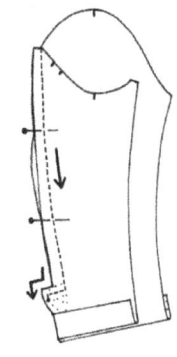

4. Press the extension towards the top sleeve and press the rest of the seam open.
I like to gradually press the seam open above the extension; alternatively you can snip into the corner of the under sleeve only to make it lie flat (a better option for very thick fabrics).

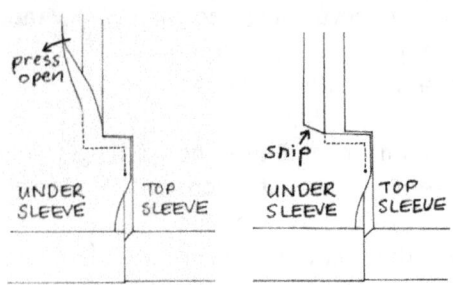

Press this seam while the sleeve is flat, then sew the front sleeve seam.

5. When you come to sewing the sleeve lining into the completed sleeves at the hem, pin the vent shut first. Begin and end sewing the lining at the vent.

6. Sew the buttons on at the end, through all the layers.

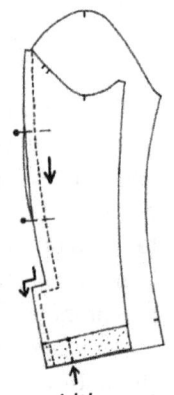

A budget method of making a (mock) vent on *lightweight* fabrics is to omit the mitred corner on the top sleeve, and sew the sleeve seam along the edge of the extension as shown. The seam is also stitched through the hem allowance in line with the sleeve seam. Press the vent extension towards the top sleeve and turn the hem up as usual.

The depth of the extension can be any width, not necessarily the same as the hem allowance. The extension need not be interfaced, to reduce bulk.

Sleeveless garments

Turning a sleeved garment into a sleeveless one doesn't necessarily entail just omitting the sleeve.

✂ The armhole will need to be made higher so your bra won't show.

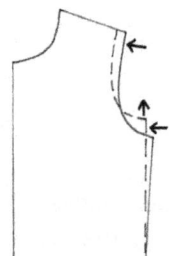

✂ The side seam will also need to be taken in slightly at the underarm so it doesn't gape.

✂ Sleeveless usually looks better if the armhole comes higher up the shoulder (so it's more cut-away), for example by 2cm (¾").

Make some facing patterns to finish the armhole (see page 97) or finish with a binding (page 22).

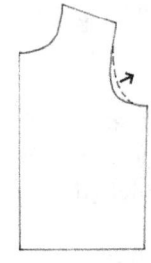 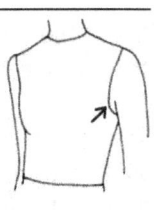

If you're large or have a large bust you might need to fill in the armhole at the front to stop it from gaping.

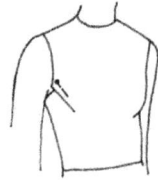 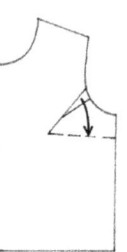

If the armhole gapes a lot, pin a dart in. On the pattern, transfer the dart to the bust by slashing along the dash line to the bust point and folding out the dart. A new dart will open along the dash line. See page 90 for more on darts.

Another solution for a gaping armhole—to use if the garment is already finished

1. Try on the garment and pin a dart in to see how much smaller the armhole needs to be.

2. Take off the garment and pin a length of 6mm (¼") wide cotton tape on the inside of the armhole, extending a few centimetres either side of the dart. Undo the dart and ease the excess onto the cotton tape, using lots of pins.

3. Using one strand of perfectly matching thread and a fine needle, handsew the cotton tape to the inside of the armhole, along each side of the tape. Fold under the ends neatly. The stitches need to be invisible on the right side. If the fabric eases well, use an iron to help shrink in any excess fullness afterwards.

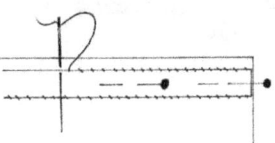

Stain removal

Every factory or fashion workroom I've worked in has had a stain removal kit—usually consisting of some baby powder, pure soap or stain removal soap, a bucket, a bottle of white spirit, eucalyptus oil and a clothes brush. Most of these things you will have at home.

Stain removal hints

When removing stains from fabric, try to use a piece of the same fabric if you can. If not, use something the same colour and lint-free. Place a pad of fabric underneath the stain to isolate it and use another piece to blot the actual stain. Work from the edges of the stain inwards. *Very important:* test solvents on a sample or an inconspicuous place before plunging in, in case it removes the fabric's colour or makes the situation worse.

Try to limit garment fittings to no more than four, if possible. Constant trying on and altering causes fabric to lose its freshness and increases the risk of stains.

Oil

Some fabrics seem to attract oil. Cover the stain with baby powder and leave (preferably overnight) to absorb the oil. Brush it off with a clothes brush. Repeat if necessary, but overnight is usually enough.

You can also remove oil with dry cleaning fluid (white spirit). Apply with a piece of the same fabric if you have some, if not use something the same colour BUT test on a sample or an inconspicuous place first.

✂ Wipe down your sewing machine with paper towel before using it to remove oil leakage.

✂ Ensure that people trying on garments aren't wearing oily moisturiser or sunscreen.

Gunk from the iron

See if you can scrape it off the fabric with a knife.
In future, invest in some iron cleaner and use it.

✂ Change your ironing board cover regularly or use a silicone appliqué mat to stop old interfacing glue fusing to your fabric.

Tailors Chalk

Brush off excess with a clothes brush. White or yellow chalk is easier to remove than blue or red.
If the marks are still there, use a small amount of water and soap.

Graphite pencil

Rub out with a plastic eraser.

Blood

Try to remove blood stains while they're fresh. For spots of blood use saliva, preferably from the same person as the blood. Thread a needle with four threads (see page 145) but don't knot the end. Wet the threads in your mouth. Pass the needle and thread through the blood spots in the same direction until the spots disappear. For large amounts of blood, use cold water and soap.

Lipstick

Lipstick is notoriously tricky to remove, especially the long-lasting type. Try a stain remover soap (for example Exit soap or Sard Wonder soap) or dry cleaning fluid (white spirit). Sometimes a plastic eraser works rubbed over the spot. You could also try glycerine on a cotton ball, wiped over the stain. Alternatively, ask at your dry cleaners—they may be able to spot clean it for you.

✂ Lipstick marks can happen at fittings—put a scarf over the person's face to cover it when taking garments off or on.

✂ Don't wear lipstick if you're in the habit of putting pins in your mouth (or don't put pins in your mouth if you're in the habit of wearing lipstick). When you put the pins in the fabric it leaves a red dot.

Chinagraph pencil

Chinagraph pencil is a waxy pencil used to mark dots for darts. It comes in several colours, and yellow or white are the easiest to remove. Try removing with dry cleaning fluid (white spirit). Red chinagraph is impossible to remove, in my experience.

Biro

Try a stain remover soap (for example Exit soap or Sard Wonder soap) or dry cleaning fluid (white spirit).

✂ Try to keep biros away from fabrics and only use pencil when you're sewing.

Stickiness

Stickiness from sticky tape or adhesive backing can be removed with eucalyptus oil BUT test it first.

Watermarks
Spray with a spray water bottle to make a less definite outline, then press with an iron and dry press cloth until the area is dry. Test it first, though.

Lint or animal hair
Use a clothes brush to brush it off. Alternatively, use sticky tape wrapped sticky side out around your knuckles and dabbed over the area. You could also use a vacuum cleaner or dust buster. If animal hair has embedded itself into the fabric, pulling the hairs out individually with tweezers may be the only thing that works.

Body odour
Wash with cold water and soap—don't use hot water or iron the area or you'll set the smell. For persistent body odour on hard to wash garments, for example the underarms of jackets, make a paste of bicarb soda and water, paint it on and leave it to dry. Brush off. Repeat if necessary.

✂ Consider making or buying some underarm shields for the garment to protect the fabric.

How to make underarm shields
Underarm shields sit astride the underarm and protect the garment from sweat. They are removed and washed instead of washing the whole garment. Choose a fabric that's soft and absorbant, for example flannelette, cotton, t-shirt knit or recycled soft, worn fabric from an old garment.

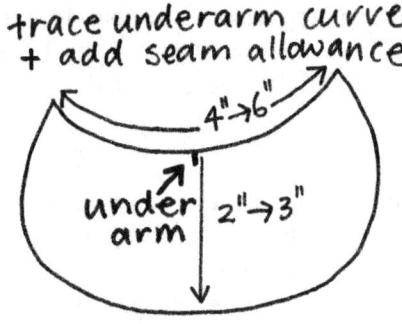

Make a pattern
The top curve of the pattern should match the underarm curve of the garment. Add a 6mm (¼") seam allowance.

To sew underarm shields
1. Cut eight (= four pairs) shapes of absorbent cotton or flannelette, to make a pair of shields.

2. With a pair held right sides together, sew the top curve with a narrow 6mm (¼") seam allowance. Press it open. Repeat with the other three pairs.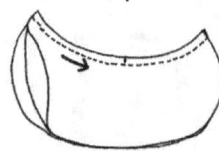

3. Take two of the seamed pieces and place them wrong sides together, matching the seam and outside edges. Overlock around the entire edge, two layers thick.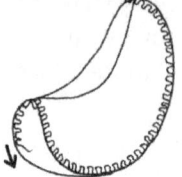

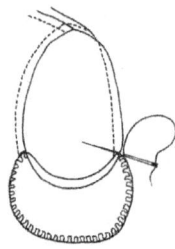

4. Sit the shield astride the underarm and tack it in place by hand on both corners.

Sleeveless shields
If the garment is sleeveless, underarm shields can be applied to the inside of the body just below the armhole and they will still offer some protection. Make the pattern in the same way as a regular underarm shield.

1. Cut four (= two pairs) in absorbent cotton or flannelette per garment.

2. Take a pair of cotton pieces and place them right sides together. Taking a 6mm (¼") seam allowance, sew around the edges leaving a small gap to turn it through. Trim the two corners and turn to the right side. Press.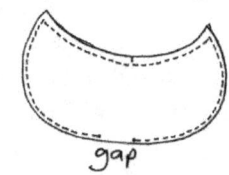

Alternatively, a slightly less bulky method is to sew the top seam only, then fold it over with the wrong sides inside and overlock all the edges together.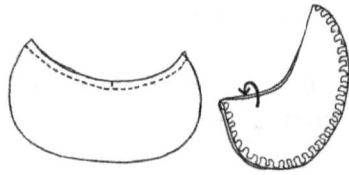

3. Attach the finished shield inside the garment by tacking it by hand along the armhole curve, making the stitches invisible to the outside.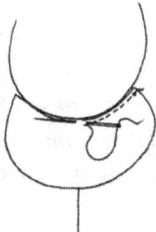

Strapless tops

Introduction............................ 343	preparing to fit....................... 344
Materials............................... 343	fitting notes............................ 344
fabrics............................ 343	after the fitting..................... 345
boning............................ 343	To sew a strapless top............. 346
fastenings..................... 344	Three other methods of
Fitting.................................... 344	sewing a strapless top............. 347

A simple strapless top plus a (separate or attached) skirt equals instant glamorous evening attire. Alternatively, a strapless top can be used as a foundation for a draped, flowing style.

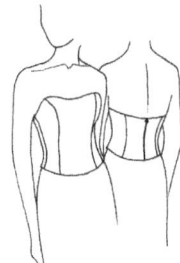

✂ A strapless top stays up by itself because it's skin tight and has boning and stiff layers inside to make it rigid.

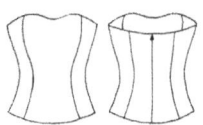

✂ A strapless top cannot have a very low back, because there would be nothing to hold the front in position (unless it's stuck to the skin with Hollywood tape).

✂ Strapless isn't the best choice for a very large bust because it doesn't really provide enough support. I suggest choosing a style with shoulder straps that are part of the top. The top will still have boning in it. The more seams the better, because more boning can be applied giving more support.

Materials
Fabrics
The **outer fabric** is your fashion fabric. A strapless top can be made from once the length if the fabric is 150cm (60") wide. For 112cm (45") wide fabric, one length is sufficient for busts 95cm (37½") and smaller; otherwise two lengths are required.

You'll need the same amount of some **firm, woven, sew-in interfacing** to give rigidity. If it seems too thin and pliable, iron on some lightweight fusible interfacing to make it firmer. As an alternative to sew-in interfacing, you could iron some firm fusible interfacing straight onto the fashion fabric if it fuses well and looks OK on the outside. Try a jacket fusing. You'll also need some **lining**; regular acetate or satin lining is fine. You'll need the same amount as the outer layer.

Boning
Strapless bodices are boned to the waist or just below, but no more than about 8 or 9cm (3½") below the waist. If it's a top that finishes just below the waist, I would extend the boning the entire length of the seam. However, some dressmakers still finish the boning at the waist.

If the strapless top is part of a dress that has a waist seam, the boning should finish at the waist. If it's a dress with no waist seam, finish the boning at the waist or 8-9cm (3⅛"-3½") below. If boning is sewn too much beyond this, the wearer won't be able to sit down comfortably or at all.

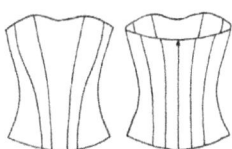

Some patterns have extra seams that can be boned for more support.

The most commonly available boning (at least in Australia) is Rigelene boning. It comes in 1.2cm (½") and 6mm (¼") widths and you can sew it straight onto the fabric. I use 1.2cm (½") for all the seams except the bust seam. For that seam I use 6mm (¼").

Another type is a flexible solid plastic 6mm (¼") boning which requires a casing—you can't stitch through it. Sometimes you can buy it with a casing already on it. If not, 1cm (⅜") bias binding makes a good casing, or the seam allowance can be stitched flat to make a channel to slot the boning into. The advantages of plastic boning are that it doesn't fray, you can insert the boning into the casings when the garment's almost finished, sometimes it's a little less $$$ and it's less likely to kink at the waist after wear.

Fastenings

The opening of the strapless bodice can be at the centre back, side or centre front, and can be done up by a zip, lacing or buttons and loops.

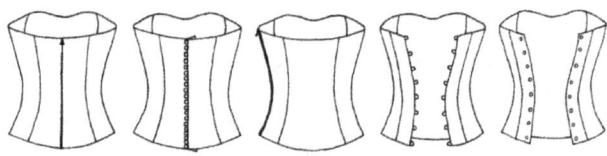

If the strapless bodice is part of a dress, a **regular or invisible zip** is fine. If the strapless bodice is a top, an open-ended zip will be required. A hook and eye at the top helps prevent strain on the zip.

Lacing is the most adjustable and is good for costumes that aren't made to fit one particular person. It gives an Olde Worlde corset look. The lacing can be threaded through small rouleau loops on the edge (see page 38) or metal eyelets punched through the fabric.

If you're going to use **buttons and loops**, don't use the elastic loops you buy by the metre—they aren't strong enough. Make rouleau loops. Cut a 2cm (¾") wide extension on the button side so you don't see flesh when the wearer is buttoned up (see page 38).

Fitting

Preparing to fit

The pattern pieces of a strapless top might look like this, or, the pattern may have more seams in it.

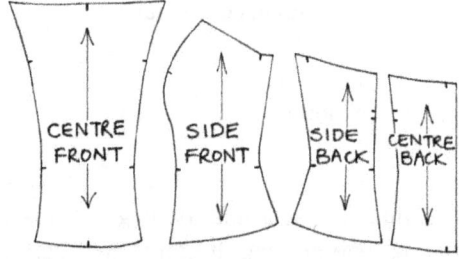

1. Measure the pattern pieces very accurately at the bust, waist and high hip. Most commercial patterns have the finished garment measurements printed on the pattern to save you from measuring. Compare the measurements to the wearer's. Don't add any ease—the measurements should be the same.

If the strapless top will finish at the waist rather than below it, determine the finished waistline at the fitting; the wearer's waist might not be in the same spot as the pattern's. For now, cut the top to finish at the hipline.

2. Make any adjustments. If the wearer has a full bust, adjust the shape of the bust before the fitting. I automatically do this alteration for busts bigger than 107cm (42"):

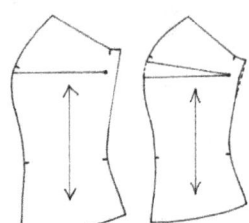

Cut the side front panel horizontally at the bust line and spread it 2.5cm (1") where it joins the centre front panel, back to nothing at the side.

Be sure to spread the pattern from the *stitching line*, not the edge of the pattern, otherwise you'll make the side seam longer.

Add 2.5cm (1") to the length of the centre front panel to make the seams the same length.
Usually 2.5cm (1") is enough.

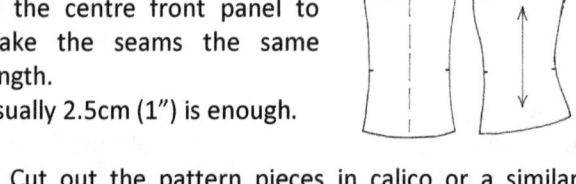

3. Cut out the pattern pieces in calico or a similar firmly-woven fabric (you cannot "tissue fit" strapless tops) and sew them together.

If the strapless top has a very V-shaped top edge (which will be on the bias and therefore unstable), sew 6mm (¼") cotton tape along the edge to stop it from stretching. Be sure to measure the length of the tape on the *pattern*, rather than the garment, which may have already stretched. I like to place a pencil dot on the tape to match it to the seams and centre front. Stitch it *on* the seam line.

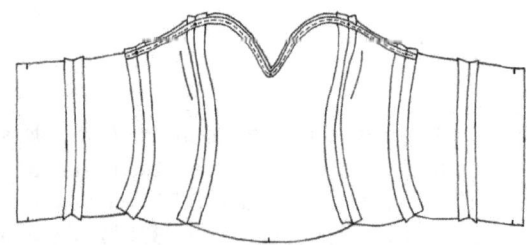

Fitting notes

✂ Fit with the right side out (seams inside). Keep the centre back seam straight—if you have to take this seam in, do it evenly all the way along.

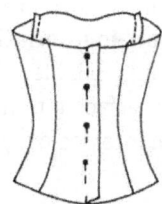

Strapless tops 345

✂ Is the wearer planning to wear a **bra**? If so, fit with the correct bra from the beginning. Pin the top to the wearer's bra for the first fitting. Is the back high enough to clear the bra? If going braless, pin the top to the wearer's (regular, unpadded) bra for the *first fitting only*—after that lose the bra.

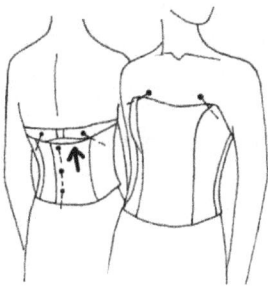

Do you need to add **bust padding**? If so, do it now (see further on this page).

✂ If you want to convert the pattern to a **laced-up back**, do the initial fitting with the whole back. Draw in where you want the laced up section to be. You'll probably need to move the side panel seams across to the sides more.

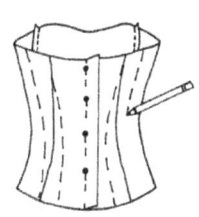

✂ Try to keep the centre front panel seam straight. If you need to take in under the bust, take it in on the side panel only. This will make the seam line slightly longer, so add any difference to the bottom of the centre front panel.

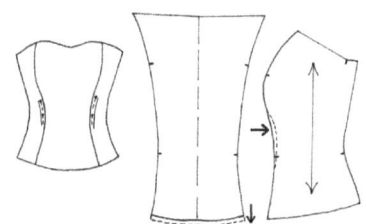

✂ If the strapless top will finish at the waistline, draw in the wearer's waistline on the calico.

✂ Don't fit the hip too tightly if the top is going over a very full skirt. You'll need to accommodate the skirt's fullness under the top.

✂ The top will firm up slightly when the alterations are sewn instead of pinned, when the top is cut in a firmer fabric and again slightly when the boning is in. So don't fit it absolutely skin tight!—just firmly.

✂ If you're making a strapless top with an open-ended zip, check your **zip length** *now* to make sure you have the right length.

✂ Take a look in the mirror to check the height of the top edge. Do you need to add a seam allowance to the top edge or is it high enough? Don't make it too high or the sides will cut into the wearer's flesh.

✂ Make any **style changes** now if you want to. The neckline and the hemline can be curved or straightened.

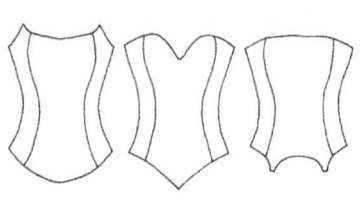

✂ If you're using a **vertically striped fabric**, the centre front panel will look better if the front seam lines follow the stripes. If the front seam lines splay out to the sides at the neckline, draw in new lines now.

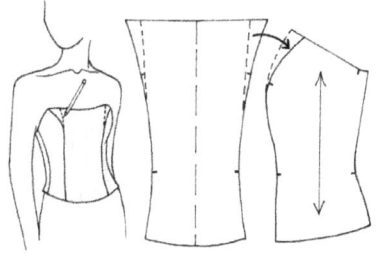

(If you *aren't* using stripes, I think having the tops of the front seam lines splaying out to the sides looks more flattering.)

✂ If you want to add **padding to the bust** to improve the shape, make or find some padding to use and put it in the top at this and every fitting. You can buy bust improvers from bra shops, or cut up an old padded bra.

To make, cut some concentric circles of polyester wadding in descending diameter. Lay them on top of one another and tack them together gently. You may only need a couple of

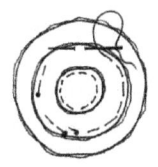

layers depending on the thickness of the wadding and the amount of padding required.

Pin the padding in place for the fitting. Sew the padding in by hand after the boning but before the lining. Stitch only through the backing so it won't show on the right side. If the fabric is fused, attach the bust padding to the seam allowances where you can.

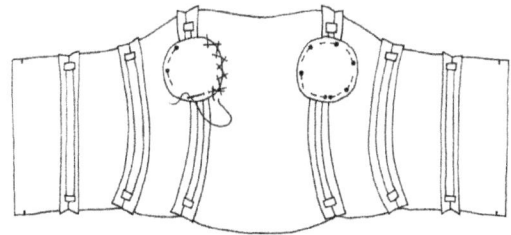

After the fitting

1. Undo the calico and transfer any changes to the pattern pieces.

2. Add any seam allowances, for example to the top edge, if required.

3. Check that the seams are the same length and the notches are in the right place, particularly on the front panel seams. An easy method is to first draw in the stitching line on the pattern. Match the stitching lines together at one end of the seam. Then, using a pencil to pivot, "walk" the top pattern piece along the stitching line until you reach the end of the seam.

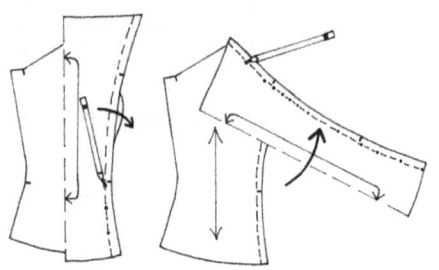

If you've taken in a seam across a diagonal, for example on the side seams, the seams will now be different lengths. Add onto the *shorter* seam rather than take it off the longer one.

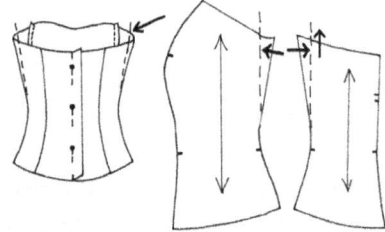

To sew a strapless top

1. Cut out all the pieces in the main fabric, the lining, and the firm woven sew-in interfacing.

2. Mount the main fabric onto the interfacing by stitching them together around the edges with a long machine stitch. Make sure both layers are wrinkle-free. I like to do the pinning at the ironing board after I've pressed each piece. Keep the pins and the stitching within the seam allowance to avoid marking the fabric. Sometimes it's easier to sew if the stiffer fabric is facing up. If you're using a fusible interfacing, securely fuse each piece instead.

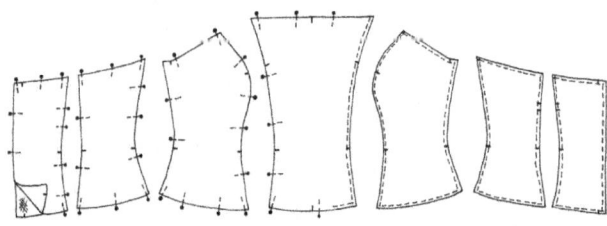

3. Sew the seams of the main pieces.

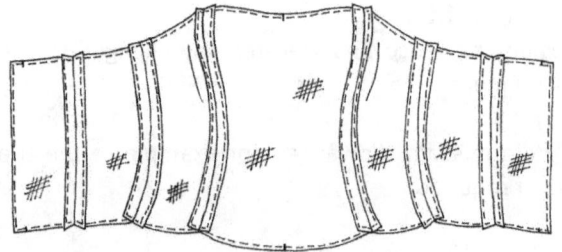

Press the seams open. There's no need to overlock the edges since they'll all be enclosed.

If the top edge is very V-shaped and liable to stretch, sew tape along the edge to stabilize it. (You would have done this at the fitting as well.) As before, measure the length of the tape on the *pattern*, rather than the garment, in case the garment has stretched.

If the top edge flares out slightly when the top is worn, sew on a shorter length of tape to ease it in.

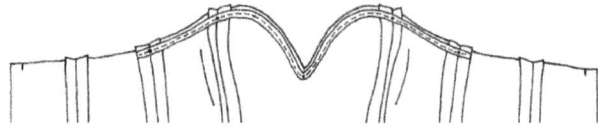

4. Sew the seams of the lining pieces. Leave a gap in one of the lining's side seams to turn the bodice through at the end.

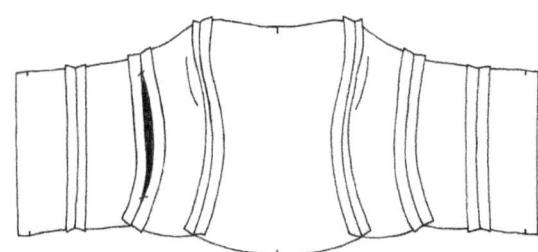

5. Check the fit.

6. Sew the boning onto the seams of the main piece. First cut the boning to the correct length. It should be the length of the seam minus the top and bottom seam allowances and 6mm (¼").

Stitch a folded piece of fabric or interfacing over the Rigelene boning at both ends. An ordinary domestic machine is capable of sewing through boning if you're careful.

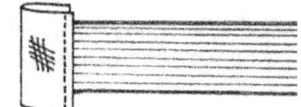

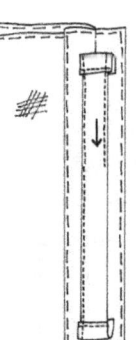

Centre the prepared boning on the opened seam.

Sew down each side of the boning, *only* on the *seam allowance*, not through to the garment.

I use 1.2cm (½") boning centred on all seams except the seam that goes over the bust. For that seam I use 6mm (¼") boning and sew it onto the centre front seam allowance *only*.

✂ The boning has a natural curve to it—I like to sew it curving *into* the body, but it really doesn't make any difference once it's being worn. The boning will re-curve in any direction.

✂ If the bodice has a **laced back**, sew boning onto the edges of the laced opening.
If the bodice has a **zip**, you may or may not sew boning to one of the edges after you've put the zip in (I usually don't because the zip has some rigidity of its own).

7. Check the fit again now the boning is sewn in. Sew in the **bust padding** if you're using it.

8. If you're making a dress, sew the skirt part on now. Attach any zips or button loops. Leave room at the top of the zip to sew on a hook and eye when the top is finished—it helps to stop strain on the zip when it's being zipped up (see page 150).

✂ If you're making a costume which will be altered to fit several different wearers in the future, sew the zip in very last of all, after the lining. Overlock the lining and main fabric zip edges separately and sew the zip in through all layers.

9. Sew the prepared lining on. Sew the top edge first and understitch it. The understitching will stop the lining from rolling to the right side.

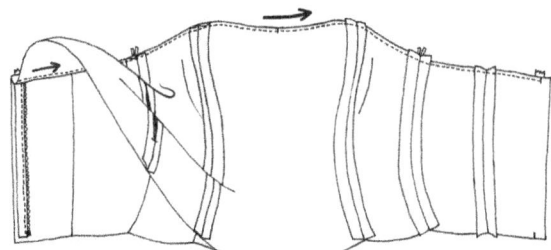

Put in **hanger loops** if required. You can attach them in the lining side seam 1.5cm (⅝") down from the top then catch them into the understitching OR sew them into the top edge and catch them in the understitching.

10. Sew the lower edge next and understitch, then the edges of the opening (next to the zip or lacing).
Turn the top through to the right side by pulling it through the gap you left in the lining seam.

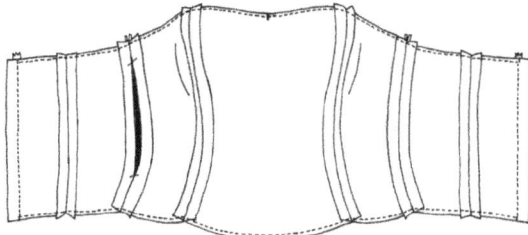

Sew up the gap in the lining—press the edges together like a pair of lips and machine them together.

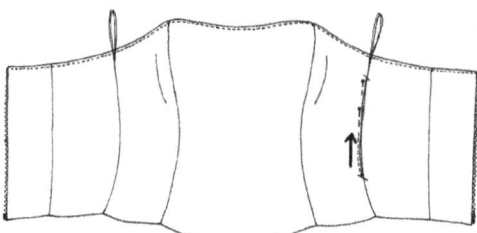

✂ If the strapless top has a very full heavy skirt attached to it, consider stitching an **inside belt** to the waist to support the skirt and stop the strapless top from being dragged down by the weight of the skirt.
Use 2.5cm (1") wide grosgrain ribbon or make a belt from the same fabric. Securely sew the belt to each seam allowance around the waist on the inside of the garment. Determine the position of the belt by trying on the dress and pinning the ribbon to the outside, marking the seam/waistline intersections. Take off the bodice and transfer the belt to the inside.
Leave a gap in the lining at each end to bring the ends of the belt through. Fasten the belt with a sturdy, flat hook and bar. When putting the strapless dress on, support the dress while you do up the inside belt, then do up the bodice.

Three other methods of sewing a strapless top

There are many other ways of making strapless tops, and everyone has their own preference. Whichever method you decide on, be prepared to take the time to get the cut and fit right. It may seem time consuming, but your efforts in checking fit and shape throughout construction will be rewarded.

Boning the lining instead of the main fabric

Often seen on ready-to-wear at the budget end of the market. I consider it a less precise method. The lining is never as firm as the main fabric and the lining's seams don't always sit perfectly in line with the garment's seams.
Press the lining seam allowance to one side and topstitch it down to form a channel. At the bottom, sew it at a right angle to meet the original seam, forming a pocket. Insert the boning into this channel. Usually 6mm (¼") boning is used, as it fits into 1cm (⅜") seam allowances. Sometimes the boning is simply stitched straight onto the lining seams, with no channel.

If you use Rigelene boning, you'll still have to cover the ends of the boning even if it's in a channel, otherwise it will eventually wear through the lining.

Boning sewn onto an inside layer
In this method, the outer fabric doesn't get mounted onto the firm interfacing—they're sewn as two separate bodices. The boning is sewn onto the stiff interfacing bodice which is then sandwiched between the lining and the outer fabric.

I've used this method and it's great for styles with complex seaming or pleating/draping in the main fabric (for example the ruched top on page 135). It's also sometimes used for strapless dresses with no waist seam.

The boning could be stitched straight onto the interfacing (my preference), or it could be inserted into a casing, or the seam allowances could be stitched to one side to form a channel into which the boning is inserted.

Stitch boning through all layers of main fabric
For a corset look, stitch the boning on through *all* layers of the fabric, not just on the seam allowances. On the right side it will look like the seams are topstitched. Be sure that the seams are pressed perfectly open before you sew the boning on.

Alternatively, you can stitch the seam allowance flat to make a channel and insert the boning into it.

Another idea is to sew boning channels separate from the seams, as a feature on the outside. They'll need to be perfectly stitched, but will provide more support.

Topstitching

Introduction 349	Troubleshooting topstitching 351
Tension, stitch length and thread 349	Directional stitching 352
A gallery of topstitching 350	how it works 352
Topstitching notes 351	some examples 352

I recall that as fashion student I was anti-topstitching! I preferred a clean look with no visible stitching whatsoever. These days I'm keen on topstitching. Topstitching is an excellent way to emphasize a construction detail, to hold seam allowances flat, to hold interfacing in position or to add interest to plain fabric. It also reinforces seams and I heard that topstitched garments require less ironing!

Seams are topstitched on the right side after pressing. Effective topstitching is straight and even.

✂ Decide on your topstitching detail at the beginning and be consistent. If you're making matching tops and bottoms, or designing a range, follow the stitching theme throughout. Which seams will you topstitch and which ones will you leave? Which style of topstitching? Usually just one style is used but occasionally more than one style is used for the same garment.

✂ The edge of the presser foot on your machine is a good guide for **6mm (¼") topstitching**. It's sometimes called footwidth stitching. If you can vary the needle position on your machine you can make slightly wider or narrower topstitching still using the edge of the presser foot as a guide. When topstitching curves, remember to watch only the part of the foot that's exactly opposite the needle.

Edgestitching or pin stitching is stitching close to the edge, about 1mm-2mm away. Edgestitching uses the edge itself as a guide. For fail-safe edgestitching, it's possible to buy an edgestitching foot for some machines—the foot has a guide that sits in the seamline.
Edgestitching is a construction stitch as well as a decoration stitch. It's used to stitch down patch pockets, sleeve plackets, shirt collars, cuffs and waistbands.

Edgestitching and footwidth stitching can be combined to make classic jeans topstitching. The edgestitched row is sewn first, then the footwidth row. It can also be achieved in one operation by using a twin needle.

For **extra-wide topstitching**, use a quilting guide-bar or screw-on gauge on your machine to help to keep it straight.

Tension, stitch length and thread

✂ Sew a test swatch and check the tension on your machine. You might need to adjust it for the topstitching if you're stitching through thicker layers of fabric or using a different thread.
If you're topstitching a reversible garment you'll need to be certain the tension is perfect both sides. Be extra-especially certain if the top and bobbin threads are different colours.
The number of thicknesses of fabric you're stitching through will slightly affect the look of the topstitching. Try, if you can, to stitch through a similar number of layers each time you topstitch the garment. Topstitching on a single layer of fabric may need a tension adjustment on the machine, or require a backing underneath to give it more substance.

✂ A slightly longer stitch is often used for topstitching (3 or 3.5, instead of 2.5), so more of the thread's surface is visible. A longer stitch shows up better; shorter stitches bury themselves in the fabric.
Having said that, a short stitch length is a reliable indicator of quality, notably on men's shirts, since it's stronger and takes longer to sew. In fact, some shirts even advertise the stitch length as one of the quality

features. A short stitch length also slows the machine down so it's easier to be accurate.

✂ You could topstitch in a contrasting, variegated or matching thread.

You may like to use a thick topstitching thread to define the stitching on heavy fabrics. I like to use Gütermann topstitching thread or strong upholstery thread. Actually I prefer upholstery thread because it seems to be less prone to abrasion as it flows through the machine, but it has a narrower range of colours. Use regular thread in the bobbin and the topstitching thread for the upper thread. Install at least a size 14 (90) machine needle, if not a 16 (100). Use the longest machine stitch length—topstitching thread looks best with a very long stitch. I find I don't need to change the machine's tension, but you might.

My domestic machine hates topstitching thread, even though it has a fair bit of grunt compared to other machines. It sounds like an old mixmaster as it chomps through the fabric. Stitching backwards is out of the question for the poor thing. Instead, I leave long ends and tie them off and/or sew them in. Straight stitch is a surer bet than zig zag. If one of the zigs or zags doesn't catch then the seam doesn't look right.

If you can't find a suitable thicker thread, try threading the machine with two strands of regular thread held together.

A gallery of topstitching

Edgestitching or pinstitching on a closed seam

Edgestitching either side of an open seam

6mm (¼") footwidth on a closed seam

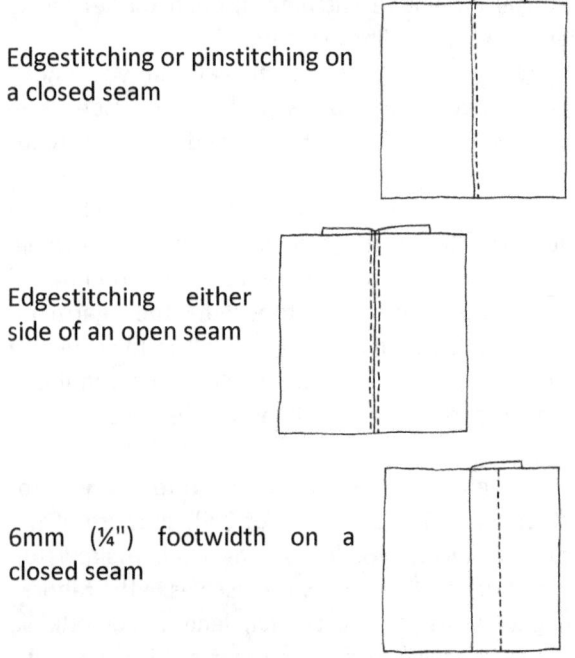

Triple jeans stitching on a closed seam

Serpentine stitch on top of an open seam

Zig zag on a closed seam

6mm (¼") footwidth either side of an open seam

Zig zag on top of an open seam

Any fancy stitch on a closed seam

Extra-wide stitching on a closed seam (you may need a wider seam allowance)

Jeans stitching—edgestitch and 6mm (¼") footwidth on a closed seam (or use a twin needle)

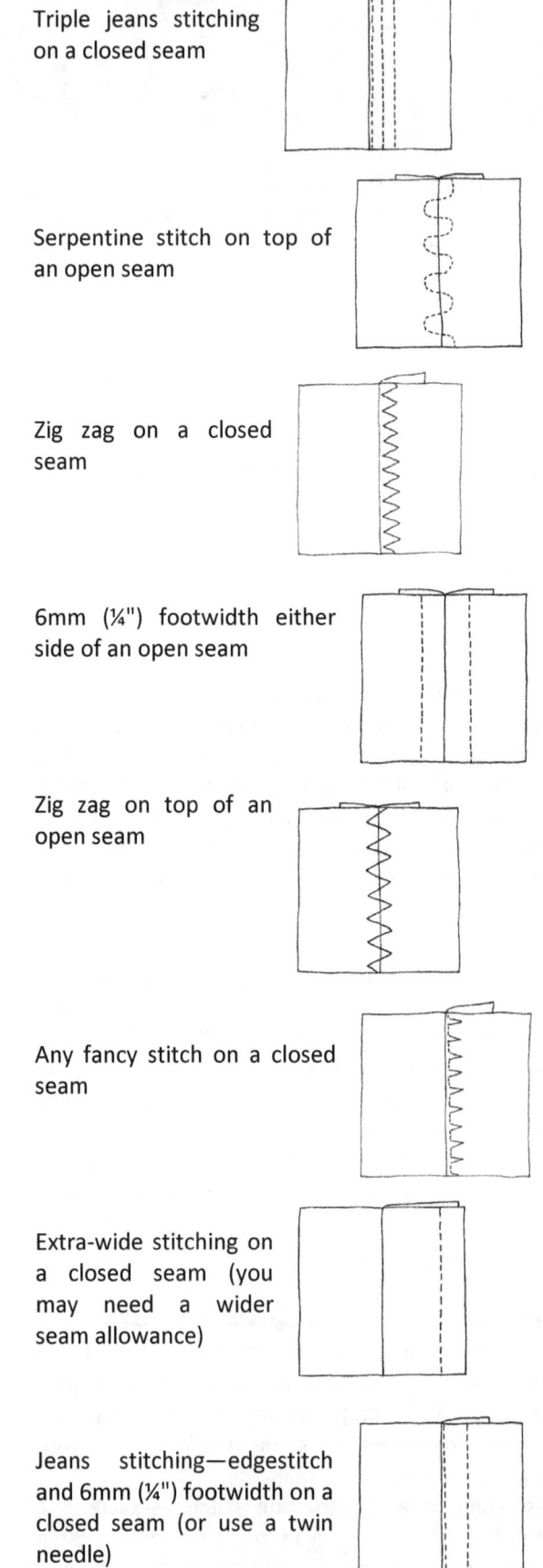

Topstitching notes

✂ On princess line garments, the seams are usually pressed towards the centre of the garment, to accommodate the way the seam curves. Therefore the topstitching will be on the centre panel (unless of course you're topstitching both sides of the seam, in which case you'll press the seam open).

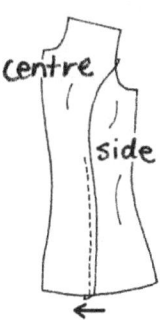

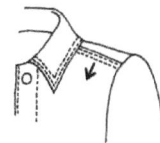 ✂ Denim shirts and denim jackets generally have the shoulder seams pressed towards the front and topstitched, to show off the topstitching.

✂ On the lapels of a jacket, both sides of the topstitched seam are visible as the lapels fold back. If you're using topstitching thread as the upper thread, remember that the right side becomes the wrong side at the break point (where the lapel turns back). Stitch the upper collar and lapel, stopping at the break point. Then flip the jacket over and continue the stitching on the right side.
As you topstitch, try to roll the edge slightly so that (what will be) the wrong side is out of sight.
If you *aren't* using topstitching thread, make sure your machine tension is adjusted properly so the stitching looks the same on both sides. You can topstitch the front edge and lapel in one operation.

✂ To correctly stitch around a lapel notch, begin topstitching from the collar, then around the lapel.

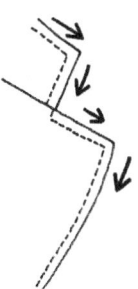 Pivot 90 degrees at the seam (or gorge line, as it's technically known), and stitch-in-the-ditch for a few stitches along the groove in the seam line. Pivot 90 degrees again at the corner and stitch for 6mm (or the width of your topstitching). Pivot a final 90 degrees and continue topstitching the lapel.

✂ To sew several rows of topstitching, stitch in alternating directions to stop the top layer from shifting.

✂ When topstitching facings down, *do* still understitch the facing first. It makes a crisp, neat edge and is easier to press.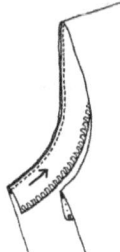

The width of the facing should be only slightly wider than the width of the topstitching, otherwise the un-anchored facing will flip back when the garment is worn and laundered. Ideally, the topstitching should land in the centre of the overlocking. I prefer to topstitch from the wrong side, with the (interfaced) facing uppermost and the garment underneath, because the firmer fabric is on top.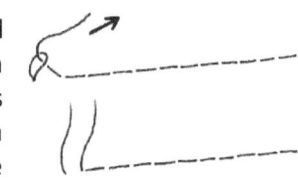

Troubleshooting topstitching
Joins in topstitching

If you backstitch at the beginning and end of topstitching it creates a thicker section of stitching. You'll also create a thicker section if you have to stop and start topstitching mid-way. It doesn't look that great, particularly with thicker thread.
Sometimes, however, you'll need to either make a join in a line of topstitching, or begin and end topstitching without backstitching.

1. Sew the topstitching, beginning and ending exactly where you want to on the right side. Cut the threads leaving long tails.

2. On the wrong side, pull the end of the bobbin thread back hard towards the stitching, exposing a loop. Use a pin to pull the loop through, to give you two tails. Tie them together and cut off the excess. Alternatively, thread them onto a handsewing needle and sew them in by hand.

Running out of topstitching thread

If you're about to run out of topstitching thread only 12cm-15cm (5"-6") from the end, tie the end of the thread onto another spool and finish topstitching—you should be able to finish before the knot reaches the eye of the needle.

Skipped stitches

Try changing the needle. The thicker the thread the larger the needle must be. Try a size 14 needle or larger and stitch slowly.

The topstitching moves the top layer of fabric

This is likely to happen on loosely woven fabrics or fabric that has been eased. It's most noticeable on checks or fabrics with a regular pattern.

On plain fabrics it gives the edge a ropey appearance.

Some possible solutions (in order of what I would try):

✂ Are you stitching in the right direction? See the section on Directional stitching, below.

✂ Try a walking foot if your machine has one.

✂ Topstitch from the wrong side (so the firmer side is uppermost). Check the tension first.

✂ Spray the area with starch, then iron dry, to stabilize the area.

Directional stitching

Directional stitching is the technique of stitching in a particular direction. Its purpose is to support the grain and prevent the fabric from changing shape or dimensions.

You'll notice the need for directional stitching when you topstitch curved or angled edges, or on loosely woven or dimensionally unstable fabrics. In one direction the topstitching will lie perfectly flat and in the other it will ripple.

Directional stitching is also applicable to regular seams, but most people notice the need for it when they topstitch.

How directional stitching works

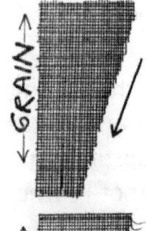

Stitching *with* the grain stops the fabric changing shape or dimensions, because it pushes the lengthwise and crosswise threads together.

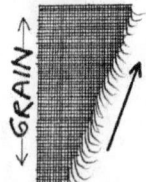

Stitching *against* the grain pushes the threads apart.

In general, if you stitch from the *wider* part of the fabric to the *narrower* part you'll be stitching with the grain.

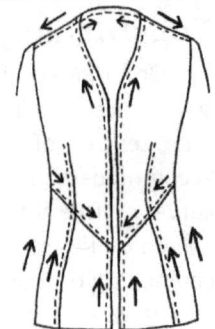

The **exception** to this principle is pile fabric. It's more important to stitch in the direction of the pile than that of the grain.

Some examples of directional stitching

✂ A curved belt (or curved waistband) needs to be stitched from the middle out to the ends.

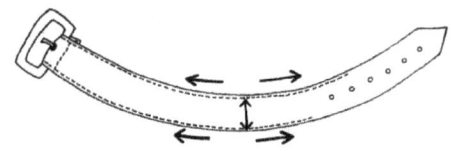

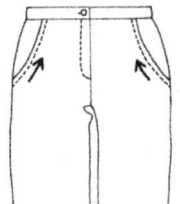

✂ Cutaway pockets on trousers need to be stitched from the bottom up.

✂ Jacket lapels are stitched from the top down.

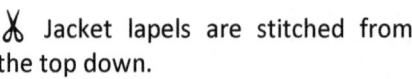

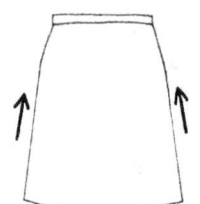

✂ The side seams of A-line skirts should be sewn from the hem up to the waist.

✂ Shoulder seams should be stitched from the neck to the shoulder.

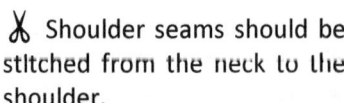

✂ The underarm seams of sleeves are best stitched from the underarm down to the wrist.

Tucks

Introduction.. 353	Some tuck variations 355
Types of tucks...................................... 353	cross tucking................................ 355
Grainline of tucks 354	mixing different tucks................ 355
Making tucks... 354	corded or piped tucks 356
Tucking a block of fabric.................. 354	movement tucks.......................... 356
method 1—classic....................... 354	curved tucks 356
method 2—factory...................... 355	pintucks with a twin needle 356
method 3—other factory........... 355	

A tuck is a stitched fold of fabric, not unlike a pleat. A tuck is usually decorative, but can be part of a garment's shaping. Tucks can be used for men's, women's or children's clothes. They are traditionally used on the front of men's formal shirts, baby's christening robes and in heirloom sewing. As a practical application, tucks at the end of sleeves and hemlines can be unpicked to make the garment longer.

  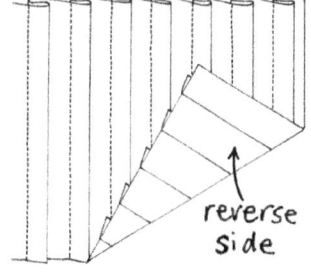

✂ Tucked fabric is stable. From the back, the tucks appear as seams. The handle of the fabric changes after tucking, becoming thicker, firmer and less pliant.

✂ Tucks can be stitched along the entire length of the fold, or only some of the way.

✂ Tucks require exact measuring, marking, folding and stitching. On fabrics liable to pucker, you'll need to hold the fabric taut as the tuck is sewn.

Types of tucks

Tucks can be any width and arranged with none, even or irregular spacing. Different types of tucks can be used together, too.

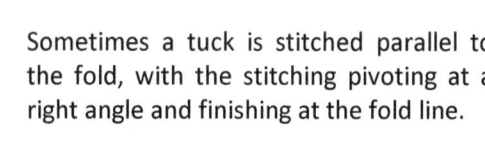

Sometimes a tuck is stitched parallel to the fold, with the stitching pivoting at a right angle and finishing at the fold line.

Pin tucks are narrow tucks, sometimes only a pin's width wide, but never wider than 3mm (⅛") from the folded edge.

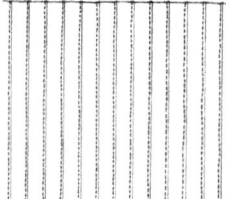

✂ Tucks work well with gathers, frills, lace insertion, cotton eyelet lace and fine sheer fabrics, especially cotton. Plain, smooth fabrics show off tucks to their best advantage, however, it's fine to use printed fabrics too.

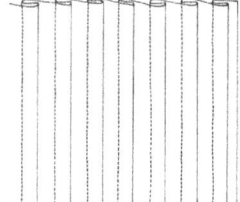

Spaced tucks are identical in width and spaced the same distance apart.

Blind tucks are tucks without visible spacing in between because the folds touch or lap over the neighbouring tuck.

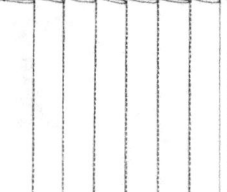

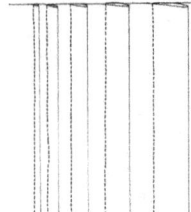

Graduated tucks are a series of tucks progressively increasing in width. The spacing between the tucks also progressively increases.

Centred tucks have two folds made by centring each tuck over its seam, rather like a box pleat.

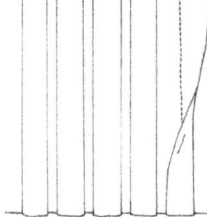

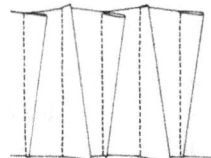

Tapered tucks are tucks sewn with straight seams not parallel to the fold.

Released tucks are also called dart tucks or partially seamed tucks. They aren't stitched along the entire length of the fold. They're used to control fullness and release it at a certain point, for example at the bust or hips. The tucks can be formed on the inside or the outside of the garment, and the fullness can be released at one or both ends. The tucks can be topstitched to help them lie flat and in the correct direction.

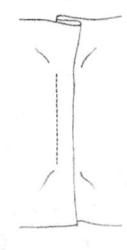

Grainline of tucks

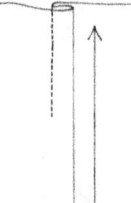

Most tucks are stitched with the straight grain of the fabric on the fold. For tucks that are purposely designed with off-grain folds and seams, choose a firm fabric, limit the length of the tucks and use a strong, good-quality thread to counter the stretchy bias.

Even though tapering tucks slant, the on-grain folds prevent the off-grain seams from stretching and snapping. With tapering tucks, you can alternate the direction from tuck to tuck.

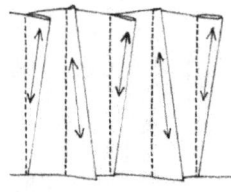

Making tucks

For small areas or few tucks, the tucks can be marked on the pattern. On the fabric, mark the top of the tuck with tiny 3mm (⅛") snips. If the tuck will be stitched along the entire length, mark the bottom with snips too.

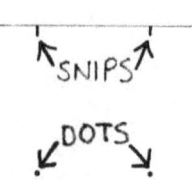

If the tuck will only be stitched part of the way, mark the bottom with dots on the right side of the fabric. The dots must be removable because they'll show. You could also use thread tacks or pins.

If the tucks are pintucks, use a single snip or dot to mark the foldline.

Fold the tuck with the right side of the fabric facing out. Bring the snips and dots together and stitch, backstitching at the ends. If the fabric is liable to pucker, hold it taut as you sew.

To press, first press each tuck flat in the direction it was sewn. Then press each tuck in the direction it will be worn. It's easier to press tucks into position from the *wrong* side, to make sure they're really flat.

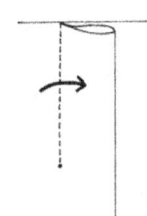

For large areas of tucks, a square or rectangle of fabric can be tucked and pressed, then the pattern laid strategically on top and cut out. The block of fabric needs to be cut perfectly on-grain, with square 90 degree corners. Calculate how much extra fabric you'll need to accommodate the tucks so the block of fabric is big enough and so you don't have waste.

Tucking a block of fabric

There are several ways to go about tucking a block of fabric.

Method 1—The classic method

This is a time-consuming method (lots of jumping up to the ironing board then back to the machine), but accurate and neat.

1. Press the fold of the first tuck in place accurately with an iron. You could fold and press the fabric over the straight edge of a heavy piece of paper, or just hold the fabric taut

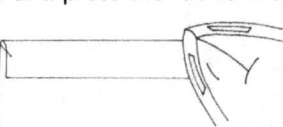

and parallel with its straight edge as you press.

2. Stitch the tuck using the lines on the needle plate of the machine as a guide, as if you were sewing a seam.
If the fabric is liable to pucker, hold it taut as you sew.

3. Press the tuck flat in the direction it was sewn first, then press it in the direction it will be worn—it's easiest to do this on the wrong side of the fabric, so you can make sure each one is pressed really flat. While you're at the ironing board, press the fold in for the second tuck, ready to sew.

Repeat this three-step process (press fold, stitch tuck, press tuck) until all the tucks have been done, making each tuck parallel with the previous one. Check that each tuck is even by measuring it if necessary.

Method 2—The factory method

This is faster than the classic method and a good one if the tucks are being made in a factory situation—you can make a pattern piece/template for the block of fabric to be tucked. It works very well on crisp fabrics that hold a crease. However, I would still use Method 1 if I was sewing at home and wanted perfect tucks or was using a hard-to-handle fabric.

1. Make a cardboard template for the tucks. If the template is to be used for several sizes, make sure it fits the largest. It might look a bit like this:

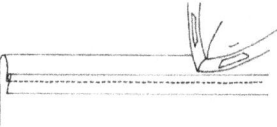

2. Use the template to mark the fold lines of each tuck, top and bottom. Mark with tiny 3mm (⅛") snips. The top and bottom snips should be in line with each other, along the straight grain of the fabric.

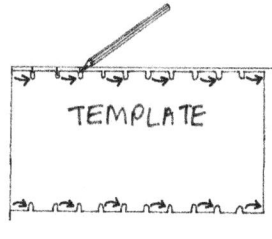

3. Sew the tucks one after the other by folding the fabric from snip to snip. You can form a crease by scraping the tightly-held fabric against the sharp edge of the table. Stitch the tuck, using the lines on the machine needle plate as a guide. If the fabric is liable to pucker, hold it taut as you sew. Press all the tucks after you've finished all the sewing.

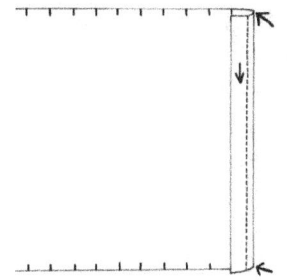

Method 3—The other factory method

If you require a great deal of tucked fabric (if designing a clothing range for manufacture, for example), it's possible to get a whole roll of fabric tucked professionally by machine.

Some tuck variations
Cross tucking

Cross tucking consists of intersecting rows of horizontal and vertical folds. The tucks can be any width and any spacing. Usually, all the tucks in one direction are sewn first, pressed, then all the tucks in the opposite direction are sewn.

Interestingly, if all the vertical tucks are stitched first, the crossover horizontal tucks will overshadow the tucks underneath (as illustrated), but when the tuck stitching alternates between vertical and horizontal, the cross tucked design appears interlaced.

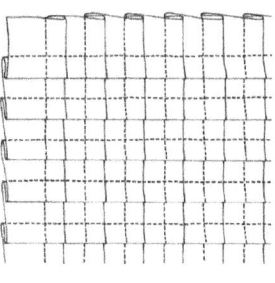

Either way, press the already-sewn tucks before changing direction. When stitching a new tuck over previous tucks, sew with the folds of the previous tucks facing *away* from the approaching presser foot.
Cross tucked fabric loses some flexibility in both directions. Thick fabrics are not suitable for cross tucking—it just gets too thick, however cross tucking is very effective on fine and sheer fabrics.

Mixing different tucks

Fold a strip of paper to plan the tuck pattern, recording on the pattern the order in which the tucks are to be sewn.

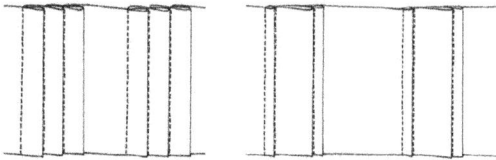

Corded or piped tucks

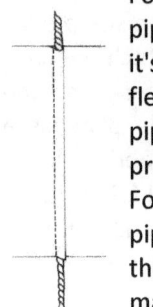

For rounded, three-dimensional tucks, piping cord can be inserted into the tuck as it's sewn. Corded tucks are stiffer and less flexible than regular tucks. Make sure the piping cord is the correct width for the proportions of the garment.

Fold the tuck into place and position the piping cord along the fold. Stitch close to the cord using a zipper foot, as if you were making piping. You might need to hold the fabric taut.

Movement tucks—tucks stitched back on themselves

Rows of plain tucks can be given a three-dimensional look by stitching perpendicularly across them, folding the tucks in alternate directions. Allow enough space between each row of stitching for the tuck to fully fold in the opposite direction.

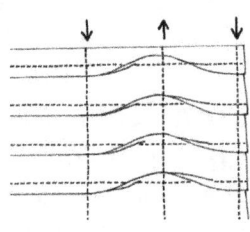

Curved tucks

Tucks that follow a curving path usually run parallel to the curving lower edge of the fabric, for example tucks around the lower edge of a flared skirt. The fabric flares below the curved tuck and the flare is progressive—the amount of flare increases with the depth and number of tucks. Obviously curved tucks cannot be deep tucks. The tucks can be blind, spaced, graduated or pintucked (see the note below for pintucks).

To accommodate the tucks, add twice the width of each tuck to the length/radius of the fabric when cutting. If the fabric is cut in segments, seam the segments together before tucking (for example a flared skirt with panels).

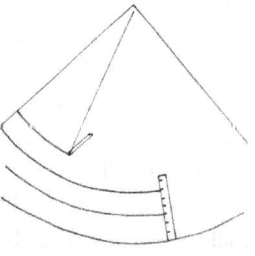

Mark the fold line for each tuck, either measuring up from the bottom edge with a ruler, or measure down from the top. If you're planning tucks on a circular or very flared skirt, level the hem on the wearer first, to make sure the tucks and hem will be parallel to the floor. Crease each tuck fold line with the tip of the iron.

Sew a line of ease stitches (either running stitches by hand or a long machine basting stitch) over the lower seam line. With the tuck folded, ease the stitching until it matches the upper seam line and pin the tuck seam lines together. Follow the upper seam line to sew the tuck, so the side to be eased is underneath.

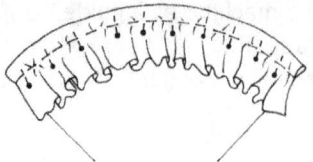

For pintucks, an ease stitch is not necessary.

Pintucks sewn using a twin needle

Pintucks can be sewn using a grooved tucking foot and a twin needle; it makes a slightly different looking tuck. Consult your machine's manual.

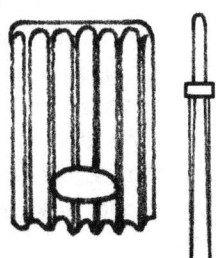

Vents and splits

for skirts and jackets

Introduction 357	method 1 lined vent 362
Vents 357	method 2 lined vent 364
Unlined vents 357	Splits 366
Back/Dior skirt vent 359	Splits within the hem allowance 367
Lining a skirt vent 360	To reinforce the top 367
Attaching lining to a skirt or jacket 361	Lining splits 367

Vents (also called kickpleats when in skirts) and splits are both design features to allow movement and help a garment be functional. They both need a seam to accommodate them and they both occur at the end of the seam.

✂ A vent or a split is an essential feature on straight (pencil) skirts to allow easy walking.

✂ Jackets, particularly blazers and men's suit jackets, may feature one or two vents at the back to allow for sitting down. Vents are also used on sleeves and bottoms of trouser legs.

✂ A vent is considered by some to be a smarter-looking and more conservative choice than a split.

✂ Splits can be used anywhere—at the sides of tops, skirts, jackets, trousers and shorts, shirts, short or long sleeves, dresses and at the front of necklines. The splits may have buttons and loops or other fastenings to do them up.

Important: if you plan to have a lining in the skirt or jacket, decide how you're going to handle the lining around the vent or split *before* starting—see page 360 for vents and page 367 for splits.

Vents

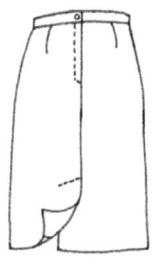

A vent is very simple to add to a **skirt** pattern. The vent can be at the back or front or both, or at one or both sides, depending on the design. One at the back is the most usual. Note on the sketch the direction of the vent opening—it's the same side as the lapped zip.

The top of the vent shouldn't be any higher than 38cm (15") measured down from the waist. Straight skirts that are 45cm (18") or shorter in length are too short to accommodate a back vent, unless you're a very short person with short legs.

Not all **jackets and coats** have back vents, but they can be added to or removed from any pattern. A single-vented (one vent in the centre) 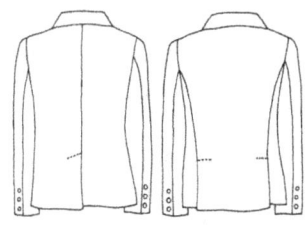 or a ventless jacket suits slim profiles. Double vents (one vent on each side) give more room for movement around the seat and are good for big men. Lined jacket vents may or may not have stitching across the top of the vent. Unlined ones generally do.

Unlined vents
Make a pattern

Draw the vent extension on the **skirt** back (or front or side) parallel to the centre back line.

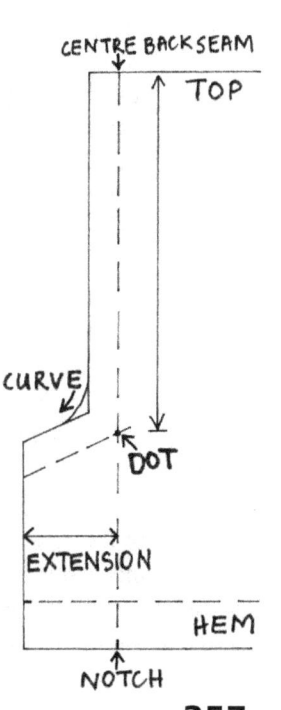

The extension **width** can be anywhere from 5cm-7cm (2"-2¾") out from the centre back *stitching* line. Anything less than this looks a bit skimpy.

If you're unsure how **long** to make the vent, it's better to make it taller and then cut it down if required. The top of the extension can be angled (as illustrated) or 90 degrees square. Curve the inside corner to make overlocking easier.

The extension is usually uninterfaced (unless it has a lining attached—see page 361), however you may decide to interface it depending on the fabric you're using.

Two important pattern markings are:

✂ A dot where the seams intersect. Mark the dot with a chalk pencil on the *wrong* side.

✂ A notch on the centre back *stitching* line at the hem. Mark it with a tiny 3mm (⅛") snip when you cut out.

Jacket vents are made in exactly the same way as skirt vents, especially on very casual jackets, but usually the underlap is double to give substance and a better look on the inside.

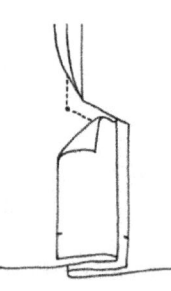

Single jacket vents fold in the same direction as skirt vents, even for men's jackets.

Here's what the pattern pieces should look like, shown with the right side of the fabric facing up (apart from the dots, which will be marked on the wrong side).

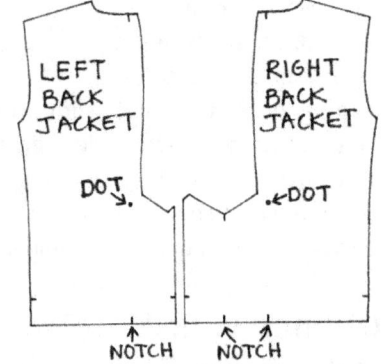

Make the vent **overlap** (the left side of the jacket) the same as described for skirts with the addition of a narrow (1cm or ⅜") hem added onto the extension. If you're planning to mitre the bottom corners, make the extension the same width as the hem.

For the **underlap** side (the right side of the jacket), simply add double the amount of extension, then a narrow 1cm (⅜") hem. The angle at the top of the second extension should mirror that of the first, so that they lay together when the second extension is folded back.

Once again, it's important to transfer the pattern markings to the fabric so you know where to pivot the stitching and fold the fabric.

Important pattern markings are:

✂ Dots where the seams intersect. Mark the dot with a chalk pencil on the *wrong* side.

✂ Notches at the centre back line at the hem to denote the fold lines on the extensions. Mark them with tiny 3mm (⅛") snips when you cut out.

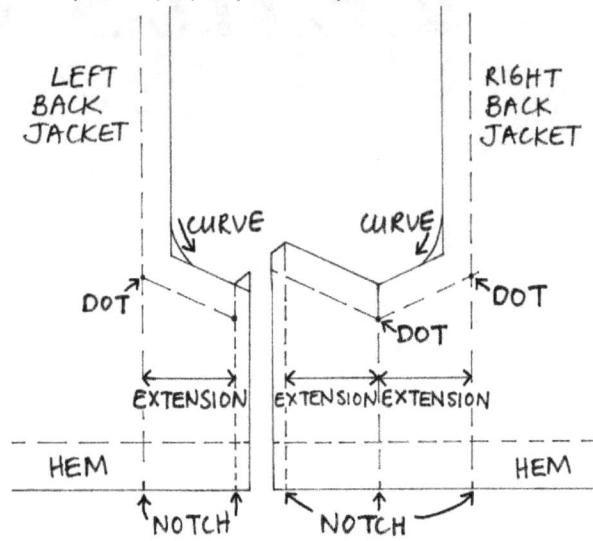

Jacket vents often have interfacing in them. Iron a strip of lightweight interfacing onto the vent extension each side. Note that you'll cut two pieces the same—*not* a pair.

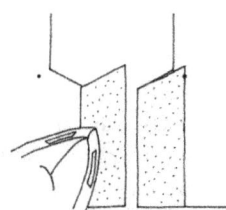

To sew an unlined vent—skirts and jackets

1. Overlock the entire centre back edge before you sew the back seam. Pivot the overlocking where the extension angles out, if you didn't cut it curved.

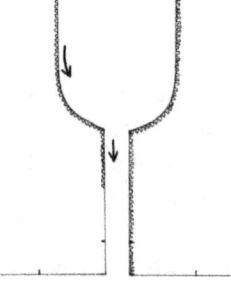

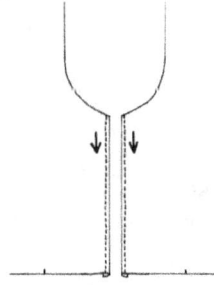

2. **Skirt vents only:** on both the extensions, turn under the width of the overlocking to the wrong side and stitch through the centre of the overlocking.

For a flatter finish on the extensions, turn under and stitch only one side of the vent—the one that will become the underneath one.

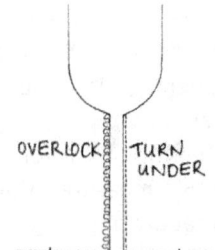

Vents and splits **359**

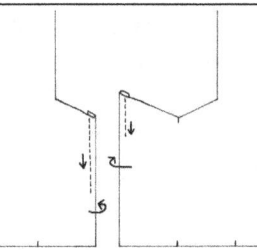

Jacket vents only: turn under the narrow 1cm (⅜") hem on each side and stitch through the centre of the overlocking.

Accurately press under the second extension on the underlap side.

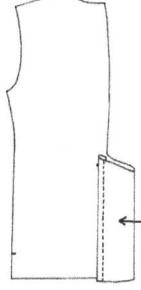

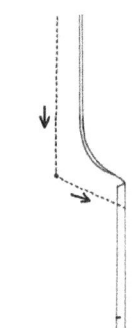

3. For both skirts and jackets, place the right sides together and sew the centre back seam, pivoting at the dot, and ending at the turned-under overlocked edges.

If you chose to have a skirt vent with only one side of the vent hemmed, remember that the unhemmed side will be longer, so don't forget and try to match them at the ends.

4. On the right side, press the folds sharply in the vent. The vent is always folded as illustrated (for both men and women) unless you're making a vent on each side of the garment, in which case you'll have one in each direction. Lay the vent flat and match the snips at the hem. From the right side, machine stitch the top of the vent extension through all layers. You should be able to feel the edge of the vent and line up your stitching with it.

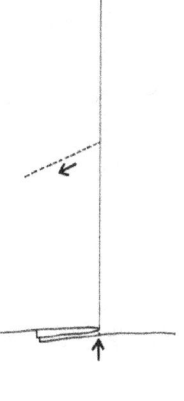

5. The seam above the vent will now be folded to one side because you've sewn the vent that way. You can leave it pressed to one side, but usually it needs to be pressed open to accommodate a zip or thick fabric. You could snip one of the seam allowances just above the vent to get it to lie open and flat, but since this weakens the seam, I always taper it open and press thoroughly.

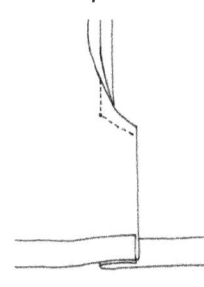

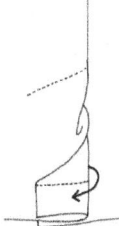

6. For the hem, overlock the lower edge first if required. The top side of the vent is bagged out by folding the vent extension back along its fold so the right sides are together. Stitch along the hem line, then turn it to the right side.

The underneath side of the skirt vent is simply turned up. Sew the bagged out side first, then turn up the other side to match. If the fabric is very thick, you can trim away any excess fabric in the bagged out section.

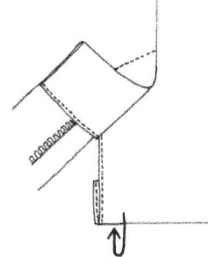

On a jacket, bag out both sides. Make sure both sides of the vent hang level at the bottom. Alternatively, on an unlined jacket you may choose to mitre the corners (see page 185).

Back pleat or Dior pleat

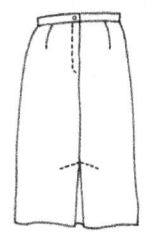

A back pleat, also known as a Dior pleat, is essentially a split backed with a panel of fabric, creating an inverted pleat. It's mostly used on skirts but you could use it for other garments.

A pattern for a back vent can easily be converted to a back pleat by simply making an extra pattern piece. The inside of the pleat looks like this:

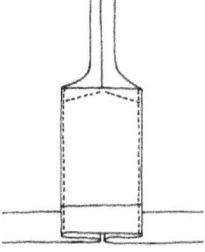

Make a pattern

The pattern for the garment is made exactly the same way as a vent (see page 357). The top of the extension can be angled (as illustrated) or 90 degrees square. Curve the inside corner to make overlocking easier.

Two important pattern markings are:

✂ A dot where the seams intersect. Mark the dot with a chalk pencil on the *wrong* side.

✂ A notch at the centre back *stitching* line at the hem. Mark it with a tiny 3mm (⅛") snip when you cut out.

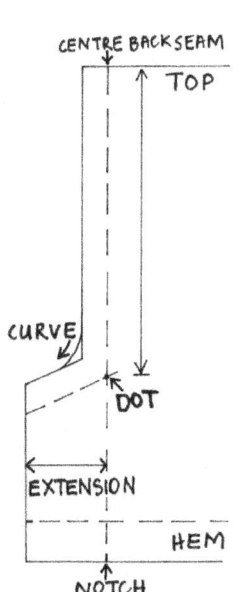

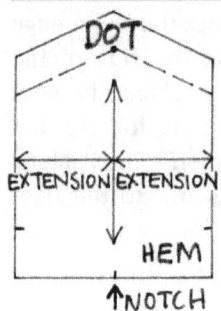

The pattern for the pleat back is simply double the vent extension. The centre of it is the same as the skirt's centre. The top of the extension needs to have the same angle as the extension on the garment (either angled as shown, or 90 degrees square). Cut one in fabric.

To sew a back pleat

1. Before sewing the back seam, overlock the entire back edge, extension and lower edge of the skirt.

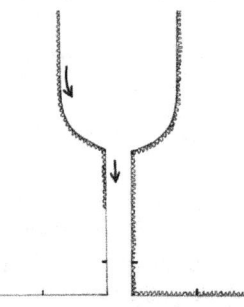

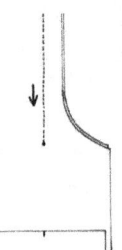
Overlock all the way around the pleat back. You should still be able to see through the overlocking the 3mm (⅛") notches you've snipped, providing you only graze the edge with the overlocker and don't trim anything off.

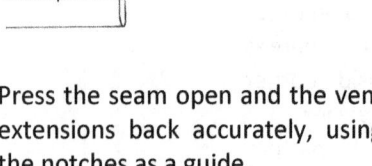
2. Hem the skirt and the pleat back (overlocking not shown for clarity).

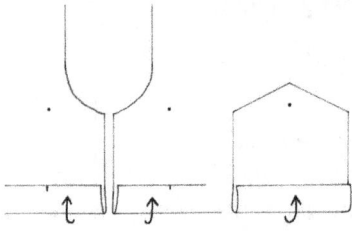
3. With the right sides together, sew the skirt centre back seam to the dot.

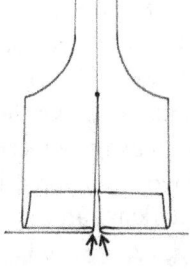

Press the seam open and the vent extensions back accurately, using the notches as a guide.

4. On the wrong side, lay the pleat back over the vent extensions and stitch them together along the top and sides. Match the lower edges carefully—I suggest starting at the hems to make sure they're perfectly matched. Note that you won't be able to sew this in one operation—you'll have to stop and start in the centre. You may prefer to only sew the sides of the pleat back now, and let the top part be sewn when you topstitch in the next step.

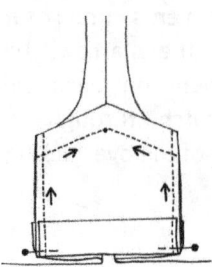

5. With the right side up, stitch the back pleat in place by sewing across the top through all layers. You should be able to feel the edge of the layers with your fingertips to guide your sewing. Depending on the shape you chose for the top of the vent, the stitching will be horizontal (for a square top) or an upside down V as shown for an angled top.

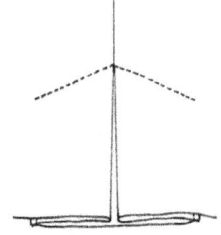

You could also invisibly handsew it inside.

Lining a skirt vent

There are several ways of tackling this, but try and plan for the lining *before* you cut the garment, because you may need to make some changes to the pattern.

Here are some options:

✂ Hem the lining as a slit the same length as the vent and leave it. This is an inexpensive and common option that manufacturers use and I use it at home too. The disadvantage is the lining is sometimes visible when the wearer walks, but less so if the vent is a very deep one, such as 6 or 7cm (2⅜" or 2¾").

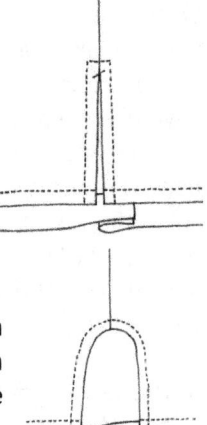

✂ Cut an upside down U-shape in the back lining, overlock, and turn under 1cm (⅜"). Manufacturers like this one too; it's simple and fast.

✂ Cut a half-lining that finishes above the back vent, so only the top of the skirt is lined. This is another low-cost manufacturing solution, but a disadvantage (apart from how the skirt looks on the inside) is that the skirt can't easily be cut out together with the lining. This idea can also be used for jackets.

Vents and splits 361

✂ Change the back vent in the skirt to a back pleat/Dior Pleat (see page 359) or a godet (page 138). Hem a slit in the back lining the same length and leave it.

✂ The back lining can be attached to the vent in one of two ways. Either of these are suitable for jackets as well as skirts. Certainly this is the most high end solution. See the instructions below.

Attaching the lining to the back vent—skirts and jackets

There are two ways of doing this, both suitable for either for a skirt or a jacket and both can be sewn by machine. These methods are not afterthoughts; you'll need to plan them in the garment before you begin cutting and sewing.

Assembly order:

For a **skirt**, sew the zip in first, make the lined vent *then* attach the lining to the zip and waist as usual.

For a **jacket**, first separately assemble the main fabric and lining as usual, then make the lined vent *first* before attaching any other part of the lining.

Ideally let the vent be the first part of the lining you sew to a skirt or jacket.

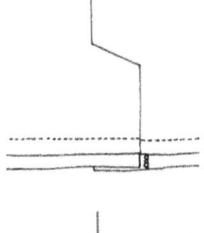

Method 1 has the vent extension cut as an identical pair in main fabric. Only lining, no fabric, is visible on the inside when the vent is finished.

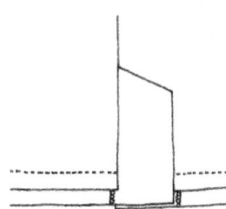

Method 2 has the underlap side of the vent cut double in fabric. The garment pieces cut in main fabric are therefore asymmetrical. Personally I think this method looks smarter.

Important: instead of being completely free hanging, the lining will be joined at the vent, so for both methods you'll need to allow extra length on the lining between the vent and the skirt waist or jacket collar. Otherwise the lining will eventually tear from sitting down and other movement because most fashion fabrics have more give than lining.

1cm (⅜") is a usual amount to add for any fabric. For stable wools such as wool gabardine add 1.5cm (⅝"), and for stretchy wools with lots of give add 2cm-2.5cm (¾"-1"). Remember to do this *before* you start drawing the vent on the lining pattern.

For a **skirt** add the amount onto the top of the waist and move the zip notch up the same amount.

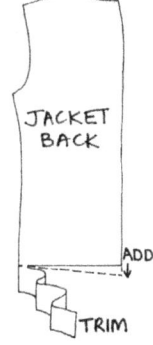

On a **jacket** add the amount onto the lower edge, blending to nothing at the sides (and as usual when converting a jacket pattern piece into a lining pattern, trim off the hem allowance). The jacket lining will need a centre back seam to accommodate the vent, instead of being cut on the fold.

A troublesome issue with lined back vents is remembering which side is left and which is right, particularly if the fabric or lining has no right or wrong side. When we say "left back" and "right back", it means the left and right when you're wearing the garment. With linings, remember that the *good* side of the lining faces to the *inside*. Label your pieces and double-check the left and right sides when making the pattern, before cutting out, and again before sewing.

Cutting tip: you can save time when cutting out the fabric or lining pieces if you cut a *pair* of the biggest side. Unpin the pattern and separate the pieces, then using the pattern for the smaller side, cut one down. However, if you don't have much fabric to work with, it's better to cut them out singly, finding the most economical placement.

Patternmaking tip: if you feel confident enough, save time and patternmaking paper by making only *one* pattern piece for left and right sides. Clearly mark the cutting lines and instructions for each side.

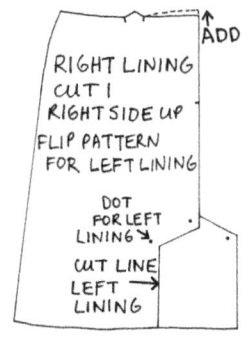

If you make *separate* pattern pieces for left and right sides, mark clearly which side is the right side up, and as an added reminder write "PTO" (Please Turn Over), circled, on the reverse side in case a piece is accidentally flipped. Also, I don't go to the trouble of drafting these pieces afresh every time I require a lined vent. Instead I just trace them off a pattern I've done previously.

Method 1 lined vent

This method is handy if you've already cut the garment out as a pair, since the left and right sides of the garment are the same.

Make a pattern for the garment

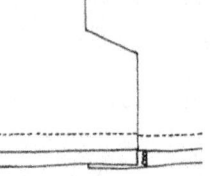

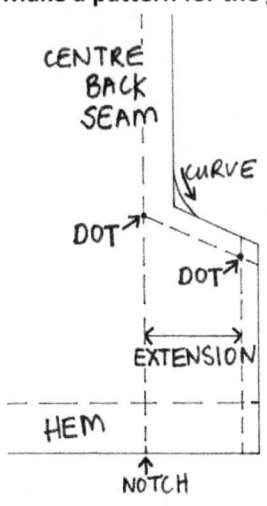

The back skirt or jacket is cut with the vent extension as illustrated. The left and right sides are cut as a pair. Be sure to mark the dots where the stitching pivots. Allow a 1cm (⅜") seam allowance along the top and side of the vent extension. You can curve the top of the vent extension to make overlocking easier if you want, but you don't have to.

Iron a strip of interfacing onto the vent extension on each side.

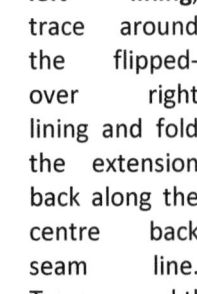

The skirt or jacket will look something like this.

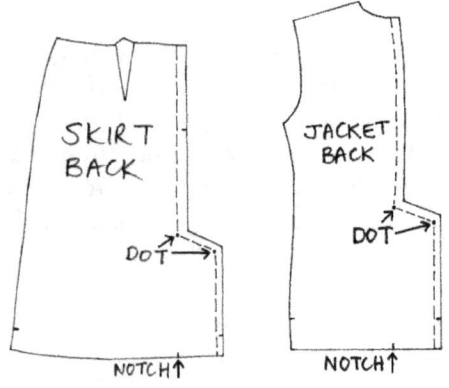

Make a pattern for the lining

Note: the lining patterns are all shown here with the right side of the fabric facing up.

Use the main fabric pattern piece you've just made to make the lining pieces. Remember to add extra length on the lining between the vent and the skirt waist or jacket collar, as described on page 361.

When you cut the lining out, if you feel nervous about confusing your left and right, cut a pair of right back linings and mark the trimming line for the left back lining, then cut when you're sure.

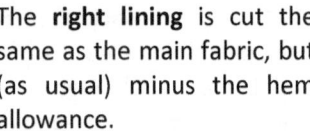

The **right lining** is cut the same as the main fabric, but (as usual) minus the hem allowance.

Be sure to mark (on the wrong side) the two dots where the stitching pivots.

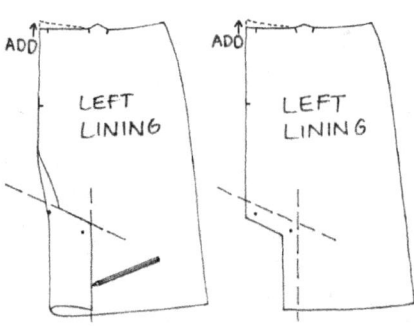

To make the **left lining**, trace around the flipped-over right lining and fold the extension back along the centre back seam line.

Trace around the edge of the vent. Add two 1cm (⅜") seam allowances to this edge = 2cm (¾") and trim the excess paper away.

Mark the two dots where the stitching pivots.

To sew a lined vent—Method 1

1. Stay stitch and clip the inside corners of the left and right linings.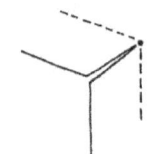

2. For skirts and jackets with free-hanging linings, overlock the entire back edges of the lining pieces and the skirt or jacket. Overlock the hem edge of the garment in readiness for sewing the hem later.
If the garment has a closed lining you won't overlock anything since it will be enclosed.

3. Hem the lining now if it's free-hanging. If you don't yet know the finished length of the garment, leave the lining hem.

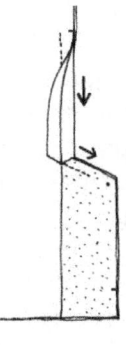

4. Sew the centre back seam, leaving an opening for the zipper if it's a skirt. Pivot at the extension's dot and sew along half of the vent extension. Snip one side of the seam to the dot to make the centre back seam lie open.

Vents and splits 363

Press the seam open and thoroughly press the fold in the vent to make it lie in place.

5. On the lining, sew the centre back seam exactly to the dot, backstitching at the dot to secure the end of the seam. Press the seam open.

6. Lay the lining on top of the garment with the wrong sides together (as the garment will be worn). Flip back the lining and match up the vertical edges of the vent extensions to each other with the right sides together.

On the left side sew from the dot down to the lining hem, backstitching carefully at the beginning.

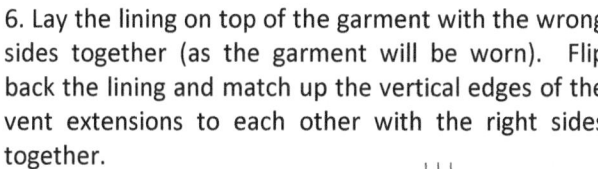

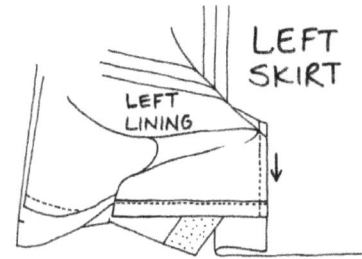

On the right side sew all the way along.

If you don't know the finished length of the skirt yet, don't sew the seams all the way down. Press both seams.
On jackets with a closed lining, don't sew these two seams all the way down—stop about 10cm (4") from the bottom.

7. Flip the top of the lining down and sew across the top of the vent through all layers, including the garment. Obviously make this row of stitching neat and straight, since everyone will see it.

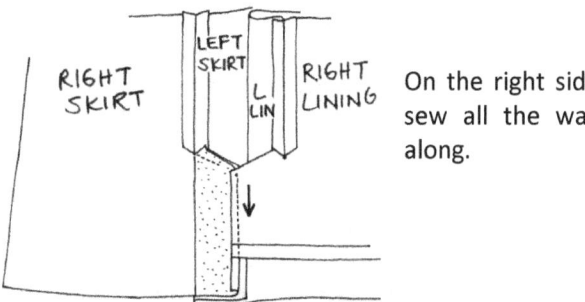

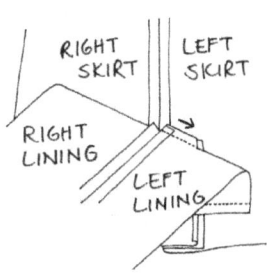

On **jackets** there's often no stitching on the outside. In this case, stitch only the lining and the vent together. Catch the top of the vent invisibly by hand to the garment to hold it in place.

Feeling nervous? You can sew this by hand from Step 6 onwards—see page 366.

8. The corners of a **skirt** hem are bagged out to finish them off. I always sew the left (outermost) side first, then the right (underneath) side to match in length.

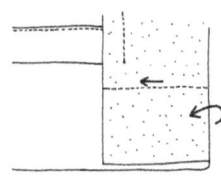

For the left side (the outermost side), fold the vent extension back along its vertical fold line, right sides together. Stitch horizontally along the hem line, then turn to the right side.

For the right side fold the hem up, right sides together, enclosing the lining and stitch the vertical seam.
Check that both sides hang level.

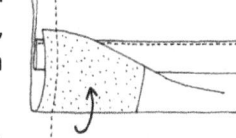

For a **jacket** with a closed lining, have the hem already interfaced and pressed up into position.

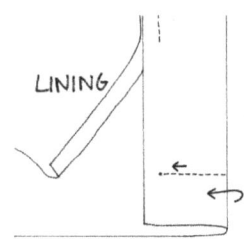

On the left side (outermost side) fold the vent extension back along its vertical fold line, right sides together. Stitch horizontally along the hem line, stopping exactly 1cm (⅜") from the raw edge. Backstitch securely.

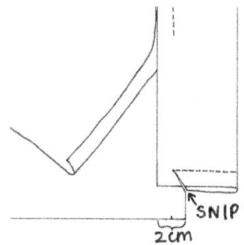

Trim off the corner as shown, leaving 2cm (¾") of fabric at the hem. Snip diagonally to the end of the stitching.

With the right sides together, sew the hem and lining together along the lower edge.

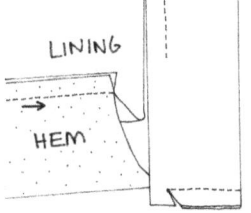

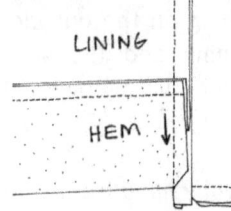

Fold the jacket hem up, right sides together, forming a pleat in the lining. Stitch the seam *exactly* to the spot you snipped to. Turn through to the right side and press.

On the right side (underneath side) sew the hem and lining to each other along the lower edge, with the right sides together.

Fold the jacket hem up, with the right sides together, forming a pleat in the lining. Stitch the vertical seam. Turn it through to the right side and press.
Check that both sides hang level.

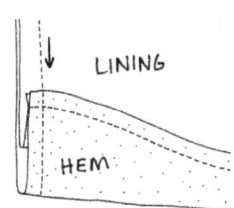

Method 2 lined vent

If I had to pick between this method and the previous one, I would say this is the smarter-looking of the two.

This method has separate left and right pattern pieces for both the lining and the main fabric.

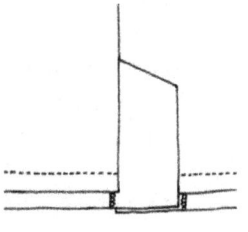

Refer to page 361 for the introductory notes.

Make a pattern for the garment

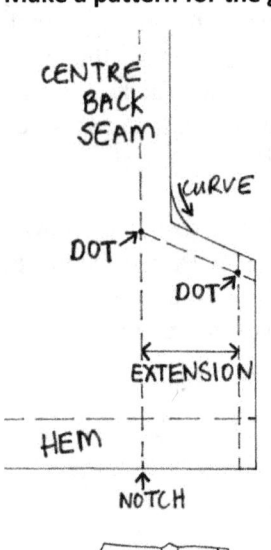

The **left** back skirt or left jacket is cut with the vent extension as illustrated. Be sure to mark the dot where the seams pivot.

Allow a 1cm (⅜") seam allowance along the top and side of the vent extension.

You can curve the top of the vent extension to make overlocking easier if you want, but you don't have to.

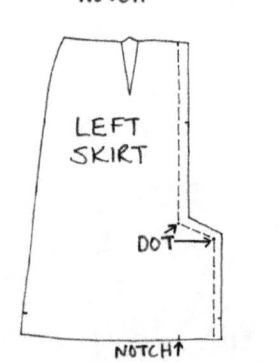
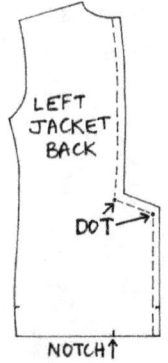

The **right** back skirt or right jacket has an extra vent extension on it. Trace around the flipped-over left back and leave extra paper for the extension. Fold back the vent extension along the centre back seam line.

Then fold back the other way along the *stitching* line of the vent extension (reminder: 1cm (⅜") seam allowance) and mark where the centre back line is on the paper. Add a 1cm (⅜") seam allowance onto this edge.

Mark dots where the stitching will pivot, and make small 3mm (⅛") notches on the edge where the fold lines are so you know where to fold.

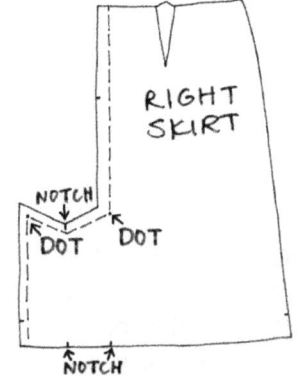

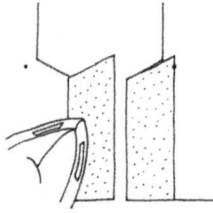

Iron a strip of interfacing onto the wrong sides of the vent extensions on each side. Note that you'll cut two pieces of interfacing the same—*not* a pair.

Make a pattern for the lining

Note: the lining patterns are all shown here with the right side of the fabric facing up.

Use the main fabric left pattern piece to make the lining pieces. Remember to add extra length on the lining between the vent and the skirt waist or jacket collar, as described on page 361, and remove the hem allowance as usual to make the lining pattern.

If you're nervous about confusing your left and right, cut a pair of right back linings and mark the line for the left back lining, then cut when you're sure.

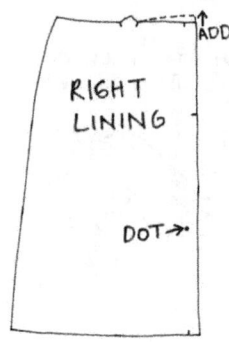

The **right lining** is cut with no vent extension at all, but *do* mark the dot in the same position as the main pieces. The centre back seam allowance can remain the same as the seam allowance on the main fabric pieces.

For the **left lining**, trace around the flipped-over left skirt pattern and fold back the extension along the

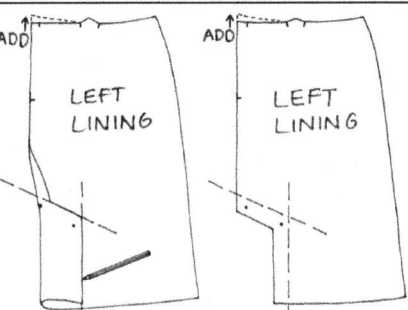

centre back *seam line*. Trace around the edge of the vent. Add two 1cm (⅜") seam allowances to this edge = 2cm (¾") and trim the excess paper away. Mark the dot where the seams intersect.

To sew a lined vent—Method 2
1. Stay stitch and clip the corner of the left lining.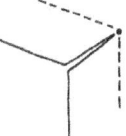

2. Overlock the entire back edges of the lining and fabric pieces. Overlock the hem edge of the garment pieces in readiness for sewing the hem later. You can skip this if you're making a jacket with a closed lining—the edges are usually left raw since they'll be enclosed.

3. If the lining has a free-hanging hem, hem the lining now. If you don't yet know the finished length of the garment, leave the lining hem.

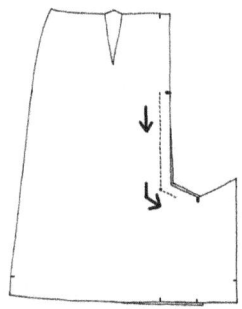

4. With the right sides of the garment together, sew the centre back seam, leaving an opening for the zipper if it's a skirt. Pivot at the dot and sew along half of the vent extension.

Don't snip the seam allowance to make the centre back seam lie open and flat, but press a fold in the seam allowance to taper it open for the zip. Accurately press the folds in the vent to make it lie in place.

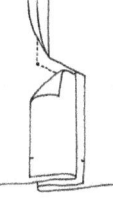

5. For the lining, place the right sides together and sew the centre back seam down to the dot, backstitching accurately at the dot to secure. Press the seam open.

6. Lay the lining on top of the skirt with the wrong sides together (in other words, as the garment will be worn).
Sew the **left lining** to the vent extension. Begin at the top left of the vent, sew across the top of the vent extension, pivot at the dot then sew vertically down the side of the vent.

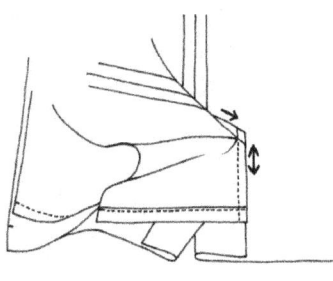

Ensure that the fold of the vent underneath is *exactly* at the point of the dot when you sew.
On a closed lining for a jacket, stop sewing this seam 10cm (4") from the bottom.

Place the **right lining** onto the vent and sew all the way down. On a closed lining for a jacket, stop sewing this seam 10cm (4") from the bottom.

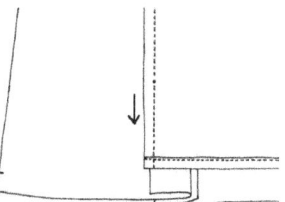

Important: note that the seam allowances of the lining and skirt or jacket will be different (unless your garment's centre back seam also happens to be 1cm).

✂ If you don't yet know the finished length of the garment, don't sew the seams all the way down. Press both seams.

7. Flip the top of the lining down and sew across the top of the vent through all layers, including the garment.

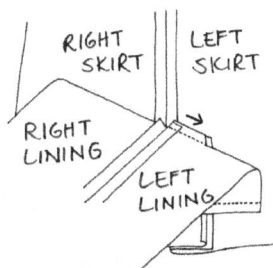

On **jackets** there's often no stitching on the outside. In this case, stitch only the lining and the vent together. The top of the vent is caught invisibly by hand to the garment to hold it in place.

Feeling nervous? You can sew this by hand from Step 6 onwards—see page 366.

8. For both corners of the **skirt** hem, bag out by folding the vent extension back along its vertical fold line, right sides together. Stitch horizontally along the hem line, then turn to the right side.

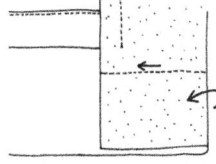

For a **jacket** with a closed lining, have the hem already interfaced and pressed up into position. Both corners are handled in the same way. I like to sew the outermost corner first, then the underneath one making sure they're the same length.

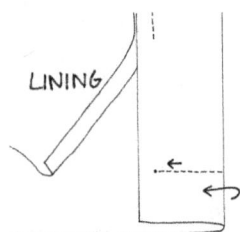

Fold the vent extension back along its vertical fold line, right sides together. Stitch horizontally along the hem line, stopping exactly 1cm (⅜") from the raw edge. Backstitch securely.

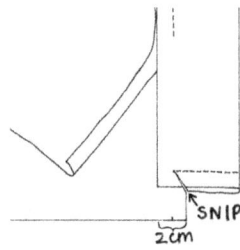

Trim off the corner as shown, leaving 2cm (¾") of fabric at the hem. Snip diagonally to the end of the stitching.

With the right sides together, sew the hem and lining together along the lower edge.

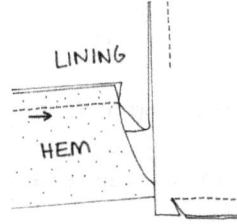

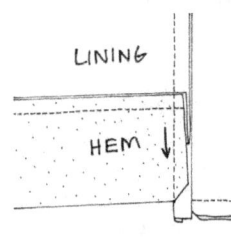

Fold the jacket hem up, right sides together, forming a pleat in the lining. Stitch the seam *exactly* to the spot you snipped to. Turn through to the right side and press. Check that both sides hang level.

Feeling nervous?
You can also sew both of these lined back vents by hand. For both methods, sew up to Step 5.

6. Ensure the vent is accurately pressed into position. For Method 1 (left picture), press back the 1cm (⅜") seam allowance on the right garment extension.

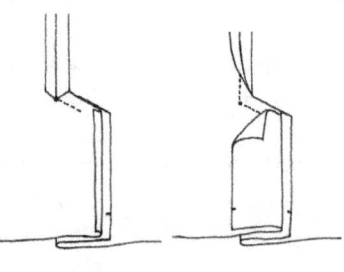

7. Machine sew across the top of the vent, attaching it to the garment (Method 2 shown).
OR
Sew it by hand to the garment using herringbone stitch for an invisible finish on the right side.

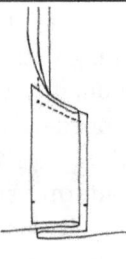

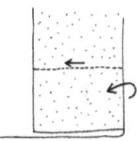

8. For **skirts**, bag out the corners of the hem as described in Step 8. For **jackets**, do this last.

9. Press under the seam allowances of the vent lining. Position it with pins onto the skirt, then hand sew around the edges (Method 2 shown).

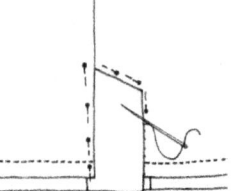

Use hidden slip stitch for an invisible finish: working from right to left, take a tiny stitch in the garment of one or two threads, then slip the needle through the folded edge.

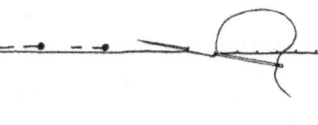

Splits
Splits are simply an unstitched area at the end of a seam, pressed open.

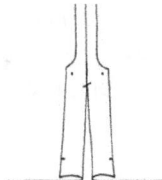

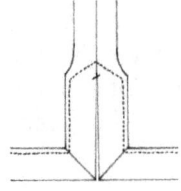

Splits can be the same width as the seam allowance but sometimes the pattern is made wider in that part, for example to accommodate wider topstitching. The corners are either mitred or bagged out.

Mitring gives a diagonal seam across the corner. Both split and hem should be the same depth.

To make a mitre, press the two sides up and make a tiny snip where they intersect. If you don't want to snip the fabric (say, if you've already overlocked the edge or already pressed under the edge in readiness for a double turned hem), insert a pin in each hem allowance where they intersect.
Pin or mark the corner. Unfold.

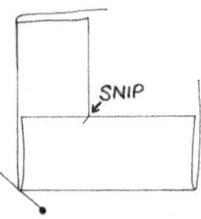

If you plan to overlock the edge, do so now before sewing the mitre. You should still be able to see the snips under the overlocking. With the right sides together, stitch from the corner point to the snips.

Trim the seam to 6mm (¼") and trim the corner. Press the seam open. Turn to the right side and press.

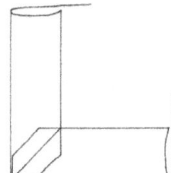

Alternatively, **bag out the corner** by folding the split extension back along its fold line so the right sides are together. Stitch horizontally along the hem line, then turn to the right side.

Splits within the hem allowance

Small splits can be made within the hem allowance, but make the splits *before* you sew the hem.

1. Overlock the raw edge of the hem, or fold under the edge if you're making a double-folded hem.

2. Stitch the garment seam, stopping one hem's width above the hem.

3. Bag out each side by folding along the hem fold line, right sides together, and stitching.

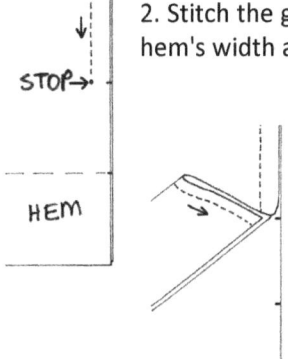

4. Turn each side through to the right side. Sew the hem.

To reinforce the top of the split

If you think the top of the split may tear from stress or strain, consider reinforcing it *before* this happens. Here are some ideas:

✂ Depending on the style of garment, you can turn the reinforcing into a feature. For example, a bar tack sewn in contrasting thread, a small triangle (or other shape) of fabric topstitched on, a jeans rivet, a bow—you get the idea.

✂ Cut a piece of grosgrain ribbon 3cm (1¼") long. Melt the ends with a flame to stop them fraying. Sew it onto the wrong side *before* you topstitch the split. Stitch each side of the ribbon separately onto the seam allowance, sewing as close as you can to the seam. The reinforcing will be invisible on the right side.

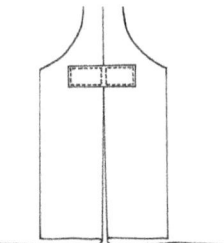

✂ An old-fashioned way to reinforce is with a hand-sewn **arrow head** on the right side. Use several strands of either a perfectly matching or a contrasting thread.

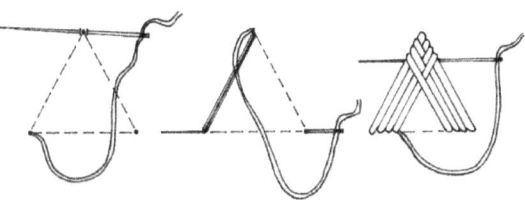

Lining splits

With splits, as opposed to vents, there's more chance of the lining peeping through the split. There are a several options for lining a garment with splits:

✂ Finish the lining higher than the top of the split. This is a good, fast option if the splits are small.

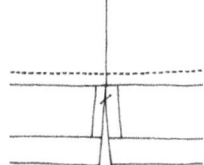

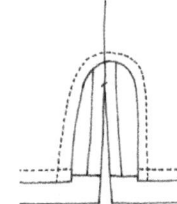

✂ Cut an upside down U-shape in the lining, overlock, and turn under 1cm (⅜"). You could sew a French tack to the top of the split and two bottom edges to stop the lining from moving (see page 173).

✂ You could also attach the lining directly to the split, either by hand or by machine.

Important: for wool and other fabrics with give, you'll need to allow extra between the top of the split and the waist. Otherwise the lining will tear when you sit down. 1cm (⅜") is usual, but for stable wools such as wool gabardine add 1.5cm (⅝") and for stretchy wools with lots of give add 2-2.5cm (¾"-1"). The amount is usually added onto the top edge of the skirt, but can be added onto the bottom edge. If you add it to the top, move the zip notch up the same amount so the extra fabric lies between the zip and split.

To attach the lining **by hand**, simply handsew the lining to the slit around the edges. Use hidden slip stitch for an invisible finish: work from right to left. Take a tiny stitch in the garment of one or two threads, then slip the needle through the folded edge.

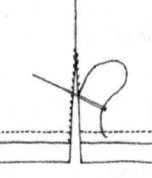

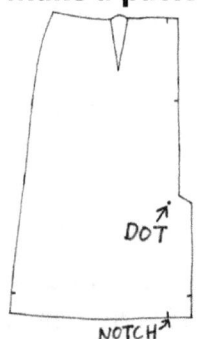

A lining attached **by machine** looks very smart on the inside. Here's how:

Make a pattern

1. On the garment, cut the splits with an extension to fold back. You could make the extension the same depth as the hem allowance—certainly do this if you plan to mitre the corners (see page 366).
Cut the left and the right sides the same.

When you cut the garment out, iron a strip of interfacing onto each of the extensions.

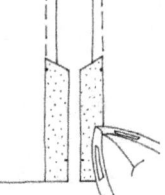

2. To find the cutting line for the lining, fold the skirt pattern back along the *seam* line and mark the edge of the slit extension.

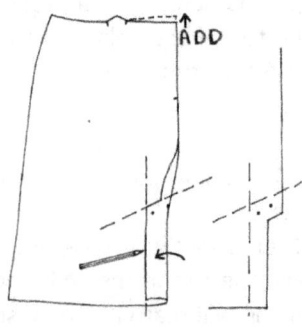

Then add two seam allowances to this edge and trim the excess away.

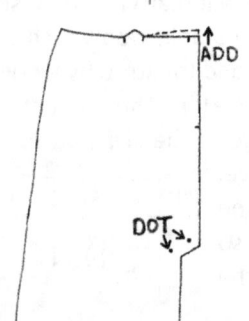

The lining pattern might look like this.
Mark the dots where the stitching pivots.

To sew lined splits

1. Stay stitch the inside corners of the lining and clip to the stitching.

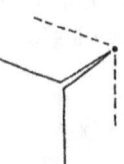

2. Overlock the centre back edges of the skirt and lining. Overlock the lower edge of the skirt in preparation for the hem.

3. Hem the lining if you know the finished length.

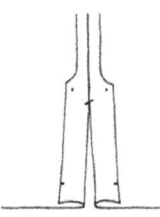

4. Sew the centre back seam to the dot at the top of the split and press it open.

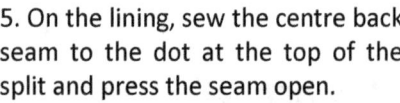

5. On the lining, sew the centre back seam to the dot at the top of the split and press the seam open.

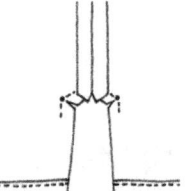

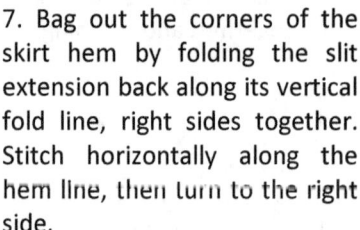

6. Sew the lining to each side of the slit, pivoting at the dots. You'll have to sew the left and right sides separately.

7. Bag out the corners of the skirt hem by folding the slit extension back along its vertical fold line, right sides together. Stitch horizontally along the hem line, then turn to the right side.

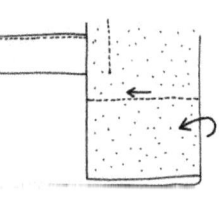

You can also mitre the corners (see page 366), which looks very smart. For a perfect corner, arrange for the hem of the lining to finish *on* the mitre seam—do the mitre before the sewing the lining hem.

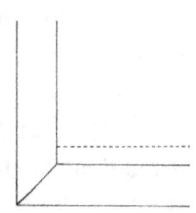

Vents and splits

Feeling unsure?
You can also sew the lining to the splits by hand. Follow the instructions up to Step 5.

6. Press back the seam allowances on the lining around the slit.

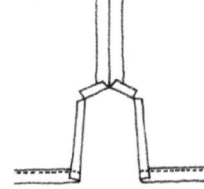

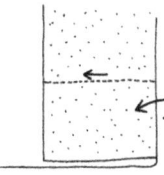

7. On the garment, bag out or mitre the corners of the hem as described in Step 7 above (or mitre them if you want to).

8. Position the lining onto the skirt, wrong sides together, matching the raw edges, and handsew in place.

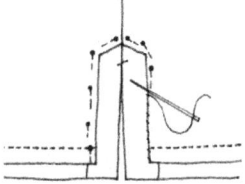

Use hidden slip stitch for an invisible finish: working from right to left, take a tiny stitch in the garment of one or two threads, then slip the needle through the folded edge.

Waistbands

Introduction 370	Simple fold-down elastic casing 386
Make a pattern 371	Decorative casing options 387
notches 371	Separate elastic casing 387
grainline 372	Elastic with a drawcord 388
other pattern notes 372	Sewn-on elastic waist 388
interfacing 372	Partially elasticized waistbands 389
To sew a waistband 373	An adjustable waistband 390
Troubleshooting waistbands 375	3 Ways to elasticize the back waist 390
Another way to sew a waistband 376	Men's waistbands 392
Banrol or Armoflexxx waistband 378	extended waistbands 392
Cut-on waistbands 379	"Your first men's waistband" 393
Cut-on waistband with Petersham 380	Another way to finish the end 395
Curved waistbands 381	Using ready-made waistbanding 395
3 ways to sew a curved waistband 382	Self-made waistbanding 396
Binding the waist 382	Men's waistband fastenings 396
Waistband using curved Petersham 383	buttons and buttonholes 396
Super-easy drawcord waist 384	hooks and eyes 397
Elastic waists 385	Adjustable waistbands 397
notes on elastic lengths 385	Concealed expandable waistband 398

A waistband is simply a band of fabric that fits around the waist to hold up and support the weight of skirts or trousers from the top.

✂ How should the ideal waistband fit? Well, most importantly, it should be *comfortable*, neither too tight nor too loose. It should look smooth and not curl, fold or wrinkle when the wearer sits down. It should support the weight of the garment properly and be in proportion to the rest of the garment.
How do you like *your* waistband to fit? Some people like a tight, supportive band. Others don't like anything firm around their waist. Do you prefer a stiffly interfaced band or a soft, natural band?

✂ Waistbands are cut the same length as the waist measurement plus a small amount of ease, usually between 1cm and 1.5cm (⅜"-⅝"). I like 1.2cm (½") for myself.

✂ A waistband can be as narrow as 1.2cm (½") finished or as wide as 8cm (3¼"), and may not sit on the actual waist of the wearer—it may be above the natural waistline or lower.

✂ The waistband is usually the last thing applied when making the garment. Zips, fly fronts, side seams and pockets should all have been finished.

✂ Parts of a waistband:

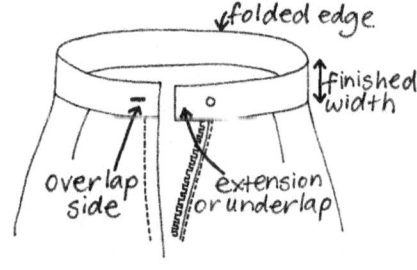

✂ Generally, the lower edge of a **classic waistband** sits *on* the waist (the waist being the narrowest part of the middle of the body).
Garment length is therefore measured from below the waistband.

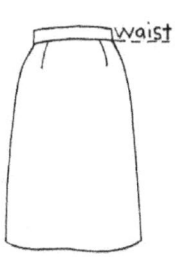

✂ Straight waistbands can be applied to **low cut waists** on skirts or trousers, providing the waistband is no wider than 1.5cm (⅝"), otherwise it won't sit close to the body.

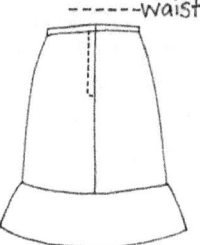

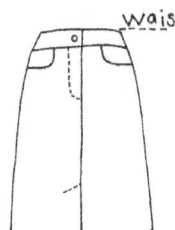

Waistbands wider than that will need to be curved with a seam on the top edge.

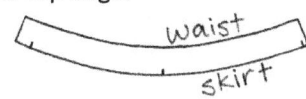

✂ **Very wide waistbands** (wider than 5cm or 2") that sit *on* the waist will need to be cut shaped to allow for the body's curves.

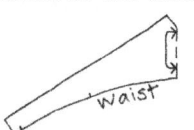 

The waistband will also need very firm interfacing and/or boning to stop it from folding over.

Make a pattern

1. Decide on the finished **width** of the waistband, for example 3cm (1¼") wide. Double this and add two seam allowances (one for each side), for example 3cm + 3cm wide + 1cm + 1cm seam allowances = 8cm.

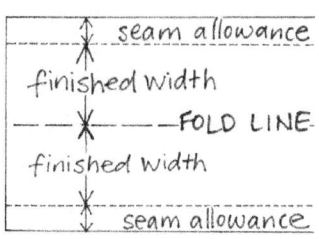

2. The finished **length** should be your waist measurement plus ease of 1cm to 1.5cm (⅜"-⅝"). For example: 71cm waist measurement + 1.5cm ease = 72.5cm. If you like a tight waistband, add only 1cm ease. The top edge of the skirt or trousers needs to be the same measurement, so measure your pattern and adjust if needed.

3. You'll need an **extension**, or underlap, on one end, so the ends of the waistband will overlap and fasten with a button or hook. The underlap is usually about 4cm (1½") long.

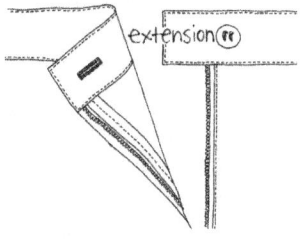

✂ If the waistband is for fly-front trousers, the extension will need to be long enough to accommodate the fly shield. If you're not sure how much longer, add extra and cut off the excess later.

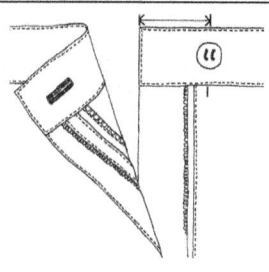

✂ Some waistbands have an underlap *and* an overlap extension. The overlap may be square or pointed. This provides a stronger and very secure closure (because there are two buttons instead of one) and works very well for trousers. Sometimes the closure is two hooks or a hook and a button.

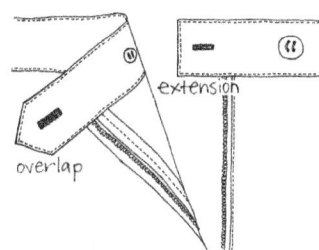

4. You'll also need **two seam allowances**—one on each end.

The waistband pattern might look like this now:

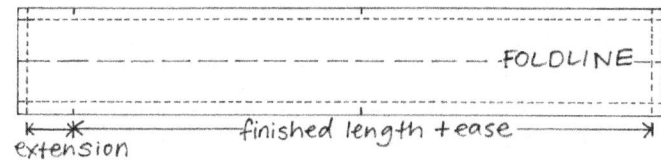

Summary of total waistband length (example):
Waist length   71cm
Ease   1.5cm
Extension   4cm
Two seam allowances   2cm   Grand total = 78.5cm

Notches

Notch the edge of the waistband with tiny 3mm (⅛") snips to mark the extension and the centre (front or back), so you know where to match the waistband to the garment.

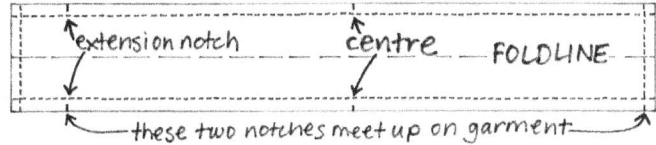

✂ If the waistband has a centre front or centre back opening, fold the waistband in half to find the opposite centre, matching the centre front or centre back points.

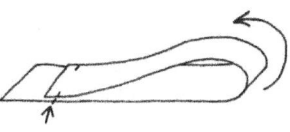

✂ For side openings, measure the pattern to find where the opposite side seam will be and mark it on the waistband.

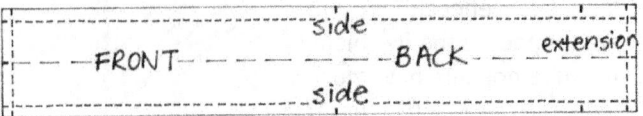

I cannot emphasize enough how important the notches are! If you don't mark them, you won't have any way of knowing where to match the waistband. The waistband could end up too big, too small or inconsistent each time you use the pattern.

Grainline

Waistbands are cut parallel to the selvedge of the fabric, because the fabric is stronger in this direction. It's also easier to ensure the waistband is cut on grain, because you can line it up next to the selvedge when you cut it out.

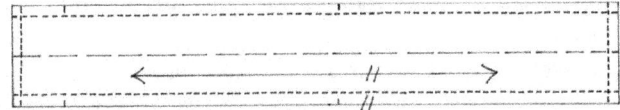

If a waistband is cut off-grain, it will ripple and twist when it's sewn.

✂ If you're short on fabric and have to cut it across the fabric (not recommended, but you might not have any choice), make sure the edge is perfectly on the crosswise grain. Either tear it straight, or else pull a thread and cut it straight (see page 69).

✂ Waistbands for pull-on stretch pants *must* have the grainline vertical so the waistband stretches with the pants and the wearer can get them on.

Sometimes stretch denim women's jeans have the grainline this way even though there's a zip and button opening. This waistband has no fusing and stretches the same as the rest of the jeans.

Other pattern notes

✂ If I'm making a waistband for myself, I don't make an actual pattern—I just record the measurements of the *finished* waistband (that is, my waist measurement plus ease). To cut the waistband, I cut a strip the correct *width*, apply the interfacing, *then* mark the centre front and extension and cut it to the correct length.

✂ When preparing for a made-to-measure fitting, I cut the waistband longer than necessary, but still mark the centre front and extension. I don't trim the ends off until after the fitting in case I want it longer.

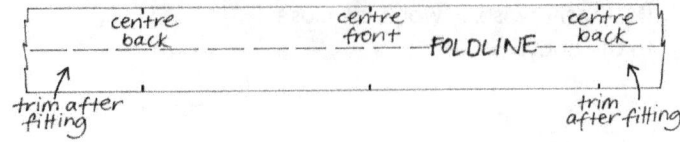

✂ Also, if I suspect (or know that) the waistband will shrink when the interfacing is ironed on, I cut the waistband to length *only after* the interfacing is applied. A loss of just 5mm can make the band a fraction too tight to be comfortable.

Interfacing

Waistbands are interfaced to make them strong and stop them folding over or wrinkling when they're worn. The interfacing you decide to use will determine how the waistband looks, feels and wears. Regular interfacing is fine to use, either fusible or sew-in.

✂ Choose something firm and sturdy for straight waistbands, remembering there'll be two layers of fabric and two layers of interfacing when the waistband is finished.

✂ For shaped waistbands, I prefer something a little softer if it's on a skirt and firmer for trousers. There'll be two layers of fabric and two layers of interfacing. You may like to choose a lighter yet crisp interfacing for the outer band and something firmer and stronger on the inner.

✂ You can buy special waistband interfacing for straight waistbands. It's variously called slotted waistband interfacing, waistband interfacing and ESL tape. It's a non-woven fusible. It has perforations to mark the central fold line and 1cm (⅜") seam allowances, resulting in sharp folds and very easy application. It's available in several different widths, in grey or white. Test a piece before using on soft or fine fabrics—it can sometimes yield a crisp, papery waistband, particularly on fine fabrics.

If you can't buy the correct width for your waistband pattern, it's fine to change the width of the waistband. Cut the waistband out the width of the interfacing, then lay the pattern on top and mark the length and the notches.

If your waistband's seam allowance is 1.5cm (⅝"), trim the waistband and garment down to 1cm (⅜") seams. Actually, I wouldn't bother trimming the top of a skirt since 5mm extra length is no big deal. Trousers I would trim because of the crotch depth.

✂ There's another type of waistband interfacing that we don't see often in Australian manufacturing. It's called Banrol by HTM or Armoflexxx Waist Shaper by McCalls/Palmer Pletsch. It's a stiff woven tape, similar to belting or buckram, and the finished width of the waistband. It sits inside the waistband and isn't stitched into any seams. Cut it the same length as your waistband minus the two end seam allowances. It produces a very firm, non-roll waistband.
The method for sewing it on is a little different and is described on page 378.

✂ On straight waistbands, press the waistband in half longways after ironing on the interfacing. It's *much* easier to sew if you do this first.

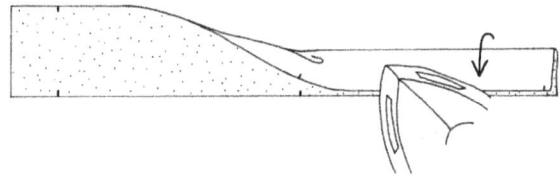

To sew a waistband

You've cut out the waistband, ironed on the interfacing, pressed it in half longways and ensured the length is marked with notches.

✂ At this point you can **check the fit** by pinning the waistband onto the outside of the waist, matching the raw edges. Place the pins on the garment side, parallel to the stitching line. When you flip the waistband up, the pins will be hidden. If you're worried about the pins, sew the waistband on with a long stitch instead.

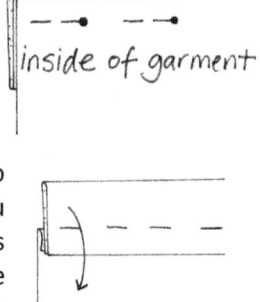

✂ Before sewing on a waistband, any beltloops or hanger tapes should be tacked or pinned in position. If you're lining the garment, have the lining all ready before you sew the waistband.

Sewing on a straight waistband is a three-step process. First, the outermost long edge of the waistband is sewn onto the waist. Then the ends are finished. Finally the remaining long edge is stitched down.

1. Decide what the inside edge of the waistband should look like, either overlocked or turned-under. Overlocking is easier and flatter, but turned-under looks neater. I recommend overlocking for thick and bulky fabrics. Overlocking is also used for budget ready-to-wear garments since it's faster. Alternatively, for a very smart finish, you could bind the edge instead of overlocking it.

If you're overlocking or binding, do it now. Do you have a 1.5cm (⅝") seam allowance on the waistband? 1.5cm on the overlocked edge is too long to look good inside the garment. I suggest trimming it to a scant 1cm (⅜"), otherwise it will flip up when the garment is washed.

To remember which edge to overlock (or bind), overlock with the *right side* of the fabric facing *up*, beginning at the *extension* end (for women's waistbands). You'll recognise this end by the extension's notches.

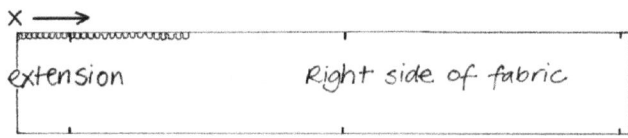

2. Position any beltloops, hanger tapes or lining now, if you're having them.

3. Place the outermost side (not the overlocked edge) of the waistband onto the right side of the garment, carefully matching the notches.

Important: allow the correct amount of waistband seam allowance to hang over the edge of the garment at each end. Don't line up the edge of the waistband flush with the edge of the garment, or you'll have no seam allowance to finish the end with and the waistband will be the wrong size.

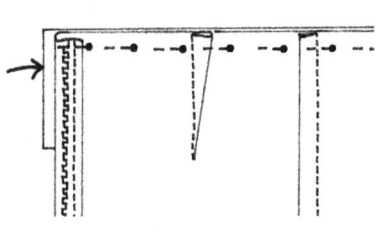

Match the notches accurately around the zip. This picture shows a lapped zip. The overlap notch should lie flush with the edge of the zip, leaving the seam

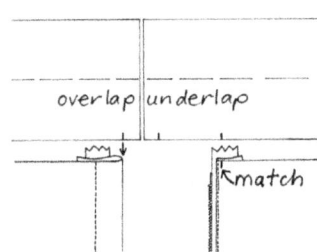

allowance hanging over the edge. The extension (underlap) notch should be slightly *in* from the garment's edge to match the garment's centre notch.

If you have a fly front, the notches will look like this:

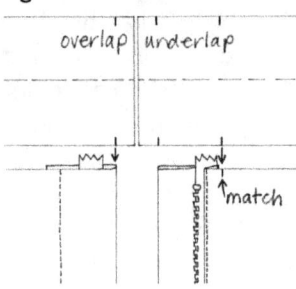

Your waistband will end up the wrong size if you fail to match the notches correctly, or at all.

✂ You may find the garment's edge is too big for the waistband, even though the waistband was cut the correct size. The garment might have stretched with handling. Fabrics such as stretch wovens and corduroy are particularly susceptible.

To remedy, un-pin the waistband and sew a line of stitching along the top of the garment, inside the seam allowance. Use a long stitch. As you sew, hold your middle finger firmly behind the presser foot.

When the fabric has bunched up (5-10cm or so along, depending how thick the fabric is), take your finger away and release the built up fabric, then put your finger back. This creates a sort of ease stitch with mini concertinas in it, and should pull in the garment's edge enough for you to attach the waistband.

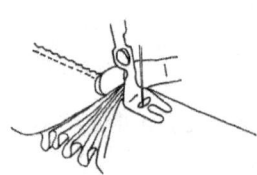

When you sew the waistband on, have the waistband on top and the garment underneath to help the machine feed the ease on the bottom layer through for you.

4. Sew with the waistband uppermost, and the garment underneath (the picture shows the garment on top for clarity).

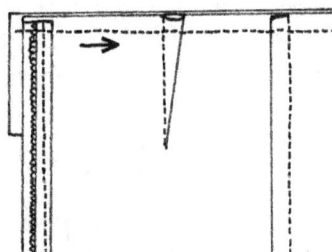

5. Press the seam and waistband *up* towards the waistband, away from the garment.

6. Perform a quality check: do up the zip and check there's a good flow-through where the ends of the waistband meet each other. If there's a difference, fix it now. Don't try to fix it by stitching another row lower or higher—the waistband will end

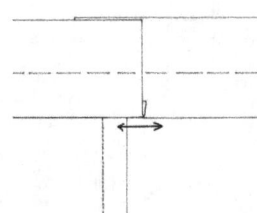

up the wrong width. Instead, note the amount to correct, unpick the section, and re-sew it. It won't take you long.

Fold the waistband along its fold line and **check the fit again** now, if required.

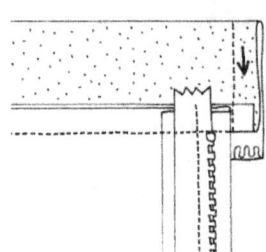

7. To finish the ends, fold the waistband in half longways, right sides together. You can measure the width of the waistband to make sure you're folding correctly.

Sew the *overlap* end first. Stitch across the end, perfectly in line with edge of the garment, with the correct amount of seam allowance hanging down.

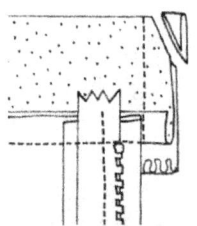

Trim the corner.

Make sure you stitch *exactly* in line with the edge of the garment. If you stitch too far away the band will have a step.

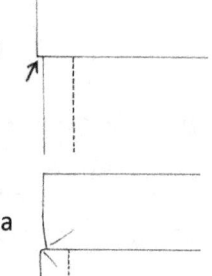

Stitching too close will make a pucker.

Turn the end through to the right side.

For the **extension** side, you can...
Stitch along the end and then along one edge (this was the text book method when I was a fashion student). I don't do mine like this; I find it hard to turn through and it always seems too narrow.

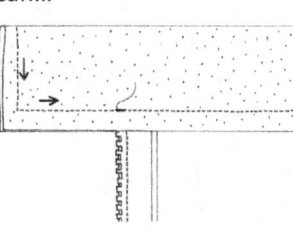

OR

Stitch only across the end (I do mine like this). Ensure the waistband stays the correct width when you fold it.

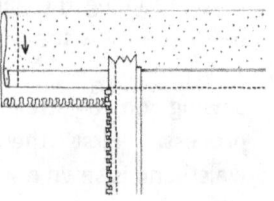

Trim off the seam allowance in the corner like you did before, and turn the end to the right side.

Do up the zip again and check that the width of the waistband is the same on each side.

Fold in the ends neatly as shown. Make your folds square and definite so this little bulky section is as neat as possible.

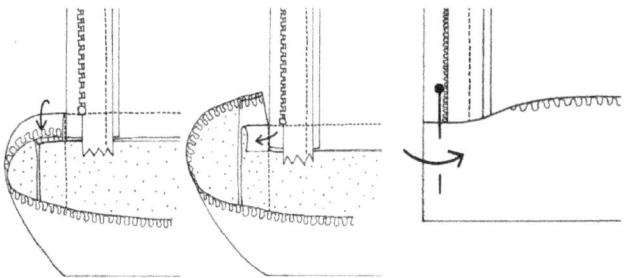

Blend the folded corner back to the unfolded overlocking. Pin the corner to hold it.

If you're turning under the edge rather than having an overlocked one, press it under now, taking about 2-3mm (⅛") less than the seam allowance.

8. Fold the waistband into position and secure with pins next to the seam line. Check to make sure you catch the back of the waistband in properly.

Check the waistband is the same width all the way around.

If the inside edge of the waistband is turned under instead of overlocked, check the back is caught in properly.

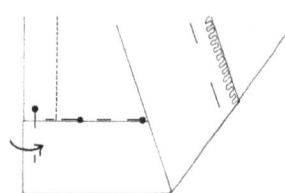

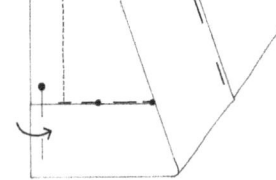

9. With the right side of the garment up, stitch-in-the-ditch. Stitching-in-the-ditch is something many people find difficult; it can be hard to keep the needle in the ditch.

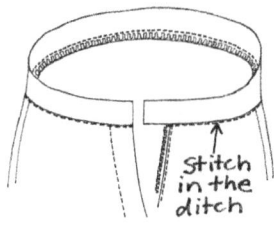

Some tips for stitching-in-the-ditch:

✂ Good pre-sewing preparation makes stitching-in-the-ditch straightforward. Press and pin along the ditch so everything lies flat and is aligned before you begin.

✂ Use perfectly matching thread so the stitches will blend in. Match the thread to the *garment*, not the waistband, if they're different colours.

✂ Start with the needle down *in* the ditch, put the presser foot down, then start sewing. That way, you're starting off already in the ditch. If your machine has variable speeds, use a slow one.

✂ As you sew, place one hand each side of the presser foot to pull the ditch flat as you sew in it. To prevent the waistband from rippling, use your hands either side to encourage the top layer to push backwards as the presser foot pushes it forwards. If rippling is a problem, stop sewing immediately because it won't improve as you go on, sorry to say. Undo the rippled section and try again.

✂ Using a zipper foot might help.

✂ Remember that no-one will be viewing your stitching up close under a bright light—it will be hardly noticeable when the garment's being worn.

Instead of stitching-in-the-ditch, you could also edgestitch the waistband, if you'd like edgestitching on it. It can make the overlocked edge hang down rather long on the inside, so either turn it under or adjust the seam allowance. You could also stitch in the ditch *and then* edgestitch.

After edgestitching the waistband down, you can continue on and edgestitch around the other edges of the waistband, if you want to. I often do this.

10. The finished waistband can have whatever topstitching you choose, or none. Bear in mind that many rows of topstitching may pull the fabric in and make the waistband smaller. I usually just edgestitch around the waistband and leave it at that.

11. Sew a button and buttonhole or a mini hook and bar to the ends. For waistbands with extended overlaps and underlaps, sew a button on the outside and a plain flat one on the inside. You can also use hooks or a combination of hooks and buttons.

Troubleshooting waistbands

The waistband doesn't fit the garment waist—either too big or too small.

✂ Did you sew all the darts and pleats?

✂ If the pattern is multi-sized, did you cut out the right size?

✂ Is the notch for the extension of the waistband in the correct spot?

✂ Check the pattern to see that both garment and waistband are cut correctly. Check that notches are in the right place.

✂ Measure the waistband and garment patterns to see if the actual pattern was correct in the first place.

✂ Did you do an alteration on the garment that affects the waist?

✂ If the garment waist is too big it might have stretched. If you've handled the garment a lot when sewing it (tried it on or done lots of unpicking), the top edge can easily stretch. If you're absolutely sure everything else is correct, you can ease the waist in before sewing the waistband on. To do this, sew a line of staystitching along the edge with your finger behind it, as described on page 374.

The waistband is too small to fit me.
✂ Did the waistband shrink when you ironed on the interfacing?
✂ Have you put on weight around the middle since you started making the garment?
✂ Is it a sewing problem—did you match the notches correctly?

The waistband on my trousers cuts my tummy in half when I sit down.
This can happen on close-fitting trousers with a waistband sitting on the natural waistline.
Is the waistband a smidge too tight? Could you make it 5mm-1cm (¼"-⅜") looser?
Another reason might be that you may not have enough height in the back rise of the actual trousers (in other words, the back might not be high enough at the back waist). As a result, when you sit down the trouser back pulls the waistband down at the back, cutting the front into your tummy.
Possible solutions to rectify this pair:
✂ Remove the waistband and make a looser one.
✂ If you have a 1.5cm (⅝") seam allowance on the waist seam, thieve 1cm (⅜") from this at the centre back to try and make the back waist higher. Unpick the back part of the waistband and shift it higher at the centre back.

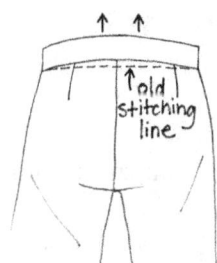
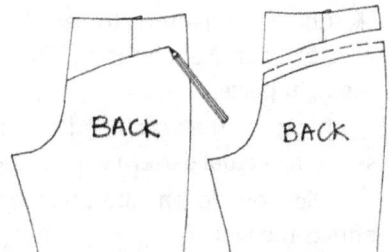

✂ If you have any spare fabric, add a back yoke. To do this, remove the waistband at the back only and undo the trousers side seams a little way. Chalk in a yoke line across the back and add a seam allowance. Cut off the yoke along the seam allowance line.
If the dart point dips below the yoke, either shorten the dart first OR remove any remaining dart value from the side seam of the back.
On the cut-off bit, mark the grainline using the pattern. Use the cut-off bit as a pattern to cut a new back yoke with a higher centre back and seam allowances as shown (you'll need to add *two* seam allowances to make up for the one you left on the trousers back).

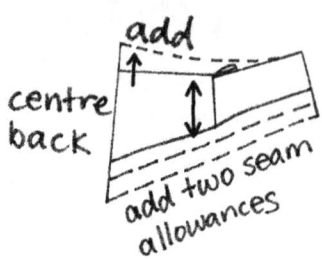

Solutions for future pairs:
✂ Loosen the waistband. Make the waistband pattern bigger and any darts, pleats or side seams correspondingly smaller so the new waistband fits.
✂ When you cut and interface the waistband, cut the waistband a little longer, iron on the interfacing and *then* cut the waistband to the correct length and add the notches. This eliminates the possibility of the waistband shrinking from the heat of the iron. Synthetic fabrics are more prone to this.
✂ Adjust the back: see how much the back pulls down on the old pair, for example 2.5cm (1"). Draw a line across the back pattern and cut along it. Split the pattern, pivoting on the side seam, and add this much in (slip a piece of paper underneath and sticky tape it to fill in the wedge). Re-draw the back crotch using a ruler, so you have a straight centre back seam again.

Another way to sew a waistband
There's another, very similar, method for sewing a waistband on. With practise it's possible to sew without using any pins, and with lots of practise both sides of the waistband will look identical.
This method is suitable for light to medium fabrics and produces a waistband with a row of edgestitching visible on the outside and inside. It yields a very clean

finish on both sides—it really suits garments like wraparound skirts. It's unsuitable for thick fabrics because *all* of the seam allowances end up inside the waistband. The garment may be lined or unlined.

In summary, the *innermost* side of the waistband is sewn onto the *inside* of the waist (instead of the outside). The ends are finished as usual. The waistband is brought over to the outermost side and stitched down on the right side. The method is actually identical to sewing a shirt cuff.

1. Cut the waistband out, interface, and fold in half longways, pressing the fold with an iron. Ensure all the notches are present.

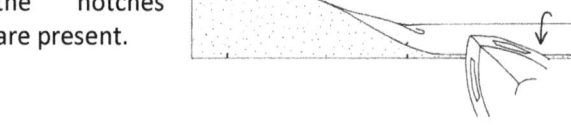

2. Position any beltloops, hanger tapes or lining.

3. Place the right side of the waistband onto the *inside* of the garment waist (instead of the outside). Ensure you've matched the notches to the centre back, centre front and extension and have the correct amount of seam allowance hanging over each end. Stitch with the waistband on top (not underneath as illustrated here for clarity).

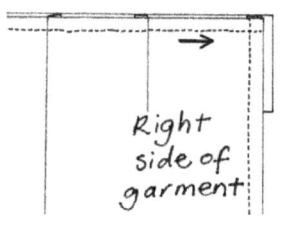

4. Press the seam and waistband *up* towards the waistband, away from the garment.

5. Perform a quality check: do up the zip and check there's a good flow-through where the ends of the waistband meet each other. If one side of the waistband is higher, do fix it now.

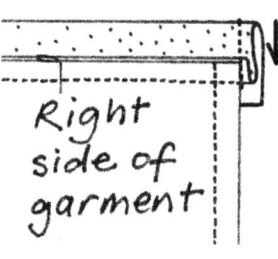

6. Finish the ends by folding the waistband back on itself (so it's inside out), and stitching across the end as illustrated. Ensure you stitch exactly in line with the edge of the garment.

For the extension side, either stitch only across the end (my preference)

OR

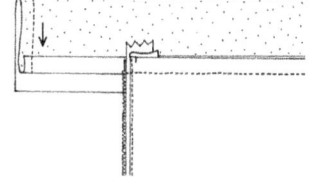

Across the end then along the long edge (textbook method).

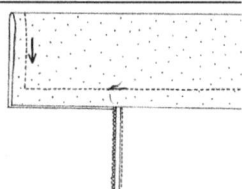

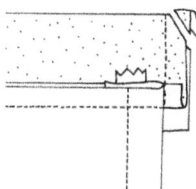

Trim off the seam allowance in the corner and turn the ends to the right side.

Do up the zip again and check that the width of the waistband is the same on each side.

7. Fold in the ends neatly and secure with a pin, as shown. Make your folds square and definite so the corners are as neat as possible. I *always* put a pin in the corner, even if I don't pin the rest of the waistband.

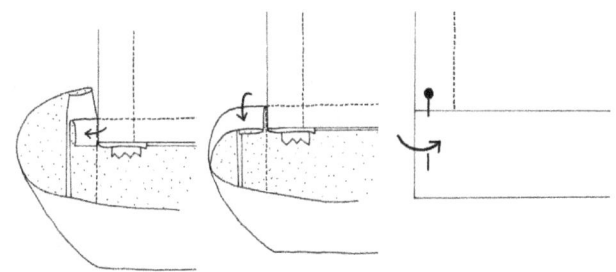

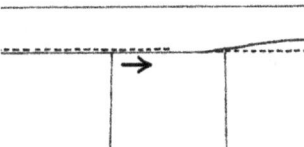

8. Bring the waistband over to the *outside* of the garment waist and edgestitch it down onto the right side, just covering the previous row of stitching. If you like, you can keep going and edgestitch around the whole waistband (I often do).

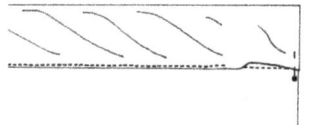

This last step is the most difficult part to execute, because the waistband can ripple if it isn't handled correctly, but it becomes easier as you practise your technique. I think using slotted waistband interfacing (page 372) makes this step a little easier because the correct seam allowance is easy to fold under.

It's important to hold the underneath layer firmly with your left hand, pulling it forward, and let the waistband "sit easy"

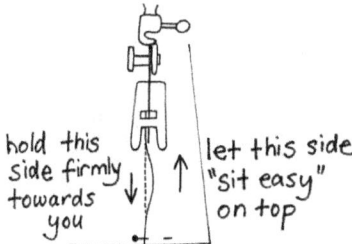

on top with your right hand.
As a sewing machine sews, the presser foot pushes the top layer of fabric forward and the feed dogs feed the underneath layer backwards. Thus, if you let a machine just sew naturally, the top layer will be longer by the time you get to the end. When applying a waistband, this is what causes the rippling effect.

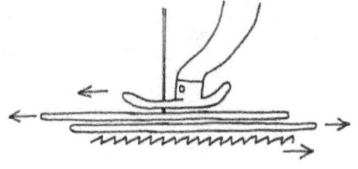

If you begin sewing and the waistband begins to ripple, stop sewing and unpick what you've done. The ripples will never go away as you sew, or with presssing. Although rippling can happen if the fabric isn't on grain, your sewing technique is a major factor. Some other things that will help reduce rippling:

✂ Ironing the waistband in half lengthways first helps to reduce rippling. I've found this to be the most helpful idea.

✂ Ease off the pressure on the presser foot if needed (there should be a knob to adjust the pressure on the top of the machine—consult your manual).

✂ Try using a walking foot, if you have one.

Banrol or Armoflexxx waistband

Banrol or Armoflexxx is a very firm sew-in waistband interfacing. It sits inside the waistband next to the outer layer, with all the seam allowances sitting behind it. Any seam allowances in front of it will cause a ridge, because the interfacing is so smooth and stiff.

1. Are you having an overlocked finish inside the waistband? If so, overlock now:
Trim back the seam allowance on the edge to be overlocked to a scant 1cm (⅜"); a 1.5cm (⅝") seam allowance is a little too long to look good inside the garment and will flip up when the garment is washed.
To remember which edge to overlock, overlock with the *right side* of the fabric facing *up*, beginning at the extension end (for women's waistbands). You'll recognise the extension end by the notches.

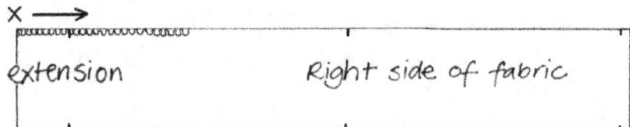

You could bind the edge for a very smart finish. If you aren't overlocking or binding, just leave it and turn under the edge to finish it in Step 6.

2. With the right sides together, stitch the waistband onto the garment. Match the notches accurately to the centre front and back and extension and be sure to leave the correct amount of seam allowance hanging over each end. Press the seam and waistband *up*.

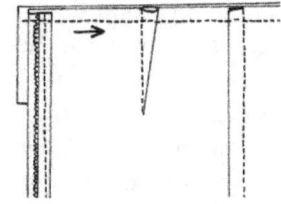

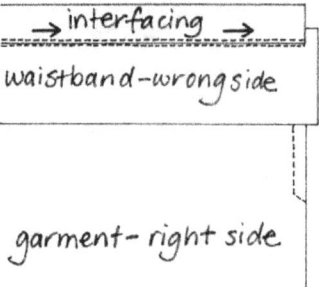

3. Measure and cut the interfacing to the same length as the finished waistband pattern (that is, without the seam allowances at each end, but *with* the extension). Stitch it onto the waist seam allowance, positioning the edge of the interfacing right next to the previous line of stitching.
Press the waistband up, then fold it in half longways, pressing it over the interfacing.

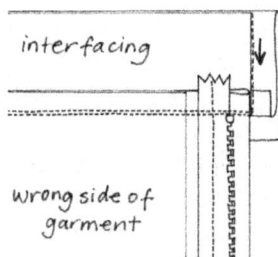

4. Finish the ends by folding the waistband back on itself, right sides together. Stitch across the end. Do the same for both ends.

5. Trim the corners, then turn the ends to the right side and fold the ends in squarely, as shown.

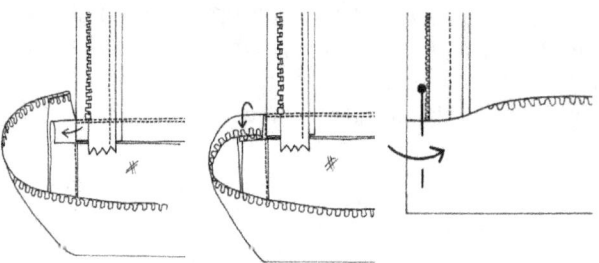

The interfacing should sit neatly inside the waistband.

6. If you haven't overlocked the inside long edge, turn it under a fraction less than the seam allowance. Pin the waistband in place along the seamline. Machine stitch-in-the-ditch the waistband in place—see page 375.

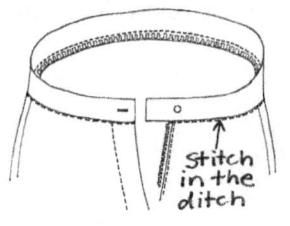

Cut-on waistbands

A cut-on waistband is simply a waistband cut in one with the garment, instead of a separate strip sewn on. A cut-on waistband can be used for *both* back and front, or *either* back or front with a regular sew-on waistband for the other side.

Make a pattern

The pattern is very simple. Decide on a finished waistband width, for example 2.5cm (1") and stick some paper to the top of your pattern. Add twice the width to the top edge, for example 5cm (2"). Extend any darts or pleats so they go straight up with parallel lines.

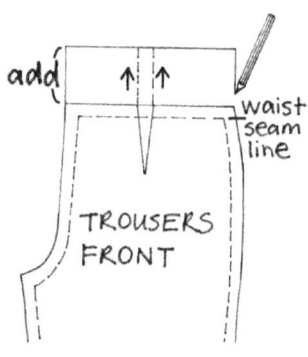

Don't be concerned about the seam allowance on the waist. The seam allowance that's already there will automatically become the seam allowance on the edge of the cut-on waistband.

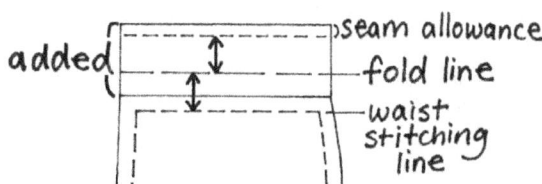

Notch each end of the fold line so you'll know where to fold.

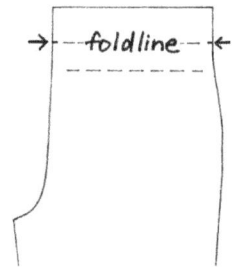

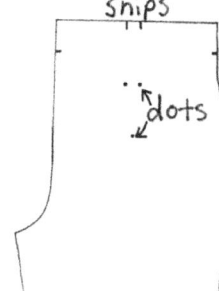

Mark darts or pleats with tiny 3mm (⅛") snips at the top edge and dots (mark the dots on the wrong side of the fabric when you cut it out).

You'll need to re-design any pockets that would finish in the waistband seam (since you won't have a waistband seam anymore). Any sort of cutaway pocket won't work.

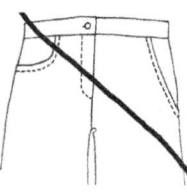

Instead, try angled welts, jet or patch pockets. You can bring the linings of jet and welt pockets all the way up to the waist to support the pocket—the thin lining won't add much bulk.

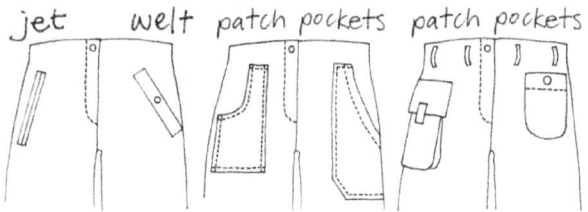

If you don't want to change the front pockets, you could use a separate sew-on waistband for the front, and add a cut-on waistband for the back only.

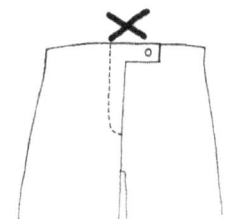

Note also that you can't have an overlap extension with a cut-on waistband. It simply won't work with the fly front.

✂ By the way, you don't have to use a zip—you could have a button fly instead. With buttons, you could have a cut-on fly facing (page 420) and cut-on fly shield (page 424) as well, since you don't need to insert a zip in anywhere.

To sew a cut-on waistband

1. Locate the foldline and press the fold in with an iron. Interface the cut-on waistband: either half of it (as illustrated), all of it, or none of it if the fabric is very thick and you don't think it needs it.

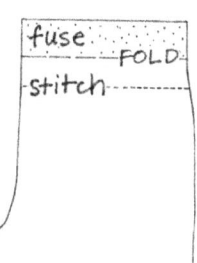

2. Sew any darts or pleats. After sewing, you may need to slash and press them open to reduce bulk.

3. Sew the pockets, side seams, crotch and fly (see below for details on sewing the fly front).

4. With the zip completed, overlock and fold down the top edge of the waist along the fold line. Stitch it in place. Add the beltloops last of all.

How to sew the fly front:
Familiarize yourself with sewing a regular fly front first (see page 419). This is sewn in the same way but with some changes in sewing order to accommodate the

cut-on waistband. These illustrations show a women's fly front (right over left). Reverse it for men.

Before you start, overlock the top edge of the cut-on waistband. Also overlock the centre front edges, where you should have a 1.5cm (⅝") seam allowance.

On the fly shield side:
1. Sew the fly shield with a 6mm (¼") seam at the top edge. Overlock together the long straight edges of the shield, as usual.

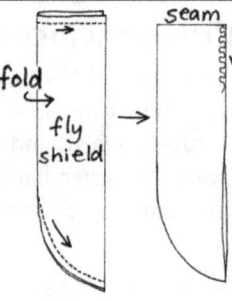

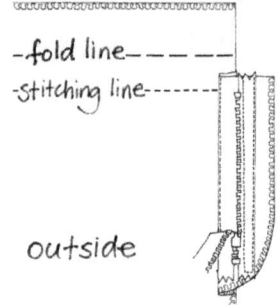

1. Begin with the fly facing side (the overlap side). Mark the waistband's stitching line on the fabric in some way, for example a chalk line, line of hand basting stitches or a row of pins.

Sit the top edge of the fly facing above the stitching line you just marked by about 1cm (⅜"). Sew the fly facing onto the front, press the seam towards the fly facing and edgestitch.

Lay the zip right side down onto the facing with the top of the zip level with the marked stitching line. Stitch the zip on as you normally would.

2. Taking a 6mm (¼") seam, stitch the shield onto the front, sandwiching the zip tape in between the shield and front as usual. The top of the *zip* should be level with the marked stitching line (tuck in the end of the zipper tape) and the top of the *shield* level with the fold line.

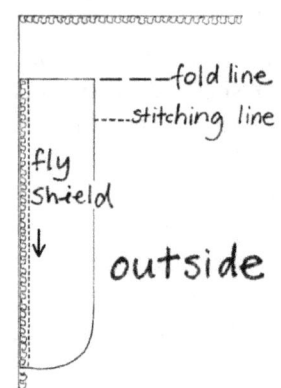

2. Fold the cut-on waistband along the fold line with the *right sides together* and stitch a vertical seam at the end right on top of the fly facing seam, as illustrated. Turn the cut-on waistband through to the right side. The fly facing will automatically turn to the wrong side at the same time.

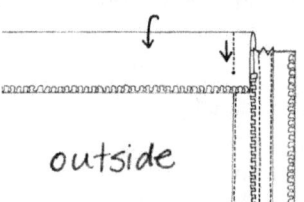

3. Fold the cut-on waistband along the fold line with the right sides together, and stitch a vertical seam with a 6mm (¼") seam allowance at the very end of the band.

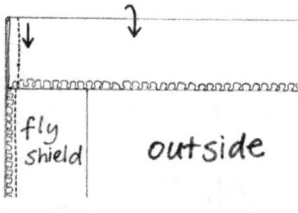

Turn the cut-on waistband through to the right side. The top of the fly shield will stand out level with the top edge of the cut-on waistband.

3. On the wrong side, tuck the corner of the waistband in neatly, blending back to the flat overlocking.

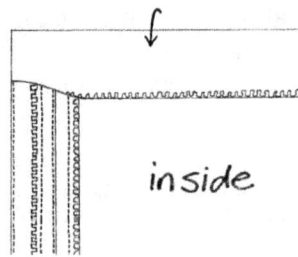

4. On the right side, edgestitch vertically along the edge of the zip as you usually would to keep everything flat.

Stitch along the waistband to hold it in position. If you don't want a line of stitching around the cut-on waistband, you could strategically tack it down at the seams and darts.

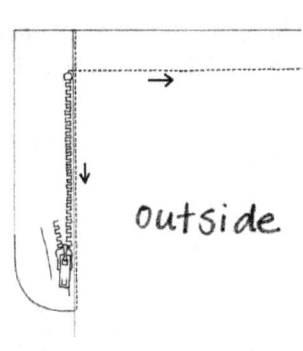

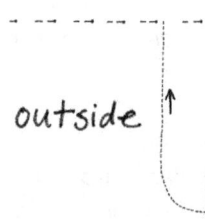

On the right side, pin the cut-on waistband in position, along the marked stitching line, ready to sew later.

On the outside of the garment, topstitch the fly front, beginning at the bottom and ending at the marked stitching line.

A cut-on waistband using Petersham

You may like to try backing a cut-on waistband with Petersham. You'll have the cut-on waistband showing at the front and a seam at the top attaching the Petersham behind it. The Petersham provides a neat finish and stiffening at the same time.

Make a pattern

Measure the width of the Petersham to determine how wide the cut-on waistband will be. Add just the width of the Petersham to the top edge of the garment. The seam allowance that's already on the garment's waist will become the seam allowance used to sew the Petersham on.

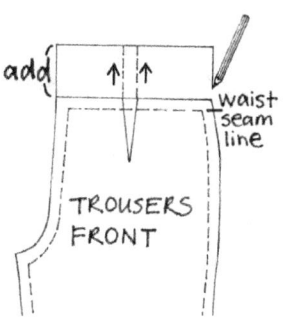

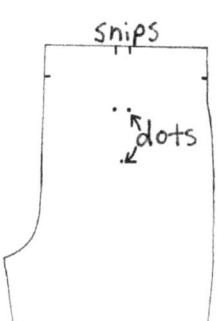

Extend any darts or pleats so they go straight up with parallel lines. Mark them with tiny 3mm (⅛") snips at the top edge and dots (mark the dots on the wrong side of the fabric when you cut it out).

To sew a cut-on Petersham waistband

1. Sew any darts or pleats.

2. Lay the Petersham on top of the raw waist edge,

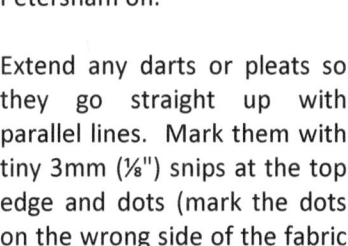

with both right sides facing up. The amount to lap the Petersham over is your original waist seam allowance. Edgestitch the Petersham on, then fold it over to the inside.

✄ If the garment has a fly front, follow the instructions on pages 379-380.

3. Stitch along the waist line to hold the Petersham down (stitch this with the Petersham uppermost and

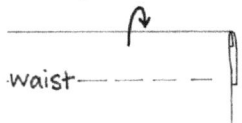

the fabric underneath), or else simply catch the Petersham in place at the side and centre back/front seams, and any beltloops. A very clean finish!

Curved waistbands

Curved waistbands are used on garments that sit below the natural waistline. The lower the waistband, the flatter the curve. A curved waistband requires a seam along the top edge since it can't be folded over. It's sewn in the same way as a regular straight waistband, with the additional step of the seam.

✄ Sometimes curved waistbands consist of one pattern piece with no vertical seams; the ends are often on the bias. Low-cut women's jeans may have this type of waistband.

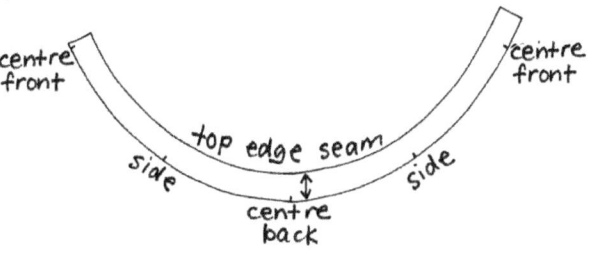

✄ More often, the waistband has side seams (for a side opening)

OR

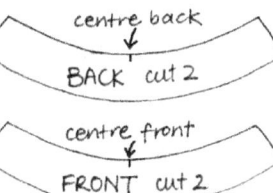

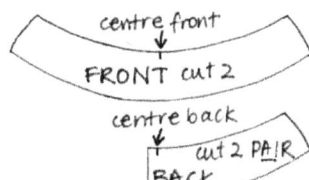

Side seams *and* a central seam (for a front or back opening).

✄ Curved waistbands have an outer band and an inner one, seamed together at the top. The outer and inner are the same pattern and both are interfaced. You can use the same interfacing for both, or you may prefer to choose a lighter interfacing for the outermost band and something firmer for the innermost.

I like to use a softer interfacing if it's on a skirt and firmer one for trousers. There'll still be two layers of fabric and two layers of interfacing in the finished waistband, same as a regular waistband.

✄ The inner waistband can have a lining attached to it, if you wish.

✄ Apply tape to the top edge to stop it from stretching when it's worn. Sew the tape on *before* you do a fitting—otherwise you won't know what size the waist should be. I like to use 6mm (¼") cotton tape, available in black or white, however, you could also use a strip of the fabric's selvedge, if it's smooth and firm.

Using the pattern as a guide, rather than the actual waistband (which may have already stretched), place the tape along the stitching line and cut it to the correct

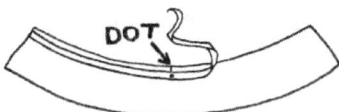

length. Mark the centre front or centre back with a pencil dot. Be exact. Include the side seam allowances.

In industry, a measurement is given for cutting the tape, according to the garment specs, rather than measuring it on the pattern each time.

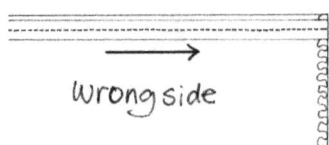

Sew the tape onto the inside of the top edge of the outer waistband, stitching with the tape uppermost and the fabric underneath. It's easiest to sew on when the seam allowance is 6mm (¼"), because you can lay the tape just next to the raw edge. Use a long stitch and sew just inside the seam stitching line, so the tape stitching will be hidden. Remember to switch the machine back before sewing regular seams.

When you sew the two waistbands together, stitch just outside this line of stitching so it won't show on the right side.

3 ways to sew a curved waistband

As with most sewing things, there are several ways of going about it. The method you choose will depend on whether you want to fine-tune the waist measurement and how little unpicking you want to do if you need to alter the garment later.

Method 1

Our bodies are round and this method sews the waist in-the-round. This gives the least amount of bulk at the sides, however, to alter the side seams requires unpicking many seams so only give it a go if you're absolutely sure the waist will fit correctly.

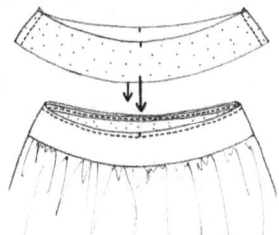

1. Sew all the side seams (garment, outer and inner waistband).

2. Cut the tape as one long piece for the whole waist, and sew it to the top edge of the outer waistband.

3. Sew the outer waistband to the garment and sew the outer waistband to the inner one at the top.

4. Stitch down the inner waistband.

Method 2

This is my preferred method. It's easy to do a fitting part way through and there'll be less unpicking than the first method if you need to alter the waist later.

1. Tape the outermost back and front waistbands separately first.

2. Attach the outer waistbands to the garment. You can do a fitting if needed now, pinning the side seams.

3. Sew the side seams.

4. Sew the side seams of the innermost waistband.

5. Sew the waistbands together at the top edge.

6. Stitch down the inner waistband.

Method 3

For the ultimate in easy-to-alter-later sewing. The front and back are sewn separately, then joined at the side seams last of all.

1. Tape the front and back outer waistbands separately.

2. Sew the front and back of the garment as separate units, including the inner and outer waistbands.

3. Sew the side seams all the way through the garment, inner and outer waistbands in one go.

4. Stitch down the inner waistband.

Binding the waist

Instead of a waistband, the top of the waist can be finished with a simple binding. It's a clean-looking, elegant finish that's ideal for hipster skirts and trousers where a narrow waistband is required. It's also great if you've run out of fabric!

✂ You can use ready-made bias binding (the wider one sold as hem facing), self-made bias binding, grosgrain ribbon or twill tape. The *finished* bound edge should be about 1cm-1.2cm (⅜"-½") wide.

✂ A binding around the waist can be the last thing sewn on a garment. The darts, side seams and zip can all have been completed.

✂ You may or may not need to stabilize the waist before applying the binding. If the garment's waist is firm without bias sections *and* you're going to be binding with something firm like grosgrain ribbon or twill tape, then I wouldn't bother. If, however, you're using bias binding, the waist edge is very curved or the fabric is prone to stretching then *do* stabilize the edge first. See Step 2 below for doing this.

1. Cut off all the seam allowance on the waist seam. Actually, on skirts I don't bother cutting it off, I just leave it. The slight extra length is no big deal. On trousers I would trim off because the crotch depth would be affected.

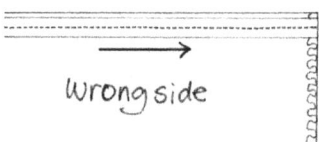

2. To stabilize the waist (optional), sew some 6mm (¼") cotton tape to the top of the waist on the inside. You could also use a narrow strip of the fabric's selvedge, if it's firm and smooth. Cut the tape to the waist measurement plus the end seam allowances so the tape will go from raw-edge-to-raw-edge. Measure the *pattern*, not the garment, because the garment might have already stretched. Sew the tape right on the top edge using a long stitch. You can measure and sew the tape individually onto the front and back, or sew the front and back together and sew a longer length of tape on. The first way is handy for fine tuning the fit, the second is less bulky. You'll be binding over the top of the cotton tape.

3. With the waist stabilized, check the fit if needed.

4. Apply the binding: **twill tape or grosgrain ribbon** can be sewn on in one operation. Iron it in half first, with one side 2mm (scant ⅛") wider than the other, to make sure you definitely catch it when you stitch it on. Lay one edge (not the 2mm longer edge; the other one) on top of the garment's edge and pin it in position. At the ends, fold the tape around the edge. Then fold the tape down and edgestitch it on.

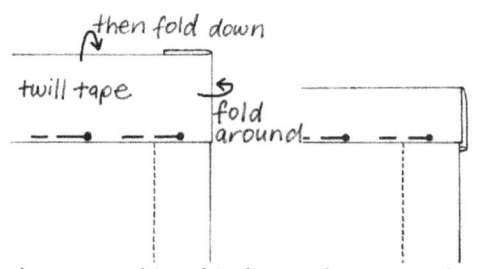

If you're using **bias binding**, place it right sides together with the garment's edge. Pin in the fold of the binding (that's where you'll be stitching). At each end, fold the binding around the edge. Stitch.
Take the binding over to the wrong side and pin it in position on the right side. Stitch-in-the-ditch to secure it (see page 375 for tips on this).

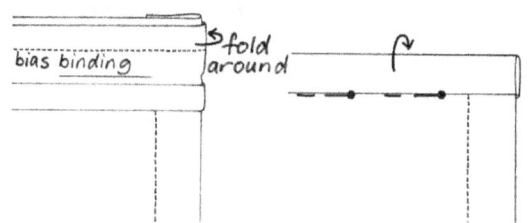

There should be room at the top of the zip to sew a hook and eye on the binding.

Waistband using curved Petersham

This is different from using a length of straight Petersham behind a cut-on waistband. In this waist finish, the curved Petersham is essentially a facing, rather than a waistband. The top edge will sit on or below the waist of the wearer. It produces a smart, clean waist finish, especially if you can get perfectly matching Petersham.

Choose some 2.5cm (1") wide curved Petersham. Cut the shorter curved edge to the same length as the garment's waistline with a seam allowance at each end. Measure the length on the *pattern*, not the garment, in case the garment has stretched.

Using pins or chalk, mark the centre and side points on the Petersham so you can match them up to the garment.

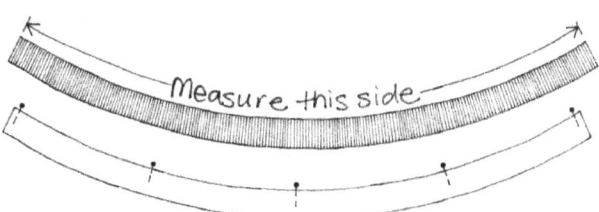

If the skirt or trousers has a zip, either invisible or regular, sew the zip *after* sewing on the Petersham. Invisible zips work best with curved Petersham, but a regular zip is possible although not quite as neat.

To sew a curved Petersham waistband

1. Trim the top of the garment so the seam allowance is 6mm (¼"). On skirts I don't bother cutting it off—I just leave it because the extra 4mm-9mm of length is no big deal. On trousers I would trim because the crotch depth would be affected.

2. If the garment is lined, baste the lining and main fabric together at the top (with their wrong sides facing in) and treat it as one layer. The Petersham will sit over the top of the lining on the inside.

3. Identify the centre front/centre back and side points of the already-cut-to-length Petersham and match to the garment. Lap the shorter curved edge of Petersham over the 6mm (¼") seam allowance on the right side of the garment. Pin the Petersham in position, then stitch close to the edge of the ribbon.

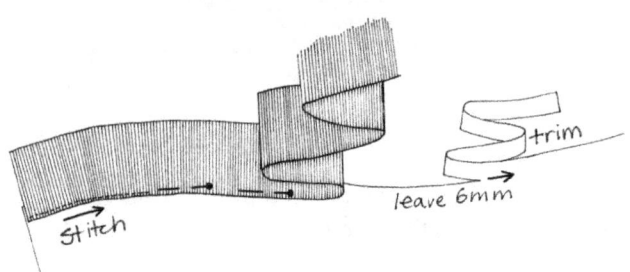

4. Turn the Petersham to the inside of the garment, allowing the edge of the garment to roll in slightly. Press. Stitch the ribbon to the garment at all seams and darts so it stays inside. You can either stitch-in-the-ditch (page 375) by machine or catch the bottom edge of the Petersham to the seam and darts by hand.

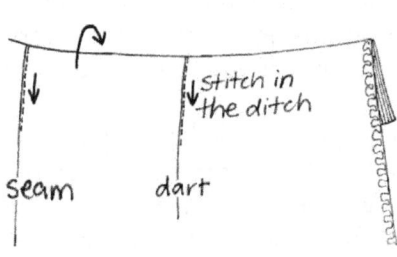

Are you using an invisible zip?

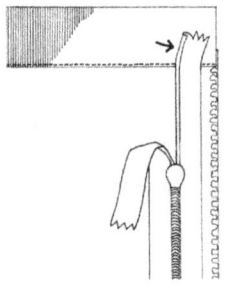

1. Sew in the invisible zip up to the ribbon. Splay out the top of the zip tape towards the raw edge as you stitch. Apply the zip about 6mm (¼") lower down if you'd like to put a hook and eye at the top.

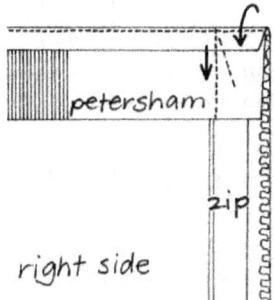

2. Undo the zip. Fold the Petersham down so it's covering the top of the zip. Using a zipper foot, stitch alongside the zipper stitching. Trim the corner off and turn to the right side. Sew a hook and eye to the top of the zip if planned.

Are you using a regular (dress) zip?
1. Fold down the tops of the zip towards the front and machine stitch in place.

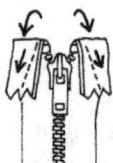

2. On the garment, fold the Petersham over so the right sides of the garment and Petersham are together.

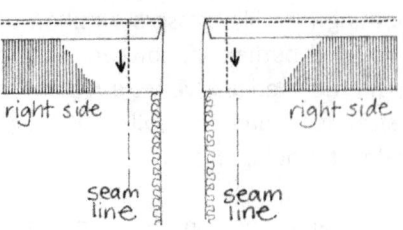

Stitch along the seam line as shown, noting that the underlap side (right picture) is stepped in by 3mm (⅛"). This is for a lapped application. For a centred application, stitch both sides the same (as the left picture). Trim the corners and turn through to the right side.

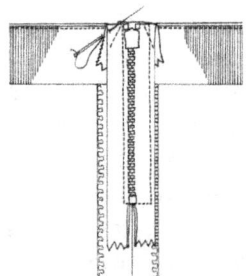

3. Sew the zip in as normal, beginning it about 6mm (¼") lower down if you'd like to put a hook and eye at the top (recommended). If required, hand sew the edges of the zip tape down inside to keep them flat, as illustrated.

Super-easy drawcord waist

A very quick and oh-so-simple drawcord waist can be made using the same fabric as the garment, with no interfacing or buttonholes required. This waist is great for simple summer trousers, shorts or skirts.

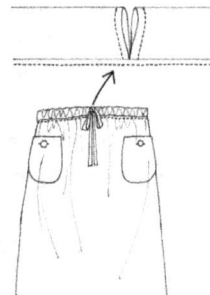

Make a pattern
1. On the garment pattern, remove any darts (simply cross them out on the pattern and don't sew them).

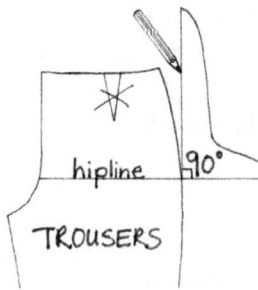

2. Check that the waist measurement is at least the same as your hip measurement, if not more (so you can get the garment on). If it's too small, square up from the sides as illustrated.

The illustration shows trousers, but it's the same for skirts.

3. Measure the *stitching line* of the waist. It's important this measurement is accurate, otherwise the waist casing won't fit.

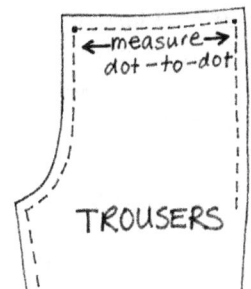

4. Cut the drawcord casing the **length** of the waist plus two seam allowances. Make the **width** 3cm-4cm (1¼"-1½") plus two seam allowances. The finished width will be 1.5cm-2cm (⅝"-¾").

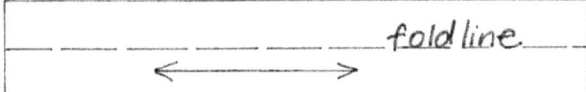

For a perfectly matching drawcord, cut a strip of the same fabric 4cm (1½") wide and about 40cm-50cm (16"-20") longer than the casing. Sew it like a long strip of beltloop (see page 6).

To sew a super-easy drawcord waist

1. Press under the seam allowance at each short end of the casing. Stitch.

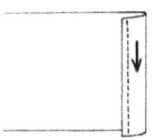

2. Iron the casing in half longways.

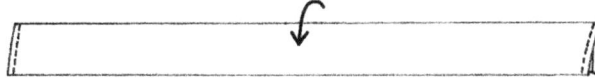

3. Stitch the casing onto the right side of the garment's waist, matching the centre front and back points. The ends of the casing should meet at the centre front. Overlock the seam.

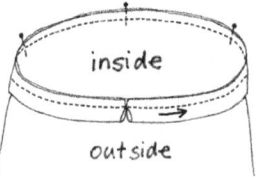

4. Press the seam towards the garment and topstitch it flat on the garment side to keep it in place. Insert the drawcord and secure it at the centre back with a few stitches to keep it from pulling out.

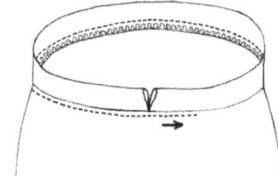

Elastic Waists

Waistbands that are all elasticized belong on pull-on garments and require no zip, button or other closure.

Since the garment will be pulled on over the hips, the waist measurement needs to be at least as big as the hip measurement in order to get the garment on, *unless* the fabric stretches.

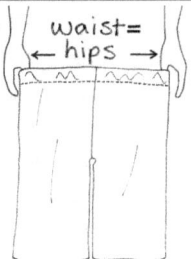

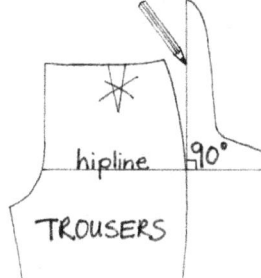

✂ To convert a skirt or trousers to an elastic waist, remove any pleats or darts (simply cross them out on the pattern and don't sew them). On non-stretch fabrics, check the waist measurement is at least the same as the hip measurement, if not more. If it's too small, square up from the sides as illustrated.

✂ As with regular waistbands, elastic waists are usually among the last things to be constructed on a garment.

✂ The width of the casing is made 6mm (¼") wider than the elastic to allow room for sewing and to allow the elastic to move easily.

✂ An all-elasticized waistband has no interfacing in it.

✂ Waistbands can be all or partially elasticized.

✂ Elastic can be inserted into the waist of a garment in several ways:
Inserted through a channel made by folding the top down and stitching.

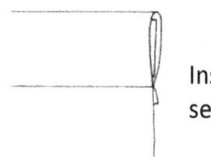

Inserted through a separate, sewn-on, casing.

The elastic can also be sewn stretched directly onto the fabric.

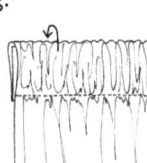

Notes on elastic lengths

To determine the correct length to cut, simply put the elastic around your waist until it feels comfortable. Allow an overlap (I always allow ½") and cut. I always note the elastic measurement on my pattern for future reference and often I tape on a small sample of the type of elastic I've used too.

You'll find the elastic measurement needed will vary slightly with the type and width of elastic. Some elastics are firmer than others and therefore need to be cut longer since they don't stretch as far. Wider elastics also tend to be firmer than narrower ones, even if they're the same type.

You might ask: "If only the back is elasticized, how long do you cut the elastic?" Measure the elastic around your waist and determine the whole waist measurement, then halve it. Add a small allowance to be stitched in at each side if required.

Simple fold-down elastic casing
Make a pattern
1. Ignore any darts or pleats on the pattern. On non-stretch fabrics, check that the waist measurement is at least the same as the hip, if not more. If it's too small, square up from the sides as shown on page 385.

2. Identify the waist stitching line. Add to this two casing widths plus 6mm (¼") to turn under, or to overlock if the fabric is thick.

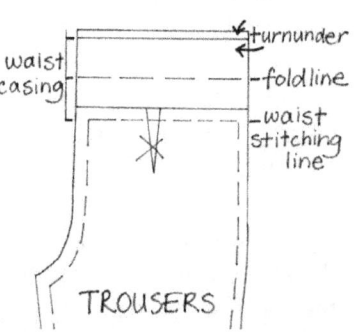

The width of the casing depends on the elastic you plan to use. Make the finished casing width 6mm (¼") bigger than the width of the elastic, so the elastic has room to move and you have space to sew it.

3. Make a small, 3mm (⅛") notch at each end of the fold line, so you'll know where to fold.

Patternmaking tip:
True the casing by folding it into position and either trimming or adding along the side. This ensures the casing will fold down correctly. You'll need to do this if the sides are angled. When you unfold the paper, the casing will have a jog on the edge.

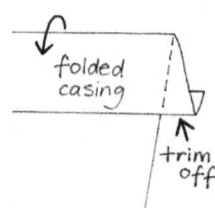

To sew a fold-down elastic casing
1. Stitch and neaten all the garment's seams. The casing is made last of all.

2. Either press under 6mm (¼") on the top raw edge, or leave it flat and overlock it (if the fabric is too thick to turn under). Press the fold line of the casing. You don't have to press the fold lines in before sewing the casing but it makes it easier to sew. You could do this right at the beginning before you start sewing (and you could press the garment's hem up too, while you're at the ironing board).

You can insert the elastic as you sew the casing, OR thread it through with a safety pin afterwards.

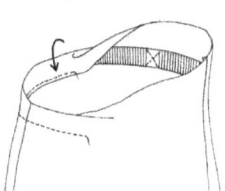 To insert the elastic as you sew, cut the elastic to length, overlap the ends and sew it in a ring.

Place the ring under the folded casing and stitch the casing edge down with the elastic inside. Use a zipper foot if needed. *Be careful not to catch the elastic in the stitching.* As you sew, move the gathering formed by the elastic out of the way.

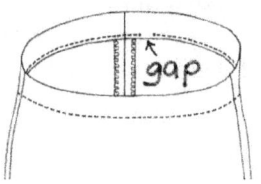

Factories like to use this method because it's faster than inserting the elastic afterwards.

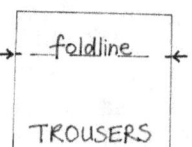 If you're threading the elastic through afterwards, stitch the casing leaving a small gap in the stitching.

Attach a safety pin or bodkin to the end of the cut-to-size elastic and thread it through. Run your hand around the casing to check the elastic hasn't twisted. Overlap the ends and stitch by hand or machine zig zag. You can leave the gap if it's small, or stitch it closed.

✂ When I sew clothes for my children, I like to leave a gap in the centre back seam so I can easily access the elastic to adjust or replace it. It only works if the centre back seam is an open seam; it doesn't work on closed seams.

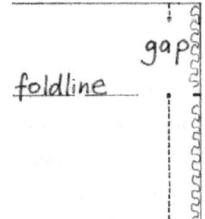 When I sew the centre back seam I stitch for 6mm (¼") from the raw edge, backstitch to secure it, then begin again at the fold line (again, backstitching securely).

I press the seam open, revealing a gap the width of the elastic. When the casing is folded into position, I have a neat slit.

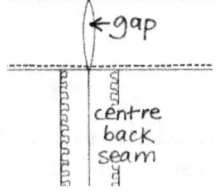

Decorative casing options

✂ The casing can contain a single piece of elastic or have multiple rows of narrow elastic.
Topstitch parallel lines of stitching along the already-stitched down casing, forming channels wide enough to accommodate narrow elastic.

✂ A decorative ruffle at the top of the casing is achieved by using a wider casing and narrower elastic.

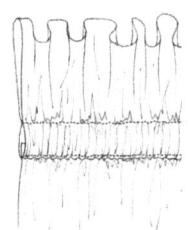

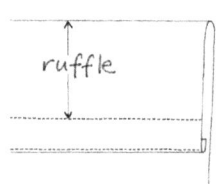

Decide on a ruffle width and add it to the casing when you make the pattern. When you sew the casing, sew a second row above the first to form the ruffle.

This idea looks cute around the bottom of puffed sleeves on little girl's dresses. It was also (briefly) used on skirt or trouser waists in the late 1980's-early 1990's, where it was called a paper bag waist. Unsurprisingly, this volume of fabric around the waistline suited few (even when worn with a bodysuit).

✂ Some people like to sew an edgestitch along the top fold of the casing to make the casing lie flat. Sometimes this is actually stitched *through* the elastic, to stop the elastic curling. Note that stitching through elastic tends to flatten it and gives it less stretch. Therefore the elastic might need to be cut shorter to allow for it.

Separate elastic casing

Why would a separate waist casing be used? It might be a more economical use of fabric, the casing might be cut in a different fabric or it could be a design feature. The top of the waist may be too curved to fold down. In a factory, the separate waistbands could be made by a different machinist while someone else makes the rest of the garment.

Make a pattern

1. Ignore any darts or pleats (simply cross them out and don't sew them). On non-stretch fabrics, check the waist measurement is at least the same as the hip measurement, if not more. If it's too small, square up from the sides as illustrated.

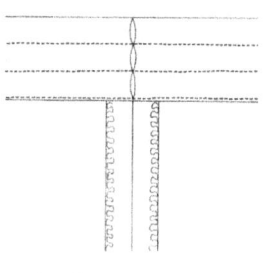

2. Identify the waist stitching line and measure the length. Regarding the waist seam allowance: make it 6mm (¼"—an overlocking width) if the entire garment is to be overlocked together. Otherwise I would suggest a 1cm (⅜") seam allowance, however, check that your overlocker can neaten a 1cm seam allowance next to thick elastic. Test it to see—if not, make the seam allowance wider, for example 1.5cm (⅝"), or otherwise insert the elastic afterwards.

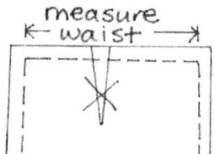

3. Make a pattern for the separate casing. The width of the casing depends on the elastic you plan to use. Make it 6mm (¼") bigger than the width of the elastic, so the elastic has room to move and you have room to sew it.
Cut the casing twice the finished **width** plus two seam allowances (the same allowance you used for the waist). Make the **length** as long as the garment's waist plus a seam allowance at each end.
The grainline usually runs longways, the same as a regular waistband.

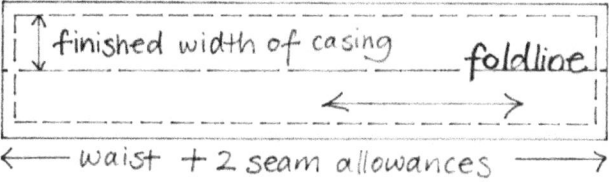

Important: if the fabric is stretchy, the grainline on the casing must run *in the same direction as the garment,* otherwise the finished garment may be too tight to pull on over the hips.

To sew a separate elastic casing

1. Cut the elastic to length, overlap the ends and sew it in a ring.

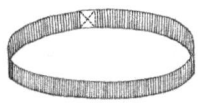

2. Press the casing in half longways with wrong sides together, matching the long raw edges.

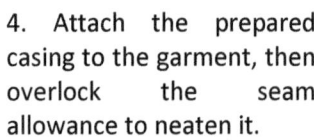

3. Sew the short ends of the casing together and press the seam open. Place the ring of elastic inside the folded casing and stitch close to the raw edges, enclosing the elastic. Use a long machine stitch and be careful not to catch the elastic in the stitching—a zipper foot works well.

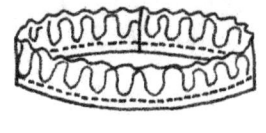

4. Attach the prepared casing to the garment, then overlock the seam allowance to neaten it.

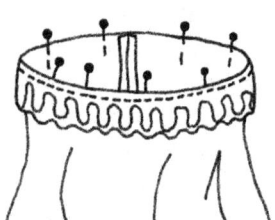

Elastic with a draw cord

Elastic is often combined with a draw cord in sports clothes such as shorts or tracksuit pants to give greater variance to the fit, or just as a design feature. The casing can be made in any way, for example fold-down, separate or elastic sewn on.

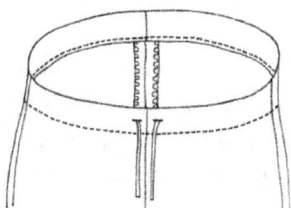

✂ The draw cord can be on the inside or outside of the garment, but inside is more usual.

✂ Make two small buttonholes (vertical or horizontal) 1cm-3cm (⅜"-1¼") apart on either side of the centre front seam to correspond with where the draw cords will emerge.
Use the pattern to work out where the buttonholes should sit, and transfer their position to the fabric.

If you're making lots, it's faster to make a cardboard template of the area. Mark the buttonhole position on the card with a hole to put a pencil through.

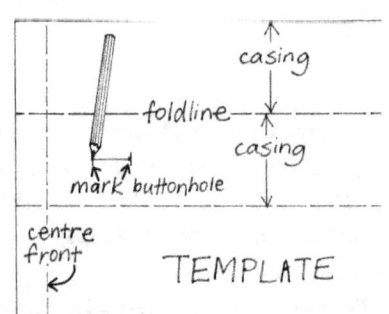

✂ Note that you'll have to make the buttonholes *before* stitching the casing in place. Put a small scrap of woven fabric behind the buttonholes as you make them, for reinforcement. Trim away the excess afterwards.

✂ The buttonholes can be horizontal or vertical.

✂ Sew the elastic and casing as normal for your chosen casing. The drawcord can be inserted at the same time as you stitch the casing, or afterwards using a bodkin or safety pin. The garment should stay up with the elastic, and the draw cord can be used to bring the waist in if needed.

✂ Another way is to cut the elastic only three-quarters of the length required, and attach draw cords on both ends. This garment will always need the draw cord to be tied to stay up.

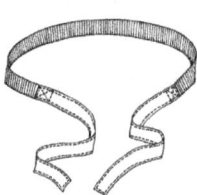

✂ Yet another option is to use draw-cord elastic. It's a soft elastic with a shoelace type draw cord through the centre.

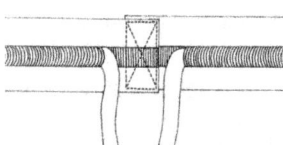

Cut the elastic to length with an overlap. Pull out the draw cord at each end, so the ends will emerge approximately where the buttonholes will be. Lap the elastic and stitch it to form a ring. Insert the draw cord ends through the buttonholes *before* sewing the elastic in the casing. Knot the ends of the cords so they don't fray.

Sewn-on elastic waist

Elastic can be stitched straight onto the garment's waist. It's often used (and works well for) stretch fabrics and gives a sporty look. It's fine to use for wovens too. A disadvantage of this method is that it's a time-consuming job to unpick if you need to replace the elastic.

It's important to consistently use the elastic width that the pattern is designed for—otherwise the garment will be longer or shorter.

Make a pattern

1. Ignore any darts or pleats (simply cross them out and don't sew them). On non-stretch fabrics, check the waist measurement is at least the same as the hip measurement, if not more. If it's too small, square up from the sides as illustrated.

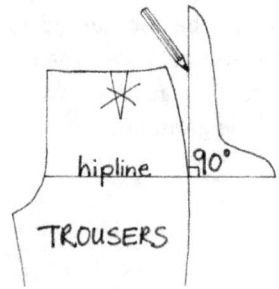

2. Add twice the width of the elastic onto the waist of the pattern. You need no seam allowance at the top because the raw edge finishes flush with the elastic edge. Note that the elastic width dictates the amount to add on.

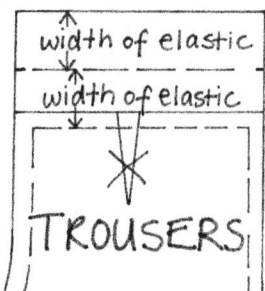

To sew a sewn-on elastic waist

1. Cut the elastic to length, overlap the ends and sew it into a ring. Fold to divide the elastic into quarters and mark, using chalk, pins or a pencil. Do the same with the garment's waist.

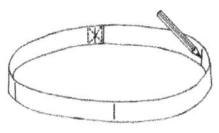

2. Place the ring of elastic onto the wrong side of the garment's waist, matching the elastic edge to the raw fabric edge. Position the join in the elastic at the centre back and match the other points.

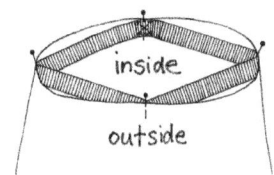

3. Overlock or zig zag the elastic to the garment's edge, stretching the elastic as you stitch so it's the same length as the garment. I find this easiest with the elastic uppermost and the fabric underneath.

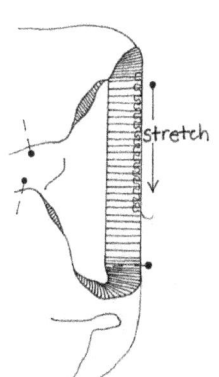

✂ I sometimes use a long straight machine stitch on the edge if I'm not sure of the fit. It can then be overlocked straight over the top later without unpicking. I also use a straight stitch if the fabric doesn't fray and I'm planning to zig zag the casing down in the next step.

4. Fold the elastic down to the inside of the garment and topstitch along the lower edge of the elastic, actually stitching through the edge of the elastic to anchor it to the garment. I do this with the right side of the garment up and the elastic underneath, but you may find it easier around the other way.

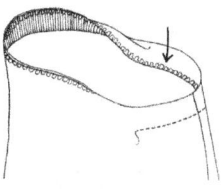

Important: Stretch it as you stitch so you're stitching flat, stretched-out elastic, otherwise the stitching will pop when it's stretched.

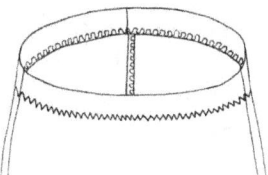

If the fabric is woven you can use straight stitch. For knits, topstitch with zig zag or stretch stitch.

Some variations:

✂ Occasionally the elastic isn't topstitched down. Instead it's stitched-in-the-ditch at the centre back, centre front and sides, or at any other seams that run through the waist. This is sometimes seen on lycra bike shorts or shorts-style swimwear bottoms, where there's little gathering from the elastic because the fabric is so stretchy.

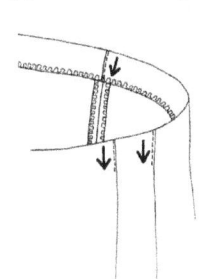

✂ Sometimes parallel rows of extra stitching are stitched through all the layers of fabric and elastic to stabilize it. Note this will make the elastic waist slightly bigger with less stretch because the elastic is flattened out with the stitching— therefore cut the elastic a little shorter if you plan to do this (sorry, only trial-and-error will determine exactly how much shorter).

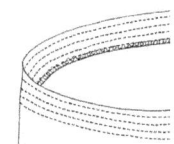

Partially elasticized waistbands

Sections of elastic can be added to regular waistbands to give a more comfortable fit. Possible areas include the sides, the side backs, the centre back or across the whole back. Try to plan the section of elastic to fit within the design and seams of the garment, for example put the elastic in between the side seam and back dart.

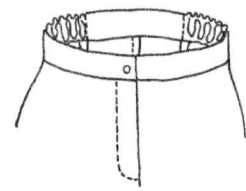

Although time consuming, sections of elastic can be retro-fitted into waistbands of finished garments by unpicking part of the waistband. It's a handy alteration if you've lost a little weight or if the waist of a garment is too big but the hips are OK.

Make a pattern

Use a regular waistband pattern (page 371) and mark where you want the elastic to go. The sections to have elastic in them aren't interfaced.

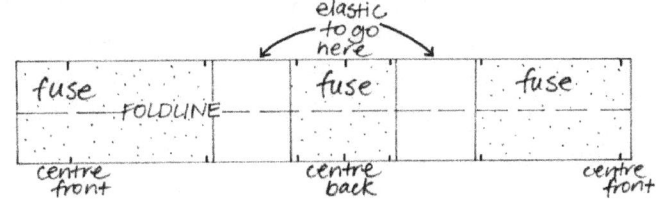

To sew a partially elasticized waistband

1. Stitch the elastic onto the innermost side of the waistband, matching the edge of the elastic to the waistband's fold.

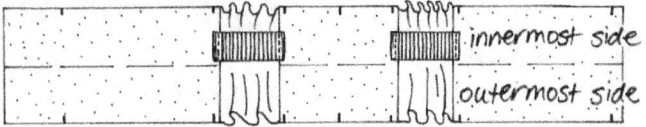

2. Sew the waistband to the garment as you usually would (pages 373-378).

3. Afterwards, the elastic can be stitched through while held stretched. This looks smart and will stop the elastic from curling, although it will make the section 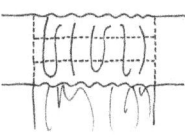 slightly bigger with less spring because the stitching flattens it out.

An adjustable waistband

Adjustable elastic waists using a special buttonhole elastic are often seen on maternity and children's clothes—obviously for maternity the elastic is at the front and for children it's at the back.

The ends of the elastic can emerge from buttonholes 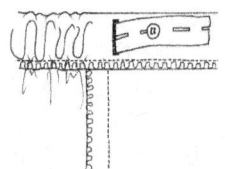 stitched on the innermost side of the waistband (as pictured here), or from gaps cleverly positioned in the side seams on the inside of the waistband (see below).

Make a pattern

You can use a regular waist band pattern (page 371) or a cut-on waistband (page 379). Note that the elasticized parts of the waistband don't have interfacing in them. Mark on the waistband where the side seams of the garment will be and make a buttonhole (the same width as the elastic) at each side of the waistband on the inside.

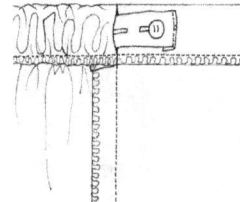

✂ If you don't fancy making buttonholes (and some people will go to extremes to avoid them), the elastic can emerge from a gap in the side seams on the waistband.

This involves making separate front and back waistbands. Interface only the parts that *won't* have the elastic.

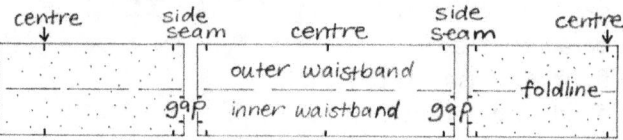

To sew an adjustable waistband

1. If the elastic is to emerge from buttonholes, make them now.

If the elastic is to emerge from gaps, sew the side seams of the waistband leaving gaps on the inner side. Backstitch securely either side of the gap.

2. Press the seam allowances open and topstitch around each gap to keep it flat.

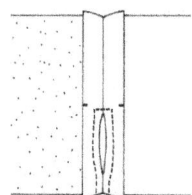

3. Decide what to do with the ends of the elastic: they can be either free hanging or stitched down onto the waistband (both are illustrated in the left column).

For free hanging ends, simply thread the elastic through the casing after sewing the waistband on. Stitch on some buttons to attach it to. If the elastic needs replacing, it can be easily done.

For stitched-down ends, thread the elastic through *before* sewing the waistband on and stitch a button on at each side. Sit the elastic flat in the casing and do up the elastic on the buttons at each end. Fold under the ends of the elastic and stitch it to the waistband. *Then* sew the waistband on. If the elastic needs replacing later, you can unpick the stitching and thread in new elastic, leaving the ends free hanging.

✂ I *have* seen waistbands with only one buttonhole and button for the elastic (and technically that's all it needs for adjustment), but it's easier to adjust the elastic if you can pull it from both ends, especially if you're wearing the garment at the time.

3 Ways to elasticize the back waist

A waistband can be elasticized at the back and not at the front. There are several ways of approaching this.

✂ The back of the garment shouldn't have any darts, since the waist shaping is being provided by the elastic in the waist. The back elastic casing can be separate or fold-down.

✂ Regular or buttonhole elastic can be used. The buttonhole elastic could emerge from buttonholes in the waistband, or gaps you've left in the side seams of the waistband.

Method 1—Separate waistband

This method has a waistband cut in one piece, with elastic running through the back. The elastic is stitched to hold it at the sides.

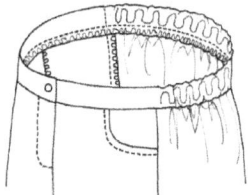

Make a pattern for a separate casing as described on page 387, or page 371 for a regular waistband. Remove any back darts (just cross them out on the pattern) and add the dart value to the back waistband, so it now fits a dartless back.
Ensure the side seam positions are marked on the waistband—this is where you'll be stitching the elastic.

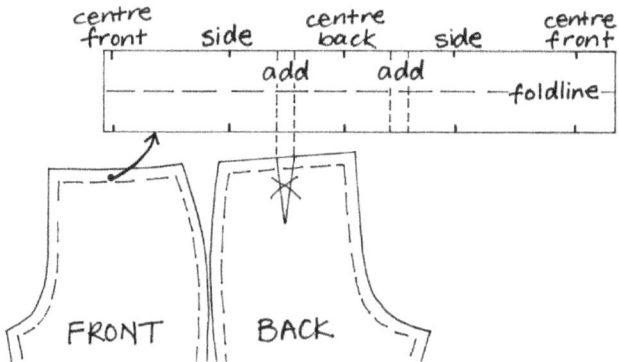

To sew, stitch the side, centre back and centre front seams of the garment. Press and neaten.
Apply interfacing on the front parts of the waistband but not the back. While you're at the ironing board, fold the waistband in half longways, wrong sides together, and press the fold.

Overlock what will be the innermost long edge of the waistband. Attach the outer long edge of the waistband to the garment, right sides together. Press the seam *up* towards the waistband.

Attach each end of the elastic to the waistband at the side seam points, on the innermost side of the waistband.

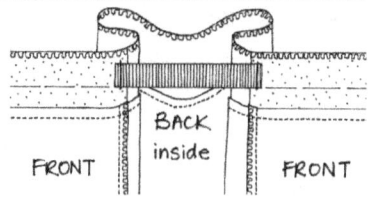

Finish the ends of the waistband if required. Fold the waistband down into position and stitch.

Method 2—A fold down casing

This method uses a fold-down casing, cut in one with the garment. Elastic is inserted through the back of the casing and secured at the sides.

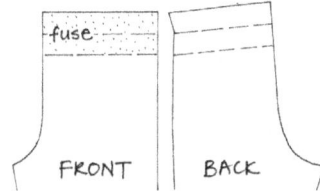

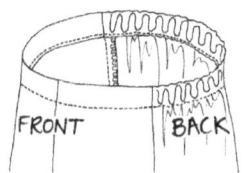

Make a pattern as described on page 386 for a fold down casing. Interface the front to give support and stop it from creasing.

To sew, sew, neaten and press all the seams of the garment, leaving the waist until last. Overlock the waist edge if needed. Attach the elastic onto the garment's side seams before stitching down the casing. Ensure the edge of the elastic is right next to the fold line of the casing. When the casing is folded into position the elastic should sit at the top of the fold.

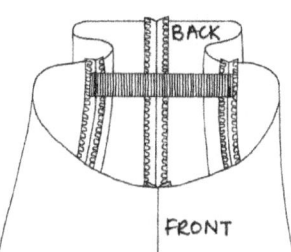

Method 3—A separate front waistband

This is a blend of the previous two methods, with the front waistband cut separately and the back folded down. It could be made around the other way, too, with the back cut as a separate waistband (and elasticized) and the front cut in one with the garment (and interfaced).

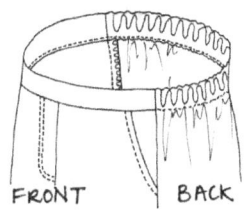

Make a pattern combining a separate casing for the front (page 387) and a fold-down for the back (page 386).

Make sure the finished waistband width is the same for back and front.

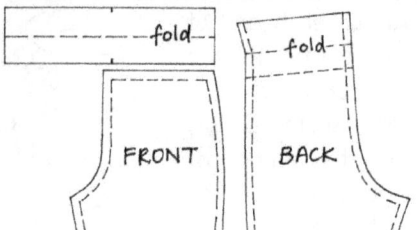

To sew, interface the front waistband and press it in half longways, wrong sides together.

Sew the centre back and centre front seams of the garment, but leave the sides undone. Press and neaten.

Stitch the waistband onto the front, right sides together. Press the seam *up* towards the waistband.

Now sew the side seams of the garment all the way through the waistband. These can be pressed open or to one side—in my illustration they're pressed towards the back. The top raw edges of the front waistband and back casing should be level.

Overlock around the top raw edge, if you haven't already.

Attach the elastic at the side seams, right next to the fold line. The top of the elastic should sit neatly

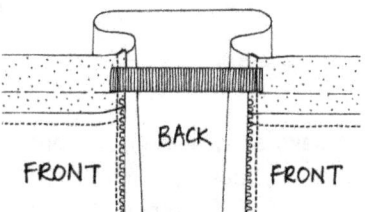

inside the fold when the waistband is finished. Fold the waistband down into position and stitch, using a zipper foot if needed.

Men's waistbands

The waistbands for men's trousers are sewn with a few differences to regular waistbands, but are certainly within reach of a home sewer's abilities.

✂ For men's garments such as jeans, shorts and work trousers, the waistband is usually made the same as a regular waistband (page 371), not the trouser waistband described here.

✂ The width of men's waistbands is much less susceptible to the whims of fashion than women's. 4cm (1½") is pretty standard.

✂ There are really only two main differences between the construction of men's and women's waistbands:

1. The waistband has a **centre back seam** to allow for any future waist

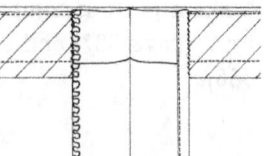

alterations. The seam allowance may be overlocked or bound to neaten it but it's always an open seam, not pressed to one side. See page 7 for the centre back beltloop solution.

The centre back seam allowance is usually about 4cm (1½") wide at the top and blends back down to the regular seam allowance where the crotch starts to curve. On the pattern, put a double notch on the crotch seam where the seam allowance starts to widen and a notch at

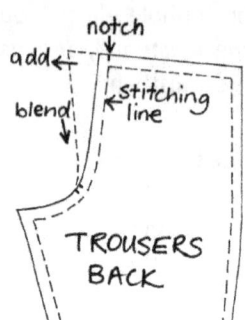

the top edge to show where the stitching line is. Sew the waistband on before neatening or sewing the centre back seam, then sew and neaten both together. This allows for easy alterations later.

2. The waistband has a **seam on the top edge**. Trouser fabric is used for the outside and the inside is cotton lining (same as the pocket linings). Either or both the inner and outer waistbands are interfaced. Sometimes pre-made waistbanding is used on the inside, available from tailor's suppliers.

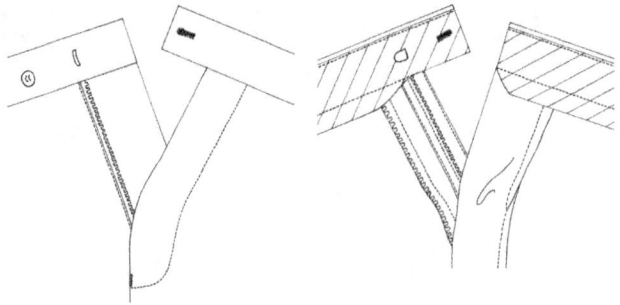

Extended waistbands

Men's trousers often have an extended left (overlap side) waistband, as shown above, featuring two fastenings—either two hooks, two buttons, or a hook and a flat button. In my experience, a waistband with an extension and two fastenings gives the best looking and most durable front finish. It's less likely to show pull lines, since the load is spread over two fastenings instead of one.

How long should an extension be? 5cm (2") is a good amount.

In super-budget men's trousers, for example work trousers, the waistband is attached using a waistband machine and the extension is simply a slightly longer waistband that's folded back and stitched.

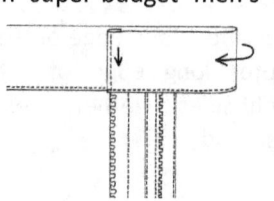

In fact, both ends of the waistband are folded back and stitched to finish them. This provides a reinforced area for the button and buttonhole.

"Your first men's waistband"

There are several ways to go about making a men's waistband, but if this is your first one, try these directions then consider one of the variations for your next pair of trousers.

This method uses the trouser fabric for the outside of the waistband, a stiff sew-in waistband interfacing and cotton pocketing fabric for the lining. The waistband lining is taken all the way to the end of the waistband, regardless of whether you have an extension on the waistband or not.

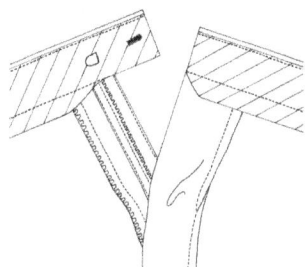

Make a pattern

1. The **left and right waistband pieces** are cut from from the trouser fabric. The width should be 4cm (1½") wide plus two seam allowances plus 6mm (¼"). For example, 4cm + 1cm + 1cm + 6mm = 6.6cm. The length of the waistband will obviously depend on the trousers—accurately measure the top of the trousers pattern to make sure the waistband will fit.
The right side will look something like this:

Notice the extra-big centre back seam allowance, to match the trousers. Snip a double notch at the back to avoid confusing it with the front extensions. The right waistband has an underlap at the centre front that's long enough to accommodate the fly shield (if you're not sure of the exact length needed, cut it longer then trim it when you sew).
The left waistband is a mirror image of the right, but with your choice of front finish (extension or none).
If you'd like an extension, add an extension and a seam allowance onto the centre front, as illustrated. If it's the same length as the fly shield extension on the right waistband, you can use the same pattern piece for both.

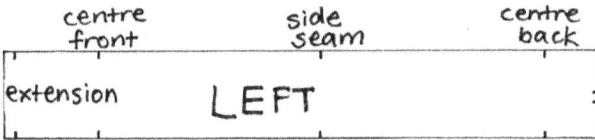

For no extension, simply add a seam allowance onto the centre front:

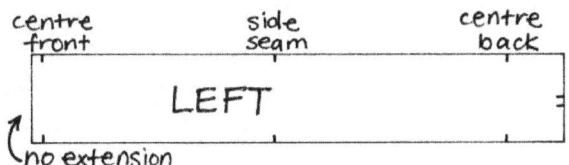

2. The **interfacing** should be the same width as the *finished* waistband, that is, 4cm (1½") wide. The interfacing needs to be a firm sew-in. You can use belting of the correct width, Armoflexxx or Banrol waistbanding or strips of buckram.
Cut the interfacing the same *length* as the waistbands, minus the front seam allowances (note that the interfacing will sit inside the front extensions). *Do* include the back seam allowance, because if you want to let the trousers out in the future, you'll need interfacing at the centre back of the waistband.

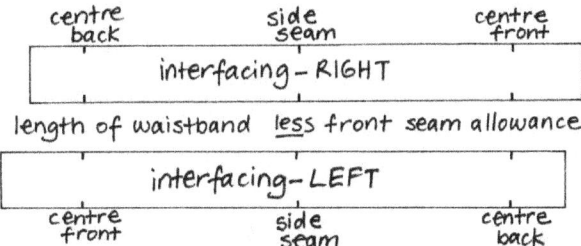

3. The waistband **lining** is cut from woven cotton fabric. If you used cotton pocket lining elsewhere on the trousers, you can use this here. Cut the lining pieces the same length as the fabric waistband, and 8.5cm (3¼") wide. It needs to be cut on the bias.

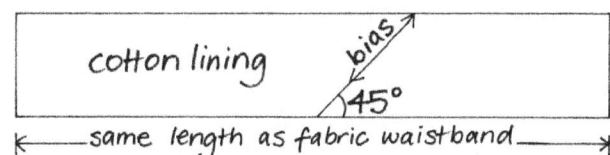

To sew a men's waistband

1. Stitch the left and right fabric waistbands to their respective sides of the trousers, right sides together. Match the notches and ensure the correct amount of seam allowance hangs over the ends.
The centre back should finish flush with no overhanging seam allowance.

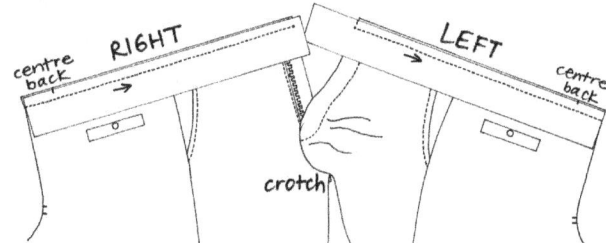

Do up the zip and check that the waistbands are level across the front zip, and alter it now if they aren't.

2. To apply the **interfacing**, sit the strip of sew-in interfacing over the seam allowance, with the edge next to the previous line of stitching. The front ends shouldn't extend into the front seam allowances.

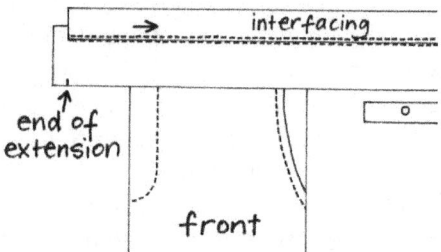

Stitch next to the edge. Press the seam allowance and waistband *up*, with the interfacing nestled in between.

3. On the **lining**, press under 2.5cm (1") along one long edge.

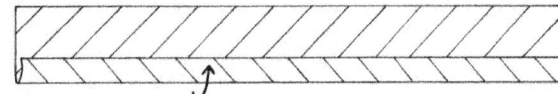

Place the unfolded edge of the lining to the top edge of the waistband, right sides together, and stitch.
Note that you'll be stitching 6mm (¼") above the top of the interfacing. Press the seam allowance towards the lining and understitch on the lining side.

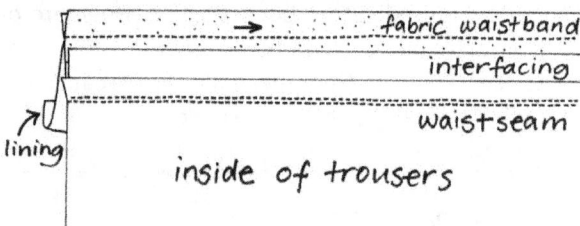

Turn the lining to the inside of the trousers. The lining will sit 6mm (¼") *below* the top folded edge. Press.

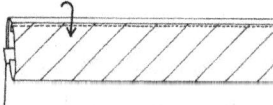

4. At the **centre back**, sew the crotch seam all the way through the waistband, accurately matching the seam junctions. Press the seam open and neaten the seam allowances with overlocking or binding.

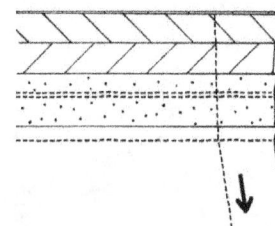

For the **front** ends, bag out the ends as you would on a regular waistband (page 374): fold the waistband back on itself, right sides together, and stitch across the ends. It's easier and more accurate to do this with the lining side underneath (not on top, as illustrated for clarity, below), so you can get the stitching exactly in line with the front edge of the trousers. You may like to measure the width of the waistband before stitching across the ends to make sure you've folded it in the right place.

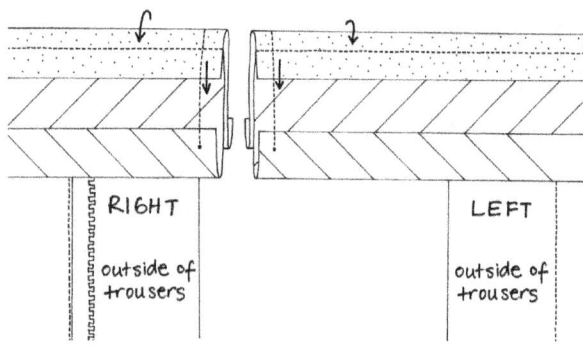

5. If you're planning to attach clamp-on hooks, do it now while you have access (see page 397).

6. After sewing, trim the corners and turn the ends through to the right sides. Fold the corners in as shown, making each fold square and neat, before securing the corner with a pin.

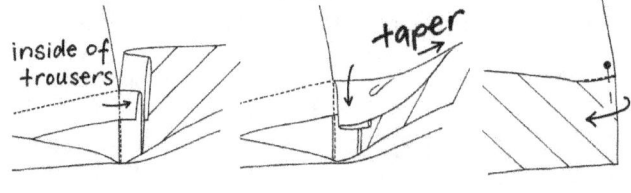

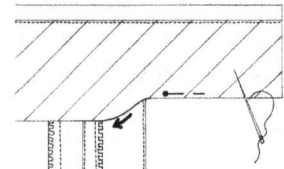

7. The lower edge of the extension can be invisibly sewn by hand for a clean look.

Alternatively, if the trousers are casual and you plan to edgestitch around the entire edge of the waistband, you can sew the extension's lower edge as part of this operation.

8. Pin and stitch-in-the-ditch (see page 375) from the right side to hold the lining in place.

9. Finish the waistband by sewing buttons and buttonholes or hooks and bars to the front opening.

Waistbands

Another way to finish the end

This is a way to sew the left (overlap) extension using

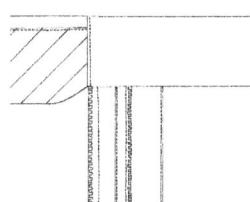

trouser fabric on *both* sides, rather than backing with lining. It gives a slightly stronger, and smarter, finish. The fabric extension finishes in line with the edge of the fly facing.

Make a pattern

Follow the instructions for making the **left and right waistband** pieces on page 393.

To the left centre front, add twice the finished extension length, for example 5cm (2") x 2, then add the width of the fly facing and seam allowance.

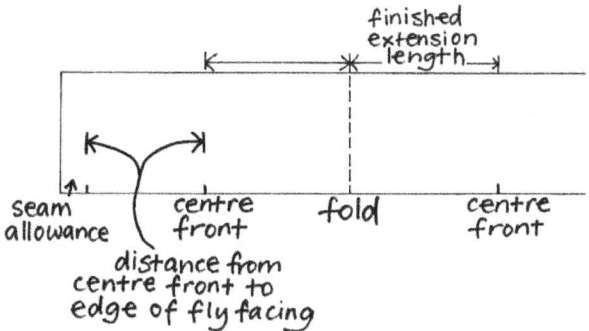

You don't have to make a pattern for the extension if you're not a patternmaking type person. Just leave lots of excess waistband at the end and trim it to size later. Leave at least 15cm (6"), or three times the extension, if you want to do it this way.

To sew the extension

1. Sew the fabric waistband onto the top of the trousers as usual, right sides together, leaving the longer extension hanging over the end of the fly front.

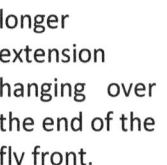
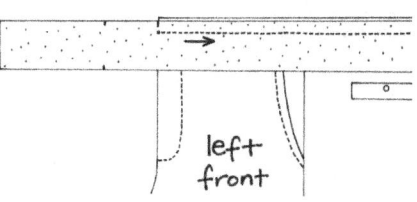

2. Stitch on the interfacing, again as usual. Take the interfacing up to the end of the *finished* extension. Press the waistband up and over the interfacing.

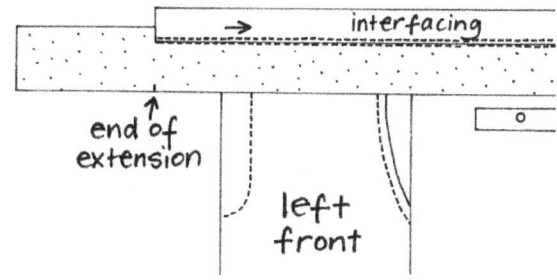

3. Fold the extension back on itself, right sides together, and stitch across the top.

Important: this seam will form the finished top edge of the waistband, so measure it up from the lower edge so it's the perfect width. The seam allowance you take will be the top edge seam allowance plus 6mm (¼").

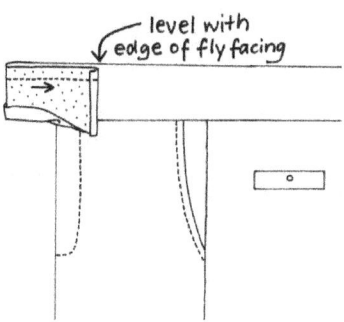

Trim off any excess length and fold back a seam allowance to bring the extension level with the edge of the fly facing inside the trousers.

4. Sew the prepared cotton lining on along the top edge, overlapping it a little onto the extension.

Note that the seam allowance will land 6mm (¼") higher than the extension seam, because the lining will be stepped down from the top edge.

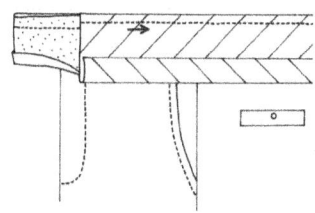

5. Turn everything through to the right way and press in place. Edgestitch the extension vertically to the lining. Press up the seam allowance on the lower edge of the extension. Insert the clamp hook and eyes if you're using them (see page 397).

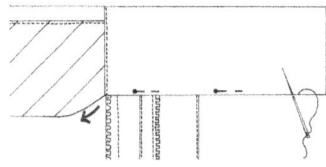

Hand sew the lower edge of the extension closed, tucking the lining in, before securing the waistband by stitching-in-the-ditch on the right side, as usual.

You could machine edgestitch the extension closed if you're edgestitching around the edge of the waistband, instead of stitching-in-the-ditch.

Using ready-made waistbanding

Ready-made men's waistbanding consists of a bias-cut cotton strip encasing a piece of firm bias-cut interfacing. It has two long folded edges: the top has a small fold-under and the lower edge has a deeper fold-under. Sometimes the waistbanding is made fancier with a line of flat piping enlivening the cotton strip and some have a rubberized insert to grip shirt tails to prevent them from becoming untucked.

The waistbanding is about 5cm (2") wide and when attached to the trousers, about 2cm (¾") of this hangs below the stitching-in-the-ditch line on the lower edge of the waistband.

In these instructions, the ready-made waistbanding is stitched (and will sit) 6mm (¼") below the top folded edge of the waistband.

Make a pattern

1. Follow the instructions for making the **left and right waistband** pieces on page 393.

2. Decide how you want to **interface** the fabric waistband, since there's already interfacing in the waistbanding. Either interface the fabric all over with a light to medium fusing, or use a firmer fusing with the seam allowances cut off so it's the same as the finished waistband. Ready-to-wear trousers often employ the second option. Take care to iron the fusing on in exactly the right spot.

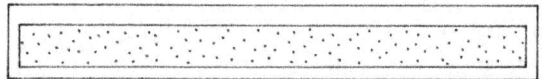

3. Cut the **ready-made waistbanding** the same length as the fabric waistband.

To sew using ready made waistbanding

1. Stitch the trouser waistband to the trousers, right sides together. Match the notches and ensure there's the correct amount of seam allowance hanging over the ends. The centre back should finish flush with no overhanging seam allowance. Do up the zip and check the waistbands are level at the front and alter it now if they aren't. Press the waistband and seam allowances *upwards*.

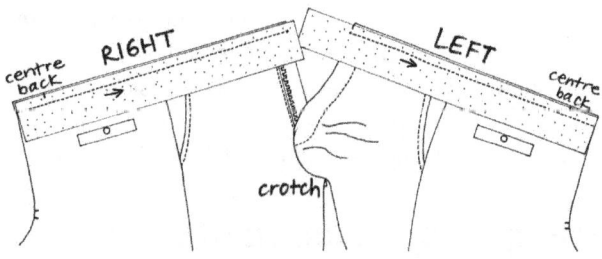

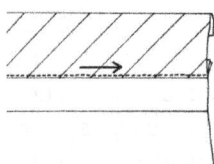

2. Lap the waistbanding over the top edge of the waistband (over the seam allowance) and edgestitch it on.

At this point the fabric waistband should measure 4.6cm (1¾") wide. It's 6mm (¼") wider than the finished measurement because the top 6mm will be innermost when the trousers are worn.

3. Fold the waistbanding to the inside to form a waistband that's 4cm (1½") wide. Press the fold along the top edge.

4. Finish the ends as described on page 394 (Step 4) and continue following the instructions to finish the waistband.

Self-made waistbanding

If you're unable to buy ready-made waistbanding, here's how to make it yourself.

You'll need:

✂ A strip of thick, woven or non-woven, non-fusible interfacing, cut 5cm (2") wide on the straight grain.

✂ A strip of 2cm (¾") wide fusible web tape, preferably the type with paper on one side because you can position it then remove the paper. If you can't get any tape, cut strips of Vlisofix (fusible web with paper, by the metre, from quilting shops).

✂ Cotton fabric for the lining, a strip cut at 11cm (4¼") wide on the bias. Cotton shirting ideal to use, as is quilting cotton or left over cotton pocket lining.

1. Lay the lining wrong side up on the ironing board. Place the interfacing in the centre of the lining, and the fusible web in the centre of the interfacing. Bond the fusible web into position and peel the paper off.

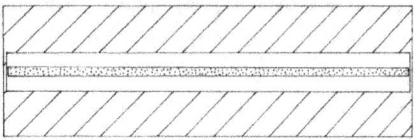

2. Fold each side of the lining up one at a time, so they overlap by 6mm (¼") in the centre. Both sides of the lining should get stuck to the fusible web, holding the raw edges in place.

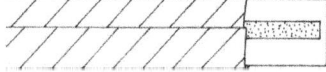

Treat the waistbanding gently until you've sewn it on.

Either long edge can be stitched to the top edge of the waistband.

Men's waistband fastenings

Buttons, hooks or a combination of both are used to fasten men's waistbands. Extended waistbands have two fastenings.

Buttons and buttonholes

If the trousers are part of a suit, make the buttonholes on the trousers match the jacket's, for example keyhole buttonholes.

Waistbands

The inside button on an extended waistband should be a flat, plain button.

Hooks and eyes

Hooks close securely and give a very clean finish to a waistband. They're never used on jeans or very casual trousers.

The hooks and eyes may need extra support—if so, add an extra layer of interfacing inside the waistband. Position one hook above the zip in the centre of the band. Position the second hook close to the edge of the extension. If it isn't close enough to the edge, the end of the extension will flap up and not lie flat.

Sew-on hooks and eyes can be attached after the waistband is completed. I like to put the hook side on first, then match the eye to it (see page 152).

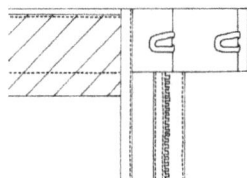

A very neat way to attach them is to arrange seams in the extension and push the hooks through the tiny gaps in the seam, sewing them on in the inside.

Clamp-on "claw" type hooks are most commonly seen on ready-to-wear trousers. They need to be installed during the construction of the waistband because you won't be able to when it's finished.

There are four parts to a clamp-on hook: two for the eye, and two for the hook. Sometimes they come in five part sets, with three parts for the hook. The outer part of each hook and eye has prongs. You'll need some needle nose pliers to bend the prongs into place.

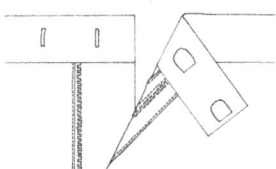

The hooks go on the overlap (left) side of the waistband and the eyes go on the underlap (right/fly shield side).

If you've never used clamp on hooks and eyes, make a sample to try them out then keep it with the hooks and eyes for future reference. Make sure you understand how the pieces fit together and which direction they go in. I like to put the hook side on first, then match the eye to it.

The waistband needs to have the lower edge open to install the hook. If you're putting a hook on an extension, keep the lower edge unstitched and hand sew it afterwards. Alternatively, some people choose to have a buttonhole at the end of the extension and a hook above the zip. That way, you can still get in to install a hook above the zip.

Do not attempt to install the hook set on a finished extension—you'll need to do it *before* the extension and waistband are finished, so you have access.

To attach the hooks: on the waistband extension, push the prongs through the inner fabric and interfacing, but not the outer waistband fabric. Make sure it faces the right way. Position the inside hook between the prongs, with the depression facing up (the folded-down prongs will sit in the depression), and use pliers to fold the prongs down over the inside hook.

To attach the eyes: do up the trouser zip and lay the hook side of the waistband over the other side, to get the placement of the eyes. Mark the point with a pencil, chalk or pin. The eyes are installed in the same way as the hook. Push the prongs through the fabric and interfacing, but not through the inside waistband fabric. Thread the holes in the backing plate over the prongs; once again the prongs will sit in the depression when folded down. Push down the prongs with pliers.

The challenge of an adjustable waistband

This chapter has seen some ways of adjusting the size of a waistband—elastic waists, partially elastic waists, and buttonhole elastic. But what if you don't want to use elastic? You may want the look of a smooth-fitting, traditional waistband with no elastic gathers.

A waistband can have adjustments to be made instantly by the wearer, for example button tabs. Other adjustments can be made by sewing, for example moving buttons or letting out the centre back seam.

Note that there's a limit to the amount you can adjust the waist of a pair of trousers—probably no more than one size (5cm or 2") at most.

Here's a gallery of some ideas:

✂ **Side tabs** are a simple thing to retrofit onto finished trousers.

You could add a button tab and a couple of buttons to bring in the sides. My husband's footy shorts have these (unbuttoned, the tabs stick out like ears). If there's a side seam in the waist you could

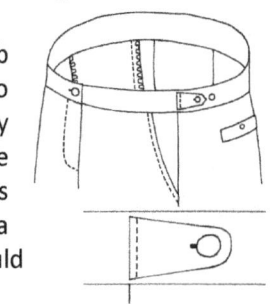

insert it into the seam; otherwise sew it on top of the waistband.

A buckle could be used instead of buttons, like a kilt.

How about a button and loop, or even Velcro? Will it be covered by a belt? If so, try and keep it as smooth and flat as you can.

✂ **Side tabs** can also be incorporated into the waistband's design. Add a channel to the back of the waistband and thread through wide elastic with fabric tabs at each end. Button the tabs to the waistband where they emerge from the channel.

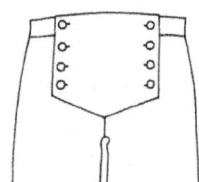

✂ This **parallel buttons** idea was sketched from a city statue, so I have no idea what the inside would look like, but I once made a pair of men's trousers with this style of opening. I put working buttonholes on both sides, not just one.

I made the inside like this:
The buttons could be moved towards the sides to make the trousers smaller.

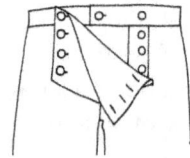

It might be more secure to make a full waistband underneath like this, but then the waistband would also need means for central adjustment.

Another take on this idea would be to have front leg seams finishing in plackets at the top with buttons and buttonholes.

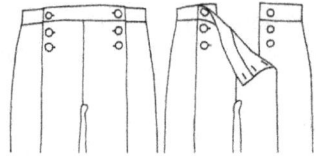

✂ Here's another idea whereby the waistband is **adjusted at the pockets**.

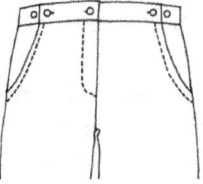

When the buttons are undone, the inside reveals a gap in the pocket bag.

You could make this the actual opening for the trousers, or merely as an option for adjustment should it be needed.

Instead of buttons, you could use hooks, Velcro, or if the waistband will be covered by a belt, a length of elastic from pocket to side seam.

Any pattern with cutaway pockets can be adapted to this style, but you'll need to make a new waistband pattern because the waistband will now be in four parts.

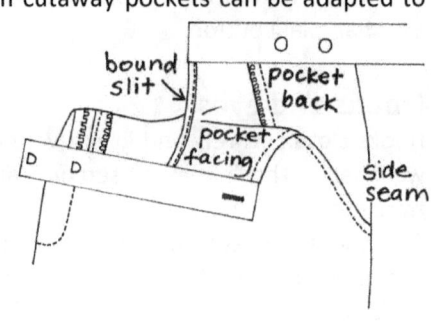

You can simply leave a gap in the pocket bags seam as shown. Overlock each side separately, then make a small hem each side of the opening.

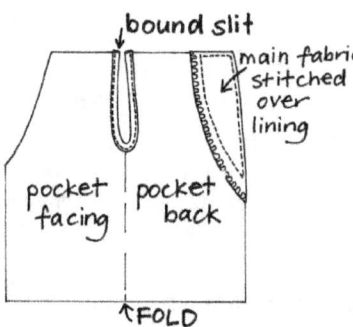

Another way is to make the pocket facing and pocket back one unit, with a bound slit on the fold line.

Concealed expandable waistband

This waistband expands with cleverly concealed elastic at each side, but looks just like a regular waistband. You can adapt an existing waistband and trouser pattern (page 393)—the style needs to have belt loops and cutaway pockets at the sides.

Before attempting this, become familiar with sewing a regular men's waistband—these instructions skip over the usual things such as finishing the ends etc.

Make a pattern

1. This type of expanding waistband has no centre back seam in the waistband like men's trousers usually do. The **back waistband** is separate to the front and is cut in one piece.

Draw in the side seam positions and add 2cm (¾") onto each side seam. These will be folded back.

Notch the beltloop positions on the waistband. If the trousers have back darts, arrange the position so the beltloops will sit over the darts.

The back waistband will look like this:

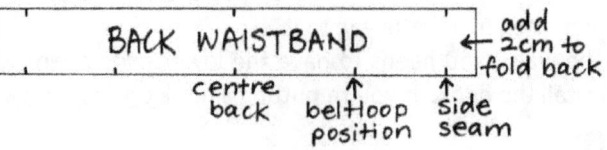

Waistbands 399

✂ This a fairly complicated construction, even if you're used to making men's waistbands. Before you start sewing, here's a sketch of the finished waistband. You may have a pair of trousers like these at home which you could look at, too.

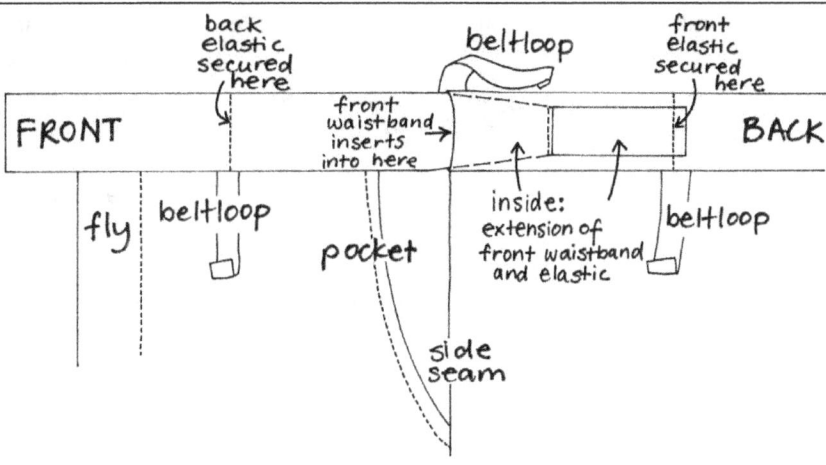

2. On the **left and right front waistbands**, mark the side seam positions with a notch and add 5cm (2") onto each side.
It will also be helpful to mark the distance from the cutaway pocket to the side seams with a notch.
As with the back, notch the beltloop positions.

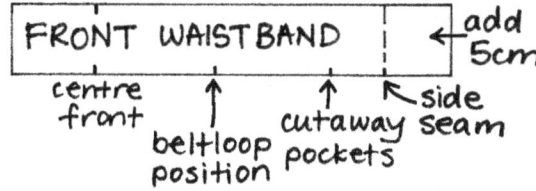

3. Adapt the **pocket** back and pocket facing by joining them together along the stitching line to make one pattern piece. Mark the fold line with a notch at the top. Cut a 6.5cm (2½") slit from the top edge, in approximately the position shown in the sketch.

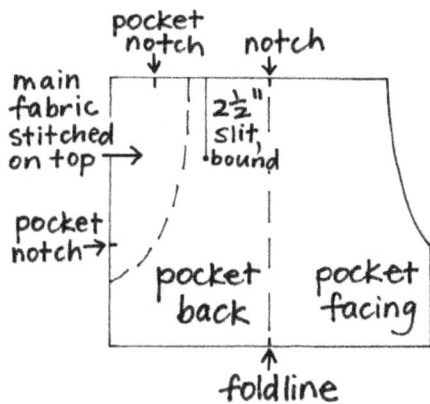

4. **Interfacing and lining.** This method requires ready-made waistbanding, where the interfacing and lining are one unit. Don't cut it to length yet. If you can't find any to buy you'll have to make some—see the instructions on page 396.
Cut some fusible interfacing the *finished* width of the waistband. Position it carefully before fusing so it sits inside the seam allowances.

5. You'll need some 2.5cm (1") wide **elastic**.

To sew an expandable waistband

1. Prepare the pocket bags by stitching the fabric on top of the pocket back.

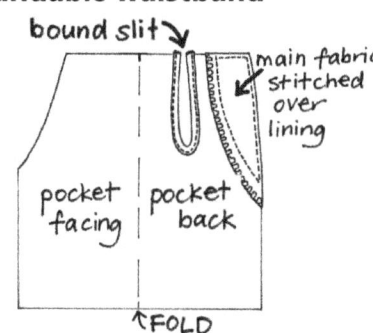

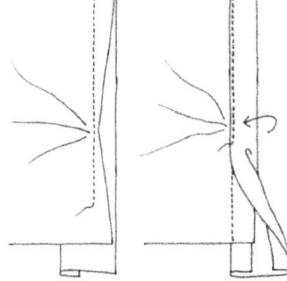

Bind the slit using a bias strip of pocket lining 3cm (1¼") wide. It's done exactly like a continuous bound placket for a shirt cuff on page 302.

2. Make the cutaway pockets in the usual way (see pages 241-244), but don't baste down the top edge.

3. Sew the side seams.

4. Overlock the top edge of the pocket back.

5. Make the beltloops (page 6) so they're ready to sew on.

6. Position the beltloops on the front and sew the front waistbands on. Sew from the centre front to the edge of the cutaway pocket. Leave the pocket back free (that's the section from the side seam to the bound slit). The rest of the pocket bag, including the other side of the bound slit needs to be stitched to the

front waistband. Press the waistband up, away from the trousers.

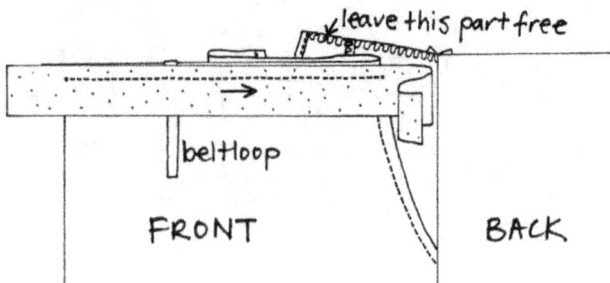

7. Sew the waistband lining to the top edge of the front waistband. Mark and sew a buttonhole in the waistband lining level with the binding on the bound slit. Make the buttonhole a generous 2.5cm (1") long, or big enough for the 2.5cm wide elastic to pass through. It's better to make the buttonhole bigger rather than smaller, otherwise the elastic will get stuck retracting. Begin the buttonhole next to the line of stitching you've just done.

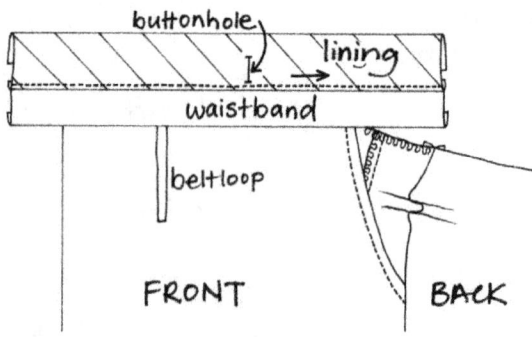

8. Measure a piece of 2.5cm (1") wide elastic—cut it about the length from the side seam to the side back beltloop. Put it aside for the moment. Bag out the front waistband at the side seam by folding down the lining over the fabric waistband (remember the lining will sit 6mm (¼") *below* the top folded edge, so don't fold it along the lining seam line). Here it will be easier if you've fused interfacing onto the waistband that's the finished width of the waistband. Sew the waistband from the pocket edge to the side seam point along the stitching line. Then, taper the waistband to the raw edge, leaving an opening of a generous 2.5cm (1") (put pins in the end to mark your goal of 2.5cm). Trim off the sides.

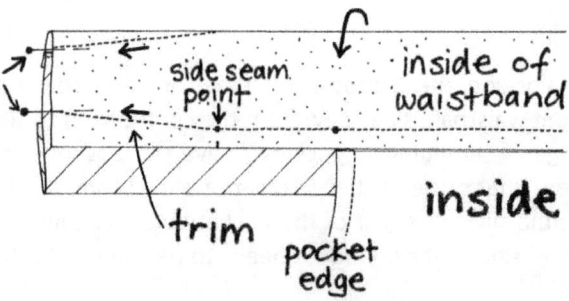

9. Turn the bagged out section to the right side after trimming. Give this area a good press now. Insert the end of the piece of elastic into the gap at the end, and stitch across to secure. It doesn't matter that the end is still raw—it will be well concealed inside the waistband. Mark the side seam position with a pin.

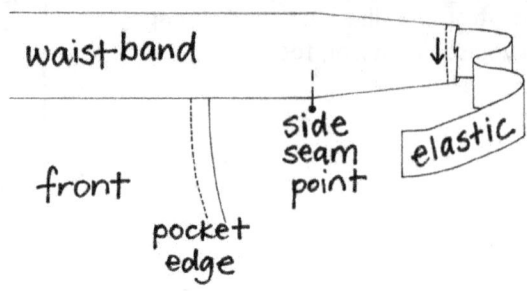

10. Time to stitch-in-the-ditch the front lining down, but before you do, cut another piece of 2.5cm (1") wide elastic for the front. It needs to reach from the front beltloop to the buttonhole you made in the lining with a bit extra at each end to stitch it in. Fold down the waistband lining into position *and at the same time* encase the piece of elastic into it. Sit the elastic about 3mm (⅛") from the top of the lining seam. Stitch the elastic vertically at the beltloop, through all layers, stitching on the right side so you can see where to stitch in relation to the beltloop. Slip the other end of the elastic out through the buttonhole and leave it hanging there for now. Finish this part of the waistband off by finishing the ends at the fly front and stitching-in-the-ditch from the right side, as you normally would when making a waistband. When you reach the pocket edge where you bagged out the waistband, and the lining is tucked up inside, angle the lining as shown.

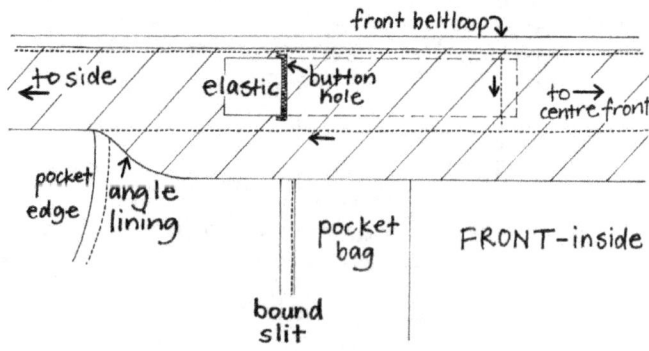

11. The front is finished; now onto the back. Sew on the beltloops and the back waistband. At the side seams, fold back the edges 2cm (¾") so the waistband is in line with the side seam of the trousers.

Waistbands 401

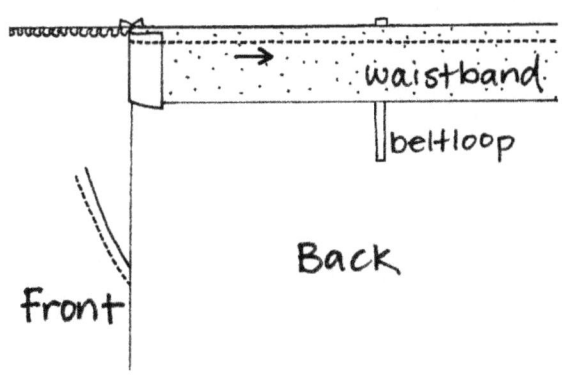

12. Position a beltloop at the *top* edge of the waistband over the side seam. Sew the waistband lining to the back waistband, leaving a length at each end a good 2.5cm (1") past the bound slit. Edgestitch the lining on the free-hanging piece so it matches the rest of the lining. Fold the lining to the inside, allowing it to sit 6mm (¼") down from the top fold, yielding a 4cm (1½)" wide waistband.

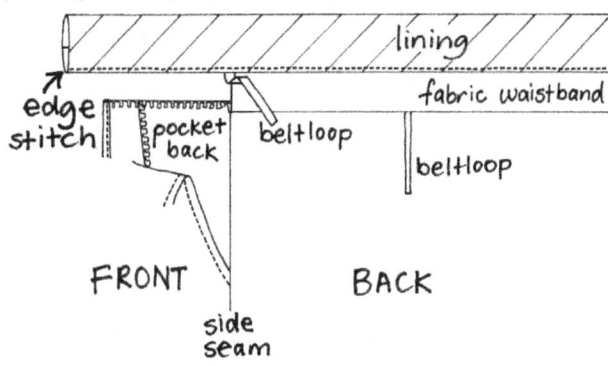

13. Lay the waistband out flat. Place the front elastic that you sewed on in Step 9 under the back waistband and pin it at the back beltloop. Sit the elastic about 3mm (⅛") down from the top of the finished waistband. Cut off any excess elastic. Check the waistband length with a tape measure, and also check the front-pocket-to-side-seam measurement. Stitch the elastic on through the outer fabric waistband only (not the lining), so the stitching will be covered when the beltloop is in position.

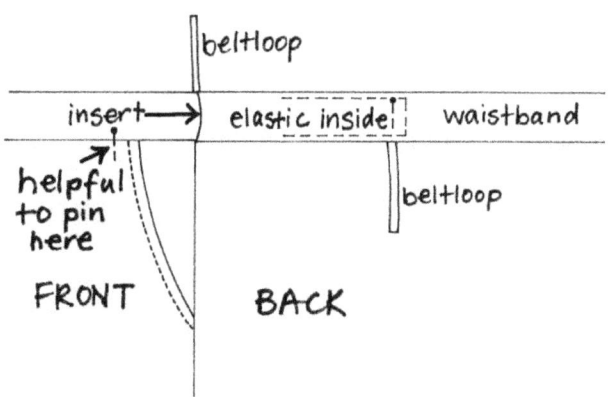

14. Fold the back waistband lining down into position. On the right side, stitch-in-the-ditch to secure the back waistband, as you normally would for a men's waistband. Stitch from side seam to side seam across the back.

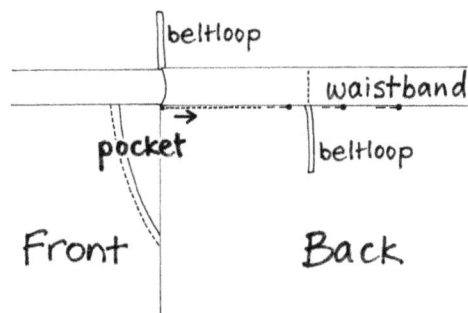

15. Turn the waistband over to sew the last part of the lining down. Lay the end of the waistband lining over the remaining section (the pocket back) and pin (this part was overlocked earlier). Fold the end of the lining under so it goes around the bound edge. Lay this over the end of the elastic that's poking out of the buttonhole, and pin together. Sew the elastic onto the folded edge. Sew the end of the waistband lining onto the top of the back pocket.

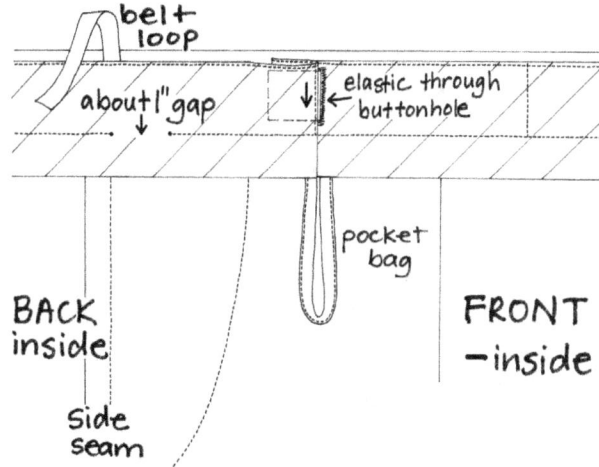

It helps to pull the elastic out once it's pinned so you have room to stitch it.

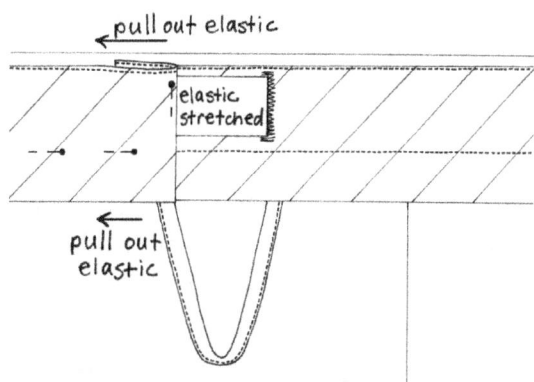

16. On the right side, stitch down the beltloops—they'll conceal the elastic stitching lines and the waistband joins in the side seams. Whew!

Zips

Types of zips 402	Further notes on regular zips 411
Parts of a zip and how it works 403	sewing a zip in by hand 411
Jammed and sticky zips 403	finishing off the top 411
Zip by the metre 403	attaching lining 414
Preparing to apply a zip 403	zips in pleats 415
Invisible zips 403	zips in stretch knits 416
invisible zip foot 404	Exposed zips 416
To sew an invisible zip 404	in woven fabric 417
Troubleshooting invisible zips 405	feature zips 418
Further notes on invisible zips 406	Fly fronts 419
industry application 406	Troubleshooting fly fronts 422
shortening 406	Further notes on fly fronts 423
the top of the zip 406	button fly front 423
supporting the top 407	concealed button fly front 423
matching a junction 407	fly front with faced top edge 424
through a waistband 407	fly front with cut-on shield 424
side zip in a dress 408	2pce fly shield with crotch binding 425
open-ended 408	mock fly front 426
Regular (dress) zips 408	Open-ended zips 427
length and shortening 408	exposed open-ended zip 428
preparing the garment 408	centred open-ended zip 429
To sew a lapped zip 409	concealed open-ended zip 430
side zip in a dress 410	Zips in fur fabric 431
To sew a centred zip 410	
Troubleshooting regular zips 411	

I'm sure that repetitive, old-fashioned practise is the key to producing a perfect zip every time, but it also helps to know the process and use a familiar machine with a good zipper foot.

When I was a fashion student we were trained to sew in a zip without using any pins, because that's how it's done in factories. We were issued with one zip and two strips of fabric and shut in a classroom for an entire (frustrating!) day with our patient teacher. We we finally got the hang of it and mastered fast unpicking at the same time!

Types of zips

There are three basic types of zipper: regular/dress zips, invisible and open-ended.

Regular zips are sold as "dress" zips. They're closed at one end. The teeth may be metal or plastic. Metal zips are stronger and more durable than plastic, but plastic ones are still pretty strong.

Invisible zips have a plastic coil that rolls inwards and disappears into the seam that it's sewn into. All you see is the tiny pull tab and no visible stitching on the outside of the garment. They're closed at one end like regular zips.

Open-ended zips are also called separating zips. They're heavier than regular zips. They open at both ends and are sewn into seams that will open completely.

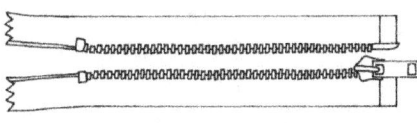

Parts of a zip and how a zip works

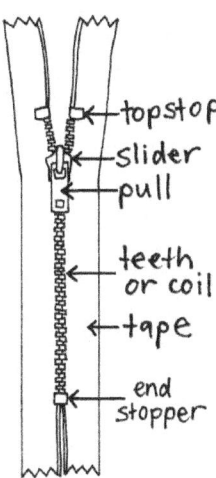

A zip consists of interlocking teeth or coils attached to tape and is operated by a slider. The coils or teeth "hook" together within the slider as it moves along the rows of teeth. Inside the slider is a curved Y-shaped channel that meshes together or spreads apart opposing rows of teeth, depending on the direction the zip is pulled.

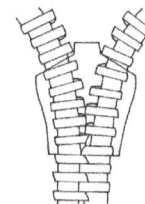

✂ Some zips have two sliders, to open or close the zip from either end.

✂ Self-locking zips have sliders that lock themselves into place wherever they are along teeth or coils, stopping the zip from pulling open. Zips for clothes are self-locking. Zips that aren't self-locking might be used for tents or soldier's sleeping bags, so they can be pulled open quickly.

Jammed and sticky zips

✂ Has the zip got hair or thread in it? Remove with tweezers. Cut your sewing threads as you go to avoid getting them jammed in the zip.

✂ Sticky zip? Apply vinegar to clean it and work the zip up and down. Lubricate the zip with one of these: tip of a graphite pencil, bar soap, petroleum jelly, olive oil on a cotton bud, baby powder, window cleaner such as Windex, wax (candle, paraffin or a crayon) then a hot hair dryer to melt the wax.

✂ Be patient when un-jamming zips—sometimes they un-jam and sometimes they don't. Hold the zipper tape straight and tight, and firmly but gently try to shift the slider.

✂ Do up the zip when you launder the garment.

✂ Don't recycle old zips into new garments—use a fresh, new zip. It isn't necessary to pre-wash zips.

Zip by the metre

You can buy continuous zip by the metre—you're usually allocated one zip slide per metre. It's often used for making things other than clothes, such as bags, tents, caravan awnings, swags and covers.

Which way the zip does up or undoes depends on which end you put the slide on. You can take a slide off and put it on the opposite end if you want the zip to close from each end with the slides meeting in the middle.

To put a slide onto the tape, first examine closely the cut end of the zipper tape and note which side has the higher tooth. If the tape is already separated, just choose one side.

Pull apart the teeth and insert each side into the slide. Wiggle them through and make sure that when they emerge the higher tooth is on the correct side.

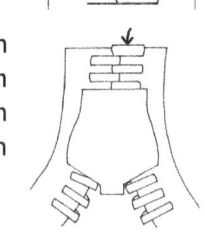

Preparing to apply a zip

✂ Zips are always inserted into open seams. That is, the seam allowance is pressed open, not to one side. The seam allowances need to be overlocked separately *before* the zip is inserted, because there won't be a chance to overlock afterwards. If the fabric is stretchy, unstable, loosely woven or cut on a curve, for example a curved side seam, stabilize the edges (before overlocking) with a strip of iron-on interfacing.

✂ Is it better to put a zip in a centre front or back seam, rather than a side seam? I'm not a great fan of side seam zippers—it's a lot of unpicking if you need to alter the garment and it's hard to get them sitting flat due to the curved edge. However, sometimes it interrupts the design to have a centre back seam, so a side seam is the only place to insert the zip. If the side seam is curved, consider stabilizing the edges (before overlocking) with a strip of iron-on interfacing.

Invisible zips

My husband finds the name "invisible" hilarious: *Invisible?* he laughs, *But I can still see it!!!*
Not everyone likes invisible zips but they're my favourite because they look, well, invisible. I rarely

use regular zips any more because I prefer invisible ones.

✂ An invisible zip can be almost one of the last things sewn on a garment. Apply it before the waistband, waist facing or neck facing.

✂ Sew the zip in *before* you sew the rest of the seam it's inserted into OR leave a generous gap in the seam to insert the zip. The seam allowance can be as small as 1cm (⅜").

✂ Because invisible zips can only be sewn in *un*zipped, you'll never use the last 2.5cm (1") of length on the zip because the slider is in the way. Therefore, buy a zip 2.5cm-5cm (1"-2") longer than the opening. I favour a 25cm (10") zip for skirts and trousers because it helps stop strain on the end of the zip.

✂ Invisible zips are mostly used on dresses or skirts. They are not used on fly fronts.

Invisible zip foot

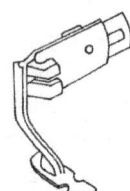

✂ It *is* possible to sew an invisible zip in using a conventional zipper foot—I do on my machine at home. I use a universal zipper foot with a screw that adjusts the left and right position of the foot.

✂ Avoid conventional zipper feet that are wide at the back—the foot won't clear the stitching and you won't be able to sew closely enough to the zip (unless you can move the needle position).

✂ However, most people find that a proper, machine-brand, invisible zip foot makes the job so much easier. They never come standard with your machine—you have to buy them as an accessory from your dealer. The foot has grooves on the sole to help hold the zipper coil open as you sew it.

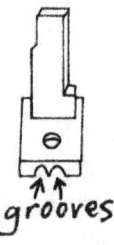

grooves

✂ A much cheaper alternative is a plastic invisible zip foot that fits some machines, or a plastic roller foot that has attachments to fit any machine. Some people use these very satisfactorily.
See what works best for you.

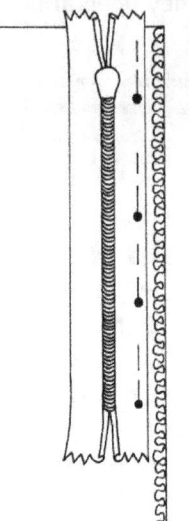

To sew an invisible zip

1. Do up the zip. The right side of the zip has a narrow groove and the zip pull. The wrong side has the coil. Position the zip onto the edge of the garment, right sides together, and pin it in place. Leave the correct seam allowance at the top. The zip tape is 1cm (⅜") wide each side. If you have a 1.5cm (⅝") seam allowance, pin the zip 5mm (scant ¼") away from the edge—you can line up the edge of the tape with the edge of the overlocking. If you have a 1cm (⅜") seam allowance, you can conveniently match the edges of the tape and fabric.

Repeat for the second side, noting that the garment will be now be inside out. Make sure the second side lines up with the first—at the top and bottom of the zip, and the bottom of the garment.

2. Using your ordinary machine foot, tack the zip in place along the edge using a long stitch for the entire length of the tape. I skip this step (I just use pins), but you'll find it easier to do for your first few zips. It's also easier if you have an inconsistent seam allowance (perhaps from alterations). Remember to turn the stitch length back.

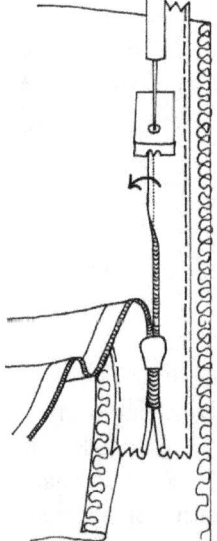

3. Change your machine to the invisible zipper foot. Undo the zip and roll back the coil of the zip with your fingertips.
Position the beginning of the zip under the foot, and plunge the needle *into* the groove, so you're starting off in the right place. Sometimes the top of the zip is curled over and glued, but you can peel it back. On one side, stitch in the groove as far as you can (until you've reached the top of the zip slide) and backstitch securely.

Even if you have a proper invisible zip foot, you'll still have to guide the machine to stitch in the right place. A proper foot will just make it easier.
Some people like to iron the groove of the zip flat with *cool* iron beforehand, to make it easier holding the groove flat.

4. Do up the zip and mark the *exact* point where the first side is stitched to, using a dot of pencil on the tape. Put a dot on the other side to match.
Use a white pencil for dark coloured zips and regular pencil for everything else.

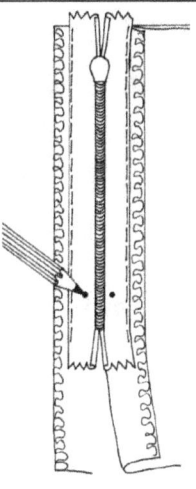

Undo the zip and sew the second side. Make sure both sides are stitched *exactly* to the same point and backstitched securely at the ends. Ensure the tops and bottoms are even. Owing to the length of the zipper foot (it might not fit between the bottom point and the slide), you might have to sew both sides of the zip from the top down.

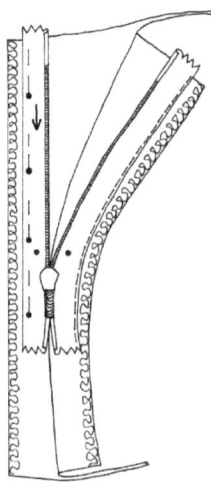

5. Sew the seam below the zip: do up the zip and match the right sides together. Taking a pin, place it through the very last stitch on each side, keeping the actual zip free. You can pin the ends of the zip tape together to keep them out of the way if needed. Change to an ordinary zipper foot.

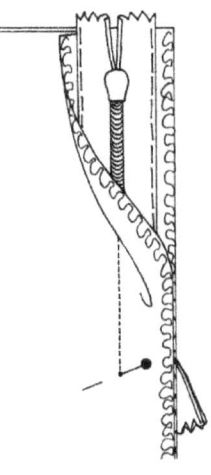

I find the best type of zipper foot for this is the universal adjustable type. Set it so the needle is *just* alongside the foot—not in the semi circular cut-out.
Begin sewing by plunging the machine's needle through where you put the pin. Whip out the pin, put the machine's foot down and sew the seam, backstitching at the beginning and taking the correct

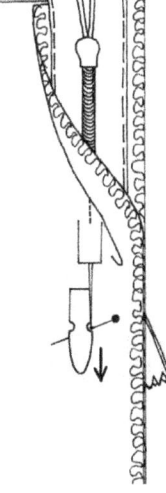

seam allowance. I sew a little of the seam with the zipper foot, but find it's easier to change back to the regular foot for the whole seam.

This can be a difficult area to get right, because there needs to be a smooth, unnoticeable transition from zip to seam. Some people like to sew the seam *up* to the bottom of the zip, but I maintain it's more reliable to begin in the exact spot where the zip ends and stitch *down*—that way you can be sure the layers won't move just below the zip.

If you have trouble backstitching here, just leave long ends to knot off later. You can make this part stronger by threading them onto a needle and backstitching by hand first, before finishing off.

Troubleshooting invisible zips

Not stitching close enough to the groove.

If you close up the zip, you shouldn't be able to see it. If you do, the remedy is easy—just sew another line of stitching closer to the zipper teeth. Starting off with the needle already *in* the groove will help you stay in the groove.

Stitching too close to the coil and catching it in the stitching.

You'll easily know if you've done this because you won't be able to do up the zip. You only need one stitch to be on the coil for the zip to jam. Unpick the offending section and re-sew.

Bottom of zip doesn't lie flat
Possible causes:

✂ One side stretched as you stitched the zip in and now the seam below the zip is longer on one side than the other. Inspect the zip, and if it appears to be sitting flat, undo the seam below the zip and let it hang where it wants to. Re-sew the seam. If the zip isn't sitting flat you've no choice but to undo the stretched side/s. Restore the stretched fabric with a steam iron and re-sew the zip, possibly with a strip of light fusing ironed onto the seam first so it won't stretch again.

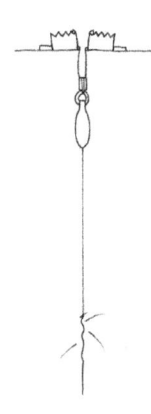

✂ You left different allowances each side at the top of the zip. To remedy, undo one side of the zip and re-sew, with the correct seam allowance at the top.

✂ The area below the zip was sewn incorrectly. A smooth transition is required between zip and seam so you can't tell where one stops and the other starts.

If you continue to have problems with this area, there's no shame in sewing it by hand. Sew the seam (by machine) below the zip up to a few centimetres short of the bottom of the zip, give it a press, then finish off by hand. Use a double strand of thread and sew it from the right side so you can see how it looks.

Further notes on invisible zips
Industry application
In some factories, the invisible zip is sewn in *after* the seam below it is sewn.

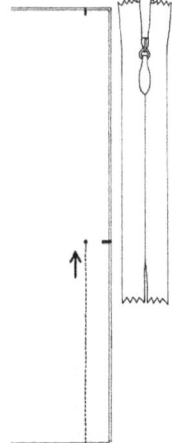

The seam is sewn to a point level with a notch and backstitched securely. The zip is sewn with each side being stitched *exactly* to the point where the seam begins.

The trouble is, the zip slide ends up on the wrong side of the garment, and has to be wiggled through. It *is* possible though and I think it's a quicker method because the machinist doesn't have to change the machine foot back and forth (it's changed with a screwdriver on industrial machines).

If there's a lining, sometimes the zip is sewn to the main and lining at the same time. The seam below the zip in each is sewn and pressed open first, giving identical length gaps for the zip. The seams are snipped to the stitching, then the lining and main are placed wrong sides together. The edges are tacked together with a long stitch and the zip is inserted into both layers together.

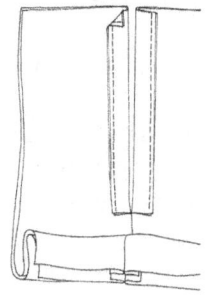

Shortening an invisible zip
If the zip is only a little bit too long, I just leave the excess hanging in the garment and only sew the length I need.

Otherwise, sew two parallel lines about 1cm (⅜") apart backwards and forwards a few times across the zipper tape 3cm (1¼") below your desired length. A regular domestic machine should be able to stitch across OK. Cut the excess zipper off below the stitching.

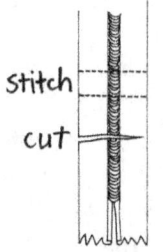

If the zip is going into a lined garment, I leave it like this, but on unlined clothes and trousers, I sew a strip of bias binding across the cut edge to stop the coil scratching on skin.

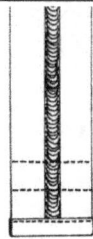

Alternatively, use a piece of the discarded tape. Trim off the coil, fold it in half longways and use it as a binding.

What to do with the top of the zip
If your garment has a **waistband**, you have no worries—simply apply the waistband as normal.

If the top is finished with a **facing** (either a waist or neck facing), and you want your garment to look horribly home-made, hand sew each side to the zip tape.

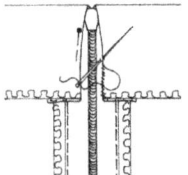

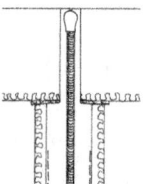

However, there's an easy machine-sewn way to finish the top:

1. Sew the invisible zip in first. Prepare the facing (fuse and overlock—see page 99) and accurately pin it into position to sew.

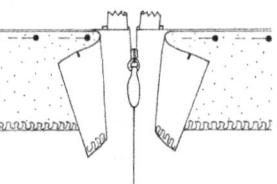

2. Unpick any tacking around the top of the zipper tape. Cut off the seam allowance at the ends of the facing. Lay the zipper *tape* on the facing and step the edge 5mm back from the freshly cut edge. Note that the garment will be longer than the facing at the moment. Sew a line of stitching through the middle of the zipper tape, using a regular zipper foot. Have the tape on top and the facing underneath, so you can see where to stitch.

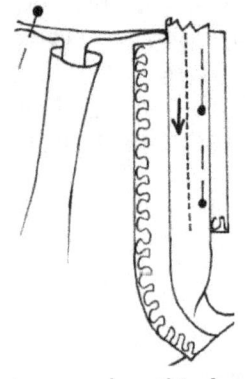

I remember this formula by thinking "half and half": half a centimetre over, stitching through half the zip tape.

3. Push the seam towards the facing. Fold vertically along the *coil* of the zip, wrapping the garment around the facing. The seams should lie on the facing. Don't catch the facing in as you fold.

Stitch the facing to the garment at the top edge, through all layers.

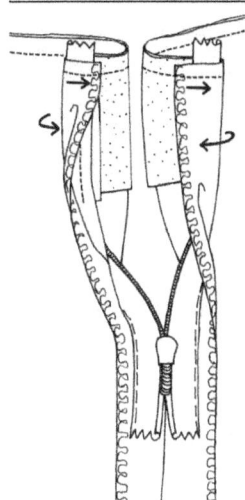

Diagonally trim the corner a little then turn the corner to the right side.

If one side of the zip is a little higher than the other, there's no need to unpick—just sew another line of stitching lower to make them the same.

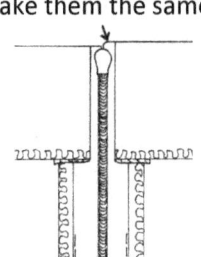

If the garment has a **lining** as well as or instead of a facing, stitch the lining to the entire length of the zip tape, tapering to nothing at the bottom.

Supporting the top of the zip

✂ To support the top of the zip with a **hook and eye**, simply sew the zip in 1cm (⅜") lower, so you have space to sew it. I don't put a hook on garments for myself—I prefer the clean look of the zip flowing all the way to the top. However, they're a good idea for strapless bodices and other tight-fitting clothes, or if you think people might be rough and careless when doing up the zip. Doing up the hook first help keeps the zip straight when it's being zipped up.

✂ Some garments have a **tab** with a button and buttonhole hidden inside at the top of the zip. Make the tab at least 1.2cm (½") wide, and insert it between the facing and the zipper tape. Put a buttonhole in the tab and sew a flat button to the garment's facing.

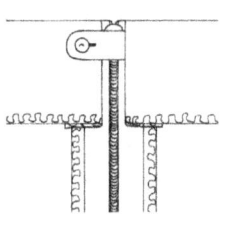

Matching a junction

If the zip has to go through a yoke or waistline seam, the sides need to be matched as you sew the zip in.
The same applies to stripes, checks and other similar patterns.
Have the seams of the junction already overlocked and pressed in the correct direction (and topstitched if desired) when you sew the zip in.

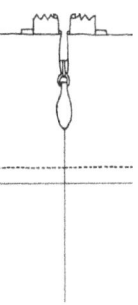

Tack and sew one side only of the zip first. Do up the zip and draw a pencil line across both sides of the zip tape at the seam junction. Match the pencil line to the junction for sewing the other side.

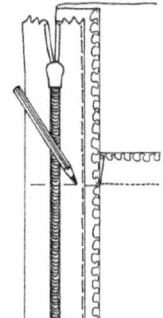

If the junction is very thick, you may need to stitch a little way away from the coil so the zip will do up easily in that spot.

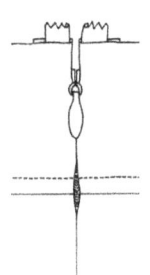

Invisible zip through a waistband

If you have a narrow waistband, for example 2.5cm (1") or narrower, you might consider stitching the zip in all the way through.
It looks very neat and saves having to sew a fastening to the waistband.

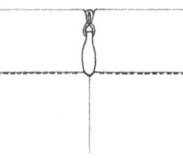

1. Interface the waistband and iron it in half lengthways, forming the crease the waistband will fold in. The short ends of the waistband should have the same seam allowance as the garment's edges.

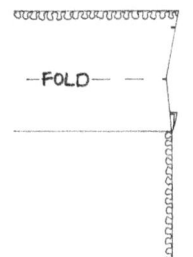

2. Sew the waistband onto the garment, right sides together. Press the seam allowance towards the waistband. Overlock the other long edge of the waistband.

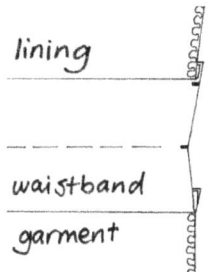

✂ If you're having a lining, attach the lining to the edge of the waistband taking 3mm (⅛") *less* seam allowance (so the lining won't get in the way when you stitch the waistband down). Overlock the seam.

3. Sew in the invisible zip in the usual way, lining up the top of the zip with the crease in the waistband.

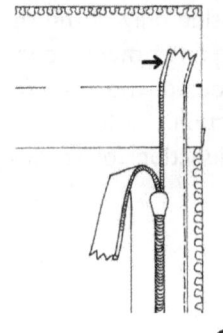

Angle the surplus zipper tape at the top towards the raw edge, as you stitch it down.
Do up the zip and check the waistband seams are level.

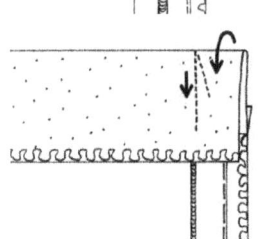

4. Fold the waistband along the crease line, right sides together, over the zip. Using a zipper foot, stitch the top of the waistband down next to the zip stitching.

If the garment is **lined**, continue stitching the lining to the zip all the way down, tapering to nothing. Repeat with the other side.
Before you trim the corner, turn it through to the right side and check the tops of the zip are level.

5. Stitch the waistband into position by stitching-in-the-ditch.

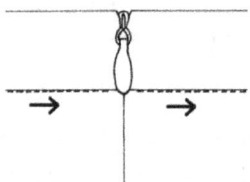

Putting a side zip in a dress

Zips in dresses go in the left side seam, with the zip pull at the top when the zip is done up. Insert the zip in the usual way, but stitch the seam below *and* above after the zip is sewn (unless it's a sleeveless dress, in which case the top of the zip will be at the underarm).

Open-ended invisible zips

Open-ended invisible zips are installed in the same way as ordinary invisible zips. The bottom stopper slides up so you can sew all the way to the bottom of the zip. When buying an open-ended invisible zip, make sure it really *is* an invisible zip—not just a light weight open-ended zip with a similar pull tab.

Regular (dress) zips

A regular zip is usually the first thing sewn on a garment, so it lies flat for you to topstitch in place. I think this zip looks best when the top of the garment is finished with a waistband or binding, rather than a facing, and I suggest using an invisible zip if you *do* have a facing. However, there are directions here for finishing the top neatly with a facing.

There are several ways to sew in a regular zip:

A **lapped application** (left) is the most common for skirts, dresses and back-opening trousers.
A **centred application** (right) is often used on furniture and cushions but is sometimes used on garments.

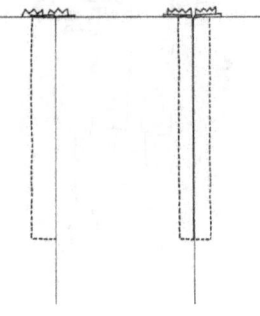

An **exposed application** (left) is used when there's no seam to insert the zip, and is sometimes the feature of a garment.
A **fly front** (right) is used on trousers.

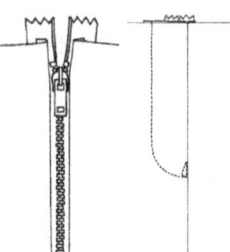

Choosing a length and shortening a zip

Try a 20cm (8") long zip for trousers or skirts. 18cm (7") is satisfactory but if you go any shorter you won't get the garment on. Back zips on dresses will need between 40cm and 55cm (16"-22"), depending on how low the back neck is.
Shortening only works on plastic zips, so choose the correct length if the zip is metal. If the plastic zip is only a little bit longer than required, for example 5cm (2"), just leave it. You can let the excess hang inside the garment. Otherwise, it depends on how the top will be finished:

✂ For a **faced** top, shorten from the bottom: sew two parallel lines backwards and forwards a few times across the zipper tape at your desired length. A regular domestic machine should be able to stitch across without problems. Cut the excess zipper off below the stitching.

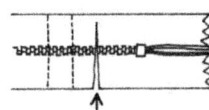

✂ If there's a **waistband** at the top, shorten from either the top or bottom. For a fly front, the zip is shortened from the top afterwards. To shorten from the top, simply leave the excess overhanging at the top and cut it off *after* stitching the waistband on (ensuring the slide is on the correct side, of course!).

Preparing the garment

If the fabric is not on the straight grain, for example a bias skirt or the centre back seam of trousers, iron a strip of fusing onto both edges. Also do this if the fabric is very light, soft, unstable (such as a knit) or loosely woven.

I don't recommend inserting a regular zip into a curved side seam—it's tricky to get a good result, but if you want to do it, iron a curved strip of fusing onto the edges to stabilize them.

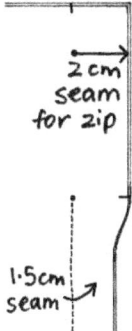

You'll need at least 1.5cm (⅝") of seam allowance to sew in a regular zip, but 2cm (¾") will make it *much* easier if you can remember to add it. Some patterns have a larger seam allowance where the zip is inserted, tapering back to a smaller seam allowance below. Others are 2cm all the way through.

To sew a lapped zip

You'll need a 2cm (¾") seam allowance to sew this zip in, but 1.5cm (⅝") will do if you're careful. With practise, this zip can be sewn without using pins.

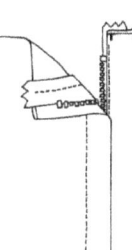

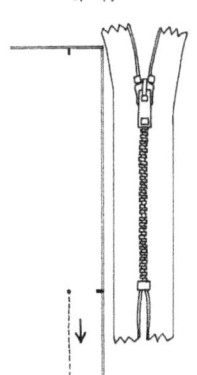

1. Overlock the edges of the garment. Mark the seam allowance at the top edges with tiny 3mm (⅛") snips.

2. Sew the seam below the zip, backstitching securely at the end (overlocking not shown here for clarity).

I always lay the zip next to the opening to ensure the seam begins *below* the end stopper.

Ideally the end stopper should be at the bottom of the opening, but if you're going to be sewing a longer (plastic) zip into a shorter opening, or you've shortened the zip by stitching across the end (and therefore have cut off the end stopper), sew the seam to give the desired length opening.

Remember to leave the correct amount of seam allowance at the top.

3. Press back the seam allowances with an iron.
On the left side, press back the full seam allowance.
On the right side, press back about 3mm (⅛") *less* than the seam allowance, so you have a small step that continues all the way down. **Important:** make sure you have a definite step at the bottom.

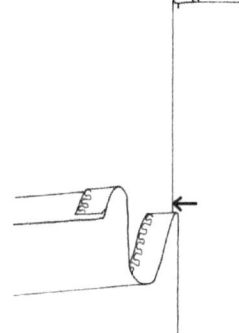

At home I iron these folds in, but in a factory the machinist scrapes the fold down the sharp edge of the table to make a crease.

4. Install the zipper foot on your machine with the needle to the left of the foot. Position the zip under the folded edge as shown and sew down the folded edge.

To avoid stretching the fabric, hold the zipper tape firmly with your left hand and let the fabric "sit easy" on top with your right hand, so you're easing the fabric onto the zip. There should be a definite step at the end of the zip so the stitching remains hidden when the second side is folded up.

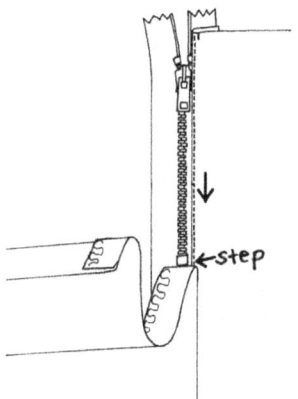

If you need to stitch past the slider, stop with the needle down, lift the presser foot and wriggle the slider past. When you reach the end, stop with the needle down in the fabric.

5. Do up the zip. With the needle down, lift the presser foot and turn the work 90 degrees so the top of the zip is to your left. Lift the needle up out of the fabric and overlap the second side of the garment onto your previous stitching. Lower the needle through the fold of the fabric and sew for about 1.2cm (½"). 1cm (⅜") won't be quite enough to clear the zip.

Don't go out too wide if you only have a 1.5cm (⅝") seam allowance. Make sure you don't hit the end stopper—sew above or below it (ideally below).

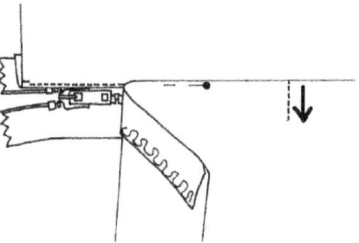

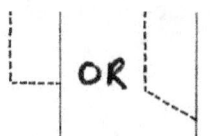

The stitching is usually sewn at 90 degrees to the seam, but sometimes it's angled, providing it clears the end stopper.

6. With the needle in the fabric, turn the work 90 degrees again so the top of the zip is closest to you. The fold of the second side should just cover your first line of stitching. Sew to about 4cm (1½") shy of the top, taking care not to stretch the fabric. The top of the zip should be level when the zip is done up, with the correct seam allowance along the top.

This second side can creep up as you stitch along and end up longer than the first side. As you sew, position your hands either side of the presser foot and try to push the top layer backwards. Most people, including me, find it difficult to get this line of stitching straight and consistent the whole way up because there's not much to line it up with. A strip of sticky tape can be used as a seam guide. Or, if your machine has a quilting bar you could try that.

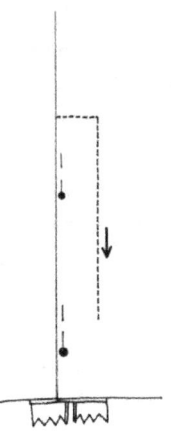

7. About 4cm (1½") before the top, undo the zip and angle the tape to the right slightly, but keep stitching in a straight line, stitching closer to the top stop. This will allow for the extra bulk of the zip pull to be hidden away. Note that you probably won't have much room, if any, to move the tape if you only have a 1.5cm (⅝") seam allowance.

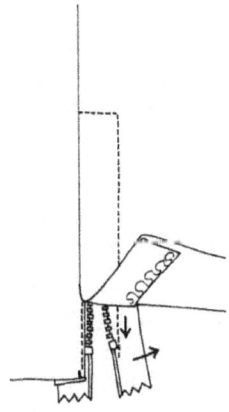

Putting a lapped side zip in a dress
Zips go in the *left* side seam of dresses, with the zip pull at the top when the zip is done up.
Actually, you don't have to use a zip in the side of a dress. You could sew a placket and do it up with press studs, vintage style. Hooks or a mini hook and bar are often sewn at the waist point.

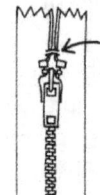

Before you sew the zip in, sew the tops of the zip tape together using a zipper foot or sew by hand. Sew the seam above and below the zip opening, securely backstitching at the ends (unless the dress is sleeveless, in which case the top of the zip will be at the underarm). Accurately press the edges of the zip opening first—it will be *much* easier to sew. If there's a zip in *both* left and right sides, for example side zip pockets, you'll need to reverse the lap for the right hand side, so you have a pair. Sew the zip in as a regular lapped zip. When you reach the top 3cm (1¼") of the zip, hold the right hand side of the zip tape and fabric together with your right hand and undo the zip with your left hand. Complete the stitching for the top 3cm, angling the top of the tab so there's room for the zip pull, then turn it 90 degrees and stitch across the top, forming a rectangle of stitching. If you can confidently sew a regular lapped zip using no pins, you can also do this using no pins.

To sew a centred zip
A centred zip isn't used as often on garments as a lapped zip, but its virtue is that it's central. You might use a centred zip in the front of a jumpsuit or pinafore. A 1.5cm (⅝") seam allowance is fine.

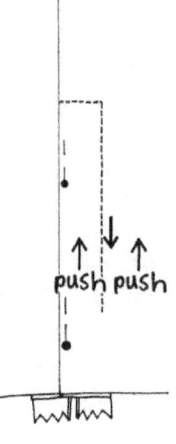

1. Overlock the edges of the garment. Mark the seam allowance at the top edges with tiny 3mm (⅛") snips.

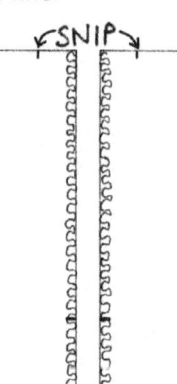

2. Sew the seam below the zip, backstitching securely at the end (overlocking not shown here for clarity).
I always lay the zip next to the opening to ensure the seam begins at the *bottom* of the end stopper on the zip.
Remember to leave the correct amount of seam allowance at the top.

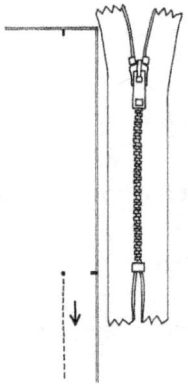

Ideally the end stopper should be at the bottom of the opening, but if you're going to be sewing a longer (plastic) zip into a shorter opening, or you've shortened the zip by stitching across the end (and therefore have cut off the end stopper), sew the seam to give the desired length opening.

3. Press the seam allowance open the whole way.

Optional: if the fabric doesn't show needle holes, you could baste the zip opening shut with a large stitch seam, then proceed with Step 4. Pull out the thread when the zip is sewn for a very even-looking centred zip.
A disadvantage with this (apart from having to unpick) is that the zip can't be unzipped as you stitch, so you can't use the machine's seam guide to sew straight. You may also find it difficult to stitch neatly past the zip pull.

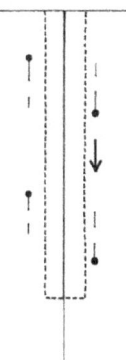

4. Pin the zip in position underneath the opening and sew it in place from the right side. The folded edges should just touch each other in the centre of the zip.
Undo the zip as you sew and use the machine's seam guide to keep your stitching straight.

Troubleshooting regular zips
(lapped and central)
Zip doesn't lie flat
The fabric has been stretched, instead of eased, as you sewed the zip in. If you don't deliberately ease the zip, the fabric will stretch all by itself.
To remedy, unpick the zip and see if you can restore the fabric by shrinking it back to size with the steam iron. It might help to run a line of hand basting along the edge to draw it up. When the fabric has been returned to its original state, fuse a strip of very light interfacing to each side to stabilize, then apply the zip again.

One side of the zip is higher than the other
The second side of the zip has stretched as the zip was sewn in.
If the high side isn't too much higher, say 6mm (¼") or less, and the zip appears to sit flat, simply trim the excess off the top. Otherwise, unpick the higher side of the zip and press with a steam iron to help restore the stretched fabric. Pin carefully and re-sew. As you sew, place one hand either side of the presser foot and try to encourage the top layer backwards, so it doesn't creep forward again. Also, check that the presser foot pressure isn't too great—adjust using the knob or lever at the top of the machine.

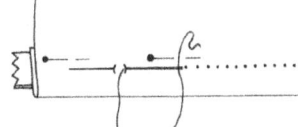

Further notes on regular zips
Sewing in a zip by hand
You can insert a regular zip using hand sewing, in a centred or lapped application. The stitch used is a variation of backstitching named prick stitch. It's also called pick stitch or half-backstitch.
To work prick stitch, backstitch so only tiny dots of stitches appear on the surface.
Hand-baste the zip in position first if you think the pins might get in the way. The hand sewn method isn't as strong as machine stitching, so for extra strength turn the garment inside out and machine stitch the edges of the zipper tape to the seam allowance. If the fabric is beaded or heavily embellished, remove the embellishments from the seam allowance before inserting the zip.
I still think invisible zips look neater, no matter how even the hand stitching, but I would use this method on heavily beaded or embroidered fabrics, where the decoration is too thick or crusty to enable a machine foot to sew.

Finishing off the top
If the garment has a **waistband**, then you have no worries. Apply the waistband as normal, but for lapped zips note where the notches match.

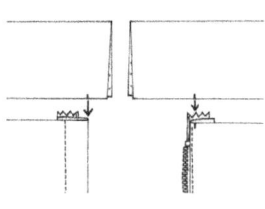

If the top of the garment is finished with a **facing**, there are several options for sewing it:

✂ The traditional home dressmaking way is to sew the zip in first, sew the facings on, then hand sew the ends of the facing into position on the inside. It's never quite satisfactory, particularly for lapped zips, because the sides of the facings get in the way of the top of the zip. It also looks horrible.

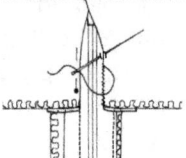

✂ A neat, quick way is to bag out the ends of the facing before inserting the zip. This is great for costumes or anything that might need altering later, because it doesn't require extensive unpicking to change the zip. This method is best for garments with a facing only—not with a lining attached to the facing. Here's how:

1. For a **lapped zip**, fold the attached facings down right side together onto the garment. Sew *on* the stitching line on the left hand side and *3mm (⅛") in* on the right hand side, forming a corner on both. Trim the corners and turn through the right way.

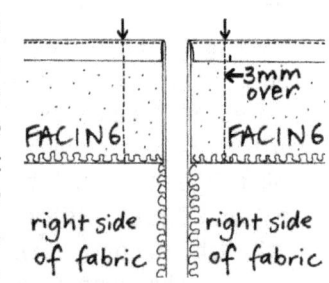

For a **centred zip**, both sides are sewn *on* the stitching line.

2. Before you put the zip in, fold the tops of the zip tapes down onto the front of the zip and stitch.

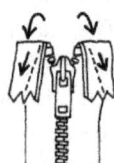

3. Insert the zip as a normal lapped or centred application. Ensure the tops of the facings are level.

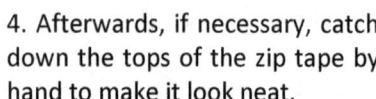

4. Afterwards, if necessary, catch down the tops of the zip tape by hand to make it look neat.

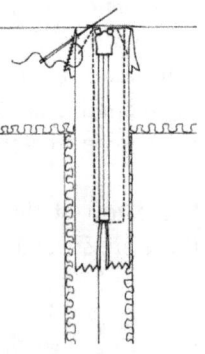

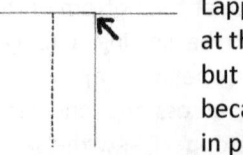

Lapped zips will have a flappy part at the top of the zip on the outside, but not much can be done about it because there's nothing to hold it in place. If there's room, you could try sewing on a hook and eye, or a small clear press stud, to hold it flat. Make space by sewing the zip in 1cm (⅜") lower down.

✂ The neatest method for a **lapped zip** involves sewing the facings and sides of the zip on first. The pattern pieces are cut in a particular way:

Begin with 2cm (¾") seam allowances on the left and right sides of the garment, and the same on the left and right facings.

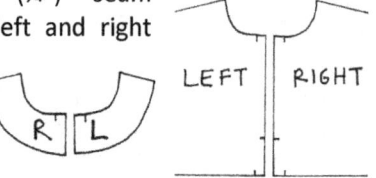

On the left side, leave the 2cm (¾") seam allowance and trim all the seam allowance plus 5mm off the facing.

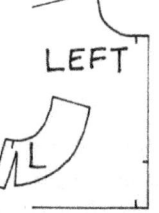

On the right hand side, trim the seam allowance back to 1.2cm (½"), and the same for the facing.

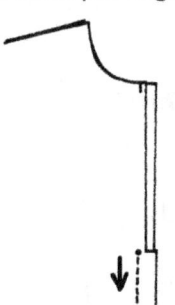

Interface and overlock the facings in the usual way before you begin sewing.

1. Sew the 2cm (¾") seam below the zip. Press open. Overlock all the edges. It's OK to round off the step on the right hand side when you overlock.
(Overlocking not shown for clarity.)

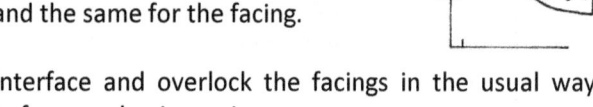

2. Fit a zipper foot to your machine. Position the zip face down on the left side matching the edges. Sew it on with a 5mm seam, splaying out the zip about 4cm (1½") from the top so the stitching runs next to the top stop (but still taking 5mm on the fabric). If you don't splay the top out, you won't have enough coverage for the zip pull when the zip is closed.

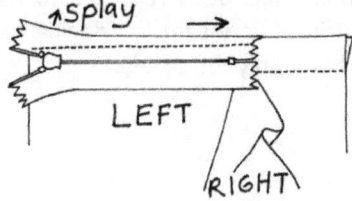

Zips regular **413**

On the right hand side, lay the zip face down matching the edges and take a 1cm (⅜") seam all the way through (no splaying at the top). You'll see the zip doesn't lie flat when it's closed.

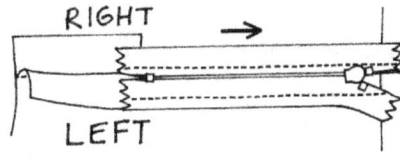

3. Attach the facings: lay the facings on their respective sides and sew them onto the zipper tape, taking a 1cm (⅜") seam for the right hand side and 5mm for the left. On the left side, match the facing edge to the garment edge, not the splayed-out zip. Note that the facing's left shoulder won't match the garment's shoulder (yet).

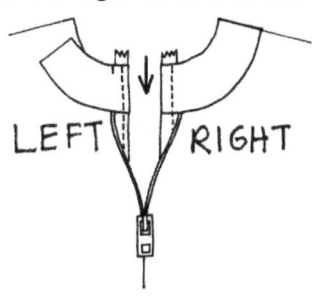

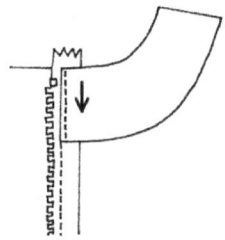

4. Press the seams towards the facings and edgestitch to hold the seam flat.

5. On the left side, fold the facing back on itself, right sides together, on the garment's centre back notch. The facing should now match the garment, but take care to fold it back in the correct spot, otherwise you won't have enough coverage for the zip pull. Do the same thing on the right side, except there's no notch—just fold it back as tightly as you can along the zip.

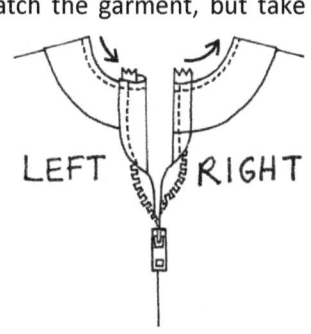

6. Sew the top edge of the facing. Turn through to the right side and check the tops are level before trimming the corners.

7. Press in the folds and sew the lapped zip in the usual way.
The zip will have a flappy part at the top—if there's room, you could sew a hook and eye, or a small clear press stud, to hold it flat. Make space by sewing the zip in 1cm (⅜") lower.

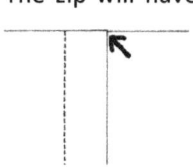

✂ The neatest method for a **centred zip** is very similar to a lapped zip but both sides are made the same.

On the garment you'll need a 1.2cm (½") seam allowance for the zip.

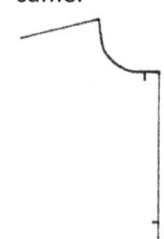

On the facings, trim off the seam allowance plus 5mm.

Interface and overlock the facings in the usual way before you begin sewing.

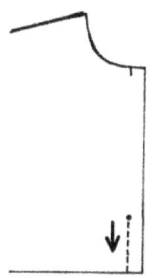

1. Overlock both edges (overlocking not shown for clarity). Sew the 1.2cm (½") seam below the zip. Press open.

2. Lay the zip face down on the garment, matching the edges. Sew the zip to each edge with a 5mm seam. About 4cm (1½") from the top, splay the edges of the zip out so the stitching runs just past the top stops. This will provide enough coverage for the zip pull when the zip is closed.

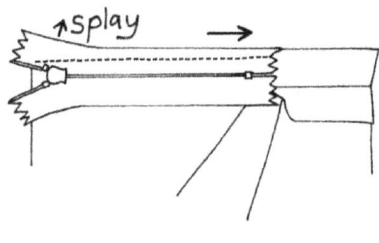

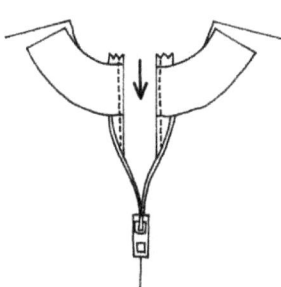

3. Lay the facings on their respective sides and stitch each onto the zip edge with a 5mm seam, following the garment edge, not the splayed out zip.

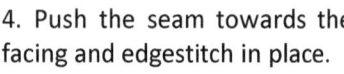

4. Push the seam towards the facing and edgestitch in place.

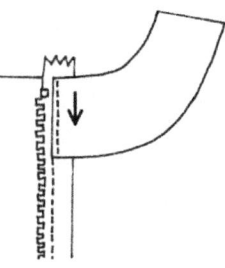

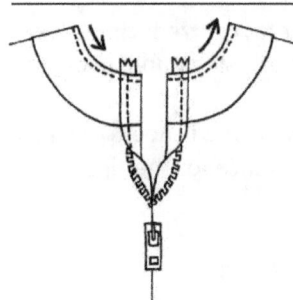

5. Fold the facings back on themselves, folding on the 1.2cm (½") notch at the top. There should be a small gap between the fold and the zip. Stitch across the tops of the facings.

6. Turn through to the right side and check the tops are level before trimming the corners.

7. Press in the folds and sew the centred zip in the usual way.

Possibilities for attaching lining
Hand sew
The edges of the lining around the zip can be pressed under and hand sewn to the edges of the zip—use two strands of thread for strength and use either a neat whip stitch (page 150 and as shown here) or hidden slip stitch (page 149).
Neaten the raw edges of the lining before you begin.

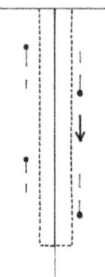

Leave a split
Turn back the edges of the lining and machine stitch around the edges. You can overlock and turn the edge under once, or turn it under twice to conceal the raw edge. The lining will hang free, not attached to the zip. This solution is the easiest, but you risk catching your toes in the lining every time you put the garment on. I often use this method for my own clothes and just get dressed carefully.

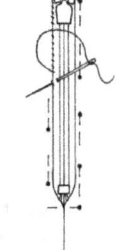

Machine stitch
Neaten all the raw edges before you begin (not shown for clarity).
Machine stitch each side of the lining to the zipper tape *after* the zip has been sewn in, but *before* the waistband is sewn on. Taper off to nothing at the bottom of the zip. Sew the seam in the lining below the zip last.
This method will give you a little extra room in the lining, because

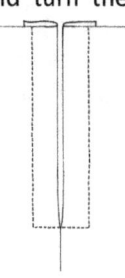

there's a gap where the zip is, so take in any extra fullness in the lining's waist in the waist tucks.

Set the zip into the lining
This is a fairly high-end manufacturing method, but isn't seen much now since most manufacturers use invisible zips. The zip must be set into the lining *before* the zip is sewn into the garment, then the zip is sewn in the usual way.
Important: make sure the zip notch is in the correct position on both lining and main fabric.
Here's how to sew it:
For a lapped zip, I recommend marking the right and wrong sides of the lining so a piece doesn't accidentally get flipped. You'll need a 2cm (¾") seam allowance on the lining.

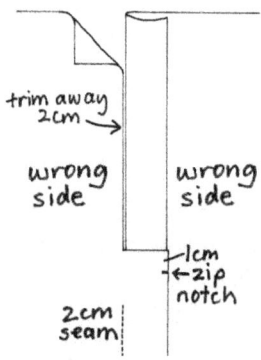

1. Trim the 2cm (¾") seam allowance off one side of the skirt lining as shown. Leave 1cm (⅜") above the zip notch.
Don't sew the seam below all the way up to the notch yet.
Leave all the edges raw at this stage.

2. With the right sides of both lining and zip facing up, stitch the zip to the lining along the very edge of the zipper tape. The *stitching* line (*not* the edge of the zip) must be 2cm (¾") from the raw edge. Sew to just below the end stopper at the end of the zip, level with the zip notch, back stitching at the end. Make sure you definitely clear the tab. Snip diagonally to the base of the stitching line.

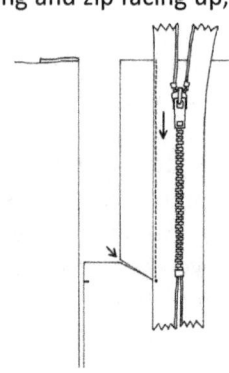

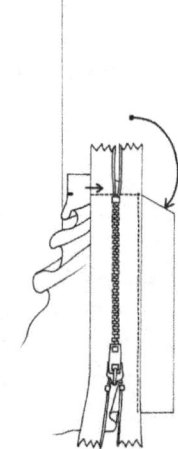

3. Pivot the zip around as shown and sew the fabric across the end of the zip, forming a neat, pucker-free corner. Avoid the end stopper.
You'll see that the wrong side of the zip will be visible from the right side of the lining.

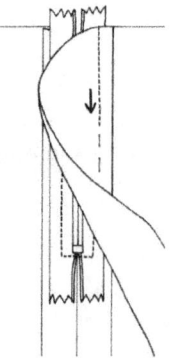

Zips regular

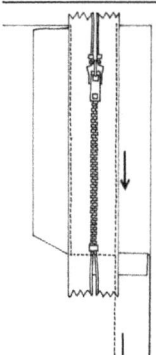

4. Sew in the remaining side of the zip to the other side of the lining, taking the correct 2cm (¾") seam allowance. Continue the stitching down to meet the seam below the zip.
There should be enough clearance to overlock the edges of the lining without the zip getting in the way.

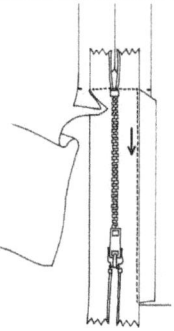 4. Flip the zip up, and stitch each long side of the zip onto the edge of the lining, taking a 1cm (⅜") seam allowance on the lining and stitching on the edge of the zip tape. Overlock the long edges.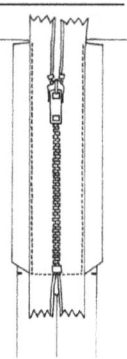

5. For strength, edgestitch around the sides. You can now insert the lapped zip into the garment as usual.

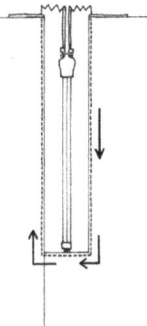

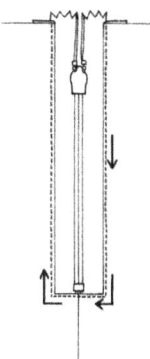 5. Edgestitch around the zip on the lining, for strength. You can now insert the centred zip into the garment as usual.

For a centred zip, any seam allowance is fine for the lining.

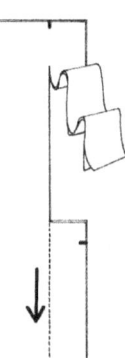 1. Trim the seam allowance off the lining where the zip will go, leaving 1cm (⅜") above the zip notch. Ensure the zip notch is just below the end stopper of the zip. Sew, press open and neaten the seam below the zip.

Zips in pleats
In pleated garments, the zip is concealed underneath a pleat.
The pleat needs to have a seam to insert one side of the zip into, as shown.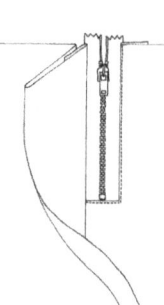

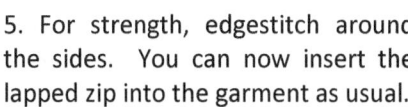

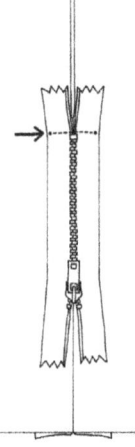

2. Lay the zip *face up* onto the *right side* of the seam, with the end stopper positioned just below the notch. Stitch across the zip just above the end stopper, using a zipper foot.

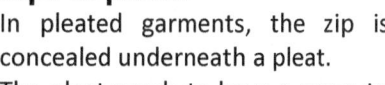

1. Trim the seam allowance off the right side of the seam as shown. Leave a 1cm (⅜") seam allowance above the zip notch.

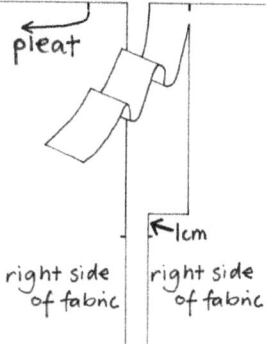

2. Place the zip *face down* onto the *right side* of the garment and stitch the zip along the very edge of the zipper tape as shown. The *stitching* line (*not* the edge of the zip) must be 2cm (¾") from the raw edge. Sew to just below the end stopper, level with the zip notch, back stitching at the end. Make sure you definitely clear the tab. Snip diagonally to the base of the stitching line.

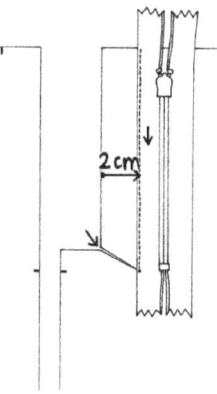

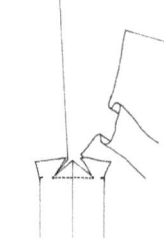 3. Snip diagonally into each end of the stitching, cutting the lining only, not the zip.

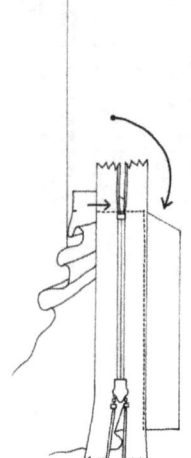

3. Pivot the zip around and sew the fabric across the end of the zip, forming a neat, pucker-free corner, avoiding the end stopper.

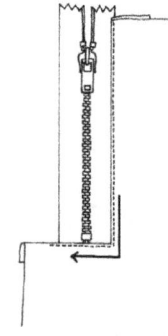

4. For strength, edgestitch around the two sides.

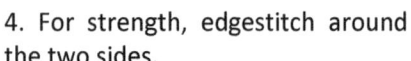

5. Sew in the remaining side of the zip to the other side of the garment, taking the correct seam allowance. There should be enough clearance to overlock the edges of the seam without the zip getting in the way—if not, overlock first.

Zips in stretch knits

If you're putting a zip in a leotard, swimsuit or anything else that will be stretched when it's worn, you'll need to insert the zip into the *stretched* opening. When the fabric stretches as the garment is being worn, the zip will sit flat. Off the figure, the fabric will relax and the zip will wave.

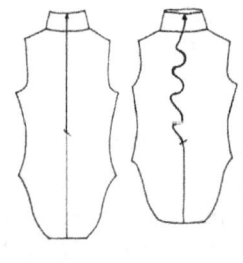

✂ How much should the fabric be stretched when the zip is inserted? An easy way is to sew enough of the garment so you can try it on. Try it on inside out. Stick a strip of sticky tape along the (now stretched) length of each side of the zipper opening. Take off the garment and sew the zip in through the sticky tape, removing the tape afterwards. This is a good method for one-offs and made-to-measures.

✂ Another way to calculate the length needed for the zip is to try the garment on, pin the opening closed, and take a measurement. This is a good method for multiple garments and clothing production. Measure the length of the zip on the (now stretched) garment and notch the seam allowance to indicate the bottom of the zip. Specify the zip length on the pattern.

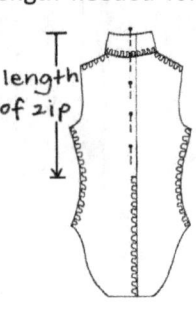

✂ To sew in the zip, pin the zip tape at regular intervals between the notch and the top of the garment. Stretch the fabric to fit the zip as you sew.

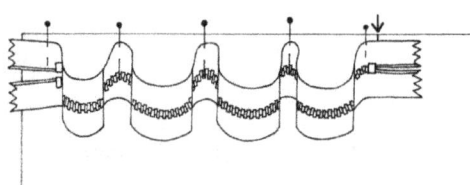

✂ You can use a straight stitch to sew the zip, because the zip will stabilize the knit.

Exposed zips

An exposed zip isn't placed in a seam, but rather a slit cut in the fabric, usually the centre front or centre back. It's used on knits and fabrics that don't ravel and is often seen on sports clothes like cycling tops. You won't need to overlock or neaten the edges in any way—just leave them. If the knit you're using ladders, cut it so the ladders run from the hem *up*, otherwise the area at the bottom of the zip is prone to laddering. (To check for laddering, cut across the fabric and tightly stretch each cut edge.)

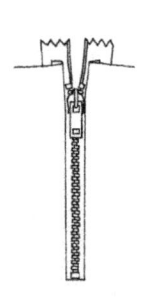

✂ This method can be used if you're retro-fitting a zip into an already-made top. It can be a good solution if you've made the neckline too small to get your head through.

✂ Before you begin, decide what you're doing with the top of the zip. If the zip is being sewn through an already attached neckband, fold the tops of the zip to the front of the zip tape and stitch down before you begin. Line up the top of the zip level with the top of the neckband when you sew it.

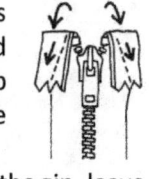

If you're attaching a collar or facing *after* the zip, leave the top of the zip as it is.

1. Lay the zip on the garment and pinpoint the exact length required, allowing for the correct seam allowance at the top and clearing the zip's end stopper at the bottom. Cut the slit for the opening to 1.5cm (⅝") short of the end. If you're feeling nervous about cutting, you can draw it in with a pencil and ruler at this stage.

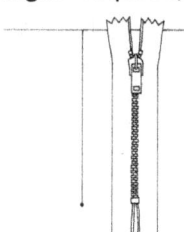

2. Lay the closed zip *face down* onto the right side of the fabric, positioned upside down so the end stopper is right below the proposed bottom of the opening.
Stitch 1cm (⅜") across the zip, using a smaller machine stitch for strength, and backstitching securely at each end. You'll need to use a zipper foot so you can get in close. Make sure this little seam is in the centre of the zip.

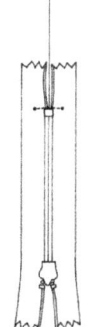

3. If you haven't already cut the slit, do so now, cutting to 1.5cm (⅝") short of the end, then snipping *exactly* to (but not through) the last stitch on each side. A triangle of fabric will form.

4. Flip the zip up towards the neck and stitch each long side to the zipper tape with the right sides of the fabric and zip together. Pin carefully first. Stitch with the zipper tape on top and sew right next to the teeth of the zip, but not *too* close in case you can't get the zip open. Some people like to stitch from the bottom up and others prefer the top down; see what suits you. Note that the raw edge and the zip tape won't be even—the zip will be wider than the fabric, but it's important that they're parallel.

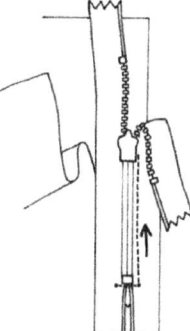

For perfect corners at the bottom, I like to sew with the fabric side up and the zip underneath, stitching from the corner up.

✂ If the zip is being sewn through a junction, such as a neckband or yoke seam, sew one side of the zip first. Then do up the zip and mark the seam line on both sides of the zip tape with a pencil to help you match the other side of the junction.

5. If desired, you can edgestitch or topstitch around the edges—it will make it much stronger.

Exposed zips in woven fabric

You can use this method for woven fabrics *or* knits. There are some interesting variations but some require forward planning, so read through the instructions before you start.

1. For garments of woven fabric, iron a strip of lightweight interfacing on the back of the slit position to stop fraying.

2. Cut a strip of fabric to use as a facing at least 3cm (1¼") longer than the zip and 5cm (2") wide. It can be the same fabric if it's light enough, or some lining fabric in the same colour. Fuse the facing with lightweight interfacing and overlock the edges (you could curve the lower corners for a neater overlock).

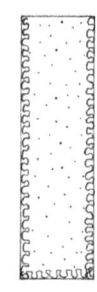

3. Mark the slit position on the wrong side of the garment and facing, but don't cut it yet. Check the slit length against the zip—the bottom of the slit should be just below the bottom zip stop, with the correct seam allowance at the top.

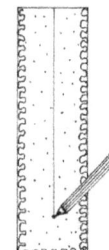

4. Lay the facing over the garment, right sides together, matching the slit positions by pushing pins through. Stitch a three sided box around the marked slit, forming neat corners at the bottom. The width of the box will depend on the type of zip (heavy or fine) and how you want the finished zip to look, but generally the opening should only expose the teeth of the zip and not too much of the tape. About 1cm (⅜") is usual.

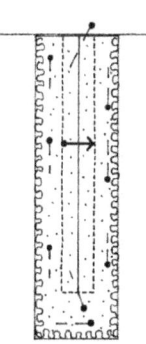

For extra strength, shorten the stitch length when you sew around the bottom corners, for example 1 or 1.5 instead of the usual 2.5.

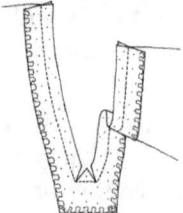
5. Cut the slit, stopping 1.5cm (⅝") short of the end. Carefully cut into each corner, cutting exactly to, but not through, the stitching. A little triangular flap will form.

6. Turn the facing through to the inside. Press the edges carefully so the facing is tucked away out of sight. It helps to first press the seam flat, then press the edges folded over. You now have a three-sided window into which the zip will be inserted.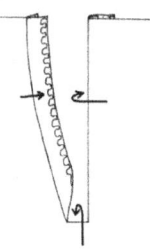

7. What happens next depends on what you want the finished product to look like:

✂ For a clean finish with no stitching visible, lay the zip face up underneath. Flip up each of the three sides and sew on top of the first line of stitching. 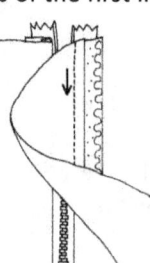 Pin it in position first to check how it looks before sewing. After sewing, the facing can be invisibly blind stitched by hand (or machine) to hold it in place and conceal the raw edges underneath.

✂ For a stitched finish, lay the zip face up underneath and pin next to the fold line. Either edgestitch with a zipper foot around the edges, or topstitch further away from the edge, or both. The wider stitching will conveniently conceal the raw edges of the slit.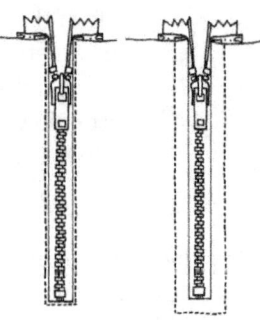

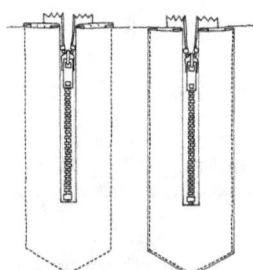 ✂ The facing can be cut a little wider, shaped and the edges stitched as a feature. It can also be applied to the outside. For both ways, neatly turn under the edges of the facing instead of overlocking them.

The facing can be any fancy shape and/or have extra topstitching.

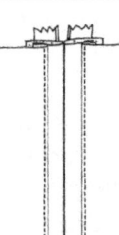 ✂ For a "bound" finish to the edges, cut the facing a little wider, for example 9cm-10cm (3½"-4") wide. Stitch the box around the slit anywhere up to 2cm (¾") wide. Press the seam allowances towards the garment. Press the edges of the facing into place. Slip the zip behind, pin, and edgestitch into place. If you prefer to have no visible stitching, stitch-in-the-ditch (page 291) along the long sides, then flip up the bottom to stitch the triangle to the end of the facing and zip.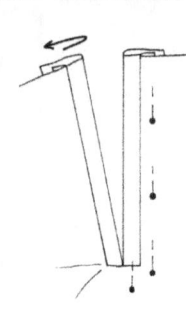

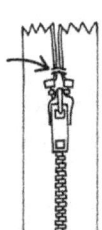 ✂ The zip can be closed at both ends, for a pocket opening or cushion cover. Before sewing the zip in, stitch together the tapes above the top stops.

✂ You can go one step further and incorporate a neck facing in with the zip facing. That way, the world will see a facing when the zip is worn open. Make a pattern by tracing off the neckline and extending it to the zip facing.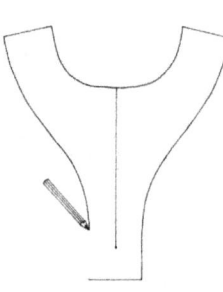

To sew, attach the facing and zip in the usual way, then turn the facing back along the zip stitching line to sew around the neckline. Trim the corner and turn through to the right side. Leave any topstitching until the very end.

Feature zips

Feature zips are a type of exposed zip where the zip is sewn straight over the opening, like an appliqué. Often the zip is metal and a contrasting colour. The zip can be sewn flat with the end tapes visible (shown on left side of zip) or just tucked under (on right side).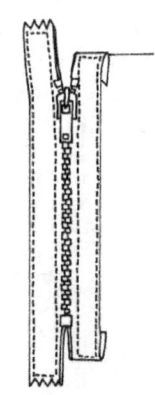

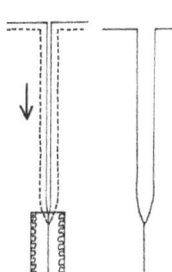

Underneath the zip, the edges can be simply trimmed back so there's no seam allowance, and overlocked. The zip is positioned over the gap.

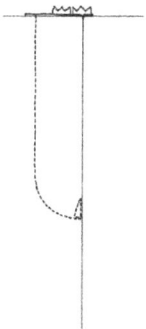

A smarter finish can be achieved with a lining or facing. Stitch the garment and lining/facing together around the edges then turn through to the right side. Sew the feature zip over the opening.

Fly Fronts

A fly front is a neat durable closing, and the traditional choice for men's trousers. It's also used for women's clothes as well. Men's fly fronts close left over right, and women's right over left (as one wears the garment).

A fly front is the first thing sewn on trousers, unless the front pocket linings are attached to the centre fronts. If so, make the pockets first.

I generally use a plastic regular (dress) zip for fly fronts. They are strong enough and light, but some people prefer to use a metal trouser zip, or a jeans zip which is even heavier.

If you use a metal zip, buy the correct length. The pattern will specify the length, but 13cm or 15cm (5" or 6") are typical lengths.

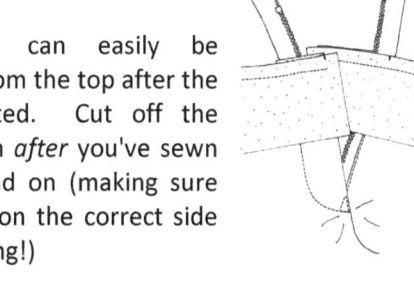

Plastic zips can easily be shortened from the top after the zip is inserted. Cut off the excess length *after* you've sewn the waistband on (making sure the slider is on the correct side of the stitching!)

Invisible zips are not used for fly fronts.

Make a pattern

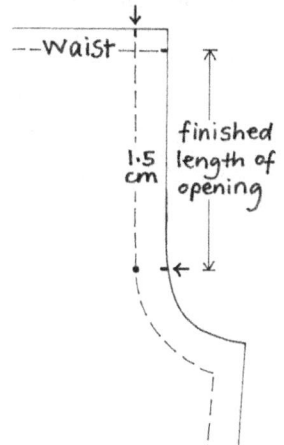

Fronts. You need a 1.5cm (⅝") seam allowance on the front. Notch the seam allowance at the top, and place another notch for the length of the zip. It's common for the centre front to be on the straight grain of the fabric, but some flat-front trousers such as jeans angle in.

Fly facing. Make the fly facing 4cm (1½") longer than your finished opening and 6cm (2⅜") wide, although it can be as narrow as 5cm (2") or as wide as 6.5cm (2½"). Draw in a pleasing curve at the bottom. The grainline is parallel with the long edges even if the front isn't on the straight grain. Note which way up the piece has to be cut—illustrated is for women's trousers; reverse it for men's. Some people cut a pair and discard the unwanted one. Cut some interfacing for the fly facing. I like to use a fairly firm interfacing—fusible jacket interfacing or a firm sew-in woven. For fusible interfacing, cut it sticky side up.

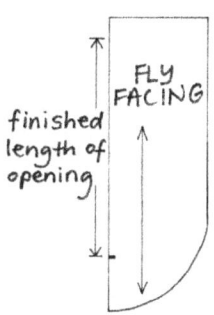

Fly shield. Make the fly shield the same length as the fly facing and 10cm (4") wide, however it can be as narrow as 8cm (3⅛") or as wide as 12cm (4¾"). Use the same curved shape as the fly facing to create the curves on the bottom edge. Fly shields on jeans are often cut as a rectangle without the curved-in section.

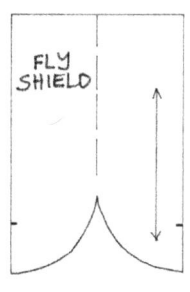

Be sure the garment's waistband extension is long enough for the fly shield. For a shield cut 10cm (4") wide, you'll need a 5.5cm (2⅛") extension on the waistband. If you're unsure, cut it longer for now and trim it when you sew the waistband.

✂ Some patterns don't have a fly shield, but I think fly shields are absolutely necessary. They protect your skin against the zip and if your zip comes undone no-one can see your undies. They do add bulk, though. If the fabric is very thick, sometimes the fly shield is lined. It's cut in two parts with a seam, with main fabric on the front and (a lighter weight) lining behind.

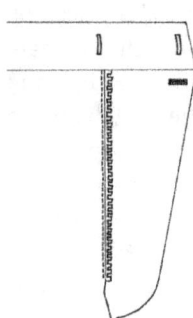

Sometimes on men's trousers, the fly shield is wider at the top than the bottom. These are always lined and are sometimes cut so the lining extends up to the top edge of the waistband (and therefore becomes the extension on the waistband). There's usually a buttonhole on it to match a button on the inside of the trousers.

✂ A **cut-on fly facing** is a good idea if you're looking for ways to reduce extra seams and bulk. Cut-on fly facings are often seen on ladies patterns but rarely on men's. The facing is cut as part of the front, therefore you won't need a separate fly facing, but you'll still need interfacing.

A cut-on fly facing can be as narrow as 3cm (1¼") or as wide as 5cm (2") from the centre front stitching line.

To save time, cut both sides with a front facing and trim the left side off leaving the regular 1.5cm (⅝") seam allowance.

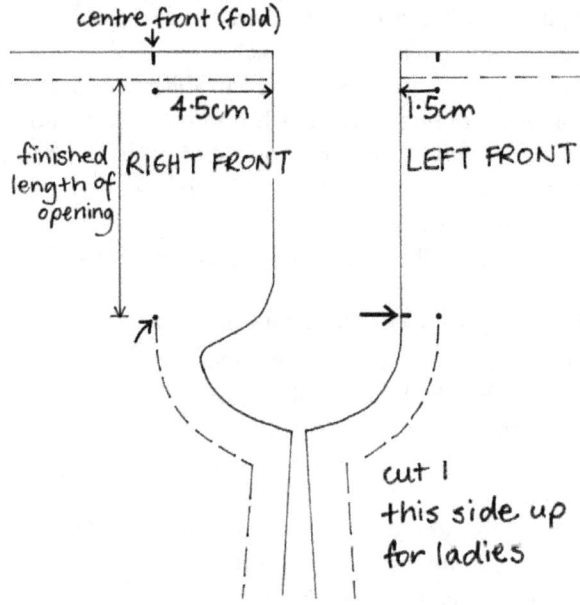

✂ **Curved fly facings** are seen on olden-days trousers for men. These days, fly fronts are applied only to the straight part of the crotch seam; the fly front stops where the seam starts to curve. On older pairs of trousers you'll notice the fly front extends into the curved section. If you want to do the fly like this, the facing and the shield will have to have curves that correspond to the front. The pattern is simple to make.

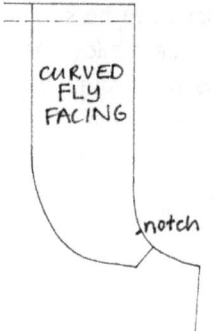

For the facing, trace around the front and draw in the desired facing shape. The bottom of the facing should extend about 2.5cm (1") beyond the zip notch.

For the fly shield, you can use the same pattern piece if the width suits you: cut a pair in the main fabric OR cut one of main and one of lining (the lining one to be the innermost).

To sew a fly front

1. Overlock the edges of the fronts. You should still be able to locate the zip notches through the overlocking.

2. Interface the fly facing and overlock the long curved edge. Occasionally the fly facing is bound with bias binding instead of overlocking. The binding fabric should be in sympathy with the trouser fabric, for example cotton bias binding for jeans or something thin and soft for fine woollen trousers.

If you have a cut-on facing, interface the area from the centre front line to the edge, then overlock the facing and crotch curve.

3. Fold the fly shield in half, right sides together, and stitch around the curve with a 6mm (¼") seam, tapering to nothing at the fold. Turn to the right side and overlock together the long, straight edges.

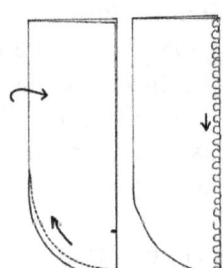

If the fly shield is in two parts, stitch them together along the entire curved edge.

If you have a rectangular fly shield, it can be angled (as shown) or squared at the bottom. Fold and stitch it, trim, then turn through to the right side. Overlock the long edge.

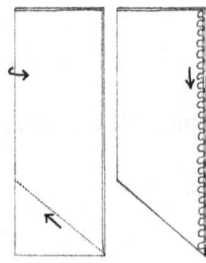

A faster but bulkier way is to fold it into shape and overlock the long edge. Sometimes jeans use this method.

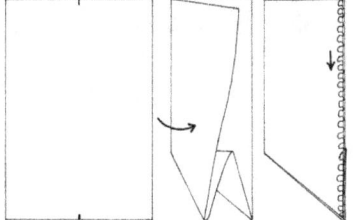

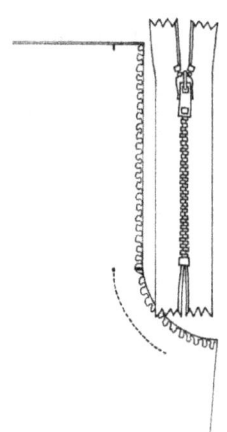

4. Double-check the zip length, making sure you'll clear the end stopper at the bottom of the zip. Sew the front crotch seam below the zip, beginning (and backstitching) at the zip notch and ending a few centimetres short of the inside leg. Take a 1.5cm (⅝") seam allowance. I always sew crotch seams with two rows of stitching, one row on top of the other, for strength, so I stitch this part twice as well.

5. Sew the facing to the front (the right front for women and the left for men—as the garment is being worn. Illustrated is women's). Take a 1.5cm (⅝") seam allowance and stitch from the exact point of the crotch seam. For accurate results, plunge a pin through the two points. Begin sewing by inserting the needle exactly where the pin is, removing the pin, then sewing the seam. Make sure you backstitch securely. If the fabric is thick, you may want to trim or grade the seam allowance back a little, either on the facing, front or both.

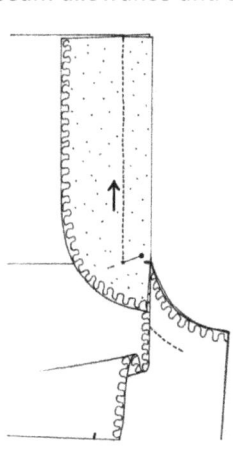

6. Press the seam allowance towards the facing and understitch the facing.

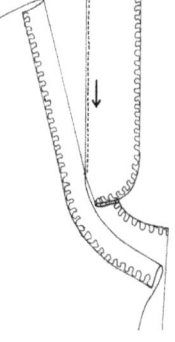

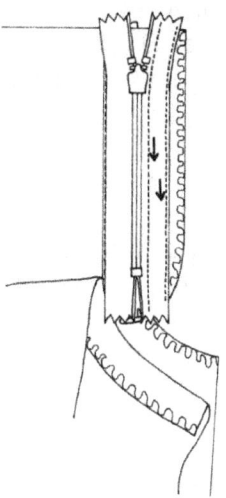

7. Place the zip *face down* onto the facing, with the edge of the tape next to the seam line, and pin into position. The end stopper should be above the point of the crotch seam. Using a zipper foot, stitch the zipper tape onto the facing as illustrated. Sew one row of stitching next to the zip teeth and another row next to the edge of the tape. Where the zip splays out at the top, stitch it as it splays—don't make it straight.

8. Fold the facing back, ready to topstitch on the right side. It is **very important** that you do not sew the free end of the zip tape down when you topstitch. I pin the tape out of the way first, so it doesn't get accidentally caught in.

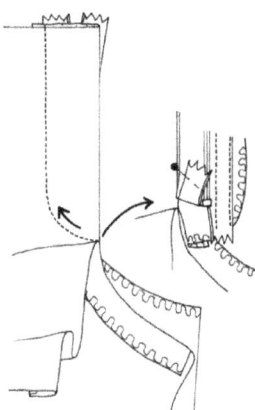

Begin sewing from the bottom, making sure you don't hit the end stopper. Stitch up to the top of the trousers. If you stitch from the top down, you'll end up with a bubble of fabric at the end.

✂ How do you get the stitching straight with a smooth curve? About ten years of everyday practise should do it. Otherwise, make a cardboard template and trace it onto the front with tailor's chalk before you stitch. Then simply follow the line and brush off the chalk afterwards.

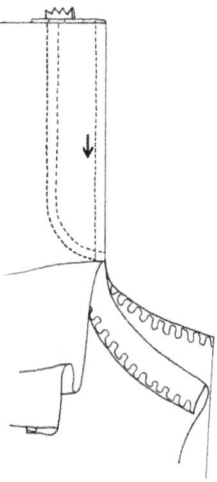

✂ If you're making jeans or heavily topstitched pants you can add extra stitching. Try a double row of curved stitching instead of one (be sure to avoid the end stopper). You can also sew a row next to the fold line—tuck the zip out of the way when you sew it.

✂ For perfect topstitching when using heavy topstitching thread, leave long threads to pull through and tie off at the back instead of backstitching at beginning and end.

9. Turn your attention to the other side of the zip. Place the prepared fly shield behind the zip. Position the shield so it covers the bottom of the zip—any excess length can be trimmed off the top. Sandwich the zipper tape between the fly shield and the front, matching all the edges. Sew together with a 6mm (¼") seam using a zipper foot. Some people find it easier to sew this part in two stages—first sewing the zipper tape to the front, then attaching the fly shield behind it.

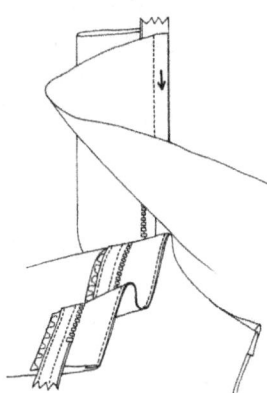

10. Edgestitch next to the zip as far down as you can. This is optional but I always do it because it helps this side to sit flat.

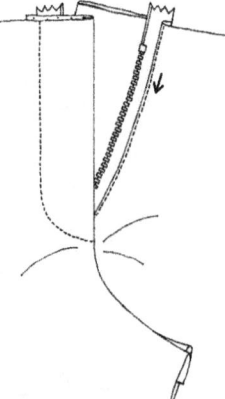

11. Reinforce the bottom of the zip with a triangle shape. Use a regular machine foot.

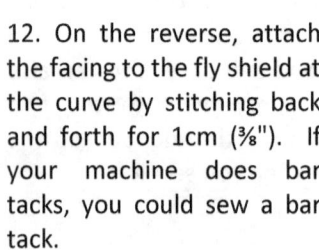

12. On the reverse, attach the facing to the fly shield at the curve by stitching back and forth for 1cm (⅜"). If your machine does bar tacks, you could sew a bar tack.

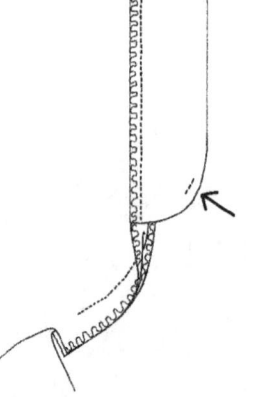

Troubleshooting fly fronts

The bottom of the fly front doesn't sit right

Possible solutions:

✂ Does it just need a press? Try unpicking the triangular stitching and the bar tack holding the shield, and give it a press.

✂ Unpick the whole shield side of the zip. Re-pin this side in position with the fly shield and check before re-sewing.

Why does it happen?

✂ The sides of the zip might not be aligned correctly before sewing, or one side might have stretched. Reduce the likelihood by pressing the facing side after topstitching, and pin and check before sewing the second (shield) side. Some fabrics are more prone to this—take extra care on unforgiving, "bouncy" or difficult-to-crease fabrics such as microfibre.

✂ Don't extend the zip into the curved part of the crotch unless you're using specially made curved pattern pieces (see page 420).

I made the fly shield too wide and my waistband extension too short, and now the waistband won't fit on

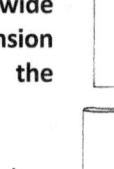

Possible solutions:

✂ If the waistband is only a fraction too short (maybe you only need a seam allowance), see if you can pinch a bit from the opposite end. So, instead of the overlap having a 1.5cm seam allowance and the extension being short by 1.5cm, both ends could have a 7mm seam allowance. Move all the notches to correspond.

✂ Do you have any fabric left? You could re-cut the whole waistband OR re-cut half the waistband and have a seam at the centre back which is a very acceptable solution OR position a join under a beltloop OR piece the waistband just under the extension section where you need it OR have side seams in the waistband and cut a new waistband front for the underlap side.

✂ You could make the fly shield narrower by tucking in the folded edge to fit. You can do this just at the top and angle the fold down, or press in the tuck down the length of the fly shield and edgestitch to hold it.

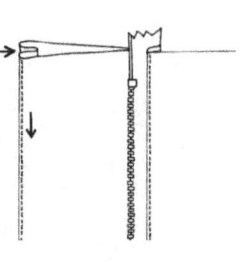

Further notes on fly fronts

Button fly front

For a button fly front, simply omit the zip. Sew the buttons to the fly shield and the buttonholes on top. Keyhole buttonholes look great.

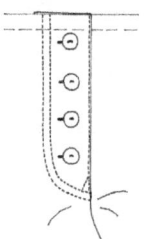

Concealed button fly front

A button fly front with concealed buttons has an extra layer with the buttonholes in it.

The pattern pieces are exactly the same as a regular fly front (page 419), with the addition of a buttonhole stand. The buttonholes are made first in the concealed piece, then it's inserted behind the fly facing. The concealed piece sits 3mm (⅛") back from the edge of the facing.

Make a pattern using the existing fly facing pattern. Trace off a copy and trim the seam allowance plus 3mm (⅛") off the long straight edge. Cut the pattern on the fold and mark in the buttonhole positions.
Cut one.
Interface behind the buttonholes if required.

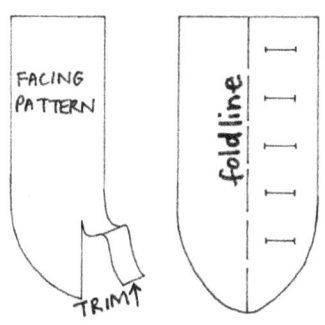

✂ The pattern can also be made in two parts, with a seam along the straight edge—you may like to use a different fabric for each. Trace off the facing pattern and trim the seam allowance back to 3mm (⅛"). This will give you a 6mm (¼") seam along the long straight edge. Cut one pair.

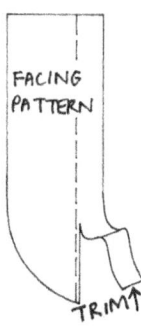

✂ You can make a more interesting concealed fly front by using a different fabric for the regular facing and the top buttonhole piece. You'll see the contrasting fabric when you "button up".
Shown is a men's (left-over-right) fly front.

Cut out the pieces as illustrated for a men's (left-over-right) fly front. Flip them over for a ladies fly front. The fly shield is cut in main fabric as usual.

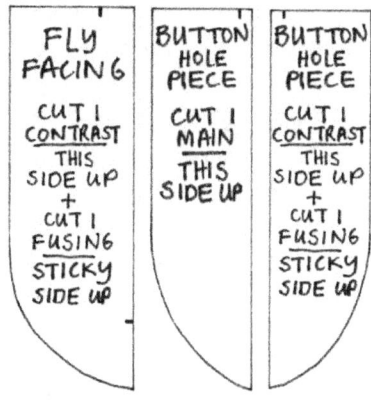

To sew a concealed button fly front

1. Interface the buttonhole stand if you think it needs it (in most cases it will).

2. If the buttonhole stand is in two pieces, lay them right sides together and sew a 6mm (¼") seam along the long straight edge. Turn to the right side and press. **Optional:** topstitch the seam.
For a one-piece stand, simply press in half with the wrong sides together. For both, overlock the curved edges together and sew the buttonholes.

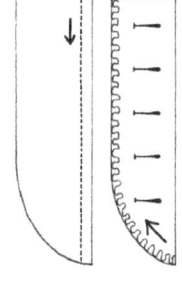

3. Attach the regular facing to the trousers and understitch as usual. Before topstitching the facing down, lay the buttonhole piece onto the facing matching the curved edges. Remember the stand will sit 3mm (⅛") back from the edge. Machine tack the buttonhole piece into place using a long machine stitch, then sew the rest of the fly front as normal.

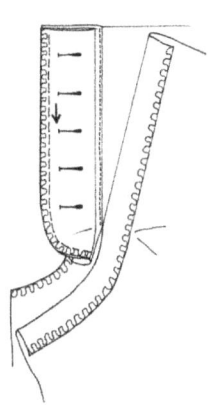

✂ **If the fabric is very thick** and tough, for example heavy denim, you can dispense with the facing. Hem the front edge of the garment that would normally be faced by turning the 1.5cm (⅝") seam allowance under twice and stitching. You can do this in topstitching thread if you're using it. The finished fold should be *on* the centre front. Slip the prepared (one-piece with no interfacing) buttonhole stand in behind, stepping it back 3mm (⅛") from the

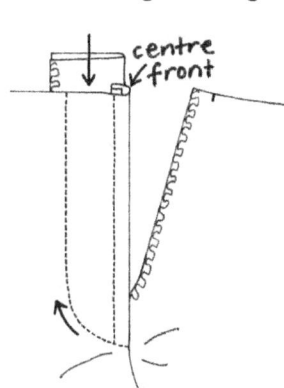

edge. Pin then stitch the curved fly shape, catching in the buttonhole stand in the process.

Fly front with a faced top edge

A fly front is most easily finished with a waistband at the top, but with a few changes you can have a fly front on garments that have a waist facing or a cut-on waistband. The top of the zip can either finish at the very top edge of the garment, or it can finish a bit lower down with a button and buttonhole at the top.

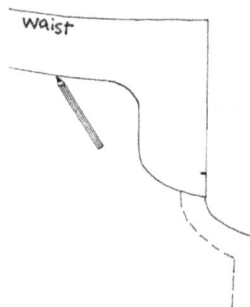

✂ If you're organised before you cut, you can turn the fly facing and the waist facing into one pattern piece. Trace around the front and draw in the waist and fly facing. The pattern would look like this.

1. Bag out the top of the fly shield by stitching a 6mm (¼") seam across the top and turning it to the right side. Ensure it's the correct length first.

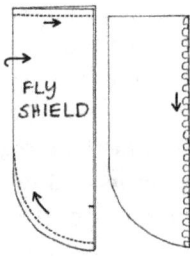

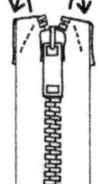

2. If you plan to have a button and buttonhole at the top, the zip needs to begin a little lower down, for example 2.5cm (1"). To tidy up the top of the zip tapes, fold and stitch them down.

3. On the **facing side**, stitch the fly facing to the garment as usual and attach the zip. Before you topstitch the fly facing down, bag out the top: turn the fly facing back and lay it *under* the waist facing as you stitch the waist facing on along the top of the garment. Trim the corner, turn through to the right side, then topstitch the fly facing.

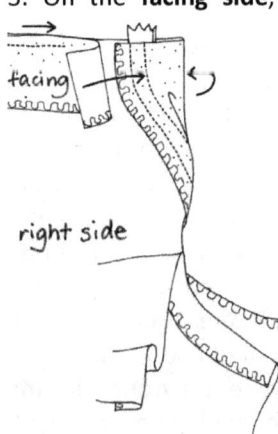

4. On the **shield side**, attach the second side of the zip and the fly shield in the usual way, making sure the two sides of the zip are level at the top. Don't edgestitch the shield yet. Turn the fly shield back as illustrated and lay the waist facing over the garment. Sew along the side and top very carefully, avoiding catching the top of the fly shield in the stitching. Turn the waist facing through to the right side and edgestitch the shield.

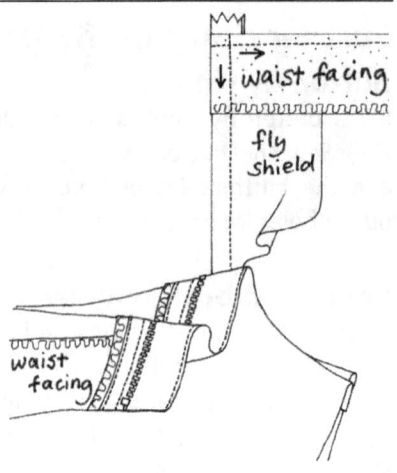

Fly front with a cut-on shield

Just as the fly facing can be cut in one with the garment (see page 420), so can the fly shield, although it isn't so common. With some forward planning, you can incorporate the back of the fly shield into the waist facing.

Make a pattern by adding the fly shield onto the front. You'll be sewing a 6mm (¼") seam sewn around the curved edge of the shield, so add that on too.

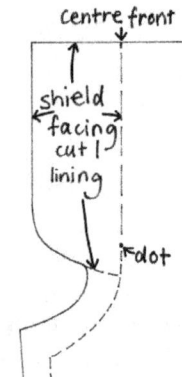

Trace off a shield facing (the back of the shield) in the same shape. The shield facing can be cut in the same fabric or lining.

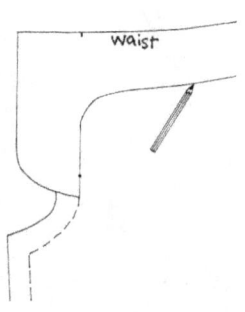

If you want to incorporate the waist facing into the shield facing, trace around the pattern and connect the facing and shield with a smooth curved line.

To sew a cut-on shield

1. Overlock the curved crotch of the garment (not shown for clarity).

2. On the right side of the garment, draw a chalk line on the shield, 1.5cm (⅝") away from the centre front.

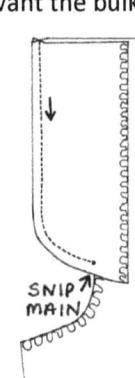

3. On the shield facing, overlock the long straight edge OR press it under 6mm (¼"). A pressed-under edge looks smarter inside, but you may not want the bulk.

4. With right sides together, sew the shield facing to the garment taking a 6mm (¼") seam. Stop sewing when you reach the edge of the garment and backstitch securely. Snip the *garment only* exactly to the stitching, and turn through to the right side.

5. Attach the fly facing and zip in the usual way.

6. On the shield, line up the edge of the zip tape on the chalk line and pin 6mm (¼") away from the tape edge. Close the zip and check the fly front lies flat and level. If not, adjust the pins. When you're satisfied, sew exactly where you pinned, stitching only through the *garment*, *not* the shield lining.

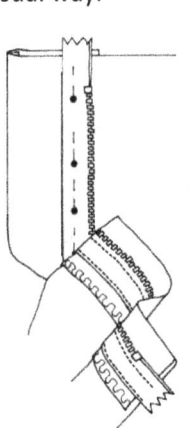

7. Flip the zip over and edgestitch in place, catching the shield lining in behind as you do.

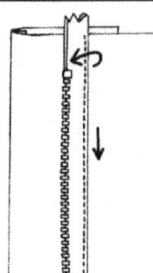

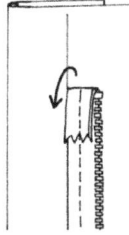

If the zip stops short of the top, such as on waist facings with a button above the zip, fold over the top of the tape as you sew to make it neat.

For regular separate waistbands or facings where the zip continues to the top, stitch the length of the tape.

Two piece fly shield with crotch binding

This type of fly shield is often seen on men's trousers. The shield pattern can be shaped to incorporate a buttonhole—the button is sewn to the inside of the fly facing. Sometimes a separate tab with a buttonhole is inserted into the shield seam instead.

To **make a pattern**, adapt the existing fly shield so it's cut in two pieces. To do this, cut it in half and add a 6mm (¼") seam allowance around the long curved edge. Cut one in main fabric.

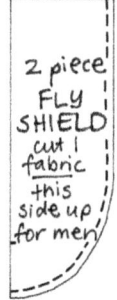

For the shield lining/crotch binding pattern, trace around the flipped-over shield and add 1cm (⅜") onto the long edge. Make the binding about 3cm (1¼") wide, and as long as the garment's front crotch curve. If you aren't sure, make it on the long side and cut off any excess later. Cut one in lining.

By "lining", I mean a strong light cotton pocket lining, not the silky lining used for lining whole garments (it's not durable enough for this).

For a buttonholed shield, shape the top as shown on both shield and shield lining.

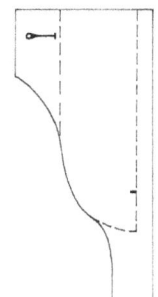

To sew a two piece shield with crotch binding

1. Place the two fly shield pieces right sides together. Match the curved side from the top and stitch with a 6mm (¼") seam until the curves diverge. Turn through and press.

2. Overlock the remaining long side of the main fabric piece. Press under 1cm (⅜") along the lining side.

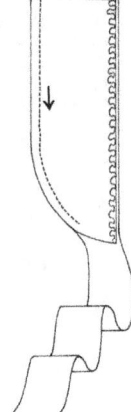

3. Sew the fly facing and first side of the zip as usual. To sew the shield on, attach only the *main fabric* side when you sandwich the zip tape between the garment and the shield.

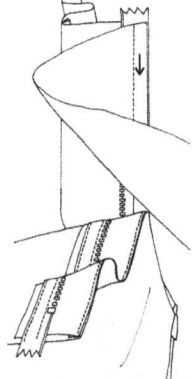

As you edgestitch along the zip, catch in the folded edge of the shield lining neatly underneath as you do.

4. When the fly is complete, use the long tail to bind the front crotch seam allowance.

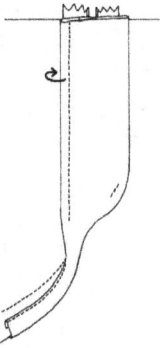

Mock Fly Front

A mock fly front has no zip and is used for boxer shorts, pyjama pants, children's trousers or to give front detail to any trousers with an elastic waist.
The front can be sewn closed, left open or opened with buttons and buttonholes.

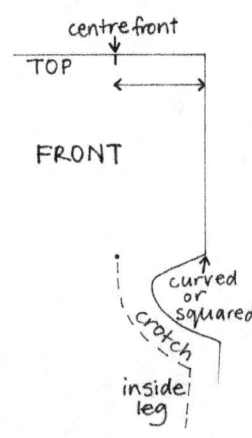

To **make a pattern**, draw a cut-on fly facing onto the front (see page 420). The extension can be as narrow as 3cm (1¼") or as wide as 5cm (2") and the corner of the extension can be curved or squared. Both left and right fronts are cut the same.

For a **mock fly that will be closed at the front**, either stitch the entire centre front seam (illustrated left), or leave a gap in the centre front (illustrated right). If you intend to leave a gap and the waist has a fold-down elastic casing, stitch from the top a few centimetres *past* the casing. Be sure to backstitch securely at each end of the gap.

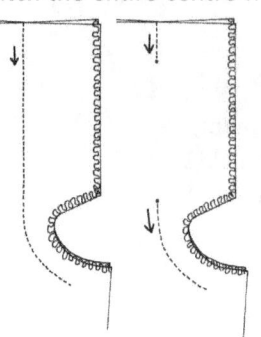

Stitching the entire centre front seam is probably a slightly faster method, but leaving a gap makes it look more like a real fly front, even though it isn't.
Sew the crotch seam with two rows of stitching, one on top of the other for strength, and overlock the edges together.

It's then a simple matter of pressing the extensions to one side and topstitching in place, just like a real fly front. Stitch from the bottom *up*, not the top down, otherwise a bubble of fabric will form at the end. If you have trouble keeping the topstitching straight, try making a cardboard template as a guide and tracing around it with chalk before stitching.

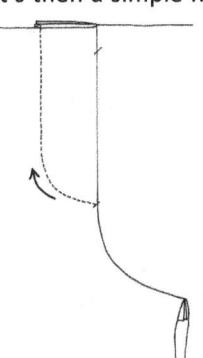

There are many ways to make a **mock fly that will open at the front**, depending on the type of fabric, whether the front will have buttons and (in industry) the cost of the garment. This closure is typically seen on pyjama pants and boxer shorts.

The least bulkiest, quickest way is to make the pattern as described above.

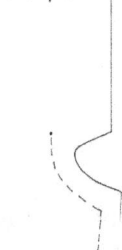

Fold one side into position like this:
The other side will fold back along the centre front, between the notch and dot.
(This is a men's front.)

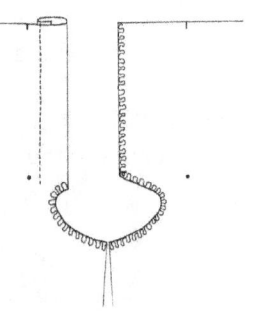

The pattern can also be designed with folded edges to support buttons and buttonholes (usually for very lightweight fabrics). The extra layers of folded fabric give a sturdier placket.

The pattern pieces may be different for each side; often the top (buttonhole) side is cut wide, and the underlap (button) side is cut narrower.

Sometimes the left and right patterns are cut the same *shape*, but with different foldlines for each side. In the illustration below, the overlap is on the right and the underlap is on the left.

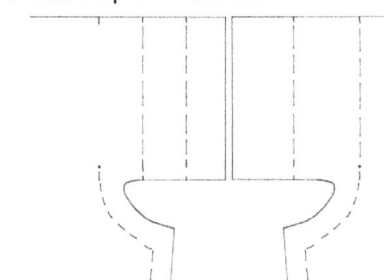

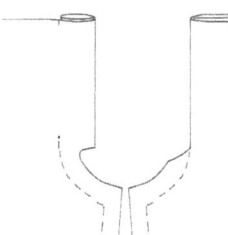

It will fold into position like this. This is a men's front.

You can see it's only suitable for lightweight fabrics, since the front will be six thicknesses when it's worn.

For a button fly, plan the folds to yield three thicknesses of fabric each. If you're having a folded placket but no buttons, you won't want three thicknesses, so make the first fold just a small amount to reduce the bulk.

I recommend folding the paper pattern pieces into position to decide on the finished width of the mock fly.

To sew, overlock the crotch seam first. Fold each side along the fold lines and press into position.

You may or may not stitch the underlap side to give a hemmed edge. If you're having buttons, you could leave it unstitched and let the buttons hold it in place. Place the right sides of the fronts together, matching the centre front points. Sew the centre front seam, leaving a gap where the mock fly will open. Be sure to backstitch securely at each end of the gap.

If there's a fold-down elastic waist casing, stitch the top a few centimetres *past* the casing.

Sew the crotch seam with two rows of stitching, one on top of the other, for strength.

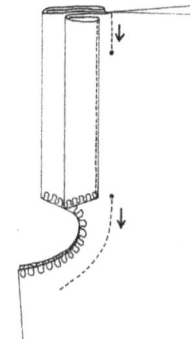

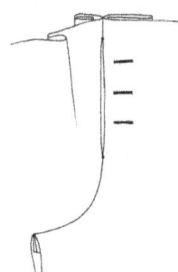

At this point, make the buttonholes if you're having them, since you won't be able to get the machine in to do them later. The buttonholes can be horizontal or vertical. You may only need one or two.

Position the fly to one side and topstitch in place. Stitch from the bottom up, not the top down, otherwise a bubble of fabric will form at the end. If you have trouble keeping the topstitching straight, try making a cardboard template as a guide and tracing around it with chalk before stitching.

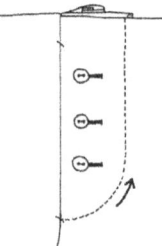

Sew on the buttons.

Open-ended zips

Open-ended zips, or separating zips, are chunkier than regular or invisible zips. They're also wider, being 3.3cm (1¼") instead of 2.5cm (1").

There are three ways of inserting them:

Exposed is the easiest and looks good.

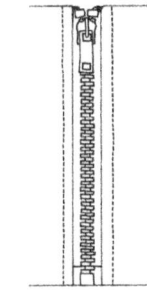

Centred has the edges of the garment meeting over the middle of the zip.

Concealed may be preferable if you don't have a perfectly matching coloured zip, or want a clean finish. The topstitching can run from top to bottom, or curve like a fly front at the bottom of the zip *if* the zip finishes above the hemline.

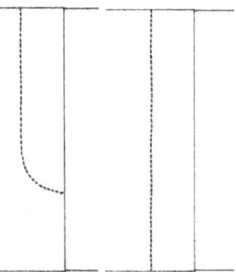

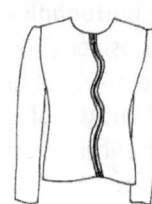 ✂ To prevent open-ended zips from forming waves when inserted, make the garment 1.2cm (½") *longer* than the zip and ease the zip in. It isn't hard to ease this amount in—you'll barely notice it. For a long-line jacket, make the garment 2cm (¾") longer.

✂ **Zip too short?**
It's considered OK, even desirable, to have two short steps with no zip at the bottom of the garment. This is handy in garment production if you're planning to use the same length zip on several sizes of garment. The sizes can be graded as usual, with slightly different length steps for each size.

If the zip is *really* too short, consider having it start a little way down from the neck, if you'll never wear it zipped up anyway.

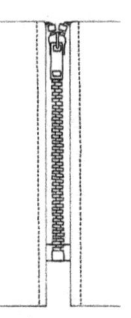

✂ **Plastic zip too long?**
There are no neat answers to shortening a plastic open-ended zip, other than buying the correct length in the first place. You could fold back the top ends and stitch them in position at the desired length, but the zip gets bulky at the top.

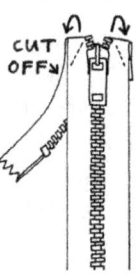

✂ **To shorten a metal open-ended zip**
1. Measure exactly how short you want the zip to be and place a mark on the zipper tape, each side of the zip teeth.

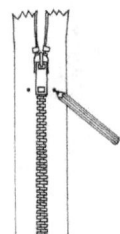

2. You'll need a pair of small pincers (similar to the ones used for removing nails, but finer) from a hardware shop or beading/jewellery making shop. Use the pincers to very carefully remove the two stops from the top of the zip. Put them in a safe place.

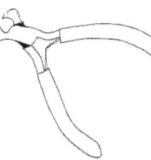

3. Still using the pincers, remove the metal teeth above the marked position, leaving about 2.5cm-3cm (1"-1¼") of tape with no teeth. Put the top stops back on. Do up the zip and double-check to see if it's the correct length. If you lose one of the top stops, just put one back on and the zip will still work. Actually,

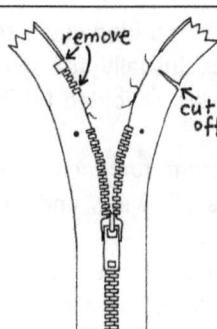 you won't need any top stops once the zip is sewn in, but you'll have to be careful until it is.

4. Cut off the excess tape at the top of the zip. Using a flame, melt off the fuzziness on the tape caused when you removed the teeth.

✂ Some zip retailers will shorten zips for you, and sometimes they can change the zip pull for you, too.

Exposed open-ended zip
Allow at least 1cm (⅜") seam allowances for the garment's edge. 1.5cm (⅝") or 2cm (¾") are fine too. Note that an exposed zip will add an extra 1cm (⅜") of width to the middle of the garment because the zipper teeth take up space. Some people compensate for this by taking slightly more seam allowance when they insert the zip, but I don't usually worry about it.

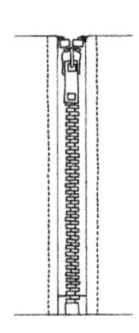

An exposed zip may or may not have a facing, but it looks neater to see a facing inside when the zip undone.

1. Overlock the edges of the garment, if there's no facing.

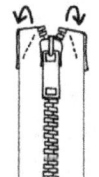

2. Fold under the ends of the tape behind the zip and stitch, so the top of the zip is level.

3. Place the zip *face down* onto the right side of the garment. Position the top and bottom of the zip with pins then pin in between. Pin with the zipper tape uppermost and the garment underneath. If the seam allowance is greater than 1cm, move the zip in accordingly so you're stitching *on* the seam line.

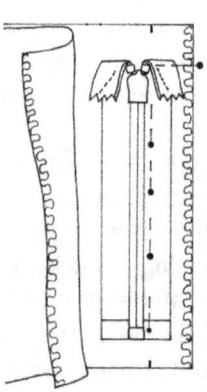

4. Using a zipper foot, stitch the zip in place alongside the teeth taking a 1cm (⅜") seam. Repeat for the other side.

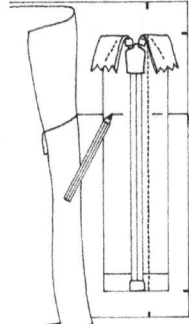

✂ If the zip passes through any **seam junctions** they need to be matched on each side. Place a mark on the tape of the zipped-up zip after sewing the first side, then use the mark to line up the seam on the second side.

5. If there's a **facing**, separate the zip and lay the facing on top of the garment, with the zip sandwiched in between. Stitch with the garment side up, on top of the previous stitching.

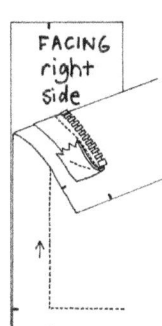

6. Sew the other parts of the garment, such as the collar and hem. If the neck edge of the garment is faced, finish it off *before* sewing the final row of topstitching on the zip in Step 7. Simply fold the garment back on itself along the front fold line, right sides together, and stitch across the top. Trim the corner and fold through to the right side.

7. Topstitch the zip at the very end. I usually stitch 6mm (¼") either side but the topstitching should match the rest of your garment. If the topstitching has to go through a band of a different colour, it looks better if you change the threads to match. For a perfect finish, leave long tails instead of backstitching and afterwards pull them through to the back and tie them off.

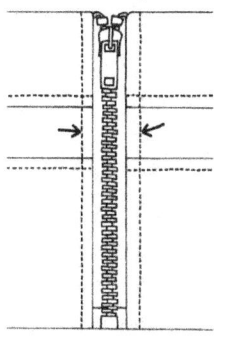

✂ On unlined jackets you could use wide herringbone twill tape as a facing.

✂ You can also have the facing on the *outside* of the jacket as a feature. Cut a strip of fabric to use as the facing, at least 4cm (1½") wide. Lay the *wrong side* of the zip onto to the *wrong side* of the garment and stitch, then lay the *right side* of the facing

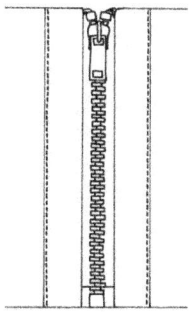

over the top, sandwiching the zip, and stitch. The facing will conceal the raw edges.
Topstitch the facing down on the right side.

Centred open-ended zip

For a centred zip you'll need at least 1.5cm (⅝") seam allowances, preferably 2cm (¾").

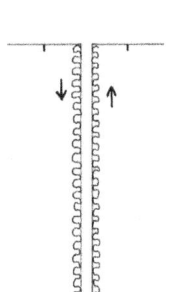

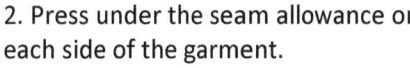

1. Overlock the edges of the garment, if there's no facing.

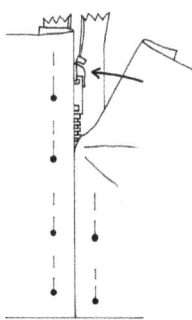

2. Press under the seam allowance on each side of the garment.

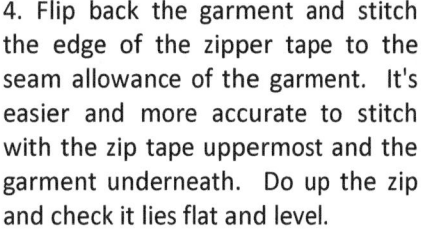

3. Position the zip under each edge, with the folded edges meeting over the centre of the zipper teeth.

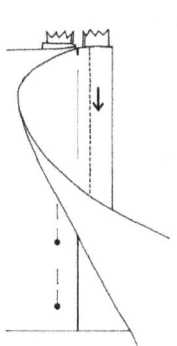

4. Flip back the garment and stitch the edge of the zipper tape to the seam allowance of the garment. It's easier and more accurate to stitch with the zip tape uppermost and the garment underneath. Do up the zip and check it lies flat and level.

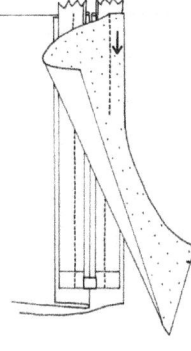

5. If you have a facing or lining, trim off all the seam allowance on the edge. Stitch the facing to the edge of the previous seam, matching it to the edge of the *zip*, taking a good 6mm (¼") seam allowance.

6. Sew the other parts of the garment such as the collar and hem.
If the neck edge of the garment is faced, finish it off *before* sewing the final row of topstitching on the zip in Step 7. Simply fold the garment back on itself, right sides together, along the front fold line and stitch around the neckline. Trim the corner and fold through to the right side.

7. Topstitch the zip at the very end, to hold it in place. Stitch about 6mm-1cm (¼"-⅜") away from the fold. If you separate the zip, you can use the seam guide on your machine to stitch straight.
If the topstitching has to go through a band of a different colour, it looks better if you change the threads to match. For a perfect finish, leave long tails instead of backstitching, and afterwards pull them through to the back and tie them off.

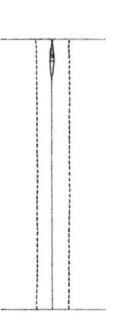

Concealed open-ended zip

A concealed open-ended zip is essentially a lapped zip. Note that the zip doesn't have to extend to the hem of the garment; indeed, on long-line jackets you might not want it to.
As with exposed and centred zips, the zip is sandwiched between the facing and the garment and topstitched into place at the end.

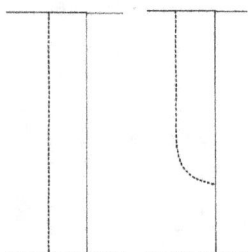

The garment will need a wrap on the side that overlaps (see page 106 for an explanation of wrap). 2cm (¾") is usual for jackets.
On the **overlap side**, add twice the 2cm wrap and a 1.5cm (⅝") seam allowance to the centre front.
On the **underlap side**, add a seam allowance of 1cm (⅜") to the centre front.

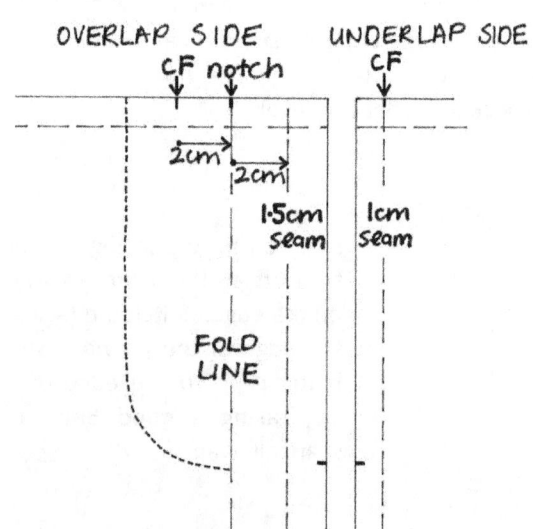

It's fine not to have a **facing** or lining behind the zip, but it looks better with one. Use the garment pattern to make the facing pattern. On the underlap side, cut the facing the same as the garment. On the overlap side, trim 1cm (⅜") off the centre front (or just fold back the excess).

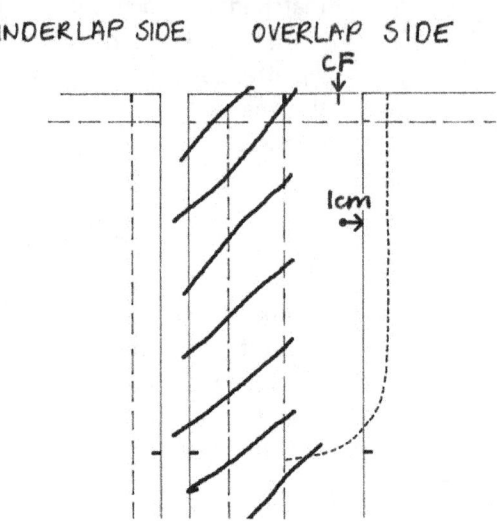

Clearly mark on the pattern pieces which way up they're to be cut, and write PTO (Please Turn Over) on the reverse in case a piece is accidentally flipped.

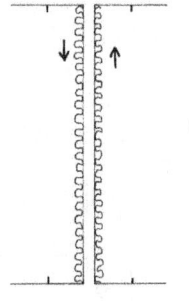

1. If there's no facing or lining, overlock the edges of the garment.

2. Place the zip *face down* onto the right side of the garment's underlap. Match the edges and sew with a 1cm (⅜") seam, using a zipper foot.
Repeat for the overlap side, taking a 1cm (⅜") seam, *even though the pattern has 1.5cm*—the difference compensates for the width of the teeth.

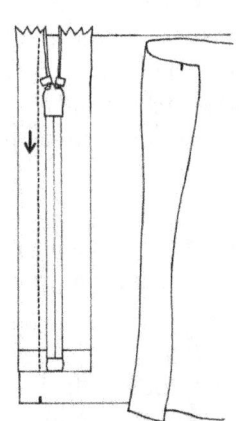

Zips open ended

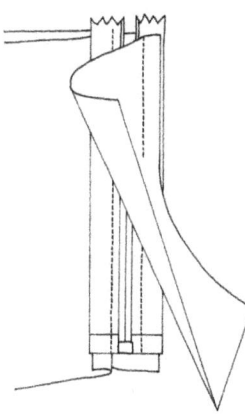

3. Separate the zip. Lay the facing or lining on the garment, with the zip sandwiched in between. Stitch with the garment side up, following the exact line of the previous stitching.

4. Press the folds in the fabric to conceal the zip. Sew the other parts of the garment such as the collar and hem. If the neck edge of the garment is faced, finish it off *before* sewing the final row of topstitching on the zip in Step 5. Simply fold the garment back on itself, right sides together, along the front fold line and stitch across the top. Trim the corner and fold through to the right side.

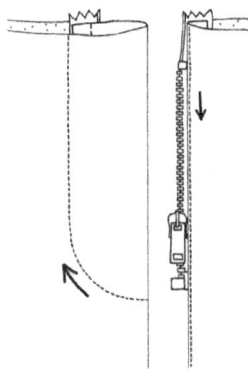

5. At the very end, topstitch the zip in place to hold it. Be sure to clear the bottom stop of the zip if you're curving the end of the topstitching like a fly front. If there's no facing, that's OK—just make sure the final row of topstitching on the overlap side catches in the zip.

You can also edgestitch the underlap side of the zip to hold it in place (optional, but I usually do). Edgestitch either the whole length of the seam or just where the zip is.

Zips in fur fabric

Fur poses the problem of fluff getting caught in the zip, as well as the thickness of the fur fabric. There are a few options for zips to help this:

✂ Sew the open-ended zip in as an exposed zip (see page 428). Afterwards smooth the fur away from the zip and topstitch 6mm (¼") away from the edge.

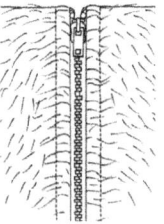

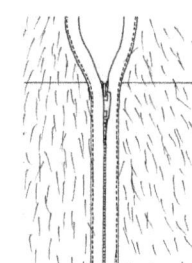

✂ Apply a binding, say 1cm (⅜") wide finished, to the zip edge, then sew the zip in behind so the edges of the binding meet in the centre of the zip. This is a good solution to jackets with hoods—the binding can go around the hood and down the fronts.

✂ Sew the zip as an exposed zip with a narrow facing, say 2.5cm (1") wide, on the *outside* of the garment, to keep the fur well away from the zip's teeth. You could also insert a strip of plain matching fabric in the centre front before sewing the zip in. If the fur is very long, trim it away under the facing to reduce bulk.

Glossary

Accordian pleats Fine, narrow, regular pleating, usually from the waistband to the hem.

Acetate A man-made cellulose shiny fabric or yarn. It dissolves in acetone. Acetate is often used as a lining fabric.

Acrylic A synthetic fibre often used as a substitute for wool. It's a warm, strong fibre that drapes well, dries quickly and requires little if any ironing.

A-line A dress or skirt shape dating from 1955, coined by Christian Dior for his spring collection. It flares from the bust or waist to form the two sides of a triangular A. The hem is the third side.

Appliqué A piece of fabric stitched on top of a larger one for decoration.

Appliqué scissors See Duck billed scissors.

Argyle A pattern of diamonds with diagonal stripes through the centres of them. Commonly knitted into socks, sweaters and vests, Argyle has its roots in Scottish culture and is alive and well today on the golfing scene. Formerly worn by men; now worn by men and women.

Armscye A patternmaking term meaning armhole.

Ascot A cravat with wide ends, worn around the neck and looped under the chin. Originally part of men's formal dress, it's now worn by women too.

Bag out To sew the edges of an area with the right sides together (forming a bag), then turn it through the right way. It's referred to as bagging out or to bag out.

Basque A wide band around the middle (waist) of a dress or at the waist of a skirt or trousers.

Basting Stitching, either by hand or machine, used to hold pieces together temporarily. The stitches are longer than a normal sewing stitch. It's also called tacking. The stitches may or may not be removed after permanent sewing.

Bateau neckline Shallow, boat-shaped neckline which runs from one shoulder to the other, the same depth back and front. It's also called a boat neckline.

Batik A form of resist dying that originated in Indonesia. Hot wax is applied to certain areas of fabric to prevent those areas from being dyed. The fabric is crushed to crack the wax and then dyed. Removal of the wax after dying leaves undyed areas covered in fine lines.

Bell bottoms Trousers that flare from the knee to the hem. Traditionally worn by sailors because they're easier to roll up when wet. Variations are flares, flared trousers or boot leg trousers.

Bermuda shorts Shorts with a straight leg that finish 5cm (2") above the knee.

Besom pocket Another name for a jet pocket.

Bias A diagonal direction in the fabric. True bias is a 45 degree angle to the lengthwise grain.

Bias cut Clothing that is bias cut has the centre front and back grainlines at 45 degrees to the straight grain of the fabric. Bias cut clothing falls in soft folds. Clothing cut on the bias is also referred to as clothing "cut on the cross" or occasionally "diamond cut" (usually for lingerie).

Bishop sleeve A long sleeve on a dress or blouse which is full below the elbow and gathered or left loose at the wrist.

Block A basic, master pattern used as a starting point for pattern adaptations. A block has seam allowances. A patternmaking workroom will have several blocks for different types of garments. Beginning with a block makes patternmaking faster and helps to ensure consistency of fit.

Blouson A blouse or jacket gathered to fall in soft folds on a band around the hips. It can be gathered on a band or by a drawcord. Usually worn as casual attire.

Bluffing An older, clothing industry word meaning understitching.

Boa A long fluffy scarf made of feathers.

Boat neckline See Bateau neckline.

Bobbin The lower thread supply on a sewing machine. It's a small spool pre-wound with thread from the reel.

Bodice The top (above the waist) part of a dress or coat. It's a term used for women's and children's clothes, not men's.

Bodkin A tool shaped like a long, blunt needle used for threading elastic or cord through a casing. It could also be used to turn rouleau or bias tubing around the right way. Some have an eye to thread the cord through and others are like tweezers that clamp onto the cord.

Boiler suit Overalls with sleeves worn as protective workwear.

Glossary 433

Boning Originally whalebone or steel, now usually nylon, strips inserted into casings used to provide support for bustier/strapless tops or corsets.

Boot legs Trousers that flare from the knee like bell bottoms, but flaring only a small amount to accommodate boots worn underneath. Circa 1990's and onwards.

Bootleggers See Deck pants.

Boucle A nubbly, textured fabric with a looped pile. From the French boucler—to curl.

Bound buttonhole A buttonhole made by stitching a patch of fabric onto the garment in a rectangle. The hole for the button is cut in the rectangle, then the patch is turned to the wrong side forming a binding at the edges.

Box pleat A pleat made of two knife pleats turned inward towards each other. The pleats are made on the wrong side resulting in a flat section on the right side. A feature of box-pleated skirts and old tunic school uniforms for girls.

Breast pocket A pocket on the breast of a shirt, jacket or coat. If there's only one pocket it's usually on the left side. It may be any type of pocket, for example a patch pocket or welt pocket.

Busk A long, flat piece of wood, ivory or whalebone which was inserted down the front of a corset.

Bustier A strapless, boned top. Originally underwear, now worn for evening wear.

Bustle Padding worn under women's skirts to make their bottoms look big and their waists look small, fashionable in the late 1800's. Often the skirt was draped over the bustle, adding to the effect. A "bustle backed" skirt can be used to describe a skirt with extra fullness or draping at the back.

Caftan or kaftan. A very simply and loosely cut ankle length garment, open at the front neck and made from only one or two pieces of fabric. It has long, wide sleeves and is pulled on over the head. It may or may not have a belt or sash. It's worn by men or women.

Camiknickers Women's underwear that combines camisole and knickers. The knickers are the French knicker/loose shorts type.

Camisole Simple tube-shaped women's underwear that covers the bust to waist and has fine shoulder straps.

Cap sleeve A small sleeve that sits on the shoulder, forming a cap. Popular for women's summer wear.

Capri pants Or just Capris. Pants tapered to the mid-calf and associated with summer resort wear. Named after the island of Capri, they became fashionable in the 1950's.

Car coat A hip-length, semi-fitted jacket, often double breasted. Styled to be convenient for driving in, it originated in the USA in the 1950's.

Carbon paper Dressmaker's carbon paper is used to transfer pattern markings such as darts and positions of pockets from the pattern to the fabric, ready for sewing. A tracing wheel is used to imprint the pattern markings through.

Catsuit All-in-one fitted stretch garment, usually with long sleeves, which is zipped or buttoned at the front from the navel to the neck. It was popular in the 1960's and was often worn with boots.

Chemise A very simple garment, usually constructed from two rectangles of fabric sewn at the shoulders and sides. Made of cotton, linen, lawn or silk, it can be collarless and sleeveless. Originally an undergarment; before the 19th century it was worn under a corset.

Cheongsam Close fitting, slim, Chinese dress for women with mandarin collar and long, short or no sleeves. It fastens with closures made of knotted fabric and has a slit at both sides to permit walking. It can be made in patterned silk brocade in rich, bright colours or plain fabrics. It's mainly worn as formal wear for important occasions or as a uniform. Also known as a mandarin gown, and in Mandarin Chinese as a qipao (pron chee-pow). The male version is the changshan.

Clapper A tailors pressing tool sometimes called a pounding block. It's a heavy, smooth piece of wood about as big as your hand and 5cm (2") thick. It's used to make seams really flat after they've been pressed.

Contour darts See Double pointed darts.

Couture A French word that translates as sewing. Haute couture means high sewing or high fashion.

Cowl neck A wide, simple, unstructured collar which drapes in soft folds around the neck.

Crêpe A type of weave with overtwisted, crinkled threads. It doesn't crease easily, drapes well and has a matt finish. It's not a strong fabric due to the overtwist.

Crew neck A plain, round flat neckline that sits close to the base of the neck. Often seen on t-shirts, windcheaters and sportswear.

Crewel Crewel needles are medium length hand sewing needles with (easy to thread) oblong eyes. They're intended for embroidery, but many people use them for all their handsewing.

Crinoline An alternative to petticoats to make skirts stand out, made from hoops to form a cage.

Croqui A fashion croqui (pronounced crow-kee) is a drawing of a figure model in various poses used as a template for sketching apparel. A croqui is traditonally taller and more slender than an average person.

Cross tucks Rows of tucks made at 90 degrees to each other.

Culottes Also called a divided skirt or pantskirt. Culottes look like a skirt but have separate legs.

Dart A way of shaping the fabric to fit the body. It's a stitched tuck of fabric which tapers to nothing at the point.

Dauber A small rolled up piece of wool fabric dipped in water and used to apply moisture when pressing.

Deck pants Sometimes called bootleggers, they're straight legged pants that are rolled up and cuffed at the knee.

Décolleté A low-necklined bodice of a dress or blouse.

Denier A unit of measure for the density of fibres. A fibre is generally considered a microfibre if it's one denier or less. The opacity of tights and pantyhose is described in denier. The lower the number the more transparent they are; less than 20 denier is sheer and 70+ is opaque.

Directional stitching A technique of stitching in a particular direction to produce a better seam, especially on loosely woven or unstable fabrics. It prevents the fabric from changing shape or rippling.

Directoire See Empire line.

Dirndl A full skirt gathered into a waistband, typical of traditional peasant costume.

Double pointed darts Sometimes called contour darts. The widest part is at the waist, tapering in either direction towards the bust and the hip, or to the fullest part of the back and hip.

Drill A strong cotton fabric, similar to denim, with a twIll weave. Used for workwear.

Duck-billed scissors Scissors with one blade wider than the other. Also called appliqué scissors. They're used for appliqué and grading seam allowances. The wide blade helps to cut through only one layer of fabric at a time.

Ease (1) Extra room which is built into a garment to allow for comfortable wearability. It's the difference between the wearer's measurements and the finished garment's measurements. (2) Ease also refers to how a seam is sewn when one side is longer than the other. One side of the seam is eased into the other side, for example to "ease the sleeve into armhole".

Edgestitching A line of topstitching sewn 2mm from a folded edge or seam. It's sometimes called pinstitching, because it's a pin width away from the edge.

Elastic Fabric made from interwoven threads of rubber, making it stretchy.

Elephant pants Women's wide cut trousers, full and flowing. Worn for evening wear in the 1970's.

Empire line High waisted women's dress with a fitted bodice ending just below the bust attached to a straight gathered skirt. Fashionable in the late 1700's and early 1800's. Sometimes empire is pronounced "om-peer". It's also known as directoire.

Epaulet Shoulder tab, originally on military coats and jackets, for decoration or for keeping military accoutrements in place.

Facing A piece of fabric used to cleanly finish the edge of a garment. It's cut the same shape as the edge it will finish. The facing is stitched to the garment's edge then turned to the inside of the garment. It doesn't show on the right side.

Fagotting Criss-cross stitch used to make a open, decorative join between two edges of fabric.

Feed dogs or feed. The zig-zag shaped metal teeth that sit under the presser foot of a sewing machine. The fabric sits between the feed dogs and the presser foot and the feed dogs move the fabric into position for each stitch. The feed dogs can be lowered to darn or for free-form quilting. They can also be changed to make the machine sew in reverse.

Felt A fabric made by matting fibres together so they permanently interlock. Felt doesn't fray and is often, but not always, wool.

Fibres All fabrics are made from fibres. It may be a natural fibre from an animal or plant, such as cotton, wool, silk or linen, or it may be a synthetic fibre like nylon, polyester, acrylic or acetate. It may be a blend of more than one type. The fibre is formed into a yarn and is knitted or woven into fabric.

Flat bed The flat, table area of a sewing machine which the fabric lies on as it's being sewn. The opposite of flat bed is free arm, where there's only a small area for the fabric to lie on. In industry, flat bed refers to a straight stitch sewing machine as opposed to an overlocker.

Flat felled seam A strong flat seam traditionally used for men's shirts. It's sewn with two rows of stitching, either manually or using a special machine foot, and results in the raw edges hidden inside.

Flounce A gathered strip of material that's sewn on the edge of a garment, for example on a hem or neckline.

Fly front A concealed zipper or buttons at the front of trousers. In men's clothes it closes left over right and in women's right over left.

Free arm A free arm sewing machine has only a small table area for the fabric to lie on as it's being sewn. It's useful for sewing small circular seams like cuffs or armholes, but it's not as fast as a flat bed machine for general sewing. Most domestic machines can convert from a free arm to a flat bed with a removable plate.

French curve A ruler in a curved shape used for patternmaking. The shape is traced to make smooth-flowing curves for necklines, armholes and style lines.

French knickers Women's underwear that resembles shorts.

French tack See Swing tack.

Frill Narrow ruffle gathered to the edge of a neckline, armhole, cuff or hem.

Frog A decorative button and loop closure made from fabric or cord. A feature of traditional Chinese dress.

Fun fur Imitation fur.

Fusing Another word for iron-on interfacing. Fusing is used to shape, stiffen, strengthen and give extra support and body to the main fabric.

Gabardine A smooth surfaced, twill weave fabric that's strong. It has fine diagonal lines in the weave.

Gangsters Wide, straight legged trousers. They're usually cuffed, and often have front waistline pleats and front creases.

Gaucho pants Named for the South American cowboys who originally wore this trouser style. They're a culottes-type garment but not designed to look like a skirt. Often banded at the waist, they flare from the hips to wide hemlines somewhere below the knee.

Gibson sleeve A very full sleeve from the shoulder to the tight wrist, often with a puff at the shoulder for added fullness.

Gigot sleeve Also called a leg of mutton sleeve. It's tight fitting from wrist to elbow, then balloons out from the elbow to shoulder, where it's gathered or pleated into the armhole.

Gilet A waistcoat, vest or sleeveless jacket that may be waist length or as long as knee length, with straight sides rather than fitted. It's an outdoor garment worn as an outer layer for warmth.

Gingham Traditionally a cotton fabric, gingham is a checked, woven pattern using two colours, one of which is white.

Godet A triangular shaped piece of fabric sewn into a garment to increase fullness around the hem. Mostly used on skirts and dresses but sometimes on other garments. A godet can be sewn into a seam or a slit in the fabric.

Gore A flared skirt panel, wider around the hem than the waist. A skirt may be sewn from four, five, six, eight, ten or more gores.

Grading A patternmaking term. Grading is a technique used to reproduce a pattern in other sizes.

Grading or layering. A method of trimming the seam allowance to remove bulk. The seam allowances are trimmed to different widths.

Grain The direction that the threads in woven fabric run in. When fabric is woven, the warp threads are positioned first on the loom and the weft threads are interlaced over and under them. The lengthwise grain is the direction of the warp threads and the crosswise grain is the weft. The lengthwise grain is referred to as the straight grain.

Grainline A line printed on the garment pattern piece to align with the lengthwise grain. It helps to position the pattern correctly on the fabric.

Grosgrain ribbon A firm ribbon with a ribbed appearance. It's used in hats as an inside hat band and as a regular ribbon or trim.

Gusset A small, triangular or diamond shaped piece of fabric which is inserted into the seams of a garment to improve fit and facilitate movement. A gusset is usually in the underarms or crotch.

Ham See Tailors ham.

Haute couture French for high sewing. Individually created, rather than mass-produced clothes. Haute couture is expensive, perfectly fitting and predominantly hand sewn.

Hem allowance The amount of fabric turned up to make a hem.

Hem An amount of fabric which is turned up at the lower edge of all garments and is held in place by a hemming stitch.

Henley shirt A casual, collarless shirt that began as uniforms worn by the rowing crews in Henley-on-Thames, England. It's often worn oversized and the sleeves may be three quarters length or long. It has a buttoned placket at the front, containing 2-6 buttons.

Hipsters Also called low-rise pants, they're trousers that sit below the natural waist. The waist may be finished with a narrow waistband or a facing. They may be worn by men or women.

H-line The sack or H-line is a dress shape introduced by Dior in 1954. With the bust up high and the waist at hip level it creates the cross bar of the letter H.

Hobble skirt A pre-WW1 skirt style introduced by Poiret. It was slim and tight to the ankle and only allowed the wearer to take the smallest of steps.

Hostess pyjamas A fashion outfit of the 1960's. A loose fitting, flowing pants outfit worn for both lounging and entertaining. Often made from silk, rayon or cotton, hostess pyjamas have a fitted top with loose-fitting culottes style pants or shorts.

Ikat fabric A fabric design that is calculated before the fabric is woven. The threads are strategically dyed to produce the pattern. Although ikat is an Indonesian word, the weaving style is common to many cultures including Indonesia, India, Japan, Thailand, Philippines, Uzbekistan and Central and South America.

Interfacing A sew-in or iron-on fabric used to stabilize the fashion fabric. It can also be used to add body, reinforce or shape a garment.

Interlining An extra layer of fabric applied to the garment or its lining to improve warmth.

Inverted pleat The reverse side of a box pleat.

Jabot A decorative frill of lace or other fine fabric falling from the base of the neck at the front. It's often seen in equestrian attire or Scottish highland dress.

Jamaica shorts Straight legged shorts that finish mid-thigh.

Jaquard Decorative weave created on the jaquard loom, descriptive of brocade or damask.

Jeans Denim trousers with a front fly zip or buttons, waistband, five pockets and stress points reinforced with copper rivets. Originally made as sturdy work trousers, they're now worn as casual wear by people of all ages.

Jerkin Hip length garment, with or without sleeves, that fastens at the sides or shoulders. It often has slits in the side.

Jewel neck A plain, round neckline that sits close to the base of the neck. Essentially the same as a crew neck, but applied to more formal clothes.

Jog An angled extension on the edge of a hem fold, dart or pleat top required for folding the fabric accurately into position once it's stitched.

Jumpsuit Trousers and a top in one, opening at the front with a zip or buttons. May or may not have sleeves.

Jute A glossy, lustrous fibre obtained from the jute plant and spun into coarse, strong threads. Used to make hessian and upholstery fabrics.

Keyhole neckline A neckline fitting closely to the sides of the neck, scooping wide and low at the front and resembling an upside down keyhole.

Kickpleat A short pleat or vent at the centre back, front or side of a skirt to allow room for walking.

Kilt An important part of men's Scottish highland dress. A traditional kilt consists of 7½ yards of tartan cloth, pleated except for the last ½ yard at each end. The unpleated "aprons" cross over each other at the front and are held in place by buckles or a large pin. Kilts have been worn as fashion garments for women since the 1940's.

Kimono sleeve A simple sleeve that's cut as an extension of the body.

Knickerbockers Loose pants that finish just below the knee. The lower edge is often gathered into a band and fastened by a buckle or button.

Knickers (1) Underpants, usually women's. (2) Abbreviation of knickerbockers.

Knife pleats A simple type of pleat with the fold facing in one direction.

Lamé Fabric woven with flat metallic threads. Popular for evening wear.

Lapel Part of the front neckline of a blouse, coat, dress or jacket that turns back.

Lawn Fine, lightweight sheer cotton. Used for underwear or delicate blouses.

Liberty bodice A sleeveless vest-like undergarment made of soft warm fabric and worn by girls in the first half of the 1900's.

Lining A lining is constructed separately of thinner, less expensive, fabric and used to finish off the inside of a garment.

Lurex A metallic fibre yarn, woven or knitted into fabric.

Madras fabric A lightweight 100% cotton fabric associated with summer clothes and originally from Madras in India. It comes in a variety of checked patterns and can have very large pattern repeats.

Magyar sleeve A long sleeve with a deep armhole cut as an extension of the body.

Mandarin collar A stand-up collar used on jackets, dresses or blouses. A feature of traditional Chinese dress.

Matelasse fabric French for quilted, padded or cushioned. Matelasse is a thick heavy textile that looks padded but actually has no padding within the fabric. It's usually 100% cotton in solid colours.

Melton Thick, smooth surfaced wool coat fabric.

Mercerised cotton Cotton treated with sodium hydroxide to bring out certain properties. First discovered by John Mercer in 1851, the process was refined by Horace Lowe in 1890. Mercerised cotton is stronger, smoother and shinier than regular cotton. It takes dyes more readily and the process shrinks the cotton fibres, tightening and smoothing the grain of the thread. It's used for sewing threads and fabric.

Microfibre A synthetic fabric woven from an extremely fine fibre of less than one denier. As a result, microfibre is resilient, crease resistant and repels stains.

Midriff The part of the body between waist and chest. A midriff top finishes at the midriff.

Mitre The diagonal line formed by connecting the inside and outside corners of two strips crossing at right angles. It's a good solution to eliminating the bulk caused by folding two edges over each other at the corners.

Moiré A water wave effect on (usually evening) fabric, for example taffeta.

Nap A brushed surface on a fabric, creating a soft, fuzzy texture that runs in one direction.

Negligee A women's nightgown or dressing gown, fancy, sheer, silky and trimmed with lace.

Nehru collar A feature of the Nehru jacket, which is straight, slim, hip length and buttoned in front to a straight, standing collar. Worn by Jawaharlal Nehru, first PM of India 1947-64.

Notch (collar) The small v in a rever collar.

Nest A patternmaking term. A nest is all of the sizes of one pattern piece stacked on top of one another. Multi-sized commercial patterns are printed in a nest for you choose the size you want.

Notches or nicks. Tiny 3mm (⅛") snips made with scissors within the seam allowance for the purpose of matching the edges of the seam when it's joined.

Notions Items other than fabric required to make a garment, for example zips, buttons and thread.

Oxford bags A trouser style worn by undergraduates at Oxford university in the 1920's. The wide hem measured about 50cm (20") and was cuffed. Also a popular pants style for women in the 1930's and 1970's.

Pad stitching A hand stitch used by tailors to mould the collar and lapels of a jacket, sewing permanent shape into it. Factories use a pad stitching machine.

Pagoda sleeve A three quarter length sleeve featuring several tiers of flounces becoming larger towards the hem. The tiers are curved to resemble a pagoda's roof, and are often trimmed with ribbons and bows. Popular in the mid 19th century.

Panne velvet Velvet with a high sheen achieved by rolling it flat. It's usually used for formal wear.

Pareo Patterned wrap-around beach skirt, similar to a sarong.

Patch pocket Pocket sewn onto the exterior of a garment, forming a patch with the top open.

Pedal pushers Mid-calf length, slim trousers.

Peg top skirt A skirt which is cut to be very full over the hips and narrow at the knee or ankle.

Peg top trousers Pants cut to be very full over the hips and narrowing towards the ankle.

Pencil pleats Continuous narrow pleats the width of a pencil used for the tops of curtains.

Pencil skirt A straight slim-fitting skirt finishing at the knee or mid-calf. It has a split or vent to permit walking.

Peplum A short length of fabric pleated, gathered or shaped and stitched onto the hem of a bodice.

Petersham A firm tape with a ribbed appearance used for stiffening or backing waistbands or belts. It may be straight or curved.

Pile A raised surface on a fabric. The pile can be cut (like velvet) or looped (like carpet).

Pinch pleats A type of pleating used for the tops of curtains, it resembles fabric that has been pinched together at intervals.

Pinking shears Scissors with tiny zig zags on the blade. To pink an edge is to cut it with pinking shears. Fabric cut with pinking shears resists fraying but is not especially robust.

Pinstitching See Edgestitching.

Pintucks Very narrow, decorative tucks, about 2mm deep, stitched by hand or by machine.

Piping A decorative, tubular trim made from a strip of bias-cut fabric wrapped around a cord. It's inserted into a seam or hem.

Placket A strip of fabric that finishes an opening or slit in a garment. Plackets are used for front or side garment openings and with shirt cuffs.

Plaid A design of woven or printed coloured bars that intersect at right angles. The design may be symmetrical or asymmetrical. Tartan is a type of plaid.

Pleat A fold of fabric held in place by stitching.

Polo neck sweater A jumper with a tubular neck that folds down onto itself. Also called a roll neck or skivvy neck. Not to be confused with the neck finish of polo shirts.

Polo shirt (Originally) tennis attire designed by tennis player Jean Rene Lacoste in c1929, when players had to wear long sleeved shirts and ties. The modern polo shirt is made from cotton knit, has two or three buttons on a front placket, a knitted collar and short sleeves.

Pounding block See Clapper.

Pressing mitt A pressing tool. A padded cushion used as a pressing area for small, curved garment areas. It has a pocket to slip your hand into.

Pret-a-porter French term for Ready to Wear. Clothes that carry a designer's label but can be bought ready-made.

Prick stitch A version of backstitch where only tiny dots of stitch appear on the surface. Also called pick stitch or half-backstitch.

Princess line A vertical seam in women's tops and dresses curving from the armhole over the bust to finish at the hem between the side seam and the centre front. The seam incorporates shaping for the bust and waist. Usually the back has matching seams. Shoulder princess line has the seam originating from the shoulder instead of the armhole.

Puffed sleeve Short sleeve gathered into the armhole of a garment to create a puff effect.

Raglan sleeve Sleeves with seams slanting diagonally from the under arm to the neck, eliminating the armhole shoulder seam.

Rajah cloth A special pressing cloth used to create a permanent crease in the fabric.

Ravel To fray.

Reinforce A line of stitching sewn to strengthen and prevent fraying, similar to stay-stitching. Reinforcing is done on a single layer of fabric before a seam is sewn. The reinforcing stops the fabric from fraying and tearing when stress is put on it.

Repeat A repeat refers to the design on patterned fabric. A repeat is the distance over which the design repeats itself. The larger the repeat, the more fabric is required in order to match the pattern on the garment.

Revers Wide lapel on a coat or jacket. A rever collar consists of a collar and lapels.

Ric rac A wavy, woven braid that's sewn on for decoration. It comes in different widths and colours.

Rigelene boning Flexible nylon boning used for strapless bodices. It's sold by the metre and comes in various widths, usually 6mm (¼") and 1.2cm (½").

Rouleau A narrow strip of material cut on the bias and sewn into a thin tube.

Running stitch A very simple, but not very strong, stitch done by hand. The point of the needle is woven in and out of the fabric before pulling the thread through. It can be used as a non-permanent tacking stitch and is sometimes used for decorative stitching.

Russia braid Sometimes called Soutache braid, it's a glossy, narrow braid with a groove down the centre. It's attached by stitching in the groove by hand or machine. Russia braid is used for cornelli, where the braid is arranged in a squiggly random design. It's also used for button loops and frog closures.

Sabrina neck Similar to a boat neck, but starting about 5cm (2") in from the shoulder for a smaller neckline.

Satin stitch Parallel stitches worked very closely together to cover an area solidly. A popular hand embroidery stitch, satin stitch can be machine made using a densely stitched zig zag.

S-bend silhouette Created by wearing a corset to produce a large, over-hanging, heavily padded bust and a small, flat waist, balanced at the back by a projecting bottom. The look culminated in full, flowing skirts, often gathered and raised onto a bustle. Popular in the late 19th and early 20th centuries.

Scallops Shallow U-shapes used to decorate and finish an edge.

Scoop neck Low, U-shaped neckline.

Seam allowance The distance a seam is sewn from the raw edge.

Seam line The stitching line. When two pieces of fabric are sewn together along the seam line, a seam is formed.

Seam roll A pressing tool. It's a firmly packed cylindrical cushion used to help press seams in narrow areas, for example sleeves or trouser legs.

Seersucker Lightweight, often cotton, fabric with a crinkly striped surfaced created by weaving together fibres of different shrinkage capabilities. Doesn't require ironing after laundering.

Selvedge or selvage. The woven, non-fraying edge of a piece of fabric that runs down both sides.

Serger American term for an overlocker machine. To serge is to sew a seam or edge with a serger.

Shank Made when a button is sewn on by winding thread between the button and garment to give a clearance when the button is done up. Some buttons already have their own shank.

Shawl collar A collar cut in one with the garment, which is turned down to form a continuous line around the back of the neck to the front.

Shears Scissors with 20cm (8") or longer blades.

Sheath Figure hugging dress with a straight skirt and any style of sleeve.

Shift A simple, unstructured dress of any length, referred to as a shift dress (or a shift).

Shirring A method of gathering used to bring in fullness and decorate parts of a garment. Shirring resembles smocking but is stretchy and machine-made. The sewing machine is threaded with regular thread at the top and the bobbin is hand wound with shirring elastic.

Shirring elastic A fine elastic used for shirring.

Skort Short, flared shorts that look like a skirt.

Slash To cut open.

Sleeve board A pressing tool resembling a mini ironing board. It clips or sits onto the real ironing board and provides a small flat surface to press narrow seams, detailed garment sections and hard-to-reach areas.

Sloper A pattern without seam allowances used for the purpose of creating other patterns.

Smocking Panel of material which is tightly gathered with decorative stitches. Smocking was traditionally used for English peasant smocks and is now often seen on the yokes of children's dresses.

Soutache braid See Russia braid.

Spencer jacket A short jacket with long sleeves reaching just below the bust. It may have a collar or be collarless. It may be single or double breasted but is usually worn done up. Worn by Jane Austen's characters.

Staystitch A line of stitching sewn to prevent the fabric stretching from being handled. It's sewn before any seams.

Stirrup pants Trousers which taper towards the ankle and have a strap, often elasticized, around the instep and under the foot. Sometimes called ski pants, they were popular in the late 1960's and the 1980's-early 1990's.

Stove pipes Trousers with straight, narrow legs.

Straight grain See Grain.

Sunray pleats Fine pleats radiating from the waistband of a skirt or dress.

Surplice neckline A false cross-over wrap-around front. The diagonal front seam is sewn up, creating a deep V neckline.

Sway back A common figure shape shared by much of the population. When viewed sideways, the person's waist dips in at the back and their bottom juts out.

Sweet heart neckline A neckline on dresses and blouses which is cut into two almost semicircular curves resembling a heart.

Swing tack Sometimes called a French tack or Paris tack. It's a thread chain about 2.5cm (1") long which connects a free hanging lining to the hem of the garment. Used on skirts, coats and jackets.

Tacking See Basting.

Tailors ham A pressing tool. A very firmly stuffed cushion with rounded edges used to help press shaped areas such as bust seams, darts or collars.

Tailors tacks A temporary thread tack used to transfer pattern markings from the pattern to the fabric. They're loose stitches made through the two thicknesses of fabric, then pulled apart and cut, leaving threads in each side. They are removed after sewing whatever they are marking.

Tartan Closely woven woollen cloth originating in Scotland, where different patterns identified individual clans. The fabric is cross banded with coloured stripes which create designs of various checked widths.

Taut sewing Holding the fabric taut as it's being sewn to prevent puckered seam.

Teddy One-piece undergarment of unstructured bodice and knickers. Similar to a one-piece swimsuit but loose.

Tencel The registered trade mark for Lyocell, which is a biodegradable fabric made from wood pulp cellulose.

Tension The tension regulates how tightly or loosely the thread is fed through the sewing machine. It's usually adjusted with a top dial, but there's also a bobbin thread tension adjusted by turning a screw.

Thimble A metal, plastic or leather protective cap for a finger used when handsewing.

Tie dye A resist method of dying fabric where the fabric is tied with string before dying. The string is untied afterwards revealing undyed areas forming a pattern. Associated with hippie clothing of the 1970's.

Tippet A small shawl, worn wound around the neck with the ends left hanging. Day or evening wear.

Toga A loose flowing garment made of a single piece of cloth covering the whole body apart from the right arm. Worn by citizens of ancient Rome.

Toile An initial mock-up of a garment in an inexpensive fabric for the purpose of checking the fit and pattern.

Topstitching Stitching done on the right side of the garment for decoration, strength or both.

Topstitching may be done by hand or by machine.

Toreador pants Tight fitting calf-length pants.

Tracing wheel Used with dressmakers carbon paper to transfer pattern markings to the wrong side of the fabric. The spikes on the tracing wheel imprint the carbon paper through. It can also be used as a patternmaking tool to imprint markings through cardboard.

Trapeze line Launched by Yves St Laurent in 1958. A wide, full, tent shape that falls free from the shoulders with a wide hem.

Trim (1) A decorative braid. (2) To cut back, for example "trim seam allowances".

Tuck A stitched pleat of any width.

True In correct alignment. To true a seam, the edge is either trimmed or added to to make it line up.

Turning Another word for seam allowance. It often refers to the seam allowances on the *edges* of a garment. For example "the neckline has 6mm turnings".

Turn of cloth The slight extra fabric taken when cloth folds or rolls over, typically for a collar or lapel. Weight roll is a less-commonly used term meaning the same thing.

Twill A type of weave. Twill weave has diagonal lines of weft threads passing alternately under and over warp threads. It's a strong weave.

Underlining A fabric applied to the wrong side of the garment to give extra strength, support or opacity. Another word for underlining might be "backing".

Understitching A line of straight stitching sewn next to the seam line (after the seam is sewn) through the inner fabric layer and seam allowance. It keeps the seam allowance and facings lying flat and in a particular direction.

Vandyke collar Large, white, lace trimmed collar that fans out over the shoulders. Sir Anthony Van Dyck (1599-1641) painted them in his portraits.

Velcro A fabric fastener made of synthetic fibres, sometimes called touch tape or hook-and-loop closure. The word Velcro is a registered trademark. Velcro consists of two fabric strips, one with soft loops on the surface and the other with tiny hooks. When the strips are pressed together, the hooks catch in the loops to fasten. They are separated by pulling them apart, making a ripping sound.

Velour A woven or knitted fabric with a thick, short pile. Knitted velour can be seen in 1970's leisure suits and science fiction uniforms.

Velvet A silk or synthetic fabric with a short cut pile and soft texture. It has a rich, lustrous appearance and is popular for winter evening wear.

Velveteen Cotton velvet, to imitate velvet.

View Each view on the front of a commercial sewing pattern envelope depicts a particular design. Each view is identified by a number or letter.

Viscose A man-made cellulose fibre derived from wood pulp. It's soft, comfortable to wear, inexpensive and dyes well. It may go by the brand name Rayon, and was originally called artificial silk or art silk.

Voile A fine, sheer, semi-transparent plain woven fabric, usually cotton.

Warp Loom threads which stretch lengthwise and are interwoven with the weft or filling threads.

Weft Crosswise threads interlaced between the warp threads on a loom to weave fabric.

Weight roll See Turn of cloth.

Wool The fibres obtained from sheep.

Woollen cloth A soft, almost felt-like cloth made from wool.

Worsted cloth A hard-wearing, smooth surfaced fabric made from wool. It's produced a little differently from woollen cloth. Before the wool is spun into a yarn, it's combed to remove any short and brittle fibres, leaving only the longer strands of the fibre. These fibres are spun with a high twist resulting in a smooth, strong, more durable, more elastic, more soil and crease resistant cloth that drapes and can be woven finely. Worsted cloth is usually more expensive than woollen cloth and is mainly used for tailored garments.

Yardage The amount of fabric required to make a garment. If the amount is in metric, it would be called a meterage. In the clothing industry, it's sometimes called a costing because it forms part of calculating how much a garment will cost.

Yardstick A wooden ruler, one yard in length.

Y-line Introduced by Dior in 1955. A slender body with a top-heavy look achieved by large collars that opened up into a V shape. The Y could also by inverted into the form of long tunics with deep slits at either side.

Yoke An upper portion of a garment, usually over the shoulders and across the upper back and front. It's joined by a seam to the rest of the garment. A yoke can also be an oversized, shaped waistband of a skirt from which the rest of the skirt hangs.

Further reading

Books

General sewing

Your sewing machine's manual
Sewing machine problem? Don't overlook the obvious book.

Reader's Digest Complete Guide to Sewing (*Reader's Digest Services Pty Ltd* 1977)
We had this book in our home when I was growing up. The 1977 edition is still considered the best and most comprehensive.

Fit for Real People by Pati Palmer and Marta Alto (*Palmer/Pletsch* 1998)
This would be one of the most user-friendly and comprehensive books on fit.

The Art of Manipulating Fabric by Collette Wolff (*Krause Publications* 1996)
An encyclopedia of techniques for the three dimensional manipulation of fabrics.

Sewing with an Overlock (Singer Sewing Reference Library) (*Cy DeCosse Incorporated* 1989)
Look past the 80's photography to find a great book on overlocking.

Claire Schaeffer's Fabric Sewing Guide (*Krause Publications* 2008)
A guide to sewing any fabric you can think of, plus inspirational photos on every page.

Specific garments

Jackets for Real People by Marta Alto, Susan Neall and Pati Palmer (*Palmer/Pletsch* 2006)
AND
Pants for Real People by Pati Palmer and Marta Alto (*Palmer/Pletsch* 2003)
Practical, generous and user-friendly.

Shirtmaking—Developing skills for fine sewing by David Page Coffin (*The Taunton Press* 1998)
AND
The Shirtmaking Workbook—Pattern, design and construction resources by David Page Coffin (*Creative Publishing International* 2015)
AND
Making Trousers for Men and Women by David Page Coffin (*Creative Publishing International* 2009)
Lots of ideas for sewing trousers and shirts, and customizing the details and look.

Sew a Beautiful Wedding by Gail Brown and Karen Dillon (*Palmer/Pletsch* 1980)
Practical advice on sewing for weddings.

Sewing for Men and Boys (*Simplicity Pattern Company Inc* 1973)
The styles might be retro, but the methods still work.

Kwik Sew series (Sewing for Baby, Sewing for Toddlers, Sewing for Children, Method for Sewing Lingerie, Swim and Action Wear, Sweatshirts Unlimited) by Kerstin Martensson (*Kwik Sew Pattern Co*)
These aren't just how-to books; they come with a master pattern sheet to make everything.

Fashion and sewing inspiration

If you visit a fashion exhibition, be sure to buy a souvenir catalogue for your inspiration library.

Fashion in Detail 1700-2000 by Claire Wilcox (*V&A Publishing* 2014)
AND
Underwear: Fashion in Detail by Eleri Lynn (*V&A Publishing* 2014)
AND
The Wedding Dress: 300 Years of Bridal Fashion by Edwina Ehrman (*V&A Publishing* 2014)
These sumptuously illustrated, hefty tomes offer close-up views of details from the richness of the Victoria and Albert Museum's famous collection.

Vintage Fashion Complete by Nicky Albrechtsen (*Thames and Hudson* 2014)

Patternmaking texts

Metric Pattern Cutting by Winifred Aldrich (*Unwin Hyman Ltd* 1985)
AND
Dress Pattern Designing, Dress Fitting, and **More Dress Pattern Designing** all by Natalie Bray (*Wiley-Blackwell* classic edition 2003)

AND
Patterncutting for Lingerie, Beachwear and Leisurewear by Ann Haggar (*BSP Professional Books 1990*)
These texts are easiest to use with a teacher. Aldrich was my textbook as a student, and Bray's books were in the reference library of several of my workplaces.

Patternmaking and inspiration
Madeleine Vionnet by Betty Kirke (*Chronicle Books* deluxe edition 2012)
THE book on Vionnet's pattern cutting. Includes small scale patterns, construction notes and biography.
AND
Vionnet by Bunka Fashion College, Japan (2009)
A companion volume to Betty Kirke's book, with scale patterns to try out.

Cut my Cote by Dorothy K Burnham (*Royal Ontario Museum* 1973)
A slim volume describing traditional clothes cut with zero waste to fit the width of the cloth.

Bias Cut Blueprints—a Geometric Method for Clothing Design and Construction by Julianne Bramson and Susan Lenahan (*Fashion in Harmony* 2014)
Easy to follow directions for making a variety of tops and dresses based on a bias-cut tube, inspired by Vionnet.

Patterns of Fashion (series of four books) by Janet Arnold (*Drama Publishers*)
Cut and construction of English historical fashion.

Drape Drape series by Hisako Sato (*Laurence King Publishing Ltd* 2012)
AND
Pattern Magic series by Tomoko Nakamichi (*Laurence King Publishing Ltd* 2010)
Japanese pattern books with patterns to draft for unusual and interesting clothes.

Style
What Not to Wear—The rules by Trinny Woodall and Susannah Constantine (*Weidenfeld and Nicolson* 2002)
Advice for women on choosing garments to suit body type and occasion.

Tim Gunn's Fashion Bible—a fascinating history of everything in your closet by Tim Gunn with Ada Calhoun (*Gallery Books* 2012)
Lively fashion advice for women and men.

Magazines
Threads (The Taunton Press)
Six issues per year of sewing articles and inspiration.

Burda Style
A monthly pattern magazine with up-to-the minute fashion styles, representing excellent value for money. Note that the patterns require tracing from a master sheet and the instructions are not illustrated.

www.seamwork.com
An online magazine with articles and patterns, produced by Colette Patterns.

Websites
www.burdastyle.com
A DIY fashion and sewing community. Buy patterns, use tutorials and read their project ideas and sewing forum.

www.patternreview.com
Read reviews of not only patterns but sewing machines, books, fabrics, expos, and more. Sewing forum, newsletters and tutorials.

www.aussew.org.au
Website for the Australian Sewing Guild—Sharing and Furthering the Art of Sewing.

www.asg.org
The American Sewing Guild—Advancing Sewing as an Art and Life Skill.

www.cutterandtailor.com
A forum (and more) for men's and women's tailoring.

www.ismacs.net
International Sewing Machine Collectors Society. Identify and discover how old your machine, accessory or sewing ephemera is, and search for a manual.

www.fashion-incubator.com
A blog with comprehensive archives on sewing and apparel manufacturing. Members may join the forum.

www.lizhaywood.com.au
Visit my sewing and fashion blog for reviews, discussion and patterns.

Index

a

adjustable waists 390, 397-398
all-in-one in-seam pockets 237
alterations for over 50's 1-4
    large bust 1-2
    rounded back 2
    close in neckline 2
    thick waist 3
    flat bum/big tum 3-4
    different sides 4
appliqué sheet 264
armhole
    sewing sleeve in 65, 333-334
    and neck facing 101-103
    fitting 334-336, 340
    measuring 338
Armoflexxx interfacing 378, 393
arms, large upper 337
arrow head 367

b

backstitch 148
backstitching, on machine 285, 297
Banrol interfacing 378, 393
bar tack 228, 230, 235, 236, 422
Barbara Hellyer 49, 309
basting 292
beaded lace 197
beading 203-206
belt loops 5-8
belts 9-16
    tie belts 9-10
    buckle belts 10-11, 12-13
    contour belts 11-12, 352
    attaching buckles 12-13
    petal belts 13-14
    plaited belts 14-16
    inside a strapless top 347
bias, definition of 17, 68
bias binding
    making and applying 22-27
    as a facing 26-27
    hemming with 156, 157, 163
    as a seam finish 287-288
    as a casing for boning 344
    to bind a waist 382-383
bias cut 17-19, 68
bias strips 20-21
binding 22-27
    to sew 23
    machine foot 23
    using tape or ribbon 24
    around curves 24
    around corners 25-26
    mitring 25-26
    binding a slit 26
    as a facing 26-27
    Hong Kong finish 288
    using seam allowance 288, 338
    bound shirt cuff placket 302-303
    around waist 382-383
blanket stitch 148-149
blind hem stitch 149-150, 159
blind hem, to sew 156-157, 159
blind herringbone stitch 149, 156
blood, removing stains 341
bodice, boned 343-348
body, measurements 75, 182-184
boning 343-344, 346
bound buttonholes 36-38
box pleats 213, 217, 313
bridal
    veils, gathering 132
    train with godet 141-142, 196
brocade 197-198
broomstick pleats 225
buckles, belt 10-11, 12-13
buckram 10, 393
bust improvers 345
butted seam 296
buttonhole elastic 390
buttonholes
    positioning 30-32
    cutting 32
    troubleshooting 32-33
    handmade 34-35
    buttonhole stitch 34-35, 148
    keyhole 35-36
    slit in seam 36
    bound 36-38
    button loops 38-40
    in men's trousers 396-397
button loops
    to make 38-40
    at centre back neck 61
    next to collar 112
    for lace 195
    for velvet 198
    with frogs 278-283
    for strapless tops 344
buttons
    to sew on 28-29
    reinforcement 29-30
    positioning 33-34
    of rouleau 279
buttons and buttonholes 28-40

c

cartridge pleats 222-224
casings
    around edge of hoods 63
    stitched on 134
    for elastic waists 384-392
carriers, belt 5-8
catch stitch 149-150, 156
Celtic ornament 283
centred zip 408, 410-411
chain piecing 293
chain weights for hems 160-161
chainstitching, unpicking 299
chalk, tailors 73, 341
channel seam 296-297
checked fabrics
    to cut 69, 80-84
    to pleat 219
    sewing, to match 290-291
Chinese closures 278-283
clapper 264
clipping curves 289-290
concealed front 110-115
concealed zip 430-431
collars 41-63
    types of 41
    parts of 42
    methods of attaching 42

fit 42-43
to change a garment's 43
flat collars 43-45
standing collars 45-52
shirt collars 46-50
men's shirt collars 48
shirt collar stays 50
mandarin collar 51
wing collar 51
Nehru collar 51-52
roll collar 52-55
rever collar 55-59, 351
neck darts in 60
tie collars 60-61
knit collars 61-62, 116-120
hoods 62-63, 431

construction, order of 64-66
contortion pleats 225
corded rouleau 278
corded tucks 356
corduroy 198-199
corners
    binding around 25-26
    of shirt collars 46
    mitred 185-189
    piping 212
    sewing 288-289
    trimming and turning 290
    of sleeve vent 338-340
    of vents and splits 357-369
cowboy shirt pockets 248-250
cowboy shirt yokes 315-316
crew neck (t-shirt neck) 61-62
crotch piecing, trousers 76-77
crotch seam binding 425-426
crotch seam, to sew 65
cufflinks 310
cuffs, shirt 300, 306-311
cuffs, trousers 161-162
curved jet pockets 248-250
curved slot seam 296-297
cut away pockets 241-245

cutting 67-84
on the bias 17-19, 72
preparing to 67-74
position pattern 72-74
using scissors 74-75
layouts 75-78
knits 79-80
stripes and checks 80-84

d

darts 85-96
bust 1-2, 88, 92, 94-96
underneath collars 60
to sew 85-86
troubleshooting 86
pressing 86-87, 266-267
double pointed 87
French darts 88
sewing by overlocker 88
in two layers of fabric 88
shaped darts 88
in interfacing 88-89
in striped fabrics 89
altering 89-90
to remove 92
in shoulder, neck 2, 93, 318
gape darts 93-94
darts in design 94-96
elbow 95, 332-333
lapped, for lace 197
dauber 265
design ease 183
Dior pleat 218, 359-360
directional stitching 352
double breasted 106
double piping 212
draping 207
drawcord waist 384-385, 388
drawcord elastic 388
dupion silk 193

e

ease (amount of in garment) 183-184, 327
ease (sewing)
    convert dart to 95
    seams with 291
    in armholes 331, 334
    elbow 332-333
Easter egg patch pockets 233
edgestitching 292, 349
elastic belts 13
elastic button loops 39-40
elastic waists 385-392
elbow darts 95, 332-333
ESL tape 168, 372
extended facings 97, 98
extension in-seam pockets 237, 239
eyelets 12

f

fabric
    preparing to cut 67-74
    prewashing 68-69
    shrinkage test 69
    straightening ends 69-70
    determining right side 70
    one-way 70
    patterned 70
    checks and stripes 80-84, 89, 290-291
    fur 160, 201-202, 431
    dupion silk 193
    tweed, novelty 193-194
    satin 194-195
    lace 195-197
    brocade 197-198
    velveteen 198-199
    panne velvet 198-199
    velvet 198-199, 269
    velour 198-199
    corduroy 198-199
    sheers 199-200, 338
    taffeta 200
    metallics 200-201

facings 97-104
using bias binding for 26-27
waist facing 65, 100-101
extended facings 97, 98
patternmake 97-99
to sew 99-100
troubleshooting 100
all-in-one 101-104
faced scallops 104
topstitching 351
top of with zip 406-407, 411-414
false hems 162-163
fast sewing 293
felling foot 294-295
finger pressing 267
fittings
    doing 65-66
    preparing for 209, 344
    afterwards 90, 298
fitting notes for
    over 50's 1-4
    bias cut 17-19
    collars 42-43, 60
    darts 88, 89-94
    gape darts 93-94
    wheelchair bound 162
    pleats 217

Index

shirt yokes 314
shoulder pads 317-318
kimono sleeve 329
raglan sleeve 330-331
armholes 334-335
set-in sleeve 334-336, 337
strapless top 344-345
flap pockets 229-231, 248, 255-257
flat collars 41, 43-45
flat felled seam 294-296
flat pattern drafting 207
fly front zips 419-427
foldback cuffs 310
French cuffs 310
French dart 88
French seam 19, 293-294
French tack 173
fringing for novelty tweed 194
frog fastenings 278-283
front button stands 105-115
    to change 105
    "wrap" explained 106
    fold-under stand 106-107
    double fold stand 107
    separate 107-108
    faced 108-109
    men's shirt 109-110
    concealed front 110-115
    placket with pleat 125
    all-in-one 126-127
front stands and tab fronts 105-129
full upper arms 337
fur
    cutting 70, 201
    hemming 160, 181
    sewing 202
    zips in 431
fusible interfacing 164-169
fusible web 160, 168

g

grosgrain ribbon
    binding with 24, 25-26
    as inner belt 347
    to reinforce splits 367
    as waistline binding 382-383
gaping armhole 340
gathering 130-137
    convert darts to 96
    amount of fabric req 130
    how to 130-131
    on heavy fabrics 130
    over long areas 131
    pressing 131, 267
    over a cord 132
    with a special foot 132
    using an overlocker 132
    smocking 132
    gathers on gathers 132
    using elastic 132-134
    shirring 133-134
    through a channel 134
    ruffles 134-135
    ruching 135
    ruched trim 135-136
    sleeves 136, 331
    from shirt yokes 136, 313
godets 138-143
    pattern for 138-139
    to sew in a seam 139
    to sew in a slit 139-140
    lining a 140
    pleated 140-141
    centre back 141-142
    with rounded tops 142
    with square ends 142
    troubleshooting 142-143
gored skirts, grainline 71
gorge line 42, 59, 351
grading seam allowances 289
grainline 71, 73
gusseted pockets 234-237
gussets, underarm 328-329

h

hand opening placket 127-129
handsewing essentials 144-152
    holding a needle 144
    thimbles 144-145
    threading a needle 145
    knotting the end 145-146
    finishing off 147
    running stitch 147
    backstitch 148
    blanket stitch 148-149
    buttonhole stitch 148-149
    hidden slip stitch 149, 157
    herringbone stitch 149, 156, 287
    blind hem stitch 149-150, 156
    whipstitch 150, 287
    press studs 150
    hooks and eyes 150-151, 397
    overcasting 287
    top of splits (arrowhead) 367
ham holder, tailors 264
header, sleeve 321, 326
hems 153-163
    lettuce leaf 19, 157
    stitches for 149-150, 156-157
    blind hem 153, 156-157, 159
    pressing 153, 267
    hem allowance 154
    determine hemline 154-155
    truing the sides 155
    sewing a hem 155-157
    narrow hems 157-159
    twin needle hem 159
    deep hems 159-160
    in pleats 160, 214-215
    fast hems 160
    in jackets 160
    in leather 160
    in fur 160
    shortening jeans 160
    rock 'n' roll t-shirt hem 160
    chain weighted 160-161
    trouser cuffs 161-162
    wheelchair trouser hems 162
    false hems 162-163
herringbone stitch 149, 287
herringbone twill tape
    binding with 24, 25-26, 382-383
    on shirt collars 48-49
    tab fronts 116, 121-122
    for seam neatening 287-288
hidden slip stitch 149, 157, 159
Hong Kong seam finish 288
hoods 62-63, 431
hooks and eyes 150-152, 397
hooks, clamp on 397

i

in seam pockets 237-241
interfacing 164-169
    behind buttonholes 30
    buying and storing 68, 167
    cutting out 74, 165-166
    darts in 88-89
    types of 164-165, 168
    where to interface 165
    applying 166-167
    troubleshooting 167
    specialty 168
    for waistbands 168, 372-373

    for jackets and coats 168-169
    Banrol/Armoflexxx 378
    men's waistbanding 395-396
interlining 171
inverted pleats 213, 218, 313
invisible seams for lace 196-197
invisible zips 403-408
invisibly applied patch pockets 232-233

j

jackets
    buttonholes 35-38
    Nehru collar 51-52
    roll collar 52-55, 60
    rever collar 55-56, 58-60, 351, 352
    concealed front 112-115
    hemming 160
    interfacing 168-169
    lining 176-181
    inside jet pocket 250-252
    shoulder pads 317-325
    sleeve header 321, 326
    2pce sleeve with vent 338-340
    back vent 357-359, 361-366
jeans
    hem allowance 154, 157
    shortening 160
    back pockets 227-228
    topstitching 349-350
    fly front 419-429
jet pockets 246-253
jump hem, lining 174, 176-178
junctions, matching 290-291, 407

k

keyhole buttonholes 35-36
kick pleats 357-366
kimono sleeves 327-329
knife pleats 213-221
knits
    neckbands 61-62
    doing fittings with 66
    cutting 79-80
    knitted collars 116, 118-120
    twin needle hem for 159
    patterns for 184
    rouleau 277
    zips in 416

knot at end of thread 145-146
knotty thread 146-147

l

lace 195-197
lacing, strapless top 344, 345, 347
ladder stitch 149
lapels, topstitching 59, 351, 352
lapped seam 296
lapped seams for lace 197
lapped zip 408-410, 411-416
large bust alteration 1-2, 344
large upper arms 337
layouts for cutting 75-78, 83-84
leather
    darts 87
    interfacing for 164
    hemming 160
    pressing 269
    "rouleau" 278
    lapped seam 296
linings 170-181
    for godets 140
    suitable fabrics 171
    interlining 171
    underlining 171
    skirts and trousers 171-173
    with facings 173
    dresses and tops 173-174
    sleeves 173-174
    pleated skirts 174, 214
    vests 175-176
    jackets 176-181, 338-340
    coat, free hanging 181
    patch pocket 228-229
    strapless top 343, 346-347
    vents 360-366
    splits 366-369
    zips 407, 414-415
lipstick, removing stains 341
loop turner 277
L square 208

m

maternity clothes 96, 125-126, 244-245, 390
measurements and ease 182-184
    taking measurements 182-183
    ease 183-184

mens clothes
    men's shirt collars 48
    collar stays 50
    shirt front stand 109-110
    trouser hems 155
    trouser cuffs 161-162
    cuff placket 303-306
    shirt cuffs 309-310
    French cuffs 310
    shirt yokes 312-316
    waistbands 392-401
    fly fronts 419-427
metallic fabric 200-201
minimum wearing ease 183
mitres 185-189
    in bias binding 25-26, 27
    for a trim or braid 185
    for a hem 185-186
    using a template 186-187
    edges 187-188
    borders 188
    bands 188-189
    splits 366-367
mock fly front 426-427
mock French seam 294
moiré taffeta 200

n

nap 70
neck darts 2, 93, 318
neck dart under collars 60
needleboard 264
needles, hand 144
negative ease 184
notch of collar 42, 59, 351
notches, on patterns 71, 78, 208

o

oil, removing stains 341
open ended zips 427-431
organ pleating 221, 224
overcasting 150, 287
overhand stitch 150, 287
overlocker 190-191
    darts 88
    gathering with 132
    rolled hem 158
    neatening 287
    over snipped edge 290
    junctions, matching 291
    unpicking 299

Index

p

panne velvet 198
party fabrics 192-206
patch pockets 226-237
patternmaking 207-210
    tools 207-208
    advice 208-210
    cataloguing patterns 208-209
    test garments 209-210
pattern pieces
    marks on 70-71
    transferring marks 78-79
    made in cardboard 207-208
patterns for things to make
    pressing mitt 272
    seam roll 273, 274
    tailors ham 275
    small shoulder pad 322
    large (coat) shoulder pad 323
    large (coat) raglan pad 324
    raglan pad 325
    sleeve header 326
Petersham 380-381, 383-384
pin tucks 353, 356
pinking shears 287
pins 73, 284-285
pipe organ pleats 221, 224
piping 211-212, 120-121
placket, hand opening 127-129
placket, front 106-127
placket, shirt cuff 300-306
plaids
    cutting 69, 80-84
    pleating 219
    sewing, to match 290-291
plain seam 284-285
pleats 213-225
    pleated godets 140-141
    hemming 160, 214-215
    lining pleated skirts 174, 214
    types of 213
    unpressed 214
    topstitched 215
    pressed 215-216
    professional pleating 215
    joining pleated pieces 216
    fitting notes 217
    inverted with underlay 218
    zips in 218, 415-416
    calulating 218-221
    sunray 221-222
    cartridge 221, 222-224
    pipe organ 221, 224
    broomstick 221, 225
    contortion 221, 225
    pockets with 231, 234-237
pockets 226-262
    patch 136-137, 226-237
    in seam 237-241
    cut away 241-245, 352, 398
    slashed 245-262
    jet 246-253
    welt 253-255
    flap 255-257
    windowpane welt 257-261
    zip 261-262
polo collar 61
pounding block 264
preshrinking fabric 68-69
press mitt 264, 270, 272
pressing 263-275
    in factories 66
    tools 263-264
    techniques 266-269
    troubleshooting 269-270
    tool patterns 272-275
pressing cloth 166, 263
prick stitch 411
princess line
    for large busts 1-2, 344
    pressing 266
    sewing curves 289
    felled seams on 295
    topstitching 351
puffed sleeves 131, 136, 331

r

raglan sleeves 327, 329-331
Rajah cloth 216, 263, 268
reinforcement buttons 29-30
Regency ornament 283
rever collar 55-60, 351
reversible garments
    vests 175-176
    shoulder pads for 319
Rigelene boning 343-344, 346
rivet buttons 28
rock 'n' roll t-shirt hem 160
roll collars 52-55, 60
rolled hems 157-159
roll line, collar 42
rouleau 276-283
    belt loops 7
    loops for buttons 38-39
    to cut and sew 276-277
    stretch fabrics 277
    loop turner 277
    in leather 278
    filled with cord 278
    ball buttons 279
    ornaments 279, 281-283
ruched trim 135-136
ruching 135
ruffles 134-135
running stitch 147

s

safari patch pockets 231
satin 32, 194-195
scalloped edge 104, 160, 296
scissors and shears 74-75
seam binding 288
seam ripper (unpicker) 298
seam roll 264, 271, 273, 274
seams 284-299
    lapped, for lace 196-197
    pressing 265-266, 286
    unpicking 270, 298-299
    pinning 284-285
    plain 284-285
    seam allowance 285-286
    neatening 286-288
    sewing corners 288-289
    sewing curves 289
    trimming 289
    clipping, notching 289-290
    understitching 290
    matching junctions 290-291, 407
    taut sewing 291
    easing 291, 334
    stitch-in-the-ditch 291, 375
    sew a folded edge 292
    tacking 292
    stay stitching 292
    stabilizing 292-293
    fast sewing 293
    other types of 293-297
    troubleshooting 297
    after a fitting 298
self-bound seam 288, 338
selvedge 67
serger 190-191
sequins 202-203, 205-206
sew-in interfacing 164-169
shanks, for buttons 29
shaped belts 11-12
shaped bias binding 24
shaped waistbands 381-384

shawl collars 52-55, 60
sheer fabric
    facings for 97
    sewing with 199-200
    armhole seam finish 288, 338
    seams for 288, 293-294
    sleeves in 338
shirring 133-134
shirt cuffs and plackets 300-311
    plackets, 7 types 300-306
    cuff pattern 306-307
    cuff, to sew 308-310
    French cuffs 310
    fold back cuffs 310
    troubleshooting 310-311
shirt yokes 312-316
shirts
    bias cut 18
    buttonholes 32, 34
    collar 46-50
    cutting layouts 77
    front stand 106-112
    maternity 125-126
    adding gathers 136, 313
    hemming 156-157
    cuffs and plackets 300-311
    yokes 312-316
shoulder darts 2, 93, 318
shoulder pads 317-326
    types of 317
    positioning 318
    in jackets 318
    for reversible garments 319
    covering 319
    adjusting pattern for 319
    making 320-325
    sleeve header 321, 326
    patterns for 322-325
silk 32, 193
skirts
    alterations for over 50's 3
    bias cut 17-19
    waist facing 65, 98-99, 100-101, 382
    cutting layouts 75-76
    adjusting flare 76
    for large figures 96
    gathered 137
    with a train 141-142, 196
    hemming 154-155
    lining 172-173
    box pleated 217
    waistbands 370-392

zips 402-416
skivvy neck 61-62
slashed pockets 245-262
sleeve board 263-264
sleeve header 321, 326
sleeveless, facing 101-104
sleeves 327-340
    elbow darts 95, 332-333
    sleeveless 101-104, 340
    adding gathers to 136, 331
    lining 173-174, 178
    kimono 327-329
    raglan 329-331
    set-in 331-340
    one and two piece 332
    set-in variations 336-337
    large upper arms 337
    in sheer fabric 338
    2pce jacket sleeve 338-340
slipstitch (hidden) 149
slits in hem 367
slot seam 296-297
slotted waistband interfacing 168, 372-373
smocking 132
spaghetti straps 276-277
splits 366-369
stand(ing) collars 41, 45-52
standing fell 288, 338
stain removal 341-342
stay stitching 292
stay tape, cotton
    darts 89
    necklines 94, 344, 346
    waists 101, 292, 383
    gathering onto 132
    cut away pockets 243
    armholes 340
steam stick 264
stretch fabrics *see knits*
strapless tops 343-348
stitch-in-the-ditch 291, 375
stitching, unpicking 270, 298-299
striped fabrics
    to cut 80-84
    darts in 89
    to pleat 219
    sewing, to match 290-291
sunray pleats 221-222
swing tack 173

t

tab fronts 116-125

    interfacing in 116
    using knitted collars 116
    simple tab front 116-119
    tab with facing 119-120
    troubleshooting 120
    with piping 120-121
    made from a slit 121-125
    free-hanging 125
table pressing 267
tacking 145, 292
taffeta 200
tailor board 264
tailors chalk 73, 341
tailors ham 263, 271, 275
tailors ham holder 264
tailors tacks 79
tape, cotton
    darts 89
    necklines 94, 344, 346
    waists 101, 292, 383
    gathering onto 132
    cut away pockets 243
    armholes 340
tapering hems 155
taut sewing 291
tartan
    cutting 69, 80-84
    pleating 219
    sewing, to match 290-291
tear-away stabilizer 101, 168, 293
test garment 209, 210
thimble 144-145
thread eyes for hooks 151
thread button loops 40
thread, securing 147
thread, topstitching 349-350
tie belt 9-10
tie collars 60-61
toile 209
topstitching 349-352
    lapels 59, 351, 352
    darts 88
    twinneedle hem 159
    pleats 215
    edgestitching 349
    how to 349-350
    gallery of 350
    notes on 351
    troubleshooting 351-352
    directional stitching 352
t-shirt neck 61-62
tracing wheel 208

troubleshooting
    binding 24
    buttonholes 32-33
    fabric shortage 75-77
    darts 86
    facings 100
    facings, all-in-one 103-104
    tab fronts 120
    godets 142-143
    knots in thread 146-147
    interfacing 167
    pressing 269-270
    French seams 294
    seams 297
    cuffs and plackets 310-311
    sleeves, set-in 334-336
    topstitching 351-352
    waistbands 375-376
    zips, invisible 405-406
    zips, regular 411
    fly fronts 422
trousers
    fitting for over 50's 3-4
    beltloops 5-7
    crotch seam 65
    cutting layouts 76-77
    hemming 155
    cuffs 161-162
    lining 171-173
    pockets 226-262
    waistband 370-401
    fly front 419-427
truing
    darts 90
    hems 155
    casings 386
tucks 353-356
    in sleeve lining 178
    types of 353-354
    making 354-355
    variations of 355-356
turn of cloth 53, 55
turn-ups, trousers 161-162
tweed, novelty 193-194
twill tape
    binding with 24, 25-26, 382-383
    on shirt collars 48-49
    tab fronts 116, 121-122
    for seam neatening 287-288
twin needle 159, 160, 356
two piece sleeve
    interfacing 169, 339
    lining for 178, 179, 339

u

under collar 42, 53, 55, 165
underarm gussets 328-329
underarm shields 342
underlining 171
understitching 290
universal zip foot 211, 404
unpicking 270, 298-299

v

velour 198-199
Velvaboard 264
velvet 198-199, 264, 292
velvet, panne 198-199
velveteen 198-199
vents and splits 357-369
    2pce jacket sleeves 338-340
    unlined vents 357-359
    back pleats 359-360
    lined skirt vent 360-366
    splits 366-369
vests, lining 175-176
V necks, adjusting 2, 93-94

w

wadding, as sleeve header 321
waistbands 370-401
    men's fastenings for 152, 396-397
    parts of 370
    types 370-371
    pattern for 371-373
    to sew 373-375, 376-378
    troubleshooting 375-376
    Banrol/Armoflexxx 378
    cut-on 379-381
    Petersham 380-381, 383-384
    curved 381-382, 383-384
    waistline binding 382-383
    drawcord 384-385, 388
    elastic 385-392
    adjustable elastic 390
    men's 392-401
    men's waistbanding 395-396
    men's adjustable 397-401
    elbow ease in seam 332
    for large upper arms 337
    to sew with vent 338-340
    pressing 269

invisible zip through 407-408
waist facing 65, 98-99, 100-101
warp 67
wearing ease 183
weft 67
welt pockets 253-257
western shirt pockets 248-250
western shirt yokes 315-316
wheelchair, trouser hems 162
whipstitch 150, 287
windowpane welt pkt 257-261
wooden clapper 264
"wrap" explained 106

y

yokes, shirt 312-316
yokes, skirt
    to make waist of bigger 3
    order of construction 65
    facing pattern for 98-99
    stabilizing waist 100-101
    with gathered skirt 137
    with pleated skirt 217
    sewing curved seam 289
    top of zip 406-407, 411-414
yokes, trouser back 376

z

zip pockets 240, 250, 261-262
zig zag stitch 287, 350
zips 402-431
    in bias garments 19
    in pleats 218, 415-416
    types of 402-403
    how a zip works 403
    jammed and sticky 403
    by the metre 403
    preparing to apply 403
    invisible zips 403-408
    shortening 406, 408, 419, 428
    regular zips 408-419
    in stretch knits 416
    exposed zip 416-418
    feature zips 418-419
    fly fronts 419-426
    mock fly front 426-427
    open-ended 427-431
    in fur fabric 431

www.ingramcontent.com/pod-product-compliance
Lightning Source LLC
Chambersburg PA
CBHW081420300426
44110CB00017BA/2335